The Villagers

By the Same Author

Richard Critchfield

The Villagers

Changed Values, Altered Lives:
The Closing of the Urban-Rural Gap

ANCHOR BOOKS
DOUBLEDAY
New York London Toronto Sydney Auckland

AN ANCHOR BOOK
PUBLISHED BY DOUBLEDAY
a division of Bantam Doubleday Dell Publishing Group, Inc.
1540 Broadway, New York, New York 10036

ANCHOR BOOKS, DOUBLEDAY, and the portrayal of an anchor
are trademarks of Doubleday, a division of Bantam Doubleday Dell
Publishing Group, Inc.

Library of Congress Cataloging-in-Publication Data

Critchfield, Richard.
    The villagers: changed values, altered lives: the closing of the urban-rural gap /
Richard Critchfield.—1st Anchor Books hardcover ed.
      p. cm.
    Includes bibliographical references and index.
    1. Villages—Case studies.   2. Villages—Cross-cultural studies.   I. Title.
HT421.C73   1994
307.76′2—dc20   94-7510
CIP

ISBN 0-385-42050-1

10 9 8 7 6 5 4 3 2 1

This neolithic peasant is the last and mightiest sleeper, before herself, whom the West has waked . . . and though today there are still fifteen hundred million not yet awakened peasants—about three quarters of the living generation of mankind—in India, China, Indochina, Indonesia, Dar-al-Islam and Eastern Europe, their awakening is now only a matter of time, and, when it has been accomplished, numbers will begin to tell.

—ARNOLD TOYNBEE, 1946

Contents

Acknowledgments

To William H. McNeill, author of *The Rise of the West;* Norman E. Borlaug, 1970 Nobel Peace Prize laureate for his work to eradicate world hunger; and George M. Foster, one of the last surviving pioneers of American anthropology's first peasant studies, I owe my most important debt: for a steady dialogue over the years, in letters, conversations and published work, on the ideas that went into this book. As Tennyson said, knowledge comes but wisdom lingers; all three, who have helped me with previous books, were seventy-seven and eighty in 1994 and still at work in their respective fields of history, agriculture and anthropology. Indeed, the contribution by Professor McNeill would be a collaboration had I not so often, I'm afraid, "constructively misunderstood" his thinking. In a letter in 1983 he wrote to me:

> I had no notion of the past dialogue that lay behind your work. Yes, indeed, the uses you have made of my stuff is the sort of constructive misunderstanding I had hoped for, and I am pleased to be able to say so to you directly.

The phrase puzzled me until I came across this passage in something he wrote in 1985:

> Really important texts are those susceptible of being richly and diversely misunderstood. An author can always aspire to that dignity.

I, of course, take full responsibility for the way Professor McNeill's wisdom is reflected in these pages.

This book, about the closing of the world's urban-rural gap, has five basic themes: traditional village society adapting to an exchange economy and commercial television culture, the religious fundamentalism it can provoke, challenges to inherited patterns of authority, cross-cultural migration and rapid agricultural change. Each is dealt with in stories and essays and they all come together in a long village portrait set in India, a country where I've spent five years since my first journey there in 1959 and whose language I speak. In breadth and scope, I believe, it is the most comprehensive of sixteen longer village studies, lasting three months to a year, and twenty-one shorter ones, many of them continued, on and off, over the last quarter-century since I began to systematically report villages in 1969.

The events in the Punjabi story up through the 1970 harvest were first described in a five-part, book-length work illustrated with over eighty photographs, *Sketches of the Green Revolution* (New York: Alicia Patterson Fund, 1970) and excerpted in *The Golden Bowl Be Broken* (1974) and *Villages* (1981); they appear here substantially revised. I have also drawn upon *Shahhat, an Egyptian* (1978) for a short passage. Articles based on research for this book have appeared in *Foreign Affairs, The Economist, International Herald Tribune, The Christian Science Monitor's World Monitor* monthly, the New York *Times* and the Washington *Post*. I particularly want to thank William P. Bundy, Rupert Pennant-Rea, Robert J. Donahue, Earl W. Foell and Mitchel Levitas. For help with global complexities, I am indebted, from *The Economist's* staff, to Brian Beedham, at present associate editor, and foreign editor 1964–89, and Barbara Beedham; John Parker, European editor, and Kerry Parker, for their hospitality in Moscow when they were assigned there and taking me to a Russian village.

My thanks to Dr. Borlaug, Masataka Minagawa, Christopher Dowswell and the Sasakawa Africa Association for funding a 1993 journey to Africa, and to the Ford and Rockefeller Foundations for supporting round-the-world research trips in 1990–91 and 1991–92 and 1993–94 research in Mexico. My thanks again to Norman R. Collins of the Ford Foundation for his steadfast encouragement. I am also grateful to Elizabeth Musser of St. Paul for her contribution.

In India, for their eyewitness accounts, I am indebted to Subhash Kirpekar of *The Times of India*, my student at Nagpur University in 1961–62, for describing Sant Bhindranwale's last interview and the Indian Army's attack on the Golden Temple of Amritsar in June 1984, and to H. Y. Sharada Prasad, former press secretary to three prime ministers of India, for telling me what happened in the garden that morning when Indira Gandhi was murdered.

For sharing their expertise on scientific agriculture, I wish to thank, met at the International Rice Research Institute (IRRI), Los Banos, Philippines: Yuan Long Ping of China's Hunan Hybrid Rice Research Center, Trinh Ton That of FAO, Klaus Lampe, Theodore Hutchcroft,

Gurdev Khush, S. S. Virmani and Susan McCouch; at the International Wheat and Maize Improvement Center (CIMMYT), El Batán, Mexico: Donald Winkelmann, Derek Byerlee, Tiff Harris, Linda Ainsworth, Bent Scovmand, Gregorio Martínez, Delbert Hess, Greg Edmeades, Sanjaya Rajaram, Robert Tripp, David Hoisington and Diego González de León. Important on Africa were two workshops sponsored by the Sasakawa Africa Association, at Airlie House near Washington, D.C., in 1992 and in Cotonou, Benin, in 1993; for various advice and information I thank Orville Freeman, Jimmy Carter, Rosalynn Carter, Denise Berry North, John Coulter, Robert Havener, Uma Lele, Patrick Orr, Marco A. Quiñones, Peter Timmer, Nathan Russell, Lukas Brader, W. T. Kang, Jean Doyen, Joyce Endeley, Hans Herren, Jean Freymond, Edward Shonshey.

For advice, suggestions, help and hospitality, I am also grateful to: Poland: Robert Bose, Gregory Vaut and Joanna Drozd of the Foundation for the Development of Polish Agriculture, Tadeusz Wolski, Szymon Bartnowski, Leszek Kruszewski, Zofia Sadowska, Teresa Borowska; Russia: Sergei Mikhailovich Skubko, Igor Drykhunov; China: Peter Wong; Egypt: Georgette Scarzella, Rose Risgallah, Muriel Allen, Kent and Susan Weeks, John and Elizabeth Rodenbeck, Clifford Nygaard, Helmi Hassan, Ahmed Lutvy; India: Rosanna Dillon Ismail, M. B. Lal, Gordon Conway, Khushwant Singh, B. G. Verghese, Mark Tully, W. A. Qazi, A. Govindan, T. S. Sohal; Nepal: Kesar Lall Shresta, Julia Chang Bloch, Todd Greentree; Thailand: Rachanida Nimmanop; Philippines: Frank Wisner, Jr., Alejandro Melchor, Amando Doronila; Korea: Sang-Bok Han, Jil Hyun Lee, Huhn Pal Moon, Byong Man Ahn, Cheong Ju Woong, Horace Underwood, Ben Kremenak; Indonesia: Bur Rasuanto, Soetedjo Moeljodihardjo; Ghana: Sydney Seho-Ahiable, Adansi Pipin Boaduo, Owusu-Bobie, Takyi Boadu Andrews, Felix, Wayne Haag; Benin: Marcel Galiba, Jackson Makweta; Washington, D.C.: Robert W. Alvord, Peggy Ann Trimble, James and Lois Critchfield, Kevin Cleaver, Peter Riddleberger, Graeme Donovan, Robert S. McNamara, Cynthia Helms, Donald Plucknett; Cambridge, Mass.: Roderick and Emily MacFarquhar; Seattle: Roy Prosterman; San Francisco: Wanda Tomczykowska. For photographic processing, I thank V. Shankar of New Delhi and Eddie and Elfriede Dyba of San Francisco.

I am greatly indebted to my interpreters: Agnes Serrano, Alek Borowski, Piotr Łapinski, Pawel Kraticz, Maciek Łaszewski, Jerzy Stefanski, Hassan Abu Sayeed, Byeong Min Yu, Kim Chyung Ok,

Myong Shin Kim, Aurelio Rendon, Mario Medina Alejandre, Pushkar, Widgna Tarma Husen, Edy Razak, Monica Mutuli, Samson Aiakora, Krishanjit Singh and Yadvender Singh. Taking leave from the Indian Institute of Mass Communications in New Delhi, Yadvender Singh was my interpreter in Punjab going back to 1973, or all stays but the first in 1970; without his courage I doubt I would have braved going back to Ghungrali at the height of Punjabi terrorism in 1991 and 1992. Also greatly appreciated is the moral support from Vice Chancellor K. M. S. Gill and Dr. Ranjit Singh of Punjab Agricultural University.

I have mentioned William P. Bundy, but I wish to particularly stress my gratitude for his analytic skill in helping me formulate my conceptual findings after twelve years of village study, in 1982, which make up the first few pages of this book.

This is my fourth book with Doubleday and I wish to thank Charles Flowers for his exceptionally fine and judicious editing. I was astonished to learn, as we neared the end of our work together, that he was only twenty-eight. I also thank Martha Levin and Charles Conrad of Anchor Books, and Susan Moldow, now with Scribner's, who, as president of Doubleday in 1990, got this book going.

Lastly, my deepest gratitude to the villagers themselves.

Grateful acknowledgment is made to the following to reprint previously published material.

Robert Redfield, from *Peasant Society and Culture*. Copyright © 1956 the University of Chicago. Reprinted by permission of The University of Chicago Press.

William H. McNeill, from *Sea Changes: American Foreign Policy in a World Transformed*, edited by Nicholas X. Rizopoulos. Copyright © 1990 William H. McNeill. Reprinted by permission of the Council of Foreign Relations Press.

Clifford Geertz, from *The Religion of Java*. Copyright © 1960 by The Free Press. Reprinted by permission of the publisher.

Clifford Geertz, from *Islam Observed*. Copyright © 1968 Yale University. Reprinted by permission of The University of Chicago Press.

Henry Habib Ayrout, from *The Fellaheen*. Copyright © 1938, Payot, Paris; 1945, R. Schindler, Cairo. Reprinted by permission of Hyperion Publishers, Ltd.

William H. McNeill, from *Mythistory and Other Essays*. Copyright © 1986 The University of Chicago. Reprinted by permission of The University of Chicago Press.

William H. McNeill, from *Fundamentalisms and Society*. Copyright © 1993 the University of Chicago. Reprinted by permission of The University of Chicago Press.

William H. McNeill, from *The Rise of the West*. Copyright © 1963 the University of Chicago. Reprinted by permission of The University of Chicago Press.

George M. Foster, from *Peasant Society: A Reader* by Jack M. Potter, May N. Diaz, and George M. Foster. Copyright © 1967 Little, Brown and Company. Reprinted by permission of Little, Brown and Company.

E. M. Forster, from *A Passage to India*. Copyright © 1924 Harcourt, Brace, & World, Inc.; copyright © 1952 by E. M. Forster. Reprinted by permission of Harcourt, Brace.

Garnett translation reprinted by permission of R.I.B. Library, Reed Book Services, a member of the Reed Elsevier group, London.

Richard Lingemann, from *Small Town America*. Copyright © 1980 Richard Lingemann. Reprinted by permission of The Putnam Publishing Group.

Robert Frost, from *Collected Poems of Robert Frost*. Copyright © 1942 Robert Frost. Reprinted by permission of Henry Holt and Company Inc.

I

The Sleeper Wakes:
An Introduction

TO EXPLORE is also to discover what we left behind. For every new experience changes our perception of what has gone before. When I set out to explore villages twenty-five years ago, Barbara Ward had just described the postcolonial world as "a new political country, unexplored, ominous, planetary in scale, and, conceivably, bordering on the end of time."

Her words have stayed in my mind, as they continue to fit the kaleidoscopic, ever-changing present. For in these twenty-five years, overcrowding on the land, all kinds of scientific advances and the nearly universal spread of television have quite abruptly ended the old, autonomous, isolated and culturally self-contained village. This book aims to illustrate this closing of the urban-rural gap, largely through the story of a village in India, which goes back close to fifty years, the last thirty-five of them, on and off, personally observed. Shorter tales deal with the triumph over Nazism, Stalinism and latter-day Communism, the rise of militant Islam, the East Asian Confucian challenge, migration exemplified by Mexicans into the United States and Africa's special farming problems, all skeins in the fabric of drastically changing village behavior.

I am a reporter who has been writing about villages, or their cultural influences, almost all my life. My hope is to leave a record, as set down by a witness, to show interested readers what life was like for a few ordinary villagers in our tumultuous times. As Arnold Toynbee saw in 1946, peasant villagers are to be found in India, China, Indochina, Indonesia, the Islamic world and Eastern Europe; I would add Africa and much of Latin America. To anyone born in 1931, as I was, in a small farming community out on the North Dakota prairie, there is just the faintest memory of villagelike dirt roads, horse-drawn farm wagons, threshers pitching bundles by hand and small farms where cows were milked, pigs fed, bread baked, vegetables canned, and chickens ran about underfoot.

As our peasant ancestors migrated from Europe—and go back three or four generations and most of them *were* peasants—hired hands stayed cheap and abundant through most of the nineteenth century. American farms didn't go from human power to horsepower in any big way until the Civil War and from horsepower to machinery until the two world wars, all in response to manpower shortages and high farm prices. So even I can remember a few horses around, still used for plowing. One of my brothers, fourteen years older, who worked around horses on farms, joined America's last horse cavalry in 1939, which patrolled the Mexican-Californian border. In Iowa, where two uncles farmed in the poor but picturesque Grant Wood country along the Wapsipinicon River, horses lasted a bit longer.

Generally in America by 1940, when I was nine, even in the remoter parts of North Dakota, highly mechanized, capitalized farming was taking over. Since 1940 the number of Americans who farm has dropped from 30 percent of the total population to less than 2 percent—it was 96 percent in 1776. In 1994, the U.S. Census Bureau classified less than 25 percent of 260 million Americans as rural—that is, living on farms or in any town of fewer than 2,500 people. This is not as extreme as in Britain, just 10 percent rural, or the whole of Northern Europe, 17 percent. But it does mean that the past half-century has seen a drastic decline of rural influences in American, and much of Western, society.

Is something being lost? And if so, what? I first saw traditional villages on a trip to Europe in 1950 when I was nineteen, in Korea as a soldier in 1954–55 and in India while teaching at Nagpur University in 1960–62. The question of cultural loss, I suppose, was gradually forming in my mind. In 1958–59 I studied *Volkskunde*, ethnography, at the University of Innsbruck; we tramped about the Alpine valleys of the Austrian and Italian Tyrol, but one soon felt the way Adela Quested did in *A Passage to India*, when she complained: "I'm tired of seeing picturesque figures pass before me as a frieze." What made the crucial difference was Vietnam. I covered the war from May 1964 to November 1967, three years and seven months, for the Washington *Star*. The first year, trying to be one's idea of a war correspondent, I covered battles; the second year, pacification; the third year, politics; and the last, the breakdown of the ordinary Vietnamese villager's Confucian culture. What began as conventional reporting ended as amateur anthropology. I had reached the conclusion that it was knowledge of culture and character, not just battles, which often changed nothing, that would decide the issue of the war.

In the fall of 1969, after a year covering the White House as the *Star*'s number two man there, I requested and was given two years' leave of absence to try an experiment: to report villages by going to live in them, what anthropologists call the "participant-observer" method. You pitch in and work silently while your interpreter writes down what the villagers do and say. The method was adapted from a technique used by Oscar Lewis in his 1959 Mexican study, *Five Families*. Lewis soon left it in favor of long taped interviews. As much as I can, I've stayed with stenographically recorded dialogue as the basis for my stories.

Over the years I did sixteen long village studies of three months to more than a year in Mauritius, India, Indonesia, Iran, Morocco, the Philippines, Nepal, Egypt, Sudan, Brazil, Mexico, Kenya, Korea and Poland, doing villages in both Upper and Lower Egypt and on the islands of Java and Bali. I went to China three times, Indonesia nine times. Other countries where village research was done include Russia; Senegal, Mali, Mauritania, Ghana and Benin in Africa; Yugoslavia, Lebanon, Turkey and Afghanistan; and in Asia: Pakistan, Bangladesh, Sri Lanka, Burma, Malaysia, Thailand, Taiwan, and besides Vietnam, Laos and Cambodia. Mind you, this was spread over a quarter-century. Eventually I added two small American farm communities, one in North Dakota and one in Iowa. And after *The Economist* asked me in 1987 to do its first survey on Britain itself, I expanded my approach to a cultural study of the West's once-greatest nation in decline.

A village, of course, is a group of people who live together tilling land, or fishing (not herding, if it is nomadic), ranging from a few households to several thousand inhabitants. The Polish village in this book, for instance, has fewer than a hundred and fifty people, while the one in India has just under fifteen hundred. Estimates of the number of villages the world over go from 1.5 million to 3 million; my guess is about 2 million. About a third are in China, another third are in India-Pakistan-Bangladesh and the rest are spread out over a hundred and fifty or so other countries.

I tend to use "villager" rather than "peasant" or "farmer" unless there is a specific reason for using the other terms. A villager is simply the inhabitant of a village, whereas modern anthropology defines a peasant much more precisely as a villager who makes a living and has a traditional way of life through cultivation of the land, producing crops mostly for his own subsistence. A farmer, who can also be a villager, as once defined by anthropologist Robert Redfield, carries on "agriculture for reinvestment and business, looking on the land as capital and commodity." In America, except in New England, where there were villagelike clusters of houses from which people went out to farm, much of the population was settled in scattered individual farms surrounding a small trading town; hence we say "small town." How to define peasants has much occupied anthropologists. Yeats may "sing the peasantry" and Oliver Goldsmith admire "a bold peasantry, their country's pride," but city people have long looked upon country people with a touch of condescension, the hardy rustic also being the uncouth hick or hayseed. Yet in Eastern Europe, for instance, "peasant" is a perfectly respectable term for a small, traditional cultivator.

Before proceeding, let me define a few more terms and offer some key concepts I use in my village work. First, I use "culture" in the anthropological sense to mean a set of rules or solutions to problems handed down from parents to children, so that each new generation does not have to start out from scratch. This is not too far from the Arnoldian sense of culture. Any culture embraces all socially transmitted behavior patterns, arts, beliefs, institutions and ideas. But at bottom culture signifies a time-tested design for living.

In a village this cultural transmission is easy to observe since fathers and mothers are physically with their sons and daughters so much of the time, in the home or in the fields. The man and the woman share the task of nurture. Not equally, because the woman is responsible for the infant, but once a child is three or four, the man's role starts to widen and he, too, becomes engaged in cultural transmission. Because the father wants help with his farm work, children learn useful chores from toddlerhood—how to collect eggs, how to milk a cow. From a very tender age they start to work and grow into the whole discipline of adulthood with little formal nurture. Handed down at the same time are religious beliefs, the agricultural moral code, respect for family ties and property, a work ethic, and subordination of self-interest to family and community solidarity. Since this happens in all villages, a great sameness in village ways exists, in both space and time. Most of the 2 million or so villages that survive today have developed similar habits, routines and outlooks.

Second, this cultural transmission is decisive in human behavior.

We are as much the result of nurture as of nature. We can no longer completely accept Emile Durkheim's idea that the human mind is a *tabula rasa*—a blank slate on which culture is written. Scientists take it for granted that there are genetic explanations for some human behavior. Others, like paleoanthropologist Richard Leakey, who traced human origins back 3 to 4 million years in Africa's Great Rift Valley, lean heavily toward nurture:

> Man is not innately anything and is capable of everything. Human beings are cultural animals and each one is the product of a particular culture.

In a 1981 interview in Nairobi, Leakey told me that humans evolved a cooperative society because hunting and gathering, and later farming, required it. Perhaps 70–80 percent of our behavior comes from inherited culture. What about the other 20–30 percent? A criminal may be born, but made worse by a violent culture. Martin Daley and Margo Wilson of McMaster University in Canada compared homicide statistics in Chicago with those in England and Wales. In all they found young men thirty times as likely as women of all ages to kill. Obviously there is something to inborn male aggressiveness, but also to the products of childhood socialization: the study found young men in Chicago thirty times more likely to kill than young men in England or Wales. Nature and nurture both always figure in, and we can benefit by knowing which is which.

Third, a concept from Aristotle, is that every creature's mode of living—that is, culture—depends on how it obtains its food. This corresponds to Leakey's theory about behavior growing out of hunting-gathering or farming. If culture is a way and view of life, it is the way that shapes the view. The technology on which our livelihood depends shapes our ideas, and the modern farmer on his tractor and the primitive cultivator with his hoe are likely to give the world and life quite different meanings.

Fourth, all villagers share something of a universal culture. In every village I've studied, prime value is given to property (land, the means of production) and family (tillers, the producers). Aside from race or level of technology, I find villagers differ most when it comes to the realm of abstract ideas, or religion. Here I define religion as the way we and our ancestors have tried to provide life and the world with metaphysical meaning. In the final pages of his *Earth in the Balance*, Al Gore says, "More people than ever are asking, 'Who are we? What is our purpose?' " As Max Weber has written, this is the ultimate question of all metaphysics. Religion is the core of any culture. (Or, in the case of a Marxist, nonreligion, though I regard Marxism as a secular offshoot of Christianity.) Religion affects everything: how hard people work, how inventive they are, their enterprise.

A fifth concept is that no substitute for the rural basis of urban culture has yet been invented. In other words, rural life is the source, and the only source, of such aspects of our culture as religious beliefs, the agricultural moral code, the institutions of family and property, and the work ethic. This concept was introduced to me by historian William H. McNeill in a letter in 1990 and we have spent many hours discussing it.

Here I must pause to say that many of the arguments in this book, once we move beyond the first four concepts, have evolved from conversations and correspondence with Professor McNeill. I first came across his work in India in 1970 when I picked up a copy of his 1963 work, *The Rise of the West*, which traces the role of agriculture, technology and cultural diffusion from their Neolithic beginnings. After reading it I headed for the Iran-Iraq borderlands and the Mesopotamian plain, where it became the bible of my village studies, the first copy so reread it literally fell to pieces. The dialogue began in 1982 after both of us were asked by William Bundy, then editor of *Foreign Affairs*, to contribute essays to its sixtieth anniversary issue. Professor McNeill is a world historian of extraordinary erudition and, as I say, I am a reporter who writes about villages, a nonintellectual writing essentially for nonintellectuals, certainly for nonacademics. Many of the paths I have explored in villages were suggested by his thinking.

A problem in village work is how much to rely on the scholarship of others, such as Henry Habib Ayrout's *The Fellaheen* in Egypt or Clifford Geertz's *The Religion of Java*, classic works about particularly exotic cultures. McNeill suggests:

> Once you read a book like those, you just see things through its eyes, it's perfectly true. But you also see things you might not otherwise understand. I don't buy the argument you should just go in totally naive and blind. It's possible. But the more you know in detail about the country or region you're looking at, the more likely you are to be perceptive about it.

I seized on Professor McNeill's concept of the rural base of urban culture at the end of a book I did three years ago on what was going wrong in the rural Midwest, *Trees, Why Do You Wait?* After quoting McNeill, I concluded:

> My main argument in this book, if you'll accept that I'm painting with a very broad brush, is that what kind of urban culture we have in America is going to depend on how many Americans farm. All culture, as we've said, has a rural origin . . . Successive generations are growing up without rural ties. This in turn produces social ills like homelessness, crime, vandalism and drug abuse . . . Rural life can have its shortcomings. Farming has always meant hard physical labor. But my main point is: farming creates societies that work. It creates a very durable and basic culture. And we need to save as many farms and small towns as we can because America's urban culture is at stake.

Too many Americans are sick of living in cities and looking at asphalt and feeling lonely—staring out an inner-city window and seeing a wall of red bricks. So much that matters—family, ethics, morals—came out of villages. People who till the soil just have organic ties with nature, physical work and each other that we don't. In a modern city a man goes off to office or factory and is insulated from his children. Chances are the woman goes off too. Too often, the young are left to learn from each other, teachers or TV. This produces a radical disjunction between generations. In cities young people may be socialized to behavior that is fundamentally antagonistic to fitting them for adult roles. Young inner-city gangs—white, black, Latino or Asian—are apprenticed to a world of gangs and crime. This is terribly costly to any society and, in turn, to the young people themselves. Few gang members live past thirty. Such loss is a very high price to pay for the failure of cultural reproduction that used to be quite spontaneous in villages.

In a talk with McNeill in 1991 I said I agreed with him, but didn't see how any substitute for the rural base of urban culture *could* be invented. He cautioned me that just because we haven't found a substitute doesn't mean we can't. But how, I asked, thinking of the way land, work and family shaped so many ways and views in villages. "We don't know," he replied. "We don't know."

A sixth and final concept, and the one which this book explores, is the closing of the urban-rural gap. This has been happening, at an accelerating pace, for some time. Toynbee used his simile of a waking sleeper for it as early as 1946. A decade later, Robert Redfield, the great University of Chicago anthropologist, predicted, "For the future it may be said that peasantry are ceasing to be." He implied such extinction was by choice: "Peasants now want to be something other than peasants."

During the 1980s television penetrated to all the villages of this book, practically to every mud hut. TV, radio, telephones, computers, all the wonders of modern communications mean that the old inequalities of information and outlook are ending with astonishing speed. TV's great power is the way it replaces words with pictures. Seeing is believing and needs no translation. It is not true that just because old village culture is in danger—and it does seem to be in danger all over the world—that we necessarily face some kind of cultural catastrophe. It certainly means a great change in the general human condition. Professor McNeill, who was Toynbee's biographer and co-worker in London and studied under Redfield in Chicago, says, "This is a very deep transformation of human life. I would rank what is happening now with man's transition from a hunter and gatherer into a settled farmer." McNeill:

> The transition to agricultural life involved very great strains. Getting adjusted. New customs. Daily life routines. All the rest of it. Think what it meant not to eat what you had but to save seed for next year. This was an enormous transformation of human behavior.

He feels that we are on the threshold of evolving new cultural patterns, but that no one can confidently predict what they might be:

> Human ingenuity is very great. In human life, just because a problem is there, it doesn't mean there's a solution in the short run. It may take a hundred years. It may take a thousand years. It doesn't mean there's a stone wall either. I tend to think of cultural change as much more of a process of random experiment than selective survival. These things that work tend to spread by imitation. And just what will work as the urban-rural gap closes isn't very clear yet.

McNeill accepts, if things go wrong, the possibility that cities can collapse into internal civil war or that epidemics can bring down human life, Bosnias, Rwandas and Somalias on a vastly bigger stage.

In the meantime, in the twenty-five years since I set out, the world has already become a radically newer political country. The stories in this book are as much a look backward as a look ahead. They begin with one about a village called Popowlany in the Polish-Russian borderlands. Communism was like a great concrete slab on top of everything. Nothing stirred. Two world wars also had the same effect on the village, so that Popowlany has preserved, right up until now, what might be called Europe's last authentic peasantry. The same is true in those areas of Bulgaria and what was Yugoslavia where, as in Poland, the peasantry's small farms were not collectivized. Democracy and free-market economics, with farms ever bigger and fewer, are likely to end this peasantry, with all its stability and stagnation, very quickly. My journey there was a chance to try to capture this way of life before it is gone forever.

The Islamic revival, which gets deeper into rage and anarchy the more it thrives, is seen in three quite different settings: two villages in Egypt—Nageh Kom Lohlah on the Upper Nile and Sirs el Layyan in the Delta—and Pilangsari village on the Indonesian island of Java. The Confucian challenge to the West is taken up in Nae-Chon, a village in South Korea, and in China's Guangdong province as China surges toward becoming perhaps the world's biggest economy in twenty to thirty years. Migration, as brought home to us by the flood of Latinos coming north, is viewed in Huecorio, a Tarascan Indian village in Mexico's central highlands. Africa's special farming problems are explored. Last is the story of Ghungrali, a Sikh Punjabi village in the area where the green revolution of scientific farming and high-yield dwarf grain had its biggest success. The story explores why, despite the prosperity that has made Punjab as rich as Southern Europe, its village culture is disintegrating, amidst caste and communal strife and armed terrorism. Ghungrali is my most comprehensive village study and its story and characters best illustrate, I believe, the social forces at play in villages today, just as its central figure, Pritam, born in 1898, personifies the traditional peasant at his best. These stories are told in the third person. Rather like a camera crew, my interpreter and I keep out of sight so that readers will see the villagers more as I saw them. I use first-person commentary only when it seems essential.

II

No culture is ever static, but in most of human history there has been much more time to adjust to change. The West, well before its post-1800 industrial revolution, had three and a half centuries from the day Luther posted his theses on the Wittenberg church door to James Watt's steam engine. The Protestant Reformation emphatically transformed Christian culture from the world-rejecting tenets of the historical Jesus to a world-affirming religion of the urban middle class, with philosophical motivations for seeking salvation primarily through hard work and a more rational control of life.

When technological change comes too fast, age-old beliefs, such as the Egyptian villager's traditional notion that the earth is flat and surrounded by sea and the mountains of Kaf, lose their basis. Among deeply religious, illiterate peasants, something like the sight of this planet on TV can make their universe incomprehensible. Such personal crises, if enough people suffer them, can produce such political eruptions as growing Hindu-Muslim violence in India or all the Islamic turmoil.

V. S. Naipaul, a gloomy but astute observer of the way peasant societies the world over are changing, particularly in India, has attributed "all the trouble in the world" to adapting to the West and its ways. "Not adapting to its tools," he said some years ago, "but trying to fit in with its ideas." I agree with Naipaul, except an anthropologist might argue that you can't separate the ideas from the tools; all culture has a technological basis. Marx would say the same thing.

The industrial revolution two hundred years ago gave the West its technological head start. It is only now that the Asians have begun to assert a technological supremacy similar to the one they enjoyed between 1000 and 1450. There could well be a seismic shift of world leadership—economic, political and cultural—underway once more. Not just in industry. In agricultural science, the Japanese have put an insect-resistant gene in rice, the Chinese invented hybrid rice, the Indians hybrid cotton, and everybody is working on hybrid wheat.

For the West, 1800 was key. From the day men followed their cattle down from Central Asia and up from Africa into the Fertile Crescent, and women invented farming and men the plow, wheel, sail and irrigation, nothing really big happened to the peasant cultivator—aside from the invention of the moldboard plow, gunpowder, the rice paddy, and adoption of American food crops after 1500—until about 1800. There were great nonfarming advances during these five to six thousand years, such as the Gutenberg printing press (actually a Chinese invention) and techniques of seafaring and navigation. But aside from the introduction from the New World of corn, potatoes, tomatoes and such, which enabled Europe to feed itself up to this day, agricultural technology remained much the same when it came to methods.

Very generally speaking, anyone cultivating land in 1800 A.D., whether in Europe, China, India or what was then the twenty-four-year-old United States of America, used about the same energy sources as the 5000 B.C. cultivator (animal power, wind, water, sun and his own muscles). He could travel much the same few miles per day (walking or sailing or by horse or carriage—the first railroads date from 1820). He used much the same material for tools (iron and wood) and fuel (firewood and draft animals). He had much the same life expectancy from birth (late thirties to early forties, about the same as a modern Afghan).

Then, in the West after 1800, everything suddenly took off. Since 1800, according to *The Economist*'s former deputy editor Norman Macrae, world population has risen sixfold, but real gross national product has risen eightyfold; the distance a person can travel a day has gone up between a hundredfold and a thousandfold; the killing area of the most effective megadeath weapon a millionfold or more; the amount of energy that can be released from a pound of matter over fifty-millionfold; and the range and volume of information technology (computers, chips, telecommunications) several billionfold. The whole world is hooked up to the same jet-and-electronics network and a closing of this 5000 B.C.–1990s A.D. technology gap is now at hand.

To date this more precisely for the villages: If the 1920s and 1930s brought decisive technological change to American agriculture, the decade of the 1970s, if often at a much lower level, was the turning point for many villagers, especially Asians. Scientific farming did not fully win acceptance by many governments until the breakthroughs in tropical plant genetics in the late 1960s. The postcolonial expansion of primary education and training abroad of large numbers of students in Western technology did not begin to pay off until the 1970s. Transistor radios came in early, but television did not reach great numbers of villagers until the 1980s. By 1992 there were 1.2 persons per television set in the United States and 1.5 per set in Japan, but there were also already 7 persons per TV set in Mexico, 9 in China, 14 in Egypt, 16 in Indonesia, 44 in India and 85 in an African country like Ghana. And even in Ghana in 1993 it was hard to find anybody who had not seen a televised boxing or soccer match or the Gulf War.

The change that really mattered came in the mentality of villagers once they saw concrete evidence of how Western technology could improve their lives. My recognition of this phenomenon dates from 1978, when after a five-year absence from Africa and Latin America, I returned to a number of Asian villages, from India to Indonesia, where I had lived in the late 1960s and early 1970s. Among the village people I knew personally, there was a marked difference: somehow, in those five years, something had happened in their minds. They felt the future would no longer simply repeat the past, as it had always done, but could be radically improved. It wasn't just agricultural techniques but reproductive technology as well: women were starting to accept the Pill and the IUD. I excitedly reported this information to *The Economist* in London, which, checking with experts in the field, held up the story for some months before deciding to print it. It appeared March 9, 1979, with the headline "A Great Change Has Started." I reported: "Times change, and men, once they have the technological means and enough years to culturally adjust, change with them." I described what was happening as "a great change in the general human condition"—that is, the rural-urban gap had begun to close.

The pace of change has steadily quickened. Its agricultural side, which thanks to Norman Borlaug and my village experience I know more about, differs from what happened in the West in three fundamental ways.

First, it is coming more than fifty years later. The mechanization of American farming, and the application of chemical and biological science to it, largely took place when I was a little boy. During this half-century-plus, man's control over matter and energy, particularly in physics and biology, and his ability to process and disseminate this knowledge, has grown and accelerated fantastically. In Asia, beginning in 1967 in Punjab, and quickly spreading all over, the biggest gains in farming have come from biological technology, advances in output per unit of land (not to be confused with "biotechnology," now universally used for genetic engineering). Biological technology —breeding better seeds and using chemicals and controlled water to grow them—does not demand, like America's mechanical technology, advances in output per man, the same substitution of capital for labor. Experience in China and India is showing that high-yield dwarf or hybrid crops are more labor-intensive, not less.

Second, peasants are involved, that is, subsistence cultivators within ancient civilizations. North America, once it was settled by

Europeans, became one of the few places on earth that never had a peasant society. Sedentary Native American tribes, among the Plains Indians and such Pueblo cultures as the Hopi and Zuni, cultivated corn, squash and beans, fished, hunted and gathered roots and berries. But once the Spanish introduced the horse, many nomadic tribes like the Sioux, mounted and armed with bow and arrow, left farming to range the grasslands hunting buffalo. As European settlement expanded, and the vanquished Indians sank into poverty, the old world cultural traditions of uprooted peasants were actively discouraged by the Yankee commercial and professional classes who ran most small towns. Novels from Willa Cather's *My Ántonia* to Sinclair Lewis's *Main Street* dramatize this uniquely American and often wrenching experience. Despite pro-rural instincts by presidents from Thomas Jefferson to Theodore Roosevelt to John F. Kennedy, the economic basis of American culture, never having been a village except in the memories of its European immigrants, in time shifted from farm and small town to city. As small towns die, so do their churches, schools and family life, with a weakening of religion, family, work ethic and a small town's sense of community.

Third, the staggeringly big populations involved and the sheer densities in some places are way beyond anything previously experienced. Village populations that doubled the past thirty years are projected to redouble in the next thirty. So that while rural overcrowding has led to a mass exodus to the cities, the absolute number of people left in villages is greater than at any time in history. In a few places—the Nile Valley, the Mexican central highlands, the island of Java, all settings in this book—absolute growth has already overshot the available land and water even with the application of all known farm science. The alternative to agriculture lies in decentralized industry. Japan, Taiwan and increasingly Java itself have industrialized through small village-based workshops which make components for central factories.

Two important things about this explosive population growth: it is a rural phenomenon, which affects cities through migration, and it is fairly recent, not really beginning until the century 1750–1850. Pestilence and famine long kept up death rates, as they might again. History has examples of radical depopulation. Egypt's people, who were no more than 7 million in pharaonic times and may have reached 20 million during the six hundred years Egypt was a Christian country ruled by Rome, fell, under Islamic rule, to 2.5 million by the time of Napoleon's invasion in 1798–1801. The Black Death claimed a third of all Europeans in 1346–49. China and Persia were drastically depopulated during Mongol invasions between 1200 and 1400, and the Aztec and Inca civilizations fell to smallpox and other diseases brought by the Spanish conquistadores. There were a billion people on earth in 1800, 2 billion by 1920, 3 billion by 1960, 6.3 billion in mid-1994; we are now going up by a billion people a year. By the end of this decade, more people will live in towns and cities than in villages, a great milestone in human history. The hopeful side of this is that in cities birth rates fall. With steep, mysterious drops in fertility in Russia and Eastern Europe since the collapse of Communism, and white birth rates falling everywhere, it is conceivable that a reverse of population growth, even an actual decline, will follow the closing of the urban-rural gap.

The explosive growth in human numbers has been lethal to other living creatures. Professor McNeill:

> Everywhere, growing human populations persist in altering the face of the earth to suit themselves, using an ever more powerful technology to cut down forests, divert watercourses, plant fields, dig mines, and in still other ways alter natural environments.

The threat of hunger, he says, is not new.

> What is new is the scale of the human assault on other forms of life, and the disturbances of atmospheric and oceanic balances that human activity has begun to make, not merely locally but also globally. Just what the consequences may be no one knows. They may turn out to be drastic.

As with the Aswan Dam in Egypt or hybrid rice in China, which needs new seeds for every crop, gains in food production have always involved increased vulnerability to breakdown. The first farmers faced risks in crop failure or plundering bandits that hunter-collectors never faced. Subsistence peasants, whether in India or in Poland, are far less vulnerable to loss of livelihood than urban populations face when political or natural disaster interrupts the flow of goods and services. Stocks in a city can never be enough.

As a historian, Professor McNeill feels it is likely the upsurge in human numbers will be checked by social and political changes long before absolute ecological limits are reached. We see over and over again how people resist getting poorer and what great measures they will undertake to avoid falling living standards. Migration and changes of occupation can relieve the problem for a while. But if this fails, collective violence usually results, as in France in 1789, Russia in 1917 and China in 1949. More recent examples are El Salvador, Peru, Lebanon and Iran, where the Ayatollah Khomeini's great following came from uprooted and jobless ex-villagers in the Teheran slums.

McNeill also reminds us that the transfer of technology, such as the West's agricultural science to the poor peasant societies, is the kind of borrowing from strangers possessing superior skills that appears to be "the principal motor of social change within civilized and simpler societies alike." As McNeill describes writing *The Rise of the West:*

> I simply set out to identify at any given age where the center of highest skills was located. By describing them and then asking how neighboring peoples reacted to such achievements, a comprehensible structure for successive periods of world history emerges, each distinguished from its predecessors and successors by a pattern of cultural flow from a dominant metropolitan center . . .

McNeill showed how from the Neolithic beginnings of grain agriculture in Mesopotamia (3000–1800 B.C.), this center of highest skills shifted to a cosmopolitan Middle East (1800–500 B.C.), the Aegean basin and Mediterranean shorelands (500 B.C.–A.D. 200) to India (200–600) and the Islamic world (600–1000).

> In the most recent millennium, world leadership oscillated toward two extremes: first the Far East (100–1500), and most recently the Far West (1500–1950).

Since *The Rise of the West* was published in 1963, McNeill says, he has grown more conscious of the slow emergence of our contemporary global society (what V. S. Naipaul calls our "universal civilization," a phrase one also finds in Toynbee). A second modification of his views from thirty years ago:

> I now believe that human culture is set in an ecological context that evolves in partial independence of cultural developments. This is notably the case with infectious diseases, as I argued in *Plagues and Peoples* (1976). Climate is another significant variable which I had previously overlooked. Deforestation, pollution, and other large-scale changes in the ecosystem may yet prove to be a third. The everchanging ratios between human numbers and resources, as currently

available for the maintenance of human life, in accordance with a particular technological and social structure, constitute still a fourth at least quasi-ecological limit upon human affairs.

McNeill sees human life and society as resting on physiological (molecules), ecological (organisms) and semiological (symbols) balances. How we act from day to day, he says, depends on symbolic messages in and out that define our consciousness. Experience of what happens when we interact with the natural world feeds back into our vocabularies and concepts in such a way as to alter and correct, refine and redefine the symbols we use to guide our further behavior. Science guides human actions today, just as theological and magical ideas did in the past. One wonders just how powerfully television will alter this process in the villagers' minds.

III

The universality of village culture struck me from the first. American anthropology discovered the peasant in Latin America, particularly Mexico, where pioneer studies were done by Redfield, Lewis and Berkeley's George Foster in the 1930s and 1940s. Dr. Foster, whose work, like that of Professor McNeill and Dr. Borlaug, spans nearly six decades, still goes back to his Mexican village at least once a year. Like them, he is a surviving link with some of the great social thinkers of this century. Redfield:

> It was by moving out of aboriginal North America into the study of contemporary village life in Middle and South America that American anthropologists came first and in large numbers to undertake the study of peasants . . . In Latin America, anthropology has moved from tribe to peasantry.

After Mexico, India next caught the anthropologists' attention, with the rest of Asia and Africa following as jet travel and America's post-World War II imperial age made the world seem a much smaller place. As McNeill suggests, it was also

> the first generation in which sufficient detachment from naive ethnocentrism has become possible, largely because the self-confidence of Western peoples was so shaken by World Wars I and II, and by the fearful prospect of World War III.

A great many village studies were published, leading Redfield to conclude that, unlike primitive tribes, many of them South Sea Islanders, the first field of anthropological study—one thinks of Margaret Mead—peasants had a universal culture. I noticed this feature right away when I began to systematically report villages. Much of the "foreignness" of a society dropped away once you entered a village. Common sense suggests that groups of people who live together and cultivate land are bound to have much in common. Oscar Handlin, in his superb study of nineteenth-century migration to North America, *The Uprooted,* wrote that "from the westernmost reaches of Europe, in Ireland, to Russia in the east, the peasant masses attained an imperturbable sameness." My experience suggests this is a global characteristic.

In the mid-1940s, E. K. L. Francis, after a study of Hesiod's famous *Works and Days* about Greek Boeotian villagers in the sixth century B.C., argued that village culture had universality not only in space but also in time.

Finally, in 1956 Robert Redfield in *Peasant Society and Culture* suggested that all peasants, past and present, shared the same view of what he called "the good life." With characteristic modesty, Redfield wrote that this "may not be good science, but it is a way to get a discussion going." Redfield compared three peasant societies: the Mayan Indians of Yucatán he himself had studied, nineteenth-century English villagers in Surrey described by George Sturt and Hesiod's ancient Greeks. Redfield found so much likeness he wrote that

> if a peasant from any one of these three widely separated communities could have been transported by some convenient genie to any one of the others and equipped with a knowledge of the language in the village to which he had been moved, he would very quickly come to feel at home. And this would be because the fundamental orientations of life would be unchanged.

Redfield's perception confirmed what I had seen in all the villages I had studied. A peasant, or villager, has a distinct way and view of life, a distinct attitude toward the universe. The peasant, as Redfield said, is a recognizable and long-enduring human type. Was the peasant villager, I began to wonder as the years went by, essentially the *only* human type—in other words, the common cultural ancestor of us all?

Where villagers differed most was in religion, and I've found five main cultural variations in villages: African, Christian, Confucian,

Hindu and Islamic. They do much to explain why villagers culturally adjust to Western ideas and technology in the way they do. Their distant ancestors must have asked, "If the world and life have a meaning, what can it be?" and come up with different answers. Myths, magic and miraculous deliverance have great appeal in all villages. When I talk about religion it is not based on formal scholarship but on how villagers presented to me their own beliefs in words and acts. I haven't named Buddhism; it decides village behavior in Thailand, Burma, Sri Lanka and among Tibetans, but is a lesser influence than Confucianism or Hinduism elsewhere. Judaism, another surviving great religion, influences only Israeli villagers, who are generally uniquely urbanized and sophisticated. I once thought of Malay-Javanese as a sixth main culture since it is syncretic, a distinctive mix of animism, Hinduism and Islam. As the Muslim revival grows stronger in Indonesia and its neighbors, it makes more sense to join it with Islam.

If something as complex as world village society could be seen as a picture, *sub-Saharan or black Africa* would stand out as something different, as something out of the picture. Africa is where the human race began and where agriculture was invented and we had our first villages. The diseases of its tropical rain forests and hot, humid regions have kept its population down to 500 million, just a tenth of mankind, and comparatively isolated. Currently, AIDS is starting to have a demographic impact in Africa too. Man was able to evolve very slowly from a hunter-gatherer—still found among Botswana's quaintly named !Kung and other tribes—into a hunter, herder and slash-and-burn cultivator because population density was so low. I experienced something of this way of life among Sudan's Nuba tribesmen in 1975, its Dinkas in 1979 and Ghana's Ashantis in 1993. The arrival of modern medicine—first with the colonial memsaabs with their Epsom salts and sanitation, then with doctors and hospitals, and most crucially with sulfa drugs and antibiotics—doomed the old way of life, but mostly only in this century.

The past fifty years has seen a mass migration toward small settled farms, or *shambas*, on ground high, wet and cold enough to grow corn. Corn has rather quickly become the main diet of black Africa. Some argue that a hybrid maize belt irrigated with presently untapped rivers could someday transform Africa into a major food producer. This reality, like harnessing the hydroelectric potential of the Himalayan snows, is a long way away. As we shall later see, Norman Borlaug has developed a package of inputs he feels could double Africa's grain production now, but he is stymied by the World Bank's opposition to subsidizing fertilizer, an ideological leftover from the Reagan-Bush era. A pressing problem is cultural adjustment, as too few African men regard farming as the key to more income. Growing food is still too often seen as the woman's task. Elsewhere in the world, men, as hunters and herders, entered farming when draft animals did. This happened in Asia six thousand years ago and in Latin America about five thousand years ago. In parts of sub-Saharan Africa it is only happening now, and even then only in areas not infested with the tsetse fly. Africa, together with the Muslim world, is the last place where population growth, at 2.9 percent compared to the global rate of 1.6 percent in 1994, shows no sign of slowing down, while growth in per capita food production keeps falling, from 2.3 percent in the 1960s to about 1.2 percent now.

In peasant villages, *Christianity* tends to mean Roman Catholicism or, in Egypt and among Slavs and Serbs, the Coptic and Orthodox churches. Protestant peasant villagers are rare outside Africa, where they are missionary converts and everyday behavior is deeply influenced by tribalism. Poland is my sole experience with European Catholic peasants. Mostly, when we talk about Christian peasant villagers, we are talking about Latin postcolonial society, where Catholicism was brought by Spaniards, as in much of Latin America and the Philippines, by Portuguese, as in Brazil, and by the French, as in a few places like Vietnam. Even imported culture seems to matter more than race; Philippine society has much more in common with Latin America than with the Filipinos' racially akin Malays. Postcolonial Latin societies, as part of their feudal inheritance, tolerate a greater degree of social inequality than any other Asian or African culture except Hinduism. Symptoms are inequitable landownership, a chronic vulnerability to peasant uprisings and military juntas to prop up hereditary landowning families. Latins have a distinct preference for city life compared with Javanese, Egyptian or Bangladeshi villagers, whose "real life" only comes in visits home, whose culture most feel is superior to that found in city slums. This may explain why Latin America in 1994 was 72 percent urban (Asia and Africa were just over 30 percent urban), even if Latin America's uprooted peasantry was crowded into the most terrible slums.

One reason so much inequality is tolerated is that, broadly speaking, Latin villagers are of two kinds: descendants of transplanted European peasantry and African slaves, as in Brazil, or Indian peoples influenced by pre-Columbian civilization who are still in an incompletely developed relationship with their urban centers of largely Spanish intellectual thought, as in Mexico. In other words, what Redfield called the "great tradition" of urban philosopher, theologian and literary man and the "little tradition" of the peasant villager don't mesh as well as they do in other cultures. The elite of any Latin society, whether in South America or in the Philippines, are always European, those at the bottom rural indigenous Indians. In Mexico this creates a dual culture, part Western, part primitive. The Latin *macho* ethic keeps women too subordinate. As with Muslims, the whole society suffers, as women, the prime teachers of small children, are the custodians of culture. Latin villages are also held back by the Vatican's continued opposition to artificial contraception. Most Catholic peasants seem as conservative as Pope John Paul II except when it comes to birth control, which practically all village women favor.

Confucianism embraces East Asia—China, Japan, Korea, Taiwan, Vietnam, Hong Kong and Singapore, and ethnic Chinese in Indonesia (7.2 million), Thailand (5.8 million) and Malaysia (5.2 million). There are 2 million Confucian-influenced Chinese in the United States and another million in Latin America. The 55 million Chinese outside of China itself are great entrepreneurs. As Roderick MacFarquhar, now at Harvard, pointed out in a seminal essay in *The Economist* in 1980: "Confucianism is as important to the rise of the East Asian hypergrowth economies as the conjunction of Protestantism and the rise of capitalism in the West." If China is the awakening giant that could dominate the twenty-first century, the deep cultural attachment all Chinese feel toward their homeland and civilization will play a big role.

Confucianism in villages is probably best seen in Korea, where from 1392 to 1910 it was the mandatory state religion; nothing else was allowed. More of an ethical system than what we think of as religion, although there is a concept of heaven, Confucianism is basically a system of harmonious, subordinate relationships based on its fundamental adage, "Filial piety is the basis of all social conduct." A Confucian society's great advantage when it comes to adapting to new technology lies in its subordination of individual interest to group interest, just as the unrestricted freedom of individual choice and its substitution of "lifestyle" over inherited culture seems to have fragmented and weakened our own. Korean villages, which I first saw as a soldier in 1954, then preserved Confucian behavior in its purest state, which today survives only among the elderly. In Taiwan I found that Confucian ways are more obscured by Taoist and Buddhist influences. But faith in social harmony achieved through subordination to one's group is a common thread in every East Asian village, including those in China, where a counter-strain of individuality paradoxically works against it.

The Japanese, in farming as in everything else, set East Asia's high-tech standards. Way ahead in biotechnology, they grow their rice with an amazing variety of mini-machines, including mechanical rice transplanters and harvesters, helicopter spraying, vinyl sheeting, concrete-banked paddies and massive use of chemical fertilizer. Most of it is designed for a part-time cultivator with two or three acres who holds another job. The ordinary Japanese may work in a factory, and drive to his fields in a car, but he still feels deep ties to a small plot of ancestral land. This is why I feel it is shortsighted for the United States to make rice such a big trade issue. Japan, already 77 percent urban and with per capita GNP in 1994 of $28,200, making it one of the richest countries on earth, needs to keep its ties to the land for its continued cultural well-being.

Uniquely, the Japanese have managed to preserve something of a traditional village in their modern urban society. Almost every Japanese belongs to a small community with a villagelike set of mutual rights and obligations. The Japanese, whose ingenious smallholder mini-machines are in all East Asia's villages, are the region's biggest aid donors, trade partners and research inventors. To make Japanese biological and mini-mechanical technology work for them, other societies must set decent farm prices, get landholdings to a similar size, educate women, get up-to-date water systems and make sure all villagers have the opportunity to learn about new techniques and try them out. Vietnam, which, like Russia and China, is dropping its totalitarian ways in agriculture, is transforming its wet rice paddy farming with amazing speed. The Vietnamese are anxious to get back into the mainstream of world society and science. Farming depends too much on the stimulus of gain and private ownership to thrive under Communism.

China, which gave us Confucianism, is the big question mark. Mao Zedong's legacy to Chinese agriculture is mixed. He gave agriculture and the peasant top priority in investment, something India has failed to do. Yet the Great Leap Forward and the Cultural Revolution, along with forced collectivization, set back scientific research for years and in 1959–61 an estimated 30 million Chinese died of famine. Whether the present pragmatism of giving the peasant sufficient incentives and quasi-ownership of land can work without the whole Communist system coming apart as it has in Russia, remains to be seen.

Hinduism, the third main village culture, affects all South Asia, not just India, because the Hindu caste system shows up in Muslim Pakistan and Bangladesh and Buddhist Nepal and Sri Lanka. Caste is highly complex but in villages it can be seen simply as a contemporary relic of an ancient tradition, common to all early civilizations, of exchanging a cultivator's labor for a share in the harvest. The system breaks down once land, labor and rent are given money values and commercialized. Caste is incompatible with modern farming.

"Well, which is it?" *The Economist* asked famously years ago. "The world's largest democracy and the light of Asia or a crumbling antheap of starving people and starved cows?" You can still ask such a question about India, even with a middle class the size of Germany. We all have mental images of India: Sabu on an elephant; Myrna Loy dying of cholera so Tyrone Power can go back and save his people; Mahatma Gandhi striding into Buckingham Palace barelegged in his dhoti. There is the fabulous India of Kipling's *Kim;* the poignant India of Satyajit Ray's *Pather Panchali;* the imperial India of *The Jewel in the Crown;* the alien India of Mrs. Moore in the Marabar Caves; the political India of Nehru and his patrician era and daughter Indira, imperious empress shot by her own Sikh bodyguards; the horrible India of Katherine Mayo's 1927 best-seller, *Mother India,* with its depictions of abused child brides, widow burning, infanticide and untouchability; and finally the exotic India of naked holy men and bejeweled maharajas, snake charmers and Gunga Din.

Individual Indians, caught up in the inhumane conditions such density of people brings, react in many ways. The middle class does what it can to pursue what Arnold Toynbee called *Herodianism:* adopting foreign ways to live, in guarded privileged enclaves, as comfortably as possible in an unavoidable situation. The only place in India that seems unchanged since I first saw it in 1959 is the fashionable tree-shaded residential area of New Delhi where India's leaders live; at times it gets surrounded by as many as 100,000 soldiers and police.

The other reaction is what Toynbee called *Zealotism*, the impulse, in seethingly overcrowded conditions, to seize on religious or ethnic differences and retreat fanatically into one's own traditional culture. We see it in the rise of fundamentalism.

In India it takes the form of Hindu rage. In a 1963 interview, Nehru told me his greatest fear for the future was "fascism":

> By this I mean revolutionary forces trying to achieve their ends by violent or subversive means. By creating an atmosphere of violence and conflict, such forces may arise from any side. They can be Communist, social fascism led by big industrialists or Hindu fascism.

In 1960–62, when I taught two years at its university, Nagpur, the centermost city in India, happened to be the headquarters of the Rashtriya Swayamsevak Sangh, or National Volunteer Corps, known as the RSS, which stressed physical training, discipline and anti-Muslim attitudes. The New York *Times* reported in 1993:

> Its ideological godfather, Madhav Sadashiv Gowalkar, spoke of Muslims as "foreign elements" who should be absorbed or driven out, adding that Nazi Germany offered "a good lesson for us in Hindustan to learn and profit by."

I met Gowalkar, now dead, a couple of times in his labyrinthine headquarters in Nagpur's old city. A thin, black-bearded, rather imposing man, he is widely thought to have ordered Mahatma Gandhi's assassination. In Richard Attenborough's film *Gandhi* an actor playing Gowalkar is briefly seen, though not identified, sitting in a horse-drawn *tonga* giving orders to the actual killer just before the assassination. Fourteen years later, not fully aware of Gowalkar's historic role, I had heated arguments with him about Gandhi's solicitude for the Muslims and his idea that all men are united under one God.

India's worst communal violence came just after partition in 1947, when India and newly created Pakistan exchanged peoples, and close to a million Hindus, Muslims and Sikhs died. Nehru's vision of a secular, democratic and unified India weathered all challenges until 1990, when Hindus, many of them RSS men, stormed a four-hundred-year-old mosque at Ayodhya on the northern plains, after Hindus all over India had been stirred up by their claim that it was the birthplace of the Hindu god Ram. For months, then and when they finally destroyed the mosque in late 1992, India was on the brink of chaos as Hindu mobs torched and looted property and people were

killed with knives, guns, swords, bombs, attacked with fire and sul-
phuric acid, even decapitated. At times it looked as if Indian society
would collapse.

Yet India has proved remarkably resilient. In 1947 it could barely
feed its 360 million people; 1.5 million Bengalis died of famine in
1943. India's steel production was just a million tons, less than a
month's output at a single American mill. Nehru, in the same 1963
interview, told me just after the U.S. Congress voted not to fund a
giant steelworks, "Everything depends on steel." He got the Russians
to build it instead. In those days three-fourths of Indian men and nine
out of ten women were illiterate. Smallpox, now eradicated, and cholera were endemic. Today India not only feeds its 918 million people
but makes jets, rockets and nuclear devices. Its computer software
engineers are in demand all over the world. Among its 150 million-
plus middle class a very rapid spread of commercial television culture
means that the glorification of material gratification as the way to
happiness is promoted all over India by pop music, TV commercials,
Bombay films and videos. As expected, there has also been a big rise
in drug and alcohol consumption and crime.

Zealotism and Herodianism always seem to go together, as we saw
in the Shah's prerevolution Iran and are seeing now in Egypt. The
have-nots mired in deepening poverty react violently against the
haves in their heedless pursuit of the consumer society. India is a
potentially rich country with vast untapped resources in land, water,
natural gas and hydroelectric potential. Yet per capita GNP in 1994
was just $310. V. S. Naipaul, who is surprisingly upbeat about India,
describes Bombay's Dharavi slum, where 600,000 people are packed
into one square mile in unsanitary conditions:

> a general impression of blackness and greyness and mud, narrow rag-
> ged lanes curving out of view; then a side of the main road dug up;
> then black mud, with men and women and children defecating on the
> edge of a black lake, swamp and sewage, with a hellish oily irides-
> cence. The stench was barely supportable.

Hindu rage draws on such poverty, envy of the better-off and
deeply seated prejudices, mainly against India's 105 million Muslims,
but also Christians and Sikhs. Yet Hindu militancy is a contradiction
in terms. The religion has evolved over four thousand years with no
single founder or ecclesiastical order. There is a whole pantheon of
gods and goddesses. Just about the only two things all Hindus share

are acceptance of the Veda, sacred scriptures brought by the Aryans in about 1500 B.C., and the caste system. There are thousands of castes in India; the main four are *Brahman* or priest; *Kshatriya,* warrior; *Vaisya,* landowner or merchant; *Sudra,* peasant or farmer; and below them the untouchables, so lowly they have no caste and perform all the most menial tasks. Gandhi called them Harijans, the Children of God. Caste has its awful side, but it has always been the glue that held India's 576,000 villages together. The Hindu militants draw their ranks from poor, educated, lower-middle-class Brahmans in the cities, a disinherited, disgruntled lot.

Islam differs from the other four cultures found in villages in two essential ways. First, unlike the Confucians, Hindus, Africans and at least the Latin Christians, Muslims are geographically dispersed. Since the fall of Communism, Islam is the only idea left in the twentieth century to claim universal relevance. One of every six of the earth's inhabitants is Muslim. They live, since the addition of the six former Soviet Muslim republics, in seventy-six or just about half the world's countries. Second, within Islam a movement has arisen in reaction to the spread of Western ideas and science that is specifically anti-Western and can be antiscience.

I have spent time in seven Muslim villages, living in one, on the Upper Nile, for more than one year and going back many times the next, and making nine trips to one in Java between 1967 and 1993, in 1979 doing an AID-funded comparative study of thirty-five Javanese villages. To me, Islam is the most living religion because it decides everything you do. Muslim villagers take the admonitions of the Koran seriously, even literally, and try to obey them in their lives. Since the Prophet Muhammad lived in the sixth and seventh centuries and was influenced by the Arab culture of his time, this imposes an almost impossible code of social conduct on contemporary life. Imagine trying to adhere literally to the teachings of Jesus in modern daily living. Islam never had its Protestant Reformation.

As in the rejection of the world voiced by Jesus in the Gospels, there is a deeply held Islamic belief in the tragic view of life: that order and reason are limited and no scientific or technological progress can enlarge them. Faith is what counts, blind faith. As Shahhat, an Egyptian I've written about, told me repeatedly, "Everything is from Allah. We cannot decide anything. Everything is from God." We forget, as Muslims do not, that Islam was the world's most scientifically advanced society from about 600 A.D. to 1000 A.D. From this once-commanding position on the heights, Muslims descended to years of subordination, and in recent centuries to outright Western domination.

During my last visit to Egypt there seemed to be a new distress and resentment bubbling away under the surface of its slums and villages. American TV shows were being heedlessly beamed into them and avidly watched. Cairo's pro-American elite was pursuing Herodianism with a vengeance, clogging the ancient downtown streets with Mercedeses. The Islamic creed of equality dictates a political need for a lot of leveling down among people with as low a per capita GNP as the Egyptians ($630) or the Sudanese ($400). The poorest Muslims are torn between wanting technological advance and longing for the imagined purity of the Islamic past, between seeking a better life in this world, or the next. The Islamic revival will surely grow the more Western ideas penetrate the villages, and in some will produce irrational revolutionary rage.

Toynbee suggested as far back as 1946 that should the world ever become deeply divided enough between its rich white north and its poor black, brown and yellow south, Islam might rise again. Toynbee saw the extinction of race consciousness among Muslims as one of the great moral achievements of Islam. There is much about the Islamic revival that seems atavistic. Still it does compel a certain admiration. Islam alone, of the world's great religions, has chosen to give battle to, rather than to accommodate, an increasingly urban, secular and scientific postreligious age. The need to believe haunts Western Christians too; there is an impulse to turn back, to find someone who says he knows the truth, to find the shrine of some new god, or cult, or citadel where there is warmth and safety, as we see among our far-right fundamentalists. This is not, to me, true faith, but rather fear of the void when faith is gone.

Eastern Islam—that is, east of Pakistan, or perhaps Bangladesh—would probably stand aloof from any attempt to unify Islam to avenge ancient resentments against the Western world. The cultural heartland of the Muslim Malay peoples is the intensely crowded Indonesian island of Java, where two-thirds of the world's fourth most populous nation lives on a little island just 620 miles long. The 190 million Indonesians are scattered over a vast archipelago and were long pagan and animist, then Hindu—Bali still is—and were finally converted to Islam. This has left their culture uniquely syncretic. The Javanese have become skilled at taking what they want from other cultures while keeping to their own genius, in art, music, even religion. At the heart of this most artistic and theatrical of all village cultures is the *wayang kulit*, or shadow play, with its gamelan orchestra and all-night puppet performances. Indeed, the main ethical rival to Islam in Java is a theatrical conception, as I shall try to illustrate, whose kindly, earthy folk wisdom is a world away from the austerity of the Koran.

Javanese, like most Malays, first fiercely resisted Western ideas. Indonesia's anti-Communist bloodbath of the 1960s (memorably dramatized in the film *The Year of Living Dangerously*) was carried out by Muslims and soldiers; its chief victims were teachers and village modernizers. Western technology too, until the early 1970s, met the same resistance. Then, quite suddenly, contraceptives and scientific agriculture won enthusiastic acceptance. Since 1973–74, rice production has jumped from 12 million to nearly 30 million tons while the population growth rate has dropped from 2.4 percent in 1977 to 1.6 percent, close to 1 percent in East Java and Bali, remarkable for a people whose per capita GNP is still $670. Indonesia, sometimes called the hidden giant, is now being transformed by its Chinese entrepreneurs, its rich natural resources and its proximity to East Asia into an economic powerhouse. Its people, particularly the Javanese, have a gift for graceful survival. This seems to come from a readiness to accept the necessary new to preserve the desirable old.

In 1969, when I first set out to systematically report on villages, I asked the World Bank where to go to look at the population crisis. "Mauritius," I was told. "It may be having the world's first true Malthusian breakdown." So I went and lived for several months with fishermen whose lagoon, on the southern Indian Ocean island, was so depleted they had resorted to spearing octopus. Today Mauritius is thriving as a tax-free zone and its population of just over a million has pretty much stabilized.

Today if I had to pick what looks like a Malthusian breakdown I'd say Nepal. In 1990, at the peak of India's Hindu-Muslim killing, I stayed up in the Himalayan kingdom until the worst of the slaughter down on the plains was over. Nepal is every escapist's dream. But it makes you wonder how much time we've got. A 1990 World Bank report on Nepal urged more extensive birth control, improved roads, extended irrigation of small farms and efforts to boost off-farm incomes, enrich diets and increase literacy. Déjà vu: this is just what the experts were saying when Nepal so eagerly invited the rest of the world into the country back in 1952.

I first went to Nepal in 1959. As I came in by land over a mountain pass and suddenly had its vistas of golden-spired temples and terraced green rice paddies spread out before me, it felt like Ronald Colman's first sight of Shangri-La. The present King Birendra's grandfather seven years earlier had thrown off the feudal Rana autocracy, ending 2,500 years of self-imposed isolation. Mount Everest was conquered in 1953. Tourism went from none to 250,000 visitors a year, while billions of dollars in foreign aid poured in. The bad old days, when ragged, barefoot Tamangs hauled Rolls-Royces and grand pianos over the mountains for the Ranas' Italianate palaces, were over. There was talk of a Switzerland of the East. Nobody dreamed the number of Nepalis would go from 9 million to 21 million by 1994, with per capita GNP stuck at $170 a year, just between Ethiopia and Bangladesh. The old Hindu-Buddhist life out in the villages, where 92 percent of Nepalis still scratch the barest existence from the soil, faces such overcrowding as to be almost unlivable.

Kathmandu still has a little of its fairy-tale look. The old barefoot porters have given way to heavy traffic, with all its air pollution. Life that revolved around religion and hereditary caste distinctions has given way to buying and selling; money is what matters. Sanitation is still awful, cholera and malaria endemic, and porno, once seen only in temple carvings, is available on video.

Yet once you get away from Kathmandu, and the few Chinese-built roads around it, and go by foot over a range of hills or two, you find yourself in the old Nepal of the 1950s, a stunning land of clear blue skies, bracing air, improbably high snowy peaks, sun-drenched ridges over misty valleys and terraces green with wheat, rice and vegetables, even if there is no longer enough to go around. I did a lot of trekking in the five years I lived in India—Jomoson, Langtang Valley, He-lambu—and the villages, half hidden in banyan trees and clumps of bamboo, seem little changed. So do the people on the paths—bronze Tamangs and Gurungs, Gurkha soldiers on leave, maroon-clad Ti-betan monks, cowherds piping flutes, old women bent double under bales of grass. Farms are getting so tiny that if you ask a villager how much land he tills, he'll tell you in square feet. Cultivation is practically all by hoe.

Poor happy countries are harder to describe than poor miserable ones. Nepalis are still cheerful but their consciousness has changed radically. An old man planting potatoes told me, "Our irrigation system failed because the minister took his ten percent, the engineer his ten percent and the village chief his ten percent, so there wasn't enough money left to buy the water pipes." Another told of police harassment in the market. A third, recalling the old hermit-kingdom days, said, "Under the Ranas if a common person tried to learn to read and write, they might jail you or kill you." This kind of talk is new in villages where everybody used to revere King Birendra as a reincarnation of the Hindu god Vishnu.

I interviewed the king in 1973, when he was twenty-nine and not long out of Eton and Harvard. It was his second year on the throne and what I remember most, aside from the Wizard of Oz look of the palace itself, was the way his elderly courtiers kept interrupting. Western diplomats say he has been caught in a web of venal intrigue ever since. His wife, Aishwarya, from the feudal Rana clan, is said to be a Marie Antoinette who opposes all change. A 1789 mood hangs about Nepal. When more than 50,000 people tried to storm the palace in 1991, the army fired and killed over fifty men and women, but then refused to shoot any more. They told the king his absolute rule was now a constitutional monarchy, which he at once with relief accepted.

Nepal's big hope is its hydroelectric potential; its melting Himalayan snows could irrigate the Gangetic Plain. A current ten-year $1 billion project is a start. But it is an old hope and, like Nepali tempers, is wearing thin. Meanwhile young trekkers from Europe, America and Japan keep coming, to pursue their own lost horizon.

IV

The idea of cultural conflicts has regained some currency since the collapse of Communism. Harvard's Samuel Huntington has written:

> Civilization identity will be increasingly important in the future, and the world will be shaped in large measure by interactions among seven or eight major civilizations. These include Western, Confucian, Japanese, Islamic, Hindu, Slavic-Orthodox, Latin American and possibly African civilization. The most important conflicts of the future will occur along the cultural fault lines separating these civilizations from one another.

In terms of village behavior I lump Western, Slavic-Orthodox and Latin American together as fundamentally Christian, and put Japan, despite its feudal past, with the Confucians. I would certainly rank African villagers, with their often superior morality, culturally equal. In *A Study of History*, Toynbee identified twenty-one major civilizations; he later expanded this to thirty-one at least. He said five were still current: Western, Byzantine, Islamic, Hindu and Far Eastern.

There are rumblings, to be sure, along the great Christian-Muslim fault that runs across Eurasia and Africa. And Americans have a habit of looking at problems in terms of the politics of the surface, instead of the cultural trends beneath the surface. This makes us slow to see long-term changes like the resurgence of Confucian East Asia or Islamic militancy or—the one that haunts us—Hanoi's strategy of subversion in Vietnam, weakening the Confucianism that was, and is, Communism's real adversary there, so that Hanoi was able to use our great military power, judo-like, against us, leaving us baffled and deeply frustrated.

But I do not see culture, village-based and religion-centered as it is, supplanting the nation-state and political ideology. A good many nations, it is true, do not really qualify as whole societies but are arbitrarily detached fragments of them. Villagers identify themselves with historically enduring cultures: they are Punjabis, not Indians; Javanese, not Indonesians; members of the Kamba or Dinka tribe, not Kenyans or Sudanese. Rather than a clash of civilizations, I prefer Toynbee's more general argument that new forms of the great Eastern religions might rise again to defeat the technologically superior West on a spiritual plane. In Britain, long the leader of the West, there is a failure of nerve, a loss of faith, a sense of decline. We begin to see some of the same self-abdication of leadership and disbelief in liberal ideals and progress in our own country.

The idea that civilizations rise and fall, grow and decay, much occupied French and German thinkers in the late eighteenth century. Oswald Spengler picked up the idea in his *Decline of the West* and argued that civilizations, like the seasons, rose and fell in conformity to a fixed timetable. Toynbee generally agreed, but he argued that the West's decline was by no means predestined. "What shall we do to be saved?" he asked.

In politics, establish a constitutional cooperative system of world government. In economics, find working compromises (varying according to the practical requirements of different places and times) between free enterprise and socialism. In the life of the spirit, put the secular superstructure back onto religious foundations.

Toynbee regarded the religious task as most important even if the other two were more urgent, and today, half a century later, they have pretty much been achieved. He felt that a spiritual failure could have fatal consequences.

> Future historians will say, I think, that the great event of the twentieth century was the impact of Western civilization upon all the other living societies of the world of that day. They will say of this impact that it was so powerful and so pervasive that it turned the lives of all its victims upside down and inside out—affecting the behavior, outlook, feelings, and beliefs of individual men, women and children in an intimate way, touching chords in human souls that are not touched by mere external material forces—however ponderous and terrifying.

Toynbee's central point was that the West had unified the earth as never before with its technology, but had failed to do the same with its religion. He believed that the majority of mankind was suffering from the same spiritual starvation that led to the rise of Christianity amid the disintegrating Greco-Roman civilization. Toynbee asked:

> Is something like this historic denouement of the Greco-Roman story going to be written into the unfinished story of the world's encounter with the West? We cannot say, since we cannot foretell the future. We can only see that something which has actually happened once, in another episode of history, must at least be one of the possibilities that lie ahead of us.

William McNeill, who has seen technology, not religion, as the prime engine of historical change, has also been influenced by Robert Redfield's anthropological view that human society is a continuum, with its more "civilized" cities, when compared with villages, being more secular, diverse and incoherent, and winning their power and wealth at a heavy price in alienation, anomie and personal isolation. The great divide, to both McNeill and Redfield, has not been so much between civilizations, or the language, history, religion, customs and institutions that make up their distinct cultures, but has been the gap between village and city, a gap both have seen as closing in the final years of the twentieth century.

Plato, in his critique of reason, contrasted the "inflamed society" of the city with the "simple society" of the peasant village. Almost all the great religions had rural origins, while all the great political ideologies came from cities. Prophets come from villages. These ideologies include Western industrial capitalism and Communist collectivism, the two main development choices offered peasant societies in the postcolonial world. Capitalism has failed to supply sufficient jobs and income, and it still remains to be seen whether free-market policies can take hold in places as poor as Africa and whether America itself can prosper without a big weapons budget. Communism, by denying villagers privately owned land, failed to provide sufficient incentives. The collapse of Communism seems definitive in Russia, but its replacement seems profoundly uncertain. Toynbee, interestingly, called Communism "another of our latter-day religions," "a leaf taken from the book of Christianity—a leaf torn out and misread."

To Aristotle, the three basic institutions of village life were property, marriage and the family. To him, Communism would have broken down because humans need the stimulus of gain and private ownership for hard work and husbandry. In *Politics* he wrote:

> That which is common to the greatest number has the least attention bestowed upon it. Everyone thinks chiefly of his own, hardly ever of the public interest . . . There is always a difficulty in living together or having things in common, but especially in having common property.

Aristotle believed the power of habit, or "second nature," was enough to defeat revolutions. I was deeply shocked on a visit to Russia in late 1991 to see how, away from the Kremlin, with its gilded domes and crosses glittering in the sunshine, such a profound pall of unease hung over Moscow.

Communism was more of a colossal failure than I had imagined, and nothing prepares you for Moscow's grandiose squalor, with its unwashed windows, mud-encrusted cars, potholed streets, beggars and drunks and prostitutes—all overlooked by Stalin's seven Gothic skyscrapers, now, I was told, plagued by cockroaches and rats. Communist-era architecture reflects the system that inspired it. So, in St. Petersburg, do the palaces of Russia's other frantic attempt to catch up with the West. Peter the Great tried in 1689–1725 and Stalin, in 1928–53. In both periods, the Russians split into those who welcomed the new ideas and those who wanted to escape the evils of Western ideas and preserve authentic Orthodox Russian culture. Again Toynbee's Zealots, the people, in Toynbee's words, who take "refuge from the unknown in the familiar" and "archaism evoked by foreign pressure."

The Slavophiles sought to keep the rural institution of the *mir*, the periodic redistribution of land to match each family's size. Peasants in old Russia felt that to enrich oneself in the marketplace by buying and selling was to cheat one's neighbors. Professor McNeill says this peasant antipathy toward buying and selling for personal gain, which I find very common in villages, may account for Russian and Eastern European anti-Semitism, since so much of trade and moneylending was left to Jews.

Today, unlike in the days of Peter the Great or even Stalin, Russia no longer has a vast peasantry. In 1914, 80 percent of Russians were peasant cultivators. In 1994, only one-third of them remain in agriculture and many, if not most, of these have been transformed from peasants into a rural proletariat—that is, hired workers on fixed times and wages like factory hands. Nonetheless, physically many of the old peasant villages remain and a majority of the Russians are children or grandchildren of peasants, so some of the old culture remains. I found that Polish and Russian villages looked alike, especially the pre-1917 wooden houses with their gardens and picket fences. And in Russia, rural churches were being reopened and pictures of the Virgin Mary and Jesus were reappearing in the houses.

On the 1991 visit one saw the same birch forests as in Poland, ablaze with yellow leaves, but in Russia the fields were full of soldiers harvesting potatoes, a sign of a starkly militarized society. There were also bent, gray figures, gleaners from the city, scavenging what few potatoes the soldiers left behind. This illustrates another change Professor McNeill sees between the 1990s and earlier times: Russia's shrinking workforce. Peter the Great and Stalin were able to shift manpower from farm to factory, he says, because the remaining peasantry could feed the Russian people. Peter did this through natural increase, Stalin through machinery on big collective farms, which, as in American agriculture, enabled fewer people to grow more food.

In about 1960 this arrangement ceased to work in Russia, which began to experience chronic food shortages. At first I used to attribute these to bad weather and temporary crop failures, but it was permanent. As McNeill points out, Russia had badly depleted both its human and its natural resources. The only surplus labor supply left consisted of Muslims, with historic apathy toward Russians, a mutual distrust heightened by the war in Afghanistan and the Islamic revival.

I found in 1991 that most Moscow families were hoarding sacks of potatoes, as they did in World War II. Queues abounded. It was ugly to see angry and apprehensive people push and shove just to take home a handful of sausages. Alarmingly little food was visibly on sale, although if Russians invited you to their homes, they would miraculously produce something like a beef roast, vegetables, salad and a bottle of cognac.

It has been said Russia needs to re-create its peasantry. Certainly it needs to redistribute collectivized land back to families. It seems inexplicable that neither Mikhail Gorbachev nor Boris Yeltsin rushed to give land back to the rural people. Anatoli A. Sobchak, St. Petersburg's mayor, said in 1992, "The main mistake has been the government has not pursued a true land reform. They should have dropped everything else and focused on giving land to anybody who is prepared to use it." By early 1994 most of Russia's 26,000 state and collective farms had reorganized into some form of share enterprise, in which each worker in theory could get land and assets to start an individual peasant farm. By July 1993, there were close to 260,000 of these in Russia, up from 49,000 in 1992 and 1,000 at the end of 1990. But they account for only 5 percent of Russia's rural population and about 4 percent of its total cropland. The holders of 41 million small garden or orchard plots, both in cities and in villages, have been given full ownership rights. But the sale and mortgage of most farmland is still highly restricted, with state-owned, state-run collective farms still heavily subsidized and running with wage-earning workers as before. An October 1993 decree confirmed and greatly expanded land rights, but without much practical effect. Unlike in China, in Russia the old system is greatly resisting family farms.

In talks with peasants, it was evident how badly Russia needed to privatize land. Villagers were eager to raise the cows and pigs that could do much to solve Russia's food problem, but they needed a little land to grow feed crops and hay.

"It's impossible to keep a cow," a forty-five-year-old irrigation worker, Igor Drykhunov, told me. He worked, as do most rural Russians, on a state farm. His house stood on a half-hectare of land. Besides cultivating a vegetable garden, he kept sheep, two pigs, geese, chickens and a goat, which he milked for about two kilograms a day. He killed one pig at Easter and another at Christmas, but the pork and much of his other produce went to feed himself, his wife and two sons. He fished when he could and dried the fish for winter. Fish were strung out like laundry in the kitchen. A year before, Drykhunov had bought a secondhand tractor from the collective farm where he worked. He used the tractor to help his friends and didn't charge for it. Evidently the old peasant ideal of equality is still very much alive in the Russian consciousness.

In 1917 Lenin promised land to the tiller. But after 1928, when collectivization began, Stalin took land back from the peasantry. He wanted to requisition grain to feed expanded numbers of industrial workers. The mechanization of agriculture allowed these workers to be recruited from the peasantry. It worked for a little more than thirty years, and then, as I've said, Russia began to be chronically short of food. Unless Lenin's promise is at last redeemed, Russia will never feed itself again. Nobody knows what an extreme disruption of a modern economy could mean, but Sarajevo suggests that mass starvation can come quickly without outside aid. Machine-based, collectivized farming is far more vulnerable to a breakdown in the input and marketing system than subsistence peasant agriculture, in which each family stores its own food.

Which is why, of course, Deng Xiaoping saw the wisdom of going back to the family farm in China. On trips in 1980 and 1983 to villages on the North China plains and in 1991 in Guangdong province near Hong Kong, I found that once you stepped inside a peasant family's household walls, property, marriage and the family mattered just as much as in any village. There were the same proudly displayed photographs, the same complaints about the expenses of weddings, the same deference shown to old people, even the same mind-numbing homemade country liquor that is, alas, the gesture of having broken the social ice from Africa to India. Unlike city workers, Chinese peasants get no pensions and look after old people at home. Garden plots used to be allocated and detached and long before Deng's reforms vegetables could be grown for sale. Every family raised a pig or two with Mao Zedong's blessing: "The pig is a fertilizer factory on four legs."

Unlike the gross neglect of nearly all public property in China, something Aristotle would nod his head over, the flowers, fruit trees and humble houses behind tall village walls were well maintained. My first trip to China was the most surprising; far from robots in blue uniforms, as one somehow expected, the villagers seemed individualistic, Confucian and civilized. This must be what Mao had in mind when he told Nixon, "I have only been able to change a few places in the vicinity of Peking." The big question about China is this very individualism, which, along with Chinese acquisitiveness and a lack of discipline, some argue, will prevent it from becoming an economic powerhouse like Japan. Now that the Soviet Union has crumbled, China is the last empire, ruling a vast land with many nonethnic Chinese within imperial frontiers. Could it come apart too, or will, as some predict, the Middle Kingdom again become the center of the earth? If Communism is to survive in China it has to adopt Deng Xiaoping's "socialism with Chinese characteristics"—Confucian-style capitalism. British sinologist Roderick MacFarquhar has put it: "Communism in China will probably end not with a bang but a whimper."

Both Russia and China leave no doubt in one's mind that a universal village culture does exist, and that the Russians want land of their own to cultivate as much as anyone else. Russia should look to Poland, where more than 80 percent of farming is still done by individual family owners, whose average farm is six hectares, half of it tilled and the rest in pasture and woods. This is enough to feed a family and sell meat and milk on the market. Poland, with an abundance of pork, veal, beef, milk, butter, cheese, grain, fruit and vegetables, has all the resilience of a peasant society. If its market economy, industry and politics are in a shambles—the disappointed Poles even elected a parliament dominated by former Communists and leftists in late 1993 —its rural people stay fed.

It is fitting that here we leave the great issues of world politics for the simple daily life of ordinary peasants in their village in the Polish-Russian borderlands. To reach for a generalization about what is happening to such villagers, as their traditional culture is dying with the century, we need to look at them in a very human way. Not in terms of a fixed state, as statistics and even factual evidence tend to do, but as individual actors caught in a vast, ongoing, dynamic revolutionary drama in perpetual kaleidoscopic movement who are making choices and taking actions to learn, adjust and survive.

"The subject of history is the life of peoples and of humanity," said Tolstoy, who argued that "great" events were the sum of innumerable small individual actions by countless numbers of people, whether they be Napoleon or the peasant Platon Karatayev. Keep in mind as we set out in a horsecart into the Polish woods on an idyllic summer day that any political system arbitrarily imposed on such villagers by cities is fated, one might say doomed, to be ephemeral. It is technology, not politics, that can permanently alter human behavior because it transforms the economic determinants of that behavior. On that much, Karl Marx was right. No political ideology, no matter how totalitarian, has ever been able to radically change village culture in any lasting way. Not Marxism-Leninism. Not Maoism.

II

Winter Nights, Summer Days: After Communism

CAST OF CHARACTERS

JÓZEF SADOWSKI, 45, peasant, Jurek's cousin
  HELENA, 70, his mother
HENRYK SADOWSKI, 67, peasant, Jurek's cousin, deported to
  Siberia, ex-Red Army
ANTONINA BOKUŃ, 60, peasant, Jurek's friend and neighbor
BOROWSKI FAMILY, Jurek's friends in Babino
  ANDRE, 27, modern farmer
  ALEK, 30, unemployed printer
  JACEK, 28, factory worker
  TERESA, 60s, their mother
JANEK, 50, peasant, a saintly fool
FERENC BOKUŃ, 70s, poor peasant
  EUGENIA, 70s, his sister

IN THE MIDDLE of the August haying there came a wet spell. It turned chilly and rained for days. The road from Popowlany down to the Narew River was thick with mud. Horsecarts slipped and slid in deep ruts left by tractors. Potholes and gullies appeared. Everybody went about drenched and with lumps of wet, heavy mud sticking to their rubber boots.

"Rain, rain. Still it rains," groaned Jurek Sadowski, getting up. He could hear the muffled cries of neighbors as they drove their cows to pasture. Jurek washed himself, snuffling and splashing at the kitchen sink. He wiped his face on the tail of his shirt, no towel being handy. Soon he was headed for the river in drizzling rain, wheeling his milk can and a pail on an old bicycle. His house was third from last. Once past the peasant farmsteads the ground sloped gently down to the Narew, two-thirds of a mile from Popowlany. Slowly the sky paled and foliage and clouds of smoke could be seen more clearly. In the bluish wet light, Jurek hurried through a dripping woods of birches, larches and willows. He came out in an open pasture, where his three cows, chained and tethered, munched on grass.

Jurek was a tall, heavy-shouldered Pole in his late forties with a long, shaggy reddish mustache and a weathered, sun-beaten face. He wore a peasant's cloth cap over his unkempt, uncut hair and a sheep-skin jacket against the rain. He was evidently strong and healthy, judging by the long strides he made and the ease with which he swung about the heavy milk can. A childhood illness had left him somewhat deaf, so his father took him out of school after only two years. He was sent to do a man's work in the fields when just nine years old. By the time he was seventeen, Jurek was the best mower in Popowlany. He could scythe a hectare of grass in a single day, twice as much as most men could do. Even now, when he cut grass, every sweep of the scythe showed his peasant's skill and strength.

His deafness made him seem gruff and taciturn. Few strangers, who thought him coarse at first, guessed he was so hard of hearing or that he was not as dour as he looked. He read lips and wore a tiny battery-powered hearing aid the government provided. Only when one spoke loudly to him from behind could one see how deaf he was. Jurek was respected in the village as a good neighbor and a pious Catholic, with a good deal of humor. When he suddenly grinned and his eyes crinkled up and he showed his uneven teeth, his whole face lit up like a small boy's.

Sadness held him much of the time. His wife, Jadwiga, as tall, hardy and good-natured as himself, after the death of their day-old son followed three miscarriages, had gone off to New York, where she now worked in a bakery in Brooklyn. "She'll come home soon," the neighbors kept telling him. But what was there in Popowlany for her to come back to? Jurek missed her terribly and tried to be as hopeful as he could. Partly Jadwiga went off to America to make money. His father, Stanisław Sadowski, had not given him the land before she went. The old man had to give up all but a third of a hectare of his land to be eligible for a retirement pension, equivalent in Polish zlotys to about sixty dollars a month. So, at last, Jurek possessed eight and a half hectares of his own, half of them tilled fields scattered about the western and southern sides of Popowlany and the rest woods and pastureland along the Narew River. Four hectares went to a sister in another village, where the father went to live. He came back once a month to collect his pension from the village postman and spend an evening saying the rosary with his circle of elderly village men.

As he went into the parish church in the nearby town of Tykocin each Sunday, Jurek stopped just inside the door to dip his fingers in the holy water, make the sign of the cross and kiss the feet of a life-size Jesus being crucified. All the men did. Sometimes after mass Jurek could be seen in the wooded cemetery on the road from Tykocin to Popowlany. He entered the wrought-iron gate and went down a long broad avenue of poplars, a tall, bent figure, cap in hand, among all the white crosses and statues of angels. There were carefully tended flowers on most of the graves and a smell of freshly dug earth. Jurek stopped at a little white monument, kneeled to pull a few weeds and stood up again to look at it for a long time. If anyone came up to him, Jurek would say in a hushed voice, "My son."

Seeing Jadwiga's unhappiness, Jurek built her a new house of cement bricks with an iron roof by taking a loan at 5 percent interest from the bank in Białystok. This city, twenty miles to the east and about halfway to the frontier with Byelarus, with the great Russian steppe beyond, had two large onion-towered Russian Orthodox churches at its center. These borderlands had changed rulers many times in the past, and Popowlany's oldest people remembered swearing allegiance to the Czar in St. Petersburg.

When Jadwiga did not return, Jurek closed off two of the house's four rooms. He lived in the large sunlit kitchen with its big white porcelain-tile stove, which kept the whole house warm in winter, and what was intended as a front parlor, where he kept a couch with pillows and a feather bed thrown across. A table with a soiled cloth faced a television set. Here Jurek took his simple meals of cheese, sausage, onions, borscht and rye bread, often washed down with a little vodka or beer. He read the Białystok paper as he ate or watched the evening TV news from Warsaw. Self-educated, Jurek kept a lively interest in what was going on in Poland and the world. Sometimes he left the set on and watched, bemused, *Dallas* or *Dynasty* before going to feed the pigs.

Jurek often swept the kitchen floor but the house was none too clean. From a back hall, full of coats and muddy boots and debris, which led out onto a porch, a steep wooden staircase rose to an attic, where clothes on wet days were hung to dry. If Jurek climbed the stairs quickly, thumping in his heavy boots, he could hear mice scurry to hide under the eaves. As in all of Popowlany's houses, there were lace curtains on the windows and large framed pictures of Jesus on most of the walls. Here a baby in Mary's lap, there an anguished man at prayer in the Garden of Gethsemane as Judas and the Roman soldiers approached. In the front room, in a gilded frame, was a print of Poland's holiest relic, the painting of the Black Madonna of Częstochowa with the saber marks on her chin left by a Swedish soldier. Most Poles believed these cuts in the picture had actually bled.

In time Jurek saved two thousand dollars to go to America. He wanted to persuade Jadwiga to come home. But every time he made the four-hour train journey to Warsaw, and applied for a visa, he was turned away. With a wife already there, a Polish clerk would tell him, he would surely overstay his visa, take a job and become an illegal immigrant. In 1987 Jadwiga sent him a thousand dollars to buy an Ursus Polish tractor. The next year came three thousand for a small Czechoslovakian Skoda car. She also sent clothes—blue jeans, flannel shirts, a fleece-lined denim jacket for doing chores in winter, a cap which said: I ♥ NEW YORK.

She never came home. But Agneshka, Jurek's cousin, whose parents lived across the road, quite often did. Agneshka went to New York in 1973 and met and married Felipe, a handsome Puerto Rican, but she kept her Polish passport. This summer they had come over with their two children. Felipe, on a short holiday, had returned to his job.

Jurek enjoyed his cousin's visits. Agneshka was a warm, generous woman of thirty-nine, plump and healthy, and always in good spirits. Everything amused her, and if a hot temper sometimes flashed, she was at once over it. The Sadowskis' three-room cement-brick house took on new life whenever Agneshka was there. Jurek was often invited to meals and the kitchen table always had a clean white cloth, flowers in the windows and a freshly baked cake to go with the coffee Agneshka always kept on the stove. Jurek, after his own simple fare, greatly enjoyed their pork cutlets, roast beef and chicken, sliced ham and cold cuts, mashed potatoes, borscht or macaroni soup, sausages, cheeses, pickles and the lettuce and tomato salads Agneshka, who worried about her figure, had introduced from America.

In the wet weather, Jurek often joined the family as they sat around the kitchen, waiting for the rain to end. If anybody came by on foot or on a tractor or horsecart, Agneshka or Zofia, her mother, would hurry to the window and pull back the curtain to see who it was. The rain ruined everything. For days it was hard for Jurek to do any sort of work except to milk the cows and feed the pigs. *"Oiy, yoi, yoi,"* he would lament, as the villagers did, as if to show how hard life was.

The muddy, dark days ended at last. Patches of bright clear blue appeared in the sky. The sun broke out, turning the weather glorious. As the sun dried the fields, Agneshka said, after being cooped up so long, she wanted to go to the woods by the river and pick hazelnuts. Her father, Mieczysław Sadowski, whom the family called Grandfather and his friends called Mietek, agreed to take her and the children in his long, narrow wooden horsecart. Long Popowlany's blacksmith, he now did little but look after his horse. They invited Jurek to come along.

When the horse was in harness, Grandfather shouted gruffly for everybody to climb on. The two children came running, and Agneshka, her light brown hair flying, climbed up to sit beside Jurek and her father, who held the reins. They set off. The horse's hooves made a loud clopping sound on the cobblestones. Marigolds, zinnias and hollyhocks, after so much rain, bloomed brightly from all the gardens. Only Jurek's was neglected, his sunflowers hanging their heavy yellow-and-brown heads so low they could hardly be seen among all the thistles and stinging nettles. Wind rustled the poplar leaves overhead. The air was fresh and fragrant. Sun flooded the road in front of them, and cawing crows circled the cart.

"Panie Boże depomoz! May God help you!" called a stout, fair man with flaxen hair who stood with a hoe in his vegetable garden. Rosy-cheeked and broad-chested, with an enormous stomach, his face wet with sweat, he looked very robust. This was Dominik Włoskowski, Jurek's closest friend since childhood. His house, more properly speaking an old wooden cabin rather than a house, was the poorest in the village. The son of a landless peasant, Dominik as a boy had gone about barefoot and in rags, with scarcely enough to eat. Now he made up for it with a gargantuan appetite.

The house had long been deserted. Somehow Dominik managed to get himself educated and as a member of Poland's United Peasant Party, an ally of the Communists for forty years, rose from one minor post in the local agricultural bureaucracy to another. In 1990 the name was changed to Polish Peasant Party, and running under its banner that May, Dominik surprised everybody by becoming Tykocin's first freely elected mayor since the 1930s. He had wrecked his car and had to take buses or cadge rides from Białystok, where he and his wife and two children in college now lived. But every Saturday, Dominik was back in his garden in Popowlany, busy from morning to night with his hoe, spade and watering pot. Sometimes he stayed overnight with Jurek, sleeping on a sofa. He and Jurek would talk politics over a bottle until the wee hours. Like most Poles, Jurek was partial to vodka, though three or four glasses made him tipsy, while Dominik could outdrink anybody for miles around.

As the horsecart rumbled by, Agneshka's son, Robert, who was nine, was excited to see a long-legged white stork standing on its nest in Dominik's chimney. Jurek said the same stork came each April and flew off to Africa in September. When a bird flitted by the cart, Grandfather turned around to tell the children, "When the swallow flies next to the ground it will rain."

Agneshka gave a peal of laughter. She knew all her father's old homilies, and she repeated another: "When the swallow flies under a cow it won't give milk."

Jurek beamed. "Oh, the old people believe everything. One believes in God, the next the Devil." Ahead was a neglected farmstead, its wood so weathered the grain in the siding stood out. Moss on an old thatched barn roof was a bright green. Geese ran about apples rotting on the grass. Grandfather told them old Ferenc, who lived there, was a lazy drunkard. Jurek agreed. "If you bring a bottle he'll drop everything. And he'll talk your ear off until the bottle's finished." He told Agneshka, "He lives with his sister these days. Eugenia came home after her husband died."

"You'll get sick if you go there," Grandfather said. "It's so dark inside. Even the roof is falling down. Many years ago when their parents were alive it was nice." He took off his cap and squinted at the nearest field, his baldness glistening in the sun. "Nobody cut this rye."

"He did cut some but he hasn't finished yet, all this rain," Jurek said. "He's mowing it with a scythe in the old way."

Grandfather snorted disapproval. "He scythes one month and hasn't finished yet!" Agneshka, seeing him squint, worried about her father. He had cataracts but was afraid to see a doctor. Zofia, just the opposite, feared catching cold so much she dressed in heavy clothes and even on a fine August day like this kept a fire going in the oven. She forever complained about her rheumatism and sinus trouble and at the slightest twinge was off to the free government clinics in Tykocin and Białystok for pills and injections and X-rays.

The cart bumped along the ruts and Popowlany was left behind. They entered a copse of birch trees and the shaded road was still muddy from the rains. It was cooler in the dappled shade. The sound of church bells tolling the hour came faintly from Tykocin, a mile away. When they came out into the bright sun of pastureland again, clumps of pale green willows and darker green reed grass showed where the river was. On both sides of the cart track were yellow foxgloves. Little blue forget-me-nots were scattered in the grass.

As soon as they entered another patch of woods, Grandfather reined in the horse and rolled his tongue, "T-r-r-r-r-r, t-r-r-r-r . . ." The cart came to a standstill. Here, all about, were hazelnut bushes, some higher than a man's head. Grandfather stayed where he was, but Jurek, Agneshka and the two children jumped off the cart and went to the bushes, going from one to the next. Robert darted every which way. Ania, a sulky fourteen-year-old, soon grew bored and wished she had stayed back with her girlfriends in the village to watch TV. The ground beneath the shadowed verge was thick with green ferns and lilies of the valley.

"If you can't see the nuts," Agneshka called to the children, "run your hand down a branch and feel them." The chestnut horse, swishing its blond mane, munched on the grass, browsed and snorted. Agneshka gave a delighted cry when she found some mushrooms and her father got off the cart to see. Robert spotted a brown hare, which darted off at once. He chased it, hoping to see it again, and whistled. Jurek was tall enough to reach up and bend down the highest branches so Agneshka could pick off the still-green fruit. It would turn reddish brown as it ripened. "Don't break any branches," she cautioned him. "Be careful."

"These look better and tastier," he said. "Oh, here's more. Those bushes on the other side in the shade."

Cries of alarm came from the children. The horse, tired of munching grass in one place, had started to go forward. Jurek shouted the familiar command, "T-r-r-r-r!" and the horse stopped. "Robert was holding a stick and that scared it," Ania tattled. Agneshka found some pink stalks of raw sorrel. "I'll cook some for supper," she said, gathering it up in her apron. She was enjoying herself.

Grandfather went back to the cart and found Ania sitting there. "Go and look for hazelnuts," he told her. She ignored him, pouting. Soon they all came back, climbed on the cart, and Grandfather picked up the reins and smacked his lips loudly, the signal to the horse to go. Agneshka told the children Jurek's land was just ahead. There had been Sadowskis in Popowlany for over four hundred years and Jurek's land was in eight places, having been handed down generation after generation. "Even if it's your own woods in Poland you must get permission to cut down a tree," Agneshka told them. "If you come upon a fallen tree, you can gather firewood from that. But you can't cut down a living tree." They stopped in Jurek's woods to look among the ferns for mushrooms. On the sunny edge of the trees there was a row of big anthills, each at the bottom of the trunk of a white-barked birch tree. The anthills throbbed with life and Robert ran to take a closer look. "They're protected too," his mother called after him, saying they were the food of near-extinct birds. "Don't destroy a hill of those big black ants or you'll go to jail!" Robert bent over an anthill. When he saw no one was looking, he gave it a kick. The insects frantically ran in all directions, trying to get away from this unexpected catastrophe.

"There are many here!" cried Jurek, bending down a hazelnut branch.

"Oh, there are many!" Agneshka came running. "Maybe we should leave some for other people who come."

"Would they leave for us?"

"Maybe we should leave a few, Jurek. If they come it will be a bad day for them if they find nothing. And these are very green. Maybe they're not ripe."

"They're ripe."

"They don't look ripe to me."

Robert chased some yellow butterflies fluttering about the ferns. Busy exploring, he spotted a squirrel eating seeds, but it ran away as soon as he got close. Then he came upon the red cap of a toadstool. He was about to pick it when Jurek came up. "That's poison," Jurek told him. "You can kill flies with it. A long time ago people would take it to the house, put sugar on it and flies would die if they landed on it. A man will also die if he eats a red toadstool." Robert wanted to take one home but Agneshka wouldn't hear of it.

Jurek sniffed about, trying to catch the smell of mushrooms. Agneshka wondered if lilies of the valley would grow if she took some seeds back to America. She bent to pick some and her face brushed into a web full of tiny spiders. She screamed, waved it aside and at once moved into a second web. "Oh, another one!" she cried, giving up. Robert found some acorns and Jurek told him they attracted wild boars from the great Puszcza of Kniszyn just a few miles away. "Boars are not dangerous unless you find a mother with a baby," he told the boy.

Robert wanted to know about the *puszcza*. It was a vast primeval forest on the Russian-Polish borderlands, Jurek told him, at least ten thousand years old, maybe older, that began near Popowlany. The villagers knew many legends about the *puszcza:* "There used to be water and swamps all over here too," Jurek told the boy. Agneshka said she well remembered how the year she left for America engineers came to Popowlany to straighten the course of the river, which had always twisted and turned, and to drain the swamps. Even now, she said, along the Narew there were wet places where the earth was soft and springy. She joked about her plumpness. "You can run, you're light," she told Robert. "When you're like me, you have to watch your step. I'm afraid I might sink into a bog."

Running ahead, Robert found some holes overgrown with reed

grass. When they caught up with him, Jurek said, "The deer make these little ditches. And then they lie down and go to sleep." Deeper in the woods, he went on, there were also foxholes dug by soldiers in the last war. He himself had come across rusted and corroded old rifles, bayonets and shells. For this region was one of the great battlefields of Europe. Napoleon's Grand Armée in its 1812 retreat from Moscow had come down the banks of the Narew River. And not thirty miles away, many mass graves had been discovered of skeletons lying face-down in rows, their hands bound behind them with barbed wire. Some might be Jews, some anti-Communists or anti-Nazis, and some were Home Army partisans executed in 1945. These woods had seen so many killings. The Russians hanged Polish insurgents from trees here in the January Revolution of 1863, when the Poles for fifteen months vainly fought to be free. "Actually," Jurek told Robert, "that's how the Sadowskis got their land." Popowlany, in the Byelarussian language, meant "place of the priests." Until 1863 the village was a feudal estate owned by some Orthodox Russian clergy. The local peasants, virtual serfs, worked for the priests five days a week and for themselves two days. When the uprising failed, the shaken Czar Alexander II put the rebels' decree to enfranchise the peasants into effect. More than fifteen hundred estates belonging to Polish nobles or the clergy were confiscated. In Popowlany the Czar's men seized the land from the priests and gave it in freehold to four peasants: Sadowski, Sakowicz, Komorowski and Bokuń. Their descendants made up most of Popowlany's people in the 1990s.

"A few of the Home Army stayed in the *puszcza* until 1957," Jurek told the boy. "They say there are still a few partisans who won't come out and linger on like ghosts haunting the forest at night." Robert's eyes grew bigger as he tried to imagine the sound of Home Army gunfire in these trees. "Wop, wop, wop!" he cried. The only reply was the sound of crickets. Jurek said the villagers had found bodies of Russian and German soldiers too. Dominik's father had discovered the remains of a Red Army soldier in uniform. "There were a lot of Russian soldiers here in 1939," Jurek said. "They thought there were many Polish soldiers here and they dug all these foxholes. But there were just a few Poles in the woods, three or four cavalrymen who rode up with their sabers and galloped off again when the Russians fired. People say one Soviet soldier came to Popowlany to make a search. The Poles tried to seize him but he escaped and they got only his machine gun. Another time a Russian was killed when he was going to the toilet. A man saw him enter a wooden outhouse and he ran and told the partisans. And they shot him."

Robert was enthralled by such talk but not Agneshka, who witnessed enough violence on 178th Street. When they got back to the cart she told Grandfather and Ania, "There are still some more hazelnuts. I told Jurek we should leave some for other people." She emptied her apron pockets into a sack half filled with hazelnuts. "I think that's enough. Don't be greedy. Lots of people come out here on Sunday."

As they headed home, Robert asked Grandfather, "Is this the way we came?"

"If you lose your way in the forest," Jurek told him, "look for moss. It only grows on the north side of a tree." Way off in the woods a ladder was leaning against a tree. Agneshka told the boy it was the forest ranger's. "To see the open spaces." They passed a man standing in a hayfield. "He's looking to see if it's dry or not," Agneshka told the children, who saw how he turned over his hay with a wooden fork. In the next field they passed a stork which was standing on one leg, very still. "He's looking for frogs," Jurek said. Dragonflies darted over the grass, and once Agneshka had her father stop so she could pick a woolly-looking herb Zofia liked to dry for medicinal tea.

It was past noon when they reached Popowlany. Ania at once rushed off to watch TV. Robert tagged along. "How good it is to be out in open country," Agneshka, looking healthy and rosy-cheeked, told Jurek. When he arrived for *obiad*, the big midday meal, the kitchen smelled of borscht. Zofia was marinating sorrel, and cabbage with salt as well, preparing for winter. Over the oven she was drying apple slices, which hung from a string like beads. "We are living in King Sas's time," joked Jurek. "Eat, drink and loosen your belt."

By the time they finished eating, dark clouds had gathered from the east and once again they felt moisture in the air. Zofia crossed herself and said, "May God give them time to gather in the hay." Jurek and Agneshka hurried out to help the neighbors. The whole village pitched in, trying to load what hay was dry onto wagons and get it into the barns before the first drops of rain.

II

The village was set back from the main Tykocin–Białystok road by a picturesque cobblestone avenue made by two rows of very old, very tall poplar trees. A white-painted, weathered sign, tipped to one side, said: POPOWLANY. Popowlany's thirty-three houses—it had fewer than a hundred and fifty people in all—faced each other across this single road, which petered out north of the village to the muddy cart track that ran down to the river. The Komorowskis and the Sakowiczes, about five or six families apiece, lived on the south side of Popowlany, the Sadowskis on the north, and the Bokuńs in a separate little colony of farmsteads a little way toward the Narew. Each house had its picket fence, most of them wooden but a few wrought iron and painted green. In summer the small gardens were ablaze with flowers and even the poorest kitchen had its fresh bouquet. Just outside the fences were wooden benches where on Sundays or saint's days, when it was a sin to work, people came to sit beside the road and gossip or bask in the sun.

Behind each house was a farmyard of cows, pigs and chickens, and sometimes geese and sheep. A few villagers, like Jurek, had cars. Almost everybody had a Russian tractor or the Polish Ursus or a locally assembled Massey-Ferguson. Practically every family still kept a horse. A long narrow strip of ancestral land extended behind most of the houses, but each family also had widely scattered fields, like Jurek, fragmented by centuries of inheritance. The farmsteads also had small "summer houses" where families cooked, ate and slept when it was too hot to use the white-tiled indoor ovens. There were grass-covered earthen potato cellars and usually a few gnarled old apple and pear trees. The older houses were made of wood, with such small doors you had to duck your head to go in and out. The newer ones were cement brick. Two with upper stories were built by men who went to America. On each front door the letters KMB and the year were scribbled in chalk, a very old custom; the initials of Kaspar, Melchior and Balthazar, the three wise men, were to tell strangers Christians dwelled therein.

The life of Popowlany flowed back and forth along this single cobbled road, men driving cattle to pasture in the morning and back to their barns at night, schoolchildren and young people who worked in factories and shops in Tykocin or Białystok walking to and from the bus stop at the crossroads. If Popowlany's people lived huddled together, they equally belonged to the district town of Tykocin. Here, more likely than not, they would be born, baptized, christened, married and buried. Here they went to school and mass on Sunday. They sold their produce at Tykocin's Tuesday market and took their grain to its government warehouse, where they bought fertilizer, feed and fuel. Here they ate a restaurant meal or got drunk on beer or vodka. They took in a film, bought a newspaper, went to an amateur theatrical, art exhibition or concert, watched a soccer match or track meet, read at the library, bought an ice-cream cone or petitioned the mayor. A sign outside the church might advertise a coming circus with "monkeys and small dogs, ponies, jugglers, acrobats on bicycles, clowns and Hula-Hoops," or issue an appeal to farmers: "Protect nature. Seek harmony between agriculture and the natural world."

The road into Tykocin was lined with tall and stately poplar trees, planted, not for their beauty, but to hold back drifting snow in winter. The hour's walk into Tykocin from Popowlany offered a panoramic view as the land sloped to the Narew. About halfway to the river extended fields of wheat, rye, triticale, potatoes and sugar beets and a few scattered farms. After that were hayfields and pastures and woods of birches, larches, willows and sycamores, and in the deeper woods, pines and firs. Poland's famous Biebrza Marsh was just fifty miles away and besides the sweeping scenery there were circling hawks, strings of white swans, wild geese and migrant ducks. If the wind stirred, poplar leaves rustled overhead, perhaps the most characteristic sound of rural Poland.

At the crossroads by Popowlany, the villagers erected an iron cross in 1980. This was two years after Poland's Karol Wojtyła had been voted God's Vicar by the elderly, mainly Italian cardinals in Rome and thrust on the world as Pope John Paul II and a year after his first triumphal visit home. Popowlany's people wanted to make a gesture of support for the Pope and of defiance of the Russian-imposed Communist regime in Warsaw. Agneshka's father did the metalwork and Jurek and a few neighbors built the concrete foundation. This was done in secret and the cross erected one night. The villagers waited for the police to come and try to force them to take it down, but nothing happened. Such things were happening all over Poland. Communism was crumbling.

Every Polish village had its cross. In Popowlany there was another, much older cross, but it was on an old cart track to Tykocin and, made of wood, was riddled with bullet holes, for Russian soldiers had used it for target practice. When someone died in Popowlany, funeral processions, led by a priest and everyone singing hymns, came on foot as far as the cross. Pallbearers sat the coffin on a wagon or on the ground. Then someone from the deceased's family would ask the village to forgive any wrong the departed might have done to them. "Please, we ask forgiveness," a family member would say. "We forgive," the villagers replied in unison. The procession resumed, sometimes still on foot, more often nowadays by car, to the cemetery in Tykocin. But the last farewell to the village was at this cross. The Catholic cemetery was on the nearest, eastern, side of town and the Jewish cemetery, now overgrown and derelict, was on the western.

Tykocin had grown up as a Jewish trading center, reaching its peak of prosperity just as Baroque architecture swept Europe from Versailles to St. Peter's in Rome, during the mid-seventeenth and eighteenth centuries. Jews in large numbers first came to Poland to escape persecution in Germany during the Crusades. In the fourteenth century, Poland's King Kazimierz III, who wanted urban expertise, offered them protection. At first Jews were a privileged class as the bringer of urban skills to a peasant society. For nearly two centuries it was quite common for blond and blue-eyed Polish peasant girls to marry a Jewish merchant and convert to Judaism as a social step upward. This ended in the sixteenth-century Counter-Reformation, when abandoning Catholicism became a crime in Polish eyes. Thereafter, to this day, "Pole" in Poland was defined as being Catholic and not being a Russian, a German or a Jew. Yet some Jews converted to Catholicism as the only way they could own land until modern times. Under the Nazis, others passed as Catholics to survive.

In Tykocin, right from the start, Jews engaged in crafts and trade and Catholic peasants farmed. There were small numbers of landowning Polish gentry and nobility too, but to join these classes took money and that meant going to the city and competing with Jews, which few villagers were equipped to do. The only real social escalation open to a poor peasant was to become a priest and rise through the Church. Tykocin's first Jewish settlers, ten families, came in 1522. They were invited as expert craftsmen from Grodno by a Polish nobleman, Olbracht Gasztold, who owned much land around Tykocin. He gave them land to settle down in, a place called Kaczorowo, set off from the Catholic town by a stream, the Meltawa. The import of advanced Jewish ideas and skills caught on particularly well in the Polish-Russian borderlands. Białystok, like Lvov and Minsk, became one of Central Europe's great Jewish cities—from it comes the bialy, a bagel without the hole.

By the mid-sixteenth century records show thirty-four Jewish households in Kaczorowo. In 1633 Poland's King Władysław IV formally acknowledged the settlement rights of their descendants. When a wooden synagogue going back to the first settlers burned down, a splendid new brick one was built in Baroque style in 1642. After the original roof was lost in one of Tykocin's many fires, a lofty red-tiled mansard roof was built which survives to this day. By the 1670s a school was set up in the vestibule of the synagogue's Great Hall, a Talmudic House was added and in the vicinity over fifty stalls and shops. Offenders against the Halakah, Jewish religious law, were jailed in the synagogue tower.

A census taken about the time of Napoleon's 1812 retreat down the Narew shows Tykocin had 4,910 people, about 90 percent of them Jewish. But decline came quickly when a new highway from Warsaw to Vilnius bypassed Tykocin and went to Białystok instead. Tykocin became a backwater, a small country town chiefly of interest for its seventeenth- and eighteenth-century Baroque architecture. After 1863 there was a harsh program of Russification. Amid pogroms and persecutions, the number of Jews fell to about fifteen hundred, half of Tykocin's people by then.

Tykocin's modern history, like Poland's, began in 1918. That year the three empires that had partitioned Poland among them for a hundred and twenty-three years—Russia, Germany and Austria—all collapsed pretty much at the same time. Marshal Józef Piłsudski, exiled to Siberia for an alleged attempt to kill Czar Alexander III, and jailed in 1900 and 1918, returned to Poland, took command of its army and on August 15, 1918, proclaimed an independent Polish republic, which he headed. It was the same date as the Assumption of the Virgin.

Two years later, in 1920, and two years after the Russian Revolution, Bolshevik armies invaded Poland. In Białystok they set up a committee of Polish Communists, who were to turn Poland into a Soviet republic. The Red Cavalry rode victoriously past Popowlany and Tykocin across eastern Poland right up to the outskirts of Warsaw. They were stopped at the Vistula River by Piłsudski and his men, who in a counteroffensive attacked the Bolsheviks' rear lines, cut them in half and drove them past Białystok.

This, which also took place in August, became known as the Miracle of the Vistula and every August 15 Tykocin celebrated Piłsudski's victory, the Virgin Mary and Polish independence together. At a special mass the priest always retold the story of how Piłsudski's soldiers shouted, as they chased the Bolsheviks, "Long live Maria! Let us die for her!" Another hero was Stefan Czarniecki, the Polish commander against the Swedes when they attacked Tykocin and destroyed the fortress-castle of King Zygmunt August on its outskirts in 1519. An enormous statue of Czarniecki holding a golden scepter, sometimes adorned by the caps of prankish schoolboys, stood in the town square, which was surrounded by poplar trees and a wrought-iron fence. Children liked to play in the grass below the statue and, going by, one could hear their cries, "Ducks, come home!" "We're afraid of the wolves!" "Why are you afraid?" "Because they want to eat us!"

The Catholic church faced the square. It was almost palatial with its twin onion towers and its many Baroque outbuildings and courts, but the basilica itself was sadly in need of repair. Its yellow porous walls of plastered brick were weather-worn and crumbling in some places. The roof was rusted. Some panes in the tower windows were missing. Yet the old tower clock kept accurate time and chimed all the hours with its bells. If the wind was right one heard them toll in Popowlany.

Tykocin's main street, which ran along the south side of the square, had been renamed from First of May to Third of May Street, this being the date of Poland's first democratic constitution in 1791. Here the eighteenth-century brick houses were the grandest in town. The most impressive of them—the Malarewicz house—was burned down by partisans in the 1950s, and only the tables and red canvas umbrellas of the ice-cream vendor stood in its place. The Malarewiczes were rich Jewish timber merchants who had lived in Tykocin for generations. The last of them were arrested and deported to Siberia by the Russians in 1939. The Russians, the Germans and the Polish Communists might have all had their headquarters there, but people still called it the Malarewicz house. Next door was another brick villa, whose cellar the Nazis used as a torture chamber. Across from the southwest corner of the square was Town Hall, where Dominik held forth in a second-floor office with a conference table and French doors that opened out onto a balcony. Toward the south was a bookstore that had replaced its old Communist texts with Stephen King, Agatha Christie, Alastair MacLean and even a biography of Yeltsin.

Then came the restaurant, a long, low building with windows across the front not easy to forget. A stranger entering would first see the lace curtains, the flower in a glass on each table, the paper napkins and frilly white aprons and starched caps of the grim-looking waitresses. Why grim? Coarse, drunken voices, swearing foully, soon gave the answer. The curtained-off door at the back led into a pub, a low haunt, that reeked of vodka, beer and tobacco smoke. Here the low-life of Tykocin was to be found. Men with bloodshot eyes and hoarse, gruff voices, who swore, shouted, mouthed oaths, cursed the barmaids or sat stupefied with throbbing heads, kept drinking from early morning on, until, not knowing when to stop, they passed out cold at the tables, heads cradled in their arms.

"*Cholera*, the plague take you, you son of a bitch!" Blasphemy and obscene references to each other's mother were plentiful. Young stalwarts of eighteen or nineteen drank as much and swore as loudly as the rest. If an old drunk was wearisomely long in making his departure, a waitress might scream at him, "I told you to go home! Nobody is going to clean up after you! You smell awful!"

"You whores! You bitches!" would come a reply. Then a shriek. "Stop that or I'll call the police!" "Call all the police in Tykocin. I don't care." An angry wife might storm in to drag off her husband. Sometimes it got too much for the younger waitress, a pale, skinny blonde who would burst into tears. Not so the older waitress, fearless and stout with frizzy yellow hair, who would rush at a drunk with a torrent of abuse, ready to flatten anyone in her path. Sometimes the whole crowd joined in singing something like "Only in Lvov City," banned by the Communists after Stalin annexed Lvov to Russia and never gave it back. All the while innocent travelers who wandered in would study the printed menu with its wide variety of dishes, not knowing nothing was ever available except *flaki*—pig intestine soup— and borscht, pork cutlets, boiled potatoes, pickles and, on good days, creamed carrots. Newcomers were soon driven to fortify themselves with vodka too.

Under Communism, every little town in Poland had such pubs, with men sitting about drinking beer and vodka at seven or eight o'clock in the morning. Among the older men, the talk always went back to World War II.

III

After German troops invaded Poland on September 1, 1939, they crossed the country with lightning speed and occupied Tykocin for two weeks. Word spread that they had killed at least eight hundred Jews in Białystok and that some villages had been put to the torch. In Tykocin itself nothing happened and then the Germans were gone.

What Adolf Hitler called the "Final Solution" did not touch Popowlany's people for two more years. On September 17 Russian soldiers crossed the frontier and entered Tykocin. The Germans, the townspeople and villagers learned, had withdrawn in accord with the Nazi-Soviet nonaggression treaty signed a month earlier. Now Stalin decreed that all "educated" Polish families under Russian occupation were to be deported to Siberia.

In Popowlany this meant anybody who could read and write. For Tykocin had been singled out by the Russians, who planned to build an airstrip just down the road from Popowlany. Tykocin, the story went, was to be turned into a military city and many of its inhabitants sent to Siberia. Some townspeople collaborated with the Russians, two of them Jewish. A merchant, Jawke Plowski, who lived in the red-brick house next to the Malarewicz family and harbored a grudge against them, sat on the committee that chose deportees, as did a trader named Rosenberg. In Popowlany this aroused hostilities going back to the 1918 Bolshevik invasion. Jurek's father, much indebted to a Jewish neighbor who taught him the cobbler's trade, joined the anti-Semitic Nationalist Party.

But Jewish families were sent to Siberia too, not just the Malarewicz family but Tykocin's doctor and his wife and children. The only Malarewicz to escape was the family's only daughter, Helena, beautiful and fair, who that summer married a Warsaw painter who showed great promise in the school of socialist realism. The father spared no expense, but her wedding shocked Tykocin, as the painter was a Catholic. Not that the Malarewiczes were Orthodox or ever went to the synagogue. The youngest of three sons, short and flaxen-haired like his sister, spent most of his time drinking vodka and playing cards. The three boys were deported with their parents. Only Helena in Warsaw escaped. Tykocin did not hear of her again for over half a century.

In modern times the old occupations generally held: Catholic Poles farmed, Jews engaged in crafts and trade. In Popowlany this exposed Jews to some hostility as the old peasant attitude was still strong that to buy and sell for personal gain went against village customs of mutual rights and obligations, such as loans without interest or hospitality without cost, expected to be met in kind. In Tykocin, Jews and Catholics lived amicably together. If the mayor was Jewish, his deputy was traditionally Catholic, or if the mayor was Catholic, his deputy would be a Jew. If the richest people in town were Jewish, so were the poorest. Except for Helena Malarewicz, no one intermarried. Separate Jewish and Catholic schools joined together in 1939, just before the war. But Tykocin's older people remembered that Jews and Catholics long before had played on the same sports teams, gone to the same dances and drunk at the same pubs, two of them owned by Catholics and four of them by Jews.

Most deportees to Siberia never came back. One who did was Jurek's cousin in Popowlany, Henryk Sadowski, a man in his late sixties. His father was arrested first. Eight months later, in April 1940, when Henryk was fifteen, Russian soldiers came and said they would take him, his mother and three sisters—seventeen, seven and four— to his father. They were loaded into a truck and driven to Białystok, where they were put into a cattle car on a freight train. Henryk: "It was already crowded with people. You could hardly get in. Some were crying. Some were screaming. Nobody knew what would happen to them. The Russians lied to everybody. We saw nothing of my father. We never saw him again. They closed the freight car doors tight and put barbed wire across them on the outside. Soldiers stood guard. There were old people. Sick people they took from their beds. Even little babies. If someone died they threw their body from the moving train. We slept on wooden shelves, tightly packed together. We had our own quilts, blankets, whatever we took from home. They let us out of the car just once every three days. Otherwise, to answer the call of nature there were little holes in the bottom of the car. They gave us almost no food or water the entire trip. Once nothing for thirteen days. A few times a decent guard brought water when we stopped at a station."

Once in Russia some small boys ran alongside the train and begged the soldiers for bread. Somebody threw them a loaf and it fell in a muddy pool of water. The children fought for it. A sergeant called out angrily, "Who gave these boys that bread? I will shoot him!" "Why, why?" Henryk and the other prisoners cried out. "Is there no bread for children in Russia?" The guards cursed them. "Shut up and be still! Plague take you!" If Henryk told this story at home, he would point to a large framed picture of Jesus hanging on his kitchen wall. "My mother even took this picture."

"All the way to Siberia and back?"

Agneshka felt it might have saved them. They were loaded on the train in Białystok on April 3 and reached Siberia on May 1. As they staggered out of the cattle car, filthy, emaciated and sick, Siberia looked desolate. In May in Popowlany the forests were green and lilacs in bloom. Here the earth was brown, the woods bare, there was snow in the ditches and a cold biting wind. The Russians gave the family a room in a kolkhoz barrack. When the commandant of the collective farm came to inspect the arrivals he saw the portrait of Jesus. "Mother, why have you brought this religious picture?" he demanded. "She was ready to be a martyr," Henryk would remember. "She carried that picture like a cross. He cursed it in foul language and told her, 'This picture is of no more consequence than that coal shovel. Less, because the shovel takes ashes out of the stove. This picture is nothing. It will not help you. You will never go back to Poland.' But he did not make her destroy it."

It was sowing season and the family was put to work in the fields. There was nothing to eat and people sold clothes and bedding to buy food, despite the bitter cold. Those deported in winter fared the worst. Stories were told in Popowlany of cattle cars being opened in Siberia by Russian soldiers who found as many as a hundred Polish prisoners frozen to death in a single piece of ice. In time the family built itself a mud hut, with branches and straw and mud. They were forbidden to go more than three kilometers from the farm. Anybody who did and was caught was put in leg irons. The guards were drunk half the time on vodka and the fields were surrounded by trackless wastes. There was a piercing wind that never seemed to stop, frost, wet snow, muddy roads, pouring rain, and when it got warm, bedbugs, cockroaches and mosquitoes. The Sadowskis did field work, reaped, gathered in the crops, threshed, dug potatoes and hauled logs. Somehow, Henryk said, they survived the strange, brutal people and hunger, cold and illness.

Rescue came because Stalin feared what would happen after the German surprise attack on Russia on June 22, 1941. He wanted allies wherever he could find them, even on a Siberian prison farm. Henryk, just seventeen, found himself in the Red Army. His mother and sisters were freed to try to make it home, which they did. A year later he was assigned to a Polish division under Colonel Zygmunt Berling. He himself did not reach Popowlany until after the war in April 1946; in 1994 his mother was long dead, one sister lived in Siekierki village down the road, another in Tykocin and a third in Chicago.

Henryk fought a year with the Russians and found them more barbaric than the Germans. "If the Germans arrested you," he would say, "you could pay them and they might let you go. The Russians put handcuffs and leg irons on prisoners and made them walk a hundred, two hundred kilometers. Many died of hunger in Russia. The Russians were the worst, worse even than the Germans." Henryk's Polish division helped liberate Berlin. He still had his old Red Army uniform and wore it every May 3, when the army veterans of Tykocin district held a parade. One of his medals, dated May 2, 1945, was inscribed in Russian: "Liberation of Berlin." When Agneshka asked when he wore the medal, Henryk's hearty wife laughed and said, "When he sleeps with me."

IV

The Poles, like people everywhere, were utterly unprepared for the full horror of Nazi Germany and the ethnic cleansing that reached its height in annihilation. When one of six elderly Jewish survivors left in Białystok in the 1990s was asked why more people didn't flee across the border into Russia, just twenty miles away, he said, "Nobody imagined what the Germans would do." *Mein Kampf,* dictated to Rudolf Hess while Hitler was in prison in the early 1920s, does clearly state that Hitler's drive into Poland would not just be to conquer the country. He wanted to annihilate the enemy and enslave survivors, to win *Lebensraum* for Germans. Such an outpouring of anti-Semitism and contempt for morality as *Mein Kampf* reads like the ravings of a madman. Once asked what he meant by "depopulate," Hitler said he intended to destroy whole nations. "Nature is cruel," he said. "It is our right to be cruel as well." What nobody imagined was that Hitler could create a political system that could psychologically transform ordinary policemen and military conscripts into mass murderers.

There was, as mentioned, warning in 1939. That fall, not just in Białystok, the Germans held more than seven hundred mass executions in which 16,000 Poles died, Jews and Catholics alike. Then after Hitler's invasion of Russia in 1941, Stalin ordered partisan warfare. Hitler countered that

> it gives us the opportunity to exterminate anyone who is hostile to us. Naturally the vast area must be pacified as quickly as possible; this will happen best through shooting anyone who even looks askance at us.

As the Wehrmacht, the regular German army, moved into Russia, Heinrich Himmler, who commanded all Nazi police, sent in behind them six thousand *Ordnungspolizei*, the Order Police, to wage what

Hitler called "a war of destruction." His decree for the invasion of Russia, code-named Barbarossa, removed acts committed by German soldiers against Russian civilians from the jurisdiction of military justice. It explicitly approved reprisals against whole villages. The Order Police were generally conscripts in their thirties and forties, who were too old for the army, and were recruited from policemen, shopkeepers, stevedores, truck drivers, construction laborers, factory workers, waiters and teachers, a real cross section of middle- and lower-class Germans. A minority belonged to the Nazi Party and a few were in the SS *(Schutzstaffel)*. Also under Himmler was the *Sicherheitspolizei*, Security Police, which included the Gestapo.

For some reason, the Nazis treated Białystok and the borderland towns and villages like Tykocin and Popowlany as if they were in Russia, not Poland. It may have been Białystok's closeness to the border, its history or the eminence of so many of its Jewish native sons: Ludwig Zamenhof, Maxim Litvinov, General Yigael Yadin, Albert Sabin, Yitzhak Shamir. In a sense, Białystok is where the Holocaust, with systematic mass murder and genocide as declared state policy, really began. The commander of Order Police Battalion 310, which went into Białystok first, took Hitler's orders to mean that all Jews, regardless of sex or age, were to be killed. This initial attack is described, drawing on court records, by historian Christopher R. Browning:

> The action began as a pogrom: beating, humiliation, beard burning, and shooting at will as the policemen drove Jews into the marketplace or synagogue. When several Jewish leaders appeared at the 221st Security Division of General Plugbeil and knelt at his feet, begging for army protection, one member of Police Battalion 309 unzipped his fly and urinated on them while the general turned his back.
>
> What started as a pogrom quickly escalated into more systematic mass murder. Jews collected at the marketplace were taken to a park, lined up against a wall, and shot. The killing lasted until dark. At the synagogue, where at least 700 Jews had been collected, gasoline was poured at the entryways. A grenade was tossed into the building, igniting a fire. The fire spread to nearby houses in which Jews were hiding, and they too were burned alive. The next day, thirty wagonloads of corpses were taken to a mass grave. An estimated 2,000 to 2,200 Jews had been killed.

A few days later, on July 8, Himmler himself, with Kurt Dalüge, the national commander of the Order Police, came to Białystok. At a review, Dalüge said his men "could be proud of participating in the defeat of Bolshevism." Four days later three thousand more young male Jews were rounded up, taken to the Białystok stadium and shot. News of these horrors had no sooner reached Tykocin than German police came to surround Kaczorowo, already crowded with Jewish refugees from the villages. The great fear was that the Germans would take everybody into Białystok.

Alicja Matusiewicz was thirteen when the Germans came the first time, fifteen when they returned. She was from a prominent Tykocin family. Her grandfather, police chief of the city of Łomza, was deported by the Russians and was never seen again. Her father, something of a local hero as one of Piłsudski's commanders against the Bolsheviks in 1920, now was among Polish prisoners in Russia allowed to form a corps and fight with the Allies under General Władisław Anders. An old Communist classmate of Alicja's had hid her in their village, where she finished school and learned German. Once the Germans reoccupied Tykocin she was ordered to report to the *Amtskommissar*, the senior civilian administrator, a Herr Letzner, and told she was to be his translator. It was a job she was to hold for more than three years. Fifty years later some old men in Popowlany claimed she had been present during interrogations where peasants were tortured and beaten. She never spoke of it. "My work as a translator," she would say, "taught me that all Germans, like all Russians, are different. Sometimes the Russian soldiers came, took food and left. They were not all bad. If somebody fell into the hands of the German police, there was no escape. Yet there were Austrian officers who talked of Mozart and Goethe."

She had not worked for Herr Letzner long before a high-ranking German officer came to see him. He and his aide had to wait for some time and talked to Alicja in German. "Where did you learn to speak German so well?" the officer asked her. "At school," she told him. "I read everything I could by Heinrich Heine. I love his poems." And she quoted, *"Ich weiss nicht was soll es bedeuten,"* half singing "The Lorelei" in a soft, low voice.

> I do not know why this confronts me
>   This sadness, this echo of pain;
> A curious legend still haunts me,
>   Still haunts and obsesses my brain.

The officer froze. *"Heine war ein Jude.* The Führer burned his books." Alicja was afraid. She had not known it. But the officer's aide broke the tension. "If such a young girl reads Heine it is proof the Poles respect German culture. It is a pity we have to kill Polish intellectuals. It would be better if Poland and Germany were fighting side by side against the damned Bolsheviks."

In the *Amtskommissar*'s office Alicja came to know that an atrocity was not necessarily a psychotic aberration. Monstrous evils were carried out in bureaucratic routine. To schedule deliveries, confiscate property, make inventories, write letters, do translations could also exterminate and enslave. It was like the signs the Germans liked to hang about: *"Sei ehrlich!" "Halte Ordnung!" "Sauberkeit ist Gesundheit."* Horror made routine. Letzner, middle-aged, with a teenage daughter Alicja's age back in Germany, himself took refuge in official routine and bureaucratic euphemisms. He spoke of *Deutsches Volk* and *Blutsgemeinschaft* and if he had doubts about Hitler's ideas on territorial expansion and racial purity he kept them to himself. He hid behind "standard operating procedure" and what he saw as the duty, discipline and competence of the loyal German civil servant. Alicja knew he hated some of the gendarmerie in Tykocin, especially a man named Joseph Schaeffer, a psychopath who caught Jewish children and shot them, who called Hitler's Barbarossa decree a "shooting license" against any Jew. Once she heard him boast to Letzner, "I have no appetite unless I kill a Pole before breakfast." Schaeffer and others tortured people in the cellar of the gendarmerie headquarters. It was next door to the Malarewicz house, where Herr Letzner had his office. "There is no hope once you fall into their hands," Alicja told her mother. The gendarmerie, the rural constables, were under an Order Police commander, first Hans Busch from 1941 to 1943 and a Herr Volkschwein from 1943 to the end of the war. Schaeffer, who also went by the name of Max, if still alive, would be in his seventies today. So would a good many of the Germans who occupied Tykocin. Some must surely be alive. "If people knew where Schaeffer was," Alicja would say, "they would go on foot to murder him. He and Nazis like him went around with guns and could shoot whoever they wanted."

After the Germans came back, normal life ended in Tykocin. There was no school. Polish offices were shut down. The peasants still farmed and apprentices were allowed to learn a trade, but that was all. The shops were closed. A little hotel by the river was turned into a prison. Catholics were shot in its courtyard, Jews in their cemetery west of town. Tykocin was soon like a penal colony. Jews fared far worse, but Catholics too were treated as *Untermenschen*, subject to random terror by Germans like Schaeffer. There was a constant danger of persecution, deportation into slave labor or being sent to a death camp. "Deep in the German soul," Alicja would say much later in life, "there is a kind of brutality."

One day a notice was posted at the synagogue that all Tykocin's Jews were to gather in the marketplace early in the morning on August 25, 1941. The head rabbi, fearing this meant Tykocin's Jews would be taken to the Białystok ghetto at last, went to the Catholic church and begged the priest to intercede with the German Wehrmacht commander on their behalf. He was the senior-ranking German military officer in Tykocin, but when the priest went to see him he said that the order had come from the Gestapo. He could do nothing.

By now thousands of Jews had been murdered in the surrounding countryside. In Jedwabne village, just a few miles from Tykocin, the Germans forced nine hundred people into a barn and set it on fire. In another nearby village, six hundred and fifty people were burned alive. Synagogues in two more villages were set ablaze. Kaczorowo was terrorized by a pogrom of beatings, killings, rapes and robberies, some said by Ukrainian criminals let loose by the Germans and later taken out to the fields and shot.

When the morning came only a few older people ventured into the marketplace. Most of the Jews remained in their houses. The market was just across the Meltawa bridge from the synagogue and not far along the poplar-shaded main street from the church. There was the morning freshness of a late-summer day. German policemen gave the old people bread, sausage and cheese. When word got around that food was being given out, hundreds of half-starved Jews poured into the square. Once there, there was no turning back. Trucks roared up, unloading Germans with fierce dogs and fixed bayonets.

Herr Letzner, hearing the trucks, told Alicja and two Polish typists that units from Order Police Battalions 309 and 316 had come to Tykocin. Soon a house-to-house search was underway. Alicja could hear shouts and screams and gunfire. The *Amtskommissar* ordered her and the clerks to get back to work. He said, "This is just an ordinary day."

The Łopuchowo Woods, a dense forest of tall birch and pine, starts four kilometers southwest of Tykocin. It was a shady, silent place, of pine needles and moss, moist earth and mushrooms, where little sun penetrated. In 1941 Jurek's grandfather happened to be the chief of one of four villages on the edge of the woods. His daughter, Helena Sadowska, who now lives in Popowlany, was then a young girl. "That day," she would say, "I remember it well. How could anyone forget? There were Germans in Tykocin but none of them lived in the villages. They came and took our grain and eggs and milk, saying it was for their soldiers on the eastern front. I remember one man complaining about Hitler. He was middle-aged and had lost two sons in the war. Some of them seemed quite human.

"One day a German from the gendarmerie in Tykocin came and he asked Father about a certain clearing in the Łopuchowo Woods. The German said Polish partisans had used the place as a gallows to hang captured German soldiers. My father said he knew nothing of it. But he knew. The Germans found the clearing themselves and came back and took my father and some village men. They were told to dig three enormous pits in the earth, each one big enough to hold hundreds of people. The Germans kept saying the pits weren't big enough. It took Father and the men days and days. They knew they were digging mass graves. On August twenty-fourth, we were told to stay away from the Łopuchowo Woods the next day. Anybody who got close, they said, would be shot. One of the Germans told my father, 'This is the place where Poles hanged Germans. And this is where we will hang the Jews.' In the morning the woods were full of Nazi soldiers with barking dogs, SS men. My sister was out cutting fodder and she saw a German on the road carrying a stick. On this stick were strung many bracelets and necklaces. My sister said it was like a string of beads. A neighbor of ours found pacifiers for babies along the road."

All day and well into the evening the villagers heard firing from the woods. Helena Sadowska said two Jewish men escaped and reached her cousin's house and asked for bread and water. Then they ran off into the woods. In a televised report on Poland's Jews in 1991, the BBC said that Tykocin's Jews, about two thousand of them, were forced into the marketplace. There the elderly, infants and sick were taken away by truck. The able-bodied were marched at gunpoint, in ranks of four across, the five kilometers to the execution site in the Łopuchowo Woods. An elderly Tykocin man told the BBC, "There was a Jewish orchestra too, marching and playing."

In Helena Sadowska's version, based largely on what the two escaped Jewish men told her cousin, many people, not just the infirm, were taken by truck to the village of Zawady. There they were taken into an old wooden schoolhouse and forced to strip as German police-men searched them for their valuables. After this, they were allowed to put their underclothes back on and were marched back to the trucks and crowded into them. People were packed in and some fainted from the heat and overloading. The truck doors were sealed and locked and the Germans attached the exhaust pipes to hoses going back inside so the fumes would asphyxiate those trapped in the truck. It was just a few kilometers from Zawady, south of Tykocin, to the Łopuchowo Woods. Some died on the way; others, the two men said, were just unconscious when a truck would back up to one of the three freshly dug pits. The trucks were equipped with hydraulic lifts so that the dead, dying, conscious and unconscious were dumped into a pit as soldiers at machine-gun emplacements fired at them. The two men had somehow managed to jump off a truck and get away from the SS men and their dogs.

Many in Tykocin said, "No one could escape Łopuchowo." Jurek's grandfather told him that after the Nazis took what gold, rings, neck-laces, watches and money they could find on their victims, they gassed them in the trucks, dumped them into the mass graves and machine-gunned anybody still alive. Helena Sadowska would ask, "If anybody got away, how could we know? They'd keep going, to Israel or America." When her father went back to the Łopuchowo Woods the next day, the Germans were gone. "The bodies were covered with something hard like rocks and over this they had dumped sand. Father came home trembling and said the sand was moving. He got some men and ran back, but by then the Germans were there again and were putting quicklime into the graves. It all happened very quickly. Just that one day. By evening the next day people said the Germans had also found and shot some men hiding in the woods and in some village houses. That is all I know. The Germans told us the same thing was going to happen to us. We were scared to death. They said if they found anybody hiding a Jew, they'd kill the whole fam-ily."

Were people buried alive? Tykocin's people fifty years later would swear, "The sand was moving." In court testimony in Germany since the war, police have described how the thin covering of overfilled mass graves did continue to move. The mass asphyxiation and use of dump trucks were used only at first. The Nazis soon shifted to what became their standard method of Nazi execution, until the shift to gas chambers at the death camps: firing squads whose victims lay on the ground. In a mass execution, as at Tykocin, victims were trucked or marched to mass graves in a forest and ordered to lie face-down in a row, with an equal number of policemen behind them. Each policeman placed his bayonet at the back of his victim's neck and fired. Two or three police companies, repeating this procedure all day and rotating the firing squads, could kill nearly two thousand people by nightfall. Almost surely, some of Tykocin's Jewish population died this way. The executioners, firing at such close range, got spattered with their victims' blood, brain tissue and bone splinters. Like Letzner, the killers used euphemisms for murder; they were not involved in slaughter but in "actions," just as taking prisoners to death camps was "resettlement." Responsibility lay with the higher-ups. It was a process of cultural conditioning. Professor Browning reports that while at first most German policemen felt revulsion, 80 percent kept shooting. "Habituation played a role as well. Having killed once already, the men did not experience such a traumatic shock the second time. Like much else, killing was something one could get used to."

There are many accounts of Poles who roused Jews from hiding places, just as there are of Poles who gave their lives trying to save Jews. If most of six million Jews went to their deaths in Poland, which had over two thousand death camps, so did six million Poles, only half of them Jews.

There is only one Jewish person whose escape from the Tykocin massacre has been confirmed beyond any doubt. He was an eleven-year-old boy, Szmul Ismach, and after the war, before emigrating to London in 1947, he provided the authorities with an account of what happened, a copy of which is now with the Jewish Institute in Warsaw. Szmul's story suggests that while the Polish villagers might have been crudely anti-Semitic, few accepted, as German policemen and soldiers did, the Nazi image of a diabolical Jewish enemy, thereby in effect justifying and becoming accessories to Hitler's crime. Szmul was born on June 21, 1930, the son of a miller, Jozef Ismach, and a woman whose maiden name was Chasia Goldsztajn. He had three brothers and a sister. Szmul's deposition begins when the Germans came back to Tykocin in 1941. Szmul says, "At first it was calm. Then they began to persecute Jews." His parents sent Szmul out to a farmer named Rakowicz, in Lesniki village. Jurek knew Rakowicz slightly, as Lesniki was just east of Popowlany. When the order came for Jews to gather in the marketplace on August 25, Szmul's whole family joined him. "My master let them stay only one night," Szmul continues in his deposition. "The next day they went to Choroszcz." This was a town nearly the size of Tykocin on the main road to Białystok. "I stayed with Rakowicz, having come for the harvest, and I remained through the winter of 1941–42. The whole village knew about me, but at this time they allowed Jews to live. Later my master grew afraid and told me to go away. This began my vagrancy, going from village to village, house to house."

From Lesniki, he went to Sawino, another village less than a mile away. There he stayed two weeks with a farmer named Sawicki, when a woman he knew came and told him someone in Choroszcz had reported his father and brother to the Germans, who shot them dead. Szmul moved on again, this time to Złotoria, a short distance away. A woman named Jackowska let him spend the night and the next day took him to her brother to work as a cowherd. This lasted only a week. A neighbor said he was a Jew.

"I was told to go out. I went back to Jackowska, spending nights at her house and during the day going to the next village of Babino to look for a place." Here he found work on a farm owned by a woman named Stypulkowska. He stayed with her for over a year. "Stypulkowska did not suspect I was a Jew," Szmul says. "Many times she told me to go to church on Sunday. I told her my clothes were too shabby. She bought me clothes and I went." Then one day in the spring of 1943, when he was out in the woods looking for two lost foals, he met a blacksmith he knew. The blacksmith warned him that the gendarmerie in Chowoszcz had traced him and were coming to kill both him and Mrs. Stypulkowska. Szmul worried about it a few days, then again fled, first to a village called Kobylin, where he was afraid to stay, and then to Makowo, where he found work with a farmer, Wnorowski.

"By now I was so much like a village boy and had learned to speak in such a country way, Wnorowski could not suspect anything. I told them my father was in Russia and I was ashamed to tend cows in my native village. That was why I was looking for a job in Makowo." Szmul says the Wnorowski family was very good to him, but like Mrs. Stypulkowska, insisted he go to mass. Just before Easter 1944 he did, avoiding the priest. Then a week after Easter, the Germans traced radio signals to a hidden receiver in Wnorowski's barn. He was secretly a partisan. "I knew nothing about it," Szmul comments. "They took us to Białystok, where I was badly beaten. They showed me a gallows where they said they would hang me. They kicked me and kept asking about the radio. But what could I say? I knew nothing. The Wnorowski family were all sent to Germany. I was left alone. That was 1944. We were lucky, because in 1943 the Germans would have just taken us behind a barn and shot us.

"In Białystok prison I almost fell into the Gestapo's hands. The Germans' Polish interpreter was suspicious of me. But I was so weak from the beatings and lack of food they set me free. Before leaving the prison I had to sign a paper saying that if I found out anything about the radio I would tell them. After I came out of prison, everybody knew the Germans let me go. After that nobody suspected I was a Jew. I went back to Babino and tended cattle for Mrs. Stypulkowska until the liberation." All this time Szmul had no idea what had happened to the rest of his family. In Białystok's archives on the Nazi occupation there was a note saying that a Chasia Ismach and her two sons reached Israel. This would be his mother. Whatever became of Szmul Ismach? Nobody in Tykocin knew.

The horror did not end with the mass murder of Tykocin's Jews. Townspeople continued to be sent to the death camps, or to Germany as slaves, or killed. Himmler's German colonization policy also decreed that children screened for Aryan traits and deemed suitable for "Germanization" should be taken off to SS orphanages. None were ever seen again and it was thought they died of neglect, hunger and disease.

Reprisals, like the mass executions, deportations and death camps, were official German policy. One hundred Poles were to be shot for every German killed. In May 1944, the Germans declared they would shoot fifteen hundred Poles for every dead German. That month Philip Schweiger, a young university-educated Wehrmacht officer, commanded the German occupation in Tykocin district. When he first came he stayed at the house of Alicja Matusiewicz, which faced the square. He took over the two front drawing rooms, and since he found Poland very cold and damp in the winter, he had Tykocin's best apprentices make him an enormous white-tiled oven, which still heated the Matusiewicz house in the winter half a century later.

One day Schweiger was driving in his car south of Tykocin on the road to Białystok. The partisans did not mean to kill him. What happened was that the pregnant wife of a partisan had been arrested and tortured and lost her baby. Her crazed husband came out of the forest, saw a German car and shot its occupant. Schweiger was the first German he met. They brought the body back to Tykocin and laid it in the church. Townspeople brought flowers. Everyone feared a reprisal. Nothing happened for three days. At last they came.

V

"It was May 27, 1944, a date, like August 25, 1941, no one in Tykocin will ever forget," Alicja Matusiewicz remembers. "The Germans surrounded the town square in front of our house at four o'clock in the morning. Other trucks and troops surrounded the whole town. Many were Gestapo with fierce dogs. The Gestapo told Herr Letzner to gather his staff. They said they were going to take away everybody sixteen or older. I was seventeen. Besides me, two older people, Kruszewski and Nakorski, worked in the office. The park was crowded with people, milling about, confused, terrified, the Germans shouting at them, dogs barking. Letzner, who was in his German civilian administrator's yellow uniform, found me and cried, *'Alles, kom, kom!* Come with me!' 'I'm not alone!' I cried. 'I have my mother and my brother. He is sixteen!'

"Herr Letzner was very frightened. With us were two women, distant cousins, who were terrified. I told him they were my aunts. *'Mein Gott! Mutter, Bruder und Tanten!'* He protested it was too many. But he opened the park gate and cried, *'Schnell! Schnell!'* We all crowded behind and followed him across the street to the Malarewicz house. Letzner told a soldier to take care of us. We were led down into a cellar. Ten people were hiding there. Several were peasants who supplied the *Amtskommissar* with bread and eggs. Others had just slipped by the Gestapo. There was great confusion. My youngest sister, who was just a child, got separated from us and she ran frantically about the park, crying and trying to find us. My grandmother didn't go to the park at all. When the SS men came to the houses they ordered the old people to stay home. Others fled out their back doors and hid along the river or in the fields. The Gestapo didn't stay long and they didn't search the houses carefully, so those who hid were safe. We stayed in the cellar until the Gestapo trucks left. They took away three hundred and seventy people in all. It was one year before the war ended. A hundred and twenty-six, most of them men, never came back.

"Schweiger had been afraid Polish partisans might come into

Tykocin to kill him. Not long before, he moved to the priests' apartments behind the church because our house was wooden and he feared they might set fire to it. He told the priests that the commander in the next town had put an iron door on his quarters. 'I'm not afraid,' he had boasted. 'I can drive safely through the woods.' People said he was a decent man for a German.

"*Amtskommissar* Letzner used to tell me, 'Alicja, you are like my daughter.' When Germans in the office would tell dirty jokes or use bad language, Letzner would reprimand them. He saved us that day." Alicja, like most of Tykocin's people, did not like to talk about the German occupation. Her small grave face, so intelligent and well bred, turned pinched and pale when she did. She almost never went to church and was like a person who had lost her faith in God and man.

Mieczysława Grabowska stayed a believer. In her sixties, just a year younger than Alicja, she was ardently religious. She was a tireless worker for the church in Tykocin, forever collecting donations, going on fasts, taking vows, making pilgrimages and acting as a lay counselor to the young. An erect, stern, still-handsome woman with finely chiseled features and grayish-blond hair, she must have been very beautiful when young. She had just turned sixteen that terrible morning. She did not even live in Tykocin in those days, but with a widowed mother and sister in Białystok. She happened to be visiting her grandmother the day Schweiger was shot and stayed on in Tykocin because she did not want to leave the old woman alone.

Her story: "It was four o'clock in the morning. We had been afraid of a reprisal for three days. Nothing happened. They said the German officer who was killed was a good man. His wife and children were visiting. When he died the whole town went to his funeral and brought flowers and paid respects to the dead. That morning the Germans surrounded Tykocin with trucks. SS men came to every house to check identification. They told us to gather in the park in front of the church. 'Take your passport and go!' they ordered us. 'Take your passport and go! *Schnell! Schnell!*' It was still dark but by the time they had gathered everybody in the park it was daylight.

"They didn't take old people and they didn't take children. Lots of people ran away. Some people thought it would be all right, as the Germans had done nothing for three days. They took the German officer back to Germany later, but the body was still in Tykocin that morning. Five trucks pulled up in front of the church. The Germans shouted at us, '*H'raus! H'raus!*' They had lots of big dogs, German shepherd police dogs. They packed us into trucks as if we were animals. In one family they arrested a young father and mother and forced them up on a truck, leaving a nine-year-old girl behind. The mother was carrying a two-month-old baby. When she wouldn't give her baby up, the Germans hit her, tore the baby out of her arms and just threw it from the truck. The little girl took the baby home but I later learned it died soon. The mother's hair turned white right afterward. The soldiers sent away children who were crying for their parents. The sixteen-year-olds like myself were taken but anybody younger could just walk away.

"They told us we were going to the Łopuchowo Woods. Everybody thought we would die like the Jews. It had been three years earlier but our fears that they would do the same to us had never left. Almost every day the Germans killed somebody in front of the monument in the park or in front of the church. Everybody was praying. The truck was headed for Łopuchowo. Then it turned and went on the highway to Białystok. We couldn't see out. Everything was closed.

"In Tykocin that day, a small German plane flew over and dropped leaflets. They said the Gestapo was going to come back and set the whole town on fire. Those who were left, mainly old people and children and some who had hid and escaped, crowded into the church that evening to say a litany to Mary, Mother of God. The old priest, seeing so many people were missing and had been taken away, collapsed at the altar. The Gestapo also seized people from three other towns, Łapy, Sokoły and Pogorzałki, and some villages. They were all taken to the central jail in Białystok.

"They opened the back of the truck and told us to get out. '*Schnell!*' they shouted, and then 'out, out! Line up! Move inside, quickly!' We were herded into the courtyard of the jail and ordered to sit around the edges. There were hundreds of people. On the left side of the courtyard there were many dead and dying people, all covered with blood. We were told we would all walk by and look at them. In the center of the courtyard four Germans with accordions were playing happy music. It was horrible."

The Gestapo's grisly use of music is another sickening aspect of Nazism. Those in front of the forced procession of Jews to the Łopuchowo Woods had to play musical instruments. Auschwitz had an orchestra that played as prisoners were marched in and out. Music blared from loudspeakers at some of the death camps and during mass executions.

Mrs. Grabowska: "Facing us across the courtyard was a long table where some German officers sat. We had to march past the dead and injured to the table, where the officers examined our passports and identification papers. As we passed the dead and dying, there was blood all over. Some of them reached out to us. The accordions were still playing. They took our passports and documents and all belts, shoelaces, rings, necklaces, watches and money. Then they said, 'Pregnant women should step forward. They will report to the doctor.' About twenty pregnant women came forward. We later found out they were kept together and sent home in six weeks. We were packed into cells, with about forty women in ours. The turnkey was a Polish policeman, who whispered he had overheard the Germans talking. He said, 'At eleven o'clock in the night planes will fly over the jail. As they roar overhead, everyone will be loaded on trucks and driven into the forest to be shot.' In the night planes came and we could hear them taking prisoners away. But the women in our cell were spared. I myself prayed the whole night.

"Four or five days went by. I lost track of time. We got so dirty. We could not change our clothes but wore them day and night and could not wash. One day we were marched into the courtyard. A Gestapo officer came and he told us, 'You are the lucky ones. You are going to Germany to work.' The men were kept separate from the women. They gave us each a loaf of bread but no water and we were loaded into cattle cars on a train. We traveled for one week. The only water was a bucketful now and then. There were no cups and not everybody got to drink. If you got a humane soldier, he might bring another bucket of water. They gave water only to women, not to the men. Women begged them to give water to the men and sometimes the Germans allowed women to run back to another freight car and give water if they knew someone had a son, husband or brother there. The first day no one died. After that there were dead every day.

"They took the men to Gross Rosen and the women to Ravensbrück. It took a week because the train kept being shunted to a side track to let German troop trains headed for the front go by. We had that loaf of bread but it was small and lasted most of us only two days. After one week we arrived at Ravensbrück. 'Out!' they shouted, not telling us where we were. They took away our papers, our clothes, and shaved off all our hair. Not only on the head. Everywhere. 'Shut up! To the bathhouse! *Schnell!'* It was freezing cold but the showers were water, not gas. Outside they threw us clothing, all different kinds of old clothes, each piece marked with a big black cross, sometimes in front, sometimes in back. And they gave everybody wooden shoes. The shoes were so heavy. And they gave us spoons. Only a spoon, no cup or bowl. You guarded that spoon like a treasure, because if you lost it, you wouldn't get another one. People tied their spoons around their necks or to a button.

"The first day somebody stole my shoes. I had to go barefoot. I asked the German woman guard what I should do. 'Nothing is missing here in the camp!' she screamed at me. 'Nothing is missing here in the camp!' I felt I was supposed to steal from someone, but I didn't want to do that. At last she gave me some shoes.

"For one month we just stayed there in the barracks, penned up in quarantine. We would be counted, twice a day, morning and evening, the live ones and the dead ones, to see if anybody was missing. Then they had a *sale*. They were selling people. Every day we would be taken out into a courtyard. *'Ausgehen!'* the woman guard would order us. Germans from outside Ravensbrück would be waiting. They came to buy women prisoners. 'Cut your fingernails, *Fräulein,'* the guard told me. 'Or bite them off. Pinch your cheeks. You are young. Maybe a rich one will take you.'

"They would take five prisoners out at a time, to be looked over by these rich Germans. They were men who owned private factories. I was in a group of twenty women who were sold to a German who owned a porcelain factory. It was in Neu Rohlau, a town in Czechoslovakia near Karlsbad. We made parts for planes. I was in Ravensbrück a month and a half."

Almost a year passed. Hitler from his bunker in Berlin was insisting that Germans must fight on to the death, but Germany was collapsing. Western and Russian armies met up in Saxony on April 25. Hitler would be dead within five days. The German factory owner decided to get rid of his workers. He did not want Russian or American soldiers to find him with slave laborers. Mrs. Grabowska said, "This was the worst time of all. It was just days before the end of the war in Europe on May 7, 1945. Besides Poles who worked in the factory, there were Gypsies, some Russian men and women and some German women prisoners, four hundred of us. German soldiers marched us away from the factory but they didn't know where to go. Anybody who tried to escape was shot. The German soldiers were all around us. We walked and walked, hungry and thirsty, for ten, eleven days. People ate grass or whatever they could along the road. The Germans themselves didn't know where to take us. We just wandered about aimlessly. Many on the march died of typhus. I promised myself never to drink water because of typhus. We ate only wet grass. The Germans were retreating. We heard the Russians were just six kilometers away, the British five kilometers."

Here, for the only time in her story, Mrs. Grabowska broke down and wept, unable to go on. It took her some minutes to regain her composure. Wiping her eyes, she continued: "The day before freedom, I will tell you what happened. When people tried to escape, the Germans would just shoot them with machine guns. On May 5, they took us into a cow pasture for the night. It started to sleet and snow, very cold and wet, and people sat up and slept, not lying down. Even so, I caught a chill and was so feverish I couldn't walk the next day. My friend, a woman from Tykocin—there were four of us still together—was holding me up. A German nudged her in the back with his machine gun. 'Leave her alone and save yourself,' he told my friend. She cried, 'Leave her alone? Never! I will never let her go!'

"She probably saved my life. By then the soldiers were shooting anybody who fell behind, stragglers nobody helped. 'If we die, we die together,' my friend said. Just hours before we got our freedom, one of the Russian men caught a hare, which he strangled and began to eat raw. A German guard came and ran his bayonet into the man's stomach and killed him. Then he laughed.

"A German truck carrying potatoes came by. Everyone begged the driver for something to eat. He stopped, but the guards shouted they would kill anybody who tried to take a potato. At that, the driver, himself a German, seized one of the guards, got his pistol away from him and held it to his head. He told the rest of the guards, 'I am responsible for my transport. Don't you try to kill anybody. They can take my potatoes. And shut up, or I'll kill you too.'

"By now German soldiers were streaming past us in retreat and they shouted at our guards that the Russians were right behind them. The guards started to gather people together to kill them. As soon as they opened fire, everybody started running. All of a sudden the shooting stopped. Somebody was shouting, 'The Russians are coming down the road!' We heard shouts of *'Alles zu Hausen gehen!'* German soldiers were running back, throwing down their rifles and trying to get away. We captives were confused. One minute it looked like we'd all be killed, the next everybody was kneeling down and praying, 'God is merciful . . . Blessed be the Lord . . .' The Germans simply left us there on the road and ran away. We didn't know what to do. We were all still wearing the striped white-and-blue flannel uniform of the concentration camps. Everybody was very thin and emaciated. I weighed just thirty-five kilos. My face was so swollen and dirty it looked like it was covered with fish scales. We had no food, nothing. We went from house to house, begging, *'Bitte, kleines Stück Brot.'* "

The Red Cross took Mrs. Grabowska to a hospital in Bratislava, where she spent a week. When she was well enough to travel, she made her own way back to Poland. At the railway station in Warsaw, she met a Jewish man she recognized from Tykocin. She was astonished he was alive. "He came up to me and called me by my first name, Mieczysława. We had gone to school together. He warned me there were Russian Army patrols in the streets of Białystok." "Be careful after curfew, as they may shoot," he told her. "Better wait until morning at the railway station." He also warned her to take only a slow local train, as some of the express trains were not stopping in Białystok but heading straight across the frontier into Russia. The next day Mrs. Grabowska found her sister in Białystok and together they went to Tykocin, walking the last twelve kilometers west on the road that passed Popowlany. She found that of the people taken away the year before, only she had so far made it home again. She also learned that in the last days of their occupation, the Germans in Tykocin turned even more brutal, killing more and more people every day and forcing others to withdraw with them, to dig fortifications during their retreat.

Almost all of Tykocin's death camp survivors suffered from arthritis or some other ailment. Piotr, a gentle, half-French old man who ran the ice-cream stall, bore jagged scars on his wrists and stomach from a Gestapo interrogation. His torturers set a vicious police dog on him, then stood and watched. "I almost bled to death," he would say. Some survivors suffered mentally. Eugenia Mocarska, an old woman who lived in a cabin near the synagogue, lost her teeth at Auschwitz. Sometimes she would tell people Nazi torturers extracted them. But she would also say, "I had some bread and the other prisoners accused me of hiding it and knocked out my teeth." If she talked about Auschwitz in a feverish, broken way, Mocarska was much more lucid about her youth, as a Catholic living in the Jewish half of Tykocin. "The Catholics and the Jews were on very good terms when I was a girl. They danced together, helped each other put up hay and harvest grain. The Jewish shopkeepers always gave credit. You got what you needed but could pay later. The Jews did not drink like the Catholics. And until the war, they went to different schools. Some Jews were rich. But many were poor and sold goods from baskets in the streets.''

Another man from Tykocin served in the *Sonderkommandos*, those who manned the gas chambers and crematoria and were usually soon put to death themselves. He said the way the arms and legs thrashed around in the fires convinced him that not all the people they shoved in the ovens were dead. Poles blamed the worst horrors on Hitler, the SS or the Gestapo. But Agneshka felt as many of Tykocin's people did: "People are afraid, now that the Germans are united, that they will be a great power again." Her father would say emphatically, "It wasn't the *Germans*. It was *Hitler*." Few agreed completely. Most felt like Alina Oldziej, a survivor of Ravensbrück, who said, "We are afraid of this united Germany. I cannot watch a film to this day where I see Germans in uniforms and helmets. We are unlikely to live until then but surely one day the Germans will come for our land." Agneshka also asked, as many have wondered, why the Jews seemed to go to the slaughter so often like sheep. But rounded up by the Germans, marched into forests, driven into ditches, stuffed into cattle cars, Tykocin's Catholics had no more success in trying to escape or resist. They all were up against the utmost evil, something far worse than any of them could conceive was humanly possible.

VI

Tykocin's first freely elected government in sixty years was not supposed to look like this. Dominik Włoskowski's Polish Peasant Party had survived under Communism by toeing the party line. Leszek Kruchevski, Mrs. Grabowska's son-in-law, was also a member and, like Dominik, had been around under the Communists. Jurek called them Flip and Flop, the one short, fat and fair, the other tall, lean and dark. "They are old keyboards," Jurek joked. "Let's see if they can play a new tune."

As mayor, the tune Dominik wanted to play was to raise morale and incomes for his constituency of peasant farmers. All but the schoolmaster in his seven-member district council worked on the land, even Leszek, who raised mushrooms in a big barn behind his house on the riverbank. All were male. Dominik's opposition, defeated in the election and now grouped into the new Society of the Friends of Tykocin, was nearly all female. Alicja Matusiewicz was one of their leaders. As Dominik saw it, his mandate was to go from Communism to capitalism at full speed. Indeed, in Tykocin, Poland's forty-five years of Communism might never have existed. Try to find a Marxist-Leninist and one always got "Oh, they were just in Warsaw." With streets renamed and statues torn down, especially the one of a Russian soldier in front of City Hall, old Stefan was the only one in town who boasted he was part of it. After a few shots of vodka at the pub he would rise and loudly declare, "I was born a Stalinist, I've been a Stalinist all my life and I'll die a Stalinist." Everybody would roar at him good-naturedly to sit down.

"What I hate most is lying," Jurek told Dominik. "And the Communists were always lying." Jurek's friend Andre Borowski, a young farmer who lived in Babino, told Jurek that when he was inducted into the Polish Army in 1985, the recruiting sergeant told him to take off his crucifix. "Well, the Communists never did anything to me," said Agneshka, who grew up under them. She did admit that government clerks were awfully rude to the farmers, telling them, "Please, wait until I finish my tea." Agneshka would go on: "Or they wouldn't even say 'Please.' Just 'Wait!' in a mean, gruff voice. They were so unpleasant that villagers didn't like to deal with them. And on a collective farm, they told you what to do all the time. 'You can't do this. You can't do that. Don't talk to him. Don't talk to her. You pick apples. You work in the orchard. You work in the road.' In Popowlany now a farmer can get up in the morning and do whatever he likes."

Andre said a lot of people like Dominik went along with the Communists to get some advantage. "Say I was a young farmer," he said. "I needed a new tractor. If I joined the Party I could get it cheaper and quicker. But if you had family abroad, especially in America, it could be very uncomfortable."

The worst, everybody agreed, were the compulsory crop deliveries in the 1950s. "If they told you to fill a quota for rye and you didn't have it, you went to jail," Jurek said. His father might have to go out and buy it. One man in Popowlany was arrested by the Tykocin militia after he failed to bring in his assigned quota. He talked them into stopping at the pub for vodka, climbed out the toilet window, bolted home, got some rye from a neighbor and took it in to the government warehouse. By the time the militiamen caught up with him, he had a receipt to wave in their faces.

Some deception was deadly. Andre's army unit was sent for training in the Ural Mountains in April 1986. The train crossed the Ukraine's Pripet Marshes, good duck-shooting country. As a cook, Andre worked outside on an open mess platform, in the fresh air. Not far from Kiev, he first saw soldiers with Geiger counters in a village they passed. His platoon leader heard a warning on the radio not to leave cows outdoors, not to drink milk and not to eat mushrooms or vegetables. What was going on? Then Radio Free Europe reported that Sweden had detected a sharp rise in radioactivity. That night a terse bulletin was broadcast from Moscow:

> An accident has taken place at the Chernobyl power station and one of the reactors was damaged. Measures are being taken to eliminate the consequences of the accident. Those affected by it are being given assistance. A government commission has been set up.

That was all. Andre's unit had passed within eighty kilometers of the Chernobyl reactor. Nobody warned them. Białystok, like Tykocin and Popowlany, were within fifty kilometers of the area worst affected by the powerful radioactive cloud that arrived over Poland on April 26, 1986. Popowlany was six hundred kilometers from Chernobyl, but its people all breathed radiation-polluted dust. In a panic, Jurek and his neighbors drank iodine until the doctor in Tykocin warned that it was useless, even harmful. Deaths from cancer over the next thirty years in Ukraine, Byelarus, Poland, Sweden, even Britain, were expected to reach tens of thousands. The catastrophic meltdown proved how demanding a technology nuclear power could be. To those like Jurek and Andre and the other villagers, it showed, when it came to secrecy and misinformation at the cost of their health and lives, just how rotten the Communist system was and how close it was to collapse.

In Tykocin the beginning of the end came eight years before, on October 16, 1978. "We took it as a sign from God," Mrs. Grabowska would say. "I'll never forget that day. I was listening to the radio and I fell asleep. All of a sudden someone was pounding on the door and screaming, 'Do you know who is elected? Ours! Ours!' People were running into the street. Everybody was hugging and crying. It was a gift from God that they chose a Pole."

Did all those Italian cardinals comprehend what they had done casting their votes for the onetime actor and poet from Wadowice, author of books on philosophy, so handsome and benevolent-looking? Pope John Paul II came to Warsaw seven months after his election. Half a million Poles gathered to see him. He did not attack Communism, as many hoped and expected. What he did do was to treat it as transient, something of short duration, something imposed. He told them they were dignified and valuable. He gave them a new spiritual confidence. From this the rest followed, the rise of Solidarity a year later and the chain of events that swept all Eastern Europe and then Russia itself and led to the death of Soviet Communism and its empire.

For a long time this outcome seemed far from certain. The day he was shot in 1981 the Pope had been fasting. To Mrs. Grabowska this saved his life. "On Fridays he only drinks a little water and eats a bit of bread. So he had an empty stomach," she told those at the church. A year later, just after the Communists in Warsaw had declared "a state of war," Mrs. Grabowska was invited to Rome to meet John Paul II. Thirty-six Poles were invited, all laymen who helped their priests counsel young people as Mrs. Grabowska did. Only twenty-eight of them, those outside Warsaw itself, got passports in time to go.

Mrs. Grabowska: "It was all at the last moment. I had two weeks to get a passport and went to the militia headquarters in Białystok. I hadn't left Poland since 1945. At first a young officer I met said it would take at least a month. When I said I had only fourteen days, he relented. Everything was ready in a week. We left from Warsaw. Józef Cardinal Glemp gave us his blessing. We took the train and were led by three priests. On the journey we learned the Pope was in Bologna. We went there and found that thousands of people had come to see him. So we made a sign. On one side we drew the Polish eagle, with a crown and the words *'Pokój i Dobro'*—'Peace and Goodness.' On the other side we pasted a picture of the Black Madonna. When Polish people in the crowd, those stranded outside Poland by martial law, saw this standard they fell to kissing the picture of the Black Madonna and weeping. Then the Pope caught sight of it and his eyes filled with tears. He arranged to meet us after the mass near a cemetery on the outskirts of Bologna. There he wept again, as did all the Polish women. We fell to our knees and he said, 'Don't cry. It's going to be better.' The touch of the Pope, it gives wings. It lifts the spirit. In Rome he arranged for us to stay at his Pilgrim's House at the Vatican. There he spoke to each of us. I can remember very little of what he said. He asked me where Tykocin was and I said it was near

Białystok. And I said I hoped he would come to us. 'We are waiting for you,' I told him."

Two years later Mrs. Grabowska again met John Paul II. When he returned to Poland she was chosen to meet him on behalf of the country's peasant women. She worked very hard for the Church. This time, Mrs. Grabowska decided to take the Pope a pig, as meat was very scarce in Warsaw. Her husband slaughtered it in the evening and she wrapped it up and hid it under a black cassock in the back seat of the Tykocin priest's Fiat. He and Mrs. Grabowska rode in front, the pig behind. It was illegal to ship meat privately and they risked arrest as black marketeers. Mrs. Grabowska: "Near Warsaw we were stopped by Russian soldiers but they waved us on. The priest had never been in Warsaw before and got lost. He said God would show us the way. Somehow we found ourselves at Cardinal Glemp's palace. We told the man at the gate, 'We have brought a pig for the Pope!' "

No one in Tykocin forgot how Russian soldiers stabled their horses in their cloister's chapel. Nor how the Communists encouraged hooligans to disturb mass, some of them so drunk they fell over when they went to kneel. On his triumphal visits to Poland in the 1980s when revolutionary fervor was at its height, the Pope received thunderous ovations wherever he went. As it turned out, the end of Communism also meant the end of the Catholic Church's unquestioned moral authority in Poland. This was not seen at once. In places like Tykocin the triumph of Solidarity was viewed above all, as it was, a triumph for the Church. It was Solidarity which voiced the cry "Down with Communism!" but everyone knew the Church harbored its activists and paid for its underground presses during the worst years. In Tykocin almost everybody went to church. The few who did not go, like Alicja's elderly mother or Alicja herself, were so exceptional everybody remarked on it. Many villagers like Jurek belonged to small circles of neighbors who gathered in somebody's parlor or kitchen on Sunday afternoons to say the rosary. Others, like Mrs. Grabowska, who suffered rheumatism from her days in Ravensbrück and as slave laborer for the Germans, made long pilgrimages on foot to holy shrines, such as to the Częstochowa monastery to pay homage to the painting of the Black Madonna. She had done it three times. Her teenage grandchildren went every year.

But many people in Tykocin, as all over Poland, objected when the government in Warsaw, without consulting Parliament, decreed that children should be taught religion at school. When Cardinal Glemp said he wanted to end the "Communist-inspired" separation of church and state, there was an outburst of angry letters, editorials and articles with headlines like "Are we ruled by the clergy?" When Catholics successfully pushed through Parliament a bill banning abortion, there was another outcry. Polls showed over half of the Polish people believed abortion should be legal as a matter of course. Few in Tykocin were surprised by this turn of events. Anticlericalism was as deeply imbued in Jurek's mind as was faith in the Virgin Mary. Had not his ancestors been virtual serfs of priests? The fight against Communism united Poles beneath the Black Madonna, the Polish crowned eagle of past kingdoms and the memories of survivors of Stalinism and the Nazis, but no longer: that battle had been won.

What mattered now was how to create capitalism. Poland's crash program to dismantle forty-five years of a state-run economy zigged and zagged, sometimes propping up old lame-duck state-owned industries and sometimes creating a "good climate" for, as one Prime Minister put it, "swindlers, crooks and thieves"—that is, emergent capitalists. No other ex-Communist country did so much so quickly to escape its past.

"To go from Communism to capitalism is not for the timid," said Dominik, who seemed to personify the unleashed invention, ingenuity and energy stirring through Poland. What Tykocin district needed, he felt, were ways to process its milk, meat and vegetable oil. He also wanted to bring telephones and paved roads to villages like Popowlany. What affected Jurek most was milk, which, together with pigs, provided his main cash income. Why not, Dominik decided, start a modern dairy? The existing milk collection system was terrible. Carts went about the villages in early morning, loading up milk cans, taking them to a crossroads and putting them on a truck to be taken to the town of Monki, thirty kilometers away. It was slow and inefficient. In summer the milk soured. The dairy in Monki sent it back and all it was good for was to feed the pigs. Sales of pigs and calves brought in more money, but milk, except in the dead of winter when the cows dried up, was a more dependable year-round source of income.

Dominik also wanted to sell off the assets of the district's bankrupt state collective farm, Stelmachowo. It had plenty of land, five hundred hectares, owned seventy cows and employed fifty workers. There were 1,300 such collective farms in Poland but Parliament couldn't decide who owned them. It wasn't too pressing, as 80 percent of Poland's farmland had never been collectivized and was already privately owned.

Full of plans, Dominik and Leszek went to Warsaw, looked around and decided that a French firm, Steripack, had what they wanted. Its equipment cost an even $1 million and could pasteurize up to 3,600 cartons of milk per hour. In a ten-hour day this would handle all the milk produced in Tykocin district. The whole project, if they could use Stelmachowo's land, might come in under $1.5 million. There was a lot of Western credit around. The European Bank offered low-cost loans. The U.S. Congress had set aside $200 million for projects in Poland that were "small," "private" and "agricultural."

As Dominik saw it, Tykocin itself would have to raise about 20 percent of the cost. In capitalism you sold shares. Mirek, the headmaster, figured there were about two thousand people in town and about six thousand more in outlying villages like Popowlany. There were only three farms in Tykocin district that were fifty hectares or more. Half of the total number, generally those along the Białystok–Warsaw highway, were eight to thirty hectares and were modern commercial farms in the sense that their owners carried on agriculture for reinvestment and as a business for profit, looking upon land as capital and commodity. The rest of the holdings, mainly along the old meandering course of the Narew River, were less than eight hectares, some of it in pasture and woods. These villagers, like Jurek, cultivated their land largely for subsistence and as part of a traditional way of life. Without money coming in from America, Dominik realized, these people would be true peasants, which gave his party its name. Both kinds of cultivators grew wheat, oats, barley, hay, triticale, potatoes and sugar beets, kept pigs and cows, sold bulls as calves for veal, and a few raised sheep and horses. What hurt since the breakup of the Soviet Union was that Tykocin district had plenty of food to sell but no buyers. Nobody in Ukraine, Byelarus or Lithuania, the nearest neighbors, had any money, nor did Russia supply the Poles with oil as barter for food anymore. Everything was being done in hard currency.

Jurek, when Dominik told him of his scheme, exclaimed, "You're crazy, crazy! Who will buy shares?" Dominik went to see Tykocin's priest, Father Tadeusz Gladkowski, a plump, balding old man in a black caftan, whose apartment behind the church was richly furnished. He agreed to tell the congregation at mass on Sunday about the dairy and urge everybody to buy shares. But he was not encouraging.

"The result of my words will not be great, I think," he warned Dominik.

"We want Tykocin to be the first town in Poland to have such a dairy," Dominik argued. "Milk is milk. It is difficult to keep more than a short time in hot weather. If we can pasteurize our milk and put it into cartons, we can sell it in Warsaw and Białystok, Zambrow and Ostrow, Mazowiecki, Łomza and Ostroleka. We want to open the dairy within two years. We figure by then everything will be in private hands in Poland."

The priest folded his hands. "The church has so many needs of its own," he said in a regretful tone. "We must raise nine million zlotys for the restoration of our Black Madonna. The frame must be regilded in Warsaw and that means a lot of money. Everything is so expensive now. It is hard to survive from one month to the next. But pork, veal, ham, wurst, it's all so expensive. Never mind, I say. Say a prayer to God."

Dominik expected everyone to share his enthusiasm for a dairy. He reckoned without the Society of the Friends of Tykocin. This circle of intellectuals, most of them women, found Tykocin drearily provincial with so many crude and coarsely ignorant peasants, who went about in dirty clothes and boots, breath smelling of vodka. The society stood for schools and better education, amateur theatricals, art exhibitions, fund raising for the library, improving the environment and piano concerts. These concerts, in the Grand Hall of the town museum, with its French doors and chandeliers and many oil paintings on the walls, ran to Chopin and his sonatas, especially the B Flat Minor and B Flat, as well as his patriotic polonaises and mazurkas. Society members saw themselves as guardians of respectability and morality in Tykocin. They were fond of sitting about in the custodian's office of the museum or in one of Alicja's drawing rooms to discuss progress, politics, literature, art and how to save the Narew River.

The Matusiewicz house was of old-fashioned design with a low, flat shingled roof and had been built by Alicja's grandfather. It had not been painted for a long time and its gray shutters were rusty. Grass grew in chinks on the stone steps. Old unpruned lilac bushes left the pillared wooden entrance in perpetual shade, and it was rare not to see a daddy longlegs crawling up the wall. Everything was dilapidated and neglected, but on the whole the house, for Tykocin, was quite grand. To ring the bell was to hear Alicja's little dog barking—then a yelp and a scuffle before the door opened. Alicja at sixty-five still looked vaguely like a schoolgirl—she moved in a youthful way, her grayish fair hair fell straight to her shoulders, her white blouse, dark skirt and cardigan could have been a school uniform. She had fine, sad eyes and an alert, intelligent expression. She was also hospitable; visitors could count on getting coffee with cake. Her reclusive husband, who looked older and wore a beret outdoors, spent much of his time at a cabin in the woods on the Bokuń side of Popowlany. Both he and Alicja were retired schoolteachers.

The drawing rooms were on either side of a dimly lit hall. They were big and gloomy with parquet floors, worn carpets and a lot of heavy mahogany furniture arranged in confusion—sofas, plush chairs, large round tables, in the west room a grand piano with raised lid and open music, velvet drapes, chests and many pictures, oil paintings with wide gilded frames. All about the rooms shelves overflowed with books, portfolios of drawings and stacks of paintings and pastels, and photographs sitting on the tables pell-mell. Alicja painted, and her portrait of Maximilian Kolbe, the priest who died at Auschwitz to save children, was in the church, just as her pictures of Jesus and the Holy Mother were in the chapel of Tykocin's cloister, now a monastic home for retired priests. Alicja carried a heavy cross. If her name came up in Popowlany, the villagers said, "She worked for the Germans. She worked for the Germans." Alicja was sensitive to this, and to what she saw as the dark side of the German character. Not long before, she was coming from Warsaw on the train when some young German students with backpacks, fresh-faced and blond, took seats across the aisle. They were laughing and joking and one of the boys said, "My father was a soldier in Poland during the war." "Did he learn any Polish?" asked one of the girls. The boy shrugged. "Only the dirty words."

Alicja was vice president of the Society of the Friends of Tykocin. Its president was Joanna Malesińska, the district nurse, a tall blond woman, taller than any of the other members. She had run against Dominik for the mayor's post and been badly defeated. A mother of six children, Joanna was one of the few society members with some claim to being a farmer. Her husband owned a few acres and milked two cows. Ewa Wroczyńska, a small, nervous woman who was curator of the museum, was secretary. They enjoyed being in opposition and called Dominik and his council the "Tykocin Mafia." While they put a political face to it, it was really Dominik's ingrained peasant uncouthness that they objected to. They thought of themselves as well-bred citizens who discussed uplifting things as they sipped tea from old china. "Dominik and his men want power," Joanna would say. "Our society works for the good of Tykocin." This was true, but it was a Tykocin of old buildings, nature and tradition. Dominik wanted to modernize farming and attract industry. He had won by a huge margin.

The society felt the town needed a local weekly newspaper with an honest viewpoint and for some years had written and printed—mimeographed—*Echo Tykocin*. Joanna wrote an editorial about Dominik's scheme:

> There are problems with the milk project.
>
> First, who will the dairy belong to if the heirs dispossessed by the Communists come back to claim the Stelmachowo estate?
>
> Second, will the machine for sterilization of the milk be big enough? Will it create environmental problems?
>
> Third, the dairy will be modern. Will it take milk from all the farmers? Half of them use traditional methods. A modern dairy must take milk of only good quality. Not every farmer has it.

Not all the society members approved of the editorial. At the next meeting a tall, untidy, scholarly-looking man who taught at the district agricultural school told the members, "You must realize we have few people who take a real interest in farming. Joanna is the only farmer in the society."

Joanna smiled. "I'll say. And there are still plenty of people like me in Tykocin who still milk by hand. How can such poor farmers buy shares? How can we finance a dairy from scratch?"

The teacher threw up his hands. "Inflation will affect the price of milk. If money loses its value, Dominik won't sell enough shares. On the other hand, if the dairy would succeed, people here might trust the idea that we can do something for ourselves. That's a big 'if.' "

Joanna nodded. "We have sunk into a kind of morass. Even a small success would be good for morale."

Ewa, the curator, brunet, fortyish, with a grave little face, spoke up. "Tykocin has a good chance for progress." She spoke in a rapid, staccato manner, as if she were afraid of being interrupted. "The town has lasted five hundred years without changing much. There are families who have lived here generation after generation. Their ancestors go back centuries. The layout of the streets hasn't changed since the sixteenth century. The architecture of many of the houses goes back to the seventeenth and eighteenth centuries. There isn't such an old historic town in a radius of hundreds of miles, in all of Białystok province. Grodno and Vilnius are very old cities but now they are in Byelarus and Lithuania. And Tykocin is surrounded by good farming country."

"The majority of the people in the district farm for a living," Joanna said. "In the election their interests won over the town's."

"Well, it's not what party you belong to," Ewa said, "as much as family and who your relatives are. That was so even under the Communists."

There was a murmur of agreement. *"Tak." "Tak, familia.* Yes, family." "It has always been that way."

Alicja interrupted, a frown on her small, serious face. "Everybody talks about Tykocin," she said, "but nobody talks about the Narew River. The fortunes of Tykocin have always come from the river. And under Communist rule all the factories in Białystok dumped their refuse into it and turned our beautiful river into a dirty and polluted canal. When I was a girl, people in Tykocin fished for a living. Who does so now? There were canoes, boats, people swam and took their vacations along the river. It was a natural reservoir, good for hay, and you could transport wood and crops by river all the way to Gdańsk. Now it's too dirty even to put your foot in. The pure waters of the Narew could be restored. But not by this government. Dominik and Leszek held office under the Communists. What did they do to stop pollution?"

Alicja's devotion to Tykocin's heritage centered on three men: Zygmunt Gloger, a nineteenth-century ethnographer famous for his four-volume encyclopedia and a geography of Poland's rivers; Zygmunt Bujnowski, a peasant who became a landscape painter and died in Tykocin in 1927 when just thirty-five; and Włodzimierz Puchalski, a nationally celebrated wildlife photographer, who died in Antarctica in 1979. Unlike Gloger and Bujnowski, Puchalski was not a Tykocin native but he kept a cabin on the Narew to photograph its wildlife; the cabin was just across the river from Jurek's woods.

Gloger's encyclopedia was once familiar to all Polish schoolchildren. A nobleman, he died in 1910 at sixty and was buried in state in Warsaw, but his wife and children were interred in a crypt in the Tykocin cemetery. Alicja was trying to save what was left of Gloger's old estate, now in ruins except for a stable and brewery. She had already done much to salvage Bujnowski's work. Her husband found one painting covering a hole in a wardrobe, another in a henhouse. Bujnowski loved Tykocin and his pictures of its church, synagogue and park, his landscapes of fields, gardens and orchards, thatched peasant huts, country houses, birch woods and moss-covered barns idealized the prewar countryside in a brooding, rhythmic linear style. Once one saw Bujnowski's pictures, one began to see Tykocin through his eyes. He redefined the town, its weather, its architecture, its scenery. The museum had forty of his works, all but two donated by the Matusiewiczes, who were given a symbolic payment in zlotys, equivalent to a dollar at the time.

"He was a peasant boy but very clever," Alicja would tell visitors. "Czar Nicholas I gave him a scholarship to study art in Kiev. During World War I he enlisted, went to the front and got shot in the head. He never wholly recovered. For years his wife sold vodka and beer in that little shop near the synagogue Mrs. Pojak has today. He would paint all day long. People thought he must be mad. When he tired of painting he'd keep busy making frames for his works. Some of the young Jewish people, who appreciated his work more, bought his paintings, but cheaply. Many he simply gave them. He died when he was so very young."

Puchalski was famous, both as a photographer and as an early environmentalist. In one of his books of photographs, *A Year in the Primeval Forest*, he says:

> After the many wars which have raged through Poland and human greed in exploiting the riches of nature, our lands are no longer covered with the dense forests of ancient oaks, beeches, maples and yew which were the hunting grounds of such kings as Władysław the Short, Kazimierz the Great and Jagiello. During the past 150 years the forest area of this country has been reduced by half. For years on end man has exploited the woods, depriving them of their finest trees. Step by step he has forced his way into the depths of the forest.

Alicja kept the keys to Puchalski's cabin on the river. His photographs were very fine: mist settling in drops on a spiderweb, a wolf in the deep snow of winter, European bison in the Białowieza Forest.

Alicja saw herself as a custodian of the past, whether preserving such treasures, laying wreaths at the Solidarity monument or even directing history plays in the castle ruins in summer so that little boys with wooden swords might be seen running about the parapets, likely as not, followed by their dogs. She even drew portraits of bearded rabbis with her pastels, so that the town's young people could better understand Tykocin's history. Dominik, without thinking much about it, was just the opposite: he looked almost wholly to the promise of the future. History, he saw instinctively, was not destiny.

One day he fired half the people on Tykocin's payroll. Rumors flew that he planned to sell the old house used by the library and that he wanted to cut down all the stately old poplar trees around the square. To some he was Lopakhin come to destroy the cherry orchard. Dominik shrugged. "The dogs bark but the caravan moves on." He admitted he had sold only seventeen shares so far, not hundreds as he had expected. "Farmers don't have the money right now," he reasoned. "Nobody can sell his grain." He didn't take *Echo Tykocin* seriously. "It's silly to oppose the dairy. And now these women are all excited about the trees around the park. Maybe I would like to cut down every other one. It's too dark. Mushrooms are growing on the roofs of the houses. Alicja loves birds and nature and that's all right, but sometimes these women go too far."

Another reason nobody was buying shares, Dominik told Jurek, was that they were already buying telephones. This was the first campaign promise Dominik had made good on. He had extended Tykocin's lines to twenty-one villages. The Białystok Telephone Company agreed to install a new cable along the Białystok–Tykocin road. It was up to each village to dig a trench in from the crossroads. Sixteen of Popowlany's families signed up for phones and for two days young men from each family pitched in. One of Jurek's cousins, Józef Sadowski, first broke the earth with a deep plow hitched to his tractor. A dozen village stalwarts, their faces red and sweaty, followed with spades. An official from the telephone company was also on hand to make sure the trench was exactly eighty centimeters deep and four meters from the edge of the road. They kept hitting the roots of the poplar trees and broke the blades of two plows, which were taken to the barn of one of the Sakowiczes to be rewelded. Then Manik Sliwonski, the beefiest youth in Popowlany, got the idea of standing on the plow and it worked well from then on.

When Agneshka and her father came to watch, Manik told them how he helped to topple the statue of the Russian soldier in front of City Hall.

"What will come next?" Agneshka joked. "A statue of Dominik?"

"What do you need a phone for?" Manik asked.

Agneshka thought. "Well, when you need to know the weather, you can call and find out."

"I can call the vet in Tykocin or my family in Białystok," one of the men said. "Or you can call to ask what is the price of fertilizer or coal." It was almost noon, and when the men started putting down their tools, Grandfather said in a loud voice, "That's enough for to-day. You should finish tomorrow." Agneshka laughed. "The big boss."

VII

After the rains of August there was a long spell of dry weather. Jurek even worried that the grass in a hayfield he owned on the opposite bank of the river was getting too dry. Once the swamps were drained, it seemed to be drier every year. Jurek decided to cut the grass and build a big smooth-sided haystack, what Polish peasants call a *stok*. He asked one of the Bokuńs, an older man, Jan, to help him, as it took a good deal of skill. They went by tractor, and when they crossed a bridge, Jurek saw how yellow the Narew's water was. It smelled like a sewer and white detergent foam floated on the surface. No fish could live in it, he thought.

A few days earlier Jurek had cut and raked the grass into twenty-one small stacks. Now he wrapped a chain around the base of each one and with the tractor dragged them back to where Jan had cut willow branches and laid them across what was left of an old haystack. "It's better we make it by this willow tree," said Jan, a wry-faced, shaggy-haired, old-fashioned peasant. "It will protect it from rain and snow.

"It looks like this good weather will hold, Jurek. My leg hurts three days before a rain and it's not hurting now. We'll have time to get the hay in." Jurek did not question this. Old villagers like Jan knew what the weather would be, what herbs cured disease, how to tell the age of a horse or a cow and all the things gained in a lifetime close to nature.

"I cut this Saturday. The grass is good and green."

"You didn't bring salt. It's better to put salt in the stack. The cows like it. Afterward they drink much water."

"I didn't want to, Jan. If you happen to give that hay to a horse, it's not good." Jurek carefully climbed to the top of the stack. It grew quickly as Jan pitched huge bundles of hay up to him to place. "I was eight years old when I made my first haystack," Jurek said.

"Who taught you how?"

"Nobody. I just watched the others."

It took them nearly three hours. When the *stok* was almost done, Jan made a tight little bundle of grass for the peak and handed it up to Jurek on a long-handled fork. Jan raked around the bottom of the stack as Jurek shaped the top and skillfully smoothed down the steep sides. "Now water won't get inside," he said, satisfied with what he had done. "You can make a thatched roof the same way. Remember when everybody had them?"

"In those days we made haystacks twice as big as this."

"They got so big we put a wooden pole in the middle. This was swampland then."

"There was so much water we sometimes came by boat." Jan discovered a pile of willow branches hidden under a tree. He swore. "*Cholera!* Plague take you! There was wood right here and I cut new." Jurek slid down the side of the haystack. He took a cloth bag from the tractor and he and Jan sat down in the willow tree's shade. Jurek took out a loaf of rye bread, some sliced ham wrapped in paper and two bottles of beer. They ate hungrily. Jan eyed the treetops, which were stirring. "The wind is rising, Jurek. Well, most people don't build *stoks* anymore. They take the hay right to the house."

"I have no place to keep it. And there's no danger of fire out here." Jurek sipped his beer, feeling contented. With eight hectares, four of them cultivated, and his cows, pigs and chickens, Jurek came close to being a true peasant. He cultivated his land mainly for subsistence, and in his faith in the Black Madonna and the rosary, the way he helped neighbors like Jan and they helped him without pay, and in many of his skills and routines, from harvesting potatoes by hand to building a haystack to killing a pig, even in the way he milked his cows, Jurek's views and ways were those of a peasantry little changed for centuries. It might be argued that Poland, as it neared the end of the twentieth century, had, along with parts of the Balkans, Europe's last authentic peasantry. Communism had failed to turn the Polish peasants into a rural proletariat, workers earning wages on big collective farms as in Russia. Yet, together with World War II, Communism had cut off Polish villages from the shift from horse-drawn machinery to tractors and combines, as happened in most Western farming in the 1930s. When Hitler invaded in 1939, two-thirds of the Poles were peasant villagers. When Communism collapsed fifty years later, 40 percent of them still were. Only in fiercely Catholic Poland did Communism so completely fail to bring land under state ownership. Nearly 80 percent of Poland's land was held, as for centuries, by peasant families, about 2.3 million of them.

Whether peasant views and ways lived on in Poland so long because religious faith, family ties and the work ethic were so strong or whether this strength came from peasant agriculture enduring so long is impossible to say. Certainly hard physical work was still the central fact of life in Popowlany, what with feeding the pigs and milking the first thing in the morning and again at night. Tractors were widely used and so were hired combines. Jurek had his Skoda, Ursus tractor and TV set. Yet horses pulled plows and trotted carts, hay got pitched with a wooden fork, wet grass was cut by scythe and potatoes gathered in wicker baskets by harvesters who crawled forward on padded knees. The same fork, the same cart, the same wicker baskets can be seen in Pieter Brueghel's sixteenth-century paintings of Flemish peasant life. The scene in Brueghel's *Haytime*, with peasants pitching loose hay up onto a horse-drawn cart, could be seen in Popowlany on any August day. When a neighbor greeted Jurek, "Let God help you," and Jurek replied, "Praise be to God," they were repeating a salutation used in Popowlany for a thousand years.

How would the village be different a thousand years ago? By the tenth century, Poland had gone from about 400,000 people at the time of Christ to more than a million, compared with 38 million today. By the tenth century, the old migratory slash-and-burn tillage had given way to cultivation of permanent plots in settled villages. Peasant holdings in the tenth-century averaged fifteen hectares, a good deal bigger than the average modern Polish farm of six hectares. Many tenth-century Polish village families owned three or four horses, a pair of oxen, a few cows, maybe a dozen sheep, several goats and six or seven pigs, again comparing favorably with today. A big difference is that vast areas, as Puchalski noted, were wooded or covered with swamps. It was not until the deforestation of the fifteenth and sixteenth centuries that the Polish countryside of mixed fields, woods and pastures took on the look it has today. Still, Polish peasants grew wheat and barley and raised cows and pigs six thousand years ago. An ox-drawn furrowing plow was used in Poland as early as 2500 B.C. Four-wheeled wooden carts like that of Agneshka's father went back to the fifth century A.D. Peasant ways had great continuity.

Jurek milked his cows in the age-old way, simply squatting down beside them. Bury, his enormous white dog, would run about sniffing and then wait expectantly as Jurek milked the first of the three cows. When he was done Jurek emptied his milk pail into a large can with a white straining cloth across the top of it. The dog ran to lick the milky froth from the cloth. Small wonder Jurek's milk was graded third class. His friend Andre Borowski, who used hygienic modern methods and came closer to being a farmer rather than a peasant, got a first-class rating and more money.

When the milking was done, Jurek would untether the cows. They ran thirstily to a marshy stream as Bury jumped about their heels and barked excitedly until Jurek shouted to him to stop. Then Jurek would head homeward, with pail and milk riding on his old bicycle. He usually met other villagers. One evening it was Janek, a poor man who lived alone on a small farm near a woods in Babino, where the Borowskis lived and Szmul Ismach had spent the last year of the war. Janek, a man of fifty, was in tatters and barefoot. His hair was tousled and he carried an old knitted cap over his shoulder. He told Jurek he had found a dead rabbit, perhaps killed by Bury or some other dog, and pulled the carcass out of his cap to show him. In it were also some ears of corn. Janek was a gentle, harmless person, always disposed to laugh and be cheerful. Jurek thought him either a saintly fool or a foolish saint.

Together they watched a black cloud of starlings swoop around the reddish western sky and down on a newly sown wheat field. Jurek cursed the birds and threw a stone at them. Janek smiled his kindly pleasant smile. "God created the birds and they have to live," he told Jurek. He had also picked some wild mustard and said he was taking it home to his flock of geese. Jurek asked if he was raising pigs. Janek laughed. "I live like a pig," he said. "You know, my mother's gone off to Białystok. She's over eighty and needs my sister to look after her." Janek was the youngest of thirteen children. The rest had gone away and his house and barn had fallen into disrepair and were in a pitiful state. Leaves blew right into the rooms but Janek didn't care. With his red sunburned cheeks and a beard as black as ink, he spent his days out of doors, always in the best of spirits. Whenever people worked in the fields, if he happened by he would stop and join them, sometimes laboring the whole day. He never accepted money.

Janek said he wanted to trade a goose for some pork. He planned to sell some goose feathers to a pillow maker in Białystok. "All is God's will, Jurek. He is wiser than man." Janek grinned. "I should sell it all and spend the money for drink. And then I'll go into the city and sweep the streets and everybody will tip their hats and say 'Good morning.' " Janek laughed, made the sign of the cross and went his way, calling back merrily, "God be willing. Have fear of God!"

The potato kept the Poles, like the Germans and the Russians, alive during two world wars. In Popowlany it fed people and pigs alike. The harvest in October was social, so many pickers worked together. By now the sky was as leaden and the earth as black as in one of Bujnowski's paintings. Agneshka and her children had flown off to New York. Jurek had enlisted the help of his cousin Józef Sadowski to pull the potato digger up and down the rows with his tractor. Also on hand were Józef's mother, Helena; Antonina Bokuń, a big, hearty neighbor; one of the Sakowicz families with two blond teenagers and an uncle who was once head of Tykocin's dreaded ORMO, secret police, but now was just a pathetic old man in a tattered uniform who drank too much; and Ferenc and Eugenia, more Bokuńs, but gaunt, bent and toothless, who lived in the tumbledown house on the way to the river. They were all spread out over several rows and crawled slowly forward, gathering up the potatoes by hand and putting them in wicker baskets. When a basket was full, they would carry it over and dump it in a large gunnysack. These sacks, set upright and lumpy with potatoes and tied at the top, stood in long rows behind the harvesters and by the end of the day looked like a graveyard of lumpy gray tombstones.

Helena Sadowska, delayed by chores, came late and stopped on the way to shake her fist at two small boys, who dropped their bicycles in the road and scrambled up a tree. She gave them a scolding and waved her stick. "You have sunflowers in your own gardens. Why do you pick mine?" The boys, each with a stolen sunflower in hand, looked at her dumbly and kept nibbling on the seeds. "They take our sunflowers," Helena complained as she joined the harvesters. "They do it every day!" She was wizened and toothless and wore a babushka. She never stopped working, and everyone knew that Józef, like seven other men in their forties who could not find wives prepared for such a life, was unlikely to marry. Józef, who had dug several rows, switched off the tractor engine and came to help. "Old women pitch hay and do everything in Popowlany," he said. "Young women want to run off to the easy life of the city," said Antonina, who also wore a peasant kerchief. As he crouched down to pick potatoes, Józef recited a poem he'd composed:

Wake up, farmer, it's almost five!
Cows are lowing, sheep bleating,
Dogs barking near the house,
Chickens clucking, pigs squealing,
All is waiting for your hand.
Wake up before your eardrums split.
Quickly, quickly, hurry up!
Sift this, pour that, clean and sweep.
It's good for a farmer to milk
Before his wife cooks breakfast.
My face is wet with sweat,
Never a chance to rest
Before it's time to plow and sow.
By the end of the day coming back from the fields
You feel like the dead.
In the house we have *flaki* soup.
You just eat and more work calls you.
Maybe it's night but you must take
The cows to the barn.
I cannot go to bed.
The cow is calving.
My wife is not too old.
She hasn't let me sleep for a week . . .

At this there was a hoot from Antonina.

The city people call us *kulak* and *burak*
But they are jealous of our gardens.
It is our fate to get kicked in the bottom.
Have I vacation even one time a year?
If only once I had a day of peace!
Amen.

"Ah, well," Józef sighed. "Now we work hard and we can't sell what we produce. Everything from Germany and the West is cheaper— milk, meat, eggs. It's a mistake for the government to allow in too much subsidized food from the West. Before, I could grow wheat and sell it. Now I can't."

"This bloody government!" cursed old Ferenc, who was working in the next row. He was as bent and toothless as his sister, with a wrinkled, weathered face like a walnut. Like the other women, she wore a kerchief, but wisps of hair had escaped, giving her a witchlike look. *"Pierdolona demokraja!* Fuck democracy! *Pierdolony Rząd!* Fuck this government!" the old woman cried, with such vehemence, her tooth-less mouth opened and shut like a hungry bird's. "This bloody government says that after a few months it will be better. Who can believe it? They've been saying that for how many years? What are they talking about in Parliament? I've never seen such hard times, even after the war. *Tak nie było!*"

"During Stalin's time, Eugenia," her brother reminded her, "if you didn't give barley, you went to jail." He gave a dry cough, and spat.

"Didn't my husband fight the Communists?" She scowled at him. All the while the two of them quickly gathered potatoes from the dirt. "He lost his health in prison."

When Jurek came up with a sack, the old man complained to him, "I can't sell my wheat. I see no way out."

Jurek grinned. "If I were you, Ferenc, I'd burn down the house and barn and take the insurance money. If I get poor enough I'll make butter and smoked ham and sell them on the streets in Białystok." In truth, Jurek had tried to make butter in Jadwiga's old spin-dry washing machine. It had made a mess and now the machine was hopelessly clogged.

"I ought to take my apples and peddle them at the frontier," the old woman said.

"With this free market maybe an American factory will come," Jurek joked.

"So kill your pigs and go there!" she scoffed. *"Oiy, yoi, yoi!* What it is to be poor!"

Jurek laughed. "Everything is okay in Popowlany. There is butter, there is meat, there is vodka!" It was true, they all got plenty to eat.

"Cholera!" cursed the old woman.

Jurek was amused to see that the old couple worked well away from the Sakowicz family. Two years before, one of the Sakowicz boys showed up in Popowlany with two prostitutes from Białystok. His mother sent them packing, but Ferenc took them in. They stayed, on and off, until Eugenia's husband in Złatoria died and she moved back home and threw them out. Once the police came and arrested the girls and took them into Białystok for medical checkups. Let go, they came back to Popowlany. God knows where they were now.

Everybody talked about how hard times were. Józef said, "America ought to give money to Poland and Poland will give Russia the food it needs."

"It used to be I could buy a tractor," Jurek said. "Now I can't. An Ursus was a thousand dollars in 1982. Now it's five times that."

"I want to sell a cow," said Józef. "But who will buy it? I must keep it at home and feed it and that costs money."

"We live very hard," Antonina agreed. "It's hard to pay for electricity and taxes. No money is coming in. Before, the dairy in Monki paid ten cents per liter for milk. This month it's less than half of that. Yesterday I got money for July. I'll be lucky to get August's in October."

Jurek told her the Borowskis were getting the equivalent of four hundred dollars a month for milk from their six cows. They drove into Białystok each morning and sold it on the street. They didn't use a dairy at all.

"Sure," Antonina said. "But they bought a car. Somebody like me has no way to get into Białystok. The bus comes too late."

"Well, the farmer always has a hard life," said Józef philosophically. "But when it costs you fifteen hundred zlotys to produce a liter of milk and the dairy just pays you four hundred, how long can you last? Young people run off to the city. And who can blame them? We old people love this land. And there are no jobs for us in the city. We like to stay in Popowlany. What can we do?" Jurek had not used enough pesticide and there were many potato bugs. These black-and-yellow-striped Colorado potato beetles were unknown in Poland until the 1950s. The Communists had claimed they were smuggled in to sabotage food production. The bugs were still called "gifts of Truman."

"If America paid us damages for all these," Józef joked, "we'd be rich."

Later in the day Antonina went to work beside Helena Sadowska and Mrs. Sakowicz. Helena told her, "I see you're bringing your cow home at night."

"We have a new calf. The pasture is not far from our house."

"Jurek leaves his cows down by the Narew at night. It's dangerous."

"He's not the only one. A man from Lesniki leaves his cows there at night too."

Antonina told them that as a girl she had worked in Lesniki for the Germans. "The village chief decided who was to go. He picked us so the Germans wouldn't take us as slave labor to Germany." Antonina remembered how a Jewish woman had left her son with them. "Adum Jozka. He was just my age. It was a pity to see him. He was so frightened. One day some Jews were marched through Popowlany and somebody recognized the boy and called to him. So the Germans took him with the others to the Białystok ghetto. I think he died there. The family had lived in Popowlany for a time before the war. They sold apples and herring."

"How we used to hide in the forest for weeks at a time," said Helena.

"We were so afraid," Antonina remembered. "One time my brother was just eight and the Germans shot at him. He ran and fell down. The Germans laughed. They thought he was dead. He was just frightened. When the Germans went away he got up and swam across the river. We found him alive in the reeds. Even now if I hear German voices I turn off the TV." Antonina worked in silence for a time, then said, "Hard as the war was, in some ways it was better. I mean, the people were better. Kinder and more decent."

Mrs. Sakowicz said her mother-in-law had just come home after two years in America.

"Does she want to go back?"

"She dreams about it. If possible she'd go there by foot." Four white swans flew across the northern sky, a sign winter was not far away. "The price of coal has gone up steeply."

"Never mind. We can cut wood."

Mrs. Sakowicz sighed. "This work isn't good. Going to America is good." Antonina said not everybody felt that way. Zofia, after a trip to New York to see Agneshka, had done nothing but complain. "She said it was noisy. Trains went right by the apartment and there were smells of gasoline and exhaust. Zofia didn't like the food. No boiled potatoes, just *pomme frites*. She was anxious about her husband in Popowlany. She couldn't work in New York, her rheumatism was too bad."

"Do you think Jadwiga will come back to Jurek? He's alone like a dog and has to make meals for himself. He needs a wife."

Antonina nodded. "It's up to them. But what does she have to come back to?"

VIII

In public Jurek always showed respect to the mayor. Among themselves, he teased Dominik and called him "Fat Man." "With your stomach," Jurek joked, "you could dress up like a priest and go from door to door collecting money." Actually Dominik had spent two years in a seminary. He might have been a priest. Instead he met his future wife and felt, as Jurek put it, "God's feeling." If the Church was the old way for a poor peasant to get ahead, under Communism it was the Party. His membership in the United Peasant Party, as a Communist ally, got him going in his career.

Dominik earned the equivalent in zlotys of three hundred dollars a month as mayor and his wife made a good wage at her factory in Białystok. But with two children in college, he patiently took the bus. In a pinch he hired Jurek to drive him around in the Skoda. Dominik had such a fat belly from his unquenchable appetite that he suffered from shortness of breath, yet he was never still and it was hard to keep up with him. The villagers enjoyed his style. A day with Jurek might begin with a look at how a new road was being resurfaced. Even before Jurek came to a stop, Dominik would be shouting out the window at the road crew. "You lazy bastards! You bums! You are capitalists now and must keep busy a full eight hours. We have a free market now, men!" He would jump out of the car and charge about, railing at everybody, all noise and bluster. The workmen were not alarmed. They knew he would praise them soon enough, saying, "Very good, men. I'm proud of you."

The future of the dairy had to await what the Polish Parliament did about collective farms like Stelmachowo. Everything state-owned in Tykocin had gone bankrupt, not just Stelmachowo but the wholesale grain, coal, seed and fertilizer dealer, the general store, the restaurant-pub, even a shoe factory, Tykocin's only big employer with a payroll of more than a hundred. Dominik had to find ways to get it all working again. He was still optimistic about the dairy. The idea of selling twenty-five- and fifty-dollar shares, he admitted, was a flop. "It didn't work and we know it," he told Jurek. Now Dominik was looking for private investors or help as humanitarian aid from the American Embassy in Warsaw. There were still plenty of avenues to explore. He was even in touch with a Tykocin-born munitions manufacturer in Gdańsk who made rockets for Iraq. "He's ready to invest in another business," he told Jurek. Something had to be done. The old state-run dairies in Monki and Białystok had gone bankrupt and were closed.

"Selling shares was a foolish idea," Jurek told Dominik. "I'd buy the shares for ten million zlotys and what would I get out of it? Who would be the owner?"

"Everybody."

Jurek scratched his head. "You are a good friend, Dominik. But sometimes you go one way and I go another way." The collapse of the dairy in Białystok had been a boon to the Borowskis. They were driving into Białoystok each morning after milking and selling about eighty liters of milk directly to housewives. They were making a fortune. Dominik objected that it wouldn't be pasteurized. "They boil at home, these housewives," Jurek said. Alek Borowski, Andre's brother, had told him, "When I take it in in the morning and sell it on the street, the women ask, 'Is that milk good? I'll try just one liter. If it's no good I'll buy no more.' Most of them are satisfied and keep coming back every day." The Borowskis used modern milking machines and kept their milk in coolers, not like Jurek.

It was Teresa Borowska, the mother, who seized the opportunity. But they had to have some way to get the milk to the city. The family's ten-year-old Fiat barely got them the mile to church in Złatoria each Sunday and it was such an eyesore that Mrs. Borowski made Andre park it out of sight down the road. Andre said he could raise the equivalent of fifteen hundred dollars for a better used car. It was his mother who brought out four thousand dollars from hiding nobody knew she had saved. It was her sixty laying hens, whose eggs, together with cheese and butter she made and sold over the years, that paid for the car.

A few years earlier, she and her husband signed over their fourteen-hectare farm to Andre so they could get their sixty-dollars-a-month old-age pensions. At the time, Andre's two older brothers were working at their trades, Alek as a printer in what was West Germany and Jacek painting flowers on glassware in a Białystok factory. After Germany was reunited, Alek lost his job and came home. Their father, crippled by an old back injury, did little but the milking. It was Teresa Borowska, a small, energetic woman, who ruled the roost. Andre argued with her a lot, but usually ended up doing what she said. Their village of Babino, south of the Białystok–Warsaw highway and about half a mile from the Narew, had better land than Popowlany, with bigger farms and richer farmers.

Mrs. Borowska, who sometimes invited him to the noon meal on Sunday, told Jurek his troubles came from living alone. "Look around. Everybody has a lot of grain stored. We don't have any because we use it all to feed the pigs and the hens. A farmer these days needs income from milk, cheese, cream, butter and eggs, besides what grain and pork he sells. For these, Jurek, you need a wife."

Andre told Jurek she saved over five hundred dollars a year from sales of eggs alone.

Jurek said it used to be that a liter of milk bought a liter of tractor fuel. After the cutoff of fuel from Russia it took eight liters. For a hundred kilos of rye he would get a hundred liters of fuel. Now he got less than twenty. And he still had to pay taxes on his house and land, contribute to his medical insurance and pension fund, pay taxes on his car and tractor and automobile insurance too. He was going deeper and deeper in debt. But so was everybody.

With the milk project on hold, tourism might be Tykocin's salvation. To promote it, Dominik decided to rebuild the old Jewish marketplace. Still cobblestoned, it was used as a bus stop and shelter. Eight small wooden shops were built to start with. Dominik had Jurek drive him over to inspect how they were coming. "This architect we hired was a blockhead," he said on the way. "I wanted our shops to be authentic. He was three months late with his blueprints. I had to draw up the designs myself. It took me two nights. I took them from Zygmunt Gloger's encyclopedia. Authentic seventeenth-century shops." They parked and went from one shop to another. "Here they'll sell fish. Next door, meat. The third will be a sex shop." Dominik laughed. "No, I'm joking. It will be a clothing shop. Then there's a bookstore and a grocery, all built in the old Jewish style."

"Who will run them?"

"Private. We will let anybody who will run a shop have a thirty-year lease." It turned out that Tadeusz Trypuć owned what was to be the butcher shop, his sidekick Witold Rudatski the fish market. Both were council members. "Didn't anybody complain?" Jurek asked. Trypuć was a beefy blond farmer with bloodshot eyes who looked like an aging prizefighter. He had spent two years as a housepainter in Connecticut and built himself a big house in Tykocin on his return. He was head of the local branch of Solidarity. Rudatski, a shorter, younger man with curly red hair, a shy manner and shifty blue eyes, was always following after Trypuć.

Dominik shrugged. "They were ready to invest."

From the market they went to the river. When the Narew was straightened disconnected segments of the old twisting river were left behind as freshwater pools. These were full of reeds and water lilies. "We want to get a stretch of the old river, with all its twists and turns, for a park where people can swim and canoe and camp," Dominik said. He pointed out an open meadow. "Here we'll have camping. It's a beautiful place for tents." A wooden dock and diving platform had already been built and some children were swimming. "People from Białystok have tested the water three times and say it's safe. And once they put the filters in at the factories in Białystok, the river water will get cleaner and cleaner." Dominik said the environmentalists were always after him, wanting to know how he would get rid of algae in stagnant water or adjust the water level. Jurek sympathized with them. Dominik had cut down half a dozen of the old poplar trees at the entrance to Popowlany and everybody was up in arms about it.

"Oh, God, I'll never hear the last of that," Dominik groaned. "Those bastards, the workmen. I gave orders only to cut down three trees and they cut six. All those clerks in my office are pricks. They don't get on well with farmers. And people in Popowlany are lazy sons of bitches." Dominik was mad because he brought some sand to Popowlany so everybody could spread it in front of their houses and it wouldn't be so muddy on rainy days. They left his share of sand in front of his house for him to spread himself.

As they drove along, Dominik said the bulldozers at the park site were uncovering a lot of bodies. "Mass graves left by the Russians and the Nazis. We keep finding them."

Another big problem in Tykocin, he said, was alcoholism. Just the previous Sunday in Babino, one of the Borowskis' neighbors, dead drunk, had almost stabbed one of his sons with a pitchfork. When his wife seized his arm, he swung at her and, just as Jurek and the Borowskis came running, threatened his wife: "Sleep with an ax under your pillow tonight because I am coming to kill you." Once sober, he begged everybody's forgiveness. Drunkenness was a big problem in villages. "It's difficult to know what to do in such cases," Dominik said. "One woman cries and complains about her drunken husband and she has a real problem. The next one is just a pain in the ass. I give them a lecture on how to live with their husbands. If there's a fight, they all come running to the mayor."

"Can you put them in jail to cool off?"

"There is no jail in Tykocin. Listen, if I could put people in jail I could fill up a prison." Jurek said he'd heard Ryszard Sakowicz from Popowlany was in jail for stealing to buy vodka. "He even took one of Zofia's chickens," which Jurek found very funny. Dominik said the *milicjanti* took him into Białystok. He laughed, and said he was reminded of the time Eduard Sakowicz, Ryszard's father, drank too much vodka and might have hung himself had not Manik Sliwonski come running with an ax to cut him down. The Sakowiczes were famous drunkards, and Jurek told about the time he was a pallbearer with Ryszard Sakowicz. "You know how it is when you're carrying a coffin, arm in arm, step by step, you have to be in unison." Ryszard, after too much vodka, was holding his cap in one hand and the coffin in the other. All of a sudden the cap fell and Ryszard reached down to get it. It threw the coffin off balance, the pallbearers lost their grip and it teetered, tipped and fell. When it hit the ground, the lid sprang open and out rolled the old man inside. The mourners, aghast, crossed themselves. Then they began to laugh. So did the weeping women and the priest. "The worse it seemed to be to laugh," Jurek said, "the harder it was to stop." The story was old and familiar to Dominik, but hearing Jurek tell it, he began to chuckle, then Jurek started to laugh too, and suddenly the two of them were laughing and shaking as if they had taken leave of their senses. Dominik got control of himself when they stopped to watch another crew paving a road. "My aim is that every farmer will get an asphalt road to his fields," he said, wiping his forehead. "We've got plenty of local stone for it."

In the village of Rzenziany they stopped at a disco just opened up by Henryk Morus, another councilman and farmer who had spent time in America. Morus had built it himself. It was a long hall of plastered-over cement blocks and a bar with tables at one end. A five-piece band came from Białystok every Saturday night. After paying the band, Morus was taking in the equivalent in zlotys of three hundred dollars. Such "cultural" activities were tax-exempt under Communism and Parliament had not yet acted on this. For Tykocin the place was a gold mine. The only decoration in the disco was a crucifix.

"Dominik won't let us sell vodka or wine," Morus's wife told Jurek. "It's just as well." Dominik and Jurek ordered beers and had just begun to drink them when two women came in and, seeing Dominik, rushed over. "We want wine!" they demanded. "We want wine!"

"The whole village should appeal, ladies. Sign a petition and I'll take it into Białystok."

"We want wine! We want wine!" they kept repeating, as if they were demented. "We women work hard. We need a drink from time to time."

Jurek nodded encouragement. *"Wino damskie, wódka męska."* Morus said he didn't want to sell wine. That and vodka only meant trouble.

As they headed back to Tykocin, they found the road workers idle.

Dominik told Jurek to stop. "Those sons of bitches are idle again!" He jumped from the car, bellowing at the men: "The bulldozer goes to another village tomorrow. You must finish up here today. *Cholera!* You just stand around!"

They stopped at Stelmachowo. The collective farm's manager, a woman, was waiting for Dominik. "Parliament must decide what's to become of us. Our nursery is not a good business. We only graft fruit trees and sell them. We can't compete with private nurseries. We pay high taxes. How can we survive?" She said they had five hundred hectares planted in grain and potatoes, besides the nursery's twenty hectares of orchards. "We don't get high enough prices for what we sell to pay for fuel and fertilizer." She told him the fifty workers at Stelmachowo averaged about sixty dollars a month in wages. "It is a very bad life," she said. "Poor conditions." While Dominik finished his business, Jurek went to see the nursery. Near the office was a white pillared gate, all that was left after the war of Stelmachowo's fifteenth-century palace, once the country home of Polish kings. A foreman took Jurek around the orchard. He was sixty and after thirty-five years at Stelmachowo was about to retire. "It's been good. We made big money before. Now we can't compete with private nurseries. We used to be able to graft twenty-five hundred cherry trees in a normal eight-hour shift."

As they drove back to Tykocin, Dominik said there was waste on a collective farm. Workers got paid whether they worked or not. "They have no incentive." As they entered Tykocin, they passed a wall where somebody had scrawled: KOMUNO WRÓĆ! COMMUNISM, COME BACK! Dominik gave a hearty laugh. Then he sobered up. "I tell you, Jurek, the situation is getting explosive. Farmers don't have enough cash to pay for their taxes, electricity, fertilizer, anything. They can't sell their milk or grain. Morale is down. Everybody blames the government. Imports are coming in from the rest of Europe. We can't sell to Russia."

The once-bustling government warehouse on the edge of town was deserted. There were piles of coal and bags of fertilizer but nobody was buying. The warehouse chief was dejected. "Nobody is creating a new system and the old one is falling apart," he said. "Out at Stelmachowo they have no money to pay taxes. They keep going by selling wood. We keep going by buying and selling bottles." As they left, Jurek asked Dominik, "If Tykocin's warehouse goes out of business, what will take its place? Who is going to buy our grain? Where will we buy fuel and fertilizer?"

"All these organizations will be private. Oh, Jurek, it is very hard to go from Communism to capitalism. You think you have it tough. You ought to hear the Communists in Białystok. They were rolling in money. How they miss the old system!"

"The world is getting crazy," Jurek said.

IX

The Society of the Friends of Tykocin, prodded by Alicja, decided to hold a conference on how to save the Narew River. They invited the head of the Polish Senate in Warsaw, the Minister of Culture and Arts, the Minister for the Protection of the Environment and the local senator. Nobody came. They had to settle for a junior officer from the Department of the Environment in Białystok. Leszek was there on behalf of the district council, raising some eyebrows. Joanna Malesińska scoffed, "Leszek is interested in making money, not saving the Narew. I'm surprised we invited him."

The conference, held at the museum, opened with a review of the river's history. The source of the Narew was a lake near Narewka village on the Byelarussian border, on the edge of the Białowieza Forest, the last of Europe's primeval woods to still have herds of wild bison. Stalin and Brezhnev hunted there. Under the Communists, Białystok became an industrial city, full of factories and high-rise housing for the workers. It drained its effluents, sewage and detergents into the Supraśl River, which emptied into the Narew a few miles east of Popowlany, so its water was a brownish yellow and poisonous-looking white foam floated on its surface. If there were heavy rains and the river overflowed its banks, this polluted water came into the fields of villages like Popowlany and Babino, killing the crops.

In an attempt to remedy this, the Communist regime between 1978 and 1981 straightened the river's course, turning it, in effect, into a canal. The government also pledged to reduce pollution from Białystok. Up until the collapse of Communism nothing had been done. One of the first promises of the new government was to remove industrial pollutants from the river waters within two years. After it left Tykocin, the Narew flowed west into the Bug, which emptied into the Vistula, Poland's longest and most celebrated river, which went through Warsaw and up into the Baltic Sea at Gdańsk.

The Narew also watered what was known as the Sea of Reeds, a wetlands unique in Europe created by receding glaciers at the end of the Ice Age: a whole series of such moraines and lakes were left in northeastern Poland around Białystok. In 1985 the Białystok government established a Narew Landscape Park of 23,000 hectares to preserve these wetlands, the habitat of one hundred and eighty-three species of migratory birds and forty-one kinds of wildflowers and water plants. Three hundred hectares of this lay across the Narew between Popowlany and Tykocin and was part of Dominik's new tourist area.

Alicja Matusiewicz wanted the Narew returned to its original meandering course. She proposed that two or three new small dams be built near Babino to reflood the wetlands and prevent them from drying out anymore and saving the Sea of Reeds. Her hope, once the water rose again, was that things would go back to their natural state. The members of the Society of the Friends of Tykocin unanimously supported this.

The project was opposed by the richer farmers. Wincenty Zimnoch, a neighbor of the Borowskis in Babino, told the conference, "We are talking about a swamp along the river with no income. Are we so rich we can waste all the money the government spent to drain our pastures?"

Dr. Boleslaw Bielicki, a professorial-looking man who had been fired as the Narew Landscape Park's first director because of his outspoken environmentalism, angrily responded. "People are fed up," he told Zimnoch. "They are tired of talking about the Communist past and what their government did. They want to talk about the future. They thought when Communism ended, it would get better. Instead it gets worse. The seven kilometers of the Narew beside Babino works as a pump and a drain for the whole river. All the water is flowing out. To me the people of Babino are very guilty. And mistaken. They think drying out the swampland will be good for their farming."

"This is only the fantasy of a man with his nose in books," Zimnoch fired back. "You were the park director under Communism. And I say to you, 'I am only a common peasant. But I am right.' " Zimnoch's son was the government veterinarian in Tykocin and Alicja suspected that the father had political influence in Białystok.

"This government in Warsaw is not strong on protecting the environment," Bielicki replied coldly. "The provincial government in

Białystok is even weaker. Only popular groups like the Society of the Friends of Tykocin really care about saving the natural world in which we must live. Before, we people in Poland could not oppose government policy. Now we can." This was enthusiastically received and a standing save-the-river committee was formed with Alicja as chairman. Its task would be to lobby the Białystok government to build two or three dams near Babino to stop further drainage of the Sea of Reeds and make sure industrial pollution of the Narew ended in the promised two years. For once, the interests of the more traditional peasant villagers along the river and those of the modern farmers near the highway separated, and Jurek sided with the Society of the Friends of Tykocin.

Many were starting to think it would be better for Tykocin if the society and Dominik joined forces. Dominik had won over Ewa Wroczyńska, the museum curator, with his plan to restore the old Jewish marketplace. "We have more privately owned shops since he became mayor," she said, "and tourism brought over thirty thousand people to Tykocin last year." Ewa was even prepared to cut down the stately poplar trees in the square, restoring it to its original bare cobblestones. Alicja was indignant. "There are many birds in those trees and the trees supply us with oxygen." Her daughter, Maria, a doctor's wife in Warsaw who was avant-garde, had just shocked everybody by making a short film about Jesus coming back to life in Tykocin and taking a boat out on the polluted river. That was going a little too far.

Even Alicja was softening toward Dominik. "He is not as bad as his Mafia. It is Tadeusz Trypuć and Witold Rudatski who are definitely persona non grata. They are neither clever nor agreeable. They are *głupi i podły*, stupid and wicked." Strong language, but she was appalled by their thirty-year leases on two of the new "little and ugly" wooden shops in the marketplace. "They are supposed to authentically resemble the old Jewish shops that once stood there. Now people are saying they are simply the monuments of Dominik, Leszek, Trypuć and Rudatski."

"The pastures along the river are already too dry," Jurek told Dominik. "It's a problem if you want to cut hay green. We need to let the water rise again."

The next time Jurek took a Sunday meal with the Borowskis he asked Alek and Jacek Borowski to show him their pastureland down by the river. Teresa Borowska, like Agneshka, feared Jurek ate badly, and while Jurek brought a bottle of vodka, she fixed barley soup, pork cutlets and roast chicken, mashed potatoes and gravy, sliced cucumbers and tomatoes, coffee and cake. It was the kind of meal you needed to walk off to survive.

Miracle of miracles, Andre had gone to America. It happened suddenly. He went to Warsaw one day, was given a visa at once—most people waited for years—and caught the first flight he could get to New York. There was just time to gather a few friends for vodka. "I think it will be lucky for me in America. And Alek will join me one day."

Alek told Jurek their mother now went about moaning and sighing, *"Boże, mój Boże!* God, my God! How I miss my Andre!" He phoned every week, always at six o'clock in the morning, it being midnight in New York. Alek told Jurek, "He found a job in Newark, New Jersey, with a Puerto Rican man who came to America fourteen years ago. He bosses Andre but he is not really the boss. The boss is an old Jewish man who owns two apartment houses. He rents to black people. If they move out Andre and the Puerto Rican go in and fix up the places for new tenants."

As they headed to the river, Jurek told them that in the old days, when he was a boy, there was peat along the Narew. "If you set fire to it, it might burn a month or two. We used peat in the stove at home. It's pretty good grass you've got here." Alek said Andre had planted it. "Before, it was all nettles and thistles." He told Jurek how the drainage of the swamplands along the Narew had split the village, some wanting to keep it as communal land, others demanding it be broken into private holdings. The daughter of a neighbor of the Borowskis had just been married and only half the village families had come. There was a lot of bad feeling.

Alek described the wedding. The church in Złatoria was full and when the time came they lit the candelabra and a girl sang Gounod's "Ave Maria" in Latin. The groom had a black mustache and thick black hair, but the bride was as blond as she could be and was veiled in a cloud of white net. After the ceremony they said a prayer at the altar and then came down the aisle to Mendelssohn's "Wedding March." There was a great crush in the vestibule as everybody crowded around the bridal couple, giving them zloty notes and congratulations. Back in Babino, the father of the bride hosted a wedding feast in his barn. There was a band from Białystok. Vodka bottles were brought round and after several toasts people were shown to seats on benches around long wooden tables where women laid out platters of ham and sausages, cold cuts, sliced beets and pickles, and all kinds of bottles—vodka, champagne, red wine, orangeade, soda pop, mineral water. Then came hot food, dish after dish: vegetable, chicken and *flaki* soup, platters of newly baked bread, fish cutlets and pork cutlets, mashed potatoes, fried potatoes, beef wrapped in cabbage leaves, a gelatin meat dish, tomatoes marinated in onions, sliced cucumbers in sour milk, and just when you thought it was over, steaming heaps of roast chicken and beef and finally ice cream, cakes, pies and cookies. Alek had never seen such food. Afterward there was dancing, and once the bride and groom swirled around the floor a few times, the whole crowd joined in. One man at their table kept saying, "The groom's father in Chicago paid for all the drinks. Ten million zlotys for the vodka alone!" All the Borowskis but Alek drifted off early, but he stayed and danced until the band stopped playing at five o'clock in the morning. His mother, getting up to milk the cows and feed the pigs, shoved him bleary-eyed into his bed.

The Borowskis' horse was grazing in the pasture. It was an old blond-maned chestnut mare named Katashka, which they never tied up but treated as part of the family. Alek asked Jurek why he didn't keep a horse anymore. "I don't need one," Jurek told him. "I'm like a horse myself." Once, after the war, he said, a man in Popowlany had hitched one of his sons to the plow.

When they reached the river they could tell from its banks how much it had fallen. "When this was swampland we had to take off our trousers to cut grass," Jurek told Alek and Jacek. "It was that wet. In the old days when the Narew was all twists and turns, the bends were deepest. Oh, watch out for those nettles."

"Nettles would be everywhere if people didn't plant grass," Jacek told him. Jurek began to sing, "Sergeant, I have a pain in my legs and there's a long way to go . . ." On the way back they met the simpleminded Janek, who said he had been helping a widow in Sawino village. She had given him a sackful of cucumbers.

"You're working too hard," Jurek joked. "You ought to get married. Let a wife look after you."

Janek laughed. "Have you an honest widow for me?" They walked together, talking about the wetlands. "We'd all have less work if we reflooded these pastures," Janek said quite sensibly. He grinned. "Maybe we should sell Poland to the Americans." He asked how Andre was doing. "Who is farming now? Who lives with Mother and

Father? Andre is the owner of the farm and he goes off to America. America! America! If I go to America I will only make jokes. The Communists used to say only the factory owners there have a good time. And many people, they go and don't have the money to come back to Poland. I know a man, he went to France. And when he came back to Poland, he had to come on foot and sleep in cemeteries. Well, some people build pyramids, some build huts. The pharaohs built pyramids to meet God, while Lazarus just rose from a pile of dirt."

They stopped and waited while Janek sat down on a large rock and kicked off his black rubber boots. He wanted to rewrap some rags he had tied about his bare feet. Then he put his boots back on. It was an old custom among the poorest peasants. "Feet get bad in rubber boots in hot weather. So I usually go barefoot." Janek grinned at Jurek. "What's the good world news?"

"How is your farm?"

"Indifferent. Sometimes I grow. Sometimes I sell. This year no crops. Nothing. I rented my land to pay my taxes. It is nothing to joke about. The ministers in Warsaw ought to come out and work with us in the fields. My God, how hard people have to work in a village! Never mind. Say a prayer to God."

X

It was over fifty years since the massacre in the Łopuchowo Woods. There were granite markers at the site, but Dominik decided Tykocin should erect a large monument of its own. He proposed this at a council meeting. Trypuć and Rudatski objected. "The Jews are rich," said Trypuć. "If they want a bigger monument, let them pay for it themselves." In recent days graffiti had appeared near the central bus station in Białystok: *"Żydzi do gazu,"* "Jews to the gas chamber." Dominik told Jurek it must be teenagers. Jurek said they got it from the old people. "In the old days all the shopkeepers were Jews. If the villagers wanted to borrow money, they went to Jews and later paid it back with interest. Jews were richer. They didn't work in the fields. That is why, among old people, there is still anger against Jews."

Dominik learned there were only seven Jews, all of them old men, left out of Białystok's prewar Jewish population of more than 60,000. When one of them died, Dominik learned he was a Malarewicz from Tykocin. He found the remaining Białystok Jews all knew him. Szymon Bartnowski, an Auschwitz survivor, who was nearly eighty, threw up his hands and exclaimed, "Malarewicz, Malarewicz, Malarewicz! Always they ask about Malarewicz! He played cards, he drank himself blind. Cards and vodka, that was Malarewicz!" Bartnowski said Malarewicz too had been almost eighty and a few years before his death he had lost his eyesight. "He was alone when he died. Nobody claimed the body at the hospital. So they sent the remains to the medical school for the students to cut up." He heaved a deep sigh. "Ah, if we'd known we'd have gone and got the body and given poor Malarewicz a decent burial." He said both of Malarewicz's parents died in Russia but one brother made it to Israel and another to Argentina. Nobody knew what had happened to the sister, Helena.

Dominik found her. He asked about her at the Jewish Institute in Warsaw. One of their officers simply looked her husband up in the phone book. He dialed and spoke. The conversation was brief. When he set down the phone, the man told Dominik, "She is a very old woman." Her husband was still alive and they lived in a fashionable part of the city, as was appropriate for an artist much celebrated for his socialist realism under the Communists. "She said she did not like her brother and had not spoken to him since before the war. Nor had she set foot in Tykocin since she left in the summer of 1939. She said she wanted nothing to do with her brother." The man paused, a little embarrassed. "Actually, her words were 'He was a dirty man.' "

Dominik ignored the protests from the other councilmen. A giant stone, nearly as high as a man and seven feet long, was excavated from some bluffs near the river and hauled to the Łopuchowo Woods. It was sunk into the earth between the three great burial pits, each now covered with grass and surrounded by black-painted iron fences. Stonecutters from Tykocin carved a memorial inscription and a Star of David. Invitations to a memorial service in the Tykocin synagogue went out to President Lech Wałęsa, other Polish notables and the head rabbi of Poland. Nobody came from Wałęsa's office, but the rabbi, who was in Israel, sent his deputy. A good many eminent people did come, officials, journalists and Jews, some from Białystok but many from Warsaw too, and there was a German radio team from Munich.

Since the synagogue was now classified as a museum and not a place of worship—who was there to go to services?—benches were set up on all sides of the roofed altar in the Great Hall. The ceremony took place on a rainy Sunday afternoon. The synagogue was so crowded, latecomers had to stand in the antechambers. Aside from

Dominik himself, Leszek, who brought his whole family and Mrs. Grabowska, represented the Tykocin council. Trypuć and Rudatski the night before had come to Jurek's house in Popowlany and over a bottle of vodka in the kitchen had drunkenly denounced Dominik. Jurek ignored them and went with Alek Borowski. To Jurek's surprise he saw that the Society of the Friends of Tykocin was out in full force. Alicja sat with her daughter, Maria, Ewa with the museum staff, Joanna with her children. There were priests in black cassocks who came in a Mercedes, and nuns too. A few of the old Jewish men from Białystok were there, one with a cane leaning on the arm of a blond and handsome grandson. Radio and TV crews hurried about with cameras and microphones. The rabbi from Warsaw, a clean-shaven, silver-haired, distinguished-looking man, led prayers for the dead. Then Waldemar Monkiewicz, Curator of the Archives on Hitler's Occupation in Białystok, tall, bookish-looking, prematurely bald, said he would read an excerpt from a document entitled "Extermination of Jews in Białystok Region in 1939 and 1941–44." In part:

> . . . The Jews were driven out of their houses into the marketplace near the synagogue. The sick, crippled, the old and small children were taken by truck to Zawady village. The Łopuchowo Woods was the place of execution. The pits in the ground were dug by the inhabitants of Łopuchowo village. So as the others would not know what was going on there, the Nazis had a Jewish orchestra play on different instruments and made the people dance.

At the end of the service, archival tapes from the Jewish Historical Museum in Warsaw were played—cantillations of prayers in Hebrew and parts of the scriptures.

When the music ended, the crowd moved in silence to their cars or to several chartered buses. It was a short journey. The road did not take them all the way. Everyone had to go on foot the last few hundred yards on a forest path covered with wet leaves and pine needles. Rain dripped from the tall, straight birches and people unfurled their black umbrellas. A clearing, vaguely defined in a foggy mist, appeared before them. Dominik and Leszek, staid and solemn in black suits, waited at the side of the enormous, now wet, stone. One by one people came up to light candles or place flowers on the earth. For a long time there was a hushed silence as more and more people came. The pine trees stirred, a few birch leaves fluttered down and rain fell softly on the umbrellas. There was a forest smell of moist earth, pine needles and moss. After some minutes Dominik blew his nose and nervously cleared his throat. His tie looked too tight and his collar seemed to be sawing his neck. He grimaced and began, his voice unnaturally loud at first.

"Dear guests, here in this place not far from Tykocin, in this forest of Łopuchowo so long ago, there occurred the greatest tragedy in Tykocin's long history. For it was here in these woods, in the place you now stand, that on a summer day, August 25, 1941, a special Nazi commando unit shot and buried more than two thousand Jews from Tykocin and its surrounding villages.

"They killed children and young people, old people, whole families. They killed innocent people. The echoes of this massacre were heard, not just in Tykocin but all over the world. And here the ground trembled. We wanted to remember those who died in this horrible mass murder. We wanted to leave a monument to the memory of those who were killed. And this monument was shaped by our own stonecutters from the rock of Tykocin's fields. Let me say, dear guests, on behalf of Tykocin's people, these words: we will never, never forget them."

That was all. After some time people began moving to the cars and buses. Dominik walked back to the police van that brought him, but seeing the *milicjantis'* uniforms and boots, he told them to go ahead, he would come by bus. Dominik was nicely dressed. It was true, as the members of the Society of the Friends of Tykocin were to say later on, as they drank tea with cream out of old china cups and ate little cakes Alicja had baked, that the sleeves of his coat were not quite long enough, that the coat itself seemed short-waisted and that his white starched shirt around his immense waist seemed alarmingly ready to burst its buttons. Yet even they could find nothing to criticize in Dominik's blunt, peasant words. Nothing could express the horror. Back in Jurek's kitchen in Popowlany, tossing off a shot of vodka, Dominik made light of his speech, though in truth he had been very frightened. "When I looked out," he told Jurek, "and saw Alicja, Ewa and Joanna standing there, I thought of pushing the stone over on them." And he gave a big laugh.

Back at the synagogue, Tykocin's amateur theatrical group, on an improvised stage set up in the vestibule, enacted scenes of prewar Jewish life. Beforehand the pale young woman director, the assistant librarian, apologized to the audience: "We had to learn what to do from books." Slides of old Tykocin were projected on a screen behind the actors. "Dear mother, I had a dream," a girl cried out as the first skit began. "A young man with dark eyes came to me and smiled . . ." The life depicted was happy. There was a wedding party. The groom held a glass of wine to the lips of his bride, who took a sip. He sipped himself and crushed the glass under his heel as the guests cried, *"Mazel tov!"* A son was born and a few scenes later it was his bar mitzvah. Women gossiped about it in the marketplace, exclaiming, *"Oiy, yoi, yoi . . ."*

When the performance was over, the young men and women who took part came down the aisle through the audience, each of them carrying an oil lamp. The little procession went out the synagogue door and into the rain. It was nearly dark when people headed home. From the synagogue tower, white prayer shawls were dropped, one by one, down to the wet dark earth.

The dead had brought the living together. Tykocin's people, having acknowledged the tragedy of their past, were poised to embrace the uncertain future. Somehow the ritual in the Łopuchowo Woods humbly reaffirmed their belief that human goodness and common decency could survive the darkest night if the survivors came together in mutual trust and respect. They would all go their own ways as before, quarreling and gossiping and carrying on, yet feeling more deeply than ever that their ties to this place, its history, their ancestors and native soil, and to each other, were truly binding, however threatened by the world outside.

Fear of Germany and Russia went with being a Pole. Trouble in either sent shudders through the borderlands. There was also the peasant's sense of enduring, going on, even in the shadow of great events and when the mighty fell. Jurek thought of the day when, walking home from his fields, he met a drunken peasant coming along in his horsecart from Tykocin. Poplar leaves rustled, the cart wheels creaked, the horse snorted and the driver, his face red and shining and his eyes bloodshot, was humming loudly and waving his hands. There was cabbage on his chin and he smelled of vodka. "Gorbachev is down!" he cried merrily. In Popowlany that night there were fears the Russians might cross the frontier, just as there were when Yeltsin faced trouble in Moscow.

Who but God knew what was in store in the future? If the Russians or Germans ever did come, Jurek thought, he'd touch a match to all he had and go. Maybe in a year or two he could join Jadwiga in America. But to stay? Could he leave the land?

Going to the Narew one October evening, the faithful Bury at his heels, Jurek cut a lonely, solitary figure. He was so much a part of the scene himself, he was just vaguely aware of the bare-looking fields, the woods, the patches of mist, the dead brown leaves and black ditches. Leaves lay thick on the road. Already it grew dark quite early. Now and then a yellow birch leaf fluttered down and wet leaves clung to his boots. On the horizon behind leafless trees flamed a broad red afterglow. The bells tolled for vespers in Tykocin, for it was Saturday night. He heard the sound of a tractor engine and of men's voices calling from places far away. Sheep and cows went by, bleating and bellowing, followed by hunched-over men in cloth caps who muttered greetings. "Let God help you." "Praise be to God."

His cows, tethered in their pasture, saw him coming and waited, impatient to be milked. Jurek, lost in thought, stood for a long time when he reached them. He gazed into the fading light. A wind came up and bent the willows by the river. Snipe rose out of the reed grass to circle and swoop with mournful cries. Bury ran off to paw and sniff at a hole left in the grass by a hare. Soon he came running back, panting loudly, his tongue hanging out, and nudged Jurek's hand to get his head stroked. Jurek felt a chill from the rising wind. Soon the sky would fill with stars. He was resigned, as country people must be, to a long, long succession of winter nights and summer days. It was God's good earth. "God is merciful," he told himself. "I will go and milk the cows."

III

Allahu Akbar:
Two Faces of Islam

CAST OF CHARACTERS

NAGEH KOM LOHLAH VILLAGE, UPPER NILE, EGYPT

SHAHHAT, 23, a fellah
FARUK, 40s, his sharecropper
SULEYMAN, 40s, a fellah
LAMEI, 50s, a rich landlord
OMMOHAMED, 45, Shahhat's mother

SIRS EL LAYYAN VILLAGE, NILE DELTA, EGYPT

HELMI, 40, a fellah
NAMAT, 39, his wife
Their children and neighbors

PILANGSARI VILLAGE, JAVA, INDONESIA

HUSEN, 55, a poor rice peasant
PA LOJO, late 60s, a comedian
SEMAR, a clown-servant puppet

SHAHHAT DREADED the yearly sugar harvest. The cane had to be loaded on freight wagons, and there were never enough to go around. Since a man's cane could be left to dry in the scorching Egyptian sun for some days, losing half its value, there could be violent fights and even killing over the wagons.

The Nile's last flood on the Theban plain had come in 1966 with the construction, which was finished in 1971, of the Aswan Dam, an earth-filled structure two miles long and seventeen times bigger than the Great Pyramid of Cheops. Also under Nasser's rule, Sombat, a feudal estate near Shahhat's village of Nageh Kom Lohlah, was broken up and its land distributed to the local fellaheen. Each fellah given land was to set aside one of his two new acres to grow sugar. This cash crop, which took a year to ripen, and was harvested from February to May, had tripled the incomes of those who were allotted land.

The government ran a large sugar refinery in the river town of Armand, ten miles south, and laid out railway tracks to the cane fields. Two of these tracks crossed Sombat, and during the harvest each fellah was allotted two freight wagons. The agricultural inspector told each man what date to cut his cane, when to bring it by camel to the nearest railway track and when to load it. Since the factory was not efficient, and the engine hauling wagons back and forth was invariably late, and since the inspector and his men were not always above favoritism, bribes or even spite, there could be trouble.

Shahhat was happiest working the half-acre of land between his house and the Ramses Canal, which brought water from Aswan. This land was all that was left of his father's inheritance. Here were Shahhat's fields of clover and onions and the family's walled garden with its grove of date palms and grape vines. These he watered with his shaduf, the well sweep Egypt's peasants have been using since early pharaonic times. At Sombat, with modern methods, all was frustration, delays and complications.

This year the cane harvest was going badly. By early April great heaps of cane could be seen by the railway tracks waiting to be loaded. "Right from the start it has not been good," Faruk, Shahhat's sharecropper, who lived nearer Sombat and kept an eye on the fields, complained. "The cane gets all dried out in the sun. Some men will get a low price, maybe only half as much as they should. Those sons of dogs at the refinery in Armand do not send the freight wagons at the promised time." Shahhat was told not to begin cutting until May 2. His acre of cane would be among the last to be cut and shipped. The Armand refinery was to shut its gates on May 10.

The harvest itself went quickly. Shahhat's brother-in-law, Kamil, agreed to help, and Shahhat hired two more men from El Kom. They cut the cane by whacking it off at the roots with a hoe, then they stripped off the green leaves and stacked it. A new custom had sprung up in the past few years: any man who cut cane all day could take home in payment that night all the fodder he could load on his donkey. Shahhat and Kamil, who soon had sore backs from cutting, often straightened up to shout, "Hello, hello, effendi! Anyone who wants fodder for his livestock, he can come and cut with us! O men and women, come! If you want to feed your family!"

Kamil's face, though he was not yet forty, was as creased and lined as an old man's, and he forever went about in a grimy old tunic, his large hands seldom clean. Quiet and taciturn in the village, he came alive in the fields, shouting, "O my God, Allah, help the poor people!" or "This day is black! Allah, send us a breeze and an army of workers from the sky!" Shahhat, in high spirits, sang as he cut, and when Kamil admonished him, saying he should sing religious songs and not love songs, Shahhat cried at the top of his lungs, "Help us, our God, we are Muslims! O our holy Prophet, be satisfied with us!"

So much shouting, accompanied by curses, coarse jokes and laughter, attracted many workers. Kamil greeted each new arrival, "Ah, we have caught another fish in our net! Come and take your share of fodder, neighbor. Did you fall from the sky or did the wind carry you here?"

"Here come some more men."

"You have sharp eyes, Shahhat."

"Wah! Pray to your Prophet! In our house the buffalo fell sick from the Evil Eye. Now you want to make me sick also with your compliments. Then no one will be found in the house or in the field."

"O men, go north to Cairo!" Kamil's voice rose from the tall cane. "This place is useless for you. O my father, I wish you had not married my mother and brought me into this world. Now you see what has become of me and weep in your graves!"

Such banter made the time pass so swiftly and attracted so many workers that by midafternoon the cane was almost half cut. A man named Suleyman, whose cane was next to Shahhat's, came to complain: "You sons of dogs are cutting your field quickly. Why, Shahhat and Kamil, when anyone passes by do you call out, 'Come, oh, come and get fodder'? You must tell whoever comes now that it is their duty to help me."

This was met with laughter and jeers. When a young boy came to join the crowd in Shahhat's field, Suleyman intercepted him and roughly grabbed him by the shoulders. "Come, let Shahhat go to the devil. *Wa-llah!* You come and work with me, not here!" The boy squirmed away and joined Shahhat's workers. Shahhat laughed and called to his neighbor, "O Suleyman, see how this boy feels safe with us! Not with you!"

"O Suleyman," Kamil joined in. "We are all poor, tired men. Our teeth are falling out from poverty!"

"Be careful, boy!" returned Suleyman, getting angry. "That Shahhat is a sodomite!" The workers roared with laughter and Shahhat retorted, "Better that than a catamite like you!" Showered with good-natured jeers and insults, Suleyman retreated to his field, cursing them.

A northerly breeze broke the oppressive heat the next day, and with an even larger number of volunteers, they finished cutting Shahhat's cane by sunset. The luckless Suleyman, whose harvest was not even half done, rained curses on them. "O you sons of dogs! Why did you go to Shahhat and not to me?"

"Praise be to God!" Shahhat exclaimed when the last of the cane had been stacked. "If it had turned cooler today I might have beaten someone. Instead of being happy we have finished, we might have ended with a funeral."

The harvesters laughed. "You are wicked, Shahhat!" one of them said. "You are like a fire that destroys everything in its path!"

That evening Shahhat was told to pick up a railway wagon the following morning at a yard a kilometer to the south. He took Faruk and at dawn they found their wagon—an open-air wagon about the size of a big truck designed to haul sugar cane. They were about to push it down the track when a voice commanded, "Take that wagon!" It was Lamei, the richest landlord around. As always, he had several men with him. As they were pushed aside, Faruk protested, "How can you take this wagon, you sons of dogs? It's Shahhat's!"

Shahhat, knowing that Lamei feared any involvement with the police or petty government officials, since his wealth invited extortion of bribes, exploded as furiously as he could, shouting, "All your fathers are dogs! I drank a bitter cup to take this wagon! Now every dog tries to take it. And I need two cars, not just the one!" He shoved one of the workers aside and struck another hard on the side of the head, knocking him away from the wagon to show Lamei he would have a fight on his hands.

"I'll kill the first one of you that touches this wagon again!" Shahhat thundered. "There is no government, no law here! Now I must rule with my fists and get twenty-five years in prison if I must kill one of you to take this wagon! But afterward I shall live proudly!"

Lamei, who was not a bad man and just wanted to get his own work done, now turned angrily on his workers. "Did I tell you to take Shahhat's car, you fools. No!" As his men fell back in confusion, Lamei offered Shahhat and Faruk cigarettes to show that this test of wills had left him with no hard feelings. Although he was said to make a profit of ten thousand pounds each cane harvest, Lamei was a simple, industrious man who labored as hard in his fields as any of his hired men.

Shahhat and Faruk wasted not a moment pushing the wagon out of the yard before someone else tried to claim it. Faruk, weakened by drink and dissipation and unaccustomed to physical labor, was soon sweating and panting, and wanted to rest.

"*Yi lan dinak!*" Shahhat cursed him, pushing against the heavy wagon harder than ever. "Your religion is bad!"

"*Yi lan dinak abook!*" Faruk retorted. "Your father's religion is bad!" He gasped, trying to catch his breath. "I may get ruptured, Shahhat, and you will be to blame!"

Pushing as hard as they could together, cursing each other all the while, they were able to move the wagon slowly forward along the track. In the morning stillness, their gasps, grunts and labored breathing were broken only by a steady exchange of insults.

"You are the son of a bad one, Shahhat."

"Shut up, you donkey!"

"Donkey! Why . . . may Allah smite you to pieces!"

"Go burn in the fire, Faruk!"

"May your father burn first!"

"Pig!"

"Pimp!"

"Bastard!"

"Christian!"

"Jew!"

"Jew, am I?" Shahhat grinned, as he gasped for breath from all the exertion of pushing the wagon. "Well, Allah must love the Jews, for he has given them everything."

In this fashion, aroused and infuriated by each other's insults and curses, time passed quickly, and Shahhat's stack of cane soon came in sight. When they reached the cane and let the wagon slide to a stop, Faruk stumbled down the bank like the survivor of a train wreck and collapsed into the pile of cane. He wiped his sweaty face with a rag and breathed heavily in and out, gasping for air. Then he turned on Shahhat.

"May your house fall down! May all your neighbors' houses fall down! May all the houses around your neighbors' houses fall down! May all the houses in your sight fall down! It's a black day I ever met you, Shahhat! You are a dirty son of a dog! You are a lazy, good-for-nothing, dirty son of a dog! I did not come to push the wagon. You know I have a bad leg. You are no good. You want everything too easily. May your house sink into the mud of the Nile and you with it!"

Shahhat, his temper exploding, squatted in the path and violently scooped up dust with his fingers, flinging it at Faruk in the Arab gesture of utmost contempt. "Take this over your head and the head of your father!" he shouted.

Faruk leaped to his feet, seized a cane stalk and raised it to strike Shahhat. "You dare to insult my father?" Seeing Faruk's face, and that so much blood had rushed to his head he turned purple and the veins stood out on his temples, Shahhat burst into laughter. He could not stop but doubled over, the laughter tumbling out until he went into a coughing, choking fit. Faruk also began to laugh as Shahhat managed to sputter, "What can I do when I see you so respectful of your father, Faruk?" For Faruk was usually full of curses for the old man. When Shahhat regained his composure, he kissed the top of Faruk's turban and the two of them set about loading cane. Before long some of Faruk's men, who had seen them from the threshing ground, came to help and the wagon was soon filled. Half the cane was still on the ground, and Shahhat saw he would need to get a second wagon somehow. Still, with at least half his sugar safely loaded, he felt more lighthearted than he had since the harvest began.

"*Le, le, le, le* . . . ?* Why, why, why, why . . . ?" he sang a popular old Arab tune on the way home. He went along the canal path in the loose-jointed, loping gait that was second nature to him when he felt carefree. Shahhat felt a sudden surge of happiness, such as sometimes overtakes us when we least expect it. The name Shahhat comes from the Arabic for "beggar," and is given to male babies to protect them from the Evil Eye if their older brothers have died in infancy, as Shahhat's had. He was barefoot, unshaven, clad in his old black tunic, his dusty gray scarf wrapped about his head, his face gritty with dust from the cane. He looked like a beggar. Shahhat did not care. When he felt a thorn in his foot, he sat down on a rock and dug it out with another thorn. He saw a lizard slither toward a puddle and threw a stone at it, and was on his way, still singing, "Why, why, why, why . . . ?"

There were no wagons at all at the freight yard the next morning. Everyone was told to go and wait by his cane, until enough wagons were provided so all could finish loading. The day was hot, without the slightest breath of air. Shahhat and the other men gathered under the shade of a large acacia tree by the railway track. Their cane had dried in the harsh May sun for three days now. Soon it would be worthless, a whole year's labor come to nothing.

In Egypt there is a mental state called *kaif.* Egyptian Jesuit priest Henry Habib Ayrout defined it as "doing nothing, saying nothing, thinking nothing." Ayrout, who studied the fellaheen, called it "a kind of wakeful passivity," a way of turning off one's mind to avoid frustration. In their impotence in the face of incompetent authority, Shahhat and his neighbors drifted into it now. From dawn to early afternoon, the men sprawled about under the acacia branches, speaking little, humming, drowsing, lost in private fantasies, a lassitude as oppressive as the drying heaps of cane along the track or the stubble fields which shimmered with heat under the vivid white sun.

Shahhat was awakened from this stupor by Lamei, who also needed a few more wagons to finish his harvest and was waiting for an engine to bring them. Lamei sat down, offered Shahhat a cigarette, took one himself, lit them and exhaled with a great sigh. "Well, do you make a living?" Lamei asked.

"*El hamdu li-llah*, praise be to God," Shahhat responded automatically. All about them the sprawling men dozed. Smoking in silence, they gazed across the stubble fields to the tree lines where the houses were and, rising above them, the upper ramparts of the great pharaonic tombs and temples, Medinet Habu built by Ramses III, the great misshapen stone Colossi of Memnon, and, higher still, the cliffs of the Libyan Desert, hazy with heat in the luminous shimmer of the faint blue distance. These cliffs rose like a wall, for the Nile Valley was really a deep flat-bottomed trough carved into the desert floor by prehistoric floods. Like the Sahara, they were of a shifting color impossible to name. Someone painting them might mix white, yellow, ocher, pink, a touch of brown, adding a pale blue as shadows appeared from the sun's westward fall. Sweeping in a majestic arc around the green fields of the Nile's western bank, they formed such a splendid natural setting it was easy to see why the pharaohs chose the Theban Plain for their greatest city.

Lamei cleared his throat and spat. "This land would be nothing without Nitrokima," he said, naming the nitrogen fertilizer that was manufactured with hydroelectric power at Aswan. Dusty and unshaven, his eyes squinting in the sun, Lamei looked as worn down by the harvest as Shahhat himself. "Our land has been cultivated since ancient times," he said. "We even use the dust of their old towns for our fertilizer. Every field is filled with bits of pottery and human bones, Shahhat. This earth is old and exhausted."

"It was a great mistake to build the Aswan Dam," Shahhat responded wearily. "The government thought it would provide more food. But the soil becomes weak. The cane was not good this year. It was a great mistake to stop the yearly flooding of the Nile. Maybe they should blow it up and let the river flood again."

Lamei chuckled. "No, no," he said in his laconic way. "Now it is good. We cultivate three crops a year and grow many things—sugar, beans, peas, clover . . . I had a hundred acres in the past and grew only the old crops—wheat, barley, lentils. Maybe I lost a fourth to rats and insects. Now with sugarcane we get ten times the profit. Before the High Dam at Aswan, the government could not help us much. Now even the poorest fellah makes two, three times what he did before."

"I am only a poor, ignorant man," said Shahhat, thinking only someone as rich as Lamei would speak as he did. Lamei predicted that someday the Nile Valley would no longer produce grain and fodder. It was a virtual greenhouse, with the world's best growing conditions. Crops like forage and sorghum could come from Sudan, wheat from Syria and Iraq. Egypt could make more growing fruit and vegetables, flowers and seeds, and selling them to Europe. "We will do what is good for Egypt," Lamei said. "And to make much money. We can do anything once we have the experience."

"No!" protested Shahhat, roused from his stupor. "We must eat from our own labor and land, Lamei. Never depend on other countries. Can our animals eat flowers? Can our families eat flowers? My buffalo must be fed from my own land."

"If the government gives us flour for bread, Shahhat, we can do anything they want."

"Never!" Shahhat's voice rose so loud he woke several of the sleeping men. "The fellaheen would never agree! Those officials in Cairo sit in a chair and have no experience. Can a minister take my hoe and cultivate my maize? No, he can only read books."

"In Cairo they say . . ."

"Leave me from Cairo! I want the good things here!"

Lamei smiled. "We cannot leave the old things easily, can we, Shahhat?"

After a while Lamei went away but Shahhat still felt upset. It was Aswan that brought the incessant field work, even in hottest summer. It had brought the diesel pumps, the fights to load cane, the feuds and frustrations. It had created the inspectors, the Lameis, the Faruks. To Shahhat, order and reason were limited. No scientific or technical progress could enlarge them; rather they made life more difficult. Shahhat told himself this land was a gift of the Nile and that without its floodwaters and silt, the land would surely someday die. His thoughts were interrupted by Suleyman's coarse voice. "Your father is not good for Allah, Shahhat! Why talk so much to Lamei? You tire our heads."

As the afternoon deepened, Shahhat went across the fields to Faruk's threshing ground and joined him for a glass of tea. Shahhat, whose eyesight was remarkably good, had not finished when he saw the first few puffs of smoke on the southern horizon. Then they heard a faint whistle. At last, coming around a bend below the freight yard, they saw the engine itself.

Shahhat counted fifty wagons. He watched transfixed as the smoking engine would move ahead a little, then let off some cars. Soon it was pulling just twenty-five, then fifteen, then it stopped at Lamei's. Shahhat realized that crowds of men must have been beside the tracks, waiting for wagons. Shahhat saw that Lamei was allotted only seven wagons, so the remaining eight were left for him and the others by the tree. But there were nine of them.

"Take care, Faruk!" Shahhat exclaimed. "They're one short! There will be a fight! C'mon, Faruk, let's run and get a wagon!"

"My legs and back are sick from yesterday," Faruk complained. "I can hardly walk."

Shahhat was off, running across the field toward the slowly advancing engine. Seeing him, the men under the tree jumped to their feet and started running up the track. Faruk looked about for his turban and sandals, but, finding neither, tore off barefoot and bareheaded, leaping over dikes and splashing through canals as if the Devil himself were behind him.

Suleyman reached the first wagon and claimed it just as Shahhat got there. Shahhat shouted at him like a madman: "Suleyman, it's mine! Yours is next! Seize it quick! We don't want a fight and there are many wagons!" Suleyman, seeing the one behind was unclaimed, ran to it. Two of Faruk's men, who followed from the fields, joined Shahhat and helped him push his wagon forward. Suleyman and some other men were so excited they lost control of their wagon and rammed it into the back of Shahhat's, forcing Shahhat and the others to jump down the embankment to avoid getting crushed. Shahhat roared at them and they let his wagon get ahead. "Push hard!" Shahhat shouted at Faruk's men. "Let's get away and load up quick!"

Faruk, who had found a donkey somewhere, was riding up and down the embankment, shouting orders and abusing everyone. "One for one, men! Take only one wagon! Mohammed, your father is a dog! Leave that one for Ala Adeen, you greedy bastard! Suleyman, no one should load his wagon until all are fairly distributed!"

"By my God, Faruk," Suleyman thundered back at him, "we'll load our wagon even if all Sombat flows with blood!"

"Take it, then, Suleyman! May your house be destroyed!"

A man rushed past Shahhat. "Help me! Help me, Shahhat!" he cried. "O my God, I must get a wagon for my father-in-law!"

Shahhat did not look back to see who it was. "I don't care about anyone!" he told the man pushing next to him. "I'll take this wagon to my cane and have done with it!"

When they reached Shahhat's field, they loaded the rest of the cane quickly as the sun set and darkness fell. The work finally done, Shahhat set out for home alone. He had never felt so tired and looked at the star-filled sky with an expression of great relief that the cane harvest, thank God, was over for another year. He felt hot and feverish and all his muscles ached. When a passing man greeted him and asked where he was going, Shahhat just managed to grin and joke: "I'm going to hell."

After supper Shahhat's head was burning. He staggered upstairs and fell into bed, turning his head to the wall. He felt dizzy, nauseated. As soon as she felt his hot forehead, his mother, Ommohamed, could not do enough for him. She feared fever more than anything. She stayed by his side, begging him to take coffee or tea. Shahhat merely shook his head and rolled back to face the wall. That evening he managed to down some beans and raw green peppers his mother prepared for him. During the night he dreamed his stomach swelled up like a giant balloon, and he awoke sweating with fright.

The fever persisted the next day. Shahhat did not stir except to stagger out to the high grass by the temple wall, returning pale and faint. Some of the neighbors, hearing Shahhat was sick, came in the evening to shake his hand and formally greet him. "*Salaamtek*, good health, Shahhat. Your illness came quickly. I hope it is not serious and will pass with peace."

His friends came to joke. "What, Shahhat? Not dead yet?"

He would manage a grin. "You'd like me to be dead?"

"Why not? If it is Allah's will." And they would laugh, cheering him up.

Shamsuddin, the student, came, making a pious virtue of it. When he left he told Shahhat he hoped he would recover in time for the Friday prayers at the mosque, as he would be delivering the sermon on "how to pray." This cheered up Shahhat as much as anything. He told Ommohamed with amusement, "What a bunch of hypocrites we have in our village! All the greediest shopkeepers will go to hear Shamsuddin tell them how to be good Muslims. *El hamdu li-llah!*"

The second night of his illness, a hot southerly wind, the dreaded khamsin, arose, so that the air became scorching and saturated with choking dust. As always when it blew in summer, there was an outbreak of fever and diarrhea all through the village. It was also the time of year when scorpions, once drowned in the Nile's annual flood, now multiplied. They could be found everywhere, on the canal path, in the road, even in the houses. Children could be fatally stung.

Ommohamed was a devout Muslim. A handsome woman, with that strong-boned kind of face that holds its looks no matter what life brings, she was forever crying, "O my God! I demand from you an invitation to Mecca! In any way, by money justly earned, before I die!"

Shahhat would listen with a wry grin, knowing what would come next.

"But I would need to take Shahhat."

"Me? I wouldn't go. Even if it cost nothing." The grin grew wider, as it did when Shahhat teased Ommohamed. When he was amused, Shahhat had an unusually broad, kind and infectious grin. He laughed, seeing his mother assume the haughty dignity she always wore when someone tried to bring her down to earth.

"If you went to Mecca," he joked, "you would come back a very pious Muslim. There would be no more drinking or cursing in the house. You would keep us to a narrow path. Who could live with you? Go to Mecca! *Yah salaam!*"

That is how they would go on. Around Ommohamed, Shahhat was humorously combative. She made her demands, arms upraised, luminous eyes flashing in her theatrical way; Shahhat resisted. She told him, "It is important to dress well, even if you have to go hungry." He habitually went about in the same faded black tunic, so full of holes his hairy chest or brown muscular shoulders showed through, the same old gray wool scarf wound about his skullcap, his bare, bony feet kicking up the dust.

On the fourth night of his illness he took a turn for the worse. His fever rose so high and his skin became so hot and dry he could not sleep, but stared silently at the ceiling as his mind drifted about.

It alarmed Ommohamed to see him lying there, eyes open, hardly taking a breath, and she asked him, "Shahhat, does your head ache much? It feels very hot."

He replied, but not at once. "I keep dreaming."

"What do you dream?"

"All sorts of things." For a time he did not speak. Then he startled her by asking, "Mother, if I died right now, the gravedigger would put me in a tomb, would he not? And the angels Munkar and Nekeer would come to examine me?"

"Yes, my son."

He spoke in such a faint, weary voice she had to lean forward to follow him. "I do so many bad things. Like drinking and chasing girls and swearing and fighting with you. And I spent that twelve pounds you gave me for seed. The two angels would not be beautiful, I think. No, they would have ugly, terrible faces. They would take me by force, beating me all the way, down to the seventh hell. And I would stay there until all my sins were gone."

"*Malesh, malesh,* never mind," said Ommohamed, wiping his hot forehead with a cloth. "Perhaps the angels would take you directly to Paradise."

Again there was a long pause. "No, no, no, no," he finally said and gave a faint chuckle. "Not like Shamsuddin. No, Munkar and Nekeer will ask me, 'Do you sometimes curse your mother?' If I say yes, they will beat me. If I say no, I become a liar and they must also beat me." He stopped speaking, closed his eyes and dozed off again. Ommohamed resolved to fetch a doctor at daybreak. Hours went by. Samah, her unmarried daughter, and the two younger boys came in and carried their bedding out to the rooftop veranda.

Samah saw her mother's face was swollen and streaked with tears, and when Ommohamed spoke, her voice broke into little sobs. "When Shahhat was born it was I and not his father who first whispered the call to prayer in his ear. Did I ever tell you that?" Ommohamed muffled her weeping with a cloth so it would not waken him and she felt his pulse and watched his chest, anxious to see that he breathed. "But, O my God, what is that time compared to now? He is my first son to live to be a man."

Around ten o'clock a quivering red glow began to fill the room. Samah came to say they were burning the cane fields, as they did each year after the harvest. Ommohamed rose and went to the door, where in a single line, going from one end of the eastern horizon to the other, at Sombat halfway to the Nile, a wall of fire rose nine or ten feet high. It scattered sparks into the air like fountains spraying fire. The whole valley seemed to have burst into flame. She could almost hear the fire crackling.

They must have waited for the khamsin to die. Everything in sight took on a quivering red light. The fire meant that all the cane was cut and loaded and taken to the refinery. The flames were a long way off, as far as Sombat, but they seemed close and threatening. Black shadows moved over the nearby fields, birds took flight, every blade of grass seemed clearly visible. Slowly the fire died and wisps of smoke began to drift over the village.

Ommohamed went back to sit by Shahhat's bed in the darkened room. As some unburnt patch of cane burst into flame, casting a red light, Ommohamed thought of the fires of hell. She shut her eyes and dozed, but even drifting off to sleep, she still saw the fiery light, like the infernal abode of *shaytans*, the devils who dwelled in the mountains of Kaf. She imagined herself in a fearful flaming landscape where Iblis, the great Satan himself—big, black, horned, hideous— was driving Shahhat into the fire with a long stick, just as he himself chased the boys if they misbehaved. Frightened, she shook herself awake, hastened to feel Shahhat's pulse, watched his chest to see if he was breathing and broke into prayers to Allah.

About two o'clock in the morning, Shahhat began to violently toss and turn, groaning and muttering unintelligible sounds. His head was burning and he moaned so loudly that Samah and the boys outside peered into the doorway, scarcely breathing, thinking Shahhat was going to die. His hoarse groans became more frequent, and Ommohamed saw his lips were trying to form the words *Allahu Akbar, Allahu Akbar . . .*

Suddenly he opened his eyes, sat bolt upright and, staring transfixed at some point in the darkness, shouted in a loud, ecstatic voice, *"Allahu Akbar! Allahu Akbar!* God is most great!"

The children shrank back. Outside, neighbors called out in alarm. Shutters were thrust back and doors opened. Dogs began to howl, babies began to cry—Ommohamed rushed to the window, flung back the shutters and cried, "No, no! Shahhat is very sick and he had a dream! It is nothing!"

When she turned around, Shahhat had fallen back on his pillows and was breathing heavily. He fought to get his breath back. Ommohamed clutched his hand and waited for him to speak. When he did, he spoke calmly, in a hoarse but excited voice, his eyes still focused on something far and distant.

He had dreamed, he said, that he was in a graveyard. He was wandering about in his old, torn black tunic among some tombs. His head hurt; he was being tormented by demons from Satan who were clawing and howling inside his head. He thought it would burst. He was sobbing and crying like a demented man, and fell against the sharp gravestones, hurting himself. It was as if some wild and angry devils, deeply miserable, whirled around inside him in fury, trying to get out.

Then there appeared before him a bearded man all dressed in white who was carrying prayer beads. This man called to him in a strange echoing voice, "Who? Who are you, Shahhat? Who are you, O Beggar? Come, come! Why do you dress in the black rags of an unclean spirit? Here, enter here!"

And they passed through an enormous gate, and at once the air was cool and inexpressibly pure and filled with such a brilliant, dazzling light Shahhat could hardly see. It blazed golden like the sun, and from this light emerged a second man, also bearded, but golden shafts of light pierced the space about him in air so swarming with blinding sparks and glittering particles that Shahhat covered his eyes with his hand. And they took his black rags and burned them. They gave him a gleaming white tunic to wear, and the second man tied a green sash, made of the richest silk, around his waist.

And they led him into a great garden filled with miraculous trees and flowers and fountains of such unutterable beauty that it gave Shahhat a sense of holiness impossible to describe. He held his breath, his heart ceased to beat and he heard a great chorus of magnificent voices rise in a thunderous shout, magical and ecstatic in its rapture: *"Allahu Akbar! Allahu Akbar!* God is most Great!" And he too joined in the tumultuous cry, shouting into the great garden and running past the dazzling flowers and fountains in the golden mist, crying with joy as inexpressible rapture filled his whole being . . .

In the torrent of Shahhat's words, in the fire in his eyes and in all his movements, Ommohamed saw such beauty that she was transfixed as if rooted to the ground and thought: It is an omen. Now he will be good. For she felt she understood the dream. The first man was the Angel Gabriel and the second the Holy Prophet himself, for only the most blessed were given the highest spiritual pleasure of beholding him, so that Shahhat was blinded by the dazzling radiance of his presence. It was he who exorcised the demons that tormented her son.

Ommohamed was so ambitious, hoped so fiercely, and yet had never found what she needed to make her happy. Now as Shahhat fell into a deep sleep, his skin cool to her touch and his fever gone, she uttered prayers of thanksgiving and felt very close to God. And she thought of the pilgrim's cry that she might someday make at Arafat, the rocky knoll at Mecca where the Prophet Muhammad preached his last sermon, *"Labayk, allahuma, labayk.* Here I am, O Lord, here I am."

Shahhat and Ommohamed, in this scene set in 1976, were expressing the deep religiosity that is the core of Muslim culture, what anthropologist Clifford Geertz has called "god-intoxicated."

To enter this world is to suspend disbelief. Copernicus, a Pole, showed us in the sixteenth century that the earth was a small planet that circled the sun, Darwin in the eighteenth that man was a biological species like any other. The space and computer age, in which galaxies and molecules are charted as never before, has utterly changed the way we see ourselves. I remember how the earth looked to the astronauts as they circled the moon on Christmas Eve 1968, quoting Genesis: "In the beginning God created the heavens and the earth . . ." Suddenly the earth looked small and fragile, the thin, white atmosphere over its bright blue surfaces bringing home the planet's unity, and the shared dangers of overpopulation destroying its habitat. We are almost as far from the idea of a personal God to whom our individual little fate matters as from my Methodist preacher grandfather's faith in a heaven of white-robed multitudes playing harps. Infinite time and space have made us insignificant.

Paleoanthropologist Richard Leakey, who has traced our origins back 3 to 4 million years, and as modern humans to Africa 150,000 years ago, says the sun is projected to last another 5 to 10 billion years, but *we* won't. "It is a certain guess," he says, "that long before the sun's energy is spent, *Homo sapiens* will no longer exist, another extinct species in Earth's history of biotic collapse and recovery." Leakey reminds us that 99 percent of all species that ever lived are now extinct and 50 percent of those left may become extinct in the next thirty years, victims of overpopulation.

Earlier I quoted Leakey's view, voiced in 1981, that "human beings are cultural animals and each one is the product of a particular culture." In the 1990s Leakey is as emphatic as ever on this point: "*Homo sapiens* is a cultural creature . . . Our view of the world, and the material trappings we enjoy in it, depend in a very direct way on what was done one generation back, ten generations back, a hundred generations back. Today we are the beneficiaries of our ancestors in a way not experienced by other species."

Consider religion. Some aspects of African tribal belief, with its closeness to nature, may go back several millennia, even if the shift from hunter-gatherer to settled farmer came much later to Africa than elsewhere, probably around 500 B.C. Some Jewish customs go back nearly 4,000 years, or, say, one hundred and sixty generations, to Abraham's departure from Ur. Aryans brought the Vedas and the caste system to India 3,500 years ago, Confucius taught harmony in China and Buddha renunciation in India 2,400 to 2,600 years ago and Jesus the love of God and man 2,000 years ago.

This leaves Islam, with the Prophet Muhammad's migration from Mecca to Medina in 622 A.D., just fifty-five to sixty generations ago, the youngest of the great religions, with inherited traits perhaps that much stronger. Islam claims 800 million to 1 billion adherents, the vast majority of them illiterate peasants like Shahhat and his mother. Shahhat, for instance, was sent, not to school, but for six years to a small local Muslim *kuttab* to memorize the Koran. The old man who taught him believed the earth was flat and surrounded by the sea and the mountains called Kaf, where good and evil jinn lived. Along with the Koran, Shahhat was taught the Hadith, or traditions of acts and nonrevealed sayings of Muhammad, and Islamic or *sharia* law. Belief in the Evil Eye, sorcery, *shaytans*, magic charms and potions were all part of Shahhat's inherited culture.

To be a Muslim, the only essentials of belief and behavior are the five pillars of Islam. These are the affirmation of faith—"There is no God but Allah and Muhammad is his prophet," five daily prayers said toward Mecca, fasting during daylight hours during the month of Ramadan, the Hajj pilgrimage to the Kaaba shrine in Mecca and the payment of a tax called *zakat*. Of these only the affirmation of faith is deemed absolutely essential.

Muslim fundamentalists demand a return to the seventh-century Arab customs that seem so barbarous and atavistic—crazed, hysterical mobs, bearded men in robes and turbans, flogged criminals, stoned adulteresses, a convicted thief's amputated hands or feet. None of this is in the Koran. The Muslim quarrel was not with Jesus but with the Christian Church for capitulating to pagan Greek polytheism and idolatry. The prophets of Israel—Adam, Noah, Abraham and Moses—are accepted, and Jesus was God's last and greatest prophet before Muhammad. From the betrayal of the One True God, or Allah, Islam retrieved the pure religion of Abraham—and in Islam's survival lies the hope of mankind.

Young militants—this is as true of Sikh fundamentalists in Punjab —try to enforce their ideas of dress, behavior and ritual with a gun (again, untrimmed beards are deemed more holy in Punjab), while ignoring the inward spiritual heart of a religion as spelled out in its scriptures. This seems to be a universal characteristic of extreme and unyielding oppositionists.

Max Weber observed that religion grows out of the human desire to work out a meaning to life. Clifford Geertz in *Islam Observed* drew a distinction between "holding religious views rather than being held by them," between being "religion-minded" without "religiosity." Fundamentalists who ideologically exploit religion so as to gain control or power over people would be "religion-minded." "As time goes on," he says, "the number of people who desire to believe, or anyway feel they somehow ought to, decreases much less rapidly than the number who are, in a properly religious sense, able to."

Geertz was writing about Islam in Morocco and Indonesia, but we see this dramatically in Christianity. In 1900 two-thirds of the world's 560 million Christians lived in Europe or North America. By 2000 two-thirds of the world's 2 billion Christians will live somewhere else, half of them Africans or Hispanics. As rich, urbanized whites lose their faith, Christianity, like Islam, is becoming a religion of the poor. Jesus is once again a liberator, a crusader against poverty and injustice.

Geertz defines true "religiosity" as "not merely knowing the truth . . . but embodying it, living it, giving oneself unconditionally to it." While in America this kind of obedience to a personal God has declined, the numbers of the "religion-minded" are up. Gallup polls show 94 percent of Americans say they believe in God, 71 percent in heaven, 53 percent in hell; 40 percent say they go weekly to a church or synagogue, 90 percent say they pray. Mainline Protestantism is down, Catholicism and Baptists are up. Fundamentalists run about 20 percent, with Bible thumpers like the Pentecostals out to save the heathen from the eternal flames of damnation. There is a streak of "religion-minded" militancy among Protestants who would excise "sexist" language from the Bible, replacing mankind with humankind, or God the father with God the creator, or in the politicization of religion as among the right-to-lifers. Some feminists object to the image of God as a benign elderly male. What is lacking is the true "religiosity" of Africans who interrupt sermons with applause or dance up to the altar, as I saw them do in Ghana in 1993.

As "god-intoxication" fades, religion becomes ideological. V. S. Naipaul in *Among the Believers* says the flaw in Islam as ideology is that, down through history, it has offered no practical solutions. "It offered only faith. It offered only the Prophet, who would settle everything but who had ceased to exist. This political Islam was rage, anarchy."

Naipaul says the Islamic revival is a reaction to the spread of Western ideas and technology, what he calls "the universal civilization." He goes on:

> It was the late twentieth century that had made Islam revolutionary, given new meaning to old Islamic ideas of equality and union, shaken up static or retarded societies. It was the late twentieth century—and not the faith—that could supply the answers—in institutions, legislation, economic systems. And, paradoxically, out of the Islamic revival, Islamic fundamentalism, that appeared to look backward, there would remain in many Muslim countries, with all the emotional charge derived from the Prophet's faith, the idea of modern revolution.

The Economist's Brian Beedham has observed that the end of the cold war left

> only one stretch of the world notably liable to produce turmoil and mayhem on a large scale in the coming 15–20 years: the approximately crescent-shaped piece of territory that starts in the steppes of Kazakhstan and curves south and west through the Gulf and Suez to the north coast of Africa. This western part of Islam is a potential zone of turbulence for a depressing variety of reasons.
>
> Except for a handful of oil-owning states, its chances of keeping its people materially happy are not good, not the worst in the world, but not all that far off. It has too many inhabitants, too little fertile land, barely the rudiments of an industrial economy . . .
>
> Worse, it does have an ideology. Now that Marxism has been lowered into its grave, Islam is the 20th century's last surviving example of an idea that claims universal relevance.

The problem, Beedham said, is not the Muslim religion itself, nor the Muslim conviction that religion ought to shape the believer's daily life. The problem is that many Muslims are "simple and emotional people" led by politicians "unscrupulously willing to use Islam as a banner, and a weapon, against the outside world."

A notable example is Sudan's Hassan al-Turabi. A lawyer with degrees from the Sorbonne and London University, the real power behind the soldiers who run Khartoum, Turabi flatly says, "Whatever the West will do, Islam will ultimately overcome . . . There is nothing else left to inspire the young, to mobilize them, to give them a vision, a sense of allegiance." Sudan's Muslim north is locked into a savage "holy war" with its Nuer, Dinka and Nuba tribes. Khartoum itself has the air of a police state with reports of arbitrary after-dark arrests, confiscated property, torture chambers and Iran-funded terrorist training centers. It is Naipaul's political Islam of "rage" and "anarchy" with a vengeance. This first erupted with fury in 1979 when the Ayatollah Ruhollah Khomeini overthrew the Shah of Iran to install the first Islamic republic based on fundamentalism ("The whole world is terrified of you," Khomeini told his military commanders, who chained young boys together at the front with Iraq so they could not escape). Then came the 1981 assassination of Anwar el-Sadat and Egypt's attempt since to accommodate fundamentalism by making its Muslim Brotherhood the de facto legal opposition, a risky strategy, as it kept someone like Sheik Omar Abdel Rahman continuing to agitate against what he deemed the enemies of Islam, and did nothing to slow the advance of Egypt's extremists. Saddam Hussein's attempt to turn the Gulf War into a war between Arabs and the West, the faithful versus infidels, only partly succeeded. Flora Lewis reported, "The ardor blazing from the eyes of ululating women in 'the Arab street,' across many countries, reflects the dream of overcoming a sense of powerlessness, wherever the dream may lead." In Algeria, foreigners and unveiled women are no longer safe from Muslim attacks.

It seems a strange fate for a religion that grew out of the Arabian desert, a land, as explorer Wilfred Thesiger described it as recently as forty years ago, which offered "silence where only the winds played" and there were people who still valued leisure, courtesy and conversation and "did not live their lives at second hand, dependent on cinemas and the wireless." Today, Arabist Peter Theroux told us in 1990, that world is gone and there is "the constant nagging presence of American food, appliances, music and politics even in the remotest Arab town or oasis."

The fundamentalists seize our attention. But there are also Muslim reformers and revivalists who stress the virtues of repentance and forgiveness—the Allah, "compassionate and merciful," that Shahhat saw in his dream. Like the Koran itself, the reformers emphasize the inward spiritual qualities of Islam. *Time* magazine's James Wilde, in an interview with Egyptian Nobel laureate Naguib Mahfouz, has written that many Arabs are aghast at Western stereotypes of them—"impoverished camel drivers, spendthrift oil sheikhs, cutthroat terrorists"—though there are plenty of all three around. Mahfouz, Egypt's greatest modern novelist, whose characters exemplify the cultural and spiritual confusion of contemporary Arabs, states, "The fundamentalists are against everything, even Islamic reformers. Let them come out into the open and show people how naked they really are, that they stand only against progress."

If Islam's renewed vitality partly comes from its anti-West character, it also reflects the enormous compulsion felt by most ordinary Muslims to work out new meaning to their lives. Overcrowding on the land and city-based radio and TV have led to a breakdown of the old ways and views. When I first visited Egypt in 1962 it had 25 million people. It will have 70 million by the end of the 1990s.

Islamic fundamentalism both feeds and is fed by this frightening upsurge of people. Most Egyptian imams, like the Pope in Rome, insist that birth control is sinful. A fellah traditionally wants at least two sons. Egypt is 55 percent rural and no peasantry has yet curbed births, just as no city population has replaced itself without immigration. With baby girls born in the 1990s going to have children of their own in another fifteen or twenty years, nothing save ecological disaster can probably stop a further redoubling of Egypt's people.

Each hectare in the Nile Valley and Delta barely fed 10 Egyptians in 1960, 22 in 1992. How can that hectare feed 44? In 1961, 1.6 million landowners averaged 3.8 acres apiece. By 1982, 2.5 million landowners averaged 2.3 acres. Despite great reclamation of the desert—over 900,000 acres in 1952–75—Egypt's cultivated area of 6 million acres has stayed almost constant over four decades. New roads, houses, factories and mosques eat up farmland at the rate of 60,000 acres a year. Farming has accounted for a third of Egypt's GNP, over a third of its labor force and most of its non-oil exports, though tourism, oil, Suez Canal tolls and workers' remittances bring in far more money. Farms along the Nile are tiny, 94 percent of them less than 5 acres. In 1992, 4.3 million agricultural workers owned no land at all.

With such intense rural overcrowding, Egypt took a giant step backward in 1992. Under laws passed from 1952 on, individual fellaheen were limited to 20 acres, rents were kept low and tenants granted open-ended, inheritable leaseholds. Rents were fixed by law at seven times the land tax. Under a new law, bitterly contested in the Egyptian Parliament, the rent figure is to be lifted in stages to twenty-two times the land tax and, by 1995, all lease contracts must be renegotiated. Owners will be free to sell without the consent of their tenants.

Roy Prosterman, a University of Washington law professor and the leading American land reform expert, calls this "both a political and an agricultural disaster." He says the reversal of Nasser's land reform "will return land rights to a new generation of landlords who are largely urban and know little of farming. The practical result will be that land will be rented out in a bidding war. Instead of protected tenants on the land as at present, paying fixed low rents and having permanent security of possession, there will be insecure sharecroppers with no incentive to invest."

Prosterman points out that Egypt's ownerlike tenants, similar to other small-farmer beneficiaries of land reforms in Taiwan, South Korea and Japan, are among the most productive farmers in the world. In both irrigated wheat and rice, scientists say, Egypt has the world's highest average yields. "It is these farmers who are now to be replaced with poorly motivated traditional sharecroppers who will perform badly, as they do in other less developed countries," Prosterman contends.

In 1987 Ommohamed at last stood at Arafat to cry, *"Labayk, allahuma, labayk.* Here I am, O Lord, here I am." During her half-day of prayer and meditation there, she felt a direct, face-to-face closeness to God she had not known before. She did not, in the event, take Shahhat, but went with a group of elderly women from nearby villages. Muslim tradition decrees that the pilgrimage should be undertaken only by those who can afford it and whose domestic obligations have been fulfilled. Ommohamed sold two *qirats* of land—about a twelfth of an acre—and got 16,000 Egyptian pounds for it, just under $5,000. Half she spent on the pilgrimage and the rest went to marry off Shahhat's younger brothers, Nubi and Ahmed. Nubi, who worked with American archaeologists near the Great Pyramids at Giza and had been trained some months in the United States as a surveyor, begged Ommohamed not to sell any land. He promised to find the money for her pilgrimage somehow. "If I wait for you," she told him grimly, "I will wait for fifty years."

That same year Shahhat left farming to become a foreman at an archaeological site, as his father had done, in Shahhat's case at Egypt's greatest pharaonic temple of Karnak near Luxor. His ambition was to become a watchman at one of the tombs in the Theban Necropolis near the village. There was too little land left to feed the family.

After she turned sixty, Hajja Ommohamed, as she was called after the pilgrimage, suddenly aged. She went from a vigorous woman with a good deal of humor to a querulous, wrinkled, bad-tempered old lady who coughed all the time. The doctor told her to stop smoking her water pipe—"I cannot give it up," she lamented. She had managed to put the title to what was left of the family's property in her name—the two acres of cane at Sombat and a date palm garden just behind her house. She ruled the roost vengefully, rarely giving her three daughters-in-law a moment's peace. Though there were nine small grandchildren about, the family no longer had a buffalo, something even the poorest fellah rarely goes without, and gone too were the old donkey, sheep and chickens.

Weary, ailing, Hajja Ommohamed spent many hours lying in the entry room of her old two-story mud-brick house, watching TV soap operas. These were mainly Egyptian, filmed in Cairo, which portrayed the fellaheen as poor and simple rustics, often as figures of fun, while the Cairenes had big cars and flashy apartments. Hajja Ommohamed also became a fan of *Falcon Crest*. If the riches of California's Napa Valley were beyond her wildest dreams, she could identify with Jane Wyman, an old woman fighting to get control of land and water rights.

Shahhat, now forty, and twice married, the father of six surviving children, lived in a small one-room mud-brick house with an enclosed courtyard on the family's ancestral land along the canal behind Ommohamed's house. His first wife, Fawzia, his first cousin, as is the custom in village Egypt, was the daughter of Ommohamed's older brother Muhammad, a watchman for Lamei. Fawzia was the mother of five of Shahhat's children. She was outraged when he sold a small clover field in front of their house to take a second, seventeen-year-old wife. Shahhat, like his father before him, now drank a good deal. Both wives took him to court for nonsupport. Everybody talked about what a heavy drinker Shahhat had become. Only Hajja Ommohamed denied it. "Nubi drinks too much, not Shahhat," she would say. "No, no. Oh, maybe sometimes. He might buy a small bottle." Shahhat seldom saw his mother, visiting her briefly once a week. The village had long grown used to the ways of mother and son and knew that, if there were violent quarrels, impassioned reconciliations would soon follow. Both were even more improvident than ever.

"Now I wake up at three o'clock in the morning," Shahhat told me on my last visit in 1992. "That's three hours before I must start work. Because I am very unhappy. Life is not so easy as before. Not only in Upper Egypt. In Cairo also." Yet Shahhat, if his work was seasonal and sometimes sporadic, was paid the equivalent of about a hundred dollars a month as a foreman, a good wage in rural Egypt. To really look at a poor fellah, we need to consider a landless laborer.

II

Helmi, in 1992 forty years old, seemed about average when I first met him two decades ago. Then just married, he farmed with his father and brother Talal on two acres, about the typical farm size in Egypt. His village, Sirs el Layyan, was fifty miles north of Cairo in the heart of the Nile Delta. As so often happens, a death in the family changes everything. The father died, willed the land to his wife, and she decided to sharecrop with Talal to get money to marry off two daughters. Helmi, with a wife and four children, found himself landless.

There are two Egypts, an Upper and a Lower, each with a character of its own. Upper Egypt has the Nile, the broad river, its narrow green banks, and pink cliffs rising to desert on either side. The Delta has its network of Nile-fed canals, densely populated mud-brick villages, many minarets, the bright green of clover and crops and the darker green of eucalyptus trees. A visitor in the Delta is struck by the fierce work ethic, the underground tile drainage, the constant procession of men leading camels, donkeys and buffaloes laden with manure or fresh dirt in an unceasing task of refertilizing the land, women working in the fields in brightly colored gowns, their heads wrapped in peasant scarves—Upper Egyptian women, who go about in long black cloaks, rarely go to the fields—and the large number of students. If Shahhat was an Upper Egyptian grasshopper—improvident, fiery-tempered, full of jokes—Helmi—docile, hardworking, ever-aspiring —was a Delta ant.

Nearly destitute, Helmi managed to rent half an acre from a neighbor. He could grow enough wheat and corn for *'aysh*, unleavened bread that has been Egypt's staple since antiquity, and enough clover to feed a buffalo and its calf, a donkey, a few sheep, rabbits and pigeons, and a flock of chickens. To save enough to send the children to school—$9 for tuition and about $15 for clothes, shoes and books for a year per child in 1992—Helmi went to Iraq and worked for seven months. He came home with $800, which he tried to double by buying and selling donkeys, but he lost it all instead. He was going back to Iraq when the Gulf War broke out. When the bodies of tortured Egyptian workers began to come back to the villages, some with their eyes gouged out, Helmi vowed he would never go back to Iraq as long as Saddam Hussein was there. To survive he found a job stamping meat and washing up at the village slaughterhouse.

It was hard if you lacked education or skill. Two neighbors, brothers who had studied accounting, went to Saudi Arabia and struck it rich; now they just came home on holidays. Another neighbor, Hajji Mahmud, worked in Saudi Arabia as a farm hand. But he had saved nearly $10,000 in five years, and now he owned five acres, beehives and a new house. So luck mattered too. Helmi's friends, Muhammad Sirhan and Salah, went to Jordan, found nothing and came back in debt.

This being Friday, Helmi rose at six o'clock, splashed some water on his face, spread out a mat and, kneeling, said his prayers, and then went to cut fodder with his sickle. He had taken to sleeping out in a shed with his buffalo, its calf, the donkey, the sheep and a small dog. Someone had poisoned seventeen of his chickens. Helmi's wife, Namat, was sure Talal had done it and wanted to go to the police. Helmi said no, they had to live side by side. "Some people love each other," he told her. "If they cook chicken, they must share it. But when there is no love, we must keep our chickens inside." Helmi's mother would follow Muslim custom when she died. "I have ten children," she said. "Each can take his share." This meant that Helmi, since four daughters got only half as much as the sons, would inherit a quarter-acre. His wife would get about the same from her parents. She told Helmi, "I'd rather have my mother and father and not the land."

The job at the slaughterhouse, its wage the equivalent of $22 a month, paid for the children's schooling. Helmi's other monthly cash expenses came to the equivalent of $12 for meat—eaten every Thursday night in Muslim custom—$10 for cloth and sandals, $2 for Helmi's roll-your-own cigarette papers and tobacco, a few cents for matches, $8 for sugar, $4 for tea, $1 for kerosene and $1.50 for soap—a total of $38.50 a month. Thus Helmi and Namat had to raise $24.50 a month elsewhere, mainly from the sale of butter, cheese and eggs.

Everybody in the village, even Helmi in his simple two-room mud hut, had television. At Muhammad Sirhan's house the set was on from morning to night. Muhammad Sirhan claimed he watched only "after dark" when work was done, but in truth he seldom missed a soccer match or a movie. "I like American films," he told Helmi. "Fighting with police, fighting with planes, fighting with cars. But *bilil, bas!* Only after dark!" Some of the more pious Muslims opposed TV and went about preaching that it was "*haram*, sinful." Even Namat felt it was a bad cultural influence. "TV is not good for young girls," she told

Helmi. "It teaches them many bad things." But she and the children kept watching.

Helmi's busiest day at the slaughterhouse was Thursday. From early morning butchers and their families brought buffaloes, twenty-seven in all, so there was a great crowd of people. A tall old man with a thin bony face, who was always smiling, went about with his knife. The victim would be hanging by its feet, which were tied together, and he slit the animal's throat at its jugular vein, so each buffalo bled to death the Islamic way. It took about a minute. Once dead, the carcass was pulled up by the hooves on chains to be skinned and butchered. Next the stomach was removed, emptied of its contents and washed. The two forequarters were separated, while the hindquarters were left in one piece. Blood flowed into troughs in the ancient stone floor. The slaughterhouse was a very old stone pavilion, open on one side like a theater, and with so many people rushing about, had the look of a pharaonic frieze. Each family worked on its buffalo, the men doing the butchering and women, bending over large iron pans full of hot water, scraping bristles, washing the meat and cleaning out the entrails. Poor women came to help in hopes of getting something for themselves. Others came with shopping bags, pots or enamel plates to buy clean intestines to stuff with rice, or a piece of lean, a chunk of fat, a bit of tripe, liver and heart while it lasted, or stomachs, heads and feet. Small boys ran about carrying hooves. One butcher, stripped down to his knee-length white cotton underwear, which was spattered with blood, did nothing but break up skulls. He stood to one side and whacked away, with the firmest of grips on his ax as its sharp blade came down again and again just inches from his bare feet. There was a smell of blood and flesh and a noisy hubbub of cleavers and knives against bone, laughter, curses, women crying to one another and a hoarse male voice shouting " 'Hammad!" in the background, such as one often heard in Egypt, maybe because so many men were named after the Prophet.

The veterinarian, a dour, stout Egyptian with glasses, who was also stripped down to his underwear, examined each carcass in turn. Helmi followed a deferential pace behind, his stamp poised in his right hand, a bright purple ink pad in his left. When the veterinarian found a buffalo fit for human consumption, he would mutter gruffly, "Stamp that animal," and Helmi would stamp it, again and again, until much of the carcass was bright purple. Three young women, veterinary students, stood by and watched. They had covered their heads with nunlike pastel-colored veils to show they were good Muslims and these and their modern clothes set them apart from the working women; one of them wore high-heeled slippers covered with pink satin, which was stained with blood and gore at the edges.

The feverish scene took place twice a week and was over in three hours. Once the crowd had left, leaving no remains behind, it was Helmi's task to scrub clean the stone floor and walls. He hosed the floor down, spattering even his face with blood, but afterward he went to his mother's house for a proper shower. At home he just washed in a bucket. This week Helmi was distressed because a health inspector had come and demanded to see his permit, required in Egypt if you sold food, worked in a café or butchered animals. Since he only went about stamping the meat once the veterinarian pronounced it edible, neither he nor the vet had thought a permit was necessary. Now they both had been summoned to appear in court, though the vet had applied for a permit for him, so Helmi hoped it would turn out all right. If he lost the job, how could he pay for the children's schooling?

Whatever happened, he was determined to educate them. Namat was illiterate, but their oldest daughter, Hanan, who had inherited Helmi's good looks, was already in the tenth grade and could even speak a little English. "I don't want our children to be fellaheen," Helmi told Namat. "We don't have land. A fellah has to work hard just to feed his family. He can't save anything. Maybe our buffalo costs us a hundred pounds to feed, and if it gives birth to a calf and the calf dies, we have lost everything."

Health was another of Helmi's worries. With so much irrigation, the Delta was cold and damp in winter and Helmi was starting to suffer from rheumatism. Twice, to ease the pain, he had gone to bedouins who lived in the Sahara near the Great Pyramids of Giza. He paid them ten pounds and they applied a red-hot poker to one of his ankles. "It was so painful I had to be held down by five strong men," he told his wife. "They hold the poker until it burns in one centimeter deep. It takes about a minute. You are screaming and shouting. It is terrible." Each winter when the rheumatism came back, Helmi told Namat he would try the local doctor's medicine first. If that failed, he would go back to the bedouins.

This day being Friday meant that at noon all the village men would go to a mosque to pray and hear a sermon. Helmi came back from cutting fodder to eat *fatar*, a breakfast of home-baked corn-and-wheat bread, broad beans, scrambled eggs, an onion and a glass of warm buffalo milk. Such village fare, because everything is so fresh, is the most delicious food in Egypt.

Afterward Helmi went to help harvest potatoes in the field of a neighbor, Ragib, who worked in town except on Fridays. Potatoes were the village's most lucrative crop. A fellah could sell 1,000 kilos for 4,000 pounds, having spent just 1,500 on fertilizer and spray, for a profit of about $800. A new kind of potatoes had been introduced from Holland. They were put in the ground for ninety days, dug up and kept in cold storage for five months, then replanted for ninety more days. When you dug them up, the old potato, brown and rotting, what the fellaheen called the *omi*, or mother, was surrounded by healthy young potatoes ready to eat.

The harvest was traditional. One man went ahead with a cow, turning over the soil with a steel-bladed wooden plow, so that loose potatoes were scattered over the surface. Ten or twelve men followed, crouching over the row and ruffling the dirt with their hands to unearth whatever potatoes might be hidden. All the good potatoes were then thrown into a row in the middle of the field to dry before being gathered up in baskets and sacked to put on donkeys to carry into market.

Like practically all field work in Egypt, it was sociable. As the group of men moved forward, squatting on their haunches and picking up the potatoes, they talked about the weather and wondered if it might rain, until the sun broke through the clouds and blue patches appeared in the sky. Unlike Upper Egypt, where it virtually never rained and even clouds were rare, it was often overcast in the Delta.

The talk turned to education. Muhammad Sirhan said that in his parents' days nobody sent girls to school. Now both he and Helmi had sisters who were teachers and nurses. "Before," Helmi told his friends, "every father wanted to have three or four sons. And he kept one or two illiterate to work as fellaheen. Now nobody wants his son to be a fellah and fathers send all their sons to school."

"If you don't have land," asked another neighbor, Salah, "how can you make a living?"

Helmi sighed. "My father wanted to keep me on the land, so he sent me to school for just three years. Then he died and left me landless."

When noon approached, the men left the field to go home and wash and put on a clean galabiya, the long cotton robe Egyptians wear, for the Friday sermon. So many new mosques had been built by villagers who had worked in Saudi Arabia, there were two right out in the fields by Helmi's house. Young imams from Al Azhar University in Cairo came out each week to deliver the sermons and Helmi chose to go hear the one who was less long-winded. The imams in town sometimes gave political harangues, but those in the villages kept to lessons from the holy Koran. Helmi and his neighbors had always been devout, but now there was a new Islamic fervor. Many more fellaheen, like Helmi, did the five daily prayers, all went to the mosque on Friday and so many made the pilgrimage to Mecca, there were now over 2 million from all over the world going each year, up from 400,000 twenty years earlier.

Alone of the harvesters, Helmi carried a bundle of potatoes home from Ragib's field, wrapping them in his galabiya. "If anyone asks he can take," he told his five-year-old son, Muhammad, who came running up the canal path to meet his father as soon as he saw him. Just as the child reached Helmi, the galabiya slipped open, spilling potatoes into the path.

"No barat feh fehah! You gave them the Evil Eye!" Helmi exclaimed. As the two of them crouched to gather up the potatoes, Helmi saw that Muhammad's shirt was torn. "Why are you always fighting with other boys?" Helmi demanded crossly. "You tear your clothes!" Muhammad hurriedly headed toward home, his shoulders hunched, afraid he might be punished. A feebleminded youth, who was standing out in a field loading dirt on his donkey, shouted at Helmi when he passed, "Don't let your son say bad things to me!" Hearing this, Muhammad took fright, looked back at his father, and his face crumpled into a sob. He began to cry, running well ahead of Helmi, one hand holding his cap on his head and the other his pants, which, tied by a string that had come undone, were falling down, exposing his bare little bottom. Tiny as he was, Muhammad was forever teasing someone, fighting or getting into trouble. Helmi scolded him as they neared the house. "I told you not to say bad things to anyone." "I don't say bad things to anybody," the child sobbed in a muffled voice and tried to stop his tears.

Namat knew what the trouble was. Muhammad had teased the retarded youth, telling him, "You're the son of Nefisa." Nefisa was indeed his mother's name, but in the village it was an insult to say so in public. "He is very naughty," Namat told Helmi. "Oh, Muhammad, why do you do bad things?" Namat was secretly pleased. Unlike her other son, who had bad eyes and was sometimes ridiculed and beaten by the other boys, Muhammad could take care of himself.

The Friday sermon was about how everyone must respect their parents and how the Prophet Muhammad paid such respect to his uncle, Omar Ibn el Katab. Afterward, back at the potato field, Muhammad Sirhan related the story of an Egyptian film he had seen on TV the night before. A dark-skinned Egyptian boxer who went to Germany and won many matches fell in love with a blond German woman. The German crowds turned against him because of the color of his skin. The film fascinated the villagers because Islam had pretty much extinguished racial consciousness in Egypt, so that it seemed strange and alien to the villagers.

By midafternoon all Ragib's potatoes had been gathered, bagged and weighed. By then they were all starved and Ragib provided a real feast. His sisters brought a round, low wooden table to the field and the men sat cross-legged around it, in the dirt. They brought many dishes from the house: roasted chicken, steamed rice, macaroni and potatoes cooked in tomato sauce and freshly baked bread. Afterward there were glasses of sugary tea. A procession of donkeys was to carry the potatoes into town.

"Give me eighty pounds and your donkey and I'll give you mine," joked Muhammad Sirhan.

"Your donkey is tired," Ragib told him.

"It's better than yours. You know, most donkeys live ten to twelve years, but if a good donkey is well treated it can last thirty."

The talk of donkeys reminded them of Helmi's loss. They would never let him hear the end of it.

"I didn't lose any money," Helmi protested wearily once again. "I worked with another man who wanted to eat my money. But that eight hundred dollars went to pay a debt to my brother. When I didn't serve in the army I owed a fine."

The men laughed, disbelieving.

"Tell us the truth, Helmi."

"Tell us how you lost on donkeys."

Helmi grimaced and look aggrieved. "I quit that job because I had to be a big liar. I started with two donkeys, sold them and bought another two. I could have gone on but that man wanted to eat my money. The whole thing lasted two, three months, *bas!* You'd have to swear to somebody, *'Wahabee!* I paid four hundred pounds for this donkey, by my God Allah.' When it was a lie. Maybe you'd paid half that. Buying and selling is that way. Somebody gets cheated. So I quit." Helmi quickly changed the subject. "Last night coming home I saw two chickens. I tried to catch them. Those chickens ran and I ran. All of a sudden they vanished! Those chickens were afreet! Evil spirits!" Everybody laughed, the donkey joke for the moment forgotten, if anything is ever forgotten long in a village.

III

Like medieval prophets, Egypt's Islamic zealots saw a divine message in the Cairo earthquake of 1992. They urged their followers to acts of violence toward whoever, in their fanatical view, had strayed from God's path. Brian Beedham, when he forecast Islamic turbulence, did not include the eastern part of the Muslim *umma* or community, or what some call Dar al Islam, the house of Islam. Turkey and Iran each have about 60 million people, and Egypt is not far behind. But most Arab countries have fairly small populations and even the five ex-Soviet Muslim republics of Central Asia have less than 50 million between them. Asia is where the big numbers are, perhaps three-quarters of all Muslims. If we look to a unified Islam, say one centering on the Gulf's oil wealth and ancient resentments against the infidel West, its driving force might not be religion, though that would create a sense of identity, but rather a multi-nation militant regionalism. This would include Pakistan, perhaps even Bangladesh, but go no further. Muslims are emerging painfully from the rural isolation of their villages and struggling to adapt to a global market economy. Fundamentalism feeds on their failures and impoverishment. The Islamic revival, like the Hindu, Sikh or any other, draws upon the frustration of youths in villages where excessive numbers of people make it impossible to replicate the ways of their parents while TV at the same time mocks them with the riches and depravity of the aliens and infidels.

The bombing of the World Trade Center by Muslim fanatics brought this home to Americans. Imams like the blind Sheik Omar Abdel Rahman preached a violent message to the young, calling for the death of infidels and the creation of a pure Islamic state in Egypt. Author Robert Stone, writing even before the terrorists were caught, captured their mentality very well:

Put yourself in the mind's eye of the bomber. Whoever he is, it's likely he first viewed the city from the air, looked out and saw the twin towers mirroring each other's dizzy rise . . . They represent an ultimate reduction of the American Dream: America as home of the unadorned Economic Man—practical, rational, powerful, even brutal. They are an expression of an aspect of America our true-believing enemies have learned to hate and fear.

Of the danger ahead, Stone wrote:

During the cold war, we lived in fear of a nuclear holocaust. Now we know that if a nuclear device ever goes off in an American city it will not likely come launched from some Siberian silo. More probably, it will have been assembled by a few people, perhaps in the guise of immigrants, in that safe house with a view of lower Manhattan. . . . The new breed of terrorist may be those whose cause we have offended perhaps by simply being what we are.

True, perhaps, for fundamentalists in the Middle East. But East and Southeast Asian Muslims benefit from their region's Confucian-led vigorous capitalist growth. They possess little Arabic and less Arab culture. There Islam is much more likely to follow a path toward peaceful symbiosis with Western civilization, as in, up to now, cosmopolitan Egypt and Turkey. It is also likely to prevail in the long run. Since the breakup of the Soviet Union, Indonesia has become the world's fourth-biggest nation. Two-thirds of the 190 million Indonesians are crowded onto the 620-mile-long island of Java, which has twice as many people as any European country. Oil-rich, timber-rich, with rice production on its fertile volcanic soil up from 12 million tons to 30 million tons in the past twenty years, and with low-wage, small-scale industry moving in from Korea and Taiwan, Indonesia lacks the popular discontent that feeds Islamic fundamentalism in Egypt.

Yet Muslim fervor is growing here too. New mosques abound on Java, young women take up the veil, over 100,000 Indonesians make the pilgrimage to Mecca, double the number of a decade ago. Islam is the official faith of 90 percent of Indonesians, who have confessed to being orthodox Sunnis for more than four hundred years. But Islam, which came with Arab traders in the fifteenth century, has never known quite what to do about Java's Hindu-Buddhist past, which began fourteen hundred years before the Arabs came and still survives on Bali. Much of the mythology and mysticism of this earlier civilization, along with much older animism, survives in Java's 40,000

villages, kept alive in all-night dance dramas and other theatrical performances, above all the *wayang kulit,* or shadow play. So that the
firebrands of Islamic fundamentalism are up against not just a revolution in living standards but, when it comes to drama, art, dance, the
ning-nong of bamboo orchestras and the shadow play's puppets, what
in Muslim Java, as in Hindu Bali, is perhaps the world's most artistic
village culture and a deeply spiritual one.

There was rain in the night, a monsoon downpour, but now the sun
was out, reflected in the rice paddies and sluggish Cimanuk River.
Mango and banana trees grew thick on its banks and hid the women
whose voices drifted up from the shoals of sand where they were
washing clothes. Along the still-muddy path by the river, the pale
blue blossoms of the *kangkung welanda,* which only blooms after dark,
had already curled up in the hot sun. A man in a conical hat guided a
wooden plow drawn by two fawn-colored cows. Near the river, in the
sun-dappled shade of the banana leaves, worked another man, bent
over, ankle-deep in mud, swinging his heavy, short-handled *patjul,* or
hoe, to break up the sticky clods of black volcanic clay.

This was Husen, a poor Javanese rice peasant in his mid-fifties. His
bare, muscular arms and back were now sinewy and stringy with age;
his face, which glistened with sweat so he could not wear his glasses
and had to squint into the sunshine, was starting to show crow's-feet
and wrinkles. He straightened up, rested his hoe and listened. Frogs
croaked. There was the distant whistle of a train, probably, he
thought, the Gunung Jati from Jakarta to Cirebon. And the din of
birdsong from Cibanteng Garden: the *derek*'s coo-coo, the *tjitji*'s high-
pitched twitter, the *ketilang*'s mournful cry. A *betjak* came down the
road, its driver pedaling fast, the pedicab's bells jingling, gong clang-
ing. Husen had been a *betjak* driver in Jakarta for nearly twenty years,
but that was long ago. He felt he had seen and known much in his
life. Married four times, he had fathered two sons—Rus, educated to
be a Muslim teacher, now a truck driver with children of his own, and
little Dahno, just two years old, the son of Husen's old age. He had
traveled to Madura and Bali and seen all the towns of Java from one
end to the other.

Husen had made his peace. Now each morning he set out from his
bamboo hut with a hoe and spent four or five hours in his rice paddy
or small banana grove. Hard work, his fate in life, had become a kind
of refuge, his solace. "I am poor but quiet," he told me on my last

visit, my ninth in over a quarter-century, in the broken English he had picked up in his years in Jakarta. "Poor but quiet. It is very important. If rich but not quiet, why for? All the time headache. Listen this, listen that. I work hard in the garden. Not baby cry, not anything. Happy, happy. I very like alone. But work hard also. If all are rich, who will work?" He could feed his wife and son but could no longer afford the clove-spiced *kretek* cigarettes he used to smoke. Now he used rolled-up *kabong* leaves from his garden.

As he worked, traffic moved along a road separated from the river by a narrow strip of fields. Cars, buses and trucks sped along in a rhythmic hum and on the roadside there were women on foot, carrying bundles of rice, vegetables and fruit (on their heads) to sell in the Jatibarang market. There were a few bicyclists, *betjaks*, even old-fashioned pony carts. What caught Husen's attention was an old dilapidated truck, overloaded, carrying trunks and scenery flats and all sorts of electric apparatus, some wrapped in tarpaulins and some just sticking out. A dozen young men in black peasant garb, and a few girls too, rode precariously on top. These were *sandiwara* actors, a village troupe going home after an all-night performance at some rich man's house. Husen imagined an old man sitting with the rest, incongruously wearing glasses, a black felt hat, suit and tie. In his memory, Husen shouted at the old fellow.

"Hello, *Pa Lojo! Arep mrana?* You want going there?"

"*Tunggo nana yah,* Husen! *Yah, yah!* Waiting there, okay?" And the truck would stop and the old man, a famous comedian in the Cirebon region, would climb down to tell Husen they were going to perform in Kliwed village that night and needed somebody who knew *pentjak*, a stylized half-fight, half-dance, to take the role of a soldier. Husen, then in his twenties, at once agreed. In *pentjak*, two opponents strike at each other with hands, feet, even knives, but pull away at the last moment so blows never land. In a mock battle, each man throws the other to the ground, attacker and victim in close rhythm. They leap about, twisting and striking martial poses. All the while the gamelan orchestra beats drums. The audience, taking sides, cheers and hisses.

Now Pa Lojo was long dead and Husen had not performed the *pentjak* in thirty years. Still, as he bent over with his hoe it all came back. A big wooden stage was set up in the garden of a villager rich enough to pay for the performance. Chairs were set up for village luminaries, children scrambled to sit on the ground up front by the orchestra, who sat cross-legged in front of their bronze chimes, flutes, bamboo xylophones, gongs and drums. Much of the audience stood in the rear. A painted canvas proscenium framed the stage and a red cotton curtain was pulled open and shut by two men hidden behind it. There were crudely painted backdrops: columns and fountains to suggest the Hindu-Buddhist world of god-kings, palaces, shrines and priests, and others with Koranic schools in simple bamboo huts and austere mosques, for the plots of *sandiwara* dramas turned on Java's conversion to Islam.

One actor in a red-caped costume and gold-painted crown, his face garishly rouged and eyes outlined like a clown's, was the king of Madjapahit, the greatest and last of Java's Hindu-Buddhist kingdoms. The villager who played him would stride back and forth, grimacing and gnashing his teeth and making faces, and when he declared it was time to pray, another actor would be carried in on a platform, his face and body painted white to resemble a Hindu idol. "Come, my subjects, let us serve our god," the king would cry. "He is the creator of this earth and lord of the universe. He is our great guru. Ask whatever you want of him." And the king and his courtiers would prance about, chanting in a comic way, "O our god, give us wealth, give us money! Oh, ho, ho, ho, give us a happy and long life!" This was slapstick, with the king and his men bumping into each other, taking pratfalls and keeping the audience laughing.

A messenger arrived. A new religion was sweeping the land. "No, no, it can't be true!" the king cried, his red mouth twisting downward and his heavily mascaraed eyes rolling this way and that. "My people going to a new religion? Never!" He demanded his soldiers be brought and told them, "Catch anyone who follows another god! Bring them here! I'll hang them from my gallows!"

After an interlude of frenzied chase music, the curtain reopened to a new painted backdrop, a humble hut in a forest. A comic actor, dressed as a peasant, declared, "Since Islam came we are free. But men are never satisfied. The more God gives them, the more they want." Soldiers rushed onstage and seized him by the arms, but the peasant ducked, squatted and pretended to defecate, to the hilarity of the village audience. "It is a new kind of fertilizer," the actor said. "If you get from the government, you have to pay. From me, it's free." More laughter at such vulgarity.

An actor in a black Muslim cap, made up to look old, came out and told the audience he was an Arab trader from Malaya and a Muslim teacher. "There are two kinds of religion," he declared. "One is created by man, the idol of the Madjapahit king. The other is sent by Allah through his messengers, the Arabs."

"What is the name of this new religion?" a soldier asked.

"Islam."

"What? Aslam? Aslim? You know it is forbidden to preach a new religion without getting a license from the village chief and paying a fee." More laughter. The scene changed to the palace but now a gallows had been erected. Soldiers led on the Arab and tied a rope around his neck. There then appeared an actor in a black wig, impersonating a woman, since in those days the young girls with the troupe, who danced in between the acts, never took speaking roles. The *bantji*, as the Javanese called a transvestite, moved with swinging hips and exaggeratedly feminine tiny steps, while the orchestra accompanied this with loud, suggestive drumbeats.

When he saw the *bantji*, the Madhapahit king cried out, "Who is this girl? I must have her! Is she a virgin? Oh, she must be a virgin. O Muslim teacher, if your daughter will marry me, I'll set you free!" Boos and hisses from the audience. But the daughter set one condition. The king must go to Mecca and bring her back a medallion. As the audience knew, he would be converted, though this would not happen for several hours more.

Husen remembered standing backstage with the other soldiers and watching Pa Lojo put his makeup on. The comedian, a man in his late sixties, dyed his hair black, as many Javanese did, and when he performed his famous role as an elderly clown-servant, had to make himself look old. He used no powder but drew wrinkles on his brown skin, using a white paste he mixed in a dish with water. He drew deft, quick lines with a piece of straw to give himself a mustache and a stubble beard. Side whiskers, arched and surprised white eyebrows and lines under the eyes came next, then he darkened his lips, eyelids and the hollows of his cheeks with lampblack, adding a few wisps of white hair escaping from the rag he tied about his head, and the familiar face of the old, much-put-upon, but patient and wise, Javanese clown-servant was complete.

A cold meal was brought to Pa Lojo and he quickly ate rice, cucumbers, vegetable soup and tea, oblivious to the cries from the stage: "Run, run! The lava is coming this way!" or the steady hum of hushed voices around him: "Why are you just sitting there? You're not dressed yet!" "Where's the comb?" When two girl dancers, who wore the gilded helmets of Hindu gods, characters from the shadow play, came on, Pa Lojo watched closely how they fluttered their hands and twisted their bodies in intricate gestures to the *ning-nong, ning-nong* of the gamelan's gongs. He was teaching them that every movement had meaning—a pointed finger flipping a sash, a sarong train kicked back by a bare foot, a hand bent backward from the wrist—and he nodded approvingly as they danced.

When the time came for him to go on, Pa Lojo took a last puff on his *kretek* and walked out alone on the stage as the audience applauded, for the old clown-servant had come to be the star of the show, overshadowing its Muslim heroes and Hindu villains. "Generally, generally," he began in his humble, apologetic style, "I am happy. I hope all the people will be happy and good in their lives. I hope that all the people, the old man and the old woman, the young boy and the young girl, are friends. It used to be boys were forbidden to gamble. Now many gamble and a few even watch *sandiwara*. Well, some people are rich. Heh-heh, a poor servant must laugh and sing to make people happy, even when he wants to cry." A few members of the audience threw rupiah notes onstage, somebody a pack of *kreteks*. "You give me?" Lojo exclaimed. "*El hamdu li-llah!* God be praised! Thank you very much. *Trimakasih.*"

A voice came from the orchestra. "Pa Lojo, what music do you like?"

"Music? I like a *lagu* like *Djoged Ramayan*. That's slow. Like me to show you? Please." The orchestra played a few bars and Lojo danced, but like a creaky old man. He stopped, but his little finger kept moving and he grasped it with his other hand.

"Have you money, Lojo?"

"Yah. I have. Fifty rupiah." He reached into his ragged trousers but his fingers came out a hole. "Oh, yah, nothing. Maybe stay at home." The banter kept up until the orchestra started to play again. At first it was a slow, classical *djoged* and Lojo moved to the beat. But the orchestra played faster and faster and he kept dancing until both the music and his steps were frenzied. "Stop!" he shrieked. "Very good, very happy, but stop!" The orchestra played all the faster. Lojo, seemingly unable to stop his feet, kept frantically moving them as he cried, "Finish! Finish! Stop those drums! *Eeeyah!* Difficult!" He seized the scenery but his feet kept moving. The audience laughed until the music stopped. One couldn't help laughing at Lojo.

Lojo came to center stage and said he was a servant in Jakarta and wanted to go home to his village. He hired three *betjaks* to take him, as his master owed him three hundred kilos of rice. The master, played by a very fat comedian, waddled onstage. "Do not forget, Lojo, you were ill for some days. You borrowed rice, a hundred kilos."

A *betjak* man strode onstage and angrily grabbed Lojo by the collar. "Hey, *mang!* Be quick. We've got three *betjaks* waiting. A long time already."

"Ah, I am sorry. Because the rich people now say my rice is only two hundred kilos. Two *betjaks* are enough." Lojo turned back to the fat man. "May I have my two hundred kilos, *tuan?*"

"Again you forget. Your wife had a baby. You got a hundred kilos to pay the midwife."

The *betjak* man returned and angrily shouted, "Hey, *mang!* Why are you taking so long?"

"*Eeeyah!* I am sorry. These rich people are very, very difficult. One *betjak* is enough. Yah, here is two cigarettes. One for you and one for the man who was waiting."

"Well, be quick!"

Lojo rushed to carry off the remaining sack. The fat master came running. "Lojo! Where are you taking that rice?" At the same time, the *betjak* men shouted from offstage, "Hurry, hurry! Be quick, old man!" "No, no, no, no!" the master said, grabbing the sack from Lojo and going away with it. Lojo looked from one to the other. "Where is my rice?" he wailed.

"Why, you . . ." His master cursed him. "Have you forgotten all the dishes you broke!" The *betjak* man came up behind Lojo, seized him by the collar, spun him around and tweaked his nose. "So you want to cheat us *betjak* drivers, do you? *Awas!* Watch out, old man! If we catch you in the street, you'll see! Nobody keeps us waiting so long for nothing!" He swung and hit Lojo in the stomach, then stamped out.

Lojo bent over, clutched his stomach and howled, "*Hiiiih! Hiiih, wah!*" He limped offstage as the audience roared with laughter and applauded. In the wings, the transvestite, in makeup but without his wig, was waiting. He doubled as the troupe's cashier and was angry. Their sponsor, who had promised to give 26,000 rupiah, now said he could pay only 12,000. "The bastard said this was all he would give for everything. I told him, 'What about the orchestra? They have to be paid too. Where is that going to come from?' The cheap bastard!"

Lojo took it calmly, unsurprised to find life mirroring what happened onstage. "Don't worry. We'll get it back. It's a debt that will be redeemed. We don't make a fuss over money." He took a few hasty puffs on a *kretek* and went back onstage. A gruff voice could be heard shouting at him. "Pa Lojo, what are you doing there?" "Picking up cigarette butts," came the squeaky reply, to the audience's laughter, as it was one of the lowliest occupations. Chinese cigarette-makers reused what tobacco was left. Lojo soon came back, his performance over, but later, when the audience got too excited and started pelting the Madjapahit king with stones, he went onstage again, to deliver a long, windy monologue on conditions in the kingdom, how crops suffered from insects and so on, until the audience fell half asleep. He knew how to whip them up or calm them down.

Husen always marveled that when morning came, the stage was torn down, scenery and equipment were loaded on the truck and the troupe was going along the road again. Perched high on the load, Lojo in the harsh morning light looked like a dried-up old schoolteacher. The girl dancers lost their allure; the Madjapahit king was just another villager. The troupe had an unkempt, seedy appearance, and yet, when the overloaded old truck let him off and wheezed down the road, Husen felt that a kind of magic went with it.

Theater was inborn in the Javanese peasant, Husen both spear-carrier and insatiable fan. Even as a small boy he improvised little bamboo prosceniums and made puppets from mango leaves. For the other children, he reenacted the story of an all-night shadow play he had seen. During harvests, there might be two or three a week and he used to see them all.

After nightfall, the bronze percussion sound of a gamelan orchestra could be heard across the Cimanuk River or from a distant tree line. Husen would slip away from home, hurrying in the darkness as the music got louder and his anticipation grew. In the cobbled courtyard of a prosperous peasant, he would dart past tea stalls where old women sold cakes and cigarettes, throwing a long black shadow behind him as he moved into the bright light of the *dalang*'s coconut-oil lamp. Sometimes Husen would pause behind the big white screen set up between pillars on a portico and watch the puppeteer unpack his puppets, sticking them upright on their tortoiseshell sticks into a fibrous banana trunk. Perhaps the *dalang* would have arranged them already and be sitting cross-legged, head bowed in prayer or puffing on a *kretek*, deeply solemn, as a *wayang* is both an art form and a village religious ceremony called a *slametan,* symbolizing the unity of those taking part, even spirits and dead ancestors.

If Husen was late he would go at once to the front of the screen, where the grown men, village notables in their black Muslim caps and sarongs, took places in a favored pavilion or in rows of comfortable low chairs where tables with tea and bananas were set before them. Like water seeking its own level, Husen and the other small boys would scramble to the front, sitting on the ground, and often drowse off or even go to sleep during the long court debates and philosophical discussions, until it was time for the battles or the clowns to come on. But sometimes Husen sat wide-eyed and watched everything, and gradually, as the years wore on, the *wayang* came to be for him, as it is to all Javanese, a truly sacred drama.

A king wrestled with demons, a holy man combated evil spirits. The flat, buffalo-leather puppets, painted in gold, reds, greens, blues and blacks, portray Hindu gods, kings, warriors and saints, buffoons and clowns, monsters, ghosts, giants and fantastic animals. They come to seem, hidden as they are on the other side of a lamplit screen, a dreamlike illusion, and their shadows, as they appear to tremble and breathe with life in the *dalang*'s hands, the reflection of that illusion. And somehow, wholly unconsciously, Husen absorbed the Hindu belief that soul, shadow, spirit and ghost are one, that the soul and God are one. And although Husen thought himself a Muslim, the teachings of the *wayang* penetrated deep into his being, and his true religion, a synthesis of Muslim, Hindu and animist beliefs, was formed.

Most of the shadow plays are tales from the Hindu epic, the *Mahabharata,* which recounts a great war between kinsmen, the five Pendawa kings and their hundred Korawa cousins, which culminates in a great battle, the Bratajuda; it is an endless struggle portrayed in the *wayang* because this final battle is never shown. The struggle is less between good and evil than between what Javanese call *alus* and *kasar* feelings, detached, effortless self-control and base animal passions. All the characters take on symbolic importance: one Pendawa king, Judistira, symbolizes how compassion weakens the will to act; another, Bima, vitality and the dangers of passionate commitment; a third, Ardjuna, cool capability and merciless justice.

The *dalang* speaks all the roles from memory, making up dialogue as he goes along, in a great variety of voices—a noble's commanding tone, a giant's rumbling bellow, the high-pitched falsetto of a princess, the nasal squeak of a clown-servant—singing when needed, and all the while kicking an iron clapper with his foot to keep up the rhythm or make sounds of war. With its court debates, quests for wisdom, battles with demons and intervals of low comedy, accompanied by the bamboo-and-bronze xylophones of the gamelan orchestra which gets louder and more frenzied as the night goes on, a shadow play, like a *sandiwara* drama, begins just after dark and lasts until dawn. The *dalang* sits cross-legged, never getting up, the whole time. A *wayang* is an acquired taste, excruciating to watch at first with the interminable dialogue in strange, squeaky voices, but you soon get hooked.

The heart of a shadow play, and indeed the soul of Java itself, is not an elegant Pendawa king, with his stylized, gilded, ornamental dress, but an old clown-servant like Pa Lojo called Semar. With his wife and many children—his sons Gareng and Petruk are best known—Semar tills a small patch of rice fields at the foot of Mount Merbabu, an extinct volcano in central Java. Physically repulsive, Semar is old and fat with an ugly face, a single wisp of white hair, an enormous behind and bulging belly. His earthy humor can be crudely vulgar, such as breaking wind to chase away his naughty children or throwing feces at his opponents.

Javanese find Semar's antics hilarious; they also revere him. Clifford Geertz calls him "the wonderfully comic and wise shadow-play clown and the greatest of all culture heroes." There is nothing like Semar in other cultures; imagine Jesus as an elderly slapstick comedian. In Geertz's words, Semar is "actually a god in all too human form" and "the guardian spirit of all Javanese from their first appearance until the end of time." In the Javanese creation myth, familiar to all villagers, for ten thousand years all Java is covered by forest except for Semar's rice paddy. When Hindu and then Muslim holy men arrive, Semar asks them:

> Why have you come here and driven my children and grandchildren out? The spirits, overcome by your greater spiritual power and religious learning, are slowly being forced to flee into craters of volcanoes or to the depths of the Southern Sea. Why are you doing this?

The priests reply they have come to bring their religions and settle Java with human beings. But they give Semar the role, for Java's entire history down to modern times, of spiritual adviser and magical supporter of all kings and princes to come.

Geertz, who studied religion in a small town in east-central Java in the 1950s, is famous for dividing it in three ways: *priyayi*, classical Hindu-Buddhist elements found among educated urban classes; *santri*, orthodox Islam, most common among traders and landowners; and *abangan*, the much more animistic folk religion of the rural peasantry. Geertz put Semar right at the center of *abangan* belief; he was "both god and clown, man's guardian spirit and his servant, the most spiritually refined inwardly and the most rough-looking outwardly." Geertz:

> Semar is said to be the eldest descendant of "He that is One" (i.e., God) . . . but Semar became a man—a fat, awkward, ugly-looking man, full of rough talk, comic stupidities, and hilarious confusions . . . Semar is the lowliest of the low . . . and, at the same time, the father of us all.

Falstaff, fat, merry and ribald, might be the closest thing in Western culture, but Semar is not boastful like Shakespeare's knight. He does symbolize earthier, more humane rural values; *priyayi* and *santri* traditions are both urban. *Sandiwara* dramas, with their live actors and Islamic conversion themes, are the main competition to shadow plays in the Cirebon region's villages where Husen lives. Pa Lojo, just like Semar, kept audiences entertained with pratfalls, mock fights, graphic jokes about bodily functions, mournful recitals of a poor man's lot and practical worldly-wise ethics. The clown-servant took over what had begun as Islamic propaganda.

Husen enjoys telling about how as a boy he would pretend he was a *dalang* to entertain his village friends. He would improvise a little theater out of bamboo and make his puppets from mango leaves. Once I asked him to show me and he said, "Okay," held up some puppets and spoke in English:

> This is Judistira, one of the five Pendawa kings, and over here is Dorna, from the Astina Kingdom. Judistira is king of Pendawa. He has four brothers. Before, both kingdoms were friends. Now they are fighting because Pendawa is poor and Astina is rich. Now Judistira is very *alus*, very kind. If somebody say to him, "Judistira, I kill you," he say, "Please, go ahead." If somebody say, "Judistira, I take your wife"—but he have no wife—he say, "Please." He has white blood, not red blood. Now Bima, his brother, is hot-blooded, many fighting. He sleeps standing up with his fists doubled. He has many wife and stabs people with his long thumbnail. Ardjuna, the third brother, he's very calm, very cold. He likes girls the best and is the nicest-looking man in

the whole world, with many, many wives. The other two Pendawa kings are twins, Nakula and Sadewa.

When it comes to Semar, Husen feels on safer ground.

His inside life is very nice, very *alus*, but outside it is not good, *kasar*. If you look at Semar, very bad, very old, very fat, very ugly. Now before, this earth was empty and Semar was the first one out. He is a god. That is why he has only one tooth. He is a god but his children are very naughty. Semar says, "Children, you must going to work in garden." But Semar's children, many going to answer the call of nature.

Husen chuckles when he tells this. As a boy he liked to stage a comedy with Gareng and Petruk trying to beat a giant but missing and hitting each other instead. Or Dorna, the Korawas' crafty and treacherous old adviser, getting accidentally burned on the nose by the bumbling Petruk's cigar. Semar's children are like the Three Stooges; Husen also had them make plays on words, easy because the words for "kiss," "sit" and "water" in the Sundanese dialect of western Java mean "drink," "go home" and "feces" in proper Javanese.

Even in middle age Husen enjoyed buying the cheap comic-book versions of *wayangs* in Jatibarang and reading them aloud to his family. "*Adjow! Adjow!* Dangerous! Dangerous!" he would say, imitating the quavering old man's voice of the ever-scheming Dorna. "Petruk has stolen the magic scepter of the Astina Kingdom!" The family would listen, utterly absorbed, as Husen took them to Fleabag Village, where Semar has his bamboo hut and rice paddy. "Come, children!" Husen would act out Semar's role. "Come, Bagong, Tjepot, Gareng, Petruk, come! I want to tell you about the new farming methods!" But instead wicked Dorna arrived with soldiers, who seized Petruk and carried him off in chains. Semar and his children went in search of Petruk and found him hanging from a tree in the forest. Bagong climbed the tree, cut the rope, and Gareng caught the body, which knocked him flat. Semar revived his son with magic and declared, "Come, Petruk, come, children. We will go deep into the forest to a holy place."

Sometimes Husen would read *Mapag Sri, The Origin of Rice*, the most popular *wayang* in his village. Like Semar, its story was not from Hindu mythology or Islamic tradition, but was native to Java. "Once upon a time, in Sura Laja, the abode of the gods . . ." Husen would begin. The story, much simplified, told of the unrequited love of a bewitched and evil-smelling prince, Budug Basuh, for a beautiful young maiden, Sri Kwatji. Sri Kwatji was repelled by Budug Basuh because he had scabies. She ran to the gods, who gave her a magic kris, a twisted Javanese dagger, but told her she must marry Budug Basuh. "No, no!" she shrieked and threw herself on the dagger. Semar and his children visited her grave and found that the first green shoots of rice were coming out. Sri Kwatji had become Dewi Sri, the goddess of rice and fertility.

When he learned what had happened, Budug Basuh in his grief threw himself on the magic dagger too, and died. The gods were to carry his coffin to the sacred Ganges and Semar warned them not to rest or open the coffin on the way. This was Husen's favorite part to tell:

> After some time one of the gods got tired of carrying the coffin and he told the others, "Let's take a rest." "No, no," they said. "Semar told us not to stop on the way." "*Tida apa apa.* Never mind. I am tired." And they put the coffin down. At once from inside came a noise— knock, knock, knick-knack, knick-knack. And forgetting what Semar had said, they opened the lid just a tiny crack to see what the noise could be and whoooOOOOSH! Out swarmed all the insects and animals who eat rice.

"And they have never left us in peace since," Husen would end his story, chuckling. Once, when his son, Rus, asked if the tale was true, Husen grinned and said, "About half-half, maybe a little more." Husen's old mother had no doubts. All her life she left a plate of rice, sauce, tea and an upturned mirror under the rice bin every night as an offering to Dewi Sri.

Both Husen and Shahhat are great storytellers, though the emotional behavior of rural Javanese and Egyptians could hardly be more different. Shahhat and his family and neighbors are continually exploding with emotion, whether laughter, anger or fear, religious or sexual passion, family feuds, anguish over demons, *shaytans* or the Evil Eye. Husen and his fellow Javanese villagers, just the reverse, try to be what they call *iklas*, a state of willed affectlessness, when, if one is ever serene, smiling and polite, nothing will happen and there will be no conflict, uncertainty or tension. This exacts a toll: unlike Egyptians, Javanese gnash their teeth in their sleep; they also gave us the phrase "run amok." *Tida apa apa* and the Arabic *malesh*, which both mean "never mind," are just about the first words you learn in their villages, though in Java it suggests keeping an unruffled tranquillity, whereas in Egypt it is often used to break up an exchange of violent abuse.

Two quite contrasting faces of a supposedly single creed, both, I think, "god-intoxicated" in the sense that religion decides daily behavior and what to expect of life and the world. The Arab's social ideal of horseman, warrior and ruler of men has to give way these days to once-despised commerce and industry, a frustration spared Indonesians, whose Islam was brought by Arab traders. Kindly, wise, earthy, comic Semar is a far cry from the stern Islamic god of war and desert; *santri* Muslims have led most of Indonesia's nationalist movements and today pose the main challenge to President Suharto's long-lived and culturally neutral authoritarian rule. The *abangan* majority out in the villages has never seriously questioned it. Clown-servants do not rebel against warrior-kings.

So long, that is, as the old *wayang* values hold. Clifford Geertz himself stirred up some excitement in 1984 by declaring, after a visit to the Javanese town where he did his research, that "the younger generation of *abangan* are becoming *santri.*" At the time this seemed to be true. There was an upsurge of Islamic orthodoxy. Even Husen, who has since backslid, started saying his prayers to Mecca five times a day and going to the mosque on Fridays. In a crisis he has always turned to Islam; when his wife suffered a miscarriage he sat by her side reciting over and over, *"La illa haillah . . . la illa haillah . . .* There is no God but Allah . . ."* Jakarta's Islamic reformers seize on such evidence that the centuries-old *abangan-santri* gap might be closing, which, if true, since Indonesia is the biggest Muslim nation, would have a profound impact on Islam. Much is made of Sunan Kalidjaga, a legendary hero who, after conversion to Islam, it is claimed, introduced the shadow play, gamelan music and the *abangan* version of Islam into Java. Older native, Hindu and Buddhist influences are ignored. One is told that the Pendawa kings symbolize the five pillars of Islam (the confession of faith, prayers, fasting, pilgrimage and almsgiving) and that Semar is the creation of Muslim missionaries intended to represent the common man.

The Egyptians, like the Javanese, are an ancient, supremely civilized people, with pharaonic, Christian and Greco-Roman influences of their own. But one probably cannot exaggerate the force of their Islamic revival, and its aversion to the West, in Egypt's villages today, or its ideological exploitation among uprooted villagers in Cairo's slums. When a densely crowded population grows faster than incomes, the great deeps of Islam stir, as is happening from Morocco to Central Asia. It is small wonder they pour into mosques in ever-greater numbers, as they do, to pray for a better life, if not in this world then in the next.

But Indonesia is prospering, with per capita income up from $240 in 1978 to nearly $700 now, the birth rate is down from 2.4 percent then to 1.5 percent, and hopes are soaring. So that wise, funny old Semar is likely to have a lot of staying power. The last time I was in Husen's village, Pilangsari, everybody chipped in to hire a *dalang* to perform the mythical story of rice; as always, Semar stole the show. Is he just a comic puppet?

Ask President Suharto and he will strenuously assert that Indonesia is a Muslim country. He can frequently be seen on television praying at a mosque. But Suharto, born a villager in a bamboo hut in central Java, comes from *abangan* roots. What TV viewers do not see, but everybody knows about just the same, are Suharto's visits from time to time to a certain sacred cave on Java's Dieng plateau. There he meditates. The cave, set in a landscape of misty volcanoes and ruined Hindu temples, is one of the spiritual dwelling places of Semar.

IV

The Heirs of Confucius:
East Asia's Challenge

CAST OF CHARACTERS

NAE-CHON VILLAGE, SOUTH KOREA,
AND GUANGDONG PROVINCE, CHINA

JADE, 22, a student
Her Parents, Confucian scholars
Mrs. KWANG, 78, villager
LEE PYONG-JIK, 83, villager
LEE CHANG-SHUP, 50s, shopkeeper
HONG, 30s, pipe fitter, commuter
Abbess, 40s, head of Buddhist nunnery
BRIAN, 23, Peace Corpsman

FORTY YEARS AGO, Jea Bi, the Valley of the Swallows, still looked to be an idyll of paddies and thatched huts. Stone-strewn fields, orchards and vineyards, the shaded greens and blues of pine-woods in mountain country, framed this world, where every bit of land, right up the terraced hillsides, was painstakingly tilled.

Spring came with the swallows. The tiny birds, migrating back, darted in and out of the village houses, and with lightning-quick wing strokes remade last year's nests under the wooden ceiling beams. Everyone welcomed them; they brought good luck. In fall there were bursting cotton pods, buckwheat white with flowers and rice and bar-ley heavy with grain. Near the village grew stalks of chilies and beans and oilseed plants. On every thatched roof, red peppers were spread to dry.

In those days, in the early 1950s, at the entrance gate to Nae-Chon village, just fifty miles southeast of Seoul but off the main roads, stood a thick wooden joss idol, eight feet high. Its upper part was carved into the face of an ugly goblin, painted green, with pop eyes and a bright red tongue sticking out between fanged teeth, meant to frighten evil spirits away. Just beside the gate were two ancient stone monuments, one to a youth who showed great filial piety to his par-ents, the other to a virtuous young woman who lost her fiancé but stayed a chaste virgin all her life. Around the low-mud-walled houses, there were patches of melons, fruit trees and flowers, and sliced pumpkins lay about, drying in the sun. Each house had its stone saucepot stand, with big earthenware jars filled with soy sauce, bean paste and red-pepper paste. Some were full of kimchi, pickled cab-bage and radishes, highly seasoned with garlic, onions, red pepper and ginger.

Nae-Chon's fields were all grouped together in the flat bottom of the valley, which rose in broad fanlike terraces. In the middle of these paddies, to scare away birds, two little boys sat on a thatched-roof platform, pulling on ropes tied with rags and making enough noise to wake the dead. Once the grain was ripe, the landscape was full of harvesters' pointed straw hats and flashing sickles. It was a rural way of life set by the gait of a jog-trotting peasant with a heavily loaded A-frame on his back. Men in the loose white garments villagers wore in those days went back and forth with buckets of nightsoil swinging from a yoke on their shoulders. What cows there were in Nae-Chon were used as draft animals. Even if some of the villagers raised chickens and pigs, they all preferred to eat fish, especially squid.

Over the hills around the Valley of the Swallows loomed the rugged, once-wooded peak of Fortress Mountain. Nae-Chon nestled in its shadow and the villagers believed the mountain protected them. Tales were told of how in the days of the Choson dynasty, savage Mongols invaded Korea, burned its palaces and Buddhist temples and built a stone fortress on top of the mountain, which they defended in fierce battles for thirty years. Peace came when Korea's Koryo kings accepted Mongol rule. This lasted until China's Ming dynasty itself overthrew the Mongols and helped a Korean, Yi Songgye, to seize the Korean throne. The Yi dynasty lasted from 1392 to 1910, ruled from a new capital, Seoul, and established Confucianism as the state religion. Buddhists were persecuted, and Korea became so culturally isolated it was called the Hermit Kingdom. Japanese conquest and a thirty-six-year colonial rule of Korea lasted until 1945. Then came North Korea's invasion in 1950, followed by hostility since, which proved the futility of trying to shut a whole society away from the rest of the world, though North Korea is still cut off.

Old Lady Kwang, a small, bent, unusually active old woman, would tell in her cracked voice how it was Fortress Mountain that saved Nae-Chon. "During the war and when Korea was under Japanese rule," she reminded the neighbors, "nobody from this village died. Almost everybody came back healthy."

One who did not was Mrs. Kwang's own husband. The Japanese took him away as a slave laborer to work in a coal mine in the north. When he returned he was feeble and broken. Hatred of the Japanese ran deep in Nae-Chon. Mrs. Kwang would narrow her eyes and say, "I am afraid the Japanese have not changed their spots very much." A few of the richer villagers went to Japan for medical treatment and many Western ideas came from Japan. Still the *waenom*, or little people, as Japanese used to be known in Nae-Chon, after three conquests of Korea, were not to be trusted. Many told harrowing stories of rape, murder and near-starvation during the war, and of girls carried off to brothels in Manchuria and never seen again. The "strong hand of Japan," in the words of Mrs. Kwang, destroyed village after village. "Not a single house was left," she said, "not a pot unbroken." Anybody who protested was executed on the spot.

Koreans could never forget they lived on an unforgiving mountainous peninsula that jutted out of Asia toward Japan. The end of the Japanese occupation in 1945 was followed by a land reform that parceled out paddies into holdings big enough to support a family, about a hectare, or two and a half acres, each. When in 1950 the villagers saw internecine war, as the Communists crossed the artificial dividing line on the 38th parallel, there was more devastation and suffering, but Nae-Chon itself was spared. There was hunger, and the villagers ate bark and roots as they always did in bad times. When they went into the town market, they saw People's Army soldiers with their red flags and Russian rifles. Everybody talked about the great American general, *Megado*, and the *bengko*, or big-nosed foreigners, he led in the United Nations forces, some as black as night. Planes bombed the nearest town and railway station, sending thick gray columns of smoke into the air.

Japanese rule and the two wars that followed preserved Korea's village peasantry right into the late twentieth century, just as the war and the Russian-imposed Communist rule did in parts of Eastern Europe like Poland. In the 1950s, certainly, Confucian doctrine determined how most of Nae-Chon's people thought and acted. To them, "filial piety" was the basis of social conduct. They believed in harmony, hierarchy, communal obligations and emphasis on the group, not the individual. A son was subordinate to his father, a wife to husband, younger brother to older brother, and subject to state. In Nae-Chon, people felt it was their duty to obey, whether the head of the family or the nation. In the "elders first" rite on New Year's Day, all family members knelt and bowed to the ground to everyone older, first grandparents, then parents, siblings and relatives, even elderly neighbors.

Ancestor worship, older even than Confucianism, meant that most village families kept careful genealogical records on bloodlines, careers, achievements, even graveyards. In the home the head of the family, the oldest male, taught Confucian ethics to its members. He set down the rules, and it was a duty and virtue to follow them. He provided food, shelter and clothing to each member, who in turn was obligated to work under his direction. His authority had an economic basis, although such elders did little work themselves. In the early 1950s when I was a soldier in Korea, one saw them going about the villages in white pajamas, loose white jackets and Korea's famous old black horsehair hats.

Life was governed by the seasons, a farmer's work prescribed in detail by the lunar calendar: 6th day of 1st moon, twist straw rope; last day of 1st moon, spread manure; 20th day of 2nd moon, plant trees; early days of 3rd moon, prepare rice seedbeds; middle of 3rd moon, cultivate barley and sow red-pepper seeds; 4th moon, transplant rice seedlings; 5th day of 5th moon, Tano festival to appease local spirits; 6th moon, weed rice paddies; 7th and 8th moons, relative leisure; 9th moon, harvest rice, sesame and buckwheat; 10th moon, thresh grain, make sauces to store in pots; 11th moon, winter solstice; 12th moon, reflect on past year's disappointments.

Like all aspects of a Korean village's Confucian culture, these yearly chores of a farming household were part of a design for living, albeit a rigid and precise one, tailored to rice-growing peasants in a hilly land with a temperate climate; the same customs and agricultural methods were followed generation after generation, so that each new group of young people were given ready-made skills and ideas. This meant that in its fundamental orientations life in Nae-Chon in the first half of the twentieth century was not very different from, say, life in the fourth century, after Confucianism arrived from China. The only thing that really alters a culture—call it Marxist determinism if you like, but, as I've said, it goes back to Aristotle—is a change in the society's economic basis. Which is why, after ten thousand years of relatively stable rural isolation, villages the world over are facing such tumultuous change today.

Custom determined the smallest acts in a traditional Confucian village. For instance, theft was condemned, but the people tolerated, even expected, that mischievous boys would raid a bean field and roast their loot at a pathside weed fire; this drew no more than a scolding from the owner. Drunkenness was frowned upon, but disorderly behavior was expected on the 15th day of the 7th moon, when villagers celebrated the last rice weeding by washing their hoes; even gambling with cards was acceptable. Drinking liquor was a venerable peasant pastime—where is it not?—and a numbing home brew, *nongju*, was taken to the fields and it was proper to serve *soju*, rice wine, to male guests in the homes.

Koreans have a flair for dance and theater and, in the old days in masked village dance-dramas accompanied by a cacophony of gongs, flutes and drums, they enjoyed making fun of normally respected Confucian scholars or Buddhist monks, who might be shown doing something outrageous, like chasing prostitutes. On New Year's Day young men also let off steam by going around the village serenading their friends with ribald old folk songs.

Even fights had their place in this orderly scheme of things. They mainly took place if somebody violated the paddy watering order or took water from another's field, a universal village phenomenon. Some villagers did sentry duty, patrolling their paddies with a shovel over one shoulder. Conflicts over irrigation water, however violent, seldom led to lasting enmity, so strong was the Confucian ideal of harmony. Some of the old village occupations I saw in the 1950s, like the making of bamboo pipes or horsehair hats, have vanished entirely, but one still finds the smithy, cobbler and carpenter, just as one does in Polish villages, or in America earlier in this century.

A dark side to Korea's Confucian society is that almost until the end of the nineteenth century, half of Koreans were slaves called *chongmin*. They were inherited and could be bought, sold, given away or killed at their owner's will. One could escape this hereditary status only through bravery on the battlefield or by buying one's way into a higher class. In Confucianism, slavery was reinforced by a strict class system. Scholar-officials came first, followed by, in order of rank, peasants, artisans and merchants. In India's caste system, peasant ranked lowest, under priests, warriors and merchants. The higher status Confucianism gives peasants, compared with Hinduism, carried over into Chinese Communism, where an ideological bias in favor of peasants was one of Maoism's chief distinctions which served China well.

At the top of Korean society were the *yangban*, scholar-officials, linked both to court and its provincial offices and to their own villages. A series of state examinations every two years, culminating in one in the Seoul palace before the king, decided one's fortune. The Confucian literati, once they made it to the top, grew their fingernails very long to show they were no longer among the sweaty, dirty-handed peasants. Some villages chipped in to educate a bright boy whose success in the imperial examinations would benefit all who helped him on his way.

Essentially, Confucianism was an ethical system that stressed virtue and devotion to family, one's ancestors, one's master and the state. The aphorisms of K'ung Fu-tzu, an obscure and frustrated official and extraordinary teacher (551–479 B.C.), were set down by his disciples a century and a half before Aristotle. They became the official ideology of China under the Han dynasty two hundred years before Christ, and lasted in China and Korea into the twentieth century, making Confucianism the longest-lasting philosophy ever devised. Some argue that Confucianism is agnostic in the sense that it lacks a personal god or belief in the afterlife and it has no priests or churches, but always works through education and example. Many Confucians, Nae-Chon's villagers among them, did pay homage to spirits of their ancestors, tried to communicate with them and believed in all sorts of good and evil supernatural beings to placate. The Confucian ideal of a superior man of the golden mean did instill authentic religious feelings of an omnipresent if vaguely defined spiritual heaven. Confucius has been called "China's greatest gift to mankind." The teachings that bear his name still call hundreds of millions of Asians to seek after harmony and righteousness. The Confucian classic *Ta Hsueh, The Great Learning*, was often quoted in Nae-Chon: "Be studious and constantly exert yourself . . ." Every family was prepared to sacrifice to educate its children, to make them into *yangban*.

Another strong cultural pull in Nae-Chon was *shamanism*, beliefs in demons, magic, healing and exorcism. There was a saying in the village that a Korean lived Confucian, got sick Shaman and died Buddhist. This animism went back at least four to five thousand years and had its roots in the origins of the Koreans' ancestral tribes from the Asian heartland. In the motifs used by Nae-Chon's two *mudangs*, or sorceresses, were the same crowns and symbols, the trees of life and antlers and bear claws, found among Tibetans and Mongolians. The *mudangs*, all the villagers believed—though not everybody would admit it—had supernatural powers to contact heavenly spirits to protect the family and Nae-Chon from evil spirits. Some villages held communal rites to honor their guardian spirit, everybody gathering with *mudangs*, musicians and dancers at an ancient shrine. At such rites they also prayed for a good rice crop.

In the quarter-century between the mid-1950s and when I next saw it in 1980, Nae-Chon itself did not change much. It was South Korea that was radically transformed. Development had to start from scratch in a poor, peasant society. Within a single generation, it was a crowded, industrial nation. Seoul looked more like Singapore every year. A six-lane superhighway ran right down the country to Pusan. In 1954, GNP was around $400 per capita. By 1980, it was nearly $4,000 and it would rise by mid-1994 to $7,000. Richer than the Portuguese and the Greeks, most Koreans had seen their lives changed beyond recognition. Those who worked on farms fell by two-thirds, while the proportion of factory jobs trebled.

The staple diet in 1954 was rice and kimchi, with a little fish and, for the poor, meat just once a year. In lean times they mixed their rice with barley. The average daily calorie intake was 2,000; by 1980 it was 3,000. Meat consumption trebled. Rice consumption per capita in villages rose by more than 40 percent. In this quarter-century, the number of doctors per 10,000 South Koreans doubled. That of dentists trebled. With better food and health care, children towered over their grandparents, a fourteen-year-old boy being four and a half inches taller than he would have been in 1954.

By 1980, virtually every village house had a television set, even if some were black-and-white, not all color as in Seoul. In the city one-third of households had washing machines; just one in ten did in the village. Industrial and commercial development was changing women's lives even more than the men's; 45 percent of them worked by 1980. Their average factory job, often low-paying, called for fifty-five hours a week, with twelve-hour shifts. But a women's movement was stirring. More than 40 percent of South Koreans over age sixty felt women should only work at home; only 13 percent of those aged fifteen to nineteen did.

In Seoul, where four of every ten Koreans lived, a great migration had taken place from the old one-story wooden houses north of the Han River, where the old walled city began, to new southern suburbs. Here families lived in small, modern apartments without elderly parents, who usually stayed behind in the villages, and with far fewer children than before. They were middle-class, many with family incomes over $1,000 a month. Wives worked and there was neither space nor time to ferment the family kimchi; it came from a supermarket. What most concerned these Koreans, as with middle-class parents the world over, was to get their children into the best schools. As the *Analects* of Confucius stated, applied learning was the key to success. By 1980 literacy in South Korea was 100 percent. Four of every ten high school graduates went on to college, a third of them women. South Korea was acquiring one of the best-educated female populations in the world, and women were changing faster than men. Yet everybody kept his or her tie to their village and went back to it on the Lunar New Year and other holidays, to see their parents and visit the graves and tombs of their ancestors. The Koreans remained Confucians at heart even if it cost them a great deal of inner turmoil.

Miss Kim, who was named Sun Mi, or Faithful Jade, but was known as Onion in Nae-Chon and Tiger to her Seoul University classmates, sat cross-legged at a tiny low table watching a pair of swallows build a nest on a ceiling beam. They flew in and out with bits of straw, almost brushing her head. Jade had tacked a piece of wood under the nesting place to catch the droppings. The little birds perched and twittered without fear, well within reach of her hands. In Japan swallows rarely nested in village houses anymore; in Nae-Chon they still did.

It was 1980 and the Valley of the Swallows had so far been spared many of the sweeping changes that were reshaping the society around it. The valley was just a few miles long and Jade could bicycle its length in fifteen minutes over a dirt road where Japanese-built railway tracks had once been. Like most of the 2.3 million hectares of cultivated land in South Korea, the valley's fields were surrounded by rugged hills, bare, Jade's parents said, after the war, but now covered with larch, oak, alder, pine, spruce and fir. Woods once again grew over three-fourths of South Korea; only 17 percent of the land was farmed. The hills, eroded since prehistoric times, were rarely higher than 1,000 meters. Mount Paektu, Korea's highest peak, was just 2,744 meters. Yet the scenery could be spectacular, with rocky pinnacles, granite cliffs, waterfalls and rapids along the streams.

One entered the Valley of the Swallows from the north over a low pass through forested cliffs. Here, high on an evergreen ridge, was Bright Cloud Temple, a Buddhist nunnery. About sixty shaven-headed, gray-robed women, many of them village girls, spent their days in study and prayer, seeking to avoid earthly suffering and find salvation in renunciation. In China or in Thailand, Buddhist temples were in the center of towns; in Korea they were in mountains and forests, reflecting the long centuries of persecution, when Buddhism was effectually banned. As Koreans looked for roots in reaction to the rapid changes they were undergoing, Buddhism enjoyed a renaissance. Bright Cloud Temple was renovated at great expense and its lands improved, so that in springtime its orchards, snowy with apricot, peach and cherry blossoms, spread down the terraced hillsides to the bright green paddies of newly planted rice shoots. A winding road, lined with Lombardy poplars, was ablaze in spring with yellow forsythia and the purples of azalea, violets and tiny irises.

If Bright Cloud Temple was like heaven, Dong Kim Leper Colony, which commanded the valley's southern ridge, was like hell. With no trees or vegetation at all, a bleak assembly of long, barrackslike poultry houses crowded about a tall and ugly red-brick church. Jade once visited it at noon and even in the bright sunshine life had deserted the place. Shreds of torn plastic sheeting fluttered from open windows. There was a stench of chicken manure. What few people she saw shrank from sight. Jade was surprised to be greeted by a tall young Texan, a Peace Corps volunteer, who said his name was Brian, though the lepers called him "Big Western One." He told her that less than half of the colony's three hundred people were lepers, and just five of these were "active" or contagious, but all Dong Kim's people shied away from strangers, ashamed and fearing their revulsion. His job, he explained, was to apply medicine every day to the lepers' ulcers, look for numbness or anesthesia, white or dark spots, an inability to close the eyes or a clawing of the hands, all signs of leprosy. Jade asked about horribly disfigured persons. Brian said, "Those are usually older ones for whom there were no drugs or money for drugs. Now they're social outcasts." He said poultry raising was something people with crippled hands could do, but he found the Koreans "fatalistic." Brian told Jade, "They tell me in the old days if a clawed hand became useless, they chopped it off."

Protected by Fortress Mountain and its outlying ramparts of nuns and lepers, Nae-Chon remained so traditional that some of its roofs were still thatched with rice straw in 1980. Most Korean villagers had by then turned to brightly painted corrugated iron or tile. Jade's own house, built by her grandfather, was reroofed with blue tile. Her family was of the old *yangban* scholar-official class. Both parents had a classic Confucian education and Jade's father had studied law in Japan. Twenty years of war and upheaval kept him from practicing and when peace came in 1953 he felt it was too late. Sixty-eight in 1980, he was content to farm and educate his children. Jade, who looked sixteen but was twenty-two, already had two years of political science behind her and aspired to study law. A small girl, with a freshly scrubbed look and long, straight black hair, she went about in blue jeans and T-shirts with American logos like "Michigan State" or "Tennis Club."

Land reform had come easily in South Korea because about a third of all farmland was held by Japanese and another third by *yangban* sympathizers of the Japanese. Thus Jade's father, who might have been a big landowner under the old regime, in the 1949–53 reform received the average-sized farm of 2.2 acres like everybody else. The descendants of Nae-Chon's *chongmin*, or slaves, were given an equal amount of land; they tended to invest in their farms and machinery rather than education. In her family, Elder Brother, as Jade respectfully called him, was thirty-two and had a good job with a cosmetics firm in the city, but he had to postpone marriage until the youngest of the family's five children, a nineteen-year-old boy, finished college. An older sister was married to a history professor at Inchon University, and another sister, after two years of college, held a civil service post in the nearby city of Suwon.

The family clung to its *yangban* status, spending all it could on education even as it lived in genteel poverty. Their house was modest, with stuccoed wattle-and-daub walls and doors and windows of paper pasted on wooden frames, which slid in grooves. Yellow linoleum covered the floors, shoes were left outside and light coming through the translucent white paper created a soft glow. Like most of the village houses, Jade's was L-shaped, with three *ondol*, or hot-floor rooms, heated from flues under the floor of stone and mud. Jade had her own desk and bookshelf, and in the three living rooms, grouped about an open wooden-floored terrace, or *maru*, there were chests, cushions, a writing table, a TV set and a cassette player. The hardest lot fell to Jade's mother, who had grown up in a houseful of servants and now spent hours each day in the damp and dimly lit old-style kitchen, with its earthen floor. On the terrace was a framed print of Millet's *The Gleaners* and a terra-cotta statue of Buddha. In the largest room were big, finely carved chests, shrines for the tablets of the dead and three seventeenth-century scrolls honoring Jade's great-grandfathers for services to the Yi dynasty. There were also albums of Jade's school days; the color snapshots were all of girls, since Confucian custom kept the sexes apart until college.

At night quilts and mattresses were taken out of cupboards and spread across the heated floor. When Jade stayed with her married sister in Inchon, she slept in a modern bed in an apartment with, as she told her mother, "washer, juicer, dryer, blender." Despite all the appliances, Jade seldom visited, as she found Elder Sister "lazy." "She orders me around," Jade complained. Jade's family ate together,

Jurek.

Janek, the foolish saint or saintly fool, from Babino near Popowlany village, Poland.

Alicja Matusiewicz, Tykocin's cultural leader who was the Germans' translator during the war.

The fiftieth-anniversary ceremony to remember Tykocin's two
thousand Jews murdered here by the Nazis on August 25, 1941. One
survivor, from Białystok, stands with his grandson and son (both blond),
while Dominik holds the speech he is about to read.

Agneshka, Jurek's cousin, in Popowlany village, Poland. In the opening scene, she, her two children, and her father go with Jurek in a horsecart to look for hazelnuts in the woods.

Shahhat as he is today (1993), Nageh Kom Lohlah village, Upper Nile, Egypt.

Hajja Ommohamed as she looks today (1993). Two of Shahhat's six
surviving children are shown with her. Nageh Kom Lohlah village,
Upper Nile, Egypt.

Helmi plowing a potato field, Sirs el Layyan village, Nile Delta, Egypt, 1992.

Husen in his banana grove, Pilangsari village, Java, Indonesia, 1970.

Puppet show, Pilangsari village, Java, Indonesia, 1992. Semar (white-faced puppet) and his children, Petruk (the tall one on the far left) and Gareng (short, face just visible), with one of the Pendawa kings.

though in many village homes men and women still took food separately. The house smelled of wood smoke, grain, kimchi and spices from the saucepot stand outside the kitchen, with its big pickle jars and vats. In moments of silence you could hear the tick of a grandfather clock brought back from Japan. Paduga, Jade's mongrel dog, might rouse himself to bark furiously at the gate if an itinerant peddler came by. It could be an old man hawking seaweed from an A-frame on his back or a youth in a flashy suit with flared pants on a Honda selling rock cassettes. The seaweed would be a side dish, along with fish, egg rolls, vegetables and kimchi or a steaming bowl of rice and a soup of vegetables and eggs.

Nae-Chon was harshly cold in winter and steamy in summer, but fall and spring were pleasant. On May nights frogs croaked from the flooded paddies, a loud chorus sometimes silenced by a disturbance that would soon begin again. In the daytime men could be heard calling *"Do-do-do!"* if their cow plowed off course. Often a newborn calf trotted alongside, scrambling and tripping over the furrows. Jade's father, like most villagers, shored up the sagging roof with new timbers. When rice transplanting time came in the 4th moon, the villagers' family members in schools or jobs in the cities came home to help and the paddies were filled with people thrusting little clumps of pale green seedlings into soft mud. There was an air of reunion as families took a noon meal of stew and squid in the fields and fathers passed around a bottle of *nongju* to all the men. In the afternoons even Jade's younger brother rolled up the black trousers of his schoolboy's uniform and joined in the work until it got dark. All day villagers trotted from seedbed to field with towels tied around their heads and heavy loads of green seedlings hung from yokes on their backs. When, at last, families walked home in the evening, the paths back to Nae-Chon were spattered with wasted bits of dropped seedlings, now past hope of bearing grain.

One day, on a visit to Bright Cloud Temple, the Abbess took Jade to see some newly painted murals on the main temple's outer walls. Upper and lower panels ran around three sides of the building like an exotic Oriental comic strip. The one on top told the familiar story of Buddha himself. There was an angel in swirling garments, resting on a cloud, and Buddha's mother, dreaming of her son-to-be on a white elephant. And then the prince, Siddhartha Gautama, raised in luxury, married at sixteen, and only at twenty-nine venturing beyond his

Nepali palace walls. A panel showed him, borne on a richly adorned palanquin, gazing upon a ragged, diseased and dying old man. The discovery of suffering led to the historic flight from wife, baby son and home. "All his life Buddha had stayed within the palace," the Abbess told Jade. "Now he went east, west, south and north and saw more poverty, death and sickness." Jade was surprised to see Buddha leaving his wife. "I did not know he was married," she said.

The Abbess moved down the granite platform around the temple. "See how he prays for the people." A panel showed Buddha under a pipal tree at Bodh Gaya; he vowed not to rise until he reached true enlightenment. At last, at thirty-six, he found the truths he sought. He was shown giving his first sermon, to the five ascetics who accompanied him, teaching them the Four Noble Truths—life is suffering, it is caused by desire, suffering can only end by extinguishing desire and this is achieved by the Eightfold Path (right views, intentions, speech, conduct, livelihood, effort, mindfulness and meditation). At last the death scene, Buddha then eighty. His followers wailed and wept, clenching their fists.

As they looked at the mural, cherry blossoms drifted down around them like pink snow; the stone was carpeted with them. The second story was Korean, about a Buddhist monk who dreamed his soul had taken the form of a half-white, half-brown ox. "You see, our minds are half good, half evil," the Abbess explained. Jade looked ahead to see that the story ended in a misty landscape of jagged mountain peaks, pinewoods, rocks and waterfalls. The monk, now a stooped old man, has reached his destination, a monastery looking like Bright Cloud Temple itself. There was a moral, the Abbess said: one will get where one is going if one follows the Eightfold Path. Inside the temple nuns were softly chanting and beating hollow drums. Jade, who wore a white blouse and pleated skirt for the visit, went inside to pray. She bowed to the ground before Buddha's smiling bronze image and lit a joss stick. She asked for peace with North Korea.

When she had met Brian, the Peace Corpsman at the leper colony, he showed her pamphlets that were floated down from North Korea by balloons in the night. One in English said, "Americans, you will die!" Jade thought of the fixed, staring eyes of the North Korean border guards she had seen at Panmunjom, on the edge of the Demilitarized Zone, barely sixty miles away. In Seoul in 1980, as in the southern city of Kwangju, perhaps two hundred miles south, rioting threatened to turn into insurrection as students and other discontented young members of the new industrial society challenged the soldiers, businessmen and technocrats who were trying to pick up the reins after the 1979 assassination of President Park Chung Hee. A relatively obscure young soldier, General Chun Doo Hwan, had assumed dictatorial powers, imposed censorship and tightened the army's grip much more than even Park had ever done. Even to Jade's father this violated Confucian ethics. The ultimate guarantee of harmony was the justness of a ruler. Confucius gave people the right, even the duty, to rise up against a tyrant.

The students had attacked Park Chung Hee as well, but Park had been careful to act in accord with Confucian strictures. Most dissidents under Park were Westernized students. The freedoms these young people in the cities held precious did not have the same appeal to an older, more Confucian-minded generation in the villages. To them, the idea of freedom of individual choice, so attractive to the young, was an alien import from the West, unfamiliar and subtly threatening the fundamental Confucian tenet of filial piety itself.

Downtown Seoul, the scene of student riots, was just twenty-five miles south of the DMZ as the missile flies, a two-minute bomber flight from North Korean air bases and within range of Russian-supplied rockets and artillery. Ever since 1978 the South Koreans kept finding tank-sized tunnels under the DMZ bored into granite as much as 240 feet down; not all could be detected. Seoul had monthly air-raid drills; everybody moved into a network of pedestrian tunnels. North Korea's old and ailing Kim Il Sung, whom some held to be crazy, had supposedly been handing over power for years to his son, Kim Chong Il. Early in 1980 there were large-scale military maneuvers in North Korea and calls for "preparedness against war."

No matter; some of Jade's fellow university students were eager to promote unification. Anti-Americanism was rife among them, the more xenophobic students claiming that American soldiers were not in Korea for its defense but to impose America's will. A mural painted on one of the university halls showed a crazed-looking Korean youth tearing apart an American flag. "Big Western One" told Jade word had come down that if anything happened, he was "just to head south to the nearest American military base." Since the nearest base was a squadron of jet fighters sure to come under attack, he was not sold on the idea. And how to get there? Everybody would be fleeing south and all he had was his bicycle.

From Kwangju came rumors that some two hundred had died, most of them young men, students. There were all-night rallies in Seoul in which effigies of Chun and other generals were burned and torchlit "grand marches for democracy." Jade, about to return to Seoul University, spoke of joining them. Her father was furious. "If you young people make more noise, another tragedy will come to Korea," he told her angrily. She bowed her head in a show of filial respect and said nothing. But she longed to join her friends in their brave clashes with riot police, with all their tear gas, shields, helmets and Darth Vader-like masks. She was not afraid. The boys she knew at the university admitted that Kim Il Sung was a megalomaniac with a million soldiers to command but vowed, "We shall be the first to sacrifice ourselves if North Korea attacks." When she repeated this to her father, he flared up: "Have I not tied my empty belt and boldly given money to send my children to universities? I'm highly literate. I have a law degree from Japan. But I am for doing one's duty to state and family and I was for the late President Park. That is all-important."

Though campus riots in Seoul were to continue to be an annual rite of spring, South Korea's politics of tear gas and Molotov cocktails were just about over. General Chun was forced to hand over power to a retired general and close friend, Roh Tae Woo, and go off to a Buddhist monastery in the mountains. Roh, when street demonstrations made such a back-room deal impossible, took a giant gamble on democratic elections and won, taking office in 1988. In five years he would establish relations with Russia and China, secure entry for South Korea into the United Nations, thaw relations with North Korea enough to sign a nonaggression treaty and host the 1988 Olympics along the way. He was to be succeeded by a directly elected civilian politician; the long years of military rule were over.

By 1990, the Valley of the Swallows' old isolation was also gone. A new paved road made it seem smaller, there were the smokestacks of a new polyurethane-foam factory, plastic sheeting warmed the rice seedbeds and litter lay about in the ditches: bottles and cans, ice-cream wrappers, plastic cartons, the refuse of a consumer society getting rich fast. All about were tarred roads, TV antennas or satellite dishes, telephone and electric wires. If grandfathers still tilled tiny two- to three-acre farms, someone in their family was sure to bring home wages from town jobs. Disposable family income had risen 400 percent in ten years. City people were getting richer even faster. The pace of migration from country to town suddenly speeded up in the

1980s, to half a million a year. The number of Koreans engaged in agriculture kept falling, from 80 percent just after the war to less than 30 percent in 1980 and under 15 percent by 1990. A few oldest sons in Nae-Chon who did their filial duty by staying on the family farm found it harder to find wives. Every year the average age of those tilling the land grew older.

The army was no longer South Korea's ruling class. The soldiers, brought to power under the Japanese military occupation, their prestige bolstered by the strict Confucianism of Park Chung Hee, who put many of them in high positions, lost their standing after Kwangju. Too many students died. The soldiers lost their ethical mandate and military rule was irreparably damaged. The brightest young men no longer wanted to enter the military academy. The new elite were businessmen and technocrats. With the end of military rule there was, as Jade's father feared, some further decline in the Confucian social order. When generals ran the state and fathers their families, it was also a place where most people did as they were told. Not anymore.

The lunar calendar still decided, as for centuries past, what was done when on the land. Rice seedbeds were still prepared in the 1990s in the early days of the 3rd moon. Until 1985 the tiny green seedlings were transplanted into flooded paddies forty days later in the 4th moon, the fields filled with people, as it took twenty-five or thirty of them to plant just a single paddy. That year three mechanical rice transplanters were introduced in Nae-Chon which did the whole village in five or six days.

A modern seedbed was made up of dirt and seeds in perforated plastic trays. Nae-Chon needed about five thousand of these trays, and the whole village pitched in for three days to prepare them, each family sending a worker. This was done in an open paved area in front of Nae-Chon's only store, a modern grocery, whose owner, Lee Chang-Shup, went about carrying a red cordless telephone. Almost everybody who came was elderly, the oldest among them, Lee Pyong-Jik, being eighty-three. He was rich by Nae-Chon's standards, with four hectares and a herd of deer, whose antlers were much valued for their recuperative powers. "I have three younger men in my house," he told them, even though they all knew his son was the principal of a school in town and his grandsons were at the university. "They say they'll come and help us. But it's difficult for them. They have their own lives. Who in the younger generation wants to be a farmer?" He himself took great pride in it. "Oh, it's a good life here in Nae-Chon. It's hard. I'm up at four-thirty. But I was born healthy." For ten years Lee Pyong-Jik held an office job in town so he could pay his son's university tuition. Now the old man had so much money he had bought each of his grandsons a new Hyundai car. But he still worked hard.

Jade's mother, now widowed, with just a twenty-eight-year-old son at home, came for her household. Everybody asked about Jade, who, she said, was in Japan, where her husband was studying Japanese. He wanted to open a school as a sideline on Cheju Island, where he had a citrus orchard. Jade had a four-year-old baby girl and rarely got back to Nae-Chon. Jade's mother told her fellow workers, "My son commutes to Suwon by bus each morning. He decided a motorcycle was too dangerous with so much traffic on the roads now. He won't work in the fields. I have to hire others to farm our land." The villagers knew her house had fallen into disrepair since the father died and Jade moved away.

As a poor widow, the mother had fallen on hard times. Still, she could always sell the land, whose value was going up so fast it had nearly doubled just that year. City people rushed to buy land as a speculative investment, but often let it lie idle and the old farmhouse and outbuildings left derelict. "A lot of good rice land goes to waste," Jade's mother lamented. "I hate to see that. I can hardly stand that."

"Once we get these seedbeds done," Lee Pyong-Jik told her, "the plowing can start. My son tells me, 'Don't work.' And I tell him, 'I have cultivated the land all my life. If I don't work, I might as well be dead. As long as I can move, I'll go to the fields.' "

A few of Nae-Chon's houses were still traditional. Jade's mother had her old sliding doors, paper windows, cushions instead of chairs, and heated floors, even if everything was wearing out. In Lee Pyong-Jik's two-year-old brick house, there was brand-new Western-style furniture in the spacious rooms and the kitchen had a modern gas stove, microwave, refrigerator and its own television set. With what he earned from his farm and his son's wages from school, the family's household income was equivalent to over $40,000 a year. Six other families were as prosperous. Nae-Chon's population had fallen; in the 1990s it had 240 people divided among 44 households, only 15 of whom farmed full-time. Average family size in South Korea had dropped from 4.6 in 1980 to 3.8 in 1990, though in Nae-Chon it was still 5.5. One old man in the village, when his son built a modern new house, refused to leave his old thatched mud-walled hut. He still lived there, without electricity or modern amenities, beside the white villa of his son, with its blue-tiled roof.

Many of the older villagers felt more comfortable with each other than with the younger generation, with its talk of clothes, sports and foreign holidays, a world they hardly knew. When they got together they liked to talk of the old days, but they grew so nostalgic, Lee Chang-Shup, who was only in his fifties, would remind them, "You make it sound romantic. Don't believe it. Remember how we lacked food and money. Life was hell. These days are heaven. Besides, the war destroyed our old way of life. Nothing can bring it back."

The old people had set up a kind of assembly line. A man shoveled dirt into trays, a woman with gloves spread the dirt evenly, another put each tray into a plastic seed feeder, Lee Pyong-Jik turned a crank that packed the dirt and seeds into the perforations, Jade's mother sprinkled more seeds into places that were missed and old Mrs. Kwang and another woman smoothed off the top of each tray with a piece of wood, pushing off excess dirt. At the end of the line two old men took the finished trays to a pile, where they were stacked until they could be loaded onto a tractor wagon to go to the fields. Only one or two of the workers were under sixty and many were in their seventies and eighties.

There was a steady murmur of conversation. "I've worked so hard I'm starting to sweat." "Who's going to carry this?" "They'll need more trays. Her husband is sick." "Tomorrow we'll take our trays to the field. Build those little bamboo arches over the rows and cover them with vinyl sheeting."

Old Mrs. Kwang sighed. She was a stooped, lively, opinionated old woman with wispy gray hair. "My mother brought me to Nae-Chon when I was married," she said, smoothing over a tray. "I was just sixteen. It was too young." "Oh, I was just fifteen and my husband fourteen," Yu-Moon-Shil, another old white-haired woman told her. "Our marriage was arranged by a go-between. He was a student in Seoul and became a civil servant and I stayed in the village and looked after everything. The house owned a lot of land so I used to hire labor to farm. It got too difficult after my husband died, so I rented out the land. He was just forty-seven. It was twenty years ago last month."

"That must have been about the time electricity came in." "There was no store when I came," said Jade's mother. "Nae-Chon had only small earthen-walled houses with thatched roofs. We didn't even eat white rice. Just barley." "Our family were among the richer peasants," said Mrs. Yu. "But the poorest people just ate the bark of trees or what herbs and grasses they could find in the spring. There was always a time of hunger before the rice harvest."

Mrs. Kwang became thoughtful, then chuckled. "Everybody in Nae-Chon sold firewood, remember? We'd gather it in the forest and carry it on A-frames into Suwon. Walking three or four hours each way. All the way into Suwon. We had those old straw shoes, and wooden shoes after the Japanese came. You had to walk all the way to Suwon to buy anything, even to buy sugar, salt or lamp oil. We never bought soap in those days. Made it ourselves out of rice skins."

Lee Pyong-Jik remembered how easily the old-fashioned roofs, thatched with rice grass, would burn. On a windy day one might catch fire and it would spread from house to house. "But everybody came and helped make a new roof if you lost yours," he said. "People were so neighborly then. Every year after the harvest, we'd go around helping people make new roofs."

"And no water!" Jade's mother joined in. "What a job that was to carry clothes all the way to the river. You know where the bus stop on the highway is now? That's where we'd wash."

"You'd have to get up at three o'clock in the morning, there was so much to do," said Mrs. Kwang. "We made everything in the village. Even cloth. Everybody had spinning wheels. Some wore cotton and some wore silk."

"But those old clothes were really lovely," Jade's mother remembered with a faded smile. "The long dresses! And no irons. Remember having to beat the wrinkles out? That was a real art."

"What was your first memory?" Mrs. Yu asked Mrs. Kwang, who had become so toothless it seemed she was never anything but aged. Mrs. Kwang thought a minute. "Just jumping about and playing in tall grass," she said. "Green grass. My mother died when I was four. I can't see her face or anything. I do remember my aunt carrying me on her back. Or maybe it was one of my brothers."

"You know what I remember?" Mrs. Yu said. "When the American soldiers came. We called them *bengko*, the big noses. When their trucks came by we'd call, 'Hello, *bengko!* Give me *chop chop!*' You know how they talked." And her voice dropped to a low bass. " '*Son-nomo betch.*' " All the old people laughed. "I was just a young girl and they gave us chocolates and chewing gum. We were very afraid of the

Americans. All the parents hid the young girls. They heard Americans were taking them."

"I heard some Americans came and demanded girls and kicked their fathers," said Mrs. Kwang.

"There was an old widow," said Lee Chang-Shup's wife, joining the conversation, "who lived with her daughter, also a widow. Both husbands were killed in the war. And the Americans came and gave the old widow some cigarettes and told her to go away. And five of those soldiers raped the young widow. It almost killed her. She stayed in bed for two months. She was very sick. They lived near Yong In." For a time nobody spoke.

"It was terrible during the war," said Mrs. Kwang. "You didn't dare go out. There were so many bodies lying along the roads."

"So many people fled south," said Jade's mother. "Fleeing the Communists. It was like when the Japanese came. We were scared to death. But they marched by on the road. Nae-Chon was spared the worst of it."

At noon Le Chang-Shup invited all of those who had been assembling the seedbeds to come to his store for cabbage soup, rice and kimchi, prepared by a young woman who worked for them. She and her husband, a pipe fitter in Suwon, were new to Nae-Chon, one of four young couples who earned their living in town but moved to the village because it was cheaper, Nae-Chon's first urban commuters. A university professor, who built a handsome villa and planted pine trees all around it, lived on the hillside up from the village, and people from Seoul had built a Baptist church retreat. The newcomers who bought land were resented, as it was city people like them who pushed land prices up.

As they ate, the young woman's husband, Hong, joined them. A young man in his thirties, Hong said his father was a farmer but he became a pipe fitter because it was better money.

"A farmer is his own boss," Lee Pyong-Jik told him sternly, with a look of disapproval.

Hong grinned. "I work freelance, so I'm on my own time too." Anyway they all knew five village farmers who now also worked full-time at the polyurethane factory. Not everybody was his own boss anymore.

Lee Chang-Shup said he heard talk Nae-Chon might be reclassified as a suburb of Singal, the nearest small town, three miles away. The others were alarmed but he was pleased. "In a town there are more cultural influences. Movies. One can see more of the world."

Mrs. Kwang shook her head. "Nae-Chon will lose its character if it gets too caught up with town life." Lee Pyong-Jik hastened to agree. Confucian tenets were already under threat.

Lee Chang-Shup shrugged, waving his cellular telephone at the old man. "They say we must respect scholars and those who study. Me, my priority is making money. If I have money, these days everybody will respect me. So I must work hard. Harder than the scholar. I must prepare for my descendants too. You old folks are too nostalgic about the past." He turned to Hong. "Don't let them tell you any different. We had hunger. We had no food. We had no money. It was not at all romantic."

The young man grinned. "I'm young. I have no experience with the old days." To change the subject, he told them about Iraq, where he worked for two years, 1982 to 1984. He was one of two hundred construction men—bricklayers, electricians, pipe fitters like himself—sent by Hyundai, one of Korea's giant corporations, or *chaebol*. Lee Chang-Shup asked about Saddam Hussein, but Hong said he wasn't into politics. "The Iraqis weren't friendly. They called us barbarians. We showed them at the 1988 Olympic Games. They saw Seoul was a modern city. Those Iraqis have money but they don't know how to spend it. You must buy a woman, pay a 'bride price,' if you want to marry. A poor man may be wifeless at sixty, while a rich man will buy three or four." He said the company gave them food at their camp on Baghdad's outskirts, but they made their own liquor. "Steamed rice. We put it with yeast and let it ferment. Twenty-four hours and it would explode. Phoom!"

They asked if he would go back. "Not to Iraq," he said. "You can make as much here at home. The value of the dollar is down. We Koreans stayed together, to keep out of trouble. A lot were caught in the Gulf War. We sent planes to bring them out." Lee Chang-Shup asked if the women were veiled. "Not at seventeen or eighteen. They're very beautiful. Once they get married they get fat and ugly. Iraqi men treat them badly. Many have no shoes and go barefoot. If they go in a car, maybe the man will allow one wife inside and the rest have to ride standing up in a wagon behind."

The women wanted to know about food, and Hong said the Iraqis mixed flour, meat and vegetables together in a big pan and cooked over a camel-dung fire and drank a lot of coffee. "The men wear long robes. Out on the desert it's so hot you can fry an egg on the hood of your car. When an animal dies, it doesn't rot, it just dries up. But it's cold at night." Hong laughed and told how he and the other Koreans played a trick on some Iraqis they knew. They went out in the desert to hunt wild dogs. "There were some dogs without owners and we killed them and cooked them and fed the Iraqis. They'd say, 'That's tasty,' and ask for more. Afterward we told them what it was." The villagers laughed, with a hasty look at Mrs. Kwang, who raised puppies to sell to a restaurant in Seoul, dog meat still being a delicacy.

Hong said he would like to go overseas again. "Why not? I'm still young. You know how secretive the Japanese are; they hide their skills and techniques so nobody can steal them. Europeans are open. You can learn from them. So I'd like to go outside to work. I have to think about getting enough money to educate my children. But two years with the Iraqis was a long time. I wouldn't go back there. There's nothing to learn from them."

Applied learning, at the heart of Confucian culture, was to Koreans the key to success. Compulsory education to age fourteen came into Korea in 1981. Yet the Western idea of the right of the individual to choose for himself directly clashes with the Confucian belief, deeply ingrained in the older generation, in the subordination of the individual for harmony's sake, whether to parents or to the state. Park Chung Hee saw this—just as Lee Kuan Yew did in Singapore—and Park worked through Confucianism, with its justification of government by a benevolent bureaucracy under a virtuous ruler who must be obeyed. Park's regime was not democratic, but it succeeded in reducing corruption and industrializing South Korea so fast that exports in 1962–72 rose at an average yearly rate of 41 percent. Park kept emphasizing the idea that a family and a state can be the same, a government's stern but benevolent rule reciprocated by its subjects in the same way a son obeys a good Confucian father. In 1979 Park wrote that

> just as a home is a small collective body, so the state is a larger community . . . A society that puts the national interest above the interests of the individual develops faster than one which does not.

In his landmark essay in *The Economist* in February 1980, "The Post-Confucian Challenge," British sinologist Roderick MacFarquhar wrote that Western global domination was threatened, not by the Russians or the Arabs, but more fundamentally by the East Asian heirs to

Confucianism, who so far provided the only real economic, political and military challenges to the Euro-American culture. MacFarquhar:

> In Tokyo last autumn, a Chinese vice-premier reportedly told his Japanese hosts: "Add your 100m to our 900m and we have a wonderful force that none can ignore or obstruct." A piece of wishful rhetoric? Perhaps. Calculated to revive Kaiser Bill's nightmare of the "yellow peril"? Possibly. A foretaste of the greatest threat to Western supremacy since the industrial revolution? Definitely.
>
> Confucianism has been the ideology par excellence of state cohesion, and it is that cohesion that makes post-Confucian states particularly formidable. . . .

MacFarquhar said the military challenge came first, from Japan in World War II, and from the Chinese, the Koreans and the Vietnamese since. Politically, he said, the challenge came from China, where "Mao Tse-tung attempted to define a new society, different from both Western democracy and Soviet-style Communism." To MacFarquhar, "this vision has been abandoned only partly and may yet be revived." In the years since, Japan has emerged as the world's industrial superpower, and richest nation, with per capita GNP in 1994 of $28,220, compared with America's $23,120. South Korea, Taiwan, Singapore and Hong Kong have made the fastest economic advance the world has ever seen, with Thailand, Malaysia and Indonesia coming up fast.

In another *Economist* survey, "When China Wakes," in November 1992, Jim Rohwer, the journal's Asia correspondent, predicted that "just a generation from now, one of the world's weightiest questions may well be how to handle a self-confident nuclear-armed China presiding over the biggest economy on earth." Rohwer quoted Napoleon's warning to the West ("Let China sleep") and Mao's declaration when the People's Republic of China was born on October 1, 1949, that "the 475 million people of China have now stood up." He also noted that Napoleon went on to add that "when China wakes it will shake the world."

Rohwer, an ex-lawyer from Berkeley, was one of the first to argue unreservedly that China is becoming a colossal economic success, though he predicts the Chinese eventually will have to choose between Communism and growth. Professor McNeill, perhaps with a historian's caution, predicts, "If the mass of Chinese ever modernized, they'd leave everybody else behind. They'd whip the Japanese." He said:

The problem is the Chinese have never been able to organize collective effort with the sort of enthusiasm and efficiency of the Japanese. There is a kind of ruthless individualism in Chinese life, a competitiveness and acquisitiveness, that may make modern large-scale industrial organization difficult. In Japan it was quite clearly a translation of the old feudal relationships, hierarchies, the duty of the *ronin* to serve the master. Some of the early entrepreneurs were themselves noblemen who could rely on the old traditions of faithfulness of their samurai. There's nothing like that in China.

In his 1980 essay MacFarquhar wrote that the significant coincidence in East Asia was culture,

> the shared heritage of centuries of inculcation with Confucianism. That ideology is as important to the rise of the East Asian hyper-growth economies as the conjunction of Protestantism and the rise of capitalism in the West. The tenets of Confucianism still provide an inner compass to most East Asians in a post-Confucian age, just as the admonitions of the Sermon on the Mount constitute the standard for the West in a post-religious era.

Professor McNeill, when asked about this, said, "It's possible. But there is a systematic difference between Japanese and Chinese society connected to the importance of feudal organization in Japan and the absence of it in China. Maybe you can have modernity without this gigantic industrial organization, Mitsubishi and the rest of it. We haven't seen that."

Toynbee describes the Japanese as being, in his terms, Zealots from the 1630s to 1860s, then reversing themselves to being "perhaps the least unsuccessful" exponents of Herodianism in the world so far. "When hard facts convinced them the Zealots' response would lead them to disaster, they deliberately veered about and proceeded to sail their ship on the Herodian tack." Mastering the West's secrets took education, and Japan's Confucian Tokugawa regime so esteemed learning that by the time of the Meiji modernizers' takeover in 1868, half of Japanese boys and 15 percent of the girls were receiving some formal schooling outside their homes; by 1908 primary education was universal. Confucian characteristics such as social discipline, hierarchical families and moral exhortation are deeply ingrained in the Japanese. MacFarquhar himself summed up his argument:

> The non-Communist East Asian states have already demonstrated that their post-Confucian characteristics—self-confidence, social cohesion,

subordination of the individual, education for action, bureaucratic tradition and moralizing certitude—are a potent combination for development purposes.

Not everyone is prepared to credit Confucianism for the shift in economic power away from Europe and North America to the western side of the Pacific Rim. Andrew Cowley, in 1991 also writing in *The Economist:*

> This cultural explanation of East Asia's rise makes some observers queasy. Not long ago Confucian societies' obsession with the veneration of elders was touted as a reason why they were condemned to remain inflexible and poor. Besides, Confucianism as it is now defined is not unique to East Asia; it is almost identical to the Calvinist work ethic described by Max Weber in 1914.

Weber, in his analysis of the Confucian scholar-official, wrote that the Confucianist saw himself, individually, as an aesthetic end in himself. But today's Zealot, acting on inherited tradition and instinct, can be tomorrow's Herodian, acting by reason to challenge an adversary by learning its weapons.

The great defender of Confucian society and prophet of its cultural primacy over the West is Lee Kuan Yew, Singapore's prime minister for thirty-one years until he stepped down in 1991. He credits East Asia's spectacular economic rise to "intangibles," which he defines as "the coherence of a society, its commitment to common ideals, goals and values." What values? Lee cites them as "belief in hard work, thrift, filial piety, national pride." In 1992, Lee Kuan Yew was behind a drive to promote Mandarin Chinese and Confucianism among Singaporeans, who were to venerate the Confucian values of order, the family and consensus, and abjure the Western idea of individual freedom of choice. Failure to do so, it was drummed in, could endanger social stability, a replay of what we saw in Jade's family in Nae-Chon.

Rohwer, in his assertion that China will probably be the biggest economy on earth within the next twenty years, makes no mention of Confucianism in his continuing articles. He does, however, quote Lee Kuan Yew on Deng Xiaoping:

> Deng knew what he was doing. That's why I think he's a great man. He opened up the system, he opened up the country and deliberately. He knew it could not be closed up again. You can't close men's minds . . .

The thrust for growth is irreversible. Also, they do not want to reverse it or they will be indicted as inefficient, as incompetent.

I know China only briefly, having just visited villages near Beijing in 1980 and 1985, as well as the cities of Guangzhou, Hangzhou, Nanjing, Shanghai and Beijing itself, and in 1991 villages in booming Guangdong province, going by myself by train, bus, ferry, foot and bicycle. I side with Arnold Toynbee, who forecast in his *Study of History* that once Western science and its applied technology lost its specifically Western character—hence, I think, the importance Asians give Confucianism—and becomes a taken-for-granted universal component of all or most societies, China and Japan and the others will have to cope with what the West has released in opening its "Pandora's box." Success in industrialization, Toynbee thought, might turn out to be less significant than "providing solutions to the problems of pollution, of resource exhaustion, and of social tension." Toynbee:

> The future may reveal a non-Western answer to a problem that was originally presented to the world by the West.

Take, for example, what has happened in China with rice, the basic food of the Chinese and much of mankind (providing 30 to 80 percent of all calories for 3 billion of the 5.5 billion people alive). China's huge food production gains go back to the massive earthworks and irrigation systems built under the Great Leap Forward of the 1950s, followed by the introduction of scientifically bred high-yield dwarf rice, wheat and other crops that spread throughout Asia after breakthroughs in tropical plant genetics in the late 1960s. China got off to a late start because it had to cross Mexican- and Philippine-bred wheat and rice with its own colder-weather, nontropical strains.

These scientific advances were one reason China reopened its doors and its ears on the West and its technology with such headlong haste. This was done by Mao Zedong himself, who invited Richard Nixon to China in 1972, followed by visits by the world's leading wheat and rice scientists in 1974. After Mao died in 1976, Deng Xiaoping offered in 1979 the Chinese peasants incentive prices for all above-quota grain surpluses and cash crops. But the money went to China's 50,000 communes—relics of orthodox Maoism and Soviet-style collectivized farming. In 1981, Deng, taking an idea as old as Aristotle, introduced the "responsibility system." This policy broke up communes as economic units into family farms which in effect rent their land. Aristotle had observed in ancient Greece that you needed the stimulus of gain for hard work and the stimulus of private ownership for husbandry and care.

Food production shot up. Given wise politics and scientific farming, the Chinese peasants outdid themselves, using hoes and sickles, often without a plow, but with the latest chemical fertilizers and pesticides. Average yields soon were up to American standards—2.5 tons of wheat per hectare to our 2.2 tons, 4.8 tons of rice to our 5 tons. China's annual wheat production more than doubled in 1978–85, from 41 to 87 million tons. Its total production of cereal grains, tubers and pulses by 1987 of 512 million tons had shot ahead of America's 298 million tons, the then Soviet Union's 287 million tons and India's 177 million tons, and have been far ahead ever since.

This achievement happened with Western science, but during this time Chinese plant breeders were working on their own advances. In 1962 they began quietly developing hybrid rice, led by a scientist from Hunan, Yuan Long Ping. He found their original quality "terrible," and it was not until 1976 that hybrids were improved enough to release to farmers. By 1992 they were grown on 60 percent of China's irrigated land and were averaging yields one ton per hectare higher than the best dwarf varieties, a 20 percent increase. This was big news in Asia and a rush was on to adapt Dr. Yuan's *japonica* cold-weather hybrids as *indica* tropical hybrids.

In 1992 I attended the world's second symposium on hybrid rice at the International Rice Research Institute (IRRI) in the Philippines— the first was in China—and several times had meals with Dr. Yuan, who was staying at the same guesthouse. In 1992 the Chinese were still the only ones growing hybrid rice, he said, except for some Vietnamese farmers in their Quang Ninh province on the border, who took the seeds across. He expected early gains in Vietnam and North Korea, followed by India and Indonesia. The hybrids allowed China to take 2 million hectares out of rice and, as Japan, South Korea and Taiwan did, diversify crops (output in oil-bearing crops doubled, cotton nearly trebled and fruit production went up by half) and shift diets from grain to more meat and milk. India, which averages just 1.7 tons per hectare with irrigated rice, compared with China's 6 tons with hybrids, is frantically trying to adapt the Chinese variety to the tropics. (Egypt, which gets 6.5 tons per hectare with old-style dwarf varieties, is still, if barely, the world's yield-per-acre champion in rice.)

So science is joining industry in our competition with the western Pacific Rim. Research in biology, physiology, biochemistry, immunology, genetics and microbiology promised a big payoff in the 1990s with higher food output at lower costs and less environmental impact (fewer rice paddies and cows to heat up Earth's atmosphere). The Japanese, too, have gained a scientific edge on the West by putting a gene in rice that kills insects but not people, and have replaced us as IRRI's biggest donors.

One important lesson to draw from China's success in hybrid rice is what it says about Chinese organizational capacity. Hybrid seeds have to be changed every crop, which means the Chinese must have a gigantic system of seed production, processing, certification and distribution, just as we do in the Midwest for hybrid corn. With the exception of the great human-ant irrigation earthworks of the 1950s, the Chinese have not been known, as Professor McNeill says, to organize efficient collective efforts on this scale. They seem to be doing so now.

Rohwer in his 1992 report said:

A visitor to China this autumn is greeted on arrival by the world's biggest economic boom. Shops are clogged with people buying consumer goods, often costly ones like Western designer clothes. Factories, offices and homes are being built as fast as round-the-clock construction crews can put them up. China's economy will have grown by some 12% this year, with industrial output by 20% or more. Despite the rich world's economic lethargy, China's foreign trade will have grown to around $170 billion this year, up from $135 billion in 1991 and from a mere $21 billion in 1978, the year the reforms began.

He reported:

Between 1978 and 1991, grain consumption of the average Chinese went up by 20%; seafood consumption two-fold; pork consumption 2½ times; egg consumption more than three-fold; edible-oil and poultry consumption four-fold. In 1981 each 100 urban households in China averaged less than one colour television among them; ten years later it was 70. In 1981 there were six washing machines for each 100 city households, in 1991 more than 80; in 1981, 0.2 refrigerators, ten years later almost 50.

Guangdong province is China's richest rural countryside, and all the new brick houses in the villages were evidence of the new prosperity, a good deal of which, as in South Korea and Taiwan, comes from family members with off-farm income from small local industry. We never quite shed certain impressions of our youth. I first saw Asian villages in 1954 as a sergeant in an Army Corps of Engineers company in South Korea. Assigned to maintain a small airstrip for a detachment of the Korean Air Force, I was in a remote mountainous valley about an hour's jeep ride from Pusan. We were isolated, our small tent encampment ringed by barbed wire and sandbagged fortifications.

It was as if we had been dropped, like Dorothy into Oz, into an exotic green world of startling beauty and serenity, "land of the morning calm," as we were forever being told. Peasants trudged about barefoot carrying huge loads on A-frames. Great numbers of them, all in pointed straw hats, would come out and work all day in the paddies, thrusting bright green rice seedlings into watery mud that reflected the sky. I was twenty-three and, except for the summer of 1950 in Europe, had never left America after a youth in North Dakota and college in Seattle. I felt that Korean life had a harmony, an accord with nature, utterly beyond anything in my experience. It was a passing, protean, strange green landscape framed in barbed wire. An absence of machines. The power of wind, water, sun, animals and human muscles. Iron and wood tools. Fields of food and forage. The kind of simple, if physically hard, village life, close to the earth, as I was to find in the next forty years of travel, that seemed to human beings the most natural, to use that sometimes loaded word, in the sense that such a village life fits the expected order of things.

As we have seen, Korean villages have lost much of that quality today. Those in Guangdong are losing it. The older people seem those most contented. Brian Beedham caught this well after a 1977 journey to China:

> Every westerner visiting China for the first time should tell himself every morning that the country he is looking at, bone-poor though much of it still is, is a science-fiction journey away from the China of warlords and foreign invasions and civil war and general chaos before 1949. All today's middle-aged Chinese can comfort themselves with the knowledge that, unlike their fathers and grandfathers, they are of no danger of starvation in a ditch; that they are in reach of at least some rudimentary medical help if a sudden pain grips their insides; and that all their children are, for the first time in history, getting an education.

In *China's Peasants,* a 1990 study of a Guangdong rural community, Berkeley's Jack and Sulamith Potter provide a graphic picture of pre-1949 China, impoverished, overpopulated, famine-prone, anarchic. It was a feudal society with a few rich scholar-officials, who also engaged in landownership and trade, lording it over the rest, with armed retainers, slavery as in Korea, low status for women and intense greed and acquisitiveness. They reported:

> Before the fall of the imperial system, in 1911, the ultimate goal was to obtain a traditional Confucian education, pass the civil service examinations, become a high official, and then enrich oneself during an official career. This was an unattainable goal for ordinary peasants . . . However, the myth of the peasant boy who started reading Confucius on the back of his water buffalo and ended up a great scholar persisted in the face of observed reality, as did the myth about the peasant who started business peddling firewood and salted fish and finally became a wealthy gentleman merchant.

One Hunanese peasant trained in Confucian classics (Chairman Mao) didn't do too badly. The Potters, in a keen insight, said the pre-Liberation villagers worked very hard but felt one could not succeed unless one was lucky, and one was lucky only if supernatural beings such as ancestral spirits or Buddhist, Taoist or Confucian temple deities, if propitiated, came to one's rescue from malevolent spirits. I found that gilded and red-painted family altars, adorned with joss sticks and ancestral portraits, were coming back into village houses, as were terra-cotta statues of Guangjing, the Buddhist goddess of mercy, just as pictures of Jesus were being rehung in Russian village homes. The Potters reported that village temples, like Russian churches, were being renovated, and costly wedding feasts, dowries and bride-prices were coming back. Old family, kinship and clan ties, along with the male head of household's authority, were being reasserted, as was the old competition to keep up materially with the neighbors.

Certainly the overseas Chinese who pack Guangzhou's luxury hotels like the Swan or China are making hay while the sun shines. The Potters reported that in Guangdong's rural industry the workers, mainly young unmarried women, were getting between $1.90 and $2.50 a day. Those I met in 1991 weren't getting much more. Guangdong is at the heart of an ethnic Chinese network that stretches across East and Southeast Asia to the American West Coast. Some 80 percent of Hong Kong's 6 million people are of Guangdong extraction, and the 21 million Chinese on Taiwan are just a short distance from Fujian, Guangdong's neighboring province. The 55 million overseas Chinese (1.8 million of them in the United States) own much of the commercial and manufacturing assets, including banks, in Malaysia, Thailand, Indonesia and the Philippines; 80 percent of Lee Kuan Yew's Singaporeans are Chinese. Almost all of them—and I met many second- and third-generation Americans visiting home—have a deep cultural attachment to the Chinese village where their ancestors are buried. The overseas Chinese are pouring a huge amount of direct foreign investment, technology and management skills into South China. With a new six-lane superhighway from Hong Kong to Guangzhou, you can reach almost every village in Guangdong in no time.

An interesting retreat to the past has come in mechanical farm technology. In 1980 and 1985 you saw a lot of tractors, even combines, on the communes. With the return of the family farm, all the plowing I saw was done with cows or buffaloes. Under Deng's "responsibility system"—that is, family-sized farms—most are just half an acre, a tiny amount of land. Agriculture has become extremely labor-intensive, 60 percent of it in China done by women. On a typical farm where I spent several days, a field was first plowed with a buffalo. Then the husband and wife used hoes to break up clods of dirt. Afterward they dug irrigation ditches in between each row. The man made several trips jog-trotting with two enormous loads of leaves yoked to his shoulders which were spread on the rows and burned, then loads of sticks, and even duck feathers, were carried in and burned. After a thin cover of commercial nitrogen fertilizer was applied, vegetable seeds were planted. In the surrounding fields, families were growing celery, peas, beans, lettuce, leeks, onions and cabbage. There was wet paddy rice, plus a few stands of bamboo, bananas or lichee nuts. Casuarina trees lined the narrow, paved country roads, which carried remarkably little traffic.

Chinese village houses are not as exotic as they are in Korea or Japan (no sliding walls, paper windows or floor cushions); there are beds and chairs and tables, and you keep your shoes on, as the floor can be bare earth. Nor are the Chinese xenophobic in the manner, under their exuberant hospitality, of the Koreans, or under their ex- quisite courtesy, of the Japanese. They *are* extremely individualist and visibly chaff under their system.

China, for all its new prosperity, is still the most totalitarian society in the world. The guardians of social morality were never far away in Guangzhou, so that on a remote country road you might come upon a dozen or so men standing in the back of a truck, white signs hung around their bowed heads, as a party cadre with a megaphone told a crowd of villagers the condemned should undergo shame and humiliation for their crimes. People's Liberation Army soldiers, in their baggy green uniforms, are as common a sight in China as Red Army soldiers in Russia. In 1994 some heavy industry was still collectively owned, with wholesale trade run by the state and the work force supervised by Communist Party cadres. Farm land was still state property, at least on paper.

Communism is by no means dead in China. This was brought home almost daily when, as I walked around a town square alone, a student or a young professional would come up to me, ostensibly to practice their English. Every time, once we were out of earshot of anybody else, an architect making the same wage as a factory worker in an assigned job he could not change, or a student denied entrance into a discipline he wanted to study, attacked the system. What in China is called "household registration," which controls housing and rations, especially denies freedom to the educated. It also sharply divides urban and rural into two fixed classes; those in cities are guaranteed employment and subsistence, whereas rural people shift more for themselves, but are forbidden to leave the land by law. (Though one can escape by joining the army or through marriage.)

Again Brian Beedham put it succinctly: "In China you work where you were born until and unless the government sends you somewhere else, and then you work there until and unless it moves you again." In 1977 he wrote what still applies:

> It has to be added that, for an unknown but very large number of Chinese, life is still an alternation between days of grinding physical labor and nights in miserably ramshackle housing. In the cities one sees men, and sometimes women, with teeth bared in the rictus of effort as they drag uphill the impossibly heavy cartloads of old iron and boulders to which they are harnessed like horses.

In 1992 one saw fewer such sights, but they were still there.

What makes Chinese Communism so unique, a hybrid between Marxism-Leninism and Confucianism, is the internal contradiction, to borrow Lenin's phrase, between the "struggle" preached by a nineteenth-century German theoretician and the "harmony" of a sixth-century B.C. Chinese sage. Mao departed from Marxist doctrine in three ways: he favored the rural peasantry and kept them on the land, he believed in perpetual revolution and he drew from China's Confucian heritage.

First, the bias toward peasants showed less in what he said—such as only poor peasants could be relied upon—than in what he did in his thirty years in power, 1949–1979. Marx hated peasants; he wanted to do away with them, turn them into a landless proletariat who worked in brigades on big mechanized collective farms like factory workers. The system broke down in Russia when a reduced agricultural labor force was unable to feed the rest of society. Unlike China, Russia also was too cold and too dry to benefit from the new high-yield tropical grain varieties that transformed Asian agriculture. Mao chose to keep about 80 percent of China's people living and working on the land, rather than turning them en masse into factory hands. Peasants were taxed lightly, provided with basic food, clothing, shelter and schools, and Mao encouraged the growth of small-scale industry in countryside communes.

This rural emphasis had one bad unintended demographic effect. Professor McNeill on a lesson of history:

> Since civilization began, town dwellers have seldom and perhaps never reproduced themselves; but in the European past, migrants from the nearby countryside, who shared much of the same cultural identity, compensated for the urban die-off, thus allowing a single people and culture to maintain itself for centuries in the same geographical area.

Only since World War II, he says, have entire nations—countries in Europe, Japan and lands of European settlement overseas—become rich and urbanized enough to see birth rates fall below replacement levels. This has happened in Russia, 75 percent urban, but not in China, just 26 percent urban, the same as in India.

In Guangdong I found in random interviews with men and women in the fields that China's one-child family system was not working. China may be manufacturing 1.3 trillion condoms a year but villagers were proud and happy to say they had three or four children, especially sons, who are bound by Confucian filial piety to look after parents in their old age. A son is an asset, while a daughter marries and goes away, after needing a dowry and bride-price. (A big abortion issue in both China and India is the marked statistical drop in female babies, down in China to 100 per every 114 boys in the 1990 census.) In September 1992, my impression that the one-child family was in trouble in the villages was confirmed by the Population Crisis Committee in Washington. It warned that flaws in birth control in both China and India made it unlikely they would be able to stabilize growth until well into the twenty-first century. The prospect was worse for India, predicted to grow from 900 million in 1993 to a catastrophic 2 billion before leveling off. China, 1.2 billion in 1993, was projected to stabilize at 1.9 billion by 2025, which, with hybrid rice and other agricultural advances, it could probably feed. Yet as long as there are villages, there are inescapably going to be rural people saying, "The more sons, the more happiness" (China) or "May you be the mother of a hundred sons" (India).

Mao's second big innovation, the idea that revolution is not a once-and-for-all event but needs to be repeated every generation, was behind the Cultural Revolution of 1966 and the Gang of Four's attempted replay in 1976. Sustained revolutions were Mao's solution to the corruptibility of Lenin's single-party system of government, which in the end proved so fatal to the Russians.

The third, probably most significant, distinction about Chinese Communism is what it takes from the Confucian heritage. The Chinese have kept the same language, the same culture and the same political identity since many of our ancestors were running around in bearskins in the forest. By adapting Communism to this Confucian culture, creating a synthesis, the Chinese have tried to resolve that inner contradiction between struggle and harmony, the rigidity of a totalitarian system and the individualist temper of the Chinese, between social justice and prosperity.

In a December 1992 article in *The New York Review of Books*, "Deng's Last Fling," Roderick MacFarquhar describes how Deng Xiaoping, who at eighty-eight spent much of his time amusing his grandchildren and playing bridge with his cronies, felt economic reform sufficiently in danger to visit Guangdong and the Special Economic Zones bordering Hong Kong and Macao. Deng gave these models of how China can absorb foreign capital, technology and management practices his blessing:

> I came to Guangdong in 1984. At that point, rural reform had been going for a few years, urban reform was just starting, and the special zones were taking their first steps. Eight years have gone by and I

would never have believed that on this visit I would find that Shenzhen and Zhuhai special zones have developed so fast. Having seen it, my confidence has increased.

As China's paramount leader since 1978, Deng deserves great credit for replacing collective farms with family-sized units, closing or privatizing much unprofitable state industry, dismantling central planning in favor of private entrepreneurship and the market, and all the while fully integrating China into the global economy. As Professor MacFarquhar summed up the visit:

> Clearly he had seen the future and it worked. The revolution had been the first step in liberating the country's productive forces, Deng said, and reform was the second; with reform, Guangdong could catch up with Asia's "four little dragons"—South Korea, Taiwan, Hong Kong, and Singapore—over the next 20 years. Deng admitted that opening up to the outside world had exposed parts of China to drugs, prostitution, and corruption and called for a crackdown on these "repulsive things." China, he said, had to emulate and surpass Singapore's strict civic spirit.

And who is Singapore's guiding light? In Rohwer's words, "Asia's wisest old authoritarian," Lee Kuan Yew. If the past thirty years have produced in East Asia "the fastest rise in incomes, for the biggest number of people, ever seen on earth," some *Kulturkampf* from the Confucians, suggesting the superiority of their ethic, was bound to come. In a late 1993 interview by Rohwer, Lee fired the first shot:

> If we follow the West in our social relations and family structures, we will be in deep trouble. In the West the Christian religion used to instil fear of punishment in hell or reward in heaven. Science and technology have eliminated that fear. So the controlling mechanism has gone awry. I am hoping that because Asian moral control is based on what is good in a secular this-world, not a spiritual after-world, we will not lose our moral bearings.
>
> The second point is we should not substitute the state for the parents or the family. If you bring a child into the world in the West, the state caters for him. That's dangerous. If you bring a child into Asia, that's your personal responsibility.
>
> As long as our society remains structured in this traditional way, we will be different. We will not allow muggers to clonk you on the head and grab your belongings and leave you dying or dead on the streets. And when you are ill you will not be abandoned, because your family are required by culture to look after you.

Surely we will be hearing a lot more of such Confucian moralism, what Brian Beedham calls "the increasingly open derision of some East Asian authoritarians," as during the 1994 caning of a young American in Singapore for vandalizing cars.

Whatever happens—and the struggle between China's reformists and Communist diehards seems likely to go on—its size and diversity suggest that China is almost bound to have a strong central, probably authoritarian, government, especially if it really does become a gigantic economic power, ten times more populous than Japan, in the next several decades. With nuclear weapons (it tested a megaton device in 1992), a vast army, a fast-growing arms industry and exports to renegade Muslims, China remains a political power to reckon with as well. Toynbee's point that China's degree of industrialization may matter less than its ability to cope with overpopulation, overuse of resources and overpollution, has military implications. Social tensions from too many people with too little land and resources have already led to two cataclysmic world wars.

Lee Kuan Yew's remarks raise a potentially worrisome aspect of the Confucian cultural challenge, buoyed by East Asia's spectacular economic dynamism: the traditional Chinese worldview of a supreme Middle Kingdom surrounded by tributary states: "There are not two suns in the sky, there cannot be two emperors on earth." The specters of a Confucian-Muslim connection or, alternatively, a Sino-Japanese axis, hostile to Western values and power and intent on supplanting them, keep being raised. What makes the future so uncertain is that the two main cultural exports of the West, embodied by China and Japan—Communism and capitalism—both had their economic basis in superior Western science and technology. This science and technology has now lost its specifically Western identity and, with Japanese, Chinese and even Indians in the lead in some fields, has become so universal it is simply taken for granted in much of the world. It was Russian technological failures that reduced Soviet Communism to ashes, even if the embers still smolder a bit. Modern technology is no longer exclusively of Western origin.

Thirty years ago Joseph Levenson, commenting on Confucianism, said, "History is process, not essence, and the past may be significant for the present without being enacted in the present." For the elderly villagers in Nae-Chon, rural survivors preparing their seedbeds and living in their memories, and for the oldest generation of Chinese, Japanese and other East Asians too, the old Confucian autocracy, bureaucracy and classics lost their grip long, long ago. Yet Confucianism is still very close to the heart of their identity. That is not so true of younger people. As their societies materially advance, increasing wealth and technology give them the same freedom of individual choice that the West, with its technological head start, experienced first. This naturally means that a younger generation will throw away a lot of the old Confucian restraints and patterns of obedience to authority. Sporadic Korean and Japanese riots, like the 1989 Tienanmen demonstrations, keep showing us that the Confucians are far from resolving authoritarian rule and the presumed harmony it brings with their young people's nonauthoritarian, unharmonious instincts. Which is why, as the Chinese say, they are fated to live in interesting times.

V

You *Can* Go Home Again: Migration

CAST OF CHARACTERS

HUECORIO VILLAGE, LAKE PÁTZCUARO, MICHOACÁN, MEXICO,
AND CALIFORNIA

AURELIO, 40, a mestizo ex-waiter
ROSENDO, 35, a Tarascan Indian canoe maker
MACARIO, 45, a Tarascan sharecropper
Other Villagers

MEXICAN VILLAGERS are a contradictory lot: warm but distrustful, idealistic but cynical, passive but violent, in times of tension, as in 1994, angry but helpless. Mainly mestizos of mixed descent, they are, some argue, Spaniards in body, Indians in mind. Anthropologists speculate that this is because what remains of pre-Columbian Indian culture out in the villages has never fully come to terms with urban Spanish ways.

This duality, which gives Mexico its mystery, its Harvard-educated modernizers and Zapatista rebels, will become familiar to us as it moves north. Mexicans call it the *reconquista,* the reconquest of what was lost when Texas won its independence in 1838, when the Oregon Territory went in 1846, and California and the Southwest changed hands in the Guadalupe Hidalgo Treaty of 1848 and the Gadsden Purchase of 1853. Despite multiple attempts, Mexico never really succeeded in populating its northern territories. The nomadic plains Indians, most notably the Apaches and the Comanches, less vulnerable than the Aztecs and the Incas to European diseases like smallpox, halted Spanish expansion. After the gold rush, Anglos outnumbered Mexicans in California about twenty-five to one.

Only now is it possible to foresee the Latinos winning these lost lands back simply by outvoting the Anglos. A growing number of Americans speak Spanish or Portuguese and possess a peasant culture strongly influenced by Roman Catholicism and a pre-Columbian Indian heritage. Fully a tenth of the 260 million Americans are now Hispanic, 80 percent of them Mexicans. They make up a third of Greater Los Angeles and over half the inhabitants in California towns like Fresno. Polls show 90 percent of them want to learn English and assimilate; a third of them marry native-born Americans, Anglo or Latino. What polls don't show is that practically every immigrant, legal or illegal, keeps close ties with one of Mexico's 96,000 villages, which range from a few houses to communities of 2,000 to 3,000 people. It is in terms of their families and these villages that most Mexican-Americans still act out their lives. (You are "Latino" if from Latin America, "Hispanic" if Spanish-speaking and "Chicano" if from Mexican ancestry born in the United States. But "Mexican" and "Mexican-American," in the context of migration, really depends on whether you feel more Mexican or American.)

Whites in America, as in Europe and Russia, stopped reproducing themselves biologically in the early 1970s. If existing rates of birth and migration stay unchanged, within twenty years Latinos will outnumber African-Americans. By 2020, says the Census Bureau, nearly 16 percent of what will be about 326 million Americans, or 51 million people, will be of Spanish descent. White Americans will become a minority, first in California, then in Texas and the Southwest. If Hispanics keep their culture and language, America will rapidly become more Latino than Anglo. For what makes Mexicans different from all previous waves of immigrants to the United States is that, not cut off by the Atlantic or Pacific Ocean, they can go home again. And they do.

Mexico is changing fast. Its birth rates have been halved in two decades and its per capita GNP of $3,470 is higher than that in Eastern Europe. Mexico is practically as urban as the United States—71 percent of its 90 million people live in towns and cities, while 75 percent of Americans do. *The Economist,* which has reported that Mexico is poised to become a rich, modern nation, argues even this is too much: "To have nearly one-third of the population living in rural areas is simply not sustainable if the country is to live up to its aspirations."

Perhaps. But my experience suggests that if Mexico is to keep what Alan Riding calls its "real strength and stability," its "ordinary Mexicans who preserve family and community traditions, whose material expectations remain secondary to their spiritual aspirations," it has to keep enough people in its villages.

The most enduring traditions of Mexicans belong to their countryside. Its maize and beans have been Mexico's staff of life since ancient times. Once the earth is plowed and seeds planted, its villagers submit to sun and rain. Piety and ties to family and village go with faith in an omnipotent God and the old ancestral order. Earlier immigrants to America were expected to readily assimilate. But the United States was much more rural then, and the Yankees who ran the small agricultural towns actively discouraged Old World customs among what was usually an immigrant peasant majority.

Those days are gone, and with them much of the rural base of our urban culture. If Mexican village ties endure, along with religious faith, family and community, America has everything to gain from such village recruits from afar, even across cultural and racial lines.

In any case, short of building a 1,950-mile fence and a symbolic Iron Curtain with Latin America, it is impossible to isolate ourselves from the problems of Mexico's villages, where there is no longer enough water and land to go around. 1994, a year that began January 1 with a Maya Indian peasant rebellion in Chiapas, Mexico's poorest state, saw land seizures, kidnapped business tycoons, bombings and the murder in Tijuana of President Carlos Salinas de Gortari's chosen successor, Luis Donaldo Colosio. At this writing his replacement, Yale-educated Ernesto Zedillo Ponce de Leon, forty-two, was favored to win Mexico's August election amid threats of "civil war" if his ruling Institutional Revolutionary Party (PRI), which has led the country for sixty-five years, stays in power. Wages in Mexico are, on the average, about one-sixth of what they are on this side of the border. Free trade will correct this in the long run. Meanwhile, the legions of legal and illegal fruit pickers, babysitters, maids, gardeners, roofers, waiters and washer-uppers will keep multiplying. Nobody knows how many are coming now, but an authoritative guess is about 850,000 a year, about half to California and another 35 percent to Texas, Florida, Chicago and New York City (where they are still out-numbered, as illegal aliens, by Italians and Poles).

Such cultural cross-pollination is not necessarily a bad thing. "Poor Mexico!" as the traditional saying goes. "So far from God, so close to the United States." Beyond politics there is a reality that decides our relationship. Mexico must sell its oil to the United States or leave it in the ground; it is our third biggest trading partner. We have to send our surplus corn to Mexico or face hungry and restless cities on our door-step. (Officially 16 percent of Mexico's people—13.5 million—are classified as living in "extreme poverty" and another 23.6 million as "poor.") Without Mexican farmhands and domestic workers, a good many Americans would be at a loss. The North American Free Trade Agreement, promising to create jobs, improve productivity and raise incomes on both sides of the border, increases Mexico's hopes of becoming a mature and prosperous democracy. Yet there is still mu-tual incomprehension. Mexicans view *el coloso* with conflicting passions of admiration and resentment. Until NAFTA, we hardly thought of Mexico at all, or vaguely, in patronizing populist put-downs like Ross Perot's—poor exploited Pedro in a sombrero dozing under a cactus while the richest Mexicans grow richer. If you happen to live in California, as I do, you see a lot more Hispanics around these days, repairing roofs, washing cars, tending lawns, waiting on tables, looking after children, tidying up, doing menial work. And last year's NAFTA debate unleashed a lot of anti-wetback outcries, like the "giant sucking sound" Perot kept hearing in an imaginary rush of American jobs to Mexico.

The first serious study of Mexican culture by an American anthropologist, Robert Redfield's *Tepoztlán—a Mexican Village*, which came out in 1930, was a warm and sympathetic study. Twenty-one years later, in *Life in a Mexican Village: Tepoztlán Restudied*, it was attacked by Oscar Lewis, an ex-student of Redfield's, who said his former professor gave Mexican village life "a Rousseauan quality which glosses lightly over evidence of violence, disruption, cruelty, poverty, disease, suffering and maladjustment." Far from Redfield's idyllic village, Lewis found Tepoztlán riven by "fear, envy and mistrust." In 1953 Redfield fought back, saying Lewis's view lacked "humanity" and that Lewis took "his own values" to Mexico. In a famous rebuttal, Redfield said:

> There are hidden questions between the two books that have been written about Tepoztlán. The hidden question behind my book is, "What do these people enjoy?" The hidden question behind Dr. Lewis's book is, "What do these people suffer from?"

Literary Americans, when they went to Mexico, looked for suffering. Lewis certainly did, in *Five Families* (1959) and *The Children of Sanchez* (1961), while his study of Puerto Ricans in *La Vida* (1966) is a good deal more optimistic. The real Sanchez, Santos Hernández Rivera, the harsh, authoritarian father in the book, who, in 1986, at eighty-four, was still kitchen manager at Mexico City's Café de Tacuba, told me Lewis tried to get at the truth in hours of tape-recorded conversation, but his four children were too young and sometimes made up the stories. "Not even half of it was true," he told me. I think Redfield was right and much of the power and beauty that lifted the Sanchez family story above mere documentary can be explained by emotions and values Lewis himself took to Mexico.

There is a good deal more suffering than joy in Katherine Anne

Porter's *Flowering Judas* (1930), Tennessee Williams's *The Night of the Iguana* (1961), Jack Kerouac's *Mexico City Blues* (1959) and B. Traven's *The Treasure of the Sierra Madre* (1935). Traven's six-novel *Coaba Cycle*, about the gruesome conditions that led to the 1910 revolution, is his major work and I have been told by Mexican writers that Traven saw their society with greater clarity and veracity than most. Hart Crane, who killed himself by jumping overboard from a ship bringing him home from Mexico, and Ambrose Bierce, who disappeared in Mexico in 1913 while reporting the revolution, both wrote darkly about it.

Suffering has also been a theme for English writers in novels about Mexico. Graham Greene's *The Power and the Glory* (1940), about a drunken, lecherous priest at a time of religious persecution who dies a Christ-like death, depicts a sinister, seedy Mexico, full of spiritual or psychological suffering. Malcolm Lowry's *Under the Volcano* (1947) is a semi-autobiographical study of the last day of an alcoholic living in Mexico who is murdered by the Mexican police and whose corpse is thrown into a ditch with that of a dead dog. Even Raymond Chandler's *The Long Goodbye* (1954), set mainly in California, has a major character vanish into Mexico, as into purgatory, in the closing pages. D. H. Lawrence, who lived in Mexico for a time in the 1920s, wrote a classic condemnation:

> It's all of a piece . . . what the Aztecs did, what Cortés did, and what Díaz did—the wholesale, endless cruelty . . . The heart has been cut out of the land. That's why hearts had to be cut out of its people. It goes on and on and always will go on. It's a land of death.

Suffering is expressed in the poetry and essays of the much-celebrated giant of the Mexican literary scene, Octavio Paz, but he also shows how it can be transcended by compassion and faith. The novels of Carlos Fuentes draw on both Spanish and Indian culture for insight into Mexican character. More familiar to most Americans are Mexican films like Robert Rodríguez's *El Mariachi*, a grubby but charming little thriller made for $7,000, and Alfonso Arau's ambitious romance, *Like Water for Chocolate*, set on a Mexican ranch in 1910, both in Spanish and unexpected hits with American audiences.

It is true there is not much in Mexican history to inspire cultural optimism. Like one of its smoking volcanoes, the country has been erupting in plagues, rebellions, massacres and defeats for three thousand years. The Maya empire, whether through peasant revolt or soil exhaustion, suddenly disappeared. The Aztecs took the murderous

Cortés for a god and lost their empire too. After the Spaniards conquered, colonized and, in a bloody struggle, gave Mexico its independence, the country lost half its territory to the United States in a war over Texas. Napoleon III even tried to foist a Hapsburg prince on Mexico as a puppet emperor, who ended up before a firing squad. Plus all the dictatorships, disasters and peasant uprisings since.

Bernal Díaz del Castillo's *True History of the Conquest of New Spain*, published in 1632—the conquest began in 1519—tells of the grandeur the conquistadores destroyed:

> . . . And when we saw all those cities and villages built on the water, and other great towns on dry land, and that straight and level causeway leading to Mexico, we were astounded. These great towns and . . . buildings rising from the water, all made of stone, seemed like an enchanted vision . . . But today all that I then saw is overthrown and destroyed; nothing is left standing.

Castillo, an eyewitness who wrote in his old age about what he could observe, described Aztec sacrifices:

> They strike open the wretched Indian's chest with flint knives and hastily tear out the palpitating heart, which, with the blood, they present to their idols in whose name they have performed the sacrifice. Then they cut off the arms, thighs, and head, eating the arms and thighs at their ceremonial banquets. The head they hang up on a beam, and the body of the sacrificed man is not eaten but given to beasts of prey . . . We know for certain, too, that when they drove us out of Mexico and killed over eight hundred and fifty of our soldiers, they fed those beasts and snakes on their bodies for many days.

Criticism has been made of some American historians that they have been what British writer Hugh Thomas calls "a little disdainful of the indigenous culture of Mexico." In his 1994 book, *Conquest: Montezuma, Cortés and the Fall of Old Mexico*, Thomas sets out to remedy this by portraying a rich, cultured civilization, though he admits human sacrifice was an essential part of it:

> At festivals there were other offerings, sometimes of animals and birds, especially quail; but on an increasingly large scale, human beings, as a rule prisoners of war or slaves especially bought for the purpose.

Thomas notes other ancient cultures practiced bloodletting. "Yet in numbers," he reminds us, "in the elevated sense of ceremony which accompanied the theatrical shows involved, as in its significance in the official religion, human sacrifice in Mexico was unique." The Aztecs, historians tell us, sacrificed and ate about 70,000 human victims a year, most of them prisoners of war, before Cortés arrived. They also had an advanced civilization in engineering, architecture, art, music, astronomy and mathematics; agriculture flourished. Much of this can be seen at the marvelous Anthropology Museum in Chapultepec in Mexico City, though there is very little about human sacrifices. In Mexican popular mythology, the Spanish conquistador is the villain, the Indian the hero. Paradoxically, after five centuries, Mexican society is still dominated by a small number of Spanish-descended *eviollos*, with mestizos making up most of the Mexican class structure, and about 8 million pure Indians at the bottom.

Caught in this dual culture, with its still incompletely developed relationship between pre-Columbian Indian ways, strongest in the villages, and urban centers of Spanish intellectual thought, the mestizos of modern Mexico can exhibit, as I mentioned at the outset, very contradictory character traits. Something in the Mexican psyche, I think, is unresolved, and it is this that keeps drawing them back to their village roots.

Huecorio, like most Mexican villages, is picturesque, spreading from the marshy shores of Lake Pátzcuaro up the stony, eroded slopes of an extinct volcano, San Miguel. A patchwork of tiny fields, enclosed by rock walls and now farmed mainly by old men or left fallow, barely provides Huecorio's 687 people with corn and beans, in ancient times and now Mexico's staff of life. Only on the lakeshore is the sometimes flooded earth rich and black. Here vegetables are grown and, like the catch of fish from the lake, sold at the market in Pátzcuaro town. A small plaza, a seventeenth-century church and cobbled streets with walled-in adobe houses are half hidden by foliage and flowering red, orange and purple bougainvillea.

I spent six months in Huecorio in 1977, going daily up San Miguel to a stony field where Aurelio, a villager in his twenties, and his grandparents, Francisco and Doña Seraphina, cultivated a little wheat and corn. I've gone back a couple of times since, most recently in 1993. Huecorio has a tractor now, jointly owned by eight men, who hire it out. There are ten TV satellite dishes, and a few flat cement roofs, deemed modern, have replaced the old red-tiled ones. MTV, motorcycles, pickup trucks, T-shirts with logos like "Keep Kids Off Drugs," *telenovelas* and soccer matches are part of a village social network that extends thousands of miles by bus, train, plane, phone, mail, fax and money order to Huecorio's young people wherever they are in the United States.

Yet you can feel the years under you. A great Tarascan Indian empire ruled this lake region until the Spanish conquest and the pure Tarascans who survived have retreated to the lakeshore or eight islands in the lake. Wheat is still cut with sickles and threshed with circling horses, ways the early Spaniards brought. In Huecorio's damp, chill church, smelling of incense, candles and gladioli, God is still petitioned to heal illness as tiny silver replicas of body parts or farm animals are pinned to the purple satin robes of a life-size wooden Jesus, painted blood streaming down his face from wounds made by the crown of thorns. *"El Señor es mi Dios y mi Salvador,"* reads a handwritten sign by his feet.

In the years since 1977, Francisco, a *rescantón*, or muleteer, who traded goods far and wide, had died. Doña Seraphina had become too old and frail to till the land, and Aurelio, now a man of about forty years of age, after eleven years as a waiter in Pátzcuaro, with a wife and four children, had twice spent months at a camp for alcoholics in the nearby village of Las Trojes. He had to give up his job. His wife had taken the children to live with her parents. Aurelio went back to stay with his mother, a seamstress, and grandmother, as he tried to get his health back. Idleness and a kind of despair weighed heavily upon him.

Aurelio and Rosendo, a Tarascan Indian a few years younger, sat on the grassy bank near the lakeshore watching another Tarascan, Macario, and his family threshing wheat. Macario's wife and two teenage sons, plump and good-humored like Macario himself, carried wheat in from the field while Macario, reins in one hand and a spinning rope in the other, led two brown horses round and round to tread on the grain. He and his family had paddled across Lake Pátzcuaro that morning in a dugout canoe from their small hamlet near Tzintzuntzan on the opposite shore.

"¡Buenos días, amigo!" Macario called cheerfully to a man coming by with a machete and saw. The man, a villager called Pelón because he was bald, said he was hurrying home to get his wheelbarrow. "I found wood in big pieces on San Miguel. I'm going home to get some tortillas." He laughed. "If I have a drink I won't come back." Huecorio's people, though they now had gas stoves, preferred the flavor of tortil-

las made over an open wood fire. It was more work for the women but also for the men, as it meant many trips up to the woods on San Miguel with a burro or wheelbarrow.

"Go!" Macario cried to the horses, and he spun his rope, making a swishing sound. "Malinche is beautiful. She comes out whenever she wants. She can give you your heart's desire. Money. Love." Macario seldom stopped talking and Aurelio and Rosendo knew Malinche was the mistress of Hernán Cortés, an Indian slave who could speak both Maya and Aztec, and had been dead four-and-a-half centuries.

"*Sí*, she was a *diablo*," Macario went on, making the sign of two horns over his head. "In Tzintzuntzan and Erongaricuaro there were no people in those days. All this was forest. Hernán Cortés, when he came to Mexico, he came for gold. And Montezuma didn't want to give it to him."

It was pleasant listening to Macario, who was so stout and cheerful and rambled on incessantly as he drove the horses round and round. Both Aurelio and Rosendo had a weary, defeated air about them, for they had just come out of Las Trojes, a nearby village where they had each spent three months at La Huerta, The Orchard, an Alcoholics Anonymous camp, though everybody just called it Las Trojes, which means "the place of grain warehouses." Aurelio spoke daily of going back to work as a waiter, and Rosendo, who had fished and made dugout canoes, of picking up his life too. But they put it off day after day, and the two of them were seen going about aimlessly in the village and surrounding fields, somehow weary and broken. When young, Aurelio wore his coarse black hair long so he looked like an Apache. Now, with his short-clipped hair, his slow walk and his defeated face, so heavy and pale and changed from the days before he began to drink, he was hardly recognizable as his old self. Rosendo was shorter in stature, still lean and sinewy, and despite a broken nose had the look of a pure Tarascan whose ancestors were warriors who undertook campaigns far from home, fearlessly held off the Aztecs, before whom everyone else crumbled, and sought no help and gave no quarter.

The bells of churches around the lake began to toll ten o'clock and Aurelio thought of their drinking friend Ladislao, who also had worked as a waiter in Pátzcuaro. Once, on a dare, Ladislao had slept overnight in Huecorio's cemetery. Now he was buried there, beside his mother. Ladislao feared nothing. Instead of greeting people with "*¡Buenos días!*" he'd say, "*¡Chinga tu madre!* Go rape your mother!"

and if a friend came up he would joke, "Give him a *chingadazo*," slang for heavy blow. At Las Trojes they told Aurelio and Rosendo that they would die too if they kept drinking.

"You see people walking around and looking healthy, and maybe the next time you see them, they're dead," Aurelio told Rosendo. "He was fine one day and gone the next." Rosendo shrugged. "Well, *la vida es una lucha*, life is a struggle," Aurelio said. Sometimes he talked of going back to Los Angeles, where he had gone to high school for three years before dropping out. It was about the time his father had left his mother for a younger wife. When he came out of Las Trojes his father had given him a pair of boots. "My mother always sent us to school so we could be someone," he told Rosendo. "She helped us all she could. But my father gives me a pair of boots. That's help? When we were little he didn't help us to go to school or anything." He too gave a shrug. "Who helps you in life? The family. Outside the family if they don't help you? Nobody."

Aurelio's father, Gregorio, was Huecorio's success story. After thirty-five years as a construction worker in Los Angeles, where he owned a house, became a union member and an American citizen, he retired and returned to Huecorio with an $800 monthly pension, $700 more in social security and what he made from four hectares, an old pickup, two cows and half a dozen pigs. Besides Aurelio and a brother in Mexico City, Gregorio had four children by his second wife in California. There were six or seven retired men like him in Huecorio. More common was Agustín, sixty-one, who got nothing from his eight years as a fruit picker in Michigan, Arkansas and Texas. Four of Agustín's five sons were in Los Angeles and were getting documents and staying in one place; they were all roofers or gardeners.

Macario, like many Tarascans, had never left Lake Pátzcuaro. "I know," he told them, swishing his rope at the horses, "here it's bad food, bad work, bad rest, bad everything. I wanted to go to the United States, but my father said, 'No *el norte*, no nothing. You stay here with your wife and eleven children.' So I say, '*Sí,* okay.' I got married when I was sixteen. Now I am forty-five."

"Eleven!" Aurelio swore. Such big families, common in the 1960s, were rare in the 1990s. Contraceptives were publicized and available, more women worked, there was more education and more migration to the United States. The birth rate was steadily dropping.

"Oh, it's a problem. I have to spend for school, bus fare, shoes, paper, everything, and it all costs pesos. Seven are now in school. My oldest boy is at the university in Morelia. It costs plenty. Everybody in Tzintzuntzan asks me how I get enough money for all the children. But it's easy. We all just keep working all the time." Macario said he was sharecropping the wheat he was threshing with an old woman in Huecorio, Doña Josefina. "Fifty-fifty. I get half the wheat and half the straw. I planted it in December and weeded it. I'll plant corn for her too. This is rich black soil by the lake. The fields in the hills are worn out. Wheat is very good here. You don't need fertilizer. You don't need water, except for corn."

Macario glanced at the sky. "The weather is getting *loco*. Every year there's not enough rain. The weather is changing. Nobody can tell if it will rain. Well, when it's time to thresh, no Mexican can be tired. It goes slowly with two horses. I have four horses at home. But how can I bring them here on the highway? *El tráfico* is too dangerous. Four horses and a pony. No burro."

"Where is Doña Josefina?" Rosendo asked.

"She is too old to come. She might get kicked by a horse." Macario laughed at his joke. "I know an Aurelio who plays in a mariachi band," he went on. "Did you go to the dance on Sunday?"

"For a little while," Aurelio said, in the humble, mild way he spoke now. Huecorio had celebrated Corpus Christi with a procession Sunday evening. The streets around the church were decorated overhead with red-and-white bunting and a band was hired, which also played for dancing outside the church until two o'clock. After the band, as rockets exploded, women carried a wooden figure of Christ, its hands and feet pierced so that nails could be driven in to suspend it from the cross. The image of the Virgin known as La Purísima, in a blue robe, was also carried, and a third group of women brought the Virgin of Guadalupe. All were decorated with green branches hung with crackers, cookies and little bananas. Many of the women, dressed in their best, wore high heels, which made walking on the cobblestones difficult. A priest came last, carrying an altarpiece of gold. Huecorio's people had been Catholic for over four centuries.

Almost everybody went to mass, confessed their sins and took part in the fiestas. Aurelio was an exception. He took no interest in the Corpus Christi procession. "That's for old people," he told Macario and Rosendo. "Old people are afraid of God. They've been bad all their life. So when they get old they have to go to church all the time so God will receive them. My grandmother, when she feels a little sick, right away she's praying." At church she would kneel, he knew, like many women, throughout the whole service.

This year, Rosendo had set off the fireworks. He told them it cost thirty-five pesos for a dozen skyrockets. He must have shot off nearly three hundred, he thought. When you figured up what it cost to pay for the fireworks, band, priest, street decorations and all the new clothes and food and drink at the fiesta, he guessed some families would be in debt for months. "Those rockets can drop and run at you and blow you up," Rosendo said. "In San Gregorio when I was a little boy, one rocket turned around and came back and hit a man in his stomach. Blew him apart."

Rosendo's broken nose came from a blow by Ladislao during a drunken fight. Rosendo, who was good-natured, bore his dead friend no grudge. He told Macario he had sold some canoes in Tzintzuntzan.

"When can I go with you to make a canoe?" Macario asked. "We'll go fifty-fifty if you like."

"Sometimes you make canoes right in the mountains where you get the logs. But I'm not doing that work now. I have to get a new license from the government." In truth, Rosendo had sold the axes and adzes he needed for hollowing and his other tools to make the gunwales, seats, squarish bow, oarlocks and stubby round-bladed oars. It had all gone to buy liquor. His wife kept him and their two children fed by selling fish and vegetables in the Pátzcuaro market, one in the long lines of Tarascan women who squatted with their baskets in front of them, crying out their wares and prices, *"Que va a llevar, marchante? What are you going to take with you, buyer?"*

"Well, well, they must know you around the islands if you used to sell canoes," Macario said.

"I don't know how I got to Huecorio after so many years on the lake," Rosendo replied. "Now there's too many fishermen and not enough fish. I was famous for making canoes until I started drinking too much. I've got an uncle in Tzintzuntzan." Macario knew the man.

"Tzintzuntzan has only two fishermen left," Macario went on. "Did you know Nacho died?"

"Poor Nacho. I used to work with him." Nacho had owned a canoe and nets and hired helpers, who shared in the catch.

"Nacho was twice married. His first wife died and he got married again to my cousin. She was fat."

Rosendo grinned. "And he was my half cousin." So they were distantly related, as Tarascans often were.

"Nacho used to work for an American." Macario held his nose and spoke in a funny nasal way. "You know how some Americans talk."

In the afternoon they helped Macario and his family load their canoe. As they paddled off, Rosendo told Aurelio, "When it's windy like this, the wind can take a canoe where it wants. You can't paddle fast enough." Church bells tolled in the lakeside villages and Aurelio could hear the faint sound of a band coming across the water. "A fiesta," he said.

"I ought to take some land like Macario and farm with the owner fifty-fifty," Rosendo said as they went along the lakeshore. "But I'd need a motor to pump water and they cost three million pesos." He asked why Aurelio didn't farm his grandmother's land up on San Miguel.

"It's dirty, it's hard farming on those stony slopes and sometimes you don't get nothing from it. You're killing yourself. I like being a waiter because you can stay clean. I can go back to work at the restaurant anytime I want. If I worked my grandma's land, who would give me money if I didn't get a crop? Would you?"

"I used to like to drink *mescal*," Rosendo said after they had walked some time in silence.

"That's strong stuff."

"*Pulque* makes you sick to your stomach. If I drink some *pulque* it's gonna make me worse. But that *caballito* will kill you." *Caballito*, "little horse," a deadly mixture of Coca-Cola and pure alcohol, was sold in a few shops in Pátzcuaro. Aurelio drank it until he got delirium tremens; he felt violent chills and nausea and it seemed like giant insects were crawling over his whole body, even into his eyes and ears, and he would start to shriek. The first few days at Las Trojes they put some alcohol in his tea. No doctors ever came. In Alcoholics Anonymous they looked after each other. *"Vivir para servir"*—"To live is to serve"—was their motto. Sometimes new arrivals were so shaky they had to be fed or given a bath or their clothes washed. A few at first ate like animals, clawing at food and stuffing it into their mouths like birds of prey. They ate simply, beans and tortillas. There was just one big hall, where they slept on the cement floor and sat and listened to each other talk for nine hours a day. They got up early, pouring buckets of cold water over their heads. Just a few of the men —there were perhaps eighty in all—worked in the camp's orchard and fields. It was like a prison, and sometimes men ran away. Aurelio had been there twice. The first time he went voluntarily, signed in by his mother; the second time his father took him after he had been jailed. Each time for three months. It was a great relief when you got out. Aurelio thought he would never want to leave Huecorio again.

It was among the pure Tarascans like Rosendo that the old folk beliefs—fear of eclipses, sorcery, evil winds and *Mal de Ojo*, the Evil Eye —were strongest, along with faith in healing herbs and the practice of *el robo*, ceremonial bride theft. Like Macario, Rosendo spoke of Malinche as if she were a real presence and not a distant historical figure. "I used to hear," he told Aurelio the next day, as they again wandered idly about Huecorio, "that when people went to gather wood, Malinche would scare them. She asked one man to take her to church, but not to look back. At the church door he turned around and looked for her. Malinche was gone. A few days later he died. She used to appear like an evil spirit."

Aurelio shrugged. "I don't believe in those things anyway." But his grandmother was a *curandera*, a medicine woman who healed with herbs and charms, but also dealt with magic candles, lucky oil, certain kinds of incense, benign, Rosendo knew, in her case, but also the tools of *brujería*, or witchcraft.

"There's a kind of ghost that comes on a horse. Another man saw him, not me. If you see him, the ghost will offer you money. You must say, 'The money God gives me is enough.' Then the man on the horse will vanish. One of my neighbors saw him about three years ago." Rosendo believed in *brujos*, or witches, and was convinced that they could take on the eyes of cats, put on wings of woven reeds and fly about looking for victims to suck their blood. He was also much closer to nature than Aurelio, a real *naturalito*, and was always the first to spot birds or wild game. Now, as he stooped to gather twigs to make a broom for his wife, he told Aurelio, "I don't have land. I ought to work for others like Macario."

"Why not go to the States?"

"I'm too lazy." In truth, Rosendo did not want to leave Lake Pátzcuaro, the only world he knew. Along the lake the two men came upon a pasture strewn with plastic bottles, beer cans, broken toys, old shoes, all kinds of trash. The debris entered the lake, along with sewage, from Pátzcuaro town, and in the rainy season, when the lake water overflowed, the waste washed up on the land. The pasture belonged to the estate of Doña Carolina, a rich widow in her eighties whose husband, a general in the revolution, was said to have taken land by force from Huecorio and never given it back. "He just took it," Rosendo said. "What could the people do? The son-in-law says no. What Doña Carolina thinks, nobody knows." Rosendo stared at the polluted fields. "Maybe that's why we're getting cholera." At the peak of the summer heat, thirty-six persons in Pátzcuaro came down with cholera and two of them, both elderly, died. Four were on Janitzio, the biggest island on the lake, which was popular with tourists. "When the cholera started, we tried to fight it," Rosendo said. "People from the islands went to see the governor in Morelia. They came with pills and injections of chloramphenicol."

"I didn't hear about it," Aurelio said.

"I didn't want anything. A doctor and nurse went from house to house. People in Huecorio drink spring water. They're safe." He waved to a group of Tarascans cutting tule reeds on a sandbar out in the water. "Go faster, men!" he called genially.

Near the village they stopped to talk to Agustín, a hardworking man who was able to get six of his eight children into college. He had just come back from Los Angeles, where he'd tried and failed for three months to find work. "It's saturated," he told them. Go north, he was telling everybody. Oregon. Washington, you could box apples and live more cheaply than in California. Even the Gulf of Alaska. He'd heard there was work to be found on salmon-fishing boats, though just in the summer. You could buy fake birth certificates, driver's licenses and social security cards in the flea market in Los Angeles for as little as $100.

The biggest danger was car accidents from the high speeds of American freeways. The bodies of so many young men got shipped home to be buried. "What about crime?" Rosendo asked. *Todo el tiempo,* all the time. But it's less a worry." "We got plenty of *ladrones* here," Aurelio said. "Between here and Lázaro Cárdenas they robbed a bus. They're stopping buses. They have guns and knives."

Agustín nodded. "Well, I tell my boys, 'Finish school and get a good job.' " There was no future in farming in the village. He had left his two acres up on San Miguel fallow. "There's not enough water and the earth is tired. It's been dry for four years. I no longer work that land. It's not worth it."

The 1990 census showed that of Huecorio's 687 people there were still about 150 farmers and 40 part-time peons, farm laborers. The rest worked as fishermen, carpenters, masons, day laborers, public employees, shopkeepers, bakers, midwives and vendors. When it came to education, 201 villagers had gone past the sixth grade but 104 hadn't finished primary school and 58 had never gone to school. One still met such children in the fields, usually boys whom nobody forced to go. Huecorio had produced three doctors, three lawyers, eight engineers and about thirty teachers, all in recent years. Those without any school were illiterate.

At any one time between a third and a fourth of Huecorio's people, mainly young men and women, were in the United States or Mexico City. Migration to California and Texas as field workers for five to six months each year began in 1943 with the *bracero* program initiated by the Americans during the farm labor shortage of World War II. That system lasted until the mid-1960s, when Congress, under pressure from organized labor, put a stop to it. Illegal migration took over. These days, if you wanted to go to *el norte*, it was a three-day, two-night bus trip from Huecorio to Tijuana. A round trip, counting fare and food, was about $300, the cheapest round-trip airfare from Guadalajara to Los Angeles in 1994 was $290.

Once in Tijuana in the old days, you took a bus east of town to Zapata Canyon, where most evenings a great crowd of Mexicans could be seen playing soccer, eating tacos and milling around, waiting for it to get dark. A mile or so to the north a few cars of the *migra*, U.S. Immigration agents, were usually parked. The border was a single strand of wire, trailing on the ground. Aurelio had once worked for a few months as a *coyote* or *pollero* (chicken carrier), who for a $300 *mordida* (bite) smuggled Mexicans across the border at night to confederates with cars who delivered them to their door in Los Angeles. "Once you got to L.A., you were free." He told Rosendo he only did it a few months. "If they caught a *pollero*, he could get five years in jail. While if the *ilegales* got picked up, the *migra* usually gave them a sandwich, orange, cookie and coffee and said, 'That's all we have to give you. Now go back.' And they'd put everybody on a bus to Tijuana." It was a daily routine.

During the three years, 1991 to 1994, Zapata Canyon, as barren as a moonscape on the American side, with houses and gardens crowded on the other, was gradually closed off by the erection of a fourteen-mile, ten-foot-high wall, which I recognized from my days in the Army Engineers in Korea as the kind of steel planking used to lay down combat airstrip runways. Already a rusted eyesore and either ridged and pierced and often with holes, it is easy to climb and one morning on a 1994 visit I saw several young Mexicans in sombreros clamber over, though chances of evading *la migra* are better at night. The most popular crossing point has shifted west of Tijuana toward the Pacific Ocean beach, where the new wall runs right into the surf. Every night hundreds cross, these days paying *coyotes* $50 just to be guided over, $2,000 for a ride into a guaranteed job in Los Angeles. On weekends Mexican sociologists are also running about, getting the migrants' data on a three-minute questionnaire and in the middle of this spectacle is the official Tijuana border crossing itself, the world's busiest, where 65 million Mexicans and Americans go back and forth each year in such crowds you rarely have to show a passport either way.

For the *ilegales*, it is a nightly cat-and-mouse game as border patrolmen roar about on motorcycles, armed with traps, radios and infrared scopes, while the Mexicans sneak through the underbrush and along riverbanks, sending out decoys and whistling and chirping to one another.

Aurelio himself had made three trips to Los Angeles. In the 1970s, sharing a $250 one-bedroom apartment with four others in the San Fernando Valley, he saved $3,000 in a year and bought a used Chevy for $940. "If you stayed in Los Angeles twenty years you'd have your own house and car. A man and woman these days can live on $200 a week. They can live on one salary and save the other. Once you come to live in Huecorio you have nothing."

Almost everybody in Huecorio had been in the United States at some time or other. A few were bitter about abuses and bribes, and those who crossed illegally into Texas told about getting knocked around by the redneck Texas Rangers, *muy mal*. Most were like Fidel, fifty, a father of nine and a veteran of eight trips as far north as Illinois, Wisconsin and Montana, who said, "I liked everything about *el norte*. Nobody treated me badly. And I said goodbye to ignorance. Best of all, you could find work." In 1994 a field worker in Huecorio was getting $10 to $15 a day, with lunch. One of Agustín's sons in Los Angeles, who helped install neon lights, got $7 an hour; another, who worked for a company that supplied shrubs and trees for Hollywood movies, made $12 an hour. Those who still worked as field hands or fruit pickers left Huecorio in the spring and came home in time for the winter fiesta season. Most felt that an eight- or ten-hour day of hard physical labor could be justified for five or six months, to save money for land, a house or whatever, back in the village. Once in Huecorio many preferred to work less and have less. As Rosendo would say, "Here we work hard three or four hours and then we rest." The great incentive was to work for food, shelter, clothing, the children's school expenses and to fulfill religious obligations.

Nothing is going to stem this tide of migration except a rise in Mexican wages from industry, which is coming with remarkable speed. The extended village networks that supply new arrivals with jobs and housing have become too large.

Wherever they are, Huecorio's people still live out their lives in relation to their families and the village. Huecorio is where they were born, baptized, confirmed and married and where they want to be buried beside their ancestors. On November 2, Mexico's Day of the Dead, families put flowers and crosses on their ancestors' graves, a yearly ceremony one also finds in East Asian society, an eerie link with the distant biological past. The villagers find satisfaction in fulfilling obligations to friends, relatives, *compadres*, and to the Virgin and the saints and enjoy seeing expectations met in consequence. Huecorio, like any Mexican village, is a place of small pleasures— listening to birds, tending potted plants on the patio, going to fiestas, breathing pure country air. There is also a good deal of despair and hopelessness, hostility and fear. But as George Foster once observed, "No village event is too minor to be a subject of interest, no personal tragedy so great but that it contains elements of humor, no community catastrophe so final but life will go on." Huecorio is where its people find the standing and dignity, safety and tranquillity they do not get in America. Materially, life is getting better all the time. In 1994 all of its 130 houses but one were still made of adobe and all but two had cement floors; 108 had running, supposedly potable, water, 56 a drainage and sewage system, 129 electricity (everybody had TV sets, videos and radios) and almost all were owned by the people who lived in them. An oddity was few refrigerators. Mexicans cling to the custom of buying fresh meat and vegetables daily. Most families don't have much money, or maybe it's because a village market is still the best place to meet and gossip.

When Aurelio and Rosendo got to the threshing ground, Macario and his family were winnowing. He and his two sons tossed grain into the air as his wife, Eréndira, named after an ancient Tarascan princess, swept away straw on the hard-beaten earth with a hand broom of twigs. Stout, dressed in an apron and *rebozo*, or shawl, a cloth protecting her hair from the dust, Eréndira looked pink-cheeked and as good-natured as her husband.

"The wind is good if it blows steadily from one direction," Macario told them cheerily as Aurelio and Rosendo took their seats on the bank. "There are too many trees here. They get in the way of the wind and make it go in circles. You know it is a great problem to cut down a tree. You have to get permission."

Macario seemed a little less ebullient today, the grueling work taking its toll. "We've been up since six for milking," he told them. "If we get up later, how can we have breakfast? I took only one sack yesterday, one thirty-kilo sack. It's more straw than wheat. I think the birds ate a lot." He yawned. "When I go fishing sometimes I'll go three days without sleeping. Just catch naps in the canoe." A horse had broken loose from his rope and Macario hurried to catch him and lead him back and tie him to a nearby tree again, as one son sifted grain in the air. "They need some water for these fields," Macario went on, when he got back to winnowing. "Some sort of irrigation."

"How would they get the water up here?" Aurelio wanted to know. "You'd need canals and a pump."

"Pumps are prohibited because the water in the lake is so low," Rosendo said. "It's been getting lower and lower for eight years now."

"Maybe it's volcanic activity," Macario speculated. Parícutin was not far from Lake Pátzcuaro. This young volcano burst forth from a cornfield one day in 1943 and kept growing and spewing forth lava for the next ten years, burying the town of San Juan Parangaricutiro and the village of Parícutin, whence its name. All the inhabitants of both escaped safely.

"Yes," said Rosendo, staring at the ground as if he could see into it, "it's bubbling beneath us all the time."

In late afternoon Macario's landowner came to inspect her harvest. Doña Josefina was a frail, bent old woman with a long face, very white hair and dangling gold earrings. Even in her worn and soiled old dress, shawl and apron, all a faded pink, she had a gracious manner. She came on the arm of a skinny teenage niece known in the village for her ill humor and haughty airs. Sure enough, as soon as they reached the threshing ground, the girl scoffed to Macario, "This is not good work." Her aunt told her to hush.

"We badly need rain when it's this dry," Macario told the old woman. "Everybody waits for rain to plant their corn. But there is no rain." After they arranged for Macario to bring their share of the wheat to the house and agreed he should prepare the land for corn, as he had been doing for years, Doña Josefina and her niece went away. Aurelio grinned and told Macario, "If there's people, there's bound to be trouble." Idling their days away and watching others work, as he and Rosendo did, was not so uncommon in villages. Huecorio was their world, everything its people did was of interest to them, its gossip and jokes their chief entertainment, "what will the neighbors say" a more potent force than fear of God or government fiat. The sense that day after day not much was going to happen gave them a comfortable feeling of changelessness and security.

Macario, who was almost done winnowing, sent the boys to water the horses and laughed that they were so stout. "When their mother was bringing them into the world, she drank too much beer," he said.

Change, when it does come to villages, comes from outside, from cities. In Mexico during 1988–92, sweeping reforms, largely engineered by Harvard-educated President Salinas, began to transform villages like Huecorio. Salinas, a former budget minister, showed a brilliant understanding of Mexico's economy and debt crisis and, unlike previous presidents, did not go in for mere populist gestures. By renegotiating Mexico's foreign debt, privatizing hundreds of state-owned companies and balancing the budget, Salinas and his team of bright new technocrats won the confidence of investors. Despite the Mayan Indian insurgency in Chiapas and a groundswell of demands for reform from peasant farmers and out-of-work laborers all over Mexico, Salinas, as the architect of NAFTA, set Mexico firmly on the road to modernization.

Trade liberalization was already well underway, with over 2,300 *maquiladora* assembly plants along the border, based on duty-free imports of components into Mexico, and growing interdependence, with Mexico supplying oil and winter produce and America corn, animal feed and jobs, and manufactures flowing both ways. Though the United States canceled tariffs on 60 percent of its imports from Mexico in 1994, other tariffs, such as corn imports into Mexico, which could drastically affect the corn-growing village peasantry, especially subsistence cultivators like the poorest Mayas in Chiapas, will not go into effect until 2008. NAFTA was expected to have winners and losers. In Mexico wages should rise, but so should productivity, as well as standards of environmental protection and safety in the workplace. Pulling off the corn tariff, even in fifteen years, will be a big gamble.

The real case for NAFTA, as set down by *The Economist:*

> Market economies work well because they constantly move resources from relatively unproductive uses to relatively productive ones. By broadening the scale of the market and increasing the pressure of competition, this powerfully enriching process of destruction and renewal can be made to work better . . . Free trade and free markets have the same virtues (they make countries better off) and the same drawbacks (people must adapt to change); they are, in fact, intimately connected and mutually reinforcing. The United States is the world's most successful economy precisely because change—mobility across space, social class and economic activity—has been greater there than anywhere else. Resist change, and the economy starts to lag.

Salinas's most fundamental reform, in terms of villages like Huecorio, was in the land tenure or *ejido* system. Mexico's land problem, like its cultural duality, is rooted in the Spaniard-Indian clash. American anthropologist Eric R. Wolf described this in *Peasant Wars of the Twentieth Century:*

> All these problems derived ultimately from the original encounter of an Indian population with a band of conquerors who had taken possession of Middle America in the name of the Spanish crown. To make use of Indian labor, the Spaniards introduced a system of large estates, *haciendas.*

The myth of the Mexican revolution was that it rid Mexico of a feudal order and established a regime based on Emiliano Zapata's cry of "Land and Liberty!" In a 1918 manifesto, Zapata declared:

> Where is the revolution going? What do the sons of the people arisen in arms propose for themselves? . . . To redeem the indigenous race, giving back its land and by that its liberty; to have the laborer in the fields, the present slave of the *hacienda*, converted into a man free and in control of his destiny through small property. . . .

In fact, the chaos of 1910–20 went through three distinct phases. First, liberal revolutionaries overthrew Porfirio Díaz, who after 1876 made Mexico a land of prosperity ruled in the interests of a few. Second, reactionaries, backed by the Catholic Church, many businessmen, big landowners and American investors, tried to restore the old order. Third, peasant rebellions broke out in north and south, crushed by a group of army generals who restored order. Zapata himself was ambushed and killed in 1919.

Out of this came *ejido* or common land, which was expropriated from big, usually Spanish-owned estates and given to Indian and mestizo villages. Communal ownership of land went back to the Aztecs, Tarascans, Mayas and other Indians, whereas the Spaniards evolved a system of debt peonage. By 1940, 16 million hectares of farmland had been redistributed. Property could be handed down from father to son and stay within a family, but could not be rented, sold or left fallow. The land was owned by the government and a bank set up to supply capital for reclamation, seeds and inputs.

The *ejido* tenure system was meant to remedy past social injustice and increase farm production. In practice it never worked very well. For Mexico is a land of spectacular mountain ranges with only a few rivers, and only 35 million of its 196.7 million hectares are deemed arable, with just 18–20 million actually farmed in 1994. Less than 5 million hectares, mostly in the far north, are irrigated. The badly eroded rain forests of the far south, about 15 percent of the country's land, get 85 percent of Mexico's rain. Even so, the Chiapas Mayas voiced anger that Salinas amended the constitution so as to stop land distribution and allow *ejidatarios*, the communal landholders, to sell their plots. Many had always been landless in a region of large estates, though some had lost ancestral land the last several decades to cattle barons. New state and federal laws to confiscate the largest landholdings and divide them were part of a March 1994 accord between the Salinas government and the peasant rebels in Chiapas.

Most villagers live on the high central plateau, 40 percent of the land, which suffers from a harsh and unpredictable climate with floods, drought and frost. There are about 2.8 million small farms, but a third are too tiny, too dry or too poor to get bank credit. About 80 percent are just two or three hectares, barely enough to grow corn and beans to feed a family. These villages, like Huecorio and Tzintzuntzan, survive through migration to the United States.

Mexico does have 600,000 modern commercial farms, which produce about 70 percent of the agricultural output. These are mainly in the fertile, irrigated coastal plain states of Sonora and Sinaloa just south of California. A legal landownership ceiling of 100 hectares was set in 1915, before big dam and irrigation projects got underway in 1925. Settlers pretty much started from scratch. There wasn't the land-to-the-tiller issue of central Mexico with its big *haciendas* and peonage.

Norman Borlaug, who first went to Mexico in 1944, offered his view on the *ejido* system to me in 1987:

> Mexico has continued to beat the drums of the 1910–20 revolution, when the message was "land to those who work it." An *ejido* holding is one to three hectares. Up in Sonora a farm is a minimum of ten to twenty hectares and some go up to a hundred-plus. Mexico's philosophy the past fifteen to twenty years should have been to get people off the land and into decentralized industry. But most industry has gone into three cities: Mexico City, Guadalajara and Monterrey. The politicians are still beating the drums to divide up the land still more. I've heard it five times from five presidents.

What Salinas did was to break with the populist past and push through a constitutional amendment to give 2.6 million farmers title to their *ejidos* and allow them to sell or rent to others, including foreigners. Salinas argued that *ejidos* had not fulfilled their promise. Production per hectare of corn in Mexico, for example, was just 1.72 tons in 1990 compared with 7.44 tons in the United States. In 1945–65, Mexico's wheat output rose eightfold, corn two and a half times and beans twofold, then stopped as population kept growing. Villages like Huecorio too often had sloped, stony, eroded land, no irrigation, no transportation, no fertilizer, no extension, late and low prices to farmers. "Mexico was back where it started," says Borlaug. "Many small landowners produce almost no surplus. Some can't even feed their families. But they love their land."

Villagers still voice loyalty to the old *ejido* system, so deeply ingrained in the popular mythology. Even so, Aurelio's grandmother lost no time in selling land to enable her to repair a leaky roof, and as Agustín said, he was leaving his poorest land up on the volcano slopes fallow. Toribio Medina Salazar, sixty-seven, a farmer in Anenecuilco, Zapata's birthplace, told an interviewer:

> Times have been tough. We barely break even and sometimes we lost money. But where would we be without land? I would never sell. Zapata fought for it, our fathers fought for it.

With 92 million people and a good deal less than an arable acre per head, the time is long past when Mexico could survive on agriculture. As mentioned, in terms of city dwellers, their incomes and growth rates, Mexico is fast becoming a nonrural society already and now has all the conditions for a sudden, steep dropoff in human fertility. Jorge A. Bustamante of the Colegio de la Frontera Norte in Tijuana, perhaps the preeminent authority on Mexican migration to the United States, told me in 1994 that over half of the migrants, legal and illegal, were now coming from cities. More than 90 percent of farm labor in California, which produces a third of America's agricultural output, is Mexican, though it is increasingly Indian, sometimes not even Spanish-speaking, as better-educated mestizos head for city jobs with Social Security and other benefits.

The danger in Mexico itself is not a return to the great feudal *haciendas*, but the same trend to ever bigger and fewer family farms such as has led to such a drastic decline in rural America. Mexico's exodus from village to city is likely to be hastened by the reform of *ejido* land and, as trade with the United States is liberalized, by ending a price support to growers of corn, Mexico's most important agricultural crop and the mainstay of its poorest villagers, of 70 percent above the world price. When this protection ends, as mentioned, in 2008, and Mexico is flooded with American corn, its economy will need to be modernized enough to provide vast numbers of displaced peasants with jobs. This may happen. But expectations are high. For instance, many of the Mayan Indian rebels in Chiapas spoke no Spanish but only one of four ancient dialects. Yet Point 11 of the failed March 1994 agreement between the rebels and Salinas government called not just for electricity, roads, potable water and such, but also "the advantages of the city like television, stoves, refrigerators, washing machines, etc." This among people whose conditions have not changed much in four or five hundred years.

In the short term the exodus of Mexican villagers to the cities or to *el norte* is bound to grow. Greater parity in wages is the only eventual solution to illegal migration from Mexico to the United States and this will take time. But I would argue, contrary to popular opinion, that this migration is both biologically and culturally a good thing for American society. Professor McNeill reminds us that "reproduction, both biological and cultural, is not automatic and unchanging." He observes: "When any notable alteration in rates of growth or decay occur, the group concerned creates critical problems for itself, and often, for its neighbors as well." The impact of Mexico's population explosion, from 20 million in 1920 to 92 million in 1994, is a good example.

It also exemplifies, if more subtly, what Professor McNeill calls "the age-old pattern of demographic circulation between town and city, rich and poor, upon which civilized society has depended since the third millenium B.C." If we take the last twenty years, we see Mexico, not long ago a peasant society, growing, and America, in terms of its aging, urbanized population of European descent, decaying and shrinking. New recruits for the American cities of tomorrow, to fill jobs and pay taxes, must come from somewhere. Earlier this century they would have come from the farms and small towns of rural America. This source has dried up and now they are largely peasants or ex-peasants from rural Mexico. Because Mexicans keep such close ties with their native villages, it injects their traditions into our cultural mainstream too.

Earlier I blamed Mexico's runaway birth rate on Catholic opposition to contraception, or on Mexican macho, or ostentatiously virile, pride in being the father of a large family. There was also a more generalized macho feeling among Mexicans that national greatness was in part greatness in numbers and that to frustrate births was to fall in with *gringo* plots to curb Mexico's destiny. History, says Professor McNeill, puts it much more simply: given enough time, villages grow, cities decline and it has always been this way unless cities recruit villagers to fill their depleting ranks. It is quite possible that Mexico, too, once it becomes sufficiently urbanized, will experience population decline. We cannot say with any exactitude when this might happen in Mexico, but when white Americans stopped replacing themselves in 1972, that is, when their annual fertility rate fell below 2.1 replacement level, the population of the United States was just over 200 million, it was 74 percent urban and per capita GNP was below $7,000, less than a third of what it is now. American Latinos, blacks and Asians are all still above 2.1—whites were 1.9 in 1994— though the Population Reference Bureau says their growth rates, too, are starting to fall. Mexico may not be so far behind. As McNeill says, "I think it's quite conceivable that fifty years from now the problem of the world will be a failure of reproduction."

In any society there is also a constant cultural flow back and forth from village and city, in Huecorio's case with Mexico City and Los Angeles. Even in the 1940s George Foster found Tzintzuntzan's local culture continually replenished by scientific and intellectual thought from the cities. Robert Redfield in his *Peasant Society and Culture*, a remarkably short and concise book originally published in 1956 but still probably the best introduction to village life, realized the villagers were affected by "teachers and exemplars who never saw that village, who did their work in intellectual circles perhaps far away in time and space." Redfield:

> When George Foster looked at Latin American villages with civilization in mind, he saw chiefly what had come into these villages from preindustrial Europe: irrigation wheels, elements of the Catholic religion from "theological and philosophical reflections of many of the best minds of history over a period of centuries," church organization, religious dramas, political institutions, godparenthood, the humoral pathology of Hippocrates and Galen, and dances and bullfights that had worked their way downward from Spanish gentry to little Indian-mestizo farmers in Mexico and Peru.

This was the genesis of Redfield's famous theory that in any culture there is "a great tradition of the reflective few" and "a little tradition of the largely unreflective many," helpful in seeing the distinction between urban literati like philosophers, theologians and scientists, and ordinary peasant villagers. Professor Foster, who lives in Berkeley, is himself best known for his theory of "limited good," the idea that in villages all good things in life are limited, so one person's success is at the expense of others, as well as for his work in Latino social institutions and medical anthropology. Foster's *Empire's Children: The People of Tzintzuntzan*, published by the Smithsonian in just a thousand copies in 1948, is, I think, the best portrait yet done about Mexican village life although it is entirely descriptive and does not grapple, as Foster's later work does, with the brooding, mysterious side of Mexican character. Octavio Paz:

> Man is alone everywhere. But the solitude of the Mexican, under the great stone night of the high plateau that is still inhabited by insatiable gods, is very different from that of the North American, who wanders in an abstract world of machines, fellow citizens and moral precepts.

With a tenth of Americans now Hispanic, most of them Mexican, mutual comprehension is getting critically important. We're not the only ones. The Europeans need to know more about Muslims, as they come to depend upon Turkish, Algerian, Tunisian, Moroccan, and Persian workers, the Russians upon Central Asians. Is there a strange, dark side to Mexicans, perhaps going back to their pre-Columbian past?

On a visit to the California-Mexico border region in 1994 I found widespread concern on both sides that anti-Mexican xenophobia was on the rise among white Americans. Dr. Bustamante was worried that after California Governor Pete Wilson blamed Mexican immigrants for everything from the state's budget crisis, tax burdens and hospital and school costs, to drug traffic and unemployment, and proposed denying government benefits to undocumented immigrants, his popularity doubled in the polls. Wilson, a Republican, sought reelection in fall 1994, but California's two Democratic Senators scrambled to get on the anti-Mexican bandwagon, Dianne Feinstein proposing a $1 border toll to pay for more border patrolmen, the supposedly liberal Barbara Boxer saying National Guard should be deployed along the porous border. (It's pretty plain on the scene that you could put Marines shoulder to shoulder the whole 1,950 miles and still lose the battle against illegal migration when 65 million people crossed both directions *legally* in 1993 at Tijuana alone.)

Some blame anti-Mexican fears on the media. Carlos Cortés, a historian at the University of California in Riverside and a direct descendant of Mexico's conqueror, has traced Hollywood's treatment of Mexicans since the first "greaser" silent film in 1908 and finds a history of portraying Mexico as "a land of chaos and menace." The classic American stereotype of a Mexican, argues Professor Cortés, is Gold Tooth in John Huston's memorable 1947 film, *The Treasure of the Sierra Madre*, "a sadistic Mexican bandit who machetes Humphrey Bogart to death and then scatters Bogart's bags of gold dust, stupidly mistaking it for sand." Cortés says Hollywood's current three basic themes on Mexico are: Anglo superiority, a "nearly pathological" Latin America "whose decadence and subhumanity pose a threat to Anglos who stumble into the south-of-the-border Hades" and the "rise of the Latino menace in the United States."

Should we fear Mexicans? Anthropologist Lola Romanucci-Ross of the University of California at San Diego feels both Redfield and Lewis were right: "Mexican expectations are so low that when the worst doesn't happen, there is cause for glee. You get both suffering and joy." Even so, after three years in a Mexico village in the 1950s she was glad to go. "The day we left I looked at my husband and said, 'Let's get the hell out of here.' You never know what the rules are. You're playing a game in a dark room. Mexico is scary."

Everybody close to the border seems to agree that migration needs to be decriminalized and regulated by treaty as it was during the *bracero* program initiated after farm labor shortages in World War II and continued until the mid-1960s. Otherwise, with politicians ready to win votes by playing upon anti-Mexican xenophobia, you risk stirring up sociopaths like Kenneth Kovzelov, a seventeen-year-old ex-skinhead taking paratroop training in San Diego in 1988, who went out and shot dead two perfectly legal Mexican farm workers on a back road in San Diego county; the judge, who gave him fifty years, called the killings "crimes of racial hatred."

Latino youth gangs in America are not more exempt than blacks from the ghetto culture of defiance, and such gangs have appeared in recent years in such unlikely agricultural centers as Topeka, Kansas, and Fargo, North Dakota. But Mexicans often succeed in re-creating their native village in a suburban *barrio* of fellow migrants from home, which means many rural ways and views are simply carried into the new setting. Cultural pluralism raises some unease; foreign-born immigrants now make up almost one out of every four California residents. Even advocates of multiculturalism such as Professor Cortés agree it is essential everyone learn English: "Education of migrant children is critical to bring them into the mainstream of opportunity." Indeed, surveys show Mexicans, Puerto Ricans and Cubans do not like to be lumped together as "Hispanics" or "Latinos" but prefer simply to be called Americans. It is also heartening to discover the pride Hispanics have in America—91 percent said in one poll they were "extremely" or "very" proud of the United States.

David Hays-Bautista at the University of California at Los Angeles has calculated that by 2030 the population of California will be 40 percent Hispanic, twice what it was in 1980. He foresees Latins being much younger and with less schooling and lower-paying jobs but paying taxes to support the aging Anglo population. Already in our greater metropolitan areas, as the Census Bureau lumps cities, suburbs and sprawl, 33 percent of 14.5 million people in Los Angeles in 1993 were Hispanic, also 33 percent of 3.2 million in Miami. Other cities: Houston, 21 percent of 3.7 million; San Francisco, 15.5 percent of 6.2 million; New York, 15 percent of 18 million; Dallas, 13 percent of 3.8 million; Chicago, 11 percent of 8 million; Washington, 5.7 percent of 4 million; Boston, 4.6 percent of 4 million; Philadelphia, 3.8 percent of 6 million; Detroit, 1.9 percent of 4.6 million.

An incentive to assimilate is provided by the way new arrivals, especially *ilegales*, are overcharged by slum landlords, overrun by neighborhood gangs who see them as easy prey since their fear of deportation keeps them from going to the police, or simply underpaid. Undocumented workers, from field hands in Oregon to garment factory workers in New York City, have been found to get less than half the $4.25 minimum wage.

We really have no choice. Any rich, urban society that is not to drift toward biological and cultural extinction, its aging, shrinking population growing poorer in the process, has to replenish its ranks with workers from poor peasant societies, subtly changing its own culture in the process. Most Mexican immigrants, legal or illegal, seem to be optimistic, hardworking, adaptable and pleased to be in the Estados Unidos, all our fears of our perpetually mysterious and frequently turbulent neighbor to the south notwithstanding. As a visiting Englishman marveled:

> They are the latest (and yet the oldest) testimony to what in European eyes has always been the most perplexing American achievement: the ability to welcome people from all over the world and make them Americans. *Que le vaya bien.*

Yet practically every Mexican in America has ties to a Huecorio somewhere, a place that Rosendo and Macario, the two pure-blooded Tarascan Indians, though very poor, chose never to leave, and Aurelio, after years in Los Angeles, felt compelled to come back to. This sense of an ancestral village to which one can always return and be renewed continues to be an altogether new aspect of the American immigrant experience.

VI

Have You Seen the Edge of the Sky? Africa's Special Farming Problems

CAST OF CHARACTERS

KAANI AND OTHER VILLAGES, MACHAKOS HILLS, KENYA

MONICA MUTULI, 29, village health worker
MZEE SILA, 88, Kamba tribal elder
MZEE KIBITI, 80s, Kamba tribal elder
JAMES ZACHARIAH NZOKA, 38, headmaster

THE SAHEL AND GHANA

NORMAN E. BORLAUG, plant breeder
JIMMY CARTER, former President
RYOICHI SASAKAWA, Japanese philanthropist
World Bank officials

THE SKY LOOKS BIGGER, the earth rawer, in Africa. As there was when we walked the Machakos Hills in Kenya, a mile high in the sky and not far from the Great Rift Valley where human life began, there is a great sense of empty, limitless space. It was 1981 and our days were spent on high windy ridges, making our way along worn, rocky red paths from *shamba* to *shamba*, for Monica Mutuli was a rural health worker and let me accompany her on her rounds of these small village farms.

Karen Blixen put this sense of space just right in *Out of Africa*. "Looking back on a sojourn in the African highlands, you are struck by your feelings of having lived for a time in the air." Africans, as they do for so many of us, aroused the admiration of Blixen, a Danish baroness. Her book had a classic portrayal of her faithful Kikuyu servant, Kamante: "His fortitude of soul in the face of pain was the fortitude of an old warrior."

Well, circumstances change. In Truman Capote's 1981 book, *Music for Chameleons*, we find Blixen, now a celebrated world literary figure under her pseudonym Isak Dinesen, having a cozy chat with Capote. "Ah, how fascinating she was," he recalled, "sitting by the fire in her beautiful house in a Danish seaside village, chain-smoking black cigarettes with silver tips, cooling her lively tongue with draughts of champagne, and luring one from this topic to that."

And Kamante? After Blixen sold her farm, left Africa in 1931 and never went back, he and her other Kikuyu were kicked off as squatters from the land. Today Isak Dinesen is long dead, her story in Africa familiar to millions from the Meryl Streep–Robert Redford movie with its stunning photography of the Kenyan landscape. When I was in Nairobi those years ago I was astonished to learn that Kamante lived on, frail, white-haired, stooped, and very old, with an ailing wife and a blind son in mud-hut poverty just outside Nairobi.

"What will happen to them if I should die?" he asked anxiously. "They are both disabled. Who can look after the other?" One wondered, seeing rather more pain than fortitude in the old man's eyes, why, from her beautiful house on the sea, the great authoress failed to look after what happened to *him*.

Our moral could be that too romantic a view of Africans may be fundamentally insensitive by blunting our ability to see their predicament as it really is. There is something psychologically fragile, angst-ridden, in the way we look at Africans even today. To some they still seem, in Joseph Conrad's words, "savage and superb, wild-eyed and magnificent." But behind the pride, the liveliness, there are those vast empty grasslands, wretched villages, malnourished children, diseases and fearful superstitions.

Africa is in deep trouble, aside from the disintegration of Rwanda into chaos and agony and such man-made famines as those in Somalia, Ethiopia and Mozambique, and the worsening ravages of AIDS, what Africans call "slim disease." Africa is the last place on earth where the population growth rate shows few signs of slowing. Instead, the rate is going up, from 2.5 percent in the early 1970s to 3 percent in 1994. Everywhere else, the output of food has continued to grow faster than population, in East Asia, a good deal faster. In Africa average annual growth in farm production was 2.3 percent in the 1960s; it fell to 1 percent in the 1990s. In seventeen of Africa's richest countries—in increasing order of income, Mali, Burkina Faso, Chad, Malawi, Zaire, Niger, Tanzania, Madagascar, Kenya, Cameroon, Sudan, Nigeria, Senegal, Zambia, Zimbabwe, Ghana and the Ivory Coast—there has been a drop in real average income from $437 a year to $334, or roughly by a fourth. Just as in part of the Muslim world, except for South Africa with its momentous 1994 election, people are getting poorer, hungrier and more desperate.

What, given its great natural potential, is going wrong in Africa?

Aside from Kenya's Machakos Hills, where I was based some weeks in the community of Kaani, in 1975 I spent six weeks in a very remote village, Neetil, in the Nuba Mountains of Sudan, and in 1977, more briefly, with the Dinkas of Sudan's great Sudd swamp. During the great drought of 1983–84, I also visited famine-struck villages in Senegal, Mali and Mauritania, and in 1993, rural Ghana and Benin. One of Africa's most fascinating characteristics is the way its varied geography preserves so many different stages of man's agricultural advance. The Sudd, a 40,000-square-mile swamp, is so fly-, mosquito-

and crocodile-plagued, so malaria-infested and wet, remote and marshy, something close to Neolithic cattle herding is carried on by its Dinka, Nuer and Shilluk tribes. Whereas the nomadic Moors and Tuaregs of Mauritania and Mali, with their camel caravans, slaves and hidden faces, are straight out of the *Arabian Nights.* Drought, the southward creep of the Sahara and the "holy war" waged by Khartoum's Islamic fanatics against the Nubas, Dinkas and others now threaten all these long-enduring ways of life.

In Machakos the villages are comparatively modern. The countryside, known as the Ukambani, the land of the Kamba tribe, is dry and hilly. There is the starved greenery, red soil and hot dusty smell so common in sub-Saharan Africa, with its hint of smoke from the thatched huts. Clouds drift across a sky that looks too big and blue to be real. At 5,000 to 7,000 feet—Monica Mutuli and I climbed up and down the hills all day going from village to village—the air was bracing. Kenya's great attraction, aside from its wildlife, is its climate. Hills, range after range of them, slope down to far-off plains, the burning desert of the Great Rift Valley, a weakness in the earth's crust broken by live volcanoes, where the earliest evidence of human life has been found. As you walk, on an exceptionally clear day as after a rain, you can see—so faint it seems part of the clouds—the sight Hemingway left so indelibly on our imaginations:

. . . there, ahead, all he could see, as wide as the world, great, high and unbelievably white in the sun, was the square top of Kilimanjaro. And then he knew that there was where he was going.

This is the country that inspired what perhaps is Hemingway's finest story; its ending captures the primordial fear Africa's strange, throbbing life can instill:

Outside the tent the hyena made the same strange noise that had awakened her. But she did not hear him for the beating of her heart.

Corn is Africa's main food crop. In Machakos, as across the continent, the twentieth century has seen a steady migration of people from the plains into the highlands wherever it is cold enough or rainy enough to grow corn, which has replaced millet, sorghum, beef and wild game as Africa's new staple diet. In Kenya, for example, 86 percent of its 27 million people are crowded onto the highest and wettest 17 percent of the land.

In Kaani village, the sun-dried corn husks, in fields edged with cactus, sisal or eucalyptus which needed little water, crackled in the ceaseless wind. Half the *shambas,* or small farms, had less than two acres of cultivated land; only half of the marginal virgin soil in Machakos had ever been tilled. A saving grace in Africa is that it is one of the few places left on earth with plenty of land. Sparse acacia and flat-foliaged thorn trees gave little shade from the powerful sun; the equator was less than a hundred miles to the north.

I grew burnt and dusty, but Monica, who made a splendid interpreter and guide, showed up each day immaculate in a freshly laundered dress, quite elegant; one I remember was brown silk with a floral pattern. I remember because on the third day I discovered she had only two dresses and rose every morning at five to bathe and wash one, using just a single basin of water, which was scarce in Machakos. And as with Sudan's Nubas and Dinkas, I soon learned again that in Africa you are forever walking, ten, twelve miles a day.

You soon recognized those farmsteads headed by single women—many of the huts tumbledown, blighted, with flaking walls and soggy thatch. Swarms of children would come to meet us and crowd about, some with shrunken limbs and protuberant bellies, their noses running, all scabs and sores, flies nestling in the corners of their eyes. Monica would stop, wipe the noses and shoo away the flies. Soon she would have the children singing noisily and happily, "If you're great and you know it, clap your hands!" Even the dustiest, most ragged little child would speak properly accented English, which was the language of the primary school.

Monica was a lovely woman, serene, gentle, yet talkative in the open, good-humored manner of Africans. In the weeks I spent going around the villages with her, she seemed at home with everyone we met, smiling and laughing easily. It was only in repose, if you caught her off guard, that her face was the very picture of human sorrow, and with reason.

She was a widow at twenty-nine. As I soon learned, a few years earlier, her husband, who earned a good wage as a salesman with a foreign company, so they could live modestly but comfortably in Nairobi, was killed in a car crash. As a Kamba, she fell under tribal law, which ruled that her children were now the property of her husband's oldest brother. A few decades earlier, he would have had rights over her too. If Monica remarried, she would lose her five children entirely. After the accident she went to their bank in Nairobi to ask about her husband's insurance. She hoped to use it to educate her children. She was told it had been paid already to the brother-in-law, with the bank manager's consent. He spent the money on land. This was too much for Monica. She broke down completely and, leaving the children with the brother-in-law's wife, she spent three months in a mental hospital in Nairobi. She had a vague memory, she once told me, of running screaming through long empty hallways.

She recovered and took a job as a clerk in a Nairobi department store. It took all her small wage to survive in one of the city's slums. So she went back to Machakos, where at least she could be with her children in the village. Eventually, after I had gone, she was able to join UNICEF as a village worker, and we have exchanged letters over the years. Perhaps her experience explained why Monica had so much empathy with village women we met. I remember what my mother once said about going hungry when my father was hospitalized during the Depression. "Nobody realized I had no money. I've always thought that was one of the best things that ever happened to me. Absolutely no money." Monica had that same empathy with poor people.

Her village headman chose her when the government asked him to send someone to be trained as a village health worker. "I was confused," Monica told me. "I asked myself, 'What could *I* do?' I thought, 'Maybe it is God's plan.' " She said her two months' training was good. When she began work, her mother asked her how she managed. "She said, 'How can you talk with all the people when you are so shy?' But me, I told her, 'I'm not afraid of men.' "

Often we joined a group of women working in the fields, perhaps threshing a mass of beanstalks with poles. Beneath the gossip and laughter there was a rustling sound as the beans popped out of the beaten stalks onto the hard earth. Some of the women might be winnowing beans; if the wind dropped, they would curse and wait, their wicker baskets poised to catch the breeze when it came back again.

I asked why they worked in groups. "We like to. It gives us strength," I was told. The ethic of mutual help is extremely strong in Kenya, as in all rural Africa, one of the happiest legacies of the tribal past. Jomo Kenyatta called it *harambee*, or pulling together. Villagers in Machakos found it natural to build their own schools, dams and roads. If villagers in Kenya wanted a school, they built it, then asked the government to find a teacher.

Usually word was sent ahead that we were coming, and when we got to a village a group of women would have gathered, probably seated on the grass under a shade tree in the schoolyard. Like Monica, the women looked well dressed, in brightly colored cottons and head scarves of orange, red, yellow, purple, green. Some carried babies in slings on their backs, and parasols to protect them from the equatorial sun. Kenyan village women, like Monica, were extremely clean, forever bathing and washing their clothes.

Monica took the roll call—Elizabeth, Agnes, Marcella, Agatha—I guessed it was a Catholic village. Mary was at home with malaria and Millika sick with backache. "Tell her not to carry so much water," Monica told them. "Let her husband do it." Everybody laughed. *That* would be the day. A woman reported that sixteen of the village's thirty-nine houses had installed new *choos*, or latrines, based on Monica's instructions; each took 112 mud bricks and was at least sixteen meters from the house, downhill. "You must talk the rest of the women into making them," Monica said. "If they just go in the bushes, flies will come and spread disease to the rest of you." Those who had built latrines were rewarded with vegetable seeds Monica had obtained from the government's Katumani agricultural research station, just outside the small town of Machakos. She handed out packets of carrots, onions, spinach, potatoes and greens. Greens were nicknamed *sukuma wiki* by the women; loosely translated, it meant "pulling through the week." "Maize and beans, *ugali* and greens," was another saying, *ugali* being cornmeal, the mainstay of the diet.

Monica said she was trying to get other seeds. She wanted the women to try growing cassava, pigeon peas, cabbage, sweet potatoes, cucumbers, and fruit such as oranges, lemons, mangoes, pawpaw, passion fruit, bananas and mulberries. Many streams flowed through the hills, and Monica told them the extension agents at Katumani said they should be growing fruit and vegetables on the banks.

She announced that the Catholic Relief Service was starting up a new program for pregnant mothers and under-fives. A family had to pay five shillings, about fifty cents, a month and they would get two kilos of fat, two kilos of millet and two kilos of dried milk. Everybody had to submit a written application. Monica handed out forms, and as they all started to fill them out, told them, "Sign your name so that your grandmother can read it." Afterward she reminded them to treat diarrhea with a mixture of sugar, salt and boiled water; to be sure to take the children in for immunization; how to weigh babies; and how to build outdoor dish racks so the sun could kill bacteria. She said she was going to get a week's training at St. John's Ambulance in Nairobi so she could teach them first aid. There would also be a weeklong farmers' training course at Katumani and this time they wanted women to come, not their husbands, if they were actually doing the farming. She also spoke about crop loans, then ended the meeting with a prayer.

As we walked on to another village, Monica told me she guessed maybe six or seven women out of ten seriously wanted to better their lot. "Much depends on the headman," she said. "If he is selfish, then the whole village may revert to every man for himself. But if the leader is good, people respond." Some men were jealous of their authority. They told Monica, "We don't want you to waste our women's time. They have to work on the land." She ignored them. "Quite often women are left out of the picture," she would tell me. "They are pushed here and there. But when you show them what they can do, they have plenty of spirit."

"Where are the men?" I would ask. We saw so few in the fields. Once we even saw a woman struggling to plow with an ox on a rocky slope. Her husband was with her, but all he was doing was walking beside her, giving commands.

"This is the problem we face here in Africa," Monica explained. "You see these women working hard in the fields? They suffer. Their husbands may be working in town, drinking beer, spending their wages, enjoying themselves. Or maybe they don't even have a job."

"In Kenya, actually, most farmers are women," said Dr. M. Thairu, one of Kenya's leading agronomists, who then ran the Katumani dry-land agricultural research center. "A family has to have both food and cash. The wife grows the food of the family and the man earns the money, either in cash crops or he goes to the city." He said that women, half of them illiterate, produced 80 percent of the corn sold in Kenya and did 100 percent of the rural marketing. We saw them flooding down from the hills on market days, armies of women streaming along the pathways in their bright cotton dresses and head scarves, heavy loads on their heads, sometimes with babies on their backs, and red, pink, yellow and orange parasols in hand.

If his center offered seed or fertilizer loans, or technical training, about 70 percent of those who signed up were women, Dr. Thairu said. His problem was how to persuade women to try something new, like the drought-resistant crops his center developed. Women were conservative; they might farm, but their husbands still made the decisions. "We can give the basic inputs—oxen, improved seeds, fertilizer

—and give these women training. But we have to put our theoretical knowledge into a package the husband will accept."

Family planners told the same story. Kenyan women, who were averaging 8.3 live children each—6.6 for all Africans—were ready to use contraceptives. The problem was the men. With a 3.9 percent annual growth, Kenya had one of the world's worst population crises. Then male attitudes changed. Since 1989 Kenya's total fertility rate has dropped 20 percent, one of the steepest falls ever observed.

Historians agree that the Neolithic woman, as the collector of roots, berries and wild grain, probably invented agriculture. Professor Mc-Neill in his *The Rise of the West* speculates:

> A critical turn must have come when collectors of wild-growing grain came to understand that allowing a portion of the seed to fall to the ground at harvest time assured an increased crop the following year. Perhaps this idea was connected with concepts of the spirit of the grain, propitiation of that spirit, and the reward that benefitted a pious harvester who left part of the precious seed behind. A second break-through occurred with the discovery that by scattering seed on suitably prepared ground, women could create grain fields even where the grasses did not grow naturally. Yet the laborious practice of breaking ground with a digging stick and covering the seed to keep it from birds may well have spread slowly, even after the prospective rewards for such labor were well understood; for hunting communities seldom re-mained long enough in one locality to engage in extended tillage.

It is generally accepted that early woman, the collector, would be the one, in these circumstances, to discover that if you dropped seeds and put some dirt over them so birds wouldn't eat them, something would grow and you wouldn't have to go so far looking for grain. Man, as the hunter and then herder and domesticator of animals, only entered farming when draft animals were introduced in the fields. Men, using animals, took over farming in much of Asia about 6,000–7,000 years ago and in what is now Latin America about 5,000 years ago. Why did this not happen on the same scale in Africa?

The oldest men in Kaani suggested part of the answer. These aging Kamba tribesmen, those born from about 1895 to 1915, easily remembered the days when a single family may have owned a thousand or more cattle and to possess just thirty or forty was to be deemed poor. And the days when elephants, zebra, antelope and giraffes were hunted and killed with traps, spears and poisoned arrows. Listening to their tales of a vanished life, if only within their lifetime, was a pleasure, like the constant hikes in the hills. We would sit around the village *duka,* a mud-brick teahouse whose walls were painted in crude and gaudy scenes. In thunderclouds and lightning bolts a black Moses received the Ten Commandments or a couple in modern dress sat beside a car with a 1977 license plate drinking from a thermos. There were more biblical scenes, men shooting hyenas, men running from a lion, a hyena attacking a flamingo. At a counter, aside from tea, a woman sold Nescafé, Lifebuoy soap, Colgate toothpaste, Kimbo shortening ("Of Kimbo Kitchen Fame"), margarine, cocoa, biscuits, ballpoint pens, liquid paraffin, Vaseline, razor blades, powdered milk, chocolate, tea, sugar, cornmeal, Strepsils, Aspro, Coca-Cola, Fanta, Tree Top orange juice, *mbaki* or local tobacco, candy, and fresh tomatoes.

The old men liked to argue which was better, the old days or the present. Mzee Kibiti, who had once been a teacher, claimed there were no poor people in his youth. "With so many cows we had plenty of milk and meat and the women would clear a patch in the bush and grow millet and sorghum." Mzee Sila, who looked like an old lion with his grizzled white beard, took the other side of the argument. "Nowadays is better," he said. "We suffered so much sickness and so many cattle died. Now there is somebody to cure you." I was reminded of Elspeth Huxley's *The Flame Trees of Thika.* Once the European memsaabs arrived with their hygiene and Epsom salts, mortality dropped and the old ways were doomed. Herding, hunting and slash-and-burn cultivation rarely supported more than 150–250 persons per square mile. Yet it had all happened within these old men's lifetimes. I found this astonishing, 10,000 years of change compressed into less than a century.

Over tea in the *duka,* we heard tales of smallpox and rinderpest epidemics, great droughts and famines, and endless tribal wars, as if Kamba history had held little else. Monica translated, since, unlike the village children, most of the old men spoke only the Kamba dialect. At least half the Kamba people perished in 1899 and 1901 when the twice-yearly rains failed five times in a row. Sila said his father told him some men chose starvation rather than kill and eat their cows. (The Dinkas lived on the milk and blood of their cattle, but, unlike Kenya's Masai, did not kill, butcher and eat them; maybe eating beef was taboo, like cannibalism, in some of the early herding societies.)

Sometimes Mzee Sila told of exciting adventures, such as raids to

pillage the cattle of the Kikuyu and Masai. "The chief had warriors—
kingole, we called them—and we had battles with the Masai for cattle.
We called it *ita,* a war for cattle, and *ita* was also the group you fought.
The wives stayed home to look after the *shamba* and the children.
The men divided into three groups, one to fight, one to look after the
cattle and one for looking on. How we would listen with longing as
boys to our fathers' tales of cattle wars. I used to despise myself
because I was almost thirty and had not killed a Masai."

The old warrior fondly remembered hunting parties. "After 1936 it
was forbidden to kill animals, but it secretly went on. There are still
antelope, baboons and hyenas in the bush a couple of miles from
here. It's too dry there to grow crops." He said baboons still plundered the bean and corn fields in Kaani village. "They screech and
make a big noise at you, but they cannot attack a man," Mzee Sila
said. Once a baboon carried off a baby; the infant wasn't injured but
died of exposure.

Sila was born in 1906. "My mother was already grown when the
wasungu came," he said, using the Kamba word for white men. "The
Arabs were still catching people to sell. The British took care of our
people, so they would not be sold. My grandfather exchanged ivory
with the British traders for cloth and beads. The British were afraid of
our arrows and spears."

When missionaries first came—those in the Machakos Hills happened to be French—the Kambas chased them away. "It was
thought," said Mzee Kibiti, "that they had come to take our land and
make us slaves."

When a mission school at last opened, the tribesmen sent only the
weakest or laziest children, those not good at herding cattle. Time
proved them the lucky ones; Jomo Kenyatta, a Kikuyu who became
an eminent anthropologist long before he entered politics, was one.
Kibiti said, "The only reason I got educated was that I was always
fighting with the other cattle boys. To punish me, my father sent me
to school."

Sila, as a tall, muscular boy, was fated to stay with the herd. "Then,
when I was still young," he said, "many cows were infected with
disease. Almost all our cattle died. My father also died at that time.
From then on we had nothing." He had stayed illiterate all his life.
Mzee Sila suddenly laughed, remembering his first encounter with a
mzungu. "I said to him, 'You white men know so much more than we,

have you found the edge of the sky?' He said that the sky has no edge and that it nowhere touches the earth. I did not believe him.''

The old men knew the name of John Kennedy. They said he was a great *mzungu* who once sent corn, cooking oil and powdered milk at a time of famine. The generation gap was wide. "The young men want to be educated," Mzee Kibiti said. "They want to wear nice clothes and be employed by the government. They don't want to dirty their hands in the earth."

Grass grew on the Kamba warpaths; the battle cries had long been stilled. Gone were the hunting parties and the great herds of cattle. The swords had literally become plowshares; village women used *pangas* to clear brush from the fields. It was when you went to a Kenya game park and, in a primal landscape, came upon a pride of lions, a lone rhinoceros or a family of giraffes, tall as dinosaurs and nibbling on the treetops, that you fully sensed what these old men had lost.

The speed of this change could be seen in the way the village headmaster, James Zachariah Nzoka, and his wife, Agnes, lived. Nzoka drove a Volkswagen, had built a modern four-room bungalow, raised Dr. Thairu's latest hybrid corn on his seven-acre *shamba* and had an orange and lemon orchard. His house was half hidden by tall hedges and shaded with eucalyptus trees. Agnes also was a teacher. "We're lucky. We're both employed," she told me. "Villagers need to build more schools so we can get the government to hire more teachers. After our students leave, there are few jobs for them. And once they go to school, they don't want to farm." Nzoka, a creature of modern Western culture, tried to bring it to his students. At school he read his pupils Shaw's *Androcles and the Lion*, and he took forty of them on a twelve-kilometer walk into town to see a film of Thomas Mann's *Joseph and His Brothers*.

As you approached Nairobi from the southeast and Machakos, across the grasslands and thorny-bush shrubs of the Kabiti Plain, in 1981 you could still glimpse the odd giraffe, zebra or ostrich just running free. About twenty miles out, the city came faintly into view, looking out of place with its tall buildings rising above the haze of traffic fumes and factory smoke. Kenya, even today, with all its political uncertainty, is still the prime symbol in Africa of what Western investment can do. It is Africa's banking, business and tourist center.

African culture is all but swamped by Westernization. Except for the odd Masai, naked under his blanket, everybody wears Western clothing, much of it rumpled and from secondhand markets. New glass-and-concrete towers, gracious British colonial architecture and parks ablaze with bougainvillea, jacaranda and flame trees make Nairobi seem a very attractive city, unless you set foot in the festering squatter camps that spread like fungus around the city's outskirts. In these really hellish quarters over half of Nairobi's people live.

In one of the worst shantytowns, Kabiro, a kindly middle-aged social worker, Mama Wahu, told me people kept coming in from the villages and throwing up shacks. There was no way to keep them out. "You can't throw away people like so much garbage," she said. Three out of four of Kabiro's men had no jobs. Wife beating, family desertion, alcoholism and dope were common. Men who did work mostly had jobs as *askaris*, or house guards; fear of the poor made protection the main employment of the poor. Wages were seldom over $45.60 a month, then the legal minimum. A monthly rent of $4.00 obtained a hut made of corrugated-iron sheeting. It was a single ten-by-ten-foot windowless, mud-floored room. Inside there was either a cot or a sleeping mat, a blanket or two, a charcoal cookstove and a few cooking pots, bowls, cups and spoons. Single women staved off starvation by buying vegetables from a truck and hawking them at a street market. Mama Wahu said she saw people eating grass, rummaging through garbage pits or sending children out to be pickpockets or to steal.

Kabiro was extremely violent. Every few weeks the body of a dead man would be found in one of its alleys, after being stabbed and robbed while staggering around at night drunk or doped. Some of the bodies were gnawed upon by hungry dogs. Mama Wahu blamed the violence on *chang'aa*, the cheapest, illicitly brewed liquor. "The men have nothing to do," she said, "so they beat up their wives out of frustration, or wander off and don't know where they are. Mothers try to hide what money they make to buy food for the children, but a man won't let go, he just won't let it go and he'll find the money and go off and get drunk."

There were six public latrines for 2,000 people, the busiest, Mama Wahu claimed, used at least 1,500 times a day. Most tragic were the aborted fetuses or even unwanted strangled babies sometimes thrown in these latrines. "The grandmothers do it," Mama Wahu said with a quiet horror. "Well, where else can they get rid of it without being seen?"

These were the most terrible slum conditions I had ever seen, worse even than the *bustees* of Calcutta. Yet right in the middle of it all, children were going to a primary school. Class was on and a young woman, who was teaching English, wrote on a blackboard: "Cows and horses walk on four legs. Little children work on two legs." She asked the little boys and girls to name English words that began with the letter *c*. There were eager cries of "cat," "cup," "cassava," "car," "cabbage," "carrot." It seemed a pathetically innocent faith in a West that, at least in Kabiro, had failed the Africans so terribly.

Nairobi buzzed with horror stories of gangs coming out at night from the worst slums like Kabiro and, armed like Mau Mau with *pangas*, waylaying pedestrians or stealing cars, often, in a weird twist, after locking the occupants in the trunk, where they might be found days later battered and barely alive. Or the gangs might invade a dinner party of Europeans and cut everybody up. Back in Machakos, you could still walk the country roads after dark from village to village in safety.

In trying to explore what is going wrong in Africa, the male failure as yet to find a new social role in settled farming seemed to me fundamental. This was changing, but slowly. One forty-year-old in Kaani village, Mutiso Mangi, said he took over farming from his wife in 1977 when he bought a team of oxen. This enabled him to plow and cultivate more land, seven acres. He prospered and built his family a new brick house. He kept away from the city. "If you go to Nairobi there's a lot of noise and nonsense," he said. He admitted, "There's still a belief that farming is for women or those who don't go to school. We have to change that."

Aside from farming, Kenya's women fetch firewood and water, keep house, cook and take care of their children, and even with life expectancies of sixty-one—up ten years the past decade—they spend much of their lives in pregnancy, birth and child rearing. Karen Blixen rightly described fortitude as an African quality. Monica Mutuli had that peculiar patient endurance that more than anything we saw or heard in our days in Machakos left me deeply impressed with the African woman. The hunter-warrior is no more; the settled farmer is not yet. Monica understood, far better than I ever could, that it would take time.

But how much time does Africa have? Seeds can survive in the desert for a hundred years. Human society is more fragile. In 1984, with a handful of European journalists led by a Senegalese PR man from the

United Nations, I toured the Sahel in the second year of the worst African drought and famine in the twentieth century. Unless the rains returned to the Sahara borderlands of Africa, we were told, a way of life that had lasted 5,000 years was ending. The largely nomadic Moors of Mauritania, like the Tuaregs of Mali, both of related Arab-Berber stock, were mostly herdsmen who camped in tents and went by camel across the Sahara sands in search of new grass springing up after rains. Camels and sheep furnished these nomads with their meat, milk, hides and skins, tents, carpets, cushions and saddles. At the oases they grew date palms and small fields of millet, wheat, yams and a few other crops.

"Our civilization is dying," Ba Aliou Ilora, secretary of Mauritania's ruling military committee, told us. It was an extraordinary trip, flying about the Sahara in a small twin-engined Otter to places few would conceivably dare to visit on their own. Ba Aliou Ilora spoke one afternoon as we sprawled on cushions around a roasting goat on a spit on the open terrace of a pink desert fortress. Africans in *Arabian Nights* outfits, the front of their sandals rising in curlicues, crawled about on their knees, serving us tea. Everybody was given a dagger, to cut off their own chunks of meat. Slavery still exists in these remote Sahara oases. Mauritania was notorious for it in the nineteenth century, when shipwrecked European sailors, famously shown in the Louvre's lurid painting *The Wreck of the Medusa*, who managed to reach shore were seized and sold to camel caravans.

During 1983–84, the Moors and Tuaregs lost at least half their livestock. Many had fled to the coastal capital of Nouakchott, a few towns along the Senegal River and Timbuktu in Mali. Others were driving their remaining cattle south into Senegal and Mali. The desolation of northern Senegal came as a shock after the swimming pools and air-conditioned French hotels of Dakar. Wells were dry and baobab and acacia trees had withered. Only old people and children were left in the villages. One man told us, "Even the vultures have fled." Out at water holes in the desert, tens of thousands of humpbacked zebu cattle jostled for a drink. Along the roads were the bleached bones and mummified corpses of thousands more.

Northern Mali was a semi-desert of failed crops, lost herds and abandoned villages. The Tuaregs had given up most of their old pasturelands. Village children could be seen clawing through anthills, searching for kernels of grain. They had the swollen bellies, sticklike limbs and yellowing hair that signal severe malnutrition and have since become so familiar from the Ethiopian and Somalian children on our TV sets. Rural hospitals in the Sahel were out of medicine and children were dying of measles for want of vaccine, although it cost only fifty cents per child.

When the rains did come at last, in 1985, the biological effect of the drought persisted. The prolonged lack of rain had touched off an explosion of leafhopper insects. A new three-inch-long beetle which caused blisters on human skin was driving millet out of northern Mali and Senegal.

It was Africa's worst drought in living memory. The West responded generously with emergency food aid. African aid from all donors worked out to about $20 a head ($44 per head in the Sahel alone). One of Africa's big misfortunes was that the breakthroughs in plant genetics that brought the green revolution to much of Asia and Latin America did not take root in Africa's soil and climate. Scientists working in Africa were confident that they could eventually adapt the new technology to African conditions, but not for some years.

Could Africa wait? The problem hit us in the face at every turn on our 5,000-mile journey through the Sahel: the blowing red dust of Africa's oldest and weakest soil. Everywhere we went people were praying for rain. We flew Air Mali back to Paris, a ten-hour flight on a creaky old plane. When we touched down at Charles de Gaulle and moved down a stairway to the tarmac, we saw it was raining. *"Il pleut,"* gasped an African woman with a baby just in front of me. A uniformed French stewardess standing below shrugged. *"Comme ça,"* she muttered, as if to say, "So what?" Rain meant nothing here, nor did it matter that the Sahara was creeping south.

In 1968 British author C. P. Snow had prophesied that within ten years

> . . . many millions of people in the poor countries are going to starve to death before our eyes . . . we shall see them doing so upon our television sets.

This had not happened as soon as expected because the green revolution's high-yield dwarf wheat, first planted on a large scale on farmers' fields in 1967, followed by dwarf rice a few years later, tripled grain output in India, and in Pakistan by 1986, two years after China, planting the same grain, had become the biggest grain-producing country in history.

Africa, paradoxically where both the human race and farming

started, has the planet's most intractable problem. Droughts keep getting longer, more severe, with sand drifting into some villages for the first time. If there is anarchy, as in Somalia, armed rabble begin to fight over food. One asks, how can Asia, with 3.2 billion of the world's 5.5 billion people, grow food surpluses on just a quarter of the earth's farmland while sub-Sahara Africa, with just 465 million people and vast land reserves, goes hungry? Why has the same Western science that has rescued Asia failed Africa?

Lack of irrigation, widespread in Asia, is one thing. Nobody knows exactly what percentage of Africa's farmland is irrigated, but it is probably between 1 and 3 percent. Other reasons given are Africa's climate, soil and topography, its lack of roads, schools and incentives. I asked Norman Borlaug, who initiated the green revolution in Asia thirty years ago, what about all that red dust one sees in Africa? The soil looks completely worn out, a fact Borlaug confirms:

> The problem is that calcium and magnesium, which make it alkaline, along with potassium, an essential plant nutrient, have been leached by higher temperatures and heavy rains over thousands of years. As a result, the soil becomes acid, its phosphorus becoming unavailable, aluminum becoming soluble and toxic to plants. Nitrogen content is low. Much of Africa is left with reddish or grayish, infertile soil incapable of sustaining a very dense population. South Africa and Zimbabwe are the only two African countries which have successfully used chemicals to restore their soil.

Dr. Borlaug explained that you had to go back to the beginning, 2 or 3 million years ago. When ice caps covered what is now Northern Europe, North America and upper Asia, the great sand sea of the Sahara formed in Africa. Further south the tropical jungle shrank to its present size. Open grassland with thorny bush, baobab and acacia trees became the characteristic landscape of Africa's east and south, then and now. In this savanna, the earliest hominid (*Australopithecus afarensis*) emerged, possibly 7.5 million years ago. Fossil footprints at Laetoli in Tanzania found by Mary Leakey were presumably made by an *afarensis* adult and child out for an upright walk 3.5 million years ago. Darwin concluded that humans and African apes had a common ancestor. Don Johanson of Berkeley's Institute of Human Origins has confirmed from fossils and a male *afarensis* skull discovered in 1994 in Ethiopia that this ancestor walked upright at least 3.5 million years ago. Richard Leakey, who talked about his book *Origins Reconsidered* in Berkeley in 1992, told us hominids migrated out of Africa into Eurasia 1 to 2 million years ago. I think they broke through the Saharan barrier by going north along the Nile. Leakey has them using fire 1 million years ago but not emerging as modern humans—*Homo sapiens*—which he feels also took place in Africa, until about 150,000 years ago. In 1994 this was challenged when Berkeley's Carl Swisher and Garniss Curtis, using new techniques to measure radioactivity in volcanic rock, were able to date some fossils in Java back 1.8 million years, suggesting the African and Asian populations of *Homo erectus* may actually have evolved separately.

So far *Australopithecus*, the first hominid, has been found only in Africa, and no one as yet seriously doubts that the ultimate origins of human beings lie in Africa. In our 1981 talk, Leakey put the emergence of settled agriculture at 10,000 years ago, a figure he still upholds. Having been at a French archaeological dig in Iran's Khuzistan province as 10,000-year-old kernels of cultivated wheat were discovered in a village site, I'd side with those who put the invention of agriculture a little earlier, about 12,000 years ago.

In Asia, starting about 5,000 years ago, the invention of wet rice paddy cultivation led to the region's own river valley civilizations, which ultimately became Hindu and Confucian. As in pharaonic Egypt, the need to control water provided the impetus for a fairly complex social organization early on. Since rice is labor-intensive, Asian populations grew large and dense. Wet rice cultivation, according to Dr. Borlaug, provides a relatively stable environment since the land is flooded so much of the year. A few inches of water protects the soil from the high temperatures and heavy rains of the tropics, whereas in Africa topsoil gets washed away. India, China and Indonesia were fertile ground for the rapid adaptation of Western farm science once Borlaug and his colleagues solved the big problem of tropical agriculture: how to apply chemical fertilizer for bigger yields without tropical long-stemmed grain growing top-heavy and falling over. Short-stemmed grain, using a dwarf gene first brought home by Dr. S. C. Salmon, an agricultural advisor to General MacArthur's occupation army in Japan, Norin #10, could be heavily fertilized without "lodging" in wind or rain.

In some places in sub-Saharan Africa, when it comes to agricultural technology, time has virtually stood still. There are still a few hunter-gatherer tribes or those like Sudan's Dinkas, who live a seminomadic cattle-herding life in the great Sudd swamp, though they do a little hoe cultivation of sorghum during the rainy season. Theirs is still a world of cattle, water, swamp, silence and naked tribesmen. As with the hunter-gatherers such as Botswana's !Kung tribe, their way of life has outlasted all others. Among the Nubas in 1975 one found Africa's most common agricultural practice. Land was so abundant, it was not private property. A family or group of tribesmen, usually males, simply cleared a patch of bush and burned the brush. Women then planted a crop of sorghum or millet with hoes and digging sticks and later weeded and harvested it. In an old tribal custom reinforced by their conversion to Islam, the Nubas were polygamous—Kuwa, whom I stayed with, had four wives, each with her own grass-thatched hut in Kuwa's thorny-bush compound and her own plot of an acre or two to feed herself and her children. Since land had no value, status among Nuba men was decided by the number of their cattle and their wives. Such slash-and-burn cultivation rarely supports more than 95 people per square kilometer, while wet rice cultivation supports about 310 people per square kilometer in Java and Bangladesh and close to 770 in China's Yangtze and Yellow river basins.

There is a temptation among economists to try to compare Africa and Asia. Harvard professor C. Peter Timmer has shown that, in 1960, seventeen sub-Saharan African sorghum- and maize-eating nations, with 144 million people among them, had per capita incomes of $437 (in 1989 dollars). Four Southeast Asian countries—Indonesia, Thailand, Malaysia and the Philippines—with 157.5 million people, had per capita incomes of $376. By 1989 the Africans had dropped to $334 a year, while the Asians were up to $762. (In 1994 it would be about $540 for the sub-Saharan Africans and $670, $1,870, $2,790 and $770 for the Asians.) Timmer, who proposed economic remedies, commented, "History did not play out as expected."

As who expected? If you are going to compare Africa and Asia, you have to go back at least 10,000 years in history and take into account vast differences in geography too. Yes, East Asia is getting richer faster, so fast it will probably be richer than most Western nations in a generation. But in the long run, I think it will be the time lag that will save Africa. As Professor McNeill says:

> A persistent paradox of all human achievement is that gains in wealth and power always involve increased vulnerability to breakdown simply because all such gains involve deliberate alternations in preexisting

"natural" relationships. This was evident among farmers from the beginning of agriculture.

A Chinese hybrid variety could fail and bring on unprecedented famine. Sophisticated Western market systems are vulnerable to large-scale disorder. Demolish the Aswan Dam and you send the artificially stored water of Lake Nasser roaring down the Nile Valley to Cairo. Or look at all the nuclear weapons scattered around. Africans may be the earth's longest-enduring humans because they have stayed closest to nature. Time will tell.

This said, what can be done to help them now? In April 1985, I put this question to Dr. Borlaug, who, it turned out, was already involved in talks with Japanese philanthropist Ryoichi Sasakawa. Sasakawa had made his fortune from parimutuel betting at speedboat races, and later shipbuilding. He had phoned Dr. Borlaug in 1984 and told him he had just given a large sum for famine relief in Africa. "But what's being done," Sasakawa wanted to know, "to improve food production as in Asia? Just feeding refugees won't solve the problem."

Borlaug, who was then seventy, told him, "I don't know anything about Africa south of the Sahara. And I'm too old to learn."

And that was that. Until Sasakawa rang back the next morning. "Listen," he said, "I'm eighty-five. I'm fifteen years older than you. We should have started yesterday. So let's start tomorrow. Let's do something."

A few months later Dr. Borlaug told me his scheme to help Africa, which I reported in the New York *Times* April 4, 1985, with a subsequent version in *The Economist* of London. "We can integrate existing knowledge about how to improve crop yields and undertake demonstration plots in Africa," he said.

His formula was simple. You start by pulling together all the available data at international agricultural research centers in Mexico and India on Africa's three main crops: maize, sorghum and millet. Then you pick one or two countries for which the data is best—Sudan and Ghana, as it turned out. Gather a few really good scientists prepared to slog it out in the African bush for a few years, have them put together a production package and start testing on acre-sized plots in grass-hut villages.

The package, Borlaug said, dealt with what variety of crops to plant, when and how to plant them, how to fertilize, how to control weeds, insects and disease and the use of moisture. On the basis of the first year's tests, you adjust the parts of the package—too much fertilizer or too little, or variety A is better than variety B—to improve it. The next year the remade package is tested on hundreds of farmers' one-acre plots. Yields must more than double to stir up enough enthusiasm among the farmers to change their old habits, which is why subsidized fertilizer in this early stage is crucial. If it all works, you go to the country's policymakers and persuade them to get fertilizer to farmers six weeks before planting, lend money to buy it (repayable after harvest) and set a guaranteed floor price so that they can afford to repay the loan.

If the governments can be persuaded, the farmers should do the rest. The whole test should last four or five years at a cost of about $5 million per country. Borlaug said it should not be tried in more than two countries at first because there were not enough scientists who knew how to make it work.

Dr. Borlaug got the $10 million he needed from Sasakawa. Why Japanese funding? Partly it was Sasakawa's personal interest. But the crisis also came just a few years after the Ford and Rockefeller Foundations, which were responsible for Asia's green revolution, phased out much of their old agricultural programs and let their scientists go. Both continued to fund the well-established global network of thirteen agricultural research centers that pool data and genetic information on crops, where Borlaug was gathering his data for the African project. New high-yield dwarf varieties had to be constantly bred to combat disease organisms and insects, along with preserving germplasm collections of the world's food crops, the centers' main job. But the network was mainly government-supported, headquartered in the World Bank's huge bureaucracy in Washington, D.C., and it lacked the flexibility of the old programs run by the foundations, which gave Dr. Borlaug the latitude he needed to move quickly in India, Pakistan and China. Some of the former ex-Rockefeller Foundation scientists formed the Winrock International Institute for Agricultural Development (set up by Winthrop Rockefeller), near Morrilton, Arkansas, but it is not a big innovator in Africa.

The Rockefeller Foundation, in a controversial move opposed by Dr. Borlaug, in 1985 dropped out of conventional plant breeding altogether and replaced that enterprise with a $9 million-a-year program in genetic engineering in rice. The Ford Foundation shifted the emphasis of its former agricultural programs to attack rural poverty, though by the 1990s it was again funding eight agricultural officers in

Africa. When I visited the International Rice Research Institute in the Philippines in 1992, I found the Rockefeller support for gene manipulation generally praised, with the caveat from the scientists involved that DNA only affects disease and insect resistance. Genetic engineering does not provide a tool for increasing yields directly. In rice this can only be done by hybrids or new varieties of self-pollinating inbreds such as a promising new plant type using germ plasm from wild Javanese *bulu* rice. The issue of support has become somewhat moot, as the Chinese, in hybrids, and the Japanese, in gene manipulation, have taken the lead away from the Americans anyway.

One ingredient was missing for the African project. In India and Pakistan in the late 1960s Borlaug had found that the most difficult battle was winning over political leaders who had to make key policy choices. It was only after he convinced Pakistan's Ayub Khan, who planted Borlaug's dwarf wheat on his own farm in 1964, that the program really went ahead in South Asia. In Africa, Borlaug told me, "once political leaders and economic planners see that crop yields can be greatly increased, and you've got the farmers all stirred up, then whoever's running the program has got to be quite a psychologist. He's got to tell the political leader, 'Here's your chance for a breakthrough.' " Which means you need somebody with plenty of clout.

President Lyndon Johnson in 1965 played a crucial behind-the-scenes role. He first sent Agriculture Secretary Orville Freeman to Rome to meet the Indian agriculture minister and warn him that India would get no more food aid until it adapted Borlaug's technology to grow more. Later Johnson repeated his threat to Indira Gandhi when the Indian prime minister visited Washington. He asked her bluntly and privately, "What I want to know is: do you want to feed your people?" He dictated what she must do. Mrs. Gandhi bitterly resented Johnson's bullying but she did what he asked. Johnson did the same thing with Egypt's Gamal Abdel Nasser, who balked. As long as Johnson was in the White House, Egypt never received another grain of American wheat.

This time Jimmy Carter volunteered to pitch in. Sasakawa was helping Carter fund Global 2000, the foundation he had set up in Atlanta. In 1985 Carter agreed to try to persuade African leaders to adopt needed policies. This has worked out well, even if Carter's participation tends to give a political tone to what is essentially an exercise in applied farm science. Carter has also pushed for a more ambitious effort than Dr. Borlaug had in mind, with projects not just in Sudan and Ghana, but also in Zambia, Tanzania, Benin, Togo and Nigeria.

The Zambia project was separately funded by BCCI, which had also given money to the Carter center in Atlanta. The program collapsed when the Abu Dhabi-based bank went under in mid-1991, ultimately landing Clark Clifford in hot water in Washington, though the case was eventually dropped. In 1990, Zambia's president, Kenneth Kaunda, promised Carter he would give farmers a fair price at harvest. Instead, to appease Lusaka's slum dwellers, he kept prices so low farmers could not pay off their fertilizer debts. "Kaunda violated his agreement with me," Carter told a workshop on Africa at Airlie House in Virginia in 1992. "He reluctantly agreed to pay the farmers if they delivered corn to the marketplace. They have not been paid for it yet." Carter monitored Zambia's election in October 1991. "Mostly because of the debacle in agriculture," Carter reported, "President Kaunda got less than 25 percent of the vote."

The savage "holy war" waged by Arab Islamic fundamentalists in Khartoum against Sudan's Nubas, Dinkas, Nuers and other black African tribes in the country's south forced Borlaug to go to Sudan in 1993 and pull his people and program out. Yet it was highly successful. "Our Sudan experience shows you can never predict what will succeed," Borlaug told me. It was supposed to focus on sorghum, but Marco Quiñones, the Mexican scientist in charge, who has been working with Borlaug since the 1940s, asked if he could spend the slack winter months working on wheat in Sudan's irrigated Gezira area between the Blue and White Niles. Sudan's sorghum output grew modestly, but its wheat production, war and all, soared from 160,000 tons to 800,000 tons harvested in March 1992, even if it has since dropped back to about 500,000 tons. Morally, one might argue that this increase helps buttress the Muslim fanatics in power, who appear, with Iranian backing, to be training terrorist and agitprop agents to try to bring down the Egyptian and other moderate, pro-Western regimes. Jimmy Carter ended his involvement in Sudan entirely, but Dr. Borlaug has kept up his ties with agricultural scientists involved in the wheat program there.

Borlaug's main testing ground has been Ghana, where corn production is up 40 percent. He told me in early 1994 that he has tried out his production package using subsidized imported fertilizer on at least acre-sized plots, with over 200,000 African cultivators in six countries taking part. Yields, he estimated, have gone up on the average two and a half times. So he has essentially done what he set out to prove: a quantum jump in crop yields, if methods and inputs, particularly nitrogen to restore soil fertility, were right, is just as possible in Africa as in Asia.

Fertilizer is the key. African farmers in 1993 used just $\frac{1}{35}$th as much fertilizer per acre as Americans and Europeans, $\frac{1}{10}$th as much as Asians and $\frac{1}{6}$th as much as Latin Americans. Or put another way, using hectares, Africans now apply 7 to 8 kilograms per hectare of chemical fertilizer—4 kilos in Ghana—compared to 93 kilos per hectare in the United States, 69 in India, 260 in China, 358 in Britain, 433 in Germany and nearly 600 in the Netherlands (all those tulips). There are only two big 1,000-ton-capacity fertilizer plants in sub-Saharan Africa, both in Nigeria. African farms are so small, few farmers can afford to buy it. Reliance on hand tools—a machete and a hoe —generally limit the amount of land a family can cultivate to a hectare, about 2.5 acres. The tsetse fly's parasites do not devastate livestock as much as they once did—less shade in the logged rain forests —but this, along with custom, means that only 16 percent of African farms depend on animal power, the reason so few men have entered farming. Only 3 percent of farms use any kind of machinery.

Dr. Borlaug argues that a tripling of fertilizer use rates must take place in the 1990s. Africa faces food deficits on the order of 40–50 million tons by 2000, or about a third of its total food needs. But to spread the new technology in time involves, at least initially, making available cheap and plentiful fertilizer, and that requires imports and subsidies.

Here Borlaug's initiative is up against resistance from the World Bank, which flatly opposes subsidized fertilizer. Practical men, John Maynard Keynes reminded us, are usually the slaves of some defunct economist. This may be what ails the World Bank's "structural adjustment" program, radical reforms that grew out of the Reagan-Bush era's hard-nosed insistence that Africans open their doors to foreign trade and investors and adopt free-market policies. It meant, among other things, ending twenty-five years of fertilizer subsidies in nearly forty African countries. Fertilizer use, already minuscule in Africa, as mentioned, dropped precipitously. Since, as the FAO says, one bag of fertilizer equals ten bags of food, so has African food production.

What the World Bank says matters in Africa because the forty-year soft loans of its International Development Agency, with 3 percent interest and a ten-year grace period, keep a lot of African governments going. Tanzania, for example, gets 77 percent of its development budget and 40 percent of its operating budget from foreign aid. I first heard about the World Bank's opposition to fertilizer subsidies at the 1992 Airlie House workshop, where Borlaug, Carter, Sasakawa's son Yohei, African finance and agriculture ministers and donors led by the World Bank met to thrash out policy issues.

Kevin Cleaver, chief of the bank's African technical department and a fairly young American economist, even questioned whether there had been enough research to produce appropriate technology for small African farmers, which made Borlaug furiously indignant. Other bank officials defended the World Bank's own "training and visit" extension system, a scheme it funded in thirty-one African countries; Borlaug said its demonstration plots—just ten meters by ten meters—were too small to be effective.

Exasperated by the World Bank's opposition, Jimmy Carter told the workshop, "God knows, if we can't do anything in agriculture in Africa, where people are starving to death, and it's getting worse every year, then I think the entire situation is hopeless. Dr. Borlaug's system works. I've seen it work. We need desperately for the World Bank to join us."

In a New York *Times* September 14, 1992, Op-Ed, "Bring the Green Revolution to Africa," subheaded "World Bank Policies Are a Huge Obstacle," which was given almost a whole page, I reported the conflict. The article was attacked by Cleaver in a letter to the *Times* published on October 3, saying it "grossly distorts the nature of World Bank assistance to African agriculture." Cleaver:

> It is true that fertilizer subsidies are often reduced under structural adjustment programs. Because Norman Borlaug's approach to agriculture, which Mr. Critchfield describes, is dependent on project-managed distribution of fertilizer supported by subsidies, such a reduction is not popular with Dr. Borlaug.

A trip to Ghana's villages in July 1993 convinced me more than ever that Borlaug was right. In Fufuo village, Ashanti tribesmen had cleared with machetes acre-sized cornfields in a logged-over rain forest. Wayne Haag, a Michigan plant breeder who was running the Borlaug initiative in Ghana, had given them Ghana-bred high-protein maize of Mexican origin called *obantampa*, "mother's milk." By applying nitrogen and potash to their badly leached soil, these Ashantis were able to triple their old harvest to 1.5 tons per acre. The equatorial forest around their fields was dank and humid, with great gray-barked kapok trees that soared to improbable heights before bursting into foliage. Tarantulas the size of a fist and black cobras scuttled and slithered under primeval ferns. Fierce black army ants, moving in a frantic river several feet wide, were said to kill everything in their path. Jungle birds screeched. It was all wet and dripping and terribly hot and green.

One of the villagers, Owusu-Bobie, told how fifteen of them had formed a group to make it easier to repay fertilizer loans—"peer pressure," he called it, speaking English, as most villagers in Ghana do. Their slash-and-burn cultivation, weeding by hoe and interplanting corn with cassava, was an age-old method, but the high-yield seeds and chemical fertilizer were new. Owusu-Bobie said they hoped to bring in a tractor in three or four years when all the stumps were dead.

The Ashantis wore used American clothing they bought cheaply, so there were a lot of faded T-shirts with logos like "Please Don't Disturb. I'm Recovering from a Rough Life." The tailgate of a truck read: "Oh, God, Help Us!" I came away haunted by so many ragged but good-humored people just surviving in their steamy jungle poverty and yet speaking in gracious, cultivated English voices. A few weeks later at a dinner party in Washington, Robert McNamara vehemently interrupted a description I was giving of Fufuo village. What set McNamara angrily off was my use of the word "hopeful."

How, he demanded, hitting the table with such force it shook the glasses, could anybody say anything about Africa was hopeful? True to his reputation, McNamara reeled off the facts: Sub-Saharan Africa's population would double in twenty-three years. Between 1960 and 1989, Africa's share of world GNP had dropped from 1.9 percent to 1.2 percent. Since 1980 its external debt had risen to $174 billion. Africans made up half the world's refugees, fleeing drought, famine or any one of seventeen or eighteen civil wars. What could be worse?

"We have to be hopeful," I repeated stubbornly. "Because these African villagers are hopeful."

At a workshop on African farming in Cotonou, Benin, at the end of July, I had heard agriculture ministers privately use words like "disaster" and "breakdown." When I asked them why they didn't criticize the World Bank openly, one said, "We have to get money from them."

"The reason I'm having this big fight with the World Bank on fertilizer subsidies," Borlaug told me in Cotonou, "is that the small

African cultivator has no choice. Now he cultivates three years and when his fertility goes down he abandons the land, moves on and chops down some more brush. And burns the vegetation. It's very harmful to the environment. The alternative is to provide the African farmer with cheap fertilizer so he can continue to work that same land. I say, rather than subsidize imported food in the cities, subsidize fertilizer for the small cultivator."

Carter, who was also at the Cotonou workshop, said Africa was forced to import fertilizer at world market prices while having to compete with rich countries which subsidize their own agriculture (the European Economic Community 38 percent, the United States 35 percent, Japan 72 percent) and dump their surpluses in Africa as food aid.

In Africa I also talked to Dr. B. T. Kang, an Indonesian at the International Institute of Tropical Agriculture in Nigeria, who after twenty-five years in Africa is considered a preeminent authority on its soils. I wanted to nail down the fertilizer subsidy issue. Dr. Kang told me that most African soils need 45 to 60 kilos per hectare of nitrogen a year. He cautioned, "It must be applied judiciously. If you can get organic matter it's best. But usually you must supplement it with chemical fertilizer and for most poor Africans it has to be subsidized." That seemed to clinch the argument, at least scientifically. Dr. Kang also said that Africa for centuries has been exporting its timber, cocoa, rubber and other natural resources to Europe and America. "So a lot of nutrients are flowing out and not being replaced." He agreed with Borlaug that the wet rice paddy cultivation of Asia, flooding the land much of the year, provides a much stabler environment, as water protects the soil from heavy tropical rains.

Wayne Haag appealed to the workshop: "We're dealing with people's lives. And we're obviously doing something wrong. Per capita food production is falling. If subsidy is a bad word, let's call it investment. But let's get improved seed and fertilizer out to African farmers."

In April 1993, the World Bank published a long strategy paper on African farming written by Kevin Cleaver. He devoted one paragraph in 140 pages to fertilizer and reiterated the bank's opposition to any form of subsidies. That August, and again in 1994, I met Cleaver in Washington. He gave me figures that showed that in nine African countries fertilizer use had actually gone up 3 percent or more a year after subsidies were removed. But these same figures showed that it dropped precipitously in fifteen other countries.

"If there were infinite resources," Cleaver said, "we'd all be for fertilizer subsidies. But extension, research, roads, schools, it's all being cut back. You have to make choices."

It was a matter of perception: scientists and economists, seeing Africa with different eyes, made different choices. But by mid-1994, in the World Bank's biggest study yet of "structural adjustment" in twenty-nine sub-Saharan countries, the best it could claim was that: "The majority of the poor are probably better off and almost certainly no worse off." Even this, bank insiders said, was deliberately cheery. "Investment won't come to Africa if it looks like a loser," said Edward Jaycox, head of the bank's African affairs. One bank official was quoted in *The Economist:* "Knowing what the truth is, self-deception has become a way of life."

The World Bank's opposition to fertilizer subsidies was becoming a mistake of tragic historical proportions. Britain's Oxfam, which has worked in Africa for decades, told the World Bank and IMF in September 1993 that its "structural adjustment" policy "can only be judged a complete failure." *The Economist* reported in March 1994:

> Disappointment crowds into the continent: unfilled bellies, untreated and untreatable disease, unschooled children and unfinished wars. Can Africa reverse this dismal trend? . . . The Africa of wretched refugee camps and bloody ethnic wars still grinds on, in Angola, Sudan, Liberia, Somalia and Burundi . . .

In theory the bank's economists such as Cleaver just want governments to spend within their means, keep their exchange rates competitive, free up prices, take off subsidies, stop meddling in business and sell off state enterprises. But applying it to agriculture at Africa's early stage of development is disastrous. "Structural adjustment," admits Ishrat Husain, the World Bank's chief economist for Africa, "is the most emotionally charged subject I have ever come across."

No wonder with so many lives at stake among people poorer at the end of the 1980s than they were at the start. The bank regards Ghana as its model reformer; its economy grew 4 percent annually in 1988–92. Not coincidentally Ghana is where Dr. Borlaug has made his biggest effort to transform agriculture, the basis of Ghana's whole economy. "Our allies," he has told me, "are going to be the Africans. It's the only way we'll get through. These theoreticians who live a comfortable life, in their air-conditioned ivory towers at the World Bank or in academia, they say you can't justify our kind of fieldwork because enough research hasn't been done. Even though we've demonstrated clearly we can double or triple yields. It's criminal not to apply what you know if you can fill empty stomachs. They say Africans can't afford fertilizer. Well, by God, they can't afford to eat either.''

After the *Times* op-ed came out, creating such an outcry from economists, Borlaug wrote to me: "It was correct and it went straight to the heart of the problem: the World Bank policy to shut off fertilizer subsidies is ridiculous.'' Borlaug, who turned eighty in 1994, was deeply frustrated and said, "We have to keep pushing, scratching, clawing, hoping to gradually win our points. I am impatient because I would like to live to see dramatic change start taking place in the African countries, and at my age I can't wait ten years. This has to happen in the next three to five.'' Too many Africans, facing hunger and upheaval and declining sympathy and generosity from rich nations preoccupied with their own troubles, can't wait either—the United States slashed its $900 million in aid to Africa in half for 1995. In a May 7, 1994 editorial on Rwanda, *The Economist* warned, "A bloodstain is spreading on the map of Africa—and on the conscience of the world.'' African civil wars are rooted in age-old tribalism, hunger and human misery. At still another workshop, in Switzerland in May 1994, the World Bank and Norman Borlaug were in agreement that African farming has got to grow at 4 percent a year for the next twenty years to avoid almost unimaginable horror. This cannot be done without improved seeds and fertilizer, that is, Borlaug's green revolution technology. Even as other donors cut back, the World Bank officials pledged that their commitment to African agriculture was as strong as ever.

The next story, the last and longest, brings together all our themes: age-old village society modernizing its farming and adapting to an exchange economy, the fundamentalist religious reaction, challenges to inherited authority and migration across cultural borders. The setting is India's Punjab, scene of Dr. Borlaug's greatest triumph and the West's biggest success in transferring its agricultural technology to a peasant society. Ghungrali's story and what happened to some of its people over the last half-century reflects, more than any other, I believe, the radical instability and its causes that lie ahead worldwide.

VII

The Banyan Tree:
The Last of the Peasants

CAST OF CHARACTERS

GHUNGRALI VILLAGE, PUNJAB, INDIA

Jats, Punjabi Sikh peasant landowners
PRITAM, 94 in 1992, a traditionalist
    SURJIT, 67, his son
    AMRIT SINGH, 92, Pritam's brother
    BAHADUR, 58, Amrit's son
    DEVINDER, 39, Bahadur's son
SADHU SINGH, d. 1979, Pritam's cousin
    CHAND KAUR, d. 1982, his wife
CHARAN, 61, Sadhu's son
    PRITAM KAUR, 60, his wife
    SUKHDEV, 38, his son
    KULDEEP, d. 1989, his son
    BEANT KAUR, 34, Kuldeep's widow
    KULWANT, 35, Charan's son
    RANI, 31, Charan's daughter
    NARINDER, 29, Charan's son
SURJIT KAUR, 63, Charan's sister, who lives in nearby
    Bhadson village

SAROOP, 70, her husband
PALA, 45, her son
KAKA, 37, her son
BULDEV, d. 1980s, Saroop's nephew
DHAKEL, 45, Charan's cousin
  SUMITRA, 56, his wife
  SARBAN SINGH, d. 1979, his father and Sadhu Singh's
    brother
  SINDAR, 46, a cousin
BASANT SINGH, 70s, Ghungrali's richest and most
  progressive farmer
SARPANCH, 61, village chief
ONE-EYE, 60s, troublemaker

Harijans, Punjabi landless laborers
MUKHTAR, 46, Charan's laborer, later bricklayer, a Chamar
POONDI, 80s, a Mazhbi of sweeper caste
  BAWA, 45, his son
GURDIAL, GURMEL, PELOO, other Chamars
BANTA, AMARJIT, SURJIT, CHANAN (d. 1992), KAPUR
  (d. 1980s), SHER (d. 1980s), other Mazhbis

Others
INDIRA GANDHI, d. 1984, Prime minister of India
SANT JARNAIL SINGH BHINDRANWALE, d. 1984, Messiah of
  Sikh fundamentalism
GURBACHAN SINGH, 50s, Ghungrali's holy man, a
  Bhindranwale follower
GURCHARAN SINGH TOHRA, 70s, powerful Sikh politician
  and uncle of Kaka's wife

PRITAM'S LIFE had spanned the twentieth century. Born in 1898, at ninety-four he was a little stooped, yet still stood over six feet two, a powerfully built, sturdy old man with muscular arms and legs. His beard had been pure white for as long as anybody could remember. He habitually wore a clean, faded blue cloth wrapped loosely about his head, peasant fashion, and when he walked the mile to his fields carried a long staff—quite an Old Testament figure. Pritam would never hear of the Sistine Chapel, but would have been humbled and amazed to learn that Michelangelo had once painted his image of God with a face, expression and physique much like Pritam's own.

It was 1992 and this morning he walked slowly, almost ploddingly, to his well, where his son Surjit and their workers were crushing sugarcane. Over one shoulder he carried a cloth bag holding a well-wrapped brass container. He could feel its warmth. He was taking his workers their morning tea, a task customarily left to servants, children or the very old. Pritam had been widowed for many years and he lived with Surjit, his grandchildren and a growing flock of little great-grand-children. Pritam was respected in the village for his upright, hard-working character and humility. He also took an interest in every-thing. Above the door of his house was the legend: "O Nanak, I am drunk with the wine of God's name day and night." Pritam rarely engaged in anger, violence or recrimination. He was not fanatic or intolerant when it came to his Sikh religion, as some of the villagers were, nor did he discriminate against lower castes and women, as so many Hindus did. Like Guru Nanak, the founder of Sikhism, Pritam was a man of gentle ways and a kindly sense of humor who relished life.

This morning, as he left his house, which faced open wheat and clover fields at the edge of Ghungrali village, Pritam could hear amplified men's voices coming from the Sikh temple, built on a hill so that its whitewashed Mogul-style dome festooned with prayer flags could be seen over all the rooftops. They were reciting from the *Guru Granth Sahib*, the anthology of sixteenth-century hymns and verses that is the Sikhs' sacred scripture. It was one of his favorite passages:

> As a team of oxen are we driven
> By the plowman, our teacher
> By the furrows made are thus writ
> Our actions—on the earth, our paper.
> The sweat of labor is as beads
> Falling by the plowman as seeds sown.
> We reap according to our measure
> Some for ourselves to keep, some to others give.
> O Nanak, this is the way to truly live. . . .

Unconsciously, Pritam took in the familiar houses of his neighbors, the usual Punjabi huddle of brick and earthen dwellings, each with high walls enclosing cattle yards, small gardens and open verandas where the women sat and cooked. The murmur of children's voices reciting a lesson in unison came from the yellow brick primary school. Beside it, in a large open ground where the earth was tinged pink with heather, was the village pond, its surface bright with green scum.

Beyond the pond rose Ghungrali's great old banyan tree, which some said was a hundred years old. What elopements, sword fights and drunken quarrels it must have seen! Its heavy branches used to spread out thirty, forty feet in each direction. Over the years dangling roots, slowly reaching the ground, took root to form new trunks to support the giant horizontal limbs. The banyan tree was so old it had become grovelike in appearance. Underneath it nothing grew and the air was shady and cool. Here twenty years ago, before everybody bought rope at a store, the village men used to gather on the ground and braid ropes from rice grass for the wheat harvest. There was plenty of gossip too.

Now the banyan tree was dying. Most of the giant old branches were bare. Hardly a week passed that one of them, rotten and decaying, did not come crashing down. The tree was a terrible eyesore just as one entered the village. Children were warned to stay well away. Worse, vultures, hideous with their dark plumage and small, naked red heads, gathered to swoop and soar above the tree, many settling in the bare branches. Nobody knew why the banyan was dying or why the voiceless vultures, with their sinister chorus of weak hisses, had come to roost in such large numbers. Vultures would not attack a man, it was said, but if they did they would go for the eyes.

"It is an ill omen," Pritam thought, disturbed by the macabre spectacle. "Something is killing the tree. Something is in the air." Pritam knew the names of all the crops and herbs around Ghungrali, all the animals and stones. He knew a red haze at sunset might mean a dust storm, that thunder and lightning from the east might mean hail. If the temperature dropped too suddenly, it was snowing in the Himalayas. "When the *bambina* bird chirrups," he told his spellbound great-grandchildren, "it will definitely rain tomorrow. It lives in holes in the earth like rats. But it is a very good bird, children, and doesn't eat our crops. And if you are really old like me, you can tell rain is coming from pains in your joints and rheumatism."

In the old days they called him Pritam Ghorawallah, Pritam the Horseman. He had always kept a horse as a youth, and when he and his fellow villagers fled to Punjab in 1947 from Lyallpur District in what was now Pakistan, Pritam brought his horse with him. In India he survived for a time by driving a *tonga*, or horsecart, in Ludhiana. He knew his livestock. "A dog's life span is about twelve years," he told the children, "but a cow, buffalo or bullock averages twenty. You can tell the age of a buffalo from its horns and teeth. First come milk teeth, then two new big ones after two and a half years, after age three and after four and a half. Once a bullock has six big teeth it is in the prime of its youth, five or six years. After that it is good for work for another six years. You first put a bullock under the yoke after it grows those first two big teeth. After eight or nine years, the teeth start getting smaller and pulling away from the gums. If these animals get really old like me, they can't walk nicely and lose their teeth."

To the children Pritam seemed to know everything. He told them sparrows would only eat grain if it was green; they found ripe grain too hard to swallow. And that herons stood on the banks of ponds at night like watchmen: "They stand on one leg and sleep with one eye and watch the water of a pond at night just like a *chowkidar*. They don't go to the treetops at night like crows and vultures do." But he did not know why the banyan tree was dying.

Ghungrali came to an end at the pond and the banyan tree. One narrow strip of paving headed east to the Grand Trunk Road, India's famed highway from Lahore to Calcutta, though the villagers thought of it as linking Delhi and the nearest Punjabi city of Ludhiana twenty miles to the north. A second paved lane headed south toward the land allotments where Pritam had his farm. As he walked along he soon left the village behind him and all about was the broad, limitless Punjab Plain, broken by clumps of trees around each well and pump house. One after another, almost identical, these small farms, most of them fifteen acres, stretched to the dusty white mist that was the horizon. In recent years eucalyptus trees had been planted and now, tall and stately, like poplars along country lanes in Europe, they lined the roads and set off one field from the next, so that the landscape was quite wooded.

The wheat was still green but starting to ripen. There were also fields of bright yellow mustard and the lush green plots of *berseem*, Indian clover grown as fodder. Along the edges of some fields marigolds and sunflowers were planted. There had been a heavy rain during the night and everything was an intensely fresh green. Pritam had been woken by flashes of lightning and peals of thunder. Now he saw where the rain and wind had whipped through some of the fields, leaving a path of fallen wheat. "It's lost," he told himself in dismay. The wheat was too ripe to stand up again. Pritam guessed the worst damage was where urea—nitrogen fertilizer—had been applied most heavily. Fields planted in PVW34, a more yellowish variety that was high-yielding but hard to thresh, had hardly lodged at all. HD2329 wheat, planted earlier, was still standing. It, too, was riper and lighter.

Pritam gave a heavy sigh. All these names. Twenty-five years ago, when what they called the green revolution had just begun, there was Khalyan Sona, PV18, 227 and later on RR21, Triple Dwarf. Now in 1992 it was Hybrid Delhi 2329, Kundam and LL711, also a durum wheat, PVW34. Insects adapted too, yields fell and new resistant varieties had to be bred as fast as new biotypes and viruses came along.

A covey of partridges, startled by Pritam's approach, rose up and flew away to more distant wheat fields. He heard the morning sound of turtledoves. A flock of black crows cawed and scolded, and flapped their wings at Pritam as they made up their minds whether to take to flight. Once they did, they flew up, one after another, and headed for their daytime roosts in Ghungrali. They would come back to the trees in the fields at dusk.

All the while Pritam saw the same thing: sky, wheat, hazy dust, a blinding white sun. The warmth of the sun felt good on his old bones. Way off to the right, water was splashing from a tube well, the outlet set high in the air so the farmer could see it from his fields, and come running if anything went wrong. In one wheat field, Pritam saw with amusement that a black pot was propped up on a stick to ward off the Evil Eye of envious neighbors.

Ahead a cart laden with dried cotton sticks came toward Pritam. A man was lying on top of the load. He had been watering his fields all night. Drowsing in the sunshine, he raised his head, saw it was Pritam and called to him. The bullocks put out their heads toward him too, and the cart gave a piercing creak.

"*Sat Sri Akal, ji!*" the man cried in the traditional Sikh greeting. "Are you hale and hearty, young man?"

"*Tik hai, maharaj, mauj hai,*" Pritam replied, chuckling. "*Kush hun.* I'm happy. *Pani lugya?* Did you finish watering?"

"Yes, all night." The man shaded his eyes with his hand. "Why is the sun so bright this morning?"

Pritam gave a little laugh. "There is so much darkness inside you." He went on and soon passed two small boys cutting fodder. They squatted side by side in a patch of lush green *berseem*, swinging their sickles. Each grasped a handful at a time and advanced slowly, rocking to each side in a squatting position, knees akimbo, leaving swaths of clover on the stubble behind them.

Pritam did not have far to go. When he turned off the lane into the pathway to his well he could hear a village boy who worked with them calling to the bullocks, "*Putchkar, putchkar.* Oh, may you die!" The bullocks, one white and one tawny, were yoked to a log. They went slowly round and round, as the log turned two rotating iron cylinders, which crushed juice from the sugarcane. Pritam's son, Surjit, a big, barrel-chested, laconic man, sat beside the crusher and fed in stalks of cane. To one side, several workers were cooking *gur*, or brown sugar. A fire had been lit in an underground pit below an enormous iron pan whose sides rested on the surface of the ground. As sugar was crushed, its juice was poured into this pan, which steamed and smoked as it concentrated into dark sticky sugar. Some would be used at home, some sold to be refined into white sugar, which was less nourishing as food. One man kept the fire going by stuffing sugarcane chaff down into it.

"*Ram bol de!* You remember God!" cried the boy as he followed the bullocks on their monotonous round with a stick.

When Pritam arrived, work stopped and the men squatted around in a semicircle while he poured the still-warm tea, milky and sugary as the Punjabis liked it, into their upraised glasses. These, dusty from staying at the well, were hastily rinsed, but were none too clean. After tea everybody went back to work and Pritam went to relieve Surgit at the crusher, where he sat on the ground to feed in the cane. Pritam was so tall that each time the bullocks made a round he had to duck his head, which he did unconsciously.

At the pit, Bawa, a husky, brown-skinned man from Ghungrali's lowly Mazhbi sweeper caste, skimmed off the scum from the steaming sugar with a giant spoon, which he poured into a wooden pail. "This will be good for my pigs," he said with a grin.

"We used to use it to distill liquor," said Surjit, who was watching him. "Now we don't." Everyone knew that Surjit drank little, but that Sudagar, Pritam's other son, who had a house apart, was a real drunkard who once scandalized the village by bringing a bottle right into the temple.

Bawa laughed, showing strong white teeth. "Now the police will catch you." He called to the other workers, who were beardless, shorn Hindus, "O Biharis, fetch more stalks for the fire!" Like most of Ghungrali's landless laborers, untouchables whom Mahatma Gandhi called Harijans, or "children of God," Bawa resented the seasonal migrant workers who came from the poorer states of Uttar Pradesh and Bihar.

Another man was approaching them, coming across the wheat fields. Wearing glasses and a dark blue turban, he was as white-bearded and tall as Pritam himself. He did not look thirty-three years younger, though he was. *"Sat Sri Akal, maharaji!"* the newcomer called in a hearty fashion. Pritam recognized Charan, the son of one of his cousins, who used to own the next farm. Now he had sold most of his land and moved away from the village. *"Sat Sri Akal!"* Pritam replied, and rose to greet his old friend. *"Kya hal chal hai?* Are you hale and hearty, Pritamji?" the other cried in a jovial manner, giving a hoarse laugh that revealed he had lost all his teeth. Charan's clothes were very white and clean in the manner of elderly Sikhs who devote themselves to prayer and attaining salvation. Pritam knew Charan to be sixty-one; he looked much older.

Charan sat down on the canal bank, spreading out a sweater to sit on, and Pritam went back to his place at the crusher. They talked about the storm in the night. "If it rains again before the harvest," Pritam said, "we could lose much. It is all in the hands of God."

"There in Chawar Khas, where I live now, they grow too much sugarcane," Charan told Pritam. "But nobody knows how to make liquor from it." He had to raise his voice over the groan of the crusher and the creak of the bullocks' yoke.

"It's been like deep winter here," Pritam said.

"It's cold where we are too. In Ludhiana last night there were so many mosquitoes." Charan said he had come by train from Uttar Pradesh and spent the night with his daughter, Rani, and her husband, Binny, who farmed near the city.

"Did I feel a raindrop?" Pritam asked.

Charan looked up. "It's only that one small cloud overhead."

"We are not salt that will melt away," Pritam said.

"Oh, your good fates," cried the boy. *"Hat, hat!"* He made a sound by pressing his tongue to the roof of his mouth and releasing it with a jerk. The bullocks picked up their pace a little.

"Your juice bucket is full."

"Yes." Pritam nodded. "Let him take a round first. We'll stop on this side. There was a procession in Ludhiana, I heard."

"I didn't see it. I came at noon and stayed at Rani's."

"There were a lot of our Sikhs in procession. Because they want to raise our taxes. Those Delhi *wallahs* are drowning the boats of the Jats."

When they emptied the bucket, Pritam told the boy to bring more cane. He told Charan, "The camel is best for crushing sugarcane. There are no Persian wheels here anymore."

"Yes, Pritamji, camels are not sold here now. In the old days we got such beautiful saddles for them." Pritam worked for a time buried in thought. Then he asked Charan, "Do you remember how your father would go here and there, gossiping and doing nothing? There were so many like that in those days. We called them 'those in white clothes.' But Sadhu Singh was a clever man. Look how he brought all those seeds and machinery from the university." He again became thoughtful. "Everybody wanted to go to America in those days. One man sold his land to go and told his father-in-law, 'You take care of your fields and I will go to America.' But who was to go and who was to take him? The poor man remained there, losing his land."

"It is enough if only we fill our bellies morning and night," Charan said. "There's no money in farming, Pritamji. I have forty acres now, but I get food only, not profit."

"How is Suka?" Pritam asked, using the nickname of Sukhdev, Charan's oldest son, who had lost his arm in a threshing accident.

"He's still drinking," Charan said, shaking his head. "Kulwant gives him half his share. Sukhdev is not doing much."

A worker came up with a fresh load of cane. "*Shabash*, my son," Pritam told him. "It is good you brought more." He pushed stalks into the crusher. "It is hot and close today. There surely will be rain."

"Now God is after our mustard."

"Do you think He's not after our wheat? With the rain it goes down and becomes shaky at the root. I fear we lost some last night." He fed some cane into the crusher, then frowned. "When we first came here from Lyallpur the people from the nearby villages would tease us because we wore white clothes. 'How can you be farmers?' they would ask. Now we have shown them."

"It's the same in Charan Khas," Charan said. "When we first moved there from Ghungrali and began sowing wheat, all the Hindus and Muslims who lived around us came and said, 'You are foolish. You will starve. Why don't you grow gram and mustard?' That first year we got twenty quintals of wheat per acre. How they were praising us then! Now they are all growing wheat. These UP *wallahs* are useless people, Pritamji. They have no money. They don't like to work hard. That's why they never tried wheat before. And I'm running to pay this and that bribe every third day. It's not like Punjab." All the Punjabis agreed that the villages down on the Gangetic Plain were poor and backward. Charan rose to his feet, saying he had to be on his way. "You still work as hard as ever, Pritamji. These youngsters can't beat you."

Pritam went with Charan as far as the road. His legs were stiff from sitting at the crusher. "Older people like me get joint pains," he said.

"It is the greed of work."

"Work can keep you healthy. An idle man gets lead in his bones. Well, Charan, in the old days there were no machines. We depended on each other and had affection for each other. Now machines have taken over. Nobody feels the same way."

"I know, Pritamji. We used to take care of each other. Not any-more."

Pritam was sorry Charan and his family had left Ghungrali. Charan had great respect for Pritam. When as Sikhs they fled for their lives from what was now Muslim Pakistan in 1947, Charan was sixteen and Pritam forty-nine. In all the years since, Charan had never known Pritam to be other than worthy. "I had four sons," Charan argued with him now. "If I had stayed in Ghungrali, how much land would each have got?" But now, Pritam thought, one is dead from a road accident and another has lost his arm. Both sons were drunk at the time. "You see what fate makes of a man," Pritam said aloud. "What he was and what he becomes? It's a joke of God. Nobody has any power over it."

"I tell my sons to keep farming and live together," Charan went on. "If they leave farming and sell the land and go to the city to work, the family will die away. In farming at least you can get your food. A farmer cannot die of hunger. I feel I have settled my children, Pritamji. God knows what will happen in India in the next twenty years with these Hindu political gangs. I can only tell my sons to stick to farming and stay together. Bad times are coming in India."

When Pritam returned to his well, he told Surjit, "Charan was foolish to leave the village. If he wanted to become a big landlord he could have bought land in Ghungrali itself. If he needed money, I would have given him a loan. He never asked. After our deaths, our children will have no ties with each other. His sons will never come back to Ghungrali. They have no ties here."

It worried Pritam that the widow of Charan's son Kuldeep had refused to leave Charan's old wellhouse in the fields after her husband was killed. She and her three small children lived in a desperate condition, barely surviving on the last two acres Charan owned in Ghungrali. By rights this land should have gone to her children, but Charan had never signed over the title to them. Pritam did not know what had happened to Charan, who did not look after his family but wandered about, making pilgrimages to Sikh holy places and affecting great piety. He left his surviving sons to fend for themselves on their newly cleared jungle land in Chawar Khas. What would become of them and the poor nearly crazed daughter-in-law and her children?

When Pritam got back to the crusher, the boy with the bullocks told him, "We'll soon be finished, Sardarji."

"Finished?" Pritam asked. "The finished are those who don't come back to this earth. We are the living."

II

Pritam's ancestral village of Bija was just across the fields from Ghungrali on the Grand Trunk Road. In 1910, when he was a boy, Pritam had gone with his family to the village of Lyallpur in the far west of Punjab, where the British colonial government was settling Jat Sikh farmers on reclaimed desert. The British, once they finally defeated them in battle in 1849, had a special affinity for the Sikhs, who in turn stayed loyal when the rest of northern India rebelled against the British Raj in the Sepoy Mutiny of 1857. Five rivers flowed onto the Punjab Plain from the Himalayas and gave it its name (*panch:* five, *ab:* water). In 1905–17 the British dug a network of canals to draw water from three of these rivers, the Ravi, Jhelum and Chenab, and here Pritam's father, a deeply indebted sharecropper at home, was given twenty-five acres, as was his brother, whose son, Sadhu Singh, was Charan's father.

The Sikh Jats who colonized what had been a barren waste had become the most prosperous peasants in Asia when, at midnight on August 15, 1947, India was partitioned into two independent nations. When word came that the new frontier would fall well to the southeast of their village of Lyallpur, even south of Lahore near the Sikh holy city of Amritsar, Pritam's family and neighbors knew they would have to flee south. Pritam told his cousin's son, Charan, then a strapping, beardless youth, "We must go through Muslim lands. This is a time when everyone holds his head in the palm of his hand, Charan. There is no way out, son. Before the bullets of those against us, you will know your own strength."

As Pritam was to tell his great-grandchildren, "We left everything. We left with empty hands." It was noon on a hot, sunny day when they fled Lyallpur. Muslims from the village began to loot the houses and seized one Sikh's bullock cart. Pritam remembered shouting to men still plowing in the fields, "Come, we're going!" and they dropped everything and came, just as they were. Charan's sister, Surjit, who was eighteen, had just given birth to her first child and, separated in the chaos from her husband, she sat in a cart with her nine-day-old baby, Pala, in her lap.

"There was danger every step of the way," Pritam recalled. "Our caravan must have been four or five miles long. Five, six hundred bullock carts moving in single file. The fields were green." Once they fought off a marauding band of Baluchi tribesmen; they put together a homemade muzzle-loading cannon and killed twelve of the attackers. The remaining Baluchis, about fifteen men, fled into an abandoned Sikh village. When they were captured and asked why they had attacked the peaceful caravan of bullock carts, the Baluchis spat in their faces and declared, "It is our will! *Allah-o-Akbar!*" After Pritam went back to the bullock carts, some of the men locked the Baluchis in a house and set fire to it.

Pritam could still see the landscape as they moved southward, green fields scorched with fire and strewn with corpses and severed heads, gore and flesh like sheep in a slaughterhouse, the wells poisoned or stuffed with bodies. Once a school friend of Charan's believed some Muslim soldiers guarding a bridge who told him he could pass to the other side provided he submitted to a search; they stripped him and cut him to pieces. Several hundred Sikhs from the steadily growing caravan trusted some Baluchi soldiers who told them to go to the main square of Jarawala town, where trucks would carry them across the frontier; instead they were mowed down by machine guns positioned on the roofs, nearly ten thousand of them.

The journey south should have taken three or four days; Pritam's family carried provisions for ten. Yet they still experienced starvation: It took twenty-seven days to reach the frontier. Across the flooded land they were met by Gurkha soldiers who told them, "You are in India now. No Muslim will attack you here." Cruelly, they had no sooner reached safety than cholera broke out, claiming Pritam's wife and Charan's youngest sister and only brother. Lacking medicine, the men tried to save them by pouring a mixture of country liquor and raw onions down their throats, but they vomited it up. At last the family reached Bija. They had covered a distance of more than two hundred and fifty miles, weaving back and forth to avoid Muslim villages and the city of Lahore.

Even in Bija there was little but desolation. Sand dunes drifted in the near-desert of stubble fields. Only a little scorched sugarcane was left standing. The Muslim villages had been looted, razed, abandoned. An uncle had taken the possessions and gathered what crops he could from fleeing Muslims. These he gave them. With his help, Pritam and a brother, Amrit, and his cousins, Charan's father, Sadhu, and an uncle, Sarban, were each allotted fifteen acres in the nearby village of Ghungrali-Rajputan. The new Indian government in Delhi was giving land left by the Muslims to Sikh Jat refugees from Pakistan.

Pritam first saw Ghungrali just after they arrived in Bija. Fifteen days earlier its Muslim population, swollen with refugees, perhaps some 15,000 to 20,000 people in all, had been massacred by Sikh mobs from Ludhiana and Hindu Dogra soldiers. The stench was terrible. Soldiers were still stuffing corpses into all the wells and sealing them with concrete. Some were burned. Not a single house was left standing. Only the shell of a brick mosque survived fire. Men were already tearing it down and stacking the bricks to make a Sikh temple. How could anybody live there?

Charan's father, Sadhu Singh, decided he could not. Nor did he intend to engage in physical labor. "I have never taken my hands out of my pockets, Pritamji, and I never shall as long as I live," he vowed. Then the land around Ghungrali was watered by Persian wheels turned by camels, which walked round and round drawing water up in buckets from deep wells. None of the Sikhs from Lyallpur had ever used one; they had irrigated with canal water. Aside from its Muslims, now entirely gone, Ghungrali also had quite a few landless Sikh Harijans, who were coming back now to rebuild their houses. One of these low-caste Sikhs agreed to farm Sadhu's allotment on a fifty-fifty basis, using looted bullocks and tools. Sadhu took his family off to Rajasthan's Ganganagar District, where the desert was being reclaimed. They stayed five years, and Pritam, who aside from farming sometimes drove his horsecart in the city to make ends meet, heard that Charan supported the family by working with the Harijans as a hired field laborer by day and tilling the family's own fields at night. Years later Charan told him, "You know, Pritamji, those hardest years of my life were also the happiest. Maybe work is good for a man."

In 1953, when consolidation of its once-scattered farms was completed and low-interest loans were made available to Ghungrali's farmers, Pritam, his brother Amrit and their cousins Sadhu, who brought his family back to Punjab, and Sarban all got tube wells and began farming four fifteen-acre farms in Ghungrali side by side. This went amiably enough, except when they quarreled over water. Once at night Pritam found Charan in a violent fight with his uncle Sarban and Sarban's young son, Dhakel, over whose turn it was to use an irrigation canal. Charan was out in the fields, his face streaked with blood and his clothes torn, shouting like a madman, "I'll rape your mother!"

Sadhu Singh, fetched from the village, arrived panting for breath and in a foul temper. "Now do whatever you want!" Sarban called to him. "We have taught your brave son a lesson, elder brother!" "I'll see who touches his water, by God!" Sadhu roared back. As the brothers abused each other and Pritam tried to calm them down, Charan staggered over to the canal and hacked away some mud with his hoe so that water flowed into his field. "Look! Look! I'm taking the water!" he cried. "I'll see who touches this water! Let's see how brave you are!"

Sadhu Singh, seeing Charan had got the upper hand, heaped scorn on his brother. "Yes, you have beaten him to the full, you and your son, but Charan is still standing there. Why didn't you leave him slain in the field?" By now Pritam saw they were all drunk. But for a long time afterward Sadhu and Sarban did not speak to each other. Only Pritam knew their reconciliation followed a secret visit by Sarban on the night before Dhakel's marriage. Sarban wept and begged Sadhu's forgiveness, imploring him, "Look, you are my elder brother. I live next door to you. My land is beside your land. If you refuse to come to Dhakel's wedding, what will my in-laws say? I shall be disgraced."

For the two older men the incident was forgotten. Sometimes, if he got drunk, Dhakel might boast, "We taught that drunkard Charan a lesson he won't forget." Or he might lament, "Oh, this liquor is a dangerous thing. We cousins were fighting like dogs that night. I'm sorry about that." In the Punjab, it was commonly said, most fights came after drinking and were over money, women, land or water.

III

"It rained and rained that year, more rain than there has been before or since." The red light of the open fire cast flickering shadows on the handsome, pockmarked face of Gurdial Singh, the leader of Ghungrali's Harijans, giving it a cadaverous, demonic appearance. It was late evening of the day in 1992 Pritam had been crushing cane and met Charan, and some of the Harijans were gathered in Gurdial's courtyard. With a poultry farm of two thousand birds, Gurdial was the richest low-caste untouchable in the village. He also headed its Congress faction, whereas most Jats belonged to Akali Dal, the main Sikh political party. Gurdial loaned money to Jats and he was as well-to-do as some of them, but as a lowly Chamar, the leatherworking caste, he lived with his fellow Harijans. The fire cast a flickering halo over the group of men and boys who huddled together, sitting or squatting, in a semicircle at the feet of Gurmel, another chamar. He and two Harijan elders sat cross-legged on a *charpoy* and, like their audience, lit a single *bidi*, or cheroot, from time to time and passed it one man to another, as Harijans do, unlike the Jats, who never smoked. Although the moon was shining, everything outside the red halo looked impenetrable and dark. The cattle in the yard were hardly noticeable in the gloom except for their munching and snuffling. Over the fire, Gurdial's wife had fixed a cauldron for boiling water and she bent over it in the smoke, waiting for the first signs of bubbles. Old Poondi, the Mazhbi barn cleaner, and his son, Bawa, sat side by side in silence, deep in thought and looking into the fire. Gurmel, once a sharecropper for Charan's uncle Sarban, was a thin, hungry-looking man who sat and absently twisted his mustaches; his shadow danced over Mukhtar, long Charan's own laborer, and at times it hid and at times revealed Mukhtar's aging but still strong face.

"In July of that year—1947—there was a rumor there would be a separate state of Pakistan for the Muslims," Gurdial said. "Except for us Harijan Sikhs, all the people in Ghungrali were Muslim. They used to tell us, 'Get your hair and beards shaved and we'll get Pakistan all the way down to Delhi.' Then after some days we came to know that the Pakistan boundary would be to the north, above Amritsar." At once, Gurdial said, rumors of Hindus massacring Muslims came from Calcutta and, within a day, from nearby villages. Muslim refugees began pouring into Ghungrali. At first the local Muslim families and the refugees decided to move to Malerkotla, a strong point the Indian Army was defending, but at the last moment a decision was taken to stand and fight. "No one had any idea how many thousands of Sikhs would come from the cities to attack here," Gurdial said. He reached into his shirt, pulled out a *bidi*, lit it, took a puff and passed it on. The fire flared up and shadows in the gloom flickered and danced.

"Aye, thousands," sighed Gurmel. "Such a cutting and harvesting." Gurdial said the Harijan women and children fled to the neighboring village of Majari, already inhabited only by Sikhs, but the Muslims kept the men back to help them guard Ghungrali. "We had to obey them," he said. "I used to come and keep people informed, going between here and Majari." Gurmel kept silent, thinking how Gurdial had made his fortune by looting.

"From dawn onward that day no one could slip away. There were seven hundred Muslim families living in Ghungrali then, and with so many refugees here there must have been fifteen to twenty thousand Muslims in all. The Muslims thought they were safe. They were ready to fight back as soon as they saw the Sikhs start to surround the village at daybreak. At two o'clock in the afternoon, Dogra soldiers opened fire. Those soldiers were all clean-shaven Hindus. A Hindu general sent them in. The Muslims had muzzle-loading rifles. They answered fire. From outside the barrage was heavier. Some Muslims had positions on the tops of houses. All the Harijan men, Mazhbis and

Chamars alike, gathered before that big iron gate that used to separate us from the Muslim quarter."

"That gate was open, I remember," Gurmel said, the scene coming back to him. "We locked our houses and gathered at that gate. This village was very strong. The Jats knew it and were afraid. They didn't dare attack without the army. At about four o'clock in the afternoon those Dogras came with machine guns. They started firing from the road to Majari. We watched them come from the tops of the houses. Thousands and thousands they were, Sikhs and Hindus and Dogra soldiers, like herds of sheep surrounding the village. Countless. Everywhere you looked you saw them coming. All the village was surrounded except the side toward Ghazipur. It was still open. Some were trying to escape."

"When the Muslims saw they couldn't cope with the heavy incoming fire," Gurdial continued, "they all ran back to their houses, as did the Harijans. The firing stopped and thousands upon thousands of men came pouring into these streets. They came running first into the streets of the Harijan side, Sikhs who demanded we give them matches and kerosene. Each Harijan had to provide them as a test of loyalty. Those Sikhs came rushing in with spears, *gandasas* and swords.

"Each of us had to give matchboxes and kerosene oil. We poured sand on our roofs to stop the fires."

Gurdial's voice rose. "The Sikhs shouted, 'Kill these kaffirs!' and there was a deafening roar of '*Jo Bole So Nihal Sat Sri Akal!* Who speaks he is full of the name of God!' We crouched in our houses. We could hear the screams of women and the shouts of our Muslim friends. 'Help us! We are being killed!' "

"It just ran like fire. Men who were hungry for generations started raping women right in the courtyards. Some of the women jumped into wells—those who wouldn't allow the touch of another man's hands. I saw a woman holding a child. They tore the baby from her and speared him in the air in front of her eyes."

Gurdial turned on Gurmel angrily. "I saw no rapes. Nobody could think of rape. It was a moment when sons forget their mothers and mothers forget their sons. It was a mass panic."

"Did you rape, Gurmel?" someone asked.

"As God may not bring lies to my tongue," swore Gurmel. "At that time I was but a soft boy. But I saw many others do it."

"Some were killed inside their houses, others while trying to escape," Gurdial continued. "Many ran into the sugarcane fields, seeking to hide. Some of the Muslims who lived in Ghungrali escaped, but most of the refugee Muslims fell, not knowing where to run. Women jumped into the wells of their courtyards or flung themselves from the rooftops into the streets. Some jumped into ponds and drowned themselves. We had the heaviest rains in memory that year and even the big pond by the banyan tree had flooded its banks."

Old Poondi, whose real name was Kishan Singh but whom everyone called "Little Bug," cleared his throat and spoke for the first time. "I ran when the attack came. Before that the Muslims wouldn't let us go."

Someone laughed. "Oh, Poondi, what a *budmash* you are!" calling him a rascal.

"No, no, Maharaj, don't say that. The wells were filled with women and there was a cutting and harvesting of human heads. I ran to a sugarcane field and hid myself there. That's all I know."

"Oh, Poondi, tell us more."

"That's all I know. I have done nothing except spend my life cleaning people's barns. That's all. *Bas!*"

But they persuaded him to go on.

"I heard the fire open from the Majari side and saw a lot of men running through the streets. I was afraid only that I may not be caught and killed. A Jat shouted at me, 'Run away! Leave the village or we'll kill you!' I ran to a sugarcane field and those hooligans started cutting and harvesting and picking up utensils and what they could find in the houses. My children were still inside my house. Pray to God they'd locked the door! I ran into that field and dug a ditch and pulled cane around me without taking my breath inside my chest, without moving or leaving that place until night. My children came searching for me in the field, afraid that someone had killed me. It was dark and there was much shrieking and yelling, 'Oh, people, we are being killed! We are being looted! Save us!' I heard the fire of a Bren gun. *Kar! Kar! Kar!* Some hungry persons were riding the women. I saw a lot, there in the dark."

Everyone looked at the tombstone in the courtyard in silence.

"There are many terrible things in the world," remarked Mukhtar.

"Many, many!" affirmed Poondi, who drew nearer his neighbors, huddling up, as if he felt a chill.

"After the attack, all of us went to Majari," said Gurdial, continuing the narrative. "Some people were taking away bales of loot on their heads."

"I also looted some grains and utensils from the Muslims," admitted Gurmel, watching Gurdial closely.

But the other made no admission. He said, "I had a round in this street. Dead bodies were jammed into the wells, the courtyards, the houses, the fields. After the attack it was three months before people stopped coming to dig in the ashes. The day after the attack the police came and made us Harijans come with them. They made us take wood and whatever we could find and burn the bodies. There were no vultures, no dogs around. Even six months later the stench in Ghungrali was terrible. Like the children, most of the women died. I would wager less than two percent of the women escaped.

"Only one of the Muslims ever came back. It was about two and a half years later. His sons had been lost in the attack and he did not know whether they'd been killed or just lost in the escape. People treated him nicely. His name was Buga Numindar."

"In Bhambadi," said Mukhtar, as if wanting to confirm some goodness in human nature, "the Sikhs protected a Muslim family which still lives there. Those four brothers who rent land near Charan's."

"If the number of Muslim families in a village was small," Gurdial said, "their Sikh neighbors usually hid them. But the Sikhs said they were afraid of this village because it was so big and they felt they must attack it. It was the custom then to send one person from each family to join in the attack; otherwise the Sikhs would kill you. Because I had been in the military both sides had the impression I must have a rifle hidden somewhere, stolen from the army, and both sides wanted me.

"After the attack, we Harijans had in mind that now we'd get the land. We told ourselves, 'Now the land is ours.' We were not even aware that there were Jat Sikh farmers living in Pakistan. But after only fifteen days the Jat refugees came. And the government gave the land to them. We were already cultivating it and had given it out to all the Harijan families. But no. They gave the land to these strangers. They confirmed how much each Jat family owned in Pakistan and gave them land accordingly. Our families had lived in Ghungrali for generations and generations. Mahatma Gandhi promised to help the Harijans. When the Jats first took over the land, they promised us two-thirds of the harvest for tilling it for them. But little by little they reduced our share. Now only twenty-two acres of common land is left to the Harijans. Even if we get a third of its earnings all the money goes to pave the roads or to the school."

Gurmel said the same thing. "We all assumed that once the Muslims were gone we would get their land. We all took possession. I harvested two hundred maunds of grams that year and plowed the fields. But we had to vacate and remained landless."

"Now all these years we are yoked by these Jats," Mukhtar grumbled.

"Oh, but there is a difference between these Jats and the Muslims," cautioned Gurdial. "Now we can touch a drinking glass of a Jat. We never dared touch a Muslim's. The Muslims hated us. A Muslim would never let a Harijan cross his threshold. We were like serfs in those days." His story ended, Gurdial looked around at his listeners. No one spoke but their eyes were still fixed on him. The men thought over what was said and how it evoked in their minds that which had been in their own lives. Alone among the audience, Mukhtar, who had nine years of schooling, might listen with skepticism, mentally noting the contradictions. But for the rest, seeing each other's faces in the halo of firelight, the massive darkness, the sense of their flat, open plain that stretched to the horizon in all directions, these and their own fates seemed in themselves so incomprehensible, even the wildest imaginings came to seem to be true. Each of them, even the youngest, had grown up aware of the crumbling Muslim graves and the sealed old wells filled with thousands upon thousands of human skeletons.

IV

In 1970, by the time he was thirty-nine, Charan was a giant of a man, almost as tall as Pritam himself. Charan's eyes were already shadowed, but underneath his bushy black eyebrows the eyes themselves sparkled with intelligence and life. When he gave his hoarse, deep laugh, he had a look of great vitality and enjoyment. Yet his asthma had worsened over the years in such a dusty land and during a bad attack, as he lay gasping in his bed, a harsh rasping sound arose deep inside his chest and throat.

Pritam worked hard in the fields beside his laborers. Charan did less and less and drank more. It was not that he was turning over the field work to his sons, as did many of the Jats. His oldest son, Sukhdev, a handsome, surly sixteen-year-old, loathed the village and farm work and wanted to join the army or the police and get away from home as soon as he could. Pritam knew that Suka, as they called the boy, cursed his father, insulted the Harijans and was insolent to his elders, but that Charan closed his eyes to it. In truth, Charan was ashamed. He suspected, rightly, that Sukhdev looked down on him as a drunken peasant with earth-soiled hands. For this reason, he could not bring himself to discipline his son. From time to time there were rumors Suka kept bad company at school. Once Pritam saw the boy hide a sword at Charan's wellhouse. He brought it up with Sadhu Singh, whose beard was turning white. Sadhu lolled around on a *charpoy* in his farmyard and drank tea and dispensed advice all day, very much the elderly patriarch. The old man regarded his grandson as a valuable ally in his disputes with Charan and he refused to let Pritam say anything ill of the boy.

Charan's second son, Kulwant, had also proved disappointing. Charan would say proudly of him, "Now this boy has a real hand for farming." Actually, like his brother, Kulwant, once his father's back was turned, refused to lift a finger to help in the fields. Half educated in Khanna, the nearest market town, like the sons of most of the newly prosperous farmers, and knowing nothing but that they were above dirtying their hands, Sukhdev and Kulwant lived for the day they would leave Ghungrali for good. God knows what fate would await them. Charan's three younger children, Kuldeep and Narinder, the two boys, and Rani, Charan's only daughter, were eager to help their father but too small for any but the most menial chores.

So Charan, like many Jats, relied on hired Harijans, above all his daily laborer, Mukhtar, whom he called Chota, or "Little One." Chota had been working for him for ten years, ever since he was a teenager. Aside from his own fifteen acres in Ghungrali, Charan had to sow, cultivate and harvest twenty-one more acres of newly cleared jungle in the village of Bhadson, twenty-seven miles away. These belonged to his sister, Surjit Kaur, whose husband, having lost his fortune in the partition, sank into opium addiction. Old Sadhu Singh managed to get the land put in Surjit's name and in a few more years her two sons would be old enough to work it. In the meantime the responsibility fell on Charan. Otherwise Sadhu had done well for his daughters, arranging their marriages to two Sikhs in Malaya, a policeman and a moneylender, both of whom would become rich. A fourth daughter was wed to a draftsman in Ludhiana and they later went to Canada. Surjit was Charan's only problem, outside his own family.

Somewhat freed from his old bondage to the land by 1970, Charan drank and caroused; he had cronies in villages for miles around. Once, for the annual April *mela* in Jarg, he took Mukhtar along, and the Harijan, riding on the fender of Charan's big Russian-made tractor, in a clean white shirt, pajamas and a pale yellow turban next to Charan's blue one, looked for all the world like another Jat. In the dusty luminous light of Punjabi country roads in the spring, there was a great flow of tractors, bullock carts and bicycles, all crowded with bobbing Sikh turbans of pink, yellow, red, saffron and green. Charan greeted everybody. "Do you have any opium pellets, young man?"

"No, I'm empty pockets." Soon they came upon Pritam, braiding rope from reeds by the side of the road. "You want to come, Pritamji?" Charan cried in his hoarse voice. "Climb on!" Pritam chuckled and looked ready to go. "My sons," he told them, "I have seen so many, many *melas*. Here we'll stay with our ears flapping, waiting to hear all the gossip. Tell me, Charan, how is your father's health? Can he still walk straight with that big tummy of his?" Charan gave a roar of laughter. "You can say anything you like. He is younger than you. But Guru is kind to him." The trip took an hour.

Their first sight of Jarg was the gleaming white Mogul-style dome of its big temple, strung with bright red banners. The way became so crowded Charan could only inch the tractor forward and white clouds of dust rose so that the white shirts of the men and the boys, the bright colors of the turbans and the green foliage of trees took on milky pastel colors. After Charan parked the tractor, he went off to find his in-laws and invite them for a drink. For who stays sober at a *mela?*

Left on his own, Mukhtar strolled about. Many men carried hockey sticks for protection since swords and sticks were banned during a *mela*. Wary policemen strolled about in twos and threes, eyes peeled for drunken fights. A man was selling bullock whips, another pythons. "Look at this godly creature," the vendor cried. "If you feed him he will look after your ancestors." Under a banyan tree a crowd listened raptly to a young man's song—"Awake, my love! Thine eyes are heavy with dreams . . ." Mukhtar saw *bhangra* dancers stamping their feet with wild exuberance, men scratching the ground before a temple to ward off disease, bangle sellers and food stands buzzing with flies and pretty girls selling sweetmeats. Outside a liquor shop with barred windows like a jail, men pushed and shoved as an amplified voice roared, "Five rupees! Five rupees! Here it is, men!"

Mukhtar bought two bottles and shoved them under his belt, Punjabi style, out of sight.

By the time he joined Charan and his in-laws in a dark and noisy cobbler's shop, they were all drunk and shouting. "I'll settle with you tomorrow!" "Who knows about tomorrow? We may die tonight!" "Have another peg!" And so it went until they staggered back to the tractor that afternoon. Two little boys with tired, begrimed faces came by playing toy trumpets and to Mukhtar, as they drove out of Jarg and his head reeled, it seemed the tooting of the little trumpets could still be heard. Over the wheat fields, around the bushes and between the clumps of trees rose a thick mist, white as milk from so much irrigation. Charan sobered up as he drove, and he felt guilty about so many failures and follies it was painful to think of them. He knew he neglected his gentle and kindly wife, that he was often remiss in helping a sister saddled in marriage to an opium addict and that he was partly to blame his sons looked down on him and were disappointing. Charan knew he was a mediocrity, a bit of a drunkard, bad-tempered, the companion of the worst wastrels in the village. And yet he felt resigned to it and looked forward to an evening's laughter over a bottle with some friends, for he knew every man must settle for what he is.

So instead of going home, Charan drove the tractor to his in-laws and there he and Mukhtar had something to eat and more to drink, from there they went to a farmer's in Bija, from the farmer's to another crony's in Majari, and so on. In short, by the time he and Mukhtar reached Ghungrali, they were so drunk they had to hold each other up on the tractor. It was already late. After he opened the gate to Charan's cattle yard, Mukhtar staggered off down the road to his hut, waving his arms and breathing heavily, "Charan is a prince. A prince among men!"

The palsied stable hand, Peloo, waked from his dreams by the tractor's roar, stumbled to the gate, and with cries and sobs from his twisted mouth, helped Charan to maneuver the tractor safely into its shed. Charan staggered out the gate, stopped and with drowsy, drunken eyes looked now at the village pond, now at the banyan tree. Jubru, his Dalmatian, came running to sniff at his master's legs. The dog growled at the night, and in his mind Charan felt that the shadows under the banyan tree, the star-filled sky and the stretch of plain had something mysterious and true to say to him. What had been had no meaning, nor did what was to come, and all he had was this matchless moment, this one moment of life. And Charan held his breath and heard Jubru's growl and the midnight silence, and he saw the pond water shimmering in the moon's pale white light, a light he had not seen before. Then he shook his head drunkenly, as if the shadows, the moonlight and the banyan tree really meant to deceive him into thinking his life was more than the mean and common thing he knew it was. "Ghosts," he whispered. "Ghosts, Jubru." He broke into a great peal of hoarse laughter as he reeled up to his house. "Ghosts! I'll eat them!"

V

Everyone said Basant Singh, the richest farmer in Ghungrali, was hard as flint. While the other villagers might fritter away their days in gossip, drink, chasing women, petty quarrels and the like, Basant Singh's thoughts never strayed from the economy of operations and returns. In matters concerning religion, politics, morality and money, he was harsh and relentless and kept a strict watch, not only over himself and his family but over his servants, field hands and neighbors, and, indeed, the entire village. God forbid that anyone should ever enter his house without being announced.

His office off the veranda of his big blue house was like Basant Singh himself and, needless to say, was the only one in Ghungrali like it: straight-backed chairs stood at attention along each wall below framed photographs of Basant Singh with such luminaries as Norman Borlaug, father of the green revolution; C. Subramanium, a former food minister; Wolf Ladejinsky, a renowned agricultural expert. After a visit to Basant Singh's farm in 1969, Ladejinsky wrote: "He is one of the few big farmers who keep detailed accounts of all his operations and has no reluctance to exhibit them. It is clear that he and many like him—even if with much smaller acreage—have taken advantage of the new technology and profited accordingly." At one end of the office, directly confronting the apprehensive visitor, was Basant Singh's desk, with its neat stacks of files, documents and government periodicals reporting the latest agricultural advances. Against the back wall, steel cabinets held a formidable collection of bound records, for Basant Singh kept detailed accounts not just of all his own farm's operations but of those of the rest of the village as well.

Every conceivable item relating to the cost of production on his own fifty-four acres was there, including amortization of everything that was amortizable, and not excluding food for the seventeen members of his family, four permanent hired men and twenty daily-wage field hands. The last item in his ledger, "Return to Management," summed up the profits of the last season; it showed a net income of 1,600 rupees per acre in the 1968–69 crop year.

Basant Singh did not need to tell his fellow villagers his business; they knew it all by heart. His success story was legendary in the nearby villages. He started out as a poor man with only eight acres when he first came to Ghungrali in 1950. He and an older brother married village girls who inherited land from their fathers. When the government built a canal through their land, Basant Singh saw to it that each of the wives was awarded 10,000 rupees for right-of-way titles. With this money, he managed to get the sole franchise for selling liquor. When new Mexican-bred dwarf wheat varieties first became available, Basant Singh was ready with capital, and the growth of his fortune was phenomenal.

In Punjab, the new seeds were first sold by Dilbagh Singh Atwal, a wheat breeder who marketed his seed crop at two to five rupees a kilo for a return of 70,000 rupees in 1964. The following year, Basant Singh, profiting God knows how from his connections at the university and the agricultural ministry, planted the first of the new wheat seeds in Ghungrali. At the harvest he sold 30,000 kilos of seed for three rupees a kilo, making 90,000 rupees. The next year he planted a still-newer variety, PV18, and sold the seeds for a profit of 70,000 rupees. When Khalyan Sona, the most popular variety in Ghungrali, came the next year and the Punjab state government purchased his entire seed crop, he made another 90,000 rupees. Now each year he sowed more and more acres in ever-newer varieties, making triple the profits of the farmers around him.

Basant Singh's neighbors grew envious, but they learned to take his advice. "The profit we get from our farm production has diminished," he would tell them in his flat calculator-machine voice. "We have to cut back in investment. The new seeds can double production. But somebody hears about it in New Delhi and they reduce the price of grain. Whenever I get a chance, I'll sell my land. There's no money in farming. Business, industry, that's the place to be. Wheat prices may be over 16,000 rupees an acre, but the yield doesn't give you the interest that a 16,000-rupee investment in industry does." To the chosen, Basant Singh would bring out his statistics and charts. "In fact, when we calculate that for the old-fashioned varieties of wheat we needed only five waterings and only half as much fertilizer, and for these new dwarf varieties eight to ten waterings and double the fertilizer, we see we have to spend double but don't get anywhere in terms of profit. Ah, the nation increases its food supply all right. But I'm not talking about the nation. I'm talking about the ordinary farmer.'' By that he meant Basant Singh.

As time went on, so obsessed was he with the economy of operations and returns, Basant Singh began to talk about Ghungrali's landless Harijan laborers not as people like Poondi and Mukhtar and Bawa but as the "labor problem." He looked forward to seeing a modern agricultural version of the trinity—the tractor, the combine and electric power—displacing hired labor to the vanishing point. What happened to the Harijans did not concern him.

A few of the more traditional landowning Jats worried about this. "Basant Singh has really done good for this village," Pritam observed, "but he's too hot-tempered with the Harijans. He has been unfair in his dealings with them."

Once Basant Singh made his fortune, he stopped selling liquor; he sold his franchise for a steep price. He became an advocate of total abstinence and prohibition, declaring, "That's the touchstone of all Ghungrali's problems—drink! All this drinking in the village is enough to make a decent person move into town." In time two factions sprang up among the village Jats: the richest, most technologically advanced and best-educated farmers rallying behind Basant Singh and a second group of younger, poorer Jats who, like Charan, spent much of their time drinking, carousing and skirmishing with one another.

At last Basant Singh announced that no one could enter his area of the village after drinking. "Now we have challenged them," he told his supporters. "I carry a rifle these days. Why? Because we'll teach anybody a lesson who dares to show up around our houses drunk and disorderly. They have no other business except drinking, those young men around Charan. Oh, Charan himself is not bad but they are an evil influence over him. Charan can't hide anywhere. They'll find him, them and their bottles, and he can't escape."

Basant Singh predicted that Charan and old Sadhu Singh would be in deep trouble in a few years. "That son is very fond of alcohol. If anybody drinks and stays sober, I don't mind. But Charan and his friends create trouble, shouting and laughing and carrying on. There is no law and order in Ghungrali. Absolutely none."

If grim, righteous, progressive Basant Singh was the richest landlord in Ghungrali, Charan, with fifteen acres and renting three more, fell just about in the economic middle of Ghungrali's sixty-five Jat land-owning families. With nine family members—he and his wife, Sadhu Singh and the old lady, two teenage sons and three smaller children, plus Peloo and Mukhtar, he had to feed eleven persons each day, to say nothing of the steady ebb and flow of guests his father was forever inviting.

During the winter *rabi* season, Charan usually raised fourteen acres of dwarf wheat, which he harvested in 1969–70 for 1,800 kilos per acre at 76 rupees per 100 kilos. He also raised clover and oats to feed his cattle: six buffaloes, two bullocks, one cow, two female calves and six small male calves. During the hot summer *kharif* season, Charan harvested about 1,200 kilos of cotton, which he sold for 136 rupees per 100 kilos, plus 5,600 kilos of corn for 52 rupees per 100 kilos, 700 kilos of mustard-oil seeds and 1,400 kilos of sugar for home consumption. Once the green revolution began, his land spiraled in value to 15,000 rupees an acre, and while the legal rate of exchange in 1970 was 7.50 rupees to the dollar, its buying power made the real value of a rupee almost equivalent to a dollar. Charan had mortgaged four acres to get a 15,000-rupee loan to build his cattle yard and a concrete cowshed at one end, which also housed his tractor. This had to be repaid to a government bank at 9 percent interest over ten years. Each year Charan and his father also borrowed about 1,200 rupees from the village cooperative to buy seeds and fertilizer; this they repaid after the wheat harvest.

Old Sadhu sometimes suggested that Charan borrow more. But Charan had seen some of his friends slide hopelessly into debt. He told his father, "The real problem is when you borrow money, like taking a loan for fertilizer, and then use it for a marriage instead. Since you haven't used the fertilizer, your crops are poor and then you are in real trouble. It's a question of management, Father. In Ghungrali, you can do well enough with ten acres to have a thresher, a tube well, three bullocks, a tractor and a laborer or two if you manage carefully. Some do."

Many did not, and in their search to find cash for the seeds, fertilizer and tractor fuel the new technology demanded, some Jats in Ghungrali began to repeat Basant Singh's talk about the "labor problem." Harijan labor accounted for half the farm expenses of every Jat.

Basant Singh wanted to mechanize all farm operations. Casting about for allies, he found them in the poorest, most marginal farmers such as One-Eye, the village gossip and troublemaker. They had a common interest in trying to weaken, if not abolish, the traditional Punjabi *jajmani* system of exchanging labor for a fixed share of the harvest.

Basant Singh stayed in the background himself while the Jats formed a thirteen-member committee to negotiate harvest wages with the Harijans. The committee, a front for the rich farmers, was composed of drunkards, opium addicts and generally shiftless Jats. It decreed that daily wages would be reduced from five rupees, plus all meals, to four rupees, without supper, breakfast or morning tea, which had been provided by a Punjabi landlord to his workers for as long as anybody could remember. When his own field hands protested, Basant Singh threw up his hands and said, "I can do nothing. It is a general village settlement and I have to abide by it." While the wage cut generated ill will, few Jats or Harijans suspected Basant Singh was conspiring to do away with the *jajmani* system in Ghungrali altogether.

This development was serious. The *jajmani* system was more than just an economic arrangement between landlord and laborer in Punjab. All over India the exchange of labor for grain and fodder provided the age-old basis of the Hindu caste system. Caste, while it offended Western ideals of equality, provided a sense of belonging to an occupational community of one's own, and had always held India's 576,000 villages together.

Sikhism emphatically condemned the caste system. The *Granth* abounds with verses attacking it, such as the second Guru, Angad's words:

> The Hindus say there are four castes;
> But they are all of one seed.
> 'Tis like the clay of which pots are made
> In diverse shapes and forms—yet the clay is the same.
> So are the bodies of men made of the same five elements.
> How can one amongst them be high and another low?

Yet in practice in Ghungrali one was born a Jat farmer-landowner or a Harijan, either a Chamar, a leatherworker, or a Mazhbi, a barn-cleaning sweeper. The Mazhbis, like Poondi and his sons, with their dark brown skin and short, sturdy stature, had converted to Sikhism earlier and historically had greater ties with the Jats. But both Mazhbis and Chamars suffered constant discrimination. They could not intermarry with Jats or eat in their homes on an equal basis. If Charan fed his workers, they sat on the ground in the courtyard, while Jats sat on chairs or *charpoys*. Nor could the two Harijan castes intermarry or eat in each other's homes. Why did the caste system endure so tenaciously in Punjab?

The Punjabi Jats, tall and fair, were relative latecomers to India. They may have been descended from Scythians, nomadic people who displaced less warlike rivals on the Eurasian steppes, seizing their lands and establishing themselves as overlords of settled cultivators. The Jats did not migrate into northern India from the plains of Central Asia until the time of Julius Caesar. Not until the collapse of the Mogul Empire in the late nineteenth century, did the Jats spread to the most fertile areas and occupy the whole of the Punjab Plain's best farming country. Even in the 1990s, divided among Pakistani Muslims, Hindus in neighboring Rajasthan and Haryana states and Sikhs in Punjab, the Jats keep some of their old warrior spirit, glorying unabashedly in the strength of arms, the number of their cattle and destruction of foes. The Jats never came under the domination of the priests and holy men of the Gangetic Plain who succeeded elsewhere in India in setting the whole spiritual, life-negating tone of intellectual life. In Ghungrali, Hindu philosophical beliefs such as renunciation and asceticism were rejected and even the Hindu doctrines of transmigration of souls from one form of life to another and supernatural rewards and punishments, both part of Sikh doctrine, were strong only among the lower castes.

So race, a quarter-century ago as today, helped to perpetuate caste, as did economics. Harijans provided cheap labor. To some degree the Jats continued as overlords of peasantries who did most of the actual cultivation. It was Mukhtar, not Charan, who toiled with hoe and sickle. Pritam, who did as much hard labor as his workers, was getting to be an exception.

Until the massacre of Muslims in 1947, Ghungrali had nearly 900 houses, with over 5,000 Muslims and nearly 1,000 Harijan Sikhs. Within two weeks of the massacre, the land was reallocated to just sixty-five Jat families. They were greatly outnumbered by one hundred and sixty Harijan families, a few of them weavers, shoemakers and blacksmiths, but most agricultural laborers. The total population on the eve of the green revolution in 1967 was 1,415. It farmed slightly more than 1,600 acres, of which all but a hundred was irrigated, sown and cultivated at any one time. Wheat, the main crop, was grown on 1,100 acres from November to April, along with smaller crops of sugarcane, oats and clover. In May a summer crop of oil seed, corn, cotton and groundnut was grown, after 1978 to be replaced by rice.

Modernization in Ghungrali began in the early 1950s with the first tube well. Water was everything in the Punjab. With it you could turn a desert into a garden. There were forty-six tube wells by 1957, ninety-five by 1962 and eventually over a hundred. At first they were run by diesel engines; in time all were electrified. New high-yield dwarf wheat was sown by every farmer in the village in November 1967. Since yields dropped after three or four years, Pritam and Charan had to get seeds of ever-newer varieties from Basant Singh, the university in Ludhiana or a government research station at Khanna. As Sadhu Singh boasted, "It's just a question of a bottle here and a bottle there."

Always in the forefront, Basant Singh bought Ghungrali's first tractor in 1962. By 1970 there were thirty-six. The use of nitrogen fertilizer went from next to nothing to more than 500 tons a year. Moderate amounts of insecticide were used. Credit first came in 1967 through a state-land mortgage bank and a village cooperative credit society. Basant Singh predicted that small Jat farmers would go under if not subsidized. "Inputs have risen in cost much faster than wheat prices," he declared. "The actual profit we are getting is diminishing. We have to cut back on expenses. Without government subsidies, those with less than fifteen or twenty acres will sink. With this legal land ceiling of thirty acres, how can a man practice economies of scale? There's so much talk of a green revolution, those politicians in Delhi think that whatever flesh they find on the farmer's bones, they have to pick it clean."

The Mazhbis, who still received grain in proportion to the number of a Jat's cattle, benefited more than the Chamars. They gathered cattle droppings in the barns, made dung cakes for cooking fuel, removed dead mules or donkeys, sang and danced at weddings, all traditional occupations, and the men also worked for wages in the fields. Not so with the Chamars. With few horses or camels left, their traditional caste occupation as leatherworkers was obsolete. Most worked as field laborers. A growing number raised buffaloes or goats and sold the milk to a new dairy in Bija. A few, like Gurdial, kept poultry. Like Basant Singh, Gurdial, as the Harijans' political leader, had something to gain from caste polarization.

Some Chamars sharecropped for an eighth of the harvest, others negotiated an annual cash payment of 1,500–1,700 rupees, and younger men like Mukhtar kept to daily wages. Mukhtar, though only twenty-three in 1970, had already worked for fifty-two of Ghungrali's Jat farmers, before settling down with Charan. This freedom to pick and choose, demanded by a new generation of Harijans, also eroded the old *jajmani* system.

At its heart were the terms of harvest. A Harijan harvester traditionally received every twentieth bale of wheat he cut and gathered. He also had the right to cut grass for his cattle on the Jats' land undisturbed. This enabled every Harijan family to get enough wheat and milk, the staples of the Punjabi diet.

To villagers like Pritam and Mukhtar, Ghungrali was not just the sum of Basant Singh's statistics, it was their whole universe. Its eighty-seven allotments could be pinned down on one of Basant Singh's maps. But it could also be seen. Here was the banyan tree, there the temple, the mill, the school, the brick houses and mud huts. Each farm could be located in terms of canals, wells, roads and trees. All of Ghungrali's men, women and children thought and acted in terms of family ties, kinship, factions, caste, mutual rights and obligations. This network extended to other Sikh villages in Punjab as Ghungrali's daughters married and moved away and were replaced by brides from dozens of surrounding villages.

Between about 1965 and 1970, Ghungrali went from subsistence agriculture to commercial farming in barely five years, a dizzyingly short time. Forced to compete with bigger landlords whose holdings operated with the latest seeds, machinery, irrigation and chemical inputs, and faced with the ups and downs of a market economy, a few like Basant Singh grew rich, some like Pritam and Charan prospered and others slid toward bankruptcy. Fearing debt and faced with the unfamiliar pressure of needing cash to buy all the new inputs, the Jats were torn between trying to cut down the cost of labor or preserving the social balances that had held Ghungrali together. Charan made the best of change; Basant Singh harnessed it; Pritam feared what it might bring.

VI

In April 1970, as the wheat ripened each day, the sky grew paler and the clouds that hung in high puffs for so long in February and March were gone. On the thirteenth day of April, what Punjabis call Baisaki, the harvest traditionally began. The sun shone hotter each day, the yellow lines on the wheat leaves widened and the heads of grain paled into yellow. The air seemed thinner, the sky mistier and there was more and more dust until the landscape faded into dull brown. On dirt roads where iron wheels broke the crust, more dust rose. By the first week of April it settled on the tractors and bullock carts. Pritam brushed it from his shoulders, while Charan had asthma attacks in the night.

Five days before Baisaki, the Jats gathered at the temple to fix the terms of payment for cutting, baling and threshing the wheat. Basant Singh's men declared they had suffered a financial loss the previous few harvests. They said the *jajmani* system was no longer economical. To offset their new costs in fertilizer and fuel, they demanded that the twentieth bale be reduced to the thirtieth bale. The poorer Jats wanted this to be a general rate. Everyone agreed, and the terms were announced over the *gurdwara* loudspeaker.

There was consternation among the Harijans, who sent back a flat rejection. "We won't go!" many Harijans cried. "Let them cut their own wheat!" One-Eye went about telling Jats, "The Harijans have insulted us." He told Pritam, "I hear the Harijans are going to the police. How can they go to the police when there is no fighting? They wrote to Indira Gandhi in Delhi. Basant Singh says they can write to anybody they like. These Harijans are getting rich off our bones. They're forgetting their place."

Once One-Eye, the troublemaker, followed the Sarpanch out to Charan's well. As village chief, the Sarpanch was worried. "Now the poor people, those Harijans who have no livelihood but daily wages, they will suffer. And it is always evil to make poor people suffer. It is those Harijans like Gurdial who are stirring up the trouble."

"Ah," One-Eye hissed, seeing an opening, "it is Gurdial Singh who is seeking to replace you as *sarpanch*. That is his game. He is very close to the police, I hear. He gives them free eggs and chickens." When they had gone Charan told Mukhtar, "That man is an evil soul. He is trying to poison the mind of the Sarpanch."

That evening when they took the tools back to the wellhouse and Charan unlocked the padlock on the door and went inside, Mukhtar heard him give a loud oath. Somebody had emptied out a drum of residue from the crushed sugarcane which Charan had been saving to distill some country liquor. Dhakel came across the fields to tell him what happened. "It was Sadhu Singh," he said, grinning. "He came last evening after you'd left and asked me to help pour it out. 'It does not behoove us,' he told me. 'It is below our dignity.' "

Charan cursed, "It would have made thirty bottles." Mukhtar stayed out in the fields that evening, going about barefoot with a hoe, opening and shutting gateways of mud, to give the wheat its final watering. He skimmed off the dirt between the stalks and threw it to make sure that the water moved to all of the field and that all of the wheat was watered evenly.

The air was heavy the next morning. The sun looked faint and wan, the sky gloomy, the dusty mist very dense and the distance hazy. Since early morning there were faint flashes of lightning. Everyone was out of sorts. Charan awoke with a hangover. Angry with his father, he had sat over a bottle with the Sarpanch until late. Now, heavy with sleeplessness, untidy, bleary-eyed, Charan rose from his *charpoy* in the cattle yard, where he and Sadhu Singh slept in hot weather, and he went over to the pump to splash cold water on his face. His father was still lying on his cot, and as usual when he first awoke, he was grumbling to himself, fussing, coughing and gazing balefully about. Seeing Sadhu in such a foul temper, Charan sent Peloo to fetch him tea. Mukhtar, who had been up watering half the night, and Kapur, a Mazhbi, came into the courtyard and Charan brightened. "Oh," he groaned to them, "I drank too much last night."

Kapur, the son of old Chanan, whom Charan much respected, laughed. "Our Charan can move lightly after a full bottle of rum. He's not affected by two bottles even."

Charan laughed. "So, come, young men," he cried hoarsely, "we must haul manure today and the weather looks bad. I'll pull the wagon up outside so you can start loading and I'll come and drive the tractor." As the two Harijans set to work, Charan's wife entered the cattle yard with Sadhu Singh's tin of morning tea. Pritam Kaur, as she was called, was a plain, gentle woman who lived mostly for her children. She suffered in silence constant nagging from Charan's mother. Sadhu Singh groaned, gave his daughter-in-law an indignant look, grumbled about how ill-served he was and sat up in bed to enjoy his tea. The sound of drums and bagpipes came from the road and Charan's wife went into the barn to unhook the shutters from a barred window so she could see outside. It was the Mazhbis playing for a group of men and women who were loading a wagon.

"Oh, Charan, it's a wedding party," she called. "It's the village watermen, the *rajas*. Oh, there's a *raja* in white clothes. How clean he looks today. How happy he appears. Oh, look, they are just leaving now. They are taking a band also. Oh, how the children are scrambling for coins!" Then, realizing she had forgotten herself in front of her father-in-law, Charan's wife held her scarf to her face and hurried from the barn. Soon a loud screech outside heralded the arrival of Charan's mother.

"There's not a drop of milk in the house!" she shouted in an angry voice. "Now you two sit here like kings and order tea all day five times each!" She swept past them, her stomach protruding from the shirt and pajamas she habitually wore, and with a great banging of pails and noisy oaths, she sat down on a stool and started to milk a buffalo.

Old Sadhu, annoyed by this outburst just as he was enjoying his morning tea, shouted back at her, "You could have arranged for more. Ask the milk sellers from the dairy, don't scream at me!"

The old lady gave a loud squawk. "Three times I sent tea to Charan yesterday and five times to you here at the barn!" She addressed the buffaloes, angrily waving an arm at her husband, "What is this man doing sitting in the barn all day and inviting people to tea? Does he drag them in from the street?"

Charan, seeing the old man's face was turning purple, tried to fend off the coming explosion. "It's none of our business," he told his mother. "Women know what's what about food. Why don't you order two kilos a day from the dairy? You know we're always short of milk this time of year."

"Harrumph!" Sadhu Singh exploded, sitting up in bed. He thundered grandly, "I will order tea ten times a day!" He was outraged to be the target of his wife's ill humor so early in the morning. "It's none of my headache to look in the milk bucket! What are you here for?" He harrumphed again, even louder.

"Why don't you stop now, Mother? You're making a scene," Charan said. "Go and milk your buffalo and arrange from tomorrow on for two extra kilos a day. That's all."

But Sadhu Singh's wrath was fully aroused now and he didn't want to let it go at that. He huffed and puffed with annoyance. Charan called to the stableboy, who had been watching the family quarrel with some interest, "Oh, Peloo, go to the house and get your breakfast and come back at once and then we'll go."

Sadhu erupted. "Why should this dirty pig eat first?" He sputtered furiously, seizing on the poor Peloo as a target. "He was roaming about all yesterday. Come, come, come, Charan, we will eat first." The old man with some effort lifted his fat body out of the cot. "You have a bottle hidden somewhere," he went on, turning on his son too. "I know what you want." His voice rose. "There should be an end to that thing!"

Charan ignored him. "Go, go, run, and come back right away, Peloo."

"Come, Charan," the old man went on, moving to the gate himself. "We'll send one of the children back in our absence. Why are you dragging your legs? Come!" Charan, angry now, remained sitting. "Let Peloo eat first," he called to his father. "He's hungry. He's been up with the cattle since four, while you were lying in your bed, and he's a poor, crippled man."

"Have the calves milked him?" Sadhu Singh roared from the gate. "What's he hungry for? He was roaming about this street and that street all day yesterday and you say he's a cripple. Ha! The dirty Chamar! He's a dog!"

Charan was too angry to speak. His father stomped down the lane muttering angrily. "I know what Charan wants. He has a bottle hidden somewhere, the dirty dog! I rape his mother! He's like a dog, wagging his tail after anyone who has a few drops of liquor. The dirty dog. I know what he wants. He'll go into the streets and beg one day, if he doesn't mend his ways." Then, feeling wide awake now and having worked up a healthy appetite, he hurried to the house.

Poondi, the Mazhbi, his wife and two daughters, attracted by the loud voices and hoping for an entertaining spectacle, came to clean the barn. As the women crouched down and began sweeping the earth with their brushes, Poondi joined Charan, seated himself on the ground near Charan's cot and lit up a cheap *bidi* cheroot. Dhakel's mother, a handsome stout woman with pink cheeks, entered the gate. "Look," she called to Charan's mother, who was still milking, "here is Poondi sitting with his legs crossed. He's enjoying life."

"Oh, I have worked enough in my life," Poondi retorted with a satisfied grin. "I have four grown sons and don't have to work any-more now. How can a person go on working till he dies?" He ex-changed good-natured banter with Dhakel's mother until the old lady screeched from her milking stool, "Poondi, your grandchild came here and destroyed our chili plant!"

"No, no," Poondi replied. "There are so many children around. It could be any. Not my grandchild. We've never brought him here. You are telling the same thing Sadhu Singh was telling. How could you have such an idea? And if some child has spoiled your chili plant, dear lady, it won't bring your house down to earth."

"Oh, that I know," called the old woman, somewhat mollified. "But you know children are very naughty. We have some pumpkin plants here. They may spoil them tomorrow."

"Give me a basket of that green fodder you have," said Poondi, needling her mischievously. "I want it for my buffalo."

The old woman gave a squawk of indignation. "You want that somebody should bring a dish of prepared food and put it into your mouth? You don't want to cook yourself? Why don't you go to the fields and cut some fodder yourself?"

Poondi chuckled. He had a deep, rich voice. Charan's mother was really a terror, he thought. "Why can't you tolerate such a small thing?" he teased her. "By evening this fodder will dry. If a poor man's buffalo eats your fodder, it won't ruin your health."

She rose and, milk pail in hand, advanced toward Poondi threaten-ingly. "You are just sitting here and gossiping and moving all day around the barns." Her voice rose to a loud screech. "Move your limbs and get some from the field, you gossipmonger!"

"Now you come with me," Poondi's wife called anxiously. "Let's go clean the other barn."

Poondi kept sitting. He thundered at his wife, "Don't make such a noise standing over there! Get along with your work! I'll reach there myself! I have legs! This gentleman is talking to me and you are just screaming over there." When his wife and the old woman had gone away, Poondi chuckled to Charan, "These women. They scream too much around here. They need to be sent to a lunatic asylum. They'd teach them some good things there, heh-heh-heh."

Outside by the manure pile, Mukhtar and Kapur were joined by Poondi's oldest son, Sher, and Gurmel, the Chamar sharecropper of Charan's cousin, Dhakel. "I heard the police are furious with the Jats," Gurmel reported to them. "They say the thirtieth bale is unreasonable and that the Jats are just trying to use force. Today some of the Harijans are going to the police station at Khanna town. Gurdial has sent one telegram to the deputy commissioner in Ludhiana and another to Prime Minister Indira Gandhi in Delhi. All the Harijans are united behind him." As a sharecropper, Gurmel said, he was not yet affected by the boycott. "I don't know what to do. That Sindar's a fool, barking vulgarity all the time, but I'm happy working with Dhakel and old Sarban Singh. They don't ask me to do too much work and they're soft-spoken." Gurmel, who was slightly hard of hearing, resented Sindar calling him "Deaf Man."

"But they're Jats. And Jats are all alike," said Sher.

"Even Charan abuses too much," Gurmel agreed. "Like he says, 'You're not my wife's brother' or 'I'll rape your sister.' "

Sher said that so far the Mazhbis were staying out of the dispute. It was just between the Jats and the Chamars. He heard the Sarpanch wanted the Jats to compromise.

"Yes, he's a good man," Mukhtar agreed. "If you get ill, he'll take you to the hospital. He and Charan are fast friends."

"It looks like trouble in the village now," Gurmel fretted, not without a touch of excitement. "The Jats are getting richer and they don't want to share it." Charan had burned off a cane field the day before and before lunch they were able to haul two loads of manure from his barn to it. The northern horizon all the while grew blacker and by noon a pale light was already flashing. It looked as if a thunderstorm was coming, and as each of them glanced up from his work, he thought: May God grant us time to gather in the wheat harvest.

At lunch the Harijan youths squatted on their haunches in Charan's courtyard and held out their hands, as was the custom, to receive *chapattis* and *alu-mutter*, a pea and potato curry. As Jats, Charan and old Sadhu sat on chairs and ate from plates at a table. The women served them, as usual waiting to eat later.

"Shall I put for all of you?" the old lady questioned as she ladled out her tasty curry onto their wheat cakes as if it were her own life's blood. Her stinginess was legendary in Ghungrali.

"Give me more *lassi*," said Mukhtar daringly, holding up his glass for more watered-down buttermilk.

"More *lassi!*" she squawked indignantly, but poured him some. As soon as she went back to the fire, Charan's wife put a plate of pickles on the ground between the Harijans. Returning, the old lady rushed to retrieve it, but as she scooped it up Mukhtar and Sher each grabbed several pickles. "Oh, that much!" she exclaimed as she hurried to put her precious pickles back under lock and key. The Harijans winked at each other.

When they went back to the fields with another load of manure, there was almost a steady drone to the north of distant rumbling thunder. A little boy of eight or nine, Pritam's great-nephew, Devinder, cried at them from Pritam's well, waving a slingshot, "Look! Look! I've killed a parrot!" Then the child put a bale of fodder on his head and hurried off in the direction of the village, a moving heap of clover with little legs below. Charan roared with laughter at the sight of him and called after Devinder, "Hurry, hurry, I rape your mother!" Then he told the Harijans, "Let's get this unloaded, brothers. It can start in minutes." Dark clouds were gathering on the left and right of the horizon, reaching toward the black northern mass. Sharply, no longer dully, came the sound of thunder. Once lightning flashed so brightly it lit up the entire plain with a strange white light.

"Come, come, men!" Mukhtar shouted. "Get your bodies wet with sweat, not rain!" He and the others shoveled manure from the wagon as fast as they were able, waving from time to time to Charan to move the tractor ahead. "Pray God there's no hail and the rain and wind don't come together," Charan shouted above the tractor's roar. Across a field at their well, Dhakel, his cousin Sindar and Gurmel were frantically trying to get their diesel engine started. Sher laughed. "One starts working and another rushes in and Sindar stands there all the time telling them what to do. Do you know why they can't fix it? The spirit of a Muslim lives at that well. His tombstone is there. That's why the engine won't go. They must please him." Sher laughed again and shouted, "Let's go, men. Show your strength! *Bas, tik hai,* Sardarji! Move ahead!"

"They've already whitewashed the grave," called Mukhtar, breathless from shoveling.

"You men are as black as Africans!" roared Charan from the tractor, though in truth Mukhtar was fairer than he was. As if reminded of this, Charan added, "If the village has a fair Harijan, we know it's a bastard." He laughed at his own joke.

Suddenly the wind nearly whipped off Mukhtar's headcloth, which flapped violently across his face. The wind tore across the plain and made a rushing noise in the wheat fields. Amid swirls of dust and flashes of light, thunder rolled over the sky from right to left, then back, ending somewhere near the village. The sky opened, flashed white, and at once the thunder roared; hardly had it ceased when there flamed such a bright flash of lightning the men for an instant saw across the fields the towers of a temple a mile away and even the rooftops and trees in Ghungrali in sharp definition. "Run for the well-house!" Charan shouted, and he turned the tractor toward the well, bumping across the stubble, wagon and all.

The rain, for some reason, was long in coming, and for this they silently thanked God, for by then the wind had died. The sky was an intense grayish green. Inside the wellhouse it was dark for midafternoon. For one last time the wind shuddered through the nearly ripe wheat and fled away somewhere. Charan stood just outside the doorway. A large cold drop fell on his forehead, another on his hand. Mukhtar saw he had left some grass out for the bullocks and thought of bringing it in, but at that moment there was a pelting and tapping on the road, the ground, the roof. The rain had come. They felt a sudden chill and dampness in the air. Charan guessed it must be snowing in the Himalayas or there was hail nearby. The temperature had dropped so fast.

"Such a storm Old Grandfather has sent us," said Sher. "The bastard must be after our wheat."

"These days," Charan said soberly, "if it's rain without wind, it's God come to earth. Rain and wind together would ruin our wheat. If the wind stays down, the profit from this rain may outweigh the loss."

Just then Gurmel came running over from Dhakel's well yard. He was soaking wet and the sleeves and back of his shirt clove to his body. Water dripped from his mustache as he went on loudly and incoherently about enmity in the village, all the while dripping water and gasping for air. Charan asked why he was shouting so.

"You do not know?" Gurmel gasped for breath. "It was declared over the loudspeaker. The Jats said, 'No Harijans can enter our fields. No Harijans can take grass from our land to feed their cattle.' It is a *boycott.*" Gurmel used the unfamiliar English word. "Because we refused to cut the Jats' wheat on the thirtieth bale."

"That's impossible," said Charan. "We can't survive in this village without a settlement. The harvest will start in a few days. In this heat the wheat will quickly shatter. We must reach a settlement. Those fools." Suddenly, with a fearful, deafening din, the sky crashed just above their heads. The men crouched and held their breath, involuntarily shut their eyes and opened them to see a blinding bright light gleaming in Mukhtar's eyes, on beads of sweat on Charan's face, along Sher's arms and glittering from the water on Gurmel's wet turban. There was another clap of thunder, louder than before. They scarcely heard it, so stunned were they by the news.

"If the Jats *boycott* us," said Mukhtar, "we must *boycott* them." There was no word for it in Punjabi. "It means I cannot work for you any longer, Gurcharan Singh."

As thunder crackled and lightning streaked the skies, Charan turned to Sher. "And you, Sher, you're a Mazhbi. You too?"

"We are all Harijans, Sardarji."

VII

As soon as the Jats banned Harijans from their fields, Gurdial, with the help of a lawyer from Ludhiana, drew up a petition and presented it to the police in Khanna. It charged that Ghungrali's Jats had been "insulting to women . . . not allowing Harijans into the fields to answer the call of nature and not allowing them into the fields or country roads and lanes for the purpose of grazing." Indian law, imbued with the teachings of Mahatma Gandhi, was, in letter if not in spirit, committed to ending untouchability and all forms of caste discrimination. If Gurdial could get the police involved, the law favored the Harijans. The Sarpanch guessed it was Gurdial's ambition to replace him as village chief. "Now the Harijans are in Gurdial's hands," he told Charan. "Once they are no longer united, he'll lose them. I'll compel the Jats to compromise on reasonable terms." But nobody listened to him.

Basant Singh won over most of the Jats. He argued, "We Jats have been suffering a heavy loss giving these laborers the twentieth bale. They have benefited more the past few years than the small Jat farmers. That's why they're creating this trouble. They've had a taste of prosperity and they want more. Well, they're not going to get it at the price of farmer after farmer going into debt."

Sadhu Singh thought the whole dispute nonsense and said so to anybody who would listen. He told Charan, "Among the Jats the real troublemakers are such fools as One-Eye, who can cut his miserable two acres of wheat himself. Among the Harijans it's those like Gurdial, who has a poultry business of his own and doesn't depend on Jat wages. The whole business is a fuss over nothing. You'll see. Once

Jade in Nae-Chon village, South Korea, 1980.

Richard Critchfield near Wanchuan village in Hopeh province on the North China Plain in June 1980, on the first of the author's three journeys in China.

Lunch while harvesting; Aurelio and his grandmother in Huecorio, a
Mexican village, 1977.

James Zachariah Nzoka and Monica Mutuli, Machakos Hills, Kenya, 1981.

Charan and family in Chawar Khas. Back row from left: Sukhdev, his wife, Kulwant's wife, Narinder's wife, and Narinder. The shed attached to the white house behind is where Charan sleeps, 1992.

Annual bullock-cart race during harvest, Punjab Plain, 1970.

Dhakel's daughter, who marries just as the *khadkus* come (1992).

Dhakel, Charan's cousin, who appears throughout the story: harvesting in 1970, kissing a Harijan girl in 1978, becoming a TV addict in 1992 and a heavy drinker.

Bawa, Poondi's son and a Mazhbi low-caste field worker, who appears throughout the story.

Pritam.

the wheat gets ripe and starts to shatter, how the Jats and Harijans will go running to each other!"

Pritam had misgivings. He warned Basant Singh, "What we sow, we shall someday reap." Basant Singh waved off such sentiment. "Either we shift to machinery or we get labor from outside, Pritamji. It's the only solution. Some say this boycott is harmful to the village. I say the poor are making more money than ever and spending it on hashish, tobacco and liquor. Bad habits, that's their real enemy."

Despite the gathering tension, daily life went on. Two days before Baisaki the Jats traditionally invited farmers from all the neighboring villages to compete in a bullock-cart race. It was a splendid day; the wheat had ripened to a pale gold, and the oats too were ripe and shone in the sunshine like mother-of-pearl. The sky was a milky blue, there was dust and white mist among the trees in the far distance. As the hot breeze came up in sudden gusts, little whirlwinds twirled through the ripe wheat. No one had watered for days now and there was little fear the wheat would lodge before it was cut.

Charan and Dhakel had goaded Sindar, the cheerful braggart, into entering the race. All morning long at Dhakel's well he fussed about importantly, washing and brushing down the bullocks and taking swigs of homemade liquor. "Oh, today you shall run like the wind," Sindar told the bullocks, breathing deeply to fill out his flat, hairy chest. "Ah, today I shall crush someone under the hooves of my bullocks. I shall ride them across the finish line like the wind. Stop, O Balda, why are you dancing so? Pour me a little, Dhakel. If I take a little now I'll get myself warmed up for the whole day and won't need more." Both he and Dhakel downed a glass apiece in the usual Punjabi single gulp. Dhakel smacked his lips and wiped his mustaches. They had made the liquor themselves and some bottles were stronger than others. "It's all right," Dhakel said. "It will serve our purpose. We don't have to spend money." And he poured himself another glass.

"Hear the doves cooing," Sindar said. "That means it will be a very hot afternoon. It's a good cart we have. Oh, today you'll see them falling in the ditches!"

"You'll break your leg." Dhakel chuckled.

"When you fight a battle, why worry about your legs and arms?" Sindar declared grandly. "We have so many other entries from our village. I don't know about the others, but nobody in Ghungrali can beat me." A crow squawked noisily in the oak branches, as if disputing this. "Kill that bastard," Sindar cursed. "I'll rape his mother."

"Just hit him with a big stone," Dhakel advised. "Then he'll understand."

Gurmel, their Harijan worker, who was cutting fodder, came over. He was worried that Sindar might get too drunk to race. "Better you go home and rest," he told him.

"Oh, Deaf Man, what should I do there? Should I grab someone's penis? We'll go straight to the race. Come, start the engine. Let's get the fodder cut. Oh, Deaf Man, if you're strong these days with all the Harijans on strike it will be good."

"I would be with them if I wasn't a yearly sharecropper," Gurmel told him. "Only those on daily wages are taking part in the boycott."

When Dhakel's father, Sarban Singh, brought them *chapattis* and curry, he said they had plenty of time before the race. The names of all the entries had to be drawn from a jug to see who went first. "Where did you get all these bottles from?" Sarban asked.

"They came up from the earth," said Gurmel with a laugh. Sarban poured some liquor into a tin mug, downed it, then wiped his beard. "Did you use all the sugar?" he asked Dhakel.

"No, we kept four jars to have plenty for the harvest."

By early afternoon the dirt road beside Basant Singh's fields was lined with hundreds of men and boys, and Basant Singh himself was walking back and forth with a rifle to make sure nobody stepped on his wheat. The sun was almost white and in the dusty luminous light everything was a pale pastel color: the wheat, the sky, the sparse acacia trees, the men in their clean white shirts and yellow, pink, pale green, red and lavender turbans.

"Clear the way! The first cart is coming now!" at last rose the shouts. "Oh, come with pomp and show!" cried the amplified voice of an announcer from the loudspeaker truck. "Come with courage, come, O Bhajan Singh of Mal Majra, come!" In a great cloud of dust and pounding hooves and cheers and shouts, the first pair of bullocks and their cart rolled down the eleven-acre-long course. At the starting line some of the entries were skittish, ready to hurtle forward. "Hold them!" cried the starter. "We'll scratch your entry if you cross the line before the flag falls." At the finish line, the announcer called out, "Mehar Singh of Bhambadi. One minute sixteen seconds! Oh, slap those boys on the back of their necks. Why are they blocking the way?"

Pritam, who was watching the race with little Devinder, kept looking about for Sindar. "I have not yet seen our Sindar go by," he told his brother's grandson. "Oh, there's Dhakel on a bicycle. Maybe he is looking for him."

Ahead on the course, Charan and his friends, who had been drinking since noon, roared with laughter as a drunken, red-faced man in a black turban came staggering down the track, waving his arms and shouting, "For God's sake, clear the way! You are masters of your wills. It is your village. But clear the way!"

"That last was very fast," said Kaka Singh, one of Charan's cronies, who had spent time in prison and was called "the Bandit." "That driver is damn good."

"Don't worry," the Sarpanch told him. "A Ghungrali *wallah* will win the next round. Look, the flag is up again."

"It's Sindar," Charan exclaimed, seeing his cousin and bursting into his hoarse laughter.

"Sindar's bullocks will take minutes, not seconds," the Sarpanch joked. "Don't think that they are the best. Oh, clear the way, you children, or ask your fathers to join the race!"

"That Isaru *wallah* got his bullocks too drunk," said the Bandit. "That's the sort of people they are. They worry about winning too much."

"One minute sixteen seconds is the best time so far."

"Come, Charan, let's slip behind those trees and have another bottle. This will go on all afternoon." The Sarpanch, red-faced and staggering, led several of them down the track, shouting as he went, "For God's sake, please clear the way, brethren. You are masters of your own wills. But clear the way!"

"Wait, Sindar's coming!" Charan cried.

The announcer's voice was deafening. "Bring that red flag up, just watch the flag. These bullocks are running eleven acres and that is something! Oh, green and red turbans, please clear the way. Now comes on line . . . Surindar Singh of Ghungrali! The flag is up! The cart is coming at full speed! Friends, clear the way. Surindar Singh, Ghungrali *wallah*, is coming! See how he flies . . . Ooop! What's happened?" The announcer was on his feet and trying to see. "Friends, clear the way! Stop running this way and that! Where is he? What? Ah-h-h-h . . . The bullocks are running toward Bhambadi across the wheat field! Clear the way! We can't see! Friends, Sindar's cart has left the road and his bullocks are headed across the wheat field. What's happened to them? Oh, he's turned them around . . . Oh, they're back on the road again! And here they come! Friends, clear the way! Now they're back on the road and the cart is coming, the bullocks are coming with great dignity. Don't worry. They'll get here someday. *Shabash, shaba-a-a-a-ash!* Surindar Singh of Ghungrali!"

A roar of laughter went up from the crowd as Sindar's cart at last rumbled across the finish line. "Time? What is the time?" men shouted hilariously. "Two minutes and five seconds," called the announcer, and there was another great roar of laughter. Charan laughed so hard he went into a coughing fit, and the Sarpanch had to hit him on the back. "Seeing Sindar race, I get drunk without liquor," Charan told his friends.

The next morning, as he braided ropes for the harvest under the banyan tree, Sindar was subdued for a change. The men worked in pairs and Sindar sat on the ground and twisted strands of reed while Gurmel, standing up and slowly stepping back, held the end of the finished rope. Mukhtar, who was braiding with Charan, told Sindar, "I heard you were ill."

Charan laughed. "He got frightened like his bullocks to see such a big crowd."

Sindar's head ached. He had gone directly from the race to Dhakel's well and polished off a full bottle. "My best time on that track was one minute and fifteen seconds," he defended himself. "That's a second less than Bhajan Singh of Mal Majra, who won. My bigger bullock got scared when so many people got in the way. If they'd just stood back and watched quietly, we'd have got the prize, by God. Next year I'll win. My bullocks will talk to the wind. Anybody who gets in the road, I'll use my sword and cut off their heads. Those that block the way. The fault lies with those bastards. Those seeds of a dog, penis of the great god, I'll rape their mothers!"

"Why are you working today?" Charan goaded him. "Better you take your rest."

"What shall I be doing? Lying on the *charpoy* and scratching my testicles?"

"At least you're up and moving about today," Charan said more sympathetically. "If you'd really lost the game, you'd be in bed the rest of your life. I myself would be scared to race a bullock cart."

"Oh, *shabash*, Deaf Man, move back quickly," Sindar called to

Gurmel. "We'll be through in half the time Charan is taking. Nobody dares beat us."

"Nobody dares beat you in the bullock races," retorted Gurmel, who wasn't going to let Sindar off too easily. "Sindar has been having diarrhea all day because he lost."

"Why should I have diarrhea?"

"Where was your cart going? Bhambadi?" The men all laughed, enjoying Sindar's discomfort.

"Even if my bullock cart falls in a well I won't have diarrhea."

The Sarpanch was approaching them and he greeted Sindar: "We should have given a prize to the man who came in last." He squatted down beside them. "Now a lot of wheat needs cutting, but who is to cut it? Wheat should be a little green at harvest. It shouldn't be over-ripe. The best thing, I think, is to go back to the old system. If your wheat is ready, everybody should come and cut it. And then the next field and the next. I'm ready to throw a big feast if people would come out and cut mine."

"God will ruin this village because you're hurting the poor," muttered Sindar.

Charan asked where the Sarpanch would get harvesters. He said he didn't know. After the Sarpanch left they settled down to braiding in silence for a while until One-Eye came by. He ignored the Harijans but spoke to Charan in his whiny, fawning way. "Do you know, Charanji, that today they stopped cleaning Basant Singh's barn, these Harijans. No telling what they will do if this keeps on."

"It doesn't matter," Sindar called to him cheerfully. "The Jats need to install underground drainage anyway. You can have manure pouring right into the fields. The Jats can dig deep ditches and when their cows and buffaloes want to piss, they can just lead them there." Sindar chuckled to himself.

"You brag too much and you were last in the race yesterday," One-Eye snarled at him. Sindar did not speak again until he had gone away, then he called to Gurmel, "Oh, *shabash*, Deaf Man, we'll beat them all. Get back, get back, we'll beat them all."

"That One-Eye," said Gurmel, "his father must have had his mother at some odd time and he's the seed of that. He's like a mad dog. If he sends his wife to my father, only then will she bear a child. The impotent bastard. That's why he abuses people. He has the worst wheat crop in the village. A real weed patch." Charan looked up, surprised to hear a Harijan defend one Jat from another.

VIII

The next day, Baisaki, Sadhu Singh went early to the village temple to pray for a good crop. He found a large crowd of Jats milling about outside. They wanted to force a showdown with the Harijans. Sadhu, who thought the whole business was nonsense, went inside, where only a few elderly Jats were praying, and ordered the *gurdwara* loudspeaker turned up full blast. Soon his prayers boomed out all over the village.

Pritam was with Basant Singh and other leading Jats under the shade of a neem tree. "We have decided to try for a settlement this morning," Basant Singh told them. "If the Harijans don't come today, it's finished." Pritam was bewildered. "I understand we've been sending them messages all morning," he said. Just then a small boy came running to say, "They are coming this way!" Then, evidently feeling the occasion called for something more, he added, "They frightened me with their eyes!"

When the Harijans arrived they formed a semicircle in front of the temple and the Jats went to face them. "Now come forward with your conditions and demands," Basant Singh declared. But his voice was drowned out by a screeching blast from the *gurdwara* loudspeaker and the wailing sound of old men's voices, Sadhu Singh's thundering above the rest.

"Turn off that loudspeaker!" Basant Singh bellowed furiously. When it was quiet, a clean-shaven young Harijan who was just out of secondary school came forward. "We want according to the field," he said in a nervous manner. "That we should be paid to reap according to the crop in each field."

"We can't form a committee to go to each and every field to decide the worth of a crop," Basant Singh snapped testily.

"Each Jat knows his wheat crop," the young man protested nervously. Then Gurdial came from the back of the group of Harijans and at once spoke with greater authority. "We have thought things over the past few days. We have decided we do not want a fixed rate but will settle field by field, farmer by farmer, as do all the Jats and Harijans in neighboring villages. We can only judge when reaching a field what payment will suit us. Now you can go and decide if that is agreeable to you."

This sounded reasonable and a murmur of approval seemed to go through the Jats. Then Basant Singh spoke even more testily than before. "If anyone wants trouble, he has no place here. We are here to get a settlement. We want a fixed rate. Some people can be cheated on a field-by-field basis."

"That depends on the man," Gurdial replied evenly. "A Jat should think about whom he is hiring. This trouble is quite serious for us. You don't allow us in your fields, a right Harijans have enjoyed in the Punjab for hundreds of years. You must decide, once and for all. Think about what you are doing to our village."

Who knows what might have happened if the Jats had done so? Instead, caught up in the heat of the moment, Basant Singh became more unyielding. "If you don't want to reach any settlement, that's up to you," he snapped to Gurdial. "You may do what you like and we will do what we like."

"You must fix rates according to each man's field. That is the way it has always been in Punjab."

"We can't do that," Basant Singh said flatly. "I have been authorized by the thirteen-member committee this morning to offer you a compromise, the thirtieth bale for a good field and the twenty-eighth bale for a bad field. Beyond that we will not budge. An individual rate for each farm would be too much trouble. Too much trouble."

"It can't be any more trouble than this village is facing now." Gurdial's voice betrayed an edge of anger. "We can't go into your fields. We can't cut grass for our cows and buffaloes . . ."

Basant Singh interrupted. "If you will not accept a generalized rate, there is no further reason to talk." For some moments there was a stunned silence. Then Basant Singh bowed his head and raised his hands, palms folded together in a formal gesture of farewell. "It is all over," he said with great finality in a harsh voice. "Finished. Now you are free to do what you will and we are free to do what we will. *Sat Sri Akal!*"

As everyone milled about, the Sarpanch came up to Charan and said, "The Harijans are very determined. I'll try to bring them around." But the Sarpanch no longer had the village under his control. Basant Singh's men quickly spread the word that the boycott stood and every Jat was to hire workers from outside. Not all the Jats went along with this. Charan's friend the Bandit got drunk and went to the Harijans, telling them, "Come and cut my wheat. Harijans are allowed in my fields. I damn this village and the Jats' decision." But Gurdial forbade anybody to go. "The Jats want to be dictators," he told his followers. "But this country is free. We want to live like free men in a free nation. They will not share their new prosperity if they can help it!"

Storming back to his fields, his rifle slung over his shoulder, Basant Singh met old Chanan, a Mazhbi who had worked for him many years. When Chanan said he would work for him no more, Basant Singh cursed him and said, "Don't get funny with me or I'll throw you off my land for good, you black seed of a dog!" Word of this incident swept through Ghungrali, much magnified in each retelling, for Chanan Singh was a respected, even saintly, old man. Resentment grew.

Sadhu Singh, prayers over, went back to his cattle yard and took a leisurely warm bath in the midday sun. He told the old lady to prepare a clean white shirt and pajamas, fresh linen and the dark blue Akali turban he wore on special occasions. Rare were the times in life when Sadhu had to rouse himself. This was one of them. He sat on a footstool by the pump, with only a wet towel around his enormous belly, pouring sudsy hot water over his back and shoulders. His brother Sarban came to say the Jats were sending a delegation to Ludhiana's railway station to hire migrant harvesters coming in from neighboring Uttar Pradesh state. "Brother," Sarban said, "you can give me your demands and deposit five rupees for bus fare for every worker you need. We are also collecting ten rupees from each Jat in case of legal battles. Suppose a person goes down the road and the Harijans start beating him on the pretext he has abused their women. Then we'll use this money to fight a court case against them."

"Uh-huh . . . h-m-m-m," Sadhu grunted absently, pouring some more warm water over his shoulders. "Yes, brother, you take an active part, don't worry. Just hand me that bucket of water. Push it a little closer. Ah, that's it. Oh, yes, it is very good if you have this arrangement. It is safer for everyone . . . Ooop! I can't reach it yet. Just push it this way. Ah, that's it. This water is not as hot as I wanted it." He bellowed, "Peloo!" Ignoring Sarban, Sadhu dipped his pitcher into the bucket and began rinsing off. He splashed his brother, who cried in exasperation, "We'll take five rupees for every harvester you need. Just give me twenty-five or thirty rupees."

"Right now?" Sadhu Singh's outraged bellow was so loud it could be heard all the way back to the house, where the old lady hastened to heat some more water, thinking that was the trouble. "I'm taking a bath!" Sadhu exclaimed, and he splashed about so gustily his brother

gave up and went away. Sadhu Singh had looked forward to spending the day on his *charpoy*, listening to the news and music on his transistor and occasionally calling for tea. Now he knew he must stir himself. He rose with surprising swiftness, hurriedly dressed in the clean clothes his wife brought, then, dispatching Peloo to the house with a message, he grabbed his umbrella and hurried across the fields toward the Bija bus stop on the Grand Trunk Road.

Charan, Mukhtar, Sindar and Gurmel, back braiding ropes under the banyan tree, watched the old man streak off. "My father really has big steps when he's going someplace," Charan said, wondering where Sadhu was headed. "After taking a bath he gets light and walks fast," was Sindar's offering. One-Eye and a crony of Charan's named Nirmal came by, headed into Ludhiana to try to hire laborers. One-Eye, in clean clothes for a change and a glass eye in the usually empty socket, told Charan they planned to bring a hundred men. "We're not hopeful of a settlement," he said. "The Harijans can't stand this for long. We'll break their will."

"Maybe they will move away, get jobs in the city," suggested Sindar.

"We won't bother our heads if they do," One-Eye retorted. "We'll bring more laborers here and give them places to live." He said he heard on the radio more than 70,000 harvest workers from Uttar Pradesh state were pouring into Ludhiana District alone. "If we don't get outside labor, these Harijans will eat us up," he said, parroting something Basant Singh kept saying. Nirmal, already bored, groaned, "We should settle and let old Basant Singh yell. What do you say? Anyway tonight we'll enjoy a good girl in Ludhiana . . ."

Once they had gone their way, Gurmel said, "If we accepted anything from drunkards like Nirmal and that one-eyed gossipmonger, we'd be fools. Who respects men like that?" He spat in their direction. "Never mind. City life is good."

"Take your children in big baskets if you go there," Sindar told him. "When they go hungry you can always throw them on the railroad tracks."

"We're afraid the Jats won't even allow our children in the village school if the boycott keeps on," Gurmel said. "Maybe I'll go to some big city after the harvest."

Sindar laughed. "If you throw cow dung in a clean sack it will still give off a bad smell. Wherever you go, they'll know you're a Chamar."

"Never mind," retorted Gurmel. "A law is coming where we'll work only eight hours a day. Then we'll apply to the government for a paved road to Khanna and we'll buy bicycles and go to town to work every day." He laughed. "You'll see Sindar's face after the harvest. He'll be black as a railway guard. This time half the Jats will die of hard work. We'll make them real skinny, cutting their own wheat. They have too much fat on them anyway."

"C'mon, Deaf Man, move back!" Sindar hooted at him. "When the harvest comes you'll get your bottom torn by stubble. Work faster. Don't let your shadow fall on me. I'll get lazy like you. *Shabash*, O, Deaf Man, *sha-a-bash!*"

When Pritam came by he noticed the roadside grass near the banyan tree was thickly overgrown. "Who would leave this lush grass by the roadside if the Chamars were allowed to cut fodder for their cattle?" He was dismayed by events. "I don't understand what is happening," he told Charan. "So much ill will. Why would Basant Singh abuse old Chanan Singh? Such a gentle old man. There must be something . . . Well, it's a dangerous day. My body tells me because of those thin clouds. It is perfectly close."

"Such things can happen without any reason, Pritamji," Charan said.

"Ah, well, whatever our leaders decide, it must be all right. I will follow them."

That evening, after cutting fodder, Charan, Sindar and Dhakel shared a bottle at Charan's well. Sindar sided with the Harijans. "It's unjust to give them the thirtieth part and the Jats know it. It's those bad farmers like that one-eyed person who make trouble and benefit. Wise men like Pritam who have good crops should tell those like One-Eye to shut up."

Dhakel was worried about where to find harvesters. "If we could get Chamars from Ghungrali, I'd pay one bale of twenty-two. Even the twentieth bale like we used to. We don't want those Hindus from Uttar Pradesh coming in. You can't depend on them. Anyone from outside the village is undependable."

Charan passed the bottle. "That Basant Singh. I think he drinks in secret and is also an opium addict."

"In the morning he takes opium and in the evening he takes liquor," agreed Sindar, who knew nothing of the kind. Charan produced a second bottle from his haystack and for some time, as they passed it around, each taking several swigs, they enjoyed abusing Basant Singh.

"Basant Singh abuses Harijans."

"Basant Singh is his own air."

"The bastard is arrogant and proud."

"He makes the lives of the Harijans a living hell."

"Fuck Basant Singh. Let's go to America."

This sobered Dhakel. "Our America is here in Ghungrali," he said.

The next day Charan tried to break the boycott, telling Mukhtar he would go back to the old *lavi* system, long abandoned in Punjab, whereby each harvester simply carried home as much grain each evening as he could put on his head. Peloo, who was listening, gurgled and clasped his twisted hands together approvingly. But Gurdial, when Mukhtar told him, turned on him angrily. "They don't even want to let our children go to school!" he cried with passion. "They want us to stay backward and illiterate!" "We're all tigers!" one of Gurdial's men shouted. "We'll go to other villages. Jats have come from Majari and Bhambadi to hire harvesters. To hell with the Jats of Ghungrali!" "C'mon!" shouted another. "In Bhambadi they are cutting on the twenty-fifth bale!" Gurdial knew he had won. "Don't go with Charan, Mukhtar. We must stay united. We'll show these Jats."

Charan came under attack too. One-Eye came rushing to demand, "What's this we hear about you hiring Mukhtar?" Nirmal was just behind him. "Don't let these Chamar bastards into your fields," he warned. "We'll provide men!"

"Where are they, then?" Charan roared at them, furious. "Bring me harvesters tomorrow or I'll take Chamars from the village!"

"We'll burn your fields!" One-Eye cried, then seeing the wrath on Charan's face, he turned and fled, shoving past Nirmal to get out the gate first.

A police inspector from Khanna came to meet Jats and Harijans in front of the temple. "Don't strangle these poor people," he warned the Jats. "Don't kill them. I'm not saying the Jats should be giving with four hands. But don't make the Harijans starve either. We want this trouble to end with a little adjustment on both sides."

He reckoned without Basant Singh. "We have already sent men to bring in laborers from outside," he told the inspector. "We have all given money. When they come here, we must put them to work. We no longer need our village Harijans."

"Then you won't prohibit them from going to the fields to answer the call of nature or moving on common lands and roads?" This was as far as police jurisdiction went. It turned out Basant Singh was offering the migrant harvesters just four rupees a day, about a fourth of what they would have got under the *lavi* system Charan proposed.

IX

There was great excitement in Ghungrali the next morning. Sadhu Singh arrived riding on a big red contraption the likes of which the villagers had never seen. It was pulled by a tractor and looked like a wooden windmill lying on its side. Sadhu looked grandly triumphant, though his face, beard, turban and clothes were covered with dust from the twenty-mile trip from Ludhiana. When the tractor came to a stop by the banyan tree, he gingerly climbed down and dusted himself off.

A crowd came running, Charan from his cattle yard. "What is it?" he exclaimed. "How much will it cost?" The old man chuckled. "It is a reaping machine, a demonstration machine from the university. It cuts an acre an hour, needs six to eight men to tie up grain and is free. If we had to pay for it, son, where would be the fun?" As everybody gathered around, Sadhu pointed out such features as the collecting reel, the scissors action and the sideways delivery band, all worked by gears as the tractor pulled the machine down a field. Then Sadhu climbed up on the tractor fender and in a roar of exhaust, flushed with triumph, he, driver, tractor and reaping machine headed for the fields.

Charan ran in search of Mukhtar, but one of Mukhtar's uncles stopped him outside the house and said to him, "Don't do this thing, Charan *Sahib*. Don't ask Mukhtar to work for you. He would be an outcast among his own people."

"Why can't I give on the old *lavi* basis?"

"It is no longer a question of payment. The truth is, there are people on both sides interested in keeping this trouble going. They can stir things up even worse."

Charan went to the Jat committee and demanded he be given workers then and there. After a hot argument, they let him have four men who had just come from Uttar Pradesh. To Charan, compared with the sturdy Punjabi Harijans, they were a sorry lot, emaciated, ragged Hindus whose heads were shaven except for a single lock at the crown for, as he had heard, Yama, their death god, to seize when they died to take their spirit. They talked in their strange tongue, bobbing their heads from side to side, as he led them back to his cattle yard. There they crouched, smoking their *bidis*, the tobacco of their cheroots tightly rolled and clipped at both ends.

Chanan, the old Mazhbi whom Basant Singh had cursed, was cleaning the barn, collecting buffalo dung in a basket. "What am I to do?" Charan asked him. "Father has brought a reaping machine from the university and I need six to eight men. If I could find Punjabis I'd give them all the wheat they could carry home each night. To hell with the thirtieth bale."

The old man squatted in the dust and scratched his beard. "We Mazhbis are not bound by what the Chamars do," he said after some time. "That Gurdial Singh is up to no good. He wants to change things . . ." He scratched the dust with a stick thoughtfully. "Twenty years ago, a Jat wouldn't drink water from a Harijan's well. There is still a Jat in Ghungrali who won't. He says it is impure."

Charan knew the man. "He's an idiot. He is also unhappy if Jats share their food with Harijans. If the fool can tell the difference between what we eat, I'll agree with him. A human being is a human being."

The Mazhbi frowned. "No, Sardara," he said, using an old form of address, "we are not happy now with all this equality."

"Why?" Charan was surprised.

"Why? In olden times after working hard if you sat for some time to take a rest, the Jats had to bring water and serve us. Now a Jat will keep sitting and tell some Harijan to bring water. He takes a full rest and has the Harijan run here and there. Now the Jats even ask us to carry their food. Would you have allowed me to touch your food twenty years ago? Let alone carry it? But now you think we are equal. Damn these new laws. Nehru was our real enemy. This government thinks it is favoring us. The fools don't realize they are putting the Harijans under great pressure."

Charan knew that Nehru, educated in the West and Mahatma Gandhi's political heir, tried to impose through India's constitution and economic central planning what he called "a casteless society with equal opportunity for all." Out in India's villages, where landless Harijans did most of the country's actual cultivation for a very low return, their untouchability was still vigorously observed by the higher, landowning castes such as Ghungrali's Jats. What had happened, and Charan agreed with old Chanan about it, was that along with enhanced legal protection, there was erosion in the age-old system of mutual rights and obligations to the Harijans' disadvantage. So that Nehru's policies, however laudable and benevolent in intent, could ring as hollow in the villages as politicians mouthing Gandhian precepts about love of one's fellow man.

Chanan continued, "Now this boycott. The Harijans of Ghungrali must bring bales of grass from other villages. It is insulting to them and insulting to you."

"There are real troublemakers in this village," Charan said.

"Yes. If our leaders don't act sensibly how can people know what is going on or what should be their attitude?"

Charan smiled. "It is all the fault of that star with a tail." Some days before, his wife had awakened him at four o'clock to see a giant comet with a long fiery tail which mysteriously appeared in the southern horizon. Older villagers spoke of it with awe and fear, saying it was an ill omen. They remembered hearing of such a star over Ghungrali only once before, in 1947 on the eve of the massacre of the Muslims. "It wanted to show its power," said old Chanan. "That star has chosen Ghungrali as its victim." He was thoughtful for a moment, then added, "Yes, yes, that star was an omen. But we are men also." The Mazhbi stood and gave Charan his hand. "Today, Charan Singh, you tried to end this foolishness. I shall have six men for you in the morning."

They made do with the four Hindus that day. Charan told his father, "I didn't go to Mukhtar."

The old man harrumphed indifferently. "Well, he's not been here, and if he's not coming, why should we keep running to him?"

The Hindus were waiting the next morning, huddled, looking bedraggled, incessantly speaking in their incomprehensible language, smoking *bidis* and eyeing all about them with misery and suspicion. Mukhtar stood by the gate, having come after all. As Charan put the bullocks under the cart's yoke and loaded on the Hindus, he asked Mukhtar, "How are things on your front?"

"Everyone has arranged to cut outside the village. Except me."

"Then you should go outside and work also." Charan at once called to the bullocks, *"Tat-tat-tat-tat-tat-tat, ta-hah, ta-hah!"* and with a creak and a groan, the cart rumbled out the gate.

The reaping machine was the creation of a member of the university's engineering faculty, Professor Verma. It might have caused a greater stir had not word gone around that day that Basant Singh was importing a brand-new combine from England, one of twenty just unloaded in Bombay. The same as a reaper in principle, a combine was much improved in performance. Those who had seen the university's two demonstration machines told how, once it cut the grain, the ears were separated from the straw, which was ejected at the back of the machine to be picked up later. The ears were riddled, the chaff blown away by a powerful fan and the grain separated. A wheat field could be "combined" while still too wet to be cut by sickle, though the grain had to be dried afterward. Basant Singh would have the first privately owned one in Punjab, perhaps in India.

Hearing this, Charan cursed him for instigating the boycott since he himself wouldn't need harvesters. "There are real hypocrites in this village," he told his father. Sadhu Singh merely shrugged. "Maybe he is a man who doesn't like to take risks. Why should we bother our heads? It is his affair."

Old Sadhu, for his part, was consumed with relief to see their wheat cut, the first in Ghungrali to be harvested. As the reaping machine's four red-painted blades rotated around and around, the grain heads were guided and swept into its sharp knives, which were given a scissors or sideways action, and made loud scraping and grinding noises. As it went around the wheat, the reaper left the cut sheaves in a regular pattern on the stubble field. All the while the old man seemed to be everywhere, prancing about like a child with a new toy.

When Professor Verma, a stout, nearsighted Hindu, came out to test its operation, Sadhu hugged him with a gleeful burst of uproarious laughter. "It's working splendidly, Vermaji! See our neighbors' ears flapping. We are always ready to try anything new. Harrumph! Now those gossipmongers are repenting!" As long as Verma stayed in the fields, Sadhu Singh strutted back and forth, shouting orders to the laborers, telling Charan to, quick, bring more water or tea, very much the hardworking farmer in command. When one of the Hindus had the audacity to complain that the reaping machine left grain standing at the corners, he bellowed at him as if he himself had been insulted, "Can anybody dare to say anything is wrong with this machine? You don't lose even a single grain!"

Aside from the fuss his father made, Charan had his hands full preventing a fight between the Mazhbis from Ghungrali and the four Hindus. The outsiders, whom the Punjabis scornfully called *bhaiyas*, or brothers, were much weaker. They did not enjoy the Punjabi diet of wheat and milk. They could not keep up with the Mazhbis but fell behind, taking twice as long to gather the sheaves into bales and tie them up. Then, if Charan or Sadhu Singh was out of sight, the Hindus would slip over to the shade of a tree, crouch with their sickles and lazily smoke their *bidis*.

To separate the workers, Charan divided them into two teams, which moved up the field behind the reaper, gathering sheaves. One Mazhbi team was led by old Chanan himself, who worked with two Sikh priests, Amarjit and Surjit Singh. They officiated at all Mazhbi ceremonies. They were big, husky men with broad shoulders, and, with their long uncut beards, looked staid and important like the warriors depicted on Sikh calendars. Indeed, they were very traditional, saintly men like old Chanan himself. Charan, as always during harvests, moved about in the manner of a genial host, telling jokes and laughing uproariously at whatever was said. "Tell me, boys," he told the priests, "whosoever gets tired I'll relieve him and he can rest." "Just take care of your *bhaiyas*," one of the priests muttered.

The second Mazhbi team was made up of young men, who joked and engaged in continuous horseplay. Their ringleader, Bawa, a son of Poondi, the barn cleaner, whose face was as black as an African's from years of labor in the sun, told Charan, "These *bhaiyas* were asking me where I was from. I said my district was Rajasthan and my village was called Fuck Them All." Bawa, who had a deep infectious laugh, kept trying to provoke the Hindus by loudly shouting abuse. "Go and tie up your *dhotis*, men, and drop your shorts. I'll take you to Fuck Them All village!" Then he would gather up the sheaves very quickly. "Hurry up, boys, we have to beat those *bhaiyas* and show them how Punjabis do it."

As the day wore on and the Hindus became steadily angrier at such baiting, Charan cursed Bawa and told them, "Now just let those boys work on their side of the field and you work on yours. That Bawa's a dangerous man. Don't let him pick a quarrel. He can eat a live pig's testicles. They are of that caste." To distract the Hindus he would tell jokes, roaring with laughter and slapping his thighs, though nobody joined in.

"We are working for a rich landlord," one of them told him. "How could these people dare say anything to us?"

"Absolutely," Charan agreed. "Nothing they can say. *Bilkool nahi.*"

"If we get angry in this foreign land, it is difficult for us to work," another threatened. But Bawa and the other young Mazhbis kept it up. Once Charan fetched a pail of water and called out, "Anyone want water?" Bawa shouted over, "Just leave a little drop on their pigtails." When Sindar came over to see the reaper, Charan left him in charge of the Hindus and stormed over to Bawa. "Listen," he warned him, "you stay four acres apart from those *bhaiyas*. Otherwise I'll play hell with you."

Sindar, glad to have a captive audience, worked alongside the Hindus, bragging of famous victories in bullock-cart races and regaling them with dirty stories. "This is the thirteenth month of the year, boys," he told them. "If you're afraid to work now, you're in trouble. If somebody commits a murder in the Punjab, he does it because of his bumper wheat crop. He can afford to spend on a lawyer."

"How many men have you killed?" asked one of the Hindus. They didn't know what to make of this tall, fierce-looking Sikh with the funny nasal voice who never stopped talking.

"I never had a bumper crop, so how could I afford a murder?" he replied, giving them a sample of his cheerful logic. "Somebody once poked somebody else's bottom but he was a Qazi—you know, a Muslim priest—and he was doing his prayers and without being disturbed he just reached back and gave a rupee to that man. And the same man poked another man's bottom but that man was a Punjabi Sikh and he cut the man in two. The poor fellow thought he could make another rupee. We tell anyone who bothers us that we are Jats and will cut them in two. We are not Qazis."

"Well, sometimes you get mad," said the tallest of the Hindus, his temper cooling down.

"That's true," readily agreed Sindar. "Everyone gets mad, but I never get mad just because I don't understand a language. These Mazhbis only talk among themselves in Punjabi. They are not insulting you. So work hard, men, show your strength!" As he rambled on and on, Sindar showed the Hindus how to stack and tie the bales. Soon they began to catch up with the two Mazhbi groups. "Oh, I rape his sister!" Sindar cursed a rock when he hit his sickle on it. "It would be better to be a woman and sit inside all day. But you know at midnight you get a foot-long penis inside you. Then you say, it would be better if I was a man. So what God has made, that is right!" He went on without a pause. "Work with an energy! Show your strength! God has made our bones of steel!" After an hour of Sindar, the Hindus had forgotten about Bawa's taunts and a fight was avoided the rest of the day. Old Chanan agreed to bring more Mazhbis the next day and Charan sent the four Hindus back to the thirteen-member committee, after giving each an evening meal and four rupees; hiring outsiders only meant trouble.

When Charan returned home that night he found his sister, Surjit, waiting for him; she was in tears. Her hired laborer, Buldev, had run away. Her husband, Saroop, was in an opium stupor. She could not engage harvesters anywhere and her wheat was beginning to shatter in the fields. Surjit was desperate. Charan had sown fourteen acres of the new dwarf wheat on her newly cleared jungle land for the first time and she felt all her hopes hung in the balance. Her two teenage sons, Pala and Kaka, had started to cut the wheat, but there was no one else. Charan felt very weary. He had trouble enough with his own harvest. Still he promised to do what he could, telling Surjit to go home and tell Saroop and the boys to cut all they could in the meantime.

In many ways, Surjit was Charan's favorite sister and the most like him. She was a strikingly handsome woman except for the hard set of her features in recent years. Like Charan, she had raven-black hair, the high color of radiant health and the same air of vitality and strength. Beside her, her husband, a once-handsome man with deep-set gray eyes and a gentle manner, looked faded, worn and old. To Charan, Surjit always spoke of Saroop with contempt, telling him her husband's opium cost only two rupees a day. "So it is all right, brother," she would say. "If you keep a laborer it's five rupees a day in our village. Whereas my husband is quite a good worker."

Surjit never admitted to her family her true affection for Saroop or that she was prepared to go through anything to keep him. Saroop had been a good catch when they married just before partition, a rich landlord's son. Unlike Charan, the uprooting had not steeled him, but made him weaker; as a refugee his whole life had crumbled, and for years he had been a slave to opium.

Even today Surjit's appearance spoke of past prosperity. Her yellow silk *salwar kameez* and frayed white wool scarf did not fit the shabby little mud hut where they lived, with its log beams at a slant and its sagging thatched roof seemingly about to collapse. Their farmstead was set in the jungle, there were jackals about at night and the nearest neighbors, whom Surjit detested, were some distance away. Everything about the place looked makeshift and mean: a cattle shed whose corrugated-tin roof was propped up by stripped tree branches, two or three hungry-looking buffaloes, string cots scattered about and piled with dusty quilts and bedding, an open hearth black with soot and buzzing with flies. Charan went there as seldom as he could and never stayed long.

When he did go he knew what she would say. First she would carry on about his drinking. "You and Father between you must spend twenty rupees by evening. You are racing to see who can ruin the family first. Ah, well, everybody has to hang himself. Oh, Charan, what is happening to you? You were so hardworking when you were young. And strong. Everybody was afraid of you. Nobody could touch your arm for fear of getting a push that would send a big man to the ground."

Then she would go on about her loneliness. "The children's grand-mother never visits us. She says she's got no company here and no new faces to see. And she's getting so fat, Charan. Fat as a pig!"

If Charan remained overnight, she would go on and on about her plans. "Now I feel a little relieved, I had to really go through hell for years together and all the time I was praying to God: *Hey, Sadhe Padshah*, O Holy King, shall I ever be able to see good days again? Now he has heard my appeal and thanks to you and father I am better off. I was only waiting for my boys to grow up. Oh, Charan, within a few years I shall be quite free of my burdens. I shall bring a bride for Pala and marry off Kaka too. I'll just be sitting on a bed in the kitchen in a few more years, sitting and sleeping in the same bed. I will get up and start churning milk early in the morning so that the children have a nice morning nap. I won't give them any trouble.

"I'll make two rooms on either side of this room here and I'll give one to Pala and his bride so they can enjoy the loneliness of their two beings. I have faith in the Maharaj. He Himself will do everything for me. You know I have a heart as big as a lioness's. One hundred people can come and stay with me. You won't see the slightest wrinkle on my forehead. Everyone brings his own food stamped by God. We are nobody in between. Oh, Charan, I have seen really bad days. Now they are over. . . ."

To himself Charan resolved to save her harvest somehow, even if he had to spirit the Mazhbis out of Ghungrali in the middle of the night. But he confided in no one except Sadhu Singh.

After Surjit left, Charan went to the cattle yard to check the tractor to see if it was ready to pull a wagonload of men out on the Grand Trunk Road. He found that his oldest son, Sukhdev, had not oiled the engine as he had been told to do. When he asked the boy about it,

Suka said he had used oil from a tin at the house. Then he changed his story, saying he got some from a bottle in the barn. Both, Charan knew, were lies. "You are lying again, my son," Charan told him sadly. "You are a big liar. Is that what you've learned from all these books? Oh, Suka, Suka. Instead of telling me the truth, that you forgot, you treat me like a fool. You should be ashamed of your dirty face. I could see the engine had not been oiled. If you go on lying and behaving in this way, you won't go anywhere in life." Suka said nothing but turned his eyes back to a schoolbook.

In contrast to Charan's sullen offspring, as they worked in the hot sun all day, the Mazhbis stayed cheerful. Charan, anxious that they stay contented and go with him to cut Surjit's wheat, was sober and genial. He went about the fields serving water, tea or glasses of buttermilk and fiercely fighting with the old lady to ensure that everybody got plenty to eat. "Here it is!" he would call out affably, serving out *chapattis* and a thick lentil curry in the fields. "Who doesn't eat of this will repent afterward!" The workers gathered under the trees by his well. In the fields with the Mazhbis, without knowing why, Charan felt pleasurably alive and contented.

The reaper finished cutting in two days and went off to another demonstration near Ludhiana, and Sadhu, exhausted, retreated happily to his cot and glasses of tea. With eleven Mazhbis on hand now, the baling went quickly. Sukhdev now became the target of Bawa's sallies. "Hey, Suka, you want a sickle so you can help us work? I've got one hidden deep in my shorts. You'll get it when it's dark."

"Don't talk rot to me, you black-faced bastard," Suka cursed him. Suka would vanish for hours on end, leaving Charan alone to fetch pails of drinking water from the well to carry out to the harvesters.

The Mazhbis continued to work in two teams, the old men and the young, and when they neared the end of a field and one or the other was not far behind, they would race to finish with shouting and good-natured banter back and forth.

"*Shabash*, boys, we have to show our strength to these old men." "Hurry, we must beat the others! They're catching up." "Here, bring that bale." "You hold mine and I'll hold yours. No, Bawa, I mean the rope." "Oh, the rope broke! I rape its mother." "Hurry, hurry, you boys! Bring more bales."

"You'll see," Bawa shouted, pushing his men to beat old Chanan's group, just a short way ahead in the next row. "We'll make them spit like stallions. Those Sikh priests like Amarjit are very tricky. They know so many ways to bring women to their beds. They'll tell them, 'Oh, dear little girl, unbutton these trousers.' If she's foolish, she'll unbutton theirs. If she's clever, he will say, 'Oh, no, my dear, I meant those trousers hanging there on the wall.' "

This made the usually grave Amarjit grin in embarrassment, and Bawa cried in triumph, "Look! Our Sikh is in high spirits again."

"*Wah, wah!*" Charan joined in exuberantly. "Go, boys, go!" Both groups of Mazhbis worked frantically now, as they always did, abreast near the end of the field. "Bring, brother!" "Hurry up!" "They should not beat us! After all, we are bearded men, Amarjit, and they are children." "Take care your long beards don't get caught in the bales, old men!" "Don't worry. We'll bring them to their knees." "Make them piss in their shorts, boys!" "Bring one more bale!" "Ah!" "Finished!" "*Shabash*, boys, now we have shown our strength to these old men!"

When both groups reached the end of the field, the old men usually a bit behind, the Mazhbis would flop down on the grassy bank, their bodies and faces drenched with sweat, gulping in the air quickly before the heat rushed back. Charan would hasten to pour water into their glasses or outstretched hands and one of the youths would boast, "The young men are better than the old in every respect."

"No, the old are real bulls. When they start they won't stop for hours. If you could see old Banta last night. How he was begging for it and his wife kicked his bottom."

"I have been where they charge one anna if it's as big as a donkey's and half an anna for smaller sizes."

"What for half an anna?"

"You wouldn't know because you are no size whatsoever. Yours is like a ladyfinger. Maybe even smaller than that."

"Oh, Bantee, Bantee, what can your wife do with a ladyfinger? She won't even know you are there."

Often the talk turned to the boycott.

"Now it's only talk," Charan would say. "But sometimes these things can lead to murders on both sides. It's nonsense."

"Boycott, boycott," Bawa joined in, repeating the strange-sounding foreign word. "When you speak that *boycott*, your whole mouth gets full of it."

On the evening of the third day, when they reached his last field, Charan told the Mazhbis to make extra-large bales, three apiece, for their payment. "These bales must be really big ones," he said, "one for every day you worked. Don't hesitate. Before, this was my farm and your labor, but now, take it, my wheat is in your hands. Be generous with your bales. Make some really big ones. Tomorrow don't say that Charan was a miser."

"No, no, Charan," old Chanan protested. "We are not that greedy." He made a moderate-sized bale and told the men to follow his example. "This is big enough. We know you are a largehearted man, a real lion. But we must not exploit your generosity."

"I'm sure you deserve these big bales. That is no untruth . . . Now shall we save my sister's wheat? What do you say, boys? It is shattering in the fields there in Bhadson village and she can get no one to help her. What do you say? You'll get the same as here all right."

After the Mazhbis talked a while among themselves, old Chanan spoke up. "We five are ready to go: Amarjit, Surjit, his son, my son Kapur and myself. Now we must finish this work. But we are ready, and ready to go, the five of us." There would be no reaper but Chanan was happy to cut in the old traditional way with sickles. The old man fiercely opposed any form of modernization. He told Charan, "These machines are awful. It's difficult to make good bales when wheat is cut by a machine."

After more talk all the other Mazhbis agreed to go also. Charan, who was relieved to see all his wheat now safely lying in bales to dry, felt very pleased. "Make your piles of bales and we'll load them on the wagon," he called. "Now it's all settled. We'll start at five."

"No," said old Chanan. "Better to go before the village stirs. We'll rise and come to your barn when the moon comes over our beds."

X

Two hours before dawn, the Mazhbis crept through the sleeping lanes of Ghungrali and gathered at Charan's cattle yard. They piled straw in his wagon and scrambled aboard as Charan started the tractor engine and roared off before any of the other Jats knew they were going. Three hours later, as the sun was rising over the fields, they arrived at Surjit's farm twenty-seven miles to the south. Along the Grand Trunk Road there was little traffic so early. Hundreds of crows, roused by the tractor engine, rose from the high branches of the old oaks along the road, to screech and caw irritably. As they neared Bhadson village, trees no longer obscured the view and they could see the sky and countryside far ahead. The Mazhbis seldom ventured far from the village, and as the tractor bumped along they looked around with curiosity. In the transparent dust, the world exposed its fairness: white mist lay unevenly around the bushes and haystacks and rose in small cloudlets. Surjit's farmstead, in the middle of a large expanse of dry, brown wheat, was reached along a narrow dirt track. Great clouds of dust rolled up from the tractor tires; the men covered their heads and noses with their shawls and blankets so as to breathe. A few hundred yards beyond the farmstead began low, flat jungle.

It was hotter in Bhadson than in Ghungrali and, perhaps because of the nearness of the jungle or the scorching wind that blew day after day, or the absence of big shade trees on the newly cleared land, the sun seemed to beat more fiercely. The air was thinner here, the sky whiter and the dust thicker; it settled on the wet backs and shoulders of the men as they worked. By late morning a gray haze of dust spread over the sky, the sun turned a livid white and hot winds unceasingly stirred the wheat. The Mazhbis tied rags over their mouths and noses to keep out the dust, and, with only their grimy wet foreheads and eyes exposed, looked like bandits or dacoits. From the edge of one field to another, fifteen men squatting on their haunches slowly moved forward, slashing away at the grain with their sickles. There were the Mazhbis, Saroop and his two sons, Pala and Kaka, and Charan. Saroop, whom Surjit had strengthened with large doses of opium, was formally the master, but he worked almost apologetically alongside the Mazhbis and gave no orders.

Everyone knew that in reality the farm was in the hands of Surjit; she arranged everything; nothing was done without her consent. Without a mechanical reaper, the Mazhbis, Saroop and his sons cut the wheat as Punjabis have done it from time immemorial, slashing their sickles at the ripe stems, grasping one handful at a time, advancing slowly, rocking from side to side on their haunches and moving steadily and rhythmically, to the end of the field, crouched low in a wide, spread-out line, nearly buried in the knee-high wheat. Sometimes they would look up as a vulture or a hawk glided on the wind high above. All day long the sickles flashed in the white sun. It was as hot as a furnace, as you could see from the glint of the sickles, from the wet faces and backs, from the salt left on their skin from sweating and the way they gathered up the swaths after cutting.

The more their muscles grew tired, the more the younger men joked and cursed and told of sexual exploits and the quieter the older men became. Charan himself, who could not mow and found his asthma much aggravated by Bhadson's dust, had somehow never seemed so full of life and energy. He ran back and forth from the house, carrying water, tea, brown sugar cakes, pails of buttermilk, steaming-hot *chapattis*, kettles of delicious potato and pea curry and sometimes even ice, for Surjit was as generous as the old lady was stingy. She worked all day over the hearth preparing the best food she could, she was so thankful to her deliverers.

As they worked, the voices of the men arose from the wheat: "Move on, O brave men. Try to be fast." "Oh, these thorny weeds, it is like the sting of a scorpion." "This wheat is dry; if your sickle is sharp it cuts easily."

Charan hovered about, as if his good humor alone sustained the brutal labor. He even joked with Saroop, whom he usually avoided. The young Mazbhis were tirelessly good-humored. "Once Bawa's uncle came and showed Bawa his penis," called Banarsi, one of them. "And the uncle asked, 'What is that, dear nephew, a dove or a snake?' And Bawa said, 'Oh, Uncle, it is a snake but only a very little one. More like a worm.'" "Oh, shameless creatures," one of the older men would call to them, "look at your elders around you and you cut such filthy jokes. Now better you stop this kind of talk."

"Race with me!" somebody would cry. "Beware, I'm coming like the wind!" Sometimes one of the young Mazbhis would start to sing, rocking on his heels as his sickle flashed in the light.

> I'm dancing like a peacock
> And my bells are jingling . . .

As they neared the end of the rows, as in Ghungrali, the men would pick up their speed, their sickles flashing. "Come, boys, show your strength! *Shabash, shaba-a-sh!* Make the parrots fly!"

When he saw Surjit bringing tea, old Chanan would shush them, and everybody would leave the field for the shade of a tree, flopping down on their backs. Always the landscape was the same: the bands of reaped wheat, the empty fields of stubble and patches still standing, crows flapping their wings and cawing to each other, the cloudless, dusty sky. The second day replaced the first, and then the third, and the air became even more stagnant with heat and stillness. Sometimes there was not a breath of wind, nor a cheering cool sound, so that even hot breezes, stirring the furnace heat, were welcome.

Old Chanan steeled his men: "We won't leave until Sister says, 'Now I cannot afford any more food for these men.'"

"I won't say that ever, Brother," Surjit told him. "You can stay here as long as you wish. I won't run out of food. After all, I am Charan's sister. I have the same blood running in my veins."

Always the talk came back to the boycott. "Some of the Jats will really be afraid now," Bawa speculated. "Their wives will tell them, 'Now, little Pritam's father, go and arrange for some Harijans to cut your wheat. You must cut it at once before it shatters or we'll starve.'"

Charan was optimistic. "Surely it will be settled by the time we reach the village." He thought it would have to end one way or another. "They may reach some compromise or there will be some killing. Ultimately they will have to stop this foolishness."

"Did you hear the new thing?" asked Bawa. "Some of the Chamars burned Basant Singh's effigy and women beat his likeness with sticks and cried, 'May he die! May he die!'"

"Who says that?"

"Women."

"Nonsense," Charan growled. "You know those gossipmongers. Those Chamars . . ."

"Never believe the Chamars," old Chanan interrupted. Even as the lowliest of the Harijans, he was opposed to any erosion of the caste system. "They are nobody's friends. Stay with your own caste. Chamars will be your friends if you go on serving them tea, but if you go to their houses and ask for tea, from that day on they'll not look you straight in the eye."

"Yes, they are a greedy lot, Uncle," echoed Bawa. "Where there is tea, Chamars are your friends."

"Bawa took too much opium," said Kapur, Chanan's son. "See how slow he cuts." As was common during a Punjabi harvest, Charan had been handing out pellets of opium to swallow to keep up one's strength and stamina.

"Bawa has a ghost inside him."

"You had that same ghost yesterday, Kapur."

In midafternoon, the Bhadson *mistry*, or carpenter, came to sharpen everyone's sickle, an old custom during harvest for which he would get grain. In an equally venerable custom, since he was from another village, the Mazhbis teased him and cracked jokes at his expense. The *mistry*, a bony, slack-jawed youth, bent over his work and pretended not to hear them.

"Oh, what is this, *mistryji?*" Bawa asked, after his sickle had already been sharpened. "It has gone dull."

"He looks dull himself. He needs sharpening."

"You should help him, Bawa. Put some energy in him."

"If he agrees, we will. He doesn't know how much energy these Ghungrali *wallahs* have. If he needs some he should come at midnight. We will all give him a drop of energy, every one of us."

Ready to fight back, the *mistry* looked at Bawa, who was sprawled out on the grassy bank. "Do you have a stomachache, boy?"

"Yes."

"If you have a stomachache, come with me. You will have to spend the night with an old man in our village. He is a real good doctor and applies his medicine at midnight. Are you ready?"

Encouraged by this daring retort and gleeful, all the Mazhbis began to taunt the poor carpenter unmercifully in high falsetto voices. Then they quieted down as Surjit came with a fresh tin of tea. She offered some to the *mistry*, who stammered something about reaching home "come what may," and dashed off amid the Mazhbis' jeers and laughter. Mystified, Surjit poured the tea, telling the workers, "Brothers, all the neighbors are jealous because we are finishing our harvest so quickly. You see, this is the first year I've grown as much wheat as my neighbors. Before, they used to graze cattle in our empty fields. Now Charan has sown all this land."

At last, as the sun was about to descend in the west, and the plain, fields and air were no longer suffocating but took on a tolerable coolness, the Mazhbis carried their sickles back to the farmhouse for the last time. Most of them flopped down on cots strewn about the yard, too tired to talk. Old Chanan came last of all. "Boys, give me your sickles," he told everybody. "Let us try to collect everything for the trip home."

"Oh, brethren, do you want to take your baths in cold water or hot?" called Charan, ever the genial host. "I shall get hot water for you. It's my duty. We'll light a fire and heat a drum of water." Charan was already quite drunk, celebrating the completed harvest. The Mazhbis, after resting, began to wander about the yard, stripping off their dusty clothes.

"Oh, Charan, what will we say to the Jats when we get home tonight?" asked Amarjit. "They will accuse us and say, 'You are running to other villages and here we are short of men. Instead of bringing men from outside, you are taking them away.' What shall we say?"

"That Charan will have to explain, not us," said old Chanan with a smile. "We will tell them Charan Singh took us out."

Charan waved a bottle at them. "Ho, ho, ho, don't worry." He shouted in his hoarse voice, *"Wahi Guruji!"* God is great!"

Some of the Mazhbis crouched around a fire. "The flames are coming out of the pit." "You used so much oil. Sprinkle some water around the edge." "I only want cold water. Shall I take a bath here or at the pump?"

The Mazhbis stripped off everything but their loincloths and poured hot water over themselves. They used no soap but rubbed their glistening, muscular bodies clean and dry with coconut oil. Charan hastened to pour a drink for old Chanan, who was still resting on a cot with another older Mazhbi, Banta. Banta downed a single shot of liquor in a gulp and, looking pleased with himself, declared loudly, "Listen to me. Charan treats us as if he were our father. It is a great honor for us. We are poor men and he is our master." Several Mazhbis drank a toast to Charan and several more came running when they saw that liquor was being served. "Charan, you are one of the finest men in the world," said old Chanan, enjoying his glass of liquor now that the work was done.

Bawa wandered over, his coarse black hair dripping wet and sticking out every which way, and his dark brown face and shiny shoulders cleaned and oiled. Charan poured him a full glass of liquor. Banta, amazed at its size, said, "Oh, Bawa, you are a naughty boy." Bawa grinned, downed the contents of the glass in one huge swig and held it out to Charan to pour another. "Be sober and enjoy your life!" cried Banarsi, coming up to join them and waving his glass in their faces. "Drink up, boys. Tomorrow you may be dead!" Bawa laughed. "Then you'll work for God. Cutting His crops in heaven."

The rest of the men milled about or sat on cots or the ground as Charan hurried back and forth refilling their glasses. Pala ran to replenish the supply of bottles from the house. "We are here because of Charan's good tongue," began Amarjit, as if he were about to give a speech, his long beard lending him a priestly aura. "The way he treats us we can sacrifice our lives for him. He is a gem of a person. . . ." He paused, thinking of what to say that would be appropriate to the occasion. "Where men work, there is God. Our Guru respected work and we are all laboring men." Surjit passed among them with a dish of her best pickled chillies, expressing to each her gratitude. Charan sensed a general feeling of well-being. "You know, my brothers," he declared in a loud voice, "I have seen many harvests in my life but I have never seen one like this. We have been three days without a fight."

"All these boys are real good workers," Chanan agreed. "No one has run off to answer the call of nature all the time or made other foolish excuses."

"Ah, the neighbors are looking across the field," Surjit said, noticing some men standing in the distance. "I don't want them to cast their evil eyes on all this pork we are going to eat. How jealous they will be! Oh, brothers, I have seen bad days but now we have a fine wheat harvest thanks to you." In her gratitude Surjit had killed and roasted a pig.

Charan poured round after round, all with great bursts of laughter. Saroop had brewed twenty-five bottles of liquor from brown sugar, a liquor which stupefied all who drank it, just as if they had been stunned by a blow to the head. It was not long before Charan and the Mazhbis sat in a great circle, exhausted, satiated, drunk and looking as rascally as any Romans at a bacchanal, especially the younger men who had not yet dressed or wound on their turbans but sat wrapped in towels as though in togas, their wet, uncombed hair plastered down. Charan was now very drunk and he jumped into the center of the circle and with a bottle in hand he roared, "I'm now at your disposal, my beloved ones. Now you will have a pig! We won't serve it on plates. We'll put it on a big platter and have it here in the middle of all of us."

Surjit spread a large white cloth on the ground and the men moved up around it, sitting cross-legged or with legs spread out in every direction, a row of precious bottles before them. It was getting dark now; soon the fire from the hearth threw red shadows on their faces. The world seemed to have shrunk to their circle, the star-filled sky and the croaking of angry frogs from the blackness of the nearest fields.

"Let me serve my friends!" Charan bellowed, and suddenly, in the warmth of the liquor, in the glistening faces of the Mazhbis, in the din and shouts and laughter, was discernible to him a great vitality, youth and revival of strength.

"Drink up!" he shouted at the top of his lungs. "Enjoy, for we only live once." And he rose to his full height, and waving his glass and so bursting with feeling that water came to his eyes, he cried hoarsely,

"I'm not happy, I'm super-happy! Happiest of all the world! I'm so happy I can jump up to the sky!"

Saroop came running from the house, arms full of bottles. "Here!" cried Charan. "Have you ever seen so many bottles? These are the young ones of the last. Who wants more?"

Surjit called to Pala to come and get the pig. At the hearth, as he strained to lift the huge platter, heaped with meat and gravy, Surjit whispered, "See the neighbors over there. How those dogs are looking with their big wide eyes! They are having heart failure to see our great kettle of pork." Pala set it in the midst of the Mazhbis and Surjit came running with a great stack of hot *chapattis*. "Do like this," Pala told them, "come and take whatever you want." At once the hungry Mazhbis fell on the food like beasts thirsting after prey, each snatching and devouring the pork as fast as he could, for few of them had meat but once or twice in a year. After some time, eating as much as they possibly could, many sat stupefied by the food and liquor with foolishly happy expressions on their faces.

Pala felt a speech was required from the host and his father was too drunk. He declared in a loud voice that startled those near him, "Brothers, you have worked hard and done everything for us. I'm too glad. If I did anything wrong, please excuse me. I'm a poor man. I did the best of my ability. I think what I served was very poor food. If I'm guilty, please pardon me." A few of them cheered and applauded and Bawa knocked over a bottle of liquor. "So, let us start for Ghungrali," at last called old Chanan. There was great confusion as the Mazhbis staggered to their feet and lurched around in the shadows. Some had to dress, others looked for their possessions, and they bumped into one another and cursed the darkness. Bawa picked up the large platter and, lifting it into the air, poured the remaining gravy down his throat. All of a sudden Surjit shrieked. Someone had stepped into a basket of baby chicks. "Oh, who has done it? Oh, God forgive me! Someone has crushed the poor little things!" Amarjit rushed to help her, crying out, "God, what a mess someone has made!" Surjit recovered herself and cried, "Only two are lost. Forget it, brothers. It was an accident. What has happened has happened."

Charan, drunk as he was, mounted to the driver's seat and shouted for everyone to climb into the wagon. Pala and Kaka came running with large heaps of straw for the Mazhbis to sit on. The tractor started with a noisy roar, Charan revving the engine. Everyone was shouting at once, Saroop staggered about the wagon shaking hands with all the

Mazhbis, and Surjit came running to give each man a piece of brown sugar. "Here, brothers," she called above the din, "take this and sweeten your mouths. Godspeed on the journey home!" Amarjit's voice rose above the others. "*A Jaikara;* I'll yell a religious cry." And his deep voice bellowed into the night:

"*Jo bole so nihal! Who speaks he is full of the name of God!*"

Everyone roared back, "*Sat Sri Akal!*"

"*Jo bale so nihal!*"

"*Sat Sri Akal!*"

The next morning in Ghungrali, One-Eye stopped Charan on the road. "Charan," he said in an ugly tone, "now we'll have to talk to you. We have an objection."

Charan whirled around. He was hurrying to the well of the Sarpanch to help his friend harvest, and his head was splitting from the revelry in Bhadson.

"Your old friends are objecting too much."

"Bring those friends to me," Charan growled at him. "Let them talk to me straight. Don't convey messages in that sneaky manner. You give an evil twist to words."

"Now, Maharaji," gasped One-Eye, taken aback. "Don't shout at me so. I fold my hands before you."

The man infuriated Charan. "Keep your evil mouth quiet!" he roared at him. "Don't always try to make trouble!" Shaken, One-Eye hurried to his fields. There he told his worker, "That Charan and his father are real crooks. They'll eat up that sister's land. Ah, what they have done to that poor girl! The tricks they've played! How they've misused her property!" His face took on a pious look. "But why should we talk? It is their own private folly."

A great crowd of men, perhaps fifty in all, had come to cut the fields of the Sarpanch. This was an old Punjabi custom called an *ahwat*, and in the evening the Sarpanch would serve a big feast for all the harvesters, with plenty of liquor. When Nirmal chided him for taking the Mazhbis to Bhadson, Charan exploded, "Are you all mad here in Ghungrali? I plowed those fields. I sowed them. It was my duty to cut the wheat."

"Now, Charan." Nirmal hastened to placate his friend. "You fly out of your clothes in a minute. I wish I'd never heard the word 'boycott.' Now the last three days there is a great rush. Everybody is demanding, 'Men, men, men!' We have only a few and demand is thirty, forty times greater. And some of the wheat is shattering."

Charan told him what One-Eye had said. "He is an evil soul. You know the saying: 'A one-eyed man is dangerous.'" Charan gave a burst of hoarse laughter and Nirmal started to laugh too, and in a moment they were laughing and slapping each other on the back as if they had taken leave of their senses. Seeing them, the Sarpanch hurried over. "No, Charan," he said, "I won't shake hands with you today. You are too sacred and have come to help us. We shall feed you good."

"Oh, don't insult me," Charan replied heartily. "It won't be the first time I've eaten good. My mother used to feed me the whole day until I was three. You can still see her udders." He gave a huge laugh. "Here, just see my body, though it's half of what it used to be. And all because one old woman had pails and pails of milk."

A mile south, near Bhambadi village, Mukhtar and two other Chamars from Ghungrali were mowing wheat, their faces burnt and glowing in the hot wind. The wheat belonged to a Hindu *pandit*. The three of them had a contract to cut and thresh it for sixty-eight kilos of grain per acre, more than they had ever earned in Ghungrali. They were talking about what they would do after the harvest.

"I don't know," Mukhtar said. He worked with a steady rhythm as he talked, grasping the stalks with his left hand and slashing the stems with his sickle in his right. "I'm hopeful the boycott won't last too many days. One thing is certain: I shall try to give my sons a good education. My parents wanted me to go on with my studies, but I couldn't master the English language. I was very poor in it, and gave up my schooling after nine years. So here I am. I'm determined my boys will not follow in my footsteps. I'm sure of one thing. No matter what happens, my children will never work for the Jats. They may be factory workers or mechanics if they don't become educated gentlemen. But I will never let them work for the Jats. Never."

"This wind is nasty. It spoils everything."

"It doesn't matter. Here we are not under any Jats. We are masters of ourselves."

"Maybe God will hear us and be kind enough to end the wind," said Uttam, a big, husky Chamar working with Mukhtar.

"We could have reached a settlement if it wasn't for Basant Singh and that one-eyed man. They want to play their own game. They are nasty fellows. But Charan is a prince, a man of silver."

"I heard he was a drunkard and abused his workers," Uttam said.

"He drinks and abuses both," Mukhtar readily agreed. "But he is always true. He stands for the right thing and disagrees when there is injustice. For that you cannot find a better man for miles around."

Mukhtar fell silent, thinking of the boycott and those responsible for it. He passed judgment on Basant Singh, One-Eye and the other troublemakers, but the more he thought, the angrier he became at Charan, Pritam, Dhakel and all the good Jats who went along with the others. For without them, where would the others be? For two days he had such thoughts, and when he and Uttam came upon Charan one evening Mukhtar's words came with unexpected harshness.

"Listen, listen, Chota," Charan called from his bullock cart as he drew abreast of Mukhtar and Uttam walking. "The harvest is almost over. It is better you reach some settlement and come back to work for me on daily wages."

"We are trying to settle," Mukhtar said.

"Then what is wrong? This dispute was over the harvest and that is almost over. If you quietly start working for me again on daily wages, everything will be all right."

"Will it? Will it be all right?"

"Are you mad? If you want that someone should come to you and beg forgiveness, then I shall come to your house this very evening. If that is all, I shall come and ask you to work for all to see."

"No, Charan. If that was all, there would never have been any trouble."

"That's what I mean. We should end this nonsense. I mean that there shouldn't be any more trouble."

"Look around you, Charan." An anger growing inside him, Mukhtar's voice rose. "Look around you. Do you think it doesn't hurt us to see the crops of our village shatter in the fields? Do you think it will be all over if only everyone apologizes to everyone? Do you think Ghungrali can ever go back to what it was? Do you think Harijans can ever again trust the Jats? Do you, Charan? Can we go back?" Mukhtar's voice had risen to such a pitch that Uttam tugged anxiously on his shoulder and said, "Let's go, Mukhtar." As they moved down the road, Mukhtar was angry, with an anger he had never known. Time would pass, and the trouble in the village, but Mukhtar's anger perhaps would not pass, but stay in his mind all his life long.

Speechless, Charan stared after him. Of all the villagers, Mukhtar was one of the best farmers, though at twenty-three he was young enough to be Charan's son. Charan knew he had such a skill and a knowledge of the land as his own sons would never possess, and that without him, his own days would become much harder. And Charan stared after him a long time, numbed by the fear that Mukhtar was right.

XI

In the lives of all men, there are times for pausing, reflecting and taking stock. This Charan did in the few days between harvesting and threshing, spending them at his well, cutting fodder, preparing the threshing ground, working alone. In the afternoons, when the hot winds came up and the sky was white with furnace heat and flying dust, he dozed on a *charpoy* in his toolshed, his only companions two sparrows who made their nest in a water pail hanging from a hook on the wall, and flew in and out the open window, feeding their young. So Charan reconciled himself and added the missed chance to break the boycott to all his other follies and failures.

Then, within a week, Sadhu Singh came with a threshing machine he had contrived to borrow free of charge from a government office. Charan was busy again. The Mazhbis, who had been cutting wheat for other Jats, returned, and old Chanan, his son Kapur, Bawa and Amarjit used hoes to cut away the stubble to make a threshing ground. Then they swept the earth clean with cotton-stick brushes. Sadhu Singh told Charan, "All it took to get the thresher was a little backslapping and six bottles of liquor." Chanan erected a curtain of jute bags sewed together to prevent dust and chaff from blowing back at the two men who would feed the grain into a revolving drum armed with steel beaters; in the front were axles with sharp little knives to quickly chop up the wheat. The Mazhbis brought bales from the fields and stacked them into an enormous pile by the threshing machine. At last they were ready to begin.

Charan climbed up on the tractor and started the engine, and then with a great shout, *"Wahi Guruji!* God is great!" he put the tractor into gear, the belt began to turn on its pulley and the hammers inside the drum started to beat down, metal screeching against metal. Chanan and Bawa, working side by side, had the most dangerous job—pushing handfuls of grain into the feeder's gnashing steel teeth, where it was quickly chewed up by the knives. On the other side of the jute curtain, Sher, who had joined the other Mazhbis at the last minute, stood with a wooden fork. The chopped-up wheat passed over rollers and shaking sieves that separated the chaff, straw and grain as a blower carried off loose strands. At last the chaff and straw were blown into the air in clouds of dust as Sher stood by to pitch them up again. Amarjit did the final winnowing, tossing wooden scoopfuls up from a stream of grain so the wind blew the rest of the dust and chaff away.

As the days wore on, two great heaps began to form by the machine, one larger and white as mother-of-pearl, and one smaller and a milky light brown—Charan's wheat harvest. No one spoke in the roaring din of the metal drum and tractor engine, but during rests they talked and joked and gossiped as much as ever.

Charan's son Sukhdev worked with them, though one day his father caught him savagely beating a bullock with a stick. "Stop that!" Charan shouted at him. "Oh, don't you see what you are doing? You are the son of a Jat, Suka, not a weaver. Why can't you handle bullocks?"

"Hush, Charan," old Chanan admonished him. "He is a child."

"Child!" Charan snorted with contempt. "He is sixteen. When I was of his age, I used to have the whole family to support as a laborer in the fields. You say he is a child . . ." He gave Sukhdev a look of disgust and turned away. "Well, let's get back to work, men."

It was the end of a break and as they moved back across the stubble field, Chanan told Sher, "Charan has been very good to us."

The younger man shrugged. "Everyone has to be more generous than before, Uncle. The old days are over."

Charan, in threshing his wheat, was again the first in the village. Some Jats found harvesters outside; others cut their own wheat. Dhakel, Sindar, Gurmel and a neighbor's sharecropper had been at it ten days. Dhakel, with his slight build, was soon exhausted and Gurmel began to feel his forty years. But Sindar, who had not run off on the eve of the harvest as expected, had proved to have surprising stamina and zest. Day after scorching day, through dust storms and whirlwinds, Sindar kept slashing away with his sickle with a vigor that surpassed all the rest. He never stopped talking: "Work with an energy! Show your strength! God has made our bones of steel!" Dhakel managed to get some of his in-laws from another village to come and cut one day. Sindar could hardly wait until they left to declare, "Today we have stomped their bottoms, those outsiders. They won't forget us the rest of their lives, that bunch of dead old ladies. Do you think it is a joke to compete with men like us?"

If Dhakel lagged behind, Sindar joked, "Do you know why Dhakel is so tired today? He was raped by us all last night. He was drunk and couldn't tell what was happening. In the morning he asked, 'Who spilled milk on my pajamas?' The poor man doesn't know he will give birth to twins next spring."

"Aaaagggh! Why do you talk all the time?" Gurmel would explode.

"Oh, Deaf Man, have you seen my sickle dance?"

"Dance! It creeps like a tortoise!"

"You say tortoise but I doubt you have eyes in your head. Didn't you see the day Dhakel's in-laws were here? Those tiny, skinny, dead old ladies, my son, will remember me for ages."

Once a family of Rajasthani beggars came. "God will give you more!" cried an old woman among them. "We are hungry. We come from a country ravaged by famine." The neighbor's sharecropper saw that one of the beggars was a handsome woman. "Oh," he told Sindar, "she can serve our purpose."

"You can take a big bale of wheat if you make our boys happy," Sindar joked with the woman. "Stay a while. Ten minutes."

Dhakel was angry with the beggars. "Shall I tell you what is what? Why should you beg when you can work? Run from here!" But Sindar gave them three bundles of wheat and they went away. The share-cropper protested. "You idiot! You should not have given her like that for nothing. Only then she could be useful to us."

"Oh, you fool," Sindar told the man. "I was cutting jokes. I didn't mean anything but a little joking. Show your strength, men! Oh, I remember one time in Isru. We were threshing. A real good girl came along to beg some grain and she brought back two more girls the next day. We had three trips each. How they were jumping like springs underneath! All were happy and all were the gainers. There was another time in Mal Majra village. . . ."

So the days passed, Sindar rambling on and on, the sickles flashing in the wheat, cutting it down stalk by stalk, row by row, field by field, acre by acre. Slowly Ghungrali changed under the hot white sun and the pall of dust. The sheaves lay row upon row in the stubble fields or the newly mown wheat would lie in swaths for the men to gather up. Every day there were clouds, it was dusty, white mist gathered in the distance. The hot wind blew in sudden gusts and never seemed to rest, surfaces became hot to the touch, the air dry in the nostrils. Day by day the threshing in Charan's fields continued, wheat and chaff tossed into the luminous light, the diesel engine droning on, the pile of precious wheat growing. The men worked carefully in the hot wind and sun, winnowing the wheat so as not to lose a single grain. Now the whole countryside grew bare and flat with only stubble fields and the green-brown foliage of the hardiest sun-baked trees. When the dust cleared as dew fell at dusk or lay on the earth in the early morning, a man could see for miles and miles. Once the wheat was gathered in, the sky seemed larger, the earth more spacious, and the men working in the brutal heat of the fields began to ponder their own significance and the meaning of it all.

Late afternoon. An hour before nightfall. The men gathered under the shade of the withered oak trees at Charan's well for the final rest of the day. Charan poured tea, and when Sindar wandered over to drink at the pump, Charan laughed and asked him to tell them some gossip. But Sindar, his face and turban and beard wet and gray with sweat and dust, for once was in no mood for banter. "I have been thinking," he told his cousin, "that it is a sin to hurt poor people. God will surely punish this village."

"A sin?" Charan laughed. "What is a sin?"

"In my eyes," called Gurmel, who was stretched out on the grass, "the greatest sin is to rape a virgin."

"The real sin," said Charan, "is to take labor by force and refuse to pay. Or if you squander your children's property, forcing them to wander on the roads."

"A man does so many sins in his life," said Sher, lighting up a *bidi.* "If you just look at someone with a bad intention, that too is a sin."

"There is one sin worse than any," Charan went on. "To show friendship with a man if you mean to destroy him. It is like helping a man in need. If he has no friends or relations, if he is shivering with cold and you give him bedding and food and make him comfortable, that is real virtue. But there must be no personal gain in it. None at all. If you do something for gain or to look good to your friends, it is nothing."

"Ho! What is all this about sins?" called the Sarpanch, coming across the field. "I have not done many sins lately but I have seen that strange star with a long white tail."

Charan shook hands and moved over on his *charpoy* to make room for his friend. "It all began with that star. They say such a star brings disaster to a village."

"Look what harm it brought to Ghungrali."

The Sarpanch chuckled. "You're right. It was there just before the boycott."

Sher gazed at the sky. "These whirlwinds will be more and more until the rains come."

"Don't worry, Sher. The whirlwinds will take your share of the grain."

"Oh, be careful with your cigarette, Sher. This hot wind is dangerous."

"Yes," said old Chanan. "It would be the greatest sin on earth to set fire to the wheat fields." Both he and Charan knew of a village years ago which caught fire and lost its entire wheat crop. "Sins . . . ," Charan mused. "It is better to speak of virtues."

"A man who lends money without interest is good," said Sher, hoping to delay the return to work.

"A man who helps others is wise," Charan agreed. "But a man who gets a loan without interest is wiser."

"It's good to scatter grain for birds."

"The birds can feed themselves," said Charan. "They are not beggars."

Sher snuffed out his cigarette. "Man says when he is alive, 'This is mine, this is my property, my wheat, my sparrows, to do with as I like.' But when he dies what does he have? We work like animals for the Jats, we go through hell. But I believe a person who does good things, his next life will be comfortable." He grinned slyly. "Let's say Charan is a bad man. He drinks. He does many bad things. Well, in the next life he'll be in my place and I'll be in his. And how I'll be taking work out of him with a whip!" All the Mazhbis laughed.

"There is no life after death," said the Sarpanch quite soberly. "People used to say there couldn't be chickens without a hen sitting on them, so there must be a God. But today there are electric incubators. Man is a seed, a fetus, a child, a man, and in the end, he dies. And nothing happens. They have cleverly cooked up these things like heaven and hell. I don't believe any of it. When you have nobody around to whom you can show happiness or anger, you can praise or curse God and satisfy yourself."

"I agree with Sarpanch Sahib," Charan said. "I don't believe in heaven and hell either. It's like this: Man has this piece of steel working as an engine. If he is missing some screw that machine will stop. In the same way if something goes wrong with our body, it stops. When the engine dies, it doesn't make any noise anymore. The same with a man's voice. When he dies, it's like you took oil out of an engine. Take it away and, *bas*, it stops."

Old Chanan was gazing off into space. "When you are dead, then everything is finished. There can't be anything after death, and yet . . ." He turned and faced Charan. "Sardarji, there are many mysteries. One night some years ago, when my wife was alive, I was lying awake. It was a cold night but for some reason I brought my *charpoy* outside to sleep under the stars. My wife told me, 'It's cold. Bolt the door from outside or it flies open.' I told her, 'All right, I'm here if you need me.' I slept and then awoke. I got up again and looked at the stars. Then I felt something and I turned around and saw my wife. I didn't speak to her. But she appeared to be standing at my bedside and looking down. I kept looking at her and wondering how she had come out. Then she went away and I went back to sleep. The next morning the door was still bolted from outside. My wife told me, 'I was inside all night. I never asked you to open the door.' And after some days she died. I have no superstitions or anything. But I can't explain it. She was alive then. It was no dream. I saw her."

The talk had grown too gloomy for Charan. "There goes a whirl-wind!" he exclaimed. "Now it's going toward the village. It will convey a message to Ghungrali: 'Now you end this boycott and thresh your wheat. Otherwise, I'll destroy it.' " They all turned to watch a spiral cloud of dust twist down the road and flee over the fields, drawing after it bits of straw, insects and feathers. The loose swaths scattered every which way and as the column rose it lifted several of Dhakel's bales into the air.

"Look! Look how it tosses those bales like feathers!"

"Oh, that piece of paper! Look how it is going higher and higher. It's in the whirlwind."

"Oh, the paper is going higher and higher."

"Oh, I see it. High as the birds. There it goes."

"It goes toward the village."

"Oh, look, now it goes toward Bhambadi."

"Yes, I'm also seeing. Now it goes toward Ghungrali again."

"Now leave that paper, boys," old Chanan told them. "It may go up ten miles in the sky. We must get back to work."

Charan laughed. "Someone is waiting for that piece of paper because he has to write a letter."

The old Mazhbi, disturbed by the conversation, studied Charan's face. "Don't you even believe in God?"

Charan shrugged. "Who knows where God lives?" he asked lightly. His eyes moved from the faces of Sindar and Gurmel to the Sarpanch, Sher, the other Mazhbis and Chanan himself, and when he spoke it was only half jokingly. "Maybe God is within all of you," he said.

Sunset was not far away and the dusty evening sky cast a pink glow on the men's faces. Old Chanan gave a cry of pleasure as he found an old forked stick he had placed on the side of an irrigation ditch during the last year's threshing and forgotten all about. Sindar had followed the others to the threshing ground and Chanan told him he had used the stick for pushing wheat into the steel hammers of the thresher after it became dangerous to do it with one's bare hands in the fading light.

"If you're so careful with this one little stick," Sindar told him, "you can save real weapons, spears and knives, for years together." Sindar hung his sickle over his shoulder, kneeled down by the threshed wheat, picked up a handful of kernels and let them sift pleasurably through his fingers.

Pritam came across the fields in the gathering dusk. "The machine works well," he told Charan, raising his voice above the din of the thresher. "Ours is an old one. It can hardly finish in two or three days what you do in a few hours. But here yours is—you have finished almost one acre since midday. Can you thresh for us? We have some bales sitting over there."

"How many are there?"

"About twelve hundred."

"You shouldn't rely on me, Pritamji, because from here I've got to go to Bhadson and thresh my sister's wheat. After that I can help you but chances are few that I'll get back before another ten days. You should not depend on me."

"All right." Pritam was weary and bewildered that evening. He and his sons and laborers had worked hard to cut their wheat. He had always believed in hard physical labor, but somehow these days, with all the new methods and machines, a man's willingness to work was no longer enough. "We'll make some other arrangement," he told Charan. "But if you help when you return, that will be good."

The old man, tall and erect as he had been in the days of his youth, moved slowly back to his fields; Charan felt sorry as he watched him go. He had never known Pritam to utter a harsh or mean word in his life.

Charan took a last look at the threshers before returning to his well, where the Sarpanch was waiting with a bottle. He watched old Chanan move patiently and steadily, pushing the grain into the grinding jaws of the thresher with his fondly rediscovered old stick. Then the tractor engine died and Chanan put down the stick and wiped his face with an expression of gratitude, as if to say this day's labor was over, praise God, and he could take his rest. Watching him, Charan thought: There may be a heaven or hell or there may not. Who can know? Or does? But one thing was certain: if there was a heaven, old Chanan was sure to go there.

On his way to the well, Charan told Suka to help the Mazhbis carry the rest of the bales to the threshing machine. The boy grappled with a heavy load, stumbled and cursed his father; he almost fell on the bale heap when he went to slide it from his head. Charan felt ashamed of his son, an heir to the fields around him. The Sarpanch called out from rinsing the glasses at the pump and Charan answered in his deep, hoarse voice that if they hurried they might be able to kill a bottle between them before the others came. Soon the workers could hear bursts of Charan's laughter drifting across the darkening fields.

At dusk in Ghungrali, crows leave the rooftops and barnyards of the village in great cawing flocks for their nighttime roosts in the trees of the fields and the ancient oaks along the Grand Trunk Road. The sun sets and dust sifts into the smoke of village fires, and the whole Punjab Plain seems to be hidden in mist. There is the smell of hay as men drive home in their bullock carts, and of dried-up grass, scorched by the sun all day long. When the moon rises, the night grows pale and dim, and the last few crows caw forlornly overhead.

Pritam's bullock cart creaked gently along in the dimness. Alert for a storm, he sensed the warm evening air was too still. Pritam was in no hurry and the cart moved slowly, coming abreast of a huddle of barefoot figures who walked softly and rapidly in the dust. One man was in front of the others, carrying a small boy in his arms. Several men and women followed him, with bundles of freshly cut grass on their heads. Pritam recognized young Mukhtar, the Chamar.

"It is not good," the old man said quietly as they went along, "the way we are treating each other. But I think it will be settled very soon."

Mukhtar did not answer. He wanted no sympathy from a Jat. He was determined that at least his sons would be free of their bondage.

"Now you go to other villages. We mind it very much." Pritam's voice quavered. "Look, we have to feed your children. Your daughters are my daughters and your sons, my sons. We must see that they are fed."

"Yes, Sardarji," Mukhtar said gently. "But it is written that we should cut the wheat of another village."

"Yes, it is written. But it will be all right in a few more days, my son."

XII

Eight years passed. It was a hot morning in April 1978. The air was still. The time had come for another wheat harvest, and at Charan's well, Kuldeep and two field hands were making *gur*. Stalks of sugar-cane had already been pressed to extract the juice, which was stored in barrels in the wellhouse. Kuldeep, Charan's third son, a heavy-shouldered, muscular youth with heavy dark eyebrows, his beard just starting to grow and an old rag tied about his curly hair, stood in the midst of smoke from a fire in an underground pit. He stirred the juice in an enormous iron pan as it slowly thickened into dark, sticky sugar. A few steps away, eyes reddened by smoke, his hired laborer, a young Hindu from Bihar, far to the east on the Gangetic Plain, fed chaff to the fire.

"White ants will eat you up, boy," Kuldeep told his worker, then he began to sing in a low voice:

> *Do Chharian di ik dholk roj Raat nu Kharke*
> *Mela Chharian da Dekh Chuhare Charr ke . . .*
> Two bachelors have a drum they beat every night.
> Watch from your rooftop the way we make merriment.
> O beloved . . .

"When it starts dripping these long strings, it's good," Kuldeep told his worker. "If it's overcooked, it won't make good white sugar." Kuldeep dipped his finger into the pan and tasted it. "If you take *gur* the size of a walnut after meals, it digests your food." Then, seeing the Bihari was idle, he told him roughly, "Quick, *bhai*, bring more husks for the fire."

"I'm doing my job," the youth muttered sullenly, casting a look at a *charpoy* in the shade of an oak tree where Charan's two eldest sons, Sukhdev and Kulwant, were sitting doing nothing. Sukhdev wore the turbaned khaki uniform of a Punjabi police constable. He had just come off duty from his post on the Grand Trunk Road. Sukhdev came over to the pan, squatted down, dipped in a finger like Kuldeep and also tasted the sugar. "We're late in making *gur*," he told Kuldeep. "If we could have sold it to the sugar refinery, we could have cut the cane and disposed of it by now."

Sukhdev and Kulwant, a student at the new liberal arts college in Khanna, were forever giving Kuldeep advice. He listened respectfully but seldom heeded it. Like many Jat Punjabis, Kuldeep regarded farming as the only respectable nonmilitary profession for a man. He was somewhat closer to Sukhdev, as Charan had arranged his and Kuldeep's marriages to two sisters, Sukhvindar and Beant, partly to save on the dowries.

"We'll crush cane tomorrow and make sugar again the day after that," Kuldeep told Sukhdev. Then he ordered the Bihari, in the rough manner he used with the migrant Hindu laborers, to go and fetch more husks. "Don't be lazy, *bhai*," he called after him. "White ants will eat you up."

Sukhdev took a sickle and went out into a nearby *berseem* field. He squatted down in the bright green clover and began to cut fodder. Soon three Harijan women came along carrying bundles of clover on their heads. They loudly chattered and giggled and their bare feet kicked up the dust. When they saw Sukhdev they slackened their pace. They enjoyed teasing a constable.

"This morning he roared like a lion," one of them called tauntingly. "Now he bleats like a lamb."

"Now he's sweating," laughed another.

"In the morning he is telling how quickly he cuts fodder. Now look! Sometimes he cuts, sometimes he stands and looks around." They burst into giggles.

"He talks much but does little."

Sukhdev, annoyed by the women's saucy banter, stopped cutting and stood up. "I'm tired and I have a backache," he told himself. He saw Kuldeep had joined the Bihari in the cane field and was waving for him to join them. Sukhdev called to Kulwant, "Go and help

Kuldeep." "I'm going home with utensils," Kulwant called back, getting on his bicycle. Kulwant studied history, geography, economics, political science and sociology, a waste of time and money in Sukhdev's eyes. White-collar jobs were hard to find in Punjab. You had to pay a big bribe just to be a bank teller. There were so many of these new arts colleges. "They create a useless person," Sukhdev would say. "Kuldeep won't dirty his hands with field work now. And what else is he fit to do?"

Not long afterwards the Bihari cried out, "Here comes Bapuji on a bicycle!" It was Sadhu Singh, who must have met Kulwant and taken his bicycle. The old man pedaled so slowly and sedately the bicycle wobbled and looked ready to fall over, but Sadhu managed to reach the well without mishap. As he dismounted and leaned the bicycle against the wellhouse, old Sadhu was a sorry sight. He was not as stout as before and he had grown quite frail. His hair and beard were unkempt, his turban askew, his whole appearance looked untidy and neglected. Charan's father had markedly aged; he was now a toothless septuagenarian. It was a surprise to see him in the fields in such hot weather. Most days he was to be seen on a cot under the shade trees by Charan's cattle yard, drowsing away, sometimes muttering to himself. If passersby greeted him, he nodded his head. He had grown very forgetful. If the old lady did not bring him his tea, he might not even ask for it.

As he tottered over to them, calling loudly, *"Sat Sri Akal!"* He seemed to have some of his old fire, especially when his look of kindly benevolence faded and he found fault with this and that. Nobody paid him any attention and he soon found an old tarpaulin in the well shed, dragged it outside and, under the shade of the oak trees, lay down, shut his eyes and was at once asleep, snoring loudly.

Now a most curious-looking figure came from the cane field carrying more husks. This was Karan Singh, a Chamar from Ghungrali, Kuldeep's other field hand. He was a flat-chested, bony man with small, dark-ringed eyes, narrow shoulders and sunken temples. What was distinctive about him was his dress, a dark blue turban with a yellow headband and iron ring around it and a short, knee-length blue tunic. A ceremonial sword and ax were strapped to his side. Any Sikh could see this was the uniform of a Nihang, or warrior for the faith. Karan Singh was one of six men in Ghungrali, four of them Jats and one other Harijan, recruited by a mysterious new holy man who had recently arrived and taken over the village temple. Little was known about Gurbachan Singh, the holy man, except that he was a follower of Sant Jarnail Singh Bhindranwale, a fanatic young preacher everybody was talking about. Bhindranwale, who was from a village not far from Ghungrali, had lately appeared at the Golden Temple of Amritsar, the Sikhs' holiest shrine. He had attacked the Nirankaris, a Sikh reformist group largely made up of merchants, calling them heretics. And he had sent men like Gurbachan Singh out to the villages to raise money and recruit Nihangs to do battle for him.

Pritam, who had seen Sadhu bicycle up, came across the fields from his wellhouse to greet his kinsman. Pritam was now eighty himself, but he was still tall, straight, firmly muscled and much healthier than Sadhu, who was actually a bit younger. Pritam was up at dawn each day to clean his cattle yard and still worked beside his men in the fields.

Seeing Karan Singh in Nihang garb, Pritam greeted him, *"Wah Guruji ka Khalsa—Wah Guruji ki Fateh!* Pure warriors are the chosen of God—Victory be to God!" The Chamar, catching the faint hint of amusement in Pritam's voice, hastened to tell him, "Nihangs are free to travel without a ticket."

"Is that so?" Pritam smiled, openly amused. "Who gives you your weapons?"

"Our Guru gives us." Old Sadhu, roused by their voices, sat up, blinked, yawned and gave a dry cough as he got to his feet. Pritam shook hands with him and pulled a *charpoy* into the shade for them to sit on. Soon they were reminiscing about the old days in Lyallpur. "Oh, how we used to sit in our bullock carts eating *gur*, eh, Pritamji?" Sadhu chuckled. "Do you remember when we used to play tug-of-war."

"Oh, yes, our team never pulled the rope without me. I used to be able to do five hundred knee bends without stopping." Pritam stood up and began doing knee bends right then and there. Sadhu protested that he might injure himself and after half a dozen Pritam sank back on the *charpoy* quite breathless. "Now these young men get tired just tying their turbans," he told Sadhu.

"Yes, these young men can't move without first taking tea." He scowled in the workers' direction.

Pritam turned serious. "Brother, the other day I was ill with fever. And I thought about you and our other old friends. And I wept, thinking I was leaving all of you."

"And why not?" Sadhu demanded indignantly. "We have lived

together since boyhood. We are of the same blood." Pritam saw his cousin was as cantankerous as ever and felt moved. He grasped Sadhu on the shoulder. "Well, thank God, Sadhu, that we are still alive and can enjoy the fruits of our young ones."

"Why shouldn't we? We worked hard for them. Well, we are lucky to have such model grandsons, no vices in them." Pritam had heard Sukhdev was hitting the bottle even if Charan himself no longer drank now that he had two daughters-in-law in the house.

"Work, work! You are meant for work!" Sadhu shouted to the group at the fire. To Pritam he said, "That *gur* is not a good color. Some of the cane must be rotten. It's rats. Nobody cares to go to the trouble of poisoning rats. How else can we ever get rid of them? It is a permanent menace to the farmers."

Pritam wholly agreed. Yet all these years Ghungrali's Jats could never cooperate to fight the rats. It was not that they had not prospered. All the village's 107 tube wells were now electrified; at night, with a light bulb glowing at each well, the Punjab Plain looked like a great city. Ghungrali had forty tractors, two small combines, and that year Basant Singh had bought the first privately owned car. Big German-made combines came in on contract to harvest. Fertilizer use was up from nothing in the 1940s to more than 800 tons a year. Some of the Jats had installed an underground piped irrigation system to prevent evaporation and cow-dung biogas plants to provide both fuel and fertilizer. Rice, first sown in the summer the year before, was an even bigger cash crop than wheat. Some Jats triple-cropped, a wheat-pulse-rice rotation made possible by a new sixty-day-maturing pulse, *mung*, which fixed nitrogen from the air and reduced the need for chemical fertilizer.

In the eight years since 1970, many of Ghungrali's old dirt tracks were paved. Bullock carts, now with rubber tires, no longer creaked. Express buses that stopped at the banyan tree took villagers directly into Chandigarh, Punjab's capital, or Ludhiana. Two doctors came on motorcycles to hold daily office hours. There was a resident Hindu nurse, who, even if she was too partial to vitamin B complex injections, gave out chloroquine for malaria.

Almost all the Jat and two Harijan families had children in college. The big new worry was how to find jobs for all the new graduates. More young people were going abroad. Letters came to Ghungrali's post office from sons or daughters in Dubai, Beirut, Munich, Toronto, St. Paul and Yuba City. Jats included TV sets in their daughters' dowries. Pritam himself had prospered. Besides his original fifteen-acre allotment, he had inherited five acres more from his father and he and his son Surjit rented five, so they farmed twenty-five acres in all. That year they had bought a new tractor.

Sadhu was mumbling and fretting. "You know, Pritamji," he said, "years ago I could challenge anybody to grip my hand. God knows how I'm still alive these days. I've taken medicine from the doctor but it's so bad it's killing me." His lips trembled and his eyes watered. "Nobody in my house wants to work. They say, 'Do you want hot tea, Grandfather?' But they come half an hour later with cold tea." There was a story he kept retelling, about an obedient family whose sons always did what their father said, fetching wood or water or cutting wheat at his command. They were rewarded with a pot of gold. A second family, which Sadhu compared to his own, was full of grumblers who questioned all the father's orders. They got nothing. "These are the types of people you see in my family, Pritamji. If you obey your elders, you'll get something in life. But nobody listens to me. God knows what fate will befall them."

With that, Sadhu declared he would bicycle back to the village. Pritam tried to discourage him. "Harrumph!" he sputtered indignantly. "I had the first bicycle in Lyallpur District, I'll have you know." He mounted Kulwant's bicycle and pedaled very stiffly, his back straight. As he turned the corner, the picture of elderly dignity, he fell over and vanished into the wheat. Pritam ran to see if Sadhu was all right. He was, and in a furious temper. Together the two old men righted the bicycle and Sadhu let Pritam wheel it as far as the paved road. On the way they met Charan and his youngest son, Narinder, a tall, skinny youth who was still in high school.

Charan's beard was gray. He left the field work to Kuldeep and spent his days going to the market in Khanna or to the university in Ludhiana, what Sadhu Singh had done before him. Like Sadhu, Charan now dressed carefully. At the well, he greeted Kuldeep and his workers and went to the wellhouse, where he gave a loud oath. Old Sadhu, when he dragged out the tarpaulin, had exposed a drum of residue from the sugar juice. "Who left this?" Charan demanded.

Narinder, with an embarrassed grin, told his father, "Kuldeep tried to make liquor from it in your absence, sir. But he could not get anything from it." Charan called the Bihari to come and pour it out. "Start the engine and run water through the canal to wash this away," he told Narinder. "If you boys want to drink, you can go to the shop and buy one, two, three bottles if you like. But I will never allow a son of mine to make this stuff at home. If the police found this, you would go to jail."

Poondi and his son Bawa came to see what Charan was making such a fuss about. "My boys don't want to work," Charan told them. "They want to make liquor only. When the government is trying to prevent it, why do they want to break the law?" Poondi winked at Bawa; everybody remembered when Charan was forever distilling liquor in his fields and what a famous drunkard he was. "Yes, Sardarji," Poondi agreed, settling down on the *charpoy*. "You are right."

"If you don't take wine, you can save money and keep your health. Why can't my sons do better work?"

"Oh, Charan, they cannot do as you did."

In truth, Charan was as disappointed as ever in his sons. Only Kuldeep had taken to farming and even he, if angry with Charan, would threaten to run off and join the army. Charan knew it would be better if, like Pritam, he went to the fields every day and worked side by side with his sons. "I'd do more but the dust in the fields comes into my chest," he told Poondi. "Indira Gandhi always went with Nehru. She learned politics from her father." He turned to Narinder. "If you fail your examinations again, what will you do?"

Charan also worried about money. Like many Jats, he was sinking into debt. He lost 28,000 rupees when some bags of fertilizer were stolen while he was in charge of the village depot and he had to make good the loss. The marriages of Sukhdev and Kuldeep, cheap as they were, as the brides were sisters and from quite a poor Jat family, cost him another 24,000. What saved him that year was the rice crop. Charan kept just two quintals for his family and sold the rest for 20,000. And land values were up, in Ghungrali to 15,000 rupees an acre. All in all, Charan guessed, whereas a farmer with ten acres in 1970 could do well and have a tube well, a tractor, bullocks and cows and two hired laborers, in 1978 you needed fifteen acres to make a go of the same thing. It was the same cost-price squeeze, leaving a smaller number of ever bigger farmers, that afflicted agriculture the world over. Punjab had an eighteen-acre legal land ceiling, but one could simply distribute titles among family members. Basant Singh did.

The only one in Charan's family to do well was his sister Surjit. After her rescue by the Mazhbis, she sold her 1970 wheat crop and invested in seeds, fertilizer and hired machinery, against all advice planting all twenty acres in cotton. The next year she bought five more acres and double-cropped wheat and rice. Now she had one of the richest farms around, the farmstead, with its big cattle barn, two Massey-Ferguson tractors and a combine, enclosed by a high brick wall. With money came status. Surjit arranged marriages for Pala and Kaka. Kaka's wife was an extremely good catch: the niece of Gurcharan Singh Tohra, a leader of the Akali Dal, the most popular Sikh political force in Punjab, and also head of the committee that ran all Sikh temples in the state. A cunning, wily old whitebeard, Tohra was a man of enormous prestige and power. Surjit and her family at once joined the Akalis and became very pious. They swore off liquor, kept their heads covered with Akali deep blue and carried symbolic *kirpans*, or swords. Surjit never rested. She drove her family as hard as ever, bullying, cajoling, generous and anxious, as if the hard times had never left her. She saw to everything and was proud and ambitious, that bed in the kitchen long forgotten.

Basant Singh, with fifty-two acres, was getting richer and richer. "We should not have small farms in Ghungrali," he told Pritam. "Fifty to a hundred acres are needed to support a tractor. Smaller farmers ought to sell their land and get out. Even a hundred acres is too small. To really mechanize, you should go to a thousand acres. And we've got to mechanize. It's the only solution to our labor problem."

XIII

At four o'clock each morning the new holy man would turn the temple loudspeaker up to its highest volume and awaken the entire village with a deafening harangue: "We are awaiting the call to march to Amritsar! Be prepared to sacrifice yourselves! All who love and believe in the holy scripture be ready to march to Amritsar and defend the Golden Temple. If the government does not arrest and hang the heretics, our leader, Sant Bhindranwale, says he will catch the Nirankari leader and put a rope through his nose and pull him through the streets! Await the call to march!"

Pritam was aghast. "It's wrong, it's very wrong," he told everyone. "The holy man should not speak such things on the loudspeaker. He should recite the scriptures only. What has he do to with politics?"

The villagers were confused about what the holy man, Gurbachan Singh, was up to; why had he come to Ghungrali? "It's all Indira

Gandhi's doing," asserted Sadhu Singh. "She has made herself Empress of India. What was democracy under Nehru is now a princely state. It's the same divide-and-rule policy we saw under the British. Pit Sikh against Sikh and those Hindus can rule in Delhi."

Pritam did not know what to think. As an orthodox Sikh, he could not defend the Nirankaris. Sikh high priests had long denounced them as heretics. Their founder, Baba Dayal Das, had preached against the tendency of Sikhs to revert to such Hindu ways as idolatry, Brahmin rituals and pilgrimages to the Ganges, which to Pritam was all to the good. But heresy crept in and Nirankaris, strong among the trading community, not only came to worship Baba Dayal Das after his death but added scriptures to the Sikh canon, an outright blasphemy.

The founder of Sikhism, Guru Nanak (1469–1538), of humble village origins, wrote the verses that make up much of the sacred scripture of the *Granth*. He was a pacifist and, in an attempt to reconcile Muslim and Hindu, taught a monotheistic creed, as well as the fundamental identity of all religions, and the realization of God through prayers, hymns and meditation. Nanak opposed idolatry, ritual, a priesthood and the caste system, and, as someone formed by village culture, believed in a strong work ethic and sharing one's goods with the poor. The word Sikh came from the Pali *Sikkha* or the Sanscrit *Shishya* meaning "disciple." Pritam closely followed Guru Nanak's teachings in his daily life.

It was Govind Singh, the tenth and last Guru two centuries later, after long persecution by the Mogul Empire and Islam, who militarized the Sikhs through a martial baptism rite, drinking the *amrit*, or sacred water, after which the initiate took the surname of Singh, or Lion, just as women became Kaur, Prince. Govind Singh created the military fraternity called the *Khalsa*, or Pure, whose ideal was the warrior saint. Govind Singh also introduced such Sikh customs as wearing a turban, carrying a dagger and never cutting the hair or beard. It was Bhindranwale's appeal to this martial side of Sikhism that captured the imaginations of young men in villages like Ghungrali. Of Gurbachan Singh, the new holy man himself, little was known. Rumor had it that this thickset, thuggish-looking Sikh with a red, beefy face and gray beard, had been thrown out of a nearby village, Mankisahib, for stealing *gurdwara* funds. Every day he demanded more and more milk, wheat and vegetables from the village women. Charan guessed he must be taking in sixty rupees' worth a day. Basant Singh was one of the few to vouch for the holy man, and everybody said this was politics.

On Baisaki, April 13, the day the harvest began and so much seemed to happen in Punjab, the Nirankaris were holding a convention in Amritsar. As Ghungrali's people later learned, at midday in the Golden Temple, Bhindranwale stood up and shouted, "We will not allow this Nirankari gathering to take place. We are going to march there and cut them to pieces!" Bhindranwale led a procession out of the temple shouting slogans against the Nirankaris. In the frenzy one of the Sikhs with him cut off the arm of a Hindu shopkeeper. Bhindranwale himself slipped away before the procession reached the convention two miles across town. When it did a battle broke out. Twelve of Bhindranwale's followers and three Nirankaris were killed in an exchange of fire.

A few days later Gurbachan Singh set up a gruesome display of twelve large photographs of the Amritsar "martyrs" in front of the altar of Ghungrali's temple. Each photograph, adorned with garlands of marigolds and smoking incense, showed the face of a dead Sikh, spattered with blood, mutilated, a few with whole faces shot away. Also displayed were newspaper clippings that portrayed Bhindranwale as the hero of the day. The holy man's predawn sermons grew louder and longer. Students complained to the Sarpanch that they couldn't prepare for their examinations. Then the villagers learned that Mrs. Gandhi's son Sanjay, with the help of Zail Singh, a Congress Party Sikh politician and ex-chief minister of Punjab, had set up a new party, Dal Khalsa, the party of the pure. It backed Bhindranwale, opposed the Akalis and called for the creation of an independent Sikh state to be named Khalistan.

The villagers were left utterly confused. "It's all politics," said Pritam. "Our holy man should keep out of it. Our old preacher was saintly. This one tells us to go and revenge those killed in Amritsar."

"Our holy man is a madman," said young Devinder, Pritam's grandnephew, with a grin. Now grown into a husky youth, Devinder had gone to college in Khanna but failed to get a BA and now he didn't want to farm. He was full of get-rich-quick schemes that never came to anything. Kuldeep agreed the holy man was mad. "Why else would he shout out his speeches so early in the morning? Those in our village become Nihangs because they get everything free from the *gurdwara*—clothes, wheat, milk, money. That's my opinion. The holy man sends his children from door to door. Who can refuse?"

The daily harangues went on. "Only those who come to worship at the temple are men," Gurbachan Singh would rail at them. "The Nihangs are real men. Those of you who arise when the sun is shining are not real men. Twelve martyrs have given their lives for Sikhism. Be ready to sacrifice!"

The first to oppose the holy man were not the Jats but the Harijans. As Mukhtar explained to Pritam: "We decided he should not do these things. We are going to start our own temple." They chose Amarjit, the pious Mazhbi who had been at the Bhadson harvest, as their preacher to read aloud scriptures from the *Granth*. But the Harijans had no copy. The *Guru Granth Sahib* was an enormous book with more than six thousand verses. On special occasions when it was read non-stop from cover to cover by relays of readers it took two days and two nights. Some readings took seven days.

A Harijan delegation led by old Chanan went to Gurbachan Singh to ask for one of the copies of the *Granth* kept at the temple. He said he had only one copy, with torn pages and a ripped covering cloth. When Chanan discovered that some pages were unreadable, they took it back. Gurbachan Singh was out but his daughter said, "There are seven extra copies. Leave that and take another." When the holy man returned, he gathered what Jats he could find and accused the Harijans of stealing the second copy. They called a meeting of the Panchayat, or village council, and Chanan challenged Gurbachan Singh: "All right, you take an oath in the temple that I have stolen a copy of the *Granth*." The holy man refused. Later Chanan told Pritam, "We decided we would not set foot in the *gurdwara* as long as he is there. He is an evil man. Now he can do nothing because we are both preaching the message of God."

"Basant Singh is to blame," Pritam told him. "His people threw out the old holy man, who was truly decent, and brought this trouble-maker here. Now how can we shunt him out?" When Pritam confronted him, Basant Singh replied harshly, "The Harijans took an old book, found the print too small to read and caused all this trouble. They're too illiterate to read the scripture anyway."

Pritam told him he was wrong. The Mazhbis, he explained, had brought the *Granth* to their new place of worship to celebrate the birthday of Ram Das, the fourth Guru, who founded Amritsar as the Sikhs' holy city. He repeated Chanan's story, and told Basant Singh, "We are all giving donations so the Mazhbis can buy a new copy of the *Granth* from Amritsar."

Poondi, as one of the oldest Mazhbis, was indignant. "How can this holy man stop us from taking the *Guru Granth Sahib?* When it itself says all human beings have the same blood running in their veins? We people look in vain to the Jats, because they don't come to our aid. Basant Singh is all praise for this holy man. But he's a bad man. You'll see. He will have to leave this village."

XIV

Pritam looked about. It was a few days later and he was out in a harvested wheat field and wanted to carry a bundle of shocks to his threshing ground. But he needed help getting it up on his head. "Help me lift this bundle, son," he called to a passing Harijan.

"No," said the man. "It is not in the contract. It is not my job to carry bundles."

Stunned, since he had known the man from boyhood, Pritam could not utter a word. He stood there dumbly, his anger rising. He was seventy-nine, an age at which most men had long since given up field work, to say nothing of lifting a heavy bundle, a job that usually took two men. "All right! Carry on!" he told the harvester. "Go cut your wheat." Back at the well he told Devinder what had happened. "These new harvesters, they won't do anything. Times are changing, son, you will see. In the future, only if Jats have sons will they get somebody to cut their wheat. Otherwise they will find no workers."

"If they won't help carry bundles, Uncle, why do you keep taking them tea? That is not in their contract."

"Because they are poor."

Pritam saw across the fields that Charan had three separate groups of harvesters—Poondi and his three sons, Mukhtar and his family and old Banta and his children. In Mukhtar's case, even his small children were cutting, which meant Charan had also contracted out his wheat harvest at so much an acre. It was the new way. Charan was at his well, and Pritam, still infuriated, went over to see him and recover himself. He told Charan, "In our day we could rely on workers. Not anymore. You have to be careful what you say to them now. They have become so touchy."

Poondi, who was getting older and spent much time at Charan's well while his sons cut wheat, was also getting more outspoken. "Oh, Pritamji, once I cut wheat for a Jat and he served the other Jats meat. For me only potatoes and vegetables. I asked him, 'Why? Did I cut less?' But don't speak. Fear God. The British were just as bad. They ruled India for a hundred years. Why did they not give the Harijans just an acre or two each? What wrong did we do them?" The two men had known each other more than thirty years. "We used to be dying the death of dogs," Poondi went on. "Slaving in the fields while the Jats enjoyed themselves. But life comes with work. Oh, Pritamji, look at you, still out in the fields at your age. Well, hard work can keep your health."

Poondi's son, Bawa, when he came to rest, also voiced the new mood of rebellion. "You remember the time Indira Gandhi sent money to us but Basant Singh objected? Some village land is supposed to be reserved for Harijans, but have we seen one acre? The Jats always say, 'We are poor. We are poor.' They don't like to spend money. Well, soon we'll all be working in town and the Jats will be cleaning their own barns and doing their own field labor. The old way of life is gone in Ghungrali, Sardarji. Before, I was against such change. Now I like it. A man must move with the times."

Such talk saddened Pritam. *Wand chako*, to share with the poor, and *sangat*, community, like *kirt karo*, hard work, were teachings of Guru Nanak and Pritam's deepest beliefs. But Guru Nanak had also crusaded against caste. Pritam was starting to see that if you took away the age-old basis for caste—the exchange of labor for grain and fodder —the old Jat-Harijan relationship lost its meaning too. Looking back, the boycott was a rude awakening for them all. Basant Singh had seen to it that field wages in Ghungrali had not risen in the eight years since. The Harijans had deserted the fields in droves for jobs in the many new factories, mills, depots and kilns opening up in Khanna and along the Grand Trunk Road.

Basant Singh kept talking about "the labor problem." To Pritam, once you came to see land, labor and rent wholly in money terms, respect for the old traditions collapsed. Pritam saw this did not bother young Jats like Kuldeep and Devinder at all. They hardly knew the old village custom of mutual rights and obligations; indeed, they scarcely knew the names of the younger Harijans. As Kuldeep saw it: "After the boycott, the Harijans never came back to work with us. Now they are all taking jobs in the oil and rice mills or at the storage depots. They do this loading and lifting work. It's hard but high-paying. They have become too greedy."

Mukhtar, who had worked the past eight years at a brick kiln, making the fifteen-mile round trip to Khanna on a bicycle, had prospered enough to buy a small plot of land and build a new house and cattle shed. He also bought his own buffalo for milk and had a Sony transistor. "It's better to work in town," he told his sons, who had been disappointing in school and worked beside him making bricks. "We only work eight hours. We get more money. And we are free. These Jats no longer rule over us. They can no longer treat us like animals. Now I can go out and work and talk to people freely." Mukhtar had cut his hair and trimmed his beard. Tall and fair, he was sometimes taken for a Jat by strangers in Khanna.

Like Pritam, a few of the older Harijans voiced regret about the passing of the old Ghungrali. Banta, now in his sixties, blamed the Jats. "If they paid us more generously, we would not go outside to work. Have I not tilled their fields for thirty years? Once the university gave Basant Singh ten shirts as prizes for a wheat crop I helped him to grow. I asked him for one shirt, but he refused to give it. He is that greedy. These days the Jats, those who have become drunkards or eat opium, sometimes even refuse to pay their workers. That never happened in the old days. It costs too much time and money to go to the police. Poor people cannot afford it. So we leave it to God. He will punish the Jats, not us." There was theft in the village and, for the first time in memory, some teenage sons of Jats tried to molest Harijan girls when they came from the fields at night. For, until now, Ghungrali's young men, in spite of all their sexual banter in the fields, were remarkably chaste when it came to actual behavior. Unmarried Punjabi women had been relatively sequestered since Mogul times, and homosexuality was condemned by Sikhism and rare among villagers who so prized the warrior's male prowess. Sexually repressed, they seemed to find an outlet in so much humorously bawdy talk.

At first the Jats were able to get what labor they needed from seasonal migrants from the much poorer states of Uttar Pradesh and Bihar, the *bhaiyas* or "brothers," as the Punjabis called them. As time wore on and new farm technology spread into the Gangetic Plain, this source dried up and only the poorest Biharis came. The new Harijan credo of "Now we are free" and "My son will never work for Jats" was not just Mukhtar's. It was sweeping all India. Atrocities against Harijans by higher castes, trying to keep them in their place, were in the papers every day. Hindu fundamentalism was on the rise. The caste system and agricultural advance were on a collision course, setting the stage for tragedy in Punjab, the green revolution's greatest success, and indeed in India itself.

This was the first year the Jats had swallowed their pride and offered their fields on contract to Ghungrali's Harijans. Gone were the large groups of men mowing side by side, joking and competing. Now there were small, scattered Harijan families squatting in the wheat with their sickles while most Jats, not mowing as before, sat idly at their wells. One day Charan's cousin Dhakel, looking for company, came over with his sickle and helped Poondi's sons Bawa and Sher cut wheat. A handsome young man with scarcely a beard in 1970, Dhakel had become very thin, his face ravaged, the Mazhbis knew, by liquor and opium. Everyone talked about how dissolute he had become. He was even said to cheat his workers and not pay them properly.

Bawa asked why he didn't cut wheat with his own harvesters, a Mazhbi family from the village. "Why should I help them?" Dhakel asked. "All the harvest is by contract this year." Dhakel smelled of liquor and there were dark rings under his eyes. "Harvesting used to be the best time of year. We all worked together as a family and we cut jokes and raced to see who could cut the fastest." Bawa asked where Sindar was these days.

"Kher village. He sold his land to buy a truck. He drives and has hired a driver also."

"Has he taken a wife? Do you hear from him?" Bawa had been told by Gurmel, Dhakel's old worker, that Sindar was in a bad state back in his village. "He takes pills, opium, wine, all those things. Look at Dhakel himself. There's nothing in his body now. He farms fifteen acres but he's never bought a tractor. It all goes for drink." Even Gurmel admitted he missed Sindar. "He called me Deaf Man and we abused each other all day and cracked jokes. It made the work go quickly."

Sher agreed. Money had taken over. The old sense of community was gone. "Nowadays Jats do not sit with us and talk with us like they did when we all worked together. There is not that old warm feeling, no."

"Charan knew how to get work from others," Dhakel said. "Kuldeep just gives orders. Workers do not stay with him long." Just then Bawa let out an oath. He had almost cut into a bird's nest. Five newly hatched sparrows were inside. "I'll tie it up with grass so their mother can find them," Dhakel said. At noon all the harvesters gathered at Charan's well. Poondi, who had brought *chapattis* and curry for his sons, offered some to Dhakel, which he took. The women among them sat some distance away, sequestering themselves from the Jat men.

Charan's youngest son, Narinder, came out of the wellhouse looking drowsy-eyed, for he had been asleep. Dhakel told him to cut fodder. "I won't start until Kuldeep comes back," the youth told him.

"And if he doesn't come?"

"I'll let the cattle go hungry."

"If no one gave food to you, how would you feel?"

"Oh, we'd hire somebody to come and cut fodder."

"Who will come for the five rupees you pay?"

"No one," said Bawa, chewing on his food. "You can easily get ten, twelve working in town."

Dhakel stretched back on the grass and yawned. "That holy man gets you up too early. All that shouting over the loudspeaker. I like to sleep to six."

Poondi laughed. "Dhakel drank too much last night. Look at his face." Dhakel, seeing Narinder trying to repair a drainage ditch, went over to show him. "Step in the water," he told the boy, "and put more mud on the bund so it becomes strong. Take mud from the far side like this." Dhakel knew Narinder had failed the eighth class for the third year in a row. Now he must learn to work in the fields.

Poondi gave an old man's dry cough. He asked Narinder, "What pills is your father taking? I may have got this disease from Charan."

"Poondi," called Narinder, "are you circumcised?"

"Oh, that operation is only for Jats. You have, what? Fifteen acres? And you are four sons and a daughter. When Charan goes, what will you each get? Three acres. What can you do with three acres? Who will give their daughter to marry you? If we Mazhbis have seven, eight or nine children, we don't bother. Each son has five barns to clean and field work. The more sons, the more money. I eat as well as a Jat. I don't owe a single rupee. This year a few Jats are even cleaning their own barns, something I thought never to see."

Poondi felt contented. "If you are good to others," he went on, "others will be good to you. For me, all people are good. I may live four years or I may live four days. You know, I've never been to Delhi. I've never been to Ludhiana. I've never seen a city. I've spent my whole life cleaning barns. Why should I go? For nothing? We are not free to roam about, we are working men. If I went to Delhi, how should I get home again?" Just then Mukhtar came with the news that a Jat on the other side of the village had refused to pay seventeen

Bihari harvesters. "After seven days he gave them nothing. They went off weeping."

"Just look what is starting to happen in our village," Poondi said, shaking his head. "If we protest and they arrest us, we'll die there in jail hungry."

"It's mostly drinkers and opium eaters who don't pay as they should," Bawa said. He laughed. "If you didn't pay us, Dhakel, we'd catch you by the feet and not let you go until you gave us our wheat."

Mukhtar had few regrets about the way Ghungrali had changed. His wife might say, "Mukhtar never goes to *melas* nowadays," but he and his family were getting seventy kilos of grain per acre to cut Charan's wheat, much more than in the old days. "I worked for Charan twelve years," Mukhtar told the Mazhbis. "And he never paid me more than five rupees a day." Yet, he felt, Charan had been good to work for. "Kuldeep never talks except to say, 'Do this' and 'Do that.' He doesn't understand his workers the way Charan did. Nowadays the Jats, once they give their fields out on contract, just sit idle. We do everything. We even bring our own food and tea. Who cares? Kuldeep gives tea with watered milk and not much sugar anyway."

But, they all agreed, their fates were still bound up with the Jats. One of Bawa's sons, Bintu, was missing three fingers from his right hand. He lost them while helping Bawa at an electrically powered fodder cutter. The Jat they were working for paid two hundred rupees, though the hospital bill came to over two thousand. "I could take him to court," Bawa said, "but it was an act of God." After Devinder's brother Toli lost five fingers the same way, Pritam wrote to the university in Ludhiana asking why fodder cutters, like threshing machines, continued to lack safety devices in Punjab. So many men lost arms and hands during threshing, some bleeding to death before they reached the hospital in Ludhiana. The law decreed that farm machines must meet standards of safety. But no one bothered.

XV

The sun rose high. It was the hottest time of the afternoon. Poondi, roused from his nap at Charan's well by voices which suddenly began to scream and shout, saw two men run in the direction of Dhakel's well but he could not at first make out what was going on. He knew they were harvesters—he could see their sickles flashing in the light. "Have you no daughter in the house!" an old white-bearded man was shouting. It was Munshi, one of Dhakel's Mazhbi harvesters. Poondi rose and hurried after him until Munshi turned back and shouted to him, gasping, "My daughter was cutting wheat alone. Dhakel went over and tried to kiss her! He has done this to us! We'll not leave him alive!" Up ahead Poondi could hear the other man, one of Munshi's grown sons, demanding, "Where is Dhakel? We want to kill him!" They passed Mukhtar and his family cutting wheat, and Poondi shouted at Mukhtar to come quick, as there was trouble at Dhakel's well.

Ahead old Sarban Singh, woken from sleep on a *charpoy*, stared at Munshi and his son drowsily; he looked to be in some kind of opium stupor.

"Have you no daughter in your house?" Munshi demanded furiously as his eyes darted around the well yard.

"What happened?" Sarban asked in a querulous voice, blinking his eyes. "Please let me know."

"My daughter was cutting alone. Dhakel went there to seize and kiss her."

At that moment Dhakel himself rose from a nearby field of uncut wheat and came to join them. He was very drunk. "What happened? What happened?" he called in a hoarse, thick voice.

Munshi's son shouted, "Come here! I'll tell you what's happened." He was a tall, lanky, bearded youth so agitated he had a fixed look in his eyes, like a madman in a frenzy. Going up to Dhakel, he swung his arm and punched him in the face. Stunned by the blow, Dhakel didn't utter a sound but staggered backward, and his nose instantly started to bleed. Munshi's son seized him by the throat and raised his sickle as if about to strike when Dhakel managed to stammer in a frightened way, breathing heavily, "Who said this? Call her, in my presence!"

Munshi ran to fetch his daughter, while his son pummeled Dhakel with his fist and jabbed him with his knee. Then he turned Dhakel around and hit him in the neck. When he struck him again, Dhakel fell and crawled backward on all fours. Sarban tried to get the youth to stop, pulling at his arm and shouting, "Leave it! Leave it!"

The girl, who looked to be about fifteen, reached the well with Munshi. She was weeping and wringing her hands, her teeth chattering. When she saw Dhakel she turned pale and huddled back and at once broke into loud sobs, pulling her sari over her face.

Poondi went up to her and said in a gentle voice, "Tell us what happened."

"He seized my arm," she sniffled, barely audible.

"Tell us who was that."

She lifted the sari away from her eyes and looked right at Dhakel, who had staggered to his feet and opened his bloodshot eyes wide. At once both Munshi and his son raised their sickles and thrust them at him. Dhakel threw up his arms to ward off the blows, catching both sickle blades with the palms of his hands, and these too started to bleed. His turban fell off, exposing a mop of tangled brown hair. He had a helpless expression and tears welled up in his bloodshot eyes as Poondi and Mukhtar pulled Munshi and his son back. "I'll not leave you alive!" the young man roared. "I'll pull your sister from your house and rape her! I'll thrust my penis into her! You should be ashamed!"

"I can go to the *gurdwara* and take an oath that I have done nothing!" Dhakel shouted in a hoarse voice.

"Leave it, leave it now and go home and we'll call the Panchayat," Poondi urged Munshi.

"Yes, leave it, leave it now," echoed old Sarban, who was still in a stupor. "And start cutting my wheat."

This enraged Munshi even more. "We'll never cut your wheat!" he shouted shrilly, straining his lungs. "Send Dhakel to the village and we will kill him! You also have a daughter in your house. If we seized her in that way, how would you feel? Dhakel has not done good to us. We will take revenge!" As he turned to go back to the village and Poondi hurried to his side, Munshi told him, "Such things have never happened in our family."

When he returned to Charan's well, where his sons were waiting, Poondi sank down on a *charpoy* and heaved a deep sigh. There was something humiliating, something insulting, to all Harijans in the village about what Dhakel had done, as if their honor was lost and Dhakel's family's too. "We live together, we eat together, we drink together," he told his sons. "If such things happen, who will work with these Jats? Munshi should keep quiet now. He should not do anything in the village."

Bawa was more hotheaded. "Why did you go there? Let this happen! Let them kill him! If this had happened with us, we would not have left Dhakel alive. We would have cut off his head then and there."

"No, no, my son," interrupted Poondi, horrified. "Munshi must go and call the village council. That is the right way. Let them decide what to do."

Mukhtar and Kuldeep joined them. Mukhtar argued that all Harijans, Mazhbis and Chamars alike, must stick with Munshi. "Unity matters now. We have to live with the Jats. Their sisters are our sisters. Why should they do these things?"

"You have to come to our fields for fodder," said Kuldeep with a frown. "This is very bad."

Charan came as soon as he heard the news, but by then Dhakel had fled across the fields in the direction of Bhambadi. "It's shameful," Charan said, shaking his head. "If I had been here, I would have beaten him myself. I could have given him two or three blows and that would have ended it. He must have been very drunk. If any of my sons did such a thing, I'd beat him mercilessly. Dhakel has three children and a fourth on the way. He's not a young boy."

"Well, Charan, nobody can match your reputation anyway," Poondi reassured him. Then with a hoot of laughter, he added, "This will be the talk of the village now. They'll all be saying it happened near Charan's well." Poondi was such a humorous, carefree soul, he never stayed grim for long.

Charan was silent, lost in thought. "What respect will our family have in the village?" Charan blamed the new way of harvesting. "An idle mind makes mischief. This would never have happened if Dhakel had been harvesting his own fields."

Poondi was right. For days Ghungrali talked of little else. The Sarpanch feared the incident might create fresh tensions between Jats and Harijans, even lead to violence. "This is a very bad thing," he told Charan. "If the Harijans are insulted like this, who will work in our fields? If such things happen, some lives may be lost. Everybody, high and low, has his self-respect."

Basant Singh, in his feud with Charan, for once sided with the Harijans. But few trusted him. As Poondi said, "Basant Singh cuts off the heads of the poor."

Pritam, as usual, tried to pour oil on troubled waters. "This is very bad," he told Charan when they met in the fields. "If Poondi and Mukhtar had not been there, those Chamars would have killed Dhakel. Some compromise must be reached. There was only one incident like this in Ghungrali before and then the woman was of bad character and at fault. Jats cannot insult Harijans like this."

Old Sadhu Singh had no sympathy at all with Dhakel. "Bad deeds never stay secret," he harrumphed. "The stink gets out. It has happened because of the bad company Dhakel keeps. Those gossipmongers who instigate quarrels are whipping it up too. Dhakel must have been under the influence of opium or some pills." He turned on Poondi, as angry and indignant as if it were all his fault. "Why did you save him?" Sadhu demanded, which Poondi answered with an embarrassed grin. "Let them take their revenge. In the old days if anyone teased a girl he would be garlanded with shoes and forced to clean the shoes at the *gurdwara* for a month. Dhakel should be given the same punishment. Only then will he understand these things." Frail as he was, the old man was as testy and peevish as ever.

Nobody knew where Dhakel was. Then news came he was hiding out in a friend's house in Bhambadi village. At last he came home, but he slept at his well and did not show his face in Ghungrali. When Charan went to see him, he sat guiltily on his *charpoy*, eyes downcast, with hanging head. When Charan pressed him to say what happened he told him in a low voice, "Really I don't know. I was not there. Believe me, I have done nothing. One of my Biharis was with me and we were cutting clover. Ask him. If I had done anything I would have run away to the fields when my father called me. But I came because I wanted to ask what happened. Immediately they attacked me with their sickles." Nobody believed Dhakel, though he never changed his story. He had been seen drunk or in an opium stupor too often.

Kuldeep, who felt all the Jats had lost face, once again talked of going away. Narinder had failed his eighth-grade examination. Kulwant was not doing well in college. Sukhdev was drinking heavily with his police cronies. Charan worried about his sons. The one child who had not disappointed him was his daughter Rani, now eighteen, who had grown up to be a lovely and intelligent woman. Charan wanted her to go to a good college in Ludhiana or Chandigarh. But when he went to talk to the women professors who ran them, he discovered the medium of instruction was English. Although Rani's entire education, in the village and at high school in Khanna, was in Punjabi, she would have to pass an entrance exam in English. There was also the problem of where she could stay in either city. Charan felt his mother would have to go with Rani, and the old lady's health, like Sadhu's, was swiftly failing. When Charan talked of his children with old Chanan, the Mazhbi advised him, "It gets difficult to maintain a family once the children are grown. But the villagers have too much love for you, Charan. You alone of the Jats have always treated me like a father."

Chanan, like Poondi, felt what Dhakel had done was worse than rape. A rape would be kept secret to avoid ruining the girl's chances of marriage. Out of respect for Charan, rather than respect for Dhakel, the two elderly Mazhbis went to see Munshi and his family. They lived in a dirty, tumbledown mud hut, a poor, wretched, unlucky family with only the daughter looking sturdy and pretty. The men, their tempers cooled, were ready to compromise.

Not Munshi's wife—a wrinkled, toothless old woman, bent and prematurely aged by grinding poverty and a lifetime of hard work. Her hatred of the Jats ran deep. "We will take our revenge!" she vowed. "If Charan gets involved, we will not spare him and his family also. I have resigned myself that one of my sons is as good as dead. Whatever the sacrifice, we'll not leave Dhakel alive!" Poondi asked if Dhakel's father, Sarban Singh, had come to apologize.

"Not a word!" she shrieked in a shrill fury, as if this rankled worst of all. "Not a word!"

XVI

Sadhu Singh died in his sleep a few months later. He left a will, giving all his land to Charan. Since he had sold one acre of his original allotment in Ghungrali, his estate came to fourteen acres. When his brother Sarban followed him within a matter of months, he died intestate, which meant everything went to Dhakel's mother. A robust, substantial woman with a strong will, she decided to go to Delhi and live with a married daughter, whose husband, a contractor, was doing well. Sarban had sold three acres of his 1947 allotment to support his opium addiction. Now the mother sold four acres more and gave four acres to a brain-injured son, Sher, a gentle, harmless soul who spent his days following Dhakel, who had long looked after him, about the well yard.

This left just four acres for Dhakel himself. Since land is everything in Punjab, most of Ghungrali's villagers felt that fate had dealt harshly with Dhakel. But with so many fathers dividing land among their sons, many of the old fifteen-acre allotments, which had enabled the Punjabis to adopt new technology so quickly, were starting to break up. No one had ever made the shift from subsistence agricul-

ture to commercial farming faster; the global rural overcrowding that
Punjab had so long escaped was only coming now.

In time the villagers even forgot Dhakel's trouble over Munshi's
daughter. Munshi and his wife and sons were eventually persuaded
by Poondi and others to drop the matter so they could marry off the
girl. Besides, Sarban Singh was dead. It all came to seem just another
chapter in what was becoming Dhakel's long downward slide.

In 1980 Charan was able to make a good match for Rani. The
groom, Binny, was a big, burly twenty-year-old, the son of a prosperous farmer on the outskirts of Ludhiana. The wedding did cause
friction with Charan's sister, Surjit. Charan went to Bhadson to get
back a golden necklace he had loaned Surjit for Pala's wedding a few
years earlier. He and his wife wanted to give it to Rani, but Surjit had
melted the necklace down and given the gold to her own daughter. Its
loss rankled and left ill feeling between Charan and his sister.

Then, soon after Rani's marriage, Charan disappeared. He simply
went off one day. Vanished. He told no one he was going, much less
where. A few days before, he had a bad quarrel with his four sons,
telling them none of them worked as they should and he did not
know what would become of them. Then he was gone. Kuldeep soon
discovered his father had borrowed seven thousand rupees from a
grain trader in Khanna against the next wheat harvest. For six months
the family heard nothing and after the harvest had little to live on. At
last his sons sold a new farm wagon of Charan's for seven thousand
rupees to Surjit's son, Kaka. Kaka, since his marriage to Tohra's niece,
was always looking for easy ways to make money and talked of going
to the Gulf or Lebanon. "Don't worry," he told Charan's sons. "We
don't have to close the deal right away. Maybe you'll find Charan in
the meantime."

One day Kulwant received a letter from a cousin, Sapooran Singh, a
retired police superintendent who lived in the Punjab town of Taran
Taran. He wrote:

> I have come to know that your father is in a village in Uttar Pradesh
> near Bareilly. Please come and I'll go with you and we'll ask him to
> come home.

The two of them set off by train. After some days they found
Charan in a remote Hindu village, Chawar Khas. He was staying with
an elderly Brahmin *zamindar*, or landlord, who owned half the village.
Chawar Khas was scarcely a village at all, just a huddle of earthen huts

in near-jungle, its thin, stunted inhabitants clad in unwashed, grayish rags. The single street was a rutted ditch, the single shop sold only grain from hemp sacks. No electricity. No dispensary. No school. It was miserable.

Sapooran Singh and Kulwant went as far as Bareilly by train; then there was an hour's trip by bus along the Grand Trunk Road. From there it was another hour's ride in a horsecart over a rough dirt track. The last two miles were on foot, through a misty jungle full of jabbering monkeys, some half as big as a man. Vultures kept circling overhead. The village was in Shahjahanpur District, in one of the most backward parts of northern India. Some of the local villages were Hindu, some Muslim; they were said to be forever at each other's throats.

Charan himself, in such a squalid setting, was dressed immaculately in white, his turban tied in the *mandari* style of a Sikh holy man. New shell-rimmed glasses perched on his nose. His beard, untied, hung in long, loose strands. He wore a gray wool vest with a gold pen in the pocket, gray stockings and polished leather shoes with laces. Everything else was the purest white: turban, neck scarf of the finest silk, jacket, shirt, pajamas. He carried a rosary in one hand.

Gone was the farmer. This was Charan the religious pilgrim. In India there is a tradition of old men leaving their families and earthly concerns to pursue their own salvation. Charan told them he had spent the past six months visiting the Golden Temple at Amritsar, where he had drunk the *amrit*, the sacred nectar of rebaptism, and gone to temples all over northern India, sleeping and eating in them without payment, as is the Sikh custom for pilgrims at their holy places. Charan said it was at Hemkunt, a Sikh shrine high in the Himalayas, that he made his decision: he would sell his land in Ghungrali and buy almost three times as much in Chawar Khas, where untilled virgin jungle land went very cheap. He would divide it into four shares so each son would get ten acres. His sons would be left, at last, on their own as he sought his personal salvation.

Charan's ostentatious piety came as a shock in Ghungrali, as he had never been at all religious. Nevertheless, Sikhism accepted the Hindu ideas of karma and transmigration of souls from one form of life to another until their ultimate union with God. A difference was that Sikhs emphasized human conduct as a way to escape the vicious cycle of life, death and rebirth. The Sikh belief was that the time to break the cycles of transmigration is when one is born a man. "Thou has been granted human form," said the fifth Guru, Arjun. "Now is the time to meet God."

Sikhism also taught that prayer was central to religious conduct, especially repeating the name of God. Charan now spent long hours listening to temple singers singing *keertan,* or hymns. He himself fingered his rosary and repeated what scriptures he had memorized, or, more often, chanted in a barely audible whisper the name of God over and over again, *"Satnaam, Wah Guru,* the True Name, the Wondrous Guru." Guru Nanak had written that repeating the name of God, like wearing clean white garments, purified the mind of impious thoughts and cleansed the soul of sin. Going about in his new clothes, Charan found he was often taken for a holy man himself. Other pilgrims would greet him, *"Babuji, Sat Sri Akal!"* and give him *prasad,* or offerings of oranges, bananas, sweet rice or *helwa,* a Punjabi sweet.

Pritam, when he came to know of it, was not impressed by Charan's "conversion," if that is what it was, or by his show of piety, any more than he had been taken in by Sadhu Singh's early-morning prayers at the Ghungrali *gurdwara.* To Pritam, love of God and one's fellow man could be judged solely by their faithful demonstration. "Whenever I feel like it I go to the temple," he told his son Surjit. "Why should I go every day just to look religious? Why lie about it? Why should I go about in white clothes if my deeds are dark?"

Pritam also saw, when Charan at last came home to the village, that every so often he would surreptitiously take a spoonful of a brown-colored mixture he called "my medicine." He kept a small bottle of it on his person and became quite ill without a regular dosage. It was, of course, opium, but Pritam spoke to no one else about it.

"The meeting is today! Sant Jarnail Singh Bhindranwale! You must all visit Dheru village and listen to his thoughts!" Since way before dawn Gurbachan Singh had been shouting this over the temple loud-speaker. Dheru was just two miles from Ghungrali and the site of a shoot-out between Bhindranwale's men and the police. A villager, Amarjit Singh, hid two fugitives, suspected of killing a Bhindranwale foe, in his house. When news of their whereabouts reached the police post in Khanna a subinspector and constable were sent to arrest them. The two men fled to the roof. When the policemen followed, the men opened fire and shot both policemen dead. Reinforcements were sent from Khanna but by then the two killers had fled. Frustrated at finding just the bodies of their colleagues, the police set fire to Amarjit's house and burned it down.

At once Bhindranwale sent word he would hold a public meeting in Dheru to raise money to rebuild Amarjit's house. A stage was erected in a stubble field and a loudspeaker installed. In Ghungrali, people were curious to see the young preacher, Charan among them. Born in 1947, the year of India's independence, Bhindranwale was the same age as Mukhtar and Dhakel.

Charan arrived early. The Punjab police were out in force, cordoning off the platform and corridor for Bhindranwale to enter, which Charan stood beside. There was a great crowd, raising a lot of dust, and while the Sikh turbans were of every color, saffron, emblem of religious persecution and martyrdom, was much in evidence. There was a stir when Bhindranwale arrived and he walked quickly in without looking from side to side, like a man pushed from behind or in pursuit of something or someone, so that his men could hardly keep up with him. The sleeves of his loose white shirt flapped as he walked. The shirt, or tunic, reached well below his knees and below it his legs and feet were bare. Charan saw he was wearing a black leather bandolier with a revolver in a black leather holster and a large curved dagger in a silver sheath. All his guard of ten men were similarly armed and carried sticks in their right hands. To Charan it was like a picture of old religious warriors.

He was quite close when Bhindranwale passed and got a good look. The Sant came first, taller than the others and taking long strides. He carried a long silver arrow in his left hand, a symbol of his religious authority. Like his men, he wore a deep blue turban tied, not in the usual jaunty Sikh way, but in tiers as in olden times. He had powerful-looking hands. He was not handsome: A pale, bony face, long untrimmed beard, beetling eyebrows and thick lashes. His left eyelid drooped, a lifelong affliction which somehow distorted his eyes, making them seem cunning and cruel. He had a large beaky nose and his partly open mouth revealed crooked, yellowish teeth. As he took a chair on the platform and faced the crowd, he smiled faintly. At the same time there was a look of distaste on his face, as if the crowd had a bad smell. He did not greet anyone else on the platform, merely smiled in his curious way and looked sly. Charan caught himself thinking that if you did not know who Bhindranwale was, you might be chary of him and suspect him of evil designs.

He rose to speak: "The police got hold of Jagdig Singh, son of

Thara Singh, made a cut in his thigh and filled it with salt!" A groan went up from the crowd, and Bhindranwale continued to list atrocities committed by the police against his men, as if two policemen had not themselves been killed just a short distance away. In a recital of police torture, his voice filled with malevolence, his face reddened, his neck muscles looked strained. "I tell you," he cried into the microphone, "we are slaves in our own country. If a Hindu dies there is an inquiry. If a Sikh dies there is no inquiry. If a Hindu dies his body is given back to his kith and kin, but if a Sikh dies his body is not given back to his people. If a Hindu is killed it is not excusable, but if a Sikh is killed the matter is scuttled."

He spoke contemptuously of Indira Gandhi as "the Brahmin's daughter." "How can he speak like that?" Charan asked the man beside him. "Don't worry," the man said. "Look at all the police they've got to protect him. They are all in it together. Mrs. Gandhi is backing him." He attacked the police themselves. "They are dacoits, thieves we must face, *choli chuk*." It was an obscene expression not usually used in public speeches. "Do not be misled by the sustained propaganda against me. I plead with you to be aware of attempts to malign me and my disciples. The newspapers are bent on turning the Sikh community against me." He grew steadily more agitated and his loose sleeves flapped as he waved his arms about. Beware of their propaganda!" he cried. "They want us to fight among ourselves like shrews. Beware."

He disavowed personal ambition, saying he did not want to be a minister in the Punjab government, nor even an assembly member. "I swear that I am prepared to receive any punishment from you if I lie. I am responsible only for the cause of Sikhism, preaching the symbols of the faith. I am to see that your beards remain intact, your hair is uncut and you do not go after the evil things in life, like alcohol and drugs." But soon he seemed to extol terrorism. "For every village you should keep one motorcycle, three young baptized Sikhs and three revolvers. These are not meant to kill innocent people. For a Sikh to keep arms and kill an innocent person is a sin. But Khalsaji, Pure Warriors, to have arms and not to get your legitimate rights is an even bigger sin. It is for you to decide how to use these arms. If you want to remove the shackles of your slavery you must have a plan."

But what plan? He did not say but his voice rose in crescendo. "I once again, with my hands folded at your feet, appeal to you—if you have not observed the five *k*'s, if you are not armed with a rifle and a

spear, you will be given the beating of your lives by the Hindus!"
The meeting came to an end as the crowd, prompted by Bhin-
dranwale's men scattered among them, shouted, *"Wah Guruji ka
Khalsa—Wah Guruji ki Fateh!* Pure warriors are the chosen of God—
Victory be to God!"

Charan was thrilled and he told Pritamji back in Ghungrali, "He
said every Sikh must carry a sharp sword. If you have just a gun or
pistol, you can run out of bullets. With a sword you don't need to carry
ammunition. Ultimately, the man with the sword will win. He also
said every Sikh should drink the *amrit."* This was to be baptized in
the pool of nectar, the Pool of Immortality, at the Golden Temple,
just as Charan had. Pritam was interested that Bhindranwale stressed
the "five *k*'s"—Guru Govind Singh's admonition to Sikhs not to cut
their hair (*kesh*) or shave their beards, to carry a comb (*kangha*), to wear
a steel bangle (*kara*) and breeches (*kuchha*) and to carry a dagger
(*kirpan*). Like the battle cry *"Raj karega Khalsa!* The Pure shall rule!"
these were symbols of those Sikhs prepared to fight their oppressors,
whether Muslims or Hindus. But, Pritam thought to himself, what
good were symbols without Sikhism's moral content and the teachings of Guru Nanak and his belief in salvation through righteous living with its work ethic, community, mutual help and sharing with the
poor? Guru Nanak fought against the very fanaticism and intolerance
this Bhindranwale preached. Nanak was gentle with a kindly sense of
humor. He was without anger, violence and recrimination, all qualities
of Bhindranwale. So why was Bhindranwale being hailed as the messiah of Sikh fundamentalism?

Pritam knew little about him. The name came from the village of
Bhindran, where the Sikh missionary movement he joined was
founded. He himself came from the village of Rode near the town of
Moga, less than twenty-five miles as the crow flies from Ghungrali.
He was the last of seven sons of Joginder Singh, a poor Jat farmer.
Bhindranwale's first name, Jarnail, was simply a Punjabi rendering of
the English word "general." Martial names were popular among Jats.

Joginder Singh, a pious man, lacked enough land for so many sons,
so he took Bhindranwale, then just seven years old, to live in the
Damdami Taksal, a Sikh seminary near Amritsar. Once Bhindranwale
became a legendary figure, his father boasted that as a small boy he
could "fell a tree in a single blow and at the same time memorize
whole chapters of the scriptures and and recite them a hundred times
a day." The Damdami Taksal was an influential school among Sikhs

founded by a Sikh hero, Baba Deep Singh, who swore to defend the Golden Temple against Muslim Afghani invaders. Baba Deep Singh raised an army of five thousand peasants but in the end the Golden Temple was overrun and desecrated. Sikh villagers still retold the legend of how Baba Deep Singh's head was cut off but he continued to fight his way into the temple with his head in one hand and his sword in the other. The Damdami Taksal had been fighting apostasy for two hundred years by the time young Jarnail Singh was sent to it. Twenty-five years later he rose to be head of the seminary. A few years after that he went to Amritsar and took on the Nirankaris as heretics.

The two policemen shot in Dheru village were the first to be killed. Now the terrorist murders began. On April 24, 1980, Baba Gurbachan Singh, the Nirankaris' leader, was shot dead at his home in Delhi. Bhindranwale's name figured in the police report and the Sant took sanctuary in the Golden Temple. Zail Singh, the Sikh politician close to Mrs. Gandhi and her son Sanjay, was now India's home minister and he told Parliament that Bhindranwale had nothing to do with the assassination. Sanjay was soon to die in an air crash while stunt flying over New Delhi, an accident with many consequences.

In August 1981, Bhindranwale came back to Isru, a village near Ghungrali, this time openly backed by Indira Gandhi's Congress Party. Charan again went and found the crowd huge this time, maybe ten thousand Sikhs. A month later there was a second murder when a Hindu editor in the Punjabi town of Jullundur was shot dead after warning in his newspaper that Bhindranwale's real aim was to lead Punjab's secession from India so it could become an independent new Sikh nation, Khalistan, Land of the Pure. Bhindranwale's reported comment on the slayings: "If those killers came to me, I would have weighed them in gold." To most Sikhs, Khalistan was a mythological golden age. Punjab, a state with just 20 million people, half of them farming, alone grew two-thirds of the wheat for India's central grain reserve. How could India ever let Punjab go?

In Ghungrali they heard on All India Radio that a warrant was out for Bhindranwale's arrest. He was taken after a gun battle in which twelve people died. The same day three Sikhs on motorcycles fired into a crowd of Hindus in Jullundur, killing four. The next day a Hindu was shot dead in Taran Taran; a police chief's office was bombed in Patiala. Young Sikh terrorists derailed a train near Amritsar, and hijacked a plane to Lahore.

As terrorism erupted all over Punjab, the villagers heard the radio report that the home minister, Zail Singh, again reassured Parliament in Delhi that there was no evidence Bhindranwale was behind it all. Then who was? "Who can doubt," Pritam asked his family, "that Indira Gandhi herself did not order Bhindranwale's release?" Word came from Delhi that Bhindranwale and a crowd of his supporters rode in triumph around Delhi in buses, many of them sitting on the roofs with AK-47s. When one of his men was shot by a rival in December 1981, the Ludhiana newspapers had pictures of Bhindranwale, Zail Singh and Rajiv Gandhi at the memorial service. When Bhindranwale came back to Punjab and Charan went to hear him speak, he listened to the preacher attack Zail Singh for dyeing his beard:

> In a village anyone who has his face blackened and sandals hung around his neck and is forced to sit backward on a donkey is being punished. He has molested someone's sister or mother. I am surprised to see in Delhi that some people have blackened their faces. Whose sisters have they molested?

It was a great insult to a man Mrs. Gandhi was about to name president of India, and soon Bhindranwale was saying Zail Singh "licked the dust off Mrs. Gandhi's sandals." Bhindranwale and his men again holed up in the Golden Temple. This time Gurcharan Singh Tohra, the old politician who headed the committee that ran all the Sikh temples in Punjab, allowed them to stay in the sanctuary of the Akal Takht, a shrine symbolizing the temporal power of God, which directly faced the glittering gold-leaf domes of the inner Golden Temple itself. The high priests protested at this sacrilege, but Tohra, a cunning old whitebeard, whose rustic village ways concealed great ambition, won the day.

This was the same Tohra whose niece had married Kaka in Bhadson. Charan soon took advantage of his influence: Tohra pulled strings to get Sukhdev into the Punjab police, helped Charan settle a property dispute and had his banker show him how to send money to his sister in Malaysia. Who knows what might have come of the connection had Charan not fallen out with Surjit.

It took time for Charan to get title to his thirty-five acres in Chawar Khas, since it was owned in small parcels by thirteen impoverished Hindus. The land, none of which was cultivated, was either jungle or barren dried earth. He would have to dig his own tube well for water.

Charan booked a freight car to carry the family's possessions by train from Ludhiana to Bareilly. From there they would have to go by a tractor-pulled wagon. He sent word to Surjit he needed his wagon back. When she did not respond, he went to the *sarpanch* of Bhadson, who at once summoned Surjit and Pala and told them to give the wagon back. Surjit, indignant and humiliated, demanded that Charan repay all his debts to her, several thousand rupees.

Outraged, he told her, "I have given you things worth far more already. The gold necklace, everything I've spent on your farm all these years—seed, fertilizer, bringing the Mazhbis to cut your wheat when you were about to lose everything." Their mother had died not long before, failing rapidly after Sadhu Singh was no longer there to quarrel with, and Charan had given all her clothes to Surjit. Now, trembling with anger, he mentioned these too, so infuriating Surjit that for some minutes they threw the bitterest oaths and accusations at each other. "Fix a date," Charan finally told her, "and we'll settle accounts."

Pala interrupted: "I've sold the wagon."

"You're lying," Charan told him. "You're a fraud and a cheat."

"If you can lie, I can too." Surjit, who had not expected the dispute to take such a furious turn, began sobbing, even as she thought of more cruel things to say. But Charan strode out and did not go back to see her again.

When Pritam heard about the fight, he caught a bus to Bhadson. "Give back the wagon and forget this matter," he told Surjit. "Charan cannot pay now."

Kaka, who had grown quite fat, told Pritam there was talk that Charan was taking opium. "In Uttar Pradesh he can get a license to grow it. Maybe that's why he's going there." Kaka himself was about to leave for Beirut, where Tohra had found him a job in a candle factory.

"Once a man gets addicted to opium it can spoil everything," Pritam said. Pala told him that his father, Saroop, who even in his seventies looked healthier than Pritam had ever seen him, had stopped taking opium after a habit of thirty years. But Saroop's nephew Buldev, a landless Jat after his parents sold their land for opium, himself got addicted. He had gone from farm to farm, working as a laborer, and was spraying malathion on cotton when he died. Pritam was appalled to hear it. "People are not aware of the dangers. They don't stay upwind and only move in one direction as they should. They ought to wear a mask. Didn't the landlord explain what the dangers were?" Pala shrugged. "Maybe Buldev took opium and grew careless." A landless Jat had no status or, as Surjit was fond of saying, "no home in the world."

Pala told Pritam he had heard that Charan had sold seven acres for three hundred thousand rupees and the house and cattle yard in Ghungrali for seventy thousand. The land at Chawar Khas cost just under four hundred thousand, paid to twelve caste Hindus and a Harijan.

Sukhdev, still at his police post on the Grand Trunk Road, went over to help the family move. He told Pritam his brothers were working hard to level the land and plant a crop. Once they harvested their first wheat crop, the worst would be over. Sukhdev said wild herds of predatory cattle came out of the jungled hills, there were great flocks of green parrots, many monkeys in the trees and masked dacoits who plundered the villages at night. He said Charan kept three big dogs, who snarled and bared their teeth at everybody, but no guns, just swords, spears and battle-axes. Pritam remembered how Charan had complained to him just before he left: "Sukhdev never gives me a single penny." It was said in Ghungrali that Sukhdev was often drunk while off duty now and beat his wife. With so much terrorism, a policeman's lot was not to be envied.

XVII

"Return your tickets! All trains have been canceled until further notice!" It was June 1, 1984, and Charan was waiting at Ludhiana station to catch a train home after picking up some wheat seed at the university. After three years of the harsh and isolated life in Chawar Khas, it was always a relief to come back to Punjab, even with the terrorists now striking almost daily in Ludhiana. "Return your tickets!" Charan listened to the loudspeaker with amazement. What was going on? Almost at once soldiers were moving out on the platform, Hindu Dogras by the look of them. The announcement left people in utter confusion. It was late afternoon, but no one was allowed to leave the station. Soon there were soldiers everywhere Charan looked. He heard some Hindus talking. There was trouble, they said, at the Golden Temple in Amritsar. A train pulled in from Pune, the Tata Express. Charan watched a young Sikh woman with three children get down. The soldiers barred their way out and said they would have to stay at the station. "How can I feed my children?" the mother demanded. The soldiers shrugged. Orders were orders.

Two of them told Charan they wanted the large dagger he carried as a pious Sikh. "Why?" he asked. "Maybe you are a man of Bhindranwale," one said. "Look," Charan protested, "that dagger is symbolic and cost five hundred rupees. How do I get it back?" They took him to an officer who had taken over the stationmaster's desk. "Do you know anybody here?" Charan had seen a policeman who worked with Sukhdev. They gave the dagger to him to keep until the curfew ended.

The passengers were stranded at the station, day after day with little food. Every morning an announcement was made over the loudspeaker that trains would run that evening, but none came. On the sixth morning Charan saw some Hindu soldiers laughing. He asked what it meant. *"Bahut kush,* very happy," one told him. "They killed Bhindranwale." Hearing this, Charan was afraid. What if the Dogras opened fire on him and the other Sikhs in the station? Nothing happened for four more days. At last, on the morning of June 10, the soldiers let people at the station leave on a goods train to Ambala. Everybody scrambled onto empty freight cars. There was just enough room to stand and it took two hours to reach the Punjabi border, where Charan caught the first train home.

In Ghungrali, June 1, hours after Charan found himself unable to leave Ludhiana station, word came that the Indian Army was sealing off the whole of Punjab. Sukhdev and some fellow constables came to say that not a bicycle or a bullock cart would be allowed to move, nor would trains, buses, trucks or cars. Nobody was to set foot on the Grand Trunk Road. They had orders to shoot on sight. The policemen told some of the villagers not to even go into the fields or cut fodder. The army was afraid, Sukhdev said, that armed Sikh villagers, carrying whatever weapons they could find, might converge on Amritsar across the fields from all directions to force the army to raise the siege. It was rumored that amid fears of a mass uprising ten thousand Hindu and Muslim soldiers had been rushed to Amritsar, which was now under twenty-four-hour curfew, and that half of the troops had encircled the Golden Temple itself.

At his well that evening, Dhakel, who had built a small house and moved his family there, turned on his television set to find Mrs. Gandhi was making an unscheduled speech. She appealed to Akali Dal leaders to call off a threatened attempt to stop grain from moving out of Punjab. She went on:

> Holy shrines have been turned into shelters for criminals and murderers. Their sanctity as places of worship have been undermined . . . And worst of all, the unity and integrity of our motherland is being challenged.

She ended with an appeal:

> Let us join hands together to heal wounds. The best memorial to those who have lost their lives is to restore normalcy and harmony in Punjab which they loved and served. To all sections of Punjabis I appeal—don't shed blood, shed hatred.

At such a time, Dhakel felt he needed a drink. The nearest liquor shop was near the Bija Bridge on the other side of the Grand Trunk Road. All India Radio said only the military could use the highway. Anybody else would be shot on sight. Dhakel and three friends decided to risk it. They crept through the fields and, when they neared the highway, dodged from tree to tree. It was still daylight and they waited for a military convoy to pass, roaring toward Amritsar at high speed. When the coast was clear they made a run for it, dashing across the highway at a low run and dodging behind more trees until they reached the liquor shop.

"Are you crazy? Run away from here!" the Hindu shopkeeper hissed at them through a crack in the door. "I'm closed." But he took the rupees he was offered and passed a bottle back. "Run from here! Don't drink here! Run away! Quick, quick!" Dhakel knew a secluded well nearby and they headed toward it, Dhakel joking, "We have to die someday. Let's enjoy first!" To their surprise, there was a whole group of Sikhs by the well, all with bottles, drinking. After a couple swigs, Dhakel felt better. They stayed at the well until dark, when they grew light-headed enough to brave the trip home.

When the army moved in, Pritam was alarmed because he knew that several thousand pilgrims would be in the Golden Temple to commemorate the martyrdom of the fifth Guru, Arjun. The Mogul emperor Jehangir, who had tortured Arjun to death, wrote of him: "In the garments of sainthood and sanctity" he had "captured many of the simple-hearted Hindus, and even of the ignorant and foolish followers of Islam, by his ways and manners, and they had loudly sounded the drum of his holiness." Jehangir said the crowds called the Sikh holy man "Guru" and "from all sides stupid people crowded to worship and manifest complete faith in him." Since villagers were pouring into Amritsar to worship Guru Arjun, surely the army would not go in shooting at such a time.

Bhindranwale ruled by fear, not by love. In the two years he and his men had been in the Golden Temple, several hundred people, mainly Sikhs, had been killed, including terrorists and policemen. Gunmen went in and out of the temple complex without hindrance. Even in Ghungrali, people knew that Bhindranwale meted out life-and-death judgments at his morning *darbars*, when he spoke to Sikh congregations, or on the roof of the big *langar*, the dining hall where meals were served to pilgrims. Bhindranwale might decide on a punishment and tell the condemned, "You know we are building a temple, so you must provide bricks, five thousand for the compound wall." Somebody might whisper into his ear, "You're letting him off too cheaply. Five thousand is nothing to him." And Bhindranwale would say, "Make that fifty thousand bricks." Not to obey was to be killed. It was said he gave his followers a daily list of people who should die. Then in the evening he would ask, "How many killed? How many killed?"

In Amritsar, the situation had become much worse in recent days. In April, Bhindranwale's chief gunman was shot by a young Sikh woman, Baljit Kaur, at an Amritsar tea shop. Bhindranwale blamed leaders of the Akali Dal Party, also holed up in the Golden Temple complex with armed men of their own. Burned and dismembered bodies began to be found in the city. The body of a woman, her breasts and genitals burned, her shins, thighs and forearms crushed, was found just outside Amritsar. The body was too badly disfigured for identification, the police said, but they thought it was Baljit Kaur. The body of her accomplice was found sliced in seven pieces by a sharp sword, the ancient punishment given a Sikh traitor. Even the owner of the tea shop was shot. Bhindranwale was heard to boast that his gunman's death had been avenged within twenty-four hours. People were being dragged before Bhindranwale in the Akal Takht, forced to confess and killed. When the carnage got too much, Tohra tried to get Bhindranwale and his men evicted from the Golden Temple but by now the priests were too terrified of them. Bhindranwale, who started out as a warrior-saint against the evil of modernity, had become criminally evil himself.

A month before the army attacked, he said, "Let them come. We will give battle, and if die we must, then we will take many of them with us. What we represent will not die with us. We will be martyrs to all Sikhs." After an early gun battle between his men and the police, Bhindranwale was quoted by the BBC as saying, "The firing shows that the government wants to insult the Golden Temple and cannot tolerate the faces of Sikhs and their way of life."

As airports closed, trains stopped running, highways were shut to traffic, telephone and telex lines went dead and reporters, camera crews and photographers, Indian and foreign, were ordered out of Punjab, Subhash Kirpekar of *The Times of India* somehow escaped the net. He was to be the last outsider to see Bhindranwale. On June 3, Kirpekar left his shoes and covered his head with a cloth at the temple entrance, walked around the large sacred pool of the Harimandir, or Golden Temple proper, to the Akal Takht, where Bhindranwale stayed upstairs. Kirpekar had heard there were about a thousand young Sikhs inside the temple armed with AK-47s, rockets, mortars, rifles and grenades. He could see some of them manning sandbagged machine-gun nests or crouched in posts on the temple's high white parapets and around its gilded domes and cupolas.

With so many pilgrims about, the air of the place was serene. Around the pool worshippers and holy men were taking baths of purification—washing away their sins. Some of the male bathers, stripped down to their shorts, still had *kirpans*, or swords, strapped to their turbans, being orthodox Sikhs who never parted with them. On the long causeway bridging the sacred pool, pilgrims kept going back and forth. Kirpekar was nervously excited about meeting Bhindranwale, who had agreed to an interview. He had never seen him before.

At the Akal Takht, once he identified himself to Bhindranwale's bodyguards and was frisked for weapons, Kirpekar was led upstairs. He had to squeeze past several Sikhs with AK-47s. Bhindranwale was waiting in a third-floor room, sitting cross-legged on a mattress. Kirpekar greeted him, *"Sat Sri Akal!"* and sat down. He asked Bhindranwale his reaction to the Indian Army's encircling the temple.

Bhindranwale shrugged. He said police had been stationed in large numbers outside the temple for two years. It was too early to say what the army was up to. Kirpekar asked, "Aren't you outnumbered? Doesn't the army have superior weapons?" Bhindranwale gave another little shrug and a faint smile. "Sheep always outnumber lions.

But one lion can eat a thousand sheep. When the lion sleeps, the birds cheep. When it awakes, the birds fly away and there is silence."

Bhindranwale looked to be a man of about fifty, though Kirpekar knew he was just thirty-seven. The Sant's drooping, half-shut eyelid gave him the appearance of a squint. When he gave one of his strange smiles and his lips slightly parted, Kirpekar saw he had bad teeth, long and neither straight nor very white. The long white garment he wore was immaculate, as was his deep blue turban. Kirpekar saw that several bearded youths seated about were dressed in the same way—blue turban, long white knee-length shirt and a black leather bandolier with sword and revolver. All the legs and feet were bare.

They were joined by an older man, tall and lean with a flowing gray beard and steel-rimmed glasses perched on an aquiline nose. Unlike the others, he wore a flowing gray silk *kurta*. He looked distinguished and carried a walkie-talkie.

"Tussi enhannoo pahchande ho?" Bhindranwale asked Kirpekar—did he know who this was? The older man sat down with them in the same cross-legged fashion. "Santji," Kirpekar replied, "I've seen him somewhere." Bhindranwale laughed and winked with his drooping eyelid. *"Ey put hay Bangladesh,* he was a big hero in Bangladesh." Kirpekar knew at once this was Major General Shabeg Singh, Bhindranwale's military adviser. In charge of the Golden Temple's defense, Shabeg Singh had been cashiered for corruption the day before he was to retire. Stripped of his rank and denied a pension, he had bitterly nursed a grievance ever since and it was he who taught Bhindranwale's men how to use modern weapons, most of them smuggled across the border from Pakistan. Kirpekar had not seen Shabeg Singh for thirteen years, but he had once been a popular figure with the press as well as a national hero.

"If you were in uniform I'd have recognized you right away," Kirpekar said in embarrassment. "But in a silk *kurta* . . ." The general would know the difference between the army and the police, that the army shot to kill. "The army has encircled the temple complex, General. What does it mean?"

Shabeg Singh's face clouded. "Subhash," he said, using Kirpekar's first name, "the attack is coming tonight." Kirpekar shot a glance at Bhindranwale, whose expression was unchanged. When the general left, Kirpekar asked Bhindranwale if he had heard Mrs. Gandhi's "don't shed blood, shed hatred" broadcast.

"I don't listen to such speeches."

"Is it your contention that Sikhs cannot live in India?"

"Yes. They can neither live in nor with India. If treated as equals it might be possible. But frankly speaking, I don't see that happening." With that, the interview was over. As Kirpekar was led down the dark, narrow staircase, again past the guards and their weapons, he heard somebody burst into a string of foul curses upstairs. He thought it was Bhindranwale's voice. Outside the Akal Takht a group of young Sikhs were reading aloud verses from the *Granth*. Farther on others were shouting slogans against the Indian government. Near the entrance, Kirpekar stopped to see Tohra, who was holding court in one of the temple hostels. "How is it," Kirpekar asked the old man, "that Bhindranwale's boys don't name you in their attacks?"

"I'm glad you noticed," Tohra smirked, stroking his beard. He's probably paying them off out of the temple donations, Kirpekar thought.

Three days later, just before sunup, the sound of prayers and the chanting of the *Granth*'s hymns in the temple died away for the first time in four hundred years. Infantrymen charged directly into the main Golden Temple gate, into heavy fire from automatic weapons, rockets and mortars. At first commandos tried to dislodge Bhindranwale's men without destroying the temple's inner sanctuary. After the rebels set up heavy machine guns in the gilded Harimandir out on the pool, seven tanks were brought in. They bombarded the three-story Akal Takht, where Kirpekar had talked to Bhindranwale; he was believed to be inside. Outside the temple, a thirty-six-hour curfew was imposed. From his nearby hotel, the Amritsar International, all night and the next morning, Kirpekar could hear explosions, gunfire and screams and shouts. Thousands of pilgrims were trapped inside by the firing of rifles, machine guns and mortars.

At last the firing stopped. Subhash was told the curfew was lifted for two hours. After that, anybody out in the street would be shot on sight. He made his way to the Golden Temple as fast as he could. The streets were full of dead bodies, great piles of men, women and children covered with blood. Near the temple Indian soldiers were loading the bodies of their fellow *jawans* onto trucks. They harshly challenged him and complained that the curfew was lifted before the army casualties were removed.

The devastation inside the temple walls was far worse than he expected. The entire front of the Akal Takht was gone, just a pillar standing. Fires had blackened its marble walls. Its gold-plated dome was badly damaged by artillery fire. The Golden Temple library, with all its sacred texts, many handwritten by the gurus themselves, was burned down, everything inside reduced to ashes. The gilded, still shimmering Harimandir was intact, though riddled by several hundred bullet holes. Inside, pages of an open copy of the *Granth* had been battered to pieces by gunfire.

The loss to Sikhism was incalculable. Not far away Kirpekar came upon the body of Bhindranwale, lying on his back on a small marble platform. Soaked in blood, he had been shot many times. One eye was open, the good eye without the drooping eyelid. He was alone and it looked as if he had been carried there. There was no time to lose and Kirpekar hurried back to his hotel. Outside the Amritsar police station, he saw policemen beating Sikhs and Hindus, pilgrims caught inside the temple. Farther on army soldiers were kicking a dozen young Sikhs who were down on their knees in the road.

Why didn't the army just starve Bhindranwale's men out? Lieutenant General Krishnaswamy Sunderji, the overall commander of the operation, affirmed that the army feared a popular uprising, just as Sukhdev had said. But who would dream Mrs. Gandhi would send the army into the Sikhs' holiest shrine and when it was full of pilgrims? And Bhindranwale's men committed terrible atrocities in the heat of battle. They threw grenades at pilgrims who tried to flee or surrender, flayed and blew up a young army officer who fell into their hands and hacked to death an army doctor who went to treat civilian casualties. Tohra, in hiding to escape such horrors, was unable to surrender until one o'clock in the morning.

How many people were killed in the temple raid, who were they and how did they die? A government White Paper ultimately put the civilian toll at just under five hundred. At least sixteen hundred people, villagers who simply went to the Golden Temple that morning to pray, were never accounted for. The day after the battle Sikh soldiers mutinied at seven places in India. In Rajasthan they shouted, "Long live Sant Bhindranwale!" and fired indiscriminately. In Bihar they commandeered a column of military vehicles and set out for Amritsar but were soon stopped.

Some said Bhindranwale declared, after the tank barrage, "Those who want to be martyrs can stay with me. Those who want to surrender can go now." No witness could ever be found who saw him die, though blurred photographs of both his body and that of Shabeg Singh, still clutching his walkie-talkie, were taken. Soon in Ghungrali, as in villages all over Punjab, word went around that Bhindranwale was alive, that like some legendary warrior of the past, he had miraculously survived and was leading the armed struggle for Khalistan from a secret headquarters, perhaps across the frontier in Pakistan. For nearly five months after the raid, Mrs. Gandhi tried to restore the traditional harmony between Sikhs and Hindus, but she never turned to traditional leaders like Tohra, whom the army had arrested. They were still in jail on October 31, 1984, when she was shot.

XVIII

Number 1, Safdarjang Road in New Delhi, where Indira Gandhi lived, was a world away from a Punjabi village like Ghungrali. A white colonial-style bungalow built by the British for one of their administrators, it was set back from the road among shade trees and a spacious garden and lawn. The walls of her study were lined with books— biographies of Malraux, Kissinger, Einstein, de Gaulle, Macmillan, and art books from Japan, India, the Met. The choice was eclectic: André Gide's *Afterthoughts on the U.S.S.R.*, Stalin's *Marxism and the National Colonial Question*, old and tattered books from childhood: Maurice Maeterlinck's *The Life of a White Ant, Cinderella* and *Problèmes d'Arithmétique*. The colors of the study were pale green, beige and ocher, and these were reflected in the carpet, the Uzbeki rug thrown across it, the impressionistic Indian landscapes and the fresh flowers on the highly polished desk. A sun-dappled Italian street scene, also pale green and ocher, hung above the desk. On it were a tiny green, orange and white flag of India, a bronze letter opener and a wicker letter basket.

About the room were many photographs: sledding and skiing in the Alps, Indira perched on a *charpoy* with Mahatma Gandhi, an autographed picture of Charlie Chaplin. There was Feroze Gandhi, a Parsi met when he was eighteen, she thirteen. He proposed on a summer day in Paris on the steps of the Sacre Coeur. When he died in 1960 she told a friend, "I feel as if my luck had run out . . ." She devoted herself to her father after that and there was a photograph with Nehru and the Kennedys at a White House dinner. Next to it was one signed: "Loving Greetings, Uncle Ho Chi Minh." There was the last picture with Nehru, on the terrace of the country house in Dehra Dun in the Himalayan foothills. After his death she wanted to go to London to look after her teenage sons, and she joined the Cabinet with great reluctance. In those days Indira was a charming, gracious, almost girlish woman and shy.

The imperious, autocratic figure *The Economist* was to call "Empress of India" came later. It was to describe her rule:

Dynast, goddess-figure, warrior-queen, Mrs. Gandhi defined and dominated the politics of her country for two decades. She took big risks, some wise, some foolish. In 1969 she split the Congress party, thereby eliminating all rivals for the next 15 years. In 1971 she broke up Pakistan, thereby making India the unquestioned superpower of the subcontinent. In 1975 she imposed an "emergency," which saved her own job at the cost of suspending Indian democracy 2½ years. And in 1984 she tackled Sikh terrorism, too late, by invading the Golden Temple in Punjab.

When she went to Amritsar and saw the ruins, she burst into tears and broke down sobbing. Once in an essay she defined culture as "intellectual development, in the arts and sciences." To Indira Gandhi, educated at Oxford, lover of Bach and French impressionists, this meant Western art and sciences and not what she called "the prejudices of our masses in the form of customs, traditions, habits, faiths, superstitions and fears." After Amritsar she told a friend:

I do not want to be a little island by myself. I mean, what's the point of living if one must do that? And I've had a full life, honestly. I'd much rather, if something was to happen, that it should happen when I'm doing something.

She refused to remove Sikhs from her bodyguard. In her study it was found she had written on a notepad:

If I die a violent death as some fear and a few are plotting, I know the violence will be in the thought and action of my assassin, not in my dying—for no hate is dark enough to overshadow my love for my people and my country; no force is strong enough to divert me from my purpose and my endeavor to take this country forward.

In her last public speech, made in the town of Bhubaneswar on India's east coast below Calcutta on October 30, Mrs. Gandhi was visibly losing her grip. She had been painfully hit by a stone on the bridge of her nose at a previous rally in Bhubaneswar and referred to it:

I am here today. I may not be here tomorrow . . . Nobody knows how many attempts have been made to shoot me, lathis [heavy sticks] have been used to beat me. In Bhubaneswar itself, a brickbat hit me. They have attacked me in every possible way.

I do not care whether I live or die. I have lived a long life and I am proud that I spent the whole of my life in the service of my people. I am proud of this and nothing else. I shall continue to serve until my last breath, and when I die, I can say that every drop of my blood will invigorate India and strengthen it. I hope that youth, women and others will all think together. They should shoulder the responsibility and it cannot be done by accepting others as leaders. Leaders come and go. . . .

That night she flew back to Delhi early. Her grandchildren had been in a car accident. "God knows," she told her aides, "it might have been an attempt on their lives."

The next morning Mrs. Gandhi had breakfast with her Italian daughter-in-law, Sonia, and her two grandchildren—Rajiv was off campaigning near Calcutta. At eight-thirty her press secretary of many years, H. Y. Sharada Prasad, went to the garden of the bungalow next door, used by Mrs. Gandhi as a prime minister's office, to see how actor Peter Ustinov and an Irish television crew were getting on. They were going to spend the morning filming an interview with Mrs. Gandhi for a series called *Peter Ustinov's People*. It was to be a busy day. Former British prime minister Lord Callaghan and his wife had an afternoon appointment and Mrs. Gandhi was giving a small dinner party for them and Britain's Princess Anne that evening. Also scheduled were meetings with the Maharaja of Jaipur and the chief minister of Nagaland. Ustinov described the scene: "We were in the garden at 8:30 and it was her idea to have the interview in the garden over a cup of tea. The tea had already been set up, the mike was in place and we were all ready. I told the press secretary we were ready and he went to fetch her."

"You go ahead and I'll be out shortly," Mrs. Gandhi told Sharada Prasad. She chose her clothes with care and that morning wore a silk saffron-colored sari. She told him a red shoulder bag should film well with it. Sharada Prasad hurried back. The gardens of the two bungalows which served as Mrs. Gandhi's home and office were separated by a wicket gate and driveway. Mrs. Gandhi loved flowers and had surrounded her own lawn with an English garden. There were roses and a lily pond and a short walk to the gate through a grove of *kadamb* trees she had planted herself. Behind them, on both sides of the sun-dappled path, were taller *kher*, neem and mango trees, and flowering bougainvilleas and palms. It was a lovely place and that morning a flock of green parrots had settled in their branches. As Mrs. Gandhi hurried toward the gate, followed by an assistant, R. K. Dhawan, she smiled at Beant Singh, a dark-skinned Mazhbi Sikh police subinspector who stood on duty before a small guardhouse, and to a constable at the gate holding a Sten gun, also a low-caste Sikh.

The subinspector drew his revolver and fired three times. Mrs. Gandhi fell to the ground. Satwant Singh, the constable at the gate, began firing wildly, emptying his submachine gun into her body, though many bullets ricocheted about, missing her. In the garden Sharada Prasad had just rejoined Ustinov and told him, "The prime minister will be with us shortly," when they heard the three shots. "It's nothing," one of the camera crew said. "Somebody bursting firecrackers." Then came the long burst of fire from the submachine gun set on automatic.

"Now that *was* something!" Ustinov cried. Sharada Prasad began to run toward the gunfire. The parrots had taken flight and frantically circled overhead. Sonia Gandhi came running from the house, as did soldiers from all over. Sonia and Dhawan cradled Mrs. Gandhi in their arms. Beant Singh, the subinspector, dropped his revolver, hung his walkie-talkie on the gate and lifted his hands over his head. "I have done what I had to do. Now you do what you have to do," he said. Soldiers from the Indo-Tibetan border police, who were guarding the house, overpowered the two Sikh bodyguards. They soon shot Beant Singh dead, but Satwant Singh lived to be tried and hanged.

There was no ambulance and Sonia and Dhawan put Mrs. Gandhi into a white Indian-made Ambassador car and drove her three miles to the All India Institute of Medical Sciences. The doctor who first attended her said she was dead on arrival. She had no pulse and her pupils did not react to light. Even so, Mrs. Gandhi was rushed to an operating room, where she was given continuous blood transfusions as doctors removed the bullets. She had been hit by at least twenty of the bullets, which punctured her liver, kidney and arm, and some arteries and veins on her right-hand side. She was not pronounced dead until two-thirty in the afternoon. Officials refused to confirm it until nearly four-thirty and All India Radio did not get permission to announce it until six that evening.

By then reprisals by Hindus upon Sikhs had begun all over Delhi. A turbaned Sikh, caught unawares by the assassination, would be seized by a frenzied mob and horribly beaten, sometimes to death.

Burning tires were thrust over the heads of other Sikhs, who died in terrible agony. Gangs of youths dragged Sikhs off buses or stopped their cars. Outside the All India Institute of Medical Sciences, as doctors worked on Mrs. Gandhi's body, mobs attacked any Sikh on the road. When Zail Singh, now president of India, arrived at the airport and heard the news and had his driver take him directly to the institute, a mob, seeing a Sikh inside, hurled stones at the presidential limousine and he barely escaped.

For forty-eight hours, the violence continued in Delhi. Mobs, some led by Congress Party politicians, roamed the streets, killing, burning and robbing Sikhs. Rajiv Gandhi was quoted as saying that "the earth trembles when a great tree falls." Trains began to pull into Delhi station with the bodies of butchered Sikh passengers. It was the horror of partition all over again. Riots spread to all the big northern Indian cities. The government was to put the death toll at just under three thousand, much of it in Delhi. Others claimed it was three times this, half in Delhi. The Hindu rage against Sikhs, India's most prosperous and progressive community, was not to be forgotten. Rajiv waited two days until he ordered the army in, just a few hours before his mother was to be cremated. The streets were almost empty when Indira Gandhi's body, laid out in a gun carriage with the face exposed, was taken to its burning ghat on the banks of the Jumuna River. Millions had poured out at the funeral processions of Mahatma Gandhi, Nehru and Lal Bahadur Shastri, but now people were too afraid.

XIX

Rani feared both for herself and for the baby she was carrying. She was five months pregnant and, as was the Sikh Punjabi custom, had come to her mother's house for the delivery. Rani was not happy in Chawar Khas with the jungle so close and full of strange animal shrieks in the night and the village so poor, with its huddle of mud huts and gawking, emaciated Hindu inhabitants.

Rani had become a tall, graceful woman, with handsome, elegant features and thoughtful eyes. Binny had left her and their small son and gone back to Ludhiana to farm. It was her second visit to Chawar Khas but the first time she was left behind without Binny. "Papa should never have come here," she told Binny before he left. "He should have stayed in Ghungrali. Or at least sent one son to try the land first. They don't get anything from these fields." It took them an all-night train trip from Ludhiana, then twelve kilometers over a rough dirt road. Binny had hired a jeep for this journey.

They did not hear of the killings in Delhi for a day. Then at noon a neighbor, Major Singh, also a Punjabi Sikh who was clearing land to farm, pedaled up on his bicycle. "Mrs. Gandhi has been shot dead!" he cried, even before he came to a stop. "By Sikhs! We are alone in this area. We fear that only." Major Singh, a big, powerful man, said he heard the news from a Hindu shopkeeper in Miranpur Katra out on the Grand Trunk Road and he had got it from the BBC. "We are happy," Major Singh declared. "The desecration of the Golden Temple is avenged. Come, make some sweets so we can eat and celebrate." When he left he warned, "Be careful. The Hindus here could turn against us."

All five of Charan's children happened to be in Chawar Khas. Besides Rani, Sukhdev had come back, quitting the Punjab police after nine years as a constable. Police posts were coming under attack by Sikh terrorists, or *khadkus* as they called themselves, and Sukhdev was afraid. Charan had built a long house, so each of his sons and his family had a separate room. Charan and Pritam Kaur had a small detached house to one side, and a lean-to of corrugated-tin sheets propped up by stripped branches served as a sleeping place for Charan, while Rani, her son and her mother shared the house. Yet everything looked makeshift, with the same feeling of jungle and isolation as in the old days in Bhadson.

At five o'clock that afternoon a Hindu schoolteacher who lived in the village came to tell Charan, "We ought to go to Delhi for Mrs. Gandhi's last rites." Charan agreed. "Be ready at six in the morning," the teacher said. Instead he came at five. "We can't go. There's mass killing in Delhi," he told Charan. "Don't leave the village now. Don't even leave your house."

Pritam Kaur said there was nothing to eat. "We have no sugar, flour or tea." Charan pedaled his bicycle into Chawar Khas, and convinced one of the Hindus to come with him as far as the Grand Trunk Road. It was a Muslim area and Charan took his sword. As they started home, a policeman stopped them. "Why are you coming here?" he demanded. "People are killing Sikhs." For three days nobody left the house, but stayed by their transistor radio. The killing of Sikhs continued, day after day, all over: Delhi, Kanpur, Patna, Varanasi, Jaipur. Eighty cities were under curfew, even Calcutta and Bombay. The only state not affected by the anti-Sikh frenzy of murder and revenge was Punjab.

Rani was shaken. "The situation is getting worse in this area," she told her mother, who was worried and told Charan, "It's given Rani a bad shock. She keeps hearing these things on the radio. Everybody talks about them. How can we keep it from her? They keep saying Sikhs are being killed, Sikh property is set on fire." About a dozen young Sikhs from five nearby farms came over. With Sukhdev, Kuldeep, Kulwant and Narinder they formed an armed band. Everybody kept a rifle or revolver ready. There were incidents now in their own district of Shahjahanpur. Then a Hindu mob burned down the house of a Sikh farmer, Kahmira Singh, a man they all knew who lived just six miles away. "His family hid in the fields," her mother told Rani. "Their Hindu neighbors and workers saved them. When you live out here it's mobs from the city you have to fear, not your village neighbors."

Rani began getting pains in her stomach. When they became more severe, Pritam Kaur told Charan, "I'm terribly afraid, but we've got to get her to a doctor." They told Kuldeep, who had grown into a tall, ruggedly handsome Sikh and the son they could most depend upon. He listened and then went into his room. When he came out they saw he had shaved and cut off his long hair. Charan was aghast. "What have you done?" he shouted at his son. "You are a Sikh! Do you want to lose your caste?" Unperturbed, Kuldeep told his father, "With the Hindus on a rampage, it's safer." He put straw in the wagon and lifted Rani up to it. Pritam Kaur cradled Rani in her arms. The trip was bumpy, and Rani was conscious but crying with pain by the time they reached the nearest doctor in Tilhar, a largely Muslim rural town. After he examined Rani, the doctor told Charan, "We cannot treat her here. You must get your daughter to the hospital in Bareilly. If you don't take her she will die."

Charan hired a car for three hundred rupees. The journey took an hour. In Bareilly, Sikh shops had been looted but nobody had been killed because the Deputy Commissioner had called in the army in time. To Charan's relief, the doctor at the hospital was a Muslim. He looked at Rani, then came out and asked them, "Do you want to save the child or the mother?" "The mother," they gasped, shocked at the question. The doctor induced childbirth with an injection and Rani's baby was born dead. After a few days a grieving Binny came to take his family home.

XX

Kuldeep worked hard at clearing and leveling the land at Chawar Khas, but he missed Punjab and never felt at home in Uttar Pradesh, where Sikhs were few. A year after the massacre, he moved back to Ghungrali with his wife and three small children. They settled into Charan's old one-room brick wellhouse until they could find something better in the village.

Dhakel was happy to have another family living nearby in the fields. Though he was poorer now, Dhakel still kept four buffaloes and three cows, and produced all the milk, cheese, eggs, grain and vegetables his family needed. In Ghungrali they might say that Dhakel was a drunkard and ne'er-do-well, but as time wore on he came not to mind. The scandal over Munshi's daughter was well in the past. If it ever came up, old Poondi would say, "In self-respect, Munshi and his sons kept it quiet. Else how could the girl find a husband? It's over now. Everybody's forgotten about it."

Dhakel still drank, but now he had a new addiction: television. He bought a set when he sold his wheat crop one year and now he watched it from his *charpoy* from the minute he opened his eyes in the morning and after chores until he closed them at night. He and his wife, Sumitra, never missed *Hum Log (We the People)*, a new soap opera. Its characters soon grew as familiar as their neighbors in Ghungrali. There was the old grandfather, Rijjak Ram, who was so upright and moral and took it so badly when his wife, Imarti Devi, died of cancer. And the drunkard father and self-effacing mother, like so many in Ghungrali. Lalloo, the oldest son, thought a big dowry would solve all his problems, and Nanhe, the younger one, forever got into scrapes. Of the three daughters, Majhli was beautiful but morally lax, Badki hardworking and Chukti studious. As Dhakel and Sumitra watched *Hum Log* day after day, the way they saw Ghungrali subtly changed, the real and the invented blurring into each other. Sometimes the pictures on the screen seemed more real than the village life outside and they would retreat into this world of flickering shadows and illusion, contented with its soothing fantasies. Maggi 2-Minute Noodles were advertised—"Fast to cook and good to eat"—and Sumitra, whose rice, *chapattis* and curries took time, found if she served noodles Dhakel was just as pleased and she could watch more TV.

Dhakel, who rented out six and a half acres of the eight belonging to him and his retarded brother Sher, just growing clover and a single acre of wheat, had time to watch seven or eight hours a day. He was not at all selective and tuned in on everything that was on—news, songs, cricket, football and hockey matches, soap operas, foreign dramas, commercials. After *Hum Log* his favorite was *Dynasty*. He worried that television created extravagant expectations in his children and he told Sumitra he knew he'd never live like Blake and Krystle Carrington or have a car. "TV is having a bad impact in Ghungrali," Dhakel would say. "It affects children also." But he didn't stop watching.

Years of homemade liquor had taken their toll. Dhakel was still in his mid-forties and while his dark brown hair was unchanged, his beard was streaked with gray and his thin face was lined. And why shouldn't he drink? he asked. "I have married off one of two daughters and have made a match for the second one. I have hardly any burdens in life. I am a grandfather. I get all the wheat, rice, vegetables and maize I need from my fields and milk and butter from my cattle. Why should I worry at all? As long as I never sell the land, I'm free to enjoy." Sumitra, who was eleven years older than Dhakel—it was an arranged marriage—showed her age even more and was turning gray.

Ghungrali itself was quieter. The troublesome holy man had been ousted, caught stealing from the temple funds. There had been some deaths. Poondi's son Sher, after years of hard work in the fields, gave it up to become a paid go-between for Harijans who had to deal with the government. He soon got fat and died of a heart attack. Dhakel heard that at his cremation Sher weighed over a hundred kilos. Old Chanan's son Kapur was also dead. After a quarrel with his wife, he poured kerosene over his head and lit a match. He ran screaming into the road, crying, "Help me! Help me!" The neighbors threw water on him when they should have tried to smother the fire. Kapur's widow was given his job as a government sweeper in Khanna. Another Mazhbi had lost both hands in a threshing machine. He was working at night and got sleepy. One hand got pulled inside by the drum's steel teeth and when he grasped it with the other, trying to pull it back, he lost both hands. Now the poor man kept alive raising pigs. On the highway one Ghungrali man was killed as he was walking along the side of the road and an overloaded truck roared up, hit a bump and fell over on him. So many people, it seemed to Dhakel, were getting killed or maimed by farm machines or on the road.

During the 1988 wheat harvest Kuldeep went back to Chawar Khas to help his brothers get the crop in. His wife, Beant, and her children did not want to go, so Charan and his wife came to Ghungrali to stay with them. On Baisaki, April 13, Charan received a telegram from Kuldeep telling him to come back at once: Sukhdev had lost his right arm in a threshing machine.

To celebrate Baisaki, Sukhdev had gone into Tilhar and joined a friend for drinks. Afterward they stopped at another friend's house for a meal and drank there too, this time *sharab*, homemade liquor. This friend mentioned he'd bought a new threshing machine but it wasn't working right. On the way home, Sukhdev saw the machine standing in a field and staggered over to take a look at it. A small boy was sitting on a bundle of wheat next to it.

"What are you doing?" Sukhdev asked him. Seeing he was drunk, the boy, afraid, said nothing. Sukhdev shrugged, started up his friend's tractor and, in a roar of exhaust, got the threshing machine going. It seemed to work all right, so he took a sheaf of grain and looked about for a stick. Seeing none, he pushed the grain in with his bare hand. At once his hand was drawn in. He couldn't pull it back. A metal knife kept slicing away, first his hand and then coming up his arm until he yanked it out just as it reached his elbow. Blood was pouring out of the stump. The child was screaming. Sukhdev fainted dead away, falling to the ground.

Sukhdev's wife, Sukhvindar, hearing the boy's screams, came running, with Kuldeep and Kulwant just behind. They tied up the arm and made a tourniquet. It took them an hour and a half to reach the Grand Trunk Road by horsecart and another hour to go by car to Bareilly. By then the arm was septic and had to be amputated up to the shoulder. Sukhdev had lost so much blood he was unconscious the whole time. They gave him blood transfusions. Kuldeep counted four bottles. But the worst was yet to come.

A year later, in 1989, one of Charan's sisters from Malaysia came home for a visit and stopped in Ghungrali to show Kuldeep and his wife, Beant, the video of her son's marriage. Kuldeep had to hire a VCR in Khanna and when the company had gone that evening he went back to return it. Dhakel's oldest son, a teenager, went with him. Afterward they joined some friends for a few beers, then climbed up on the roof of a three-wheeled Tempo scooter-taxi to go home. Just then another of Kuldeep's friends, also from Ghungrali, came by on his scooter and offered Kuldeep a ride on the pillion. Kuldeep climbed down to the road, jumped on the back of the scooter, and the two young Sikhs roared off into the night down the Grand Trunk Road. They had gone only about a mile when the scooter hit a pot-hole and Kuldeep was thrown off, right into the path of an oncoming truck. The truck, which was going very fast, did not stop but gave a jolt as a set of wheels went over Kuldeep's body, and then sped off into the darkness. A moment later a bus headed for Ghungrali from Ludhiana came by. It slowed down to pass and in its headlights the passengers could see Kuldeep lying on his back in the road. His body was untouched except for the upper abdomen where the truck tires had gone and this was crushed and flattened almost to the pavement. Traffic was stopped. Police soon came from Khanna with a photographer. He took photos of Kuldeep from all angles with a flashbulb. Kuldeep's eyes were slightly open and his lips parted to show his teeth. He had died instantly.

Dhakel was at home watching TV when some men came to tell him Kuldeep had been in a bad accident out on the Grand Trunk Road. Dhakel ran to borrow Pritam's tractor and headed for the scene. Seeing him go, Beant came to ask Sumitra, "What's happened? Is something wrong? Where is Dhakel going on the tractor? Why has Kuldeep not come home?" Sumitra said nothing, but soon Devinder came to tell Beant that Kuldeep was dead. She rushed to the hospital in Khanna but they would not let her see Kuldeep. By then they were performing an autopsy and had cut incisions across his chest and upper forehead. Dhakel, who had reached the scene before the body was taken away, had burst into weeping and had to be led to the side of the road by some children. Ajit Singh, a farmer from Ghungrali, told Dhakel that his son, Dhira, had been driving the scooter and was unhurt. He gave Dhakel two thousand rupees to hire a Maruti van to drive to Chawar Khas and bring the family back.

Charan was in Bareilly when he heard the news, so he caught the first train, stopping only at a friend's house in Ludhiana to eat, and reaching Ghungrali two hours before Dhakel arrived with the rest of the family. Kuldeep was brought home. At the last rites, his handsome young face was exposed, his head and body covered by a white shroud. Sikh tradition forbids lamentation and breast-beating. Beant, dazed with grief, her lips trembling and her eyes filled with tears, sat quietly beside her husband. In hushed voices Ghungrali's people recited in unison the familiar morning prayer from the *Granth Sahib*. The funeral pyre was lit by Kuldeep's oldest boy, a seven-year-old.

Charan was to take the ashes to the Beas River, an old Sikh custom. Beant refused to go with the family back to Chawar Khas. She said she and her children would never leave Ghungrali.

XXI

The death of Kuldeep, the one son he felt had not failed him, coming so soon after Rani's miscarriage and Sukhdev's loss of his arm, left Charan broken. He blamed himself, these events somehow in his mind tied to the move to Chawar Khas, as if they would never have happened had the family stayed in Ghungrali. From the tall, impressive-looking Jat, full of vitality and humor, Charan suddenly aged into a frail, gaunt, forgetful old man. Not only had he lost all his teeth, but his hair and beard, now pure white, grew untended. By his voice and manner one took him to be almost as old as Pritam. He was a sorry sight, but it was not this visible decline that saddened Pritam so much as what seemed the decay of his moral sense and intelligence too. It was as if Charan, his world shattered, no longer believed in the old rules he had always lived by.

For a time this decay was concealed by his piety. Charan was spending more and more time at Sikh temples and shrines, and he told Pritam, "In the Golden Temple, more than anyplace else, I feel the presence of God." There was always the hum of praying voices and the rise and fall of hymns from the *Granth*, backed by the beat of *tabla* drums. Charan liked to spend the whole day there. First he would strip to his underwear and bathe in the sacred pool, with the reflection of the Golden Temple shimmering on its surface. Then he would walk around the pool, bare feet on white marble, meditating and repeating the name of God. Halfway around he would pay some rupees for holy *prasad*, or *helwa*, and take the sweet across a marble walkway to the Harimandir, the temple's inner sanctum built out over the pool, with its blazing golden interior as its gilded, mirrored and filigreed ceilings and walls glittered in the light of ornamented lamps. Here a priest cut the sweet and gave half of the offering back to Charan to eat. Again he would sit and recite holy verses under his breath:

> . . . So when sin soils the soul
> Prayer alone shall make it whole.
> Words do not the saint or sinner make.

> Action alone is written in the book of fate.
> What we sow that alone we take . . .

Charan told Pritam how the Akal Takht had been completely re-built, with all its marble pillars, filigree and mirrorwork painstakingly replaced, just as the Harimandir had been restored to its original state. All the old houses around the temple complex had been demolished to make way for a new garden—and to make the temple less defensible. For the terrorist struggle was not over. The death toll, far from ceasing after the attack on the Golden Temple and Mrs. Gandhi's assassination in 1984, kept rising, four thousand five hundred dead in 1990, six thousand in 1991, maybe more than twenty thousand Punjabis, Sikhs and Hindus killed since the two policemen were shot in Dheru village near Ghungrali in 1980. There were said to be at least a hundred different armed terrorist bands in Punjab in 1992, all claiming that their aim was an independent Sikh state of Khalistan. Every day saw twenty to thirty people shot, stabbed, blown up or otherwise killed somewhere in Punjab, though Ludhiana and the villages around it like Ghungrali were the worst hit.

Charan was among those who claimed that Bhindranwale was still alive. "All those who are committing this terrorism must have some big leader behind them," he reasoned to Pritam. "Maybe it is Bhindranwale." Had not, Charan argued, the police surrounded the town of Moga that time when it was rumored Bhindranwale was coming there? And had not armed Sikhs once more occupied the Golden Temple in 1988 and shot a senior police officer to shouts of *"Khalistan zindabad!* Long live Khalistan!" until Rajiv Gandhi's forces starved them out?

"Bhindranwale was right," Charan would say with a hoarse sigh. "He said Sikhs were slaves of Hindus." To Pritam, part of Charan's decline was the way he did not seem sure of what was true and what was false. As time wore on, his descriptions of the three times he had seen Bhindranwale in person had become more and more fanciful: "He looked like Guru Govind Singh and his face was so bright you could not look him directly in the eyes. When you spoke to him, you had to look down. Always he came with his bodyguards, ten men with rifles. Always he made very fiery speeches, saying you should carry a sword with you, carry guns with you, drink the *amrit* and be baptized, and respect women on pain of death."

Pritam would listen for a while and then say firmly, "Bhindranwale is dead."

But Charan just went on, uninterested in hearing something sensible. "If Bhindranwale is dead, why do they still come and search villages for him? The other day over a thousand people came to Khadoorwar village near Amritsar to hear him. And a huge number of police came to mount a search for him. The soldiers say they killed Bhindranwale. Why don't the police believe them?"

In Pritam's view, many, even most, of the terrorists in Punjab were unemployed college-educated youth, frustrated sons, like Kulwant, of Jat farmers. Punjab's green revolution went on—wheat yields had gone up every year since 1975 as ever more dwarfed varieties came in. But the margin of profit was down, the size of holdings was down and the aspirations of these young Sikhs, partly driven by the television in the villages now, were way up. A few of them made their way to America, England or Canada by hook or crook and Punjabi taxi drivers became not uncommon in cities such as New York and London. When all else failed at home, a gun offered a way out. K. P. S. Gill, a Jat who served twice as Punjab's police chief and was long at the top of the terrorists' hit list, said the young rebels had "love of a good gun, a good faith, and abhorrence of surrender." Pritam thought this to be true of most *khadkus*. He hoped the worst atrocities, like the mass shootings of migrant Hindu workers or random firing into crowded city markets, were not done by real Sikhs at all. There were rumors these might be the work of Pakistani commando squads who came across the frontier disguised in beards and turbans to stir up Hindu-Sikh enmity.

"Who is to tell who is who?" Pritam would ask. What characterized much *khadku* behavior was a fanatic enforcement—with guns—of what they felt Sikh social conduct should be. This was inspired by Bhindranwale's preaching, and cassettes of his speeches were widely circulated in the villages. As self-appointed guardians of Sikh morality, the *khadkus* forbade opium, alcohol and tobacco and things like cheating on exams. They discouraged the extraction of dowries from the parents of brides, which went down well with hard-pressed fathers. In some villages, the *khadkus* even dispensed justice, settled land disputes, gave orders to civil servants and levied income taxes. Generally their activities were more criminal: they got money by robbing banks and extorting protection money from merchants, Hindu and Sikh alike.

They were quick on the trigger. After they called for a ban on radio broadcasts in the Hindi language in Punjab, they shot dead the state director of All India Radio. Hindi broadcasts promptly stopped. When the *khadkus* said all government work in the state should be conducted in Punjabi, not in English, frightened civil servants made the switch at once. Journalists were told not to translate *khadku* as "terrorist," but as "militant," "freedom fighter" or "mujahideen." Punjabi newspapers fell in line as more than two dozen journalists were killed, one of them beheaded. Jeans, skirts and saris were banned; young women were to wear the long shirt and baggy pants of the traditional *salwar kameez*. Work on digging a canal to take water from Punjab to neighboring Haryana ended after two engineers on the project were killed. The Sikhs had genuine grievances. Three Congress Party leaders everybody knew led mobs to kill Sikhs in the 1984 Delhi massacre —H. K. L. Bhagat, Sajjan Kumar and Jagdish Tytler, all of them members of Parliament at one time and two of them former cabinet ministers—had never been tried. Nor had any official investigation ever been made of the massacre itself.

Both police and *khadkus* had an interest in keeping their shooting war going. Jeeps full of stern-faced Sikh policeman manning machine guns roared by in clouds of dust, as everybody else scrambled to get out of the way. The *khadkus* scared people out of money, but so did the police, grabbing innocent villagers and then charging them to get released. Both sides profited.

Few in Ghungrali had ever seen a *khadku*. In Chawar Khas four of them once came to Charan's house to tell his sons if the Hindus ever gave them any trouble to let them know. Once, when Charan stayed overnight in Ghungrali, he was awoken about one o'clock at night by five shots. The farmer he was staying with hurried to turn out a light in his courtyard and make sure the gate was bolted. "Shooting like that is a warning," he told Charan. "They may or may not come back. Don't speak of this. Everybody in Ghungrali has heard those shots. But no one must speak of it. That would only bring trouble."

When the mother of a friend died, Devinder went in a truck with him to another village to notify her friends and relatives. They found the village dark. Nobody would open their gates. Devinder told his father, "All the villagers were thinking we were *khadkus*. I was afraid they'd fire at us from the houses. That is the situation in the villages now."

At last, in the dead of night, the *khadkus* came to Ghungrali. No one but a new priest at the temple saw their faces. They spoke over the loudspeaker and went away. They told the villagers to observe the birthdays of all the gurus and said that both the Jat and Harijan *gurdwaras* were good. Everyone knew the *Granth* condemned the caste system. They recited a hymn:

> There are ignoble among the noblest
> And pure among the despised.
> The former shalt thou avoid,
> And be dust under the foot of the other.

One of the *khadkus*, who sounded very young, declared, "No dowry," saying, "If a man has given his daughter, he has given everything." This went down well with Dhakel when Pritam told him about it the next day in the fields. Dhakel's daughter, a pretty, pale young thing gave a loud wail. She was about to be married and protested, "If you don't give me a trunk, Bapuji, how can I store my clothes?"

"Oh, if you only knew how it used to be," her mother told her. "If a groom felt his father-in-law gave too small a dowry, losing him respect in his village, he might leave his bride. Now the *khadkus* make him stay with her his whole life." Sumitra quite approved of them.

The wedding took place one day at sunrise a few weeks later. Dhakel had rented and put up a red *shamiana*, or canvas tent, just beside his house in the fields. The wedding party, or *barat*, of the bridegroom and his friends from Khanna, which would have come by horseback not many years ago, arrived in a Maruti van. Hymns were sung and the bride and groom were asked to sit in front of a copy of the *Granth* as a Sikh priest told them the obligations of married life. The bride, who wore a red *salwar kameez* embroidered in gold and a good deal of gold bangles and jewelry, looked dazzled; she kept her eyes shyly downcast, without so much as a sidelong glance at the groom. He was a handsome young Sikh in a brown suit and tie, a red bejeweled turban and a garland of marigolds, who carried a long gold-sheathed ceremonial sword. After Dhakel's daughter followed him around the *Granth* four times, each of them holding the end of a scarf, the priest pronounced them man and wife. The ceremony over, Dhakel, red-faced and weaving, staggered up and congratulated them in a very loud voice. Everybody saw he was drunk. He had been hitting the bottle since early morning.

A feast was served and despite the *khadkus'* prohibition of a dowry, a tractor and wagon followed the Maruti van back to Khanna and

Dhakel's daughter went off to her new home at noon with a TV set, a dining table and chairs, a double bed, five sets of bedding, twenty-five *salwar kameezes* and all the gold jewelry she was wearing. It was a small wedding partly, just six people in all. The local *khadkus* had decreed there could be no more than eleven.

No sooner had the wedding party gone than another Maruti van pulled up on the paved road. Four Sikhs got out. Three of them began walking toward Dhakel's well. Pritam and some other guests had already left but many were still sitting about the string cots, eating and talking. There were Sukhdev and Kulwant and their wives, Beant and her children, one of Pritam's married grandsons who taught in Khanna, Dhakel's mother from Delhi with her daughter and son-in-law, the slow-witted Sher, Charan's wife, Pritam Kaur, and Dhakel's two sons and two married sisters and their husbands. It was still quite a crowd.

The party had been about to break up and Charan was at Dhakel's well to wash some clothes as the three strangers approached. They had untied, loose-hanging beards and blue, green and gray turbans tied in the old tiered way. Two looked to be in their early twenties, the third in his thirties. All three wore bandoliers and the oldest carried an AK-47 while the other two had revolvers: *khadkus*.

The older one greeted Charan. "*Sat Sri Akal*, Bapuji!" He looked about. "Who is Dhakel?"

Hearing his name, Dhakel came from the well. He had taken a bath and had dressed but had not yet put on his turban and his mop of tangled wet brown hair gave him a drunken, rakish look. "*Sat Sri Akal*," he greeted the strangers, guessing what they were.

They did not return his greeting. "Why, Bapuji, have you been drinking?" the older man demanded harshly.

Dhakel, who feared what they might do, looked frightened. He managed to sputter, "Son, I have been drinking as there is a party at my house. To celebrate my daughter's marriage." He gave the man an imploring look, blinking unhappily. "But I won't drink again."

"No, don't drink again in the future. If you do we will come back and kill you."

Dhakel turned pale and tried to speak, but nothing came out. He strained his throat and croaked hoarsely, "I won't drink now. I swear it."

The *khadku*, noticing Charan's white pious man's getup, hailed him, "*Bapu, Sat Sri Akal! Satnaam, Wah Guru ka Khalsa! Wah Guruji ki*

Fateh! The True Name, the Wondrous Guru of the Pure! Victory be to God! The Sikhs will rule!" Charan managed to mumble the appropriate responses and the three men left down the lane. Nobody said a word until they reached their van and drove off. Then all the wedding guests began talking at once.

"If they killed everybody who drinks, they'd have to kill all the people in Punjab," scoffed Sukhdev, who was himself a little drunk.

"Are you shivering, Dhakel?" asked Devinder.

Dhakel grinned with relief and embarrassment. "I was feeling a little scared."

Kulwant recognized one of the gunmen, who had been in his class in college in Khanna.

"How did they know Dhakel was drinking?" somebody asked.

"They have their information."

"They've got their informers in the villages."

"No," Dhakel interrupted, getting control of himself. "My oldest son and I had a fight. Maybe he talked in Khanna about his father drinking too much. I'll bet a *khadku* overheard him."

"Their faces were reddish," said Charan. "They were very thin but strong-looking. Bhindranwale's followers have an office in Samrala. That's only six, seven miles from Khanna."

"Nobody makes liquor from sugarcane anymore," said Devinder, who was enjoying the excitement. "They're afraid the *khadkus* will find out about it."

"If not the *khadkus*, the police."

"The *khadkus* have frightened off so many wineshops on the Grand Trunk Road. They killed the owner of a wineshop in Dheru."

"Oh, the wineshops close but they reopen soon enough if there's money to be made."

"I heard," said Dhakel, "that if the *khadkus* catch you making liquor, they pour out all the bottles into a bucket and push your head into it."

For three weeks Dhakel kept his word that he would never touch another drop. The whole time he was tormented by thirst. At last he took a little wine. Right away it bolstered his courage. *"Koi bat nahi,* never mind," he shrugged. "If your life is going to be short you might as well enjoy it." And he took a huge swig. And then another.

XXII

Even with all the terrorism, it was go, go, go in Punjab. Agriculture and small industry boomed. Sikhs pursued the good life. Village sports meets became very popular, as if relief was found in soccer and track and field events. Even old Indian games like *kabaddi* were revived, and tugs-of-war. Ghungrali held its first bullock-cart race in twenty years.

The Sarpanch, who soon went off to run a pizza parlor in Toronto, in 1986 at last convinced the Jats to distribute some of Ghungrali's communal land to the Harijans. Eight acres were divided among 182 Harijan families; each was given a plot. Basant Singh went to court to stop this and lost. Fifty-five families built new houses. The rest stayed up in the old Harijan quarter of Ghungrali and used the land to grow fodder and vegetables. In a trade-off, the Harijans agreed the Jats could take another eight acres for a sports stadium. A Singh Sports Association was formed, and Devinder, now thirty-nine, was elected as its president. The sports area, two soccer fields with a brick grandstand in between, was named the Guru Hargobind Sports Complex after the sixth Guru. Somebody had the idea that he had visited Ghungrali three hundred years ago. Devinder, one of those cheerful optimists who never seem to make a go of anything, having by now failed at a knitting mill, dairy and truck farm for ladyfingers, ran the sports association well until one day forty thousand rupees turned up missing. He was voted out, but still he always had a place at the judges' stand at meets, nattily dressed in suit and tie, with an in-charge look.

Pritam brought three of his great-grandsons to see the tug-of war, which he found in sad decline. "These young men get tired in five minutes," he told the boys. "Dadaji," the youngest addressed him, tugging at his shirt, so Pritam had to bend way down, "I don't want to go to school."

"You have to go." Pritam smiled at the child with affection.

"But I have to sit there a long time. I like to go around with you." The tug-of-war began, with two teams of big, muscular Sikhs straining to wrest the rope from the other side. "In the old days we had to pull all the men over the line," Pritam told the children. "Sometimes it took an hour. These young men today, they're not wrestling, they're not doing yoga, they're out drinking and carousing. We used to cry, 'Show your strength, men! Show your power!' Now in five minutes they finish the game. What can they shout now? Oh, how we would cry, 'Give your full power, men! *Jor Lagho Subhash! Jo Bole So Nihal!* He who speaks is full of the name of God!' Nowadays you see the first few being pulled across the line only. Well, children, in our time we worked hard in the fields. These young men, they can hardly cut fodder now. They hire workers to cut it for them." The children were proud of their great-grandfather, so tall and fit at ninety-four.

After the tug-of-war he took the boys to watch some of the field events. They saw a great big man lie down in the grass and let a tractor run over his stomach. Another man pulled a tractor forward with a rope he held in his clenched teeth. When they went to watch a muscular-looking girl toss the shot put, the little boys said nobody would want to marry her. Pritam smiled. "That husband must also be very strong."

When it was time for the bullock-cart race, a crowd of men and boys lined the route, a dirt road north of the stadium. The racecourse was just seven acres long, not eleven acres as in the last bullock-cart race all those years before. Then it was held in April. But now it was January, when the days are crisp and sunny in Punjab but the nights are cold and everything is still green. Tall eucalyptus trees, planted all over Punjab in the 1980s, lined the country roads, like poplars in Europe. Fields of bright green wheat and clover were broken by yellow patches of mustard and marigolds, and sunflowers grew on the edges. Everything was very green.

"Clear the way!" an announcer shouted over a loudspeaker. "The first is coming now! Oh, come with pomp and show!" With a blood-curdling shriek from the driver to spur his bullocks on, a pounding of hooves and clouds of dust, the first cart hurtled past them. "Rape your mother!" the driver cried to his bullocks. "Run fast! Oh, may you die! I'll put you in the fire!" The horns of the bullocks were decorated with bits of bright orange and green cloth and flowers, and as they came at full speed the drivers would lean far forward to throw their weight over the tongues of the wooden carts. All howled at their bullocks like men possessed. "If they go like that," Pritam explained to the children, "the bullocks must go together, not one to one side and the other to the other side." As the races went on, one cart tipped over and two more went into wheat fields. The drivers were thrown to the ground but were unhurt as their bullocks just kept going, dragging the empty carts behind them.

Pritam was enjoying himself. He kept a firm hold on the hands of the two smallest boys to make sure they stayed well back from the track. In a roar of shrieks and pounding hooves, another cart hurtled by. All the time the voice kept shouting over the loudspeaker. "Bring that red flag up, just watch the red flag. Now it's number twelve, Ajit Singh of Majari. Look how the bullocks come. Like air. Look with your full eyes wide open but clear the way . . . Slow! These bullocks are running seven acres. Now, Sardar sahib, take the red flag up. Our starter today is an old army officer and he knows how. He can kill a battalion with just one flag. *Shabash! Shab-a-a-a-ash!* Kaptaan Singh of Isru is coming. He's running like a railway train. Look at that man over there. He's making mischief. Oh, black-turbaned man, don't make mischief. *Shabash.* We have two stopwatches here. Look at your watches, judges. It all depends on what you feed your bullocks, friends. Ghee and good grains. Spend good money on your bullocks and you'll get good results and honor too . . ."

"Oh, that one was not too good," Pritam said. "He used the pins too much. The one before was better. The bullocks picked up their stamina and ran. You only enjoy the bullocks running when they're brave. Now keep watching, boys. See how much time they take. But where are the young men from our village?"

". . . The carts are coming at full speed. Watch with pleasure and wide eyes, but clear the way. They're coming again. *Shabash, shaba-a-a-ash!* Now the red flag will go up, the white flag will go down and they'll start running. Watch out for the flag. Mohinder Singh's cart is flying. How he runs! *Shabash, shaba-a-a-ash!* Oh, brethren clear the way!" A man from another village had the victorious speed of 37.4 seconds. He won ten thousand rupees, donated by a Ghungrali Sikh who worked in Germany. Pritam told the children he had just sold two old bullocks and would buy two bullock calves. "Maybe you can race them someday." At the stadium, as they headed home, a woman was singing, in a humorous, bantering way, "Don't speak to me like that. I'll go home to my parents . . ." Some girls were dancing. "If we get a drunk for a husband, what can we do?" the dancers sang merrily, beating on tambourines. "If we get a husband who beats us, what can we do?"

XXIII

Charan kept up his wanderings. "He is roaming around the country," old Banta, the Mazhbi, told Pritam one day. "For a long time he doesn't go to his village. Sometimes he shows up at the Golden Temple and sometimes at the temple in Bija. A very bad thing, he didn't go to his son Narinder's marriage." Pritam had first been dismayed by Charan's behavior when, on his way to Ghungrali when Kuldeep died, he stopped at a friend's house in Ludhiana for a meal. When Narinder married a Sikh girl from Tilhar in 1991, Rani and Binny and their children came from Ludhiana and all the bride's relatives came from Punjab, but Charan was missing. Charan's story was that he went to Ludhiana to buy clothes for the wedding, as was customary for the groom's father to do, fell ill and was unable to reach Chawar Khas in time. In truth, as he confided to Pritam, he deliberately stayed away fearing his sons would get drunk and abusive.

Charan no longer made any attempt to conceal his opium addiction from Pritam. He carried the small bottle of brownish liquid with him everywhere, became shaky and sick without a spoonful now and then and lamented he couldn't do without it. The more his addiction to opium grew, the more he stayed away from his family. "My children don't listen to me," he complained to Pritam in a whining voice, wringing his hands. "They show me no respect. I don't like to stay long at Chawar Khas. I get relief by traveling and going to the temples. I want to go to heaven. I listened to my father, but my children don't listen to me. Sukhdev treats me very badly, and Kulwant is not much better." Sukhdev, unable to do much work since he lost his right arm, was drinking heavily and he and Charan often quarreled and said disagreeable things to one another. One day coming from Tilhar, Sukhdev had been irritated, and he pulled Charan's beard in anger and poked a finger in his eye so that it was bloodshot for days. After this, Charan went about solemn and dignified, as if wishing his family to understand that for him religion was the supreme interest in life. But he was unable to keep this up all the time; his spirits fell, and he consumed more and more opium. Kulwant and Narinder, forced to knuckle down and work hard just to survive, had become tall, gaunt, taciturn men with faces lined beyond their years. To avoid quarrels, the family had "three fires." Kulwant and Sukhdev and their families lived apart, Narinder and his young bride with Charan and Pritam Kaur.

Sometimes Kulwant and Narinder too felt bitterness and vexation toward Charan for bringing them to such a harsh place and they went to their father and spoke to him cruelly. The fact that his sons cursed him, and wished him ill, caused Charan pain. And so he traveled, usually carrying no luggage, just a cloth bag over his shoulder containing oil, soap, a change of linen, a blanket, a comb, a brush and a pair of sandals. He rose early each day to wash his white garments so they could dry in the hot Indian sun before he dressed. From his white scarf to his leather shoes, Charan's clothes were expensive, and for the first time in his life, he was fastidious in his dress. As a pilgrim he discovered Baru Sahib, a remote Sikh ashram in the Himalayan foothills, where the tenth Guru, Govind Singh, had gone to pray. A former leader, Sant Teja Singh, who had a master's degree from Harvard, believed in combining Sikh spiritual teaching with modern Western science and the ashram ran a boarding school for five hundred students with English as the language of instruction. Many Sikh temples and pools were built by men and women volunteers in what Sikhs call *kaar sewa*, free labor. At Baru Sahib, Charan, who had done no physical labor for years, joined in, carrying wicker baskets of wet cement on his head with the other volunteers and chanting the whole time, *"Satnaam, Wah Guru!* The True Name, the Wondrous Guru!" "As my body allows, I will carry," Charan told himself, and though he looked like a toothless old septuagenarian with his loose-hanging white beard, it somehow agreed with him. Once, when one of his sisters came from Malaysia to visit two sons at medical school in South India, Charan and Pritam Kaur, though uninvited, made a fifty-eight-hour train and bus journey to see her. One of the students told Charan, "If I get married, you can visit us in Kuala Lumpur. But you must give up opium. If they find any on you, you can be hanged for it." Pritam Kaur, who had hardly ever traveled before, told Rani when they got home, "The train went so close, I was afraid it might fall into the sea." Once, at a station, a young tea vendor ran off with Charan's good shoes, and he had to wear a pair of sandals he was taking back for Narinder. Usually Charan traveled alone, often to Baru Sahib and even beyond, to where the Himalayas rose vast and majestic. Sometimes his eyes would search this horizon as if he feared to see some unknown power which had brought so much ruin in his own life and the lives of his children. The last years had passed so bleakly and barrenly.

XXIV

Ten o'clock in the morning, the day our story began. It was late February 1992 and warming up, but the countryside was still green. Charan was back in Ghungrali, and after leaving Pritam and the men making sugar, he headed across the fields toward his old wellhouse. As he neared it, he could see the figure of Beant, Kuldeep's widow, standing in the doorway and holding her back with both hands, following him with her eyes. She stood for a long time without moving, then as he got closer, she looked about with indifference and scorn, and went inside. To Charan this was an intentional insult by his daughter-in-law. Disturbed and upset by the slight, he went on to Dhakel's well.

"*Veerji*, brother!" Dhakel hailed him warmly. He was cutting fodder and came out of the clover to shake Charan's hand. "*Sat Sri Akal!* How is everybody in UP? How are your children? How are you pulling on?"

Charan answered in the same jocular tone. "Are you drinking? More or less?" He gave a hoarse laugh, thinking of the *khadkus* that day. "Are you drinking less, Dhakel?"

Dhakel gave him a big grin. "Not yet. But I'll give it up this year." He pulled a *charpoy* into the shade of his neem trees and they sat down.

Charan shook his head and looked sanctimonious. "Being a religious man, I preach against drinking." Dhakel laughed this time. "I don't want to listen," he said, throwing up his hands. "You know I never go to the temple anymore."

Charan became sober. He told Dhakel he had come to Ghungrali the previous day to sell three of his remaining five acres. The buyer was Ajit Singh, the father of the youth who was driving the motor scooter when Kuldeep was killed. He had collected a hundred and forty thousand rupees from him and would get three hundred and ten thousand more after the April wheat harvest. Dhakel at once wondered how Beant would react. She was farming Charan's last five acres in Ghungrali with the help of her five brothers. One of them, Amrick, stayed with Beant and the children at the wellhouse. Their parents were fairly poor for Punjabi Jats, owning a small ten-acre farm in

Tundha village, twenty-five miles from Ghungrali. Two of her brothers owned a combine and made their living going about with ten Bihari laborers from March until May, harvesting on contract. The brothers, Dhakel knew, would be furious with Charan.

Charan had repeatedly asked Beant to bring the children and come to live in Chawar Khas, but she steadfastly refused. Soon after Kuldeep's death, he had even proposed that she marry Narinder, who was then twenty-seven, just a year younger than she was. "That way," Charan argued, "you'll have two acres here in Ghungrali and fourteen in Chawar Khas."

"Only if you put the sixteen acres in my name," she told him.

"That we cannot do."

Beant was sterile. After her third child, she and Kuldeep decided she should undergo a tubal ligation. She could have no more children, which meant she was almost certain never to remarry. If she did, under Punjabi law, she would lose both children and any claim to Kuldeep's land.

"You see how she's treating me," Charan protested to Dhakel. "She didn't even greet me." The relationship was complicated by Sukhdev's marriage to Beant's sister, Sukhvindar, whom he treated badly. Charan told Dhakel he could do nothing now with Sukhdev and was afraid of him. Lately, since losing his arm, Sukhdev was spending more and more of his time at Chawar Khas at the hut in a guava orchard of Sant Mani Baba, a neighbor who let his hair grow long and claimed to be a Hindu *sadhu*, or holy man. Now the two of them sat on a mat in front of the hut with a water pipe and smoked *ganja*, hashish, all the day. Sukhdev's son, Manjindar, a bright, handsome boy almost twelve, was afraid of his father too and slept at night beside Charan or his wife, especially since Sukhdev had come home in a stupor one night and tried to set Sukhvindar's bed on fire.

When Rani learned what Charan had done she was very upset. "Beant cannot survive on two acres," she told Binny. Her eyes welled up with tears. "After Kuldeep's death, our family fell apart. If Kuldeep were alive, Papa would never sell any more land in Ghungrali."

"Charan has only sold the shares of Kulwant, Sukhdev and Narinder," Binny reminded her. As heirs, the shares were rightfully theirs in Punjabi law.

"Yes," Rani agreed, thinking how hard a widow's lot could be. "And they weren't getting anything from Beant's harvests. But what is Sukhdev giving her for the six acres Kuldeep left in Chawar Khas?" In fact, this land was lying idle and she got nothing from it. Narinder farmed twelve acres, six of his own and three each for Charan and Pritam Kaur. Kulwant farmed nineteen acres, a good-sized farm; besides the six acres from Charan he bought three acres on his own and rented ten more. Like Pritam, Rani was not impressed by Charan's ostentatious piety. "He should care for his grandchildren first. When they are settled, it will be time to pray to God. How Beant is surviving, God knows. She has nothing. The children are dirty and in rags. It is a great shame for Papa." Rani wrote to her father and pleaded with him to at least give Beant's children legal title to the two acres that were left.

It may have been his intention. After he received Rani's letter, Charan went back to Ghungrali and headed directly to the fields. This time, as he approached the wellhouse, Beant came outside but did not greet him and instead sprang toward him with clenched fists. "Why have you come here?" she shrieked. "Give us money! Are you happy to see us in such a state!" She went on hysterically, her voice rising to a piercing scream. "I want your beard to catch fire! Don't think I am alone in the world! My brothers will kill you!" She went into an ungovernable rage, and flew at him like a thing possessed.

As Charan backed away, Amrick, a thin, bony-faced man in a soiled turban, came out of the wellhouse, followed by Beant's frightened children. "We are five brothers," he cursed Charan. "If one of us dies in Beant's cause, we won't bother. We'll rape your granddaughters." The two of them denounced Charan so loudly, Dhakel's wife, Sumitra, heard them from her house and rushed over to see what was going on. By then Charan was striding away across the fields, as if the furies of hell were after him. Sumitra found Beant on a *charpoy*, sobbing uncontrollably. "If Charan had stayed five minutes more," she cried to Sumitra, gasping for breath, "we would have taken him by his beard and pulled him down."

Pritam, who also heard the shouting, came to see what was wrong. Seeing him, Beant, her wet face twisted in fury, again began cursing Charan. "Either I will die or I will kill Charan," she cried like a madwoman. "He must give title of this land to my children!"

Shocked and distressed, Pritam tried to calm her. "No, no, we will press Charan to do it. We'll take him to the *patwari* in Bija and get him to sign the papers. It makes me weep to see the condition of this family. Don't worry. We won't let Charan leave the village. Charan's wife must press him too. And she should come and visit you. How can you live without land?"

"We don't want that land in Chawar Khas," Beant sobbed. "I'll never take my children back to that jungle." She could hardly speak. "We want this land only."

Dhakel joined them and Pritam told him, "I have two sons. My younger son looks after me and pays me too much respect and I live with him. My older son drinks and doesn't like me. But I gave them each half my land. It is Charan's duty to help these children." The two little boys and the little girl, who had come out of the wellhouse, looked about to cry too, and they looked at their hysterical mother with wide, frightened eyes.

"Even if my children die," Beant gasped, "I won't leave this land." Just then another of Beant's brothers arrived, pulling up to the wellhouse on a motorcycle, his wife riding on the pillion. They had just been at a wedding, they said, and Sukhvindar and Sukhdev were there too. This brother, who wore a suit and was calmer than Amrick, greeted Pritam and Dhakel and told them, "These are the children of Kuldeep. They need money to survive."

"Until he gives us title, we can't believe what Charan says," said Beant, growing calmer herself.

Pritam nodded. "Otherwise it's just talk, talk, talk."

"Rani also pleaded with him," Beant said. After some time Sukhvindar approached through the fields. She said Sukhdev had stayed behind and was getting drunk, so she had come ahead. "Kulwant and Narinder are working very hard in Chawar Khas," she told Pritam. "It is a miserable place. It will take years to make that farm pay. I have so little money I sent my daughter home to my parents so she could go to school. Manjindar must bicycle all the way to Miranpur Katra, an hour's trip each way. It's the nearest school." Sukhvindar was a plain, homely woman like Beant, but she seemed to have a more agreeable nature. "If Kuldeep were alive, Charan would not have sold those three acres," she went on. "Now, whatever he does, he must not sell the last two. If Charan's wife would come here and stay for some days, she'd win more respect. She must get him to transfer the land. Everybody says this land must go to his grandchildren and no one else."

She was right. Why was Charan behaving this way? "It's the opium," Pritam said wearily. "Charan doesn't know his own mind anymore."

"He must give power of attorney to Beant until the children are twenty-one," Sukhvindar continued. "They are of the same blood as Charan. Kuldeep was his son."

"The whole village must catch hold of Charan and force him to transfer this land," Pritam told her. He sat there, buried in thought. "Kuldeep was working very hard. He paid respect to everyone. What a great tragedy that he died. This family would have stayed together. Now it is falling apart."

Beant started sobbing again. "I lost my husband to drink." She pulled herself together and sat up, her voice resolute. "Charan is just making excuses. He must give us title and end relations with us."

Pritam nodded, still thoughtful. "Charan has become very pious. But the truly good never take opium."

Sukhvindar told him about the *sadhu* in Chawar Khas. "I tell Sukhdev not to smoke *ganja* or drink. But he won't stop." She sounded resigned to her husband's self-destruction. Maybe she welcomed it as a relief to get away. As he headed back to his well, Pritam was hailed by Dhakel's wife, who asked him to come and take tea. Over tea, Pritam speculated how Sadhu Singh might have handled things. "I remember one time Sadhu went to Surjit Kaur to help her sell her wheat crop. 'No, no,' she told him. 'Go home. We'll sell it ourselves.'" Pritam smiled, amused by the memory. "You never knew but that Sahdu might sell you too."

Sumitra laughed and refilled his glass with milky sweet tea. With a glance toward Beant, who was still sitting outside the wellhouse, she told Pritam in an undertone, "I heard her and that brother of hers cursing Charan and calling him a lot of bad names. That's when he ran off. I say if somebody asks to take something from someone, they'd better be polite."

"Yes. One must be polite."

"She doesn't let her children come over here. Oh, Pritamji, I'm praising you that you're sitting peacefully in your house getting good respect from your family. I told Beant Kaur not to call Charan bad names. She should talk politely. And ask her brother to speak properly to Charan." She narrowed her eyes. "I advise her, but she doesn't like to take advice. Charan sold that land to Ajit Singh, whose son drove the scooter that Kuldeep was riding on when he was killed. Now Beant is cursing Ajit Singh's family also. One of them came and told me, 'Tell her if she and her brothers are giving us bad names, we will kill somebody.'"

That night Sukhdev came back drunk, having stopped after the wedding for more liquor at the same Ajit Singh's house. He at once provoked Beant's suspicions that they were conspiring to get their hands on her two acres too. He told her, "Only when Bapu gives us title to our land in Chawar Khas will I agree to give these children title here." Beant flew into another rage and told her sister, loud enough for Sukhdev to hear, "Tell your husband if I don't get title to this land I will kill myself and my children. Our blood will be on his hands!" The family's ruin seemed complete.

XXV

One day a great branch of Ghungrali's old banyan tree broke off and crashed down. The noise could be heard all over the village. When several more branches rotted away and fell, what was left was a dreadful sight. Only a few large branches still had leaves on them. Vultures came and perched on them, as if waiting for them to die and fall too. Pritam and Basant Singh went to look at it. Village boys were playing games in the fallen banyan branches. Many other branches, old, enormous and gnarled, were half suspended in the air, still sprouting green leaves. Pritam told the boys not to play there. The rest of the tree could go at any time.

"There's too much water in the roots," Basant Singh declared. "Never mind. We have so many eucalyptus trees now. We like the look of them. It's good for cultivation. They dry up water quickly. We can use them to build houses and as firewood."

Everybody speculated about why the banyan tree was dying. It was such a disagreeable spectacle. The pond itself was now covered with green scum, and the tree beside it, just as you entered Ghungrali, was the very picture of dissolution and decay. Especially now that so many black vultures had come to sit in the last surviving branches or to wheel and circle in the sky. Some said the roots had drowned, flooded by so much irrigation in Punjab the past twenty years. Others argued just the opposite, that the groundwater level was falling, drying the roots out. These said there was so much overpumping in Punjab, it faced a return to the near-desert it had once been. Pritam could well remember how it all looked when they had come from Pakistan, sand dunes drifting over the Grand Trunk Road and hardly any traffic on it. Just about the only local crop was a little groundnut. The little fodder and grain that grew were cut by squatting men with sickles. Camels turned waterwheels. The commonest tree was the sparse acacia. You never heard a tractor then. Just the creak of bullock-cart wheels or the caws of crows or the gentle popping sound of the village flour mill.

In those days the banyan tree was huge and splendid with large green oval leaves, reddish fruit and all the roots that dropped from overhead branches to form new twisted trunks. To Pritam, the dying tree was an ill omen. Pritam, at his great age, was reconciled to his own fate. It was Ghungrali and its younger generations that concerned him. When he confided his feelings about the tree to Dhakel, the younger man grinned and told him, "It's just old age, Pritamji. The roots are coming out of the earth. Vultures come and sit in what's left of the branches. And vulture droppings kill a tree. Vultures never sit in a small tree. No, it was great and it's dying and vultures go for dead things."

"I don't know, son," Pritam told Dhakel, "it may be a sign. To me the old years in Pakistan were best. When we shifted here we had to work very hard and it was getting to be a good life again. Then came the boycott in 1970, and in the last two or three years this terrorism has ruined everything. First people grew apart and now they grow afraid. They no longer love each other. How can they love God? Back when we were young in Lyallpur, there was more love among men. After the harvest, if one farmer was still left cutting, everybody went to help him without thought of reward. If people were poor we shared what we had with them. Law and order were very good. If someone took too much water for irrigation, they fined him and took him to jail."

Dhakel did not know. Ghungrali was all the life he had ever had. "Surely not everything was better, Pritamji." No, he hadn't meant that, Pritam said. "In the old days my family only had two books in the whole house, and one was the *Guru Granth Sahib*. Now, as you see, Dhakel, our house is full of books, especially from my grandson, the teacher."

"Now we have TV."

Pritam knew how much Dhakel watched it. "I never look at it," he told him. Then, not wanting to hurt Dhakel's feelings, he hastened to say, "I want to save my eyesight." In truth, Pritam disliked the way television disrupted family life. "At home when I was young," he said, "our whole family ate together. Now it is different. They don't wait for each other." Dhakel had a solution for that: "In our house we all eat in front of the TV."

It was Dhakel who told Pritam that Surjit, Charan's sister, had suffered a stroke. He heard she could walk and talk a little. Pritam left for Bhadson at once, though his family objected. With eight grandchildren and twenty-odd great-grandchildren the house was full of boys and girls who doted on him. They did not like him to go away, worried about him the whole time he was gone and rejoiced when he came home. Even at his age, Pritam liked to go off by himself sometimes, independent and free-spirited as he was.

It was not a long bus journey, less than an hour. Pritam found that Bhadson had greatly prospered. Its farmhouses, often imposing brick structures with two stories, were set freestanding in the fields. As in Ghungrali, the fields were green with wheat and clover and yellow with patches of mustard. Here too eucalyptus trees lined the roads. The Punjabi landscape, once so drab, had become scenic.

He found Surjit sitting outdoors on a cot in the shade of a neem tree, a white wool shawl wrapped around her shoulders. Like Charan's, her hair had gone completely white and she too looked gaunt, her face slightly twisted from the stroke. When she saw Pritam, she burst into tears. Pritam embraced her and sat down beside her, putting an arm protectively around her shoulders. There were tears in his eyes as well, because they were old friends, because Surjit and Charan had fallen out over money and because Pritam saw her once again as a young mother fleeing Lyallpur in a bullock cart, a newborn baby in her arms. "Oh, you've come, you've come, Pritamji," she kept saying in a faint voice, her lips trembling. He had known her since she was born.

Everything about the farm spoke of prosperity. The substantial brick house was plastered and painted pink, like one in the city. There were many barns, a substantial number of tethered cattle and buffaloes and two big tractors under a great mango tree. Surjit's son Pala, now a big, heavy-shouldered man, joined them and did much of the talking. Surjit clung tightly to Pritam's hand. "Stay the night," she repeated. "Stay the night." Women from the family came out to an open fire and began to prepare tea and a meal. Pala said their land was divided three ways, six acres to a son with his parents keeping three acres in their name. He had already bought an acre from Kaka, who, when he came home from Lebanon set up a travel agency and foolishly promised to provide visas to Germany. He could not deliver and two angry customers filed a case with the police, a judge ruled that Kaka had to pay them fifty thousand rupees, and to get the money he had to sell Pala the acre of land. When Kaka joined them, Pritam saw how pale and flabby he looked, not like a farmer at all, but with puffy, swollen cheeks and a shawl wrapped about him like an old man. His turban was the deep blue of Tohra's Akali Party. It was soon evident that whereas Pala took great pride in the farm, Kaka pined for Lebanon, where he had cut his hair, shaved off his beard and worn European clothes. He brought out some photographs to show Pritam.

"Can you survive on five acres?" Pritam asked Kaka, who had a wife and several children. Pala, to Kaka's evident annoyance, answered for him: "If he works hard, he can." You could see who ruled the roost. Kaka had ten cattle and Pala himself fourteen; their younger brother Bawa also had ten. This meant the brothers' days were spent cutting fodder, taking the cattle out to graze, bringing them back, feeding them, milking them, yoking and unyoking them to a cart or a plow and bedding them down. Such large herds would give time at their Bhadson farm its rhythm. Kaka would have little time to think about Beirut. Each brother had his own motorized tube well from underground piped irrigation, and when Pala took Pritam out to see the farm, he marveled at how modern it was. Saroop, looking fit for a man who had been addicted to opium for so many years, joined them in the fields and Pala said his father had not touched opium for a decade. They knew Charan was taking it. It was Pala's theory that that was why he had moved his family to Chawar Khas, since in Uttar Pradesh one could get a license to grow opium. "You know, Pritamji," Pala said, "there was a police case pending against Kuldeep when he died. He was caught at the Punjab border smuggling in opium." Pritam had not known and was sorry to hear it. He shook his head and told Pala, "Once you get addicted to opium, you can spoil a whole family."

When they returned to Surjit, Pritam told her about the land dispute between Charan and Beant, and of Charan's ignominious flight across the fields. He had not been seen in Ghungrali since. He also told her of Charan's wandering and the way Sukhdev cursed him and wished him ill. Hearing of so much bitterness and vexation, Surjit grew quite agitated, her overflowing eyes full of emotion. "He must give the land in Ghungrali to the grandchildren," she told Pritam in a trembling, passionate voice. "That Charan must do." Pritam asked about her condition. She said that the day of the stroke, she had been cooking for harvesters all day. She spent many days in the hospital. Charan had not come once.

Pritam was grieved to hear all this. Life was too short for families to be so disagreeable and cruel to one another. "Forget what he owes you," he told Surjit. "Charan cannot pay you now. He is taking opium. He will ruin his family. Don't ask anything from him. He won't give. Forget it now." Surjit listened to his words and wept, ashamed of her quarrel with Charan on top of all his other troubles. "He is your brother," Pritam ended quietly. "Not anyone else."

In spite of Surjit's entreaties to stay the night, Pritam took a late-afternoon bus back to Ghungrali so as not to worry his family. Once police stopped the bus and came aboard to search for weapons. They said the *khadkus* had entered and opened fire in a village nearby. To Pritam's surprise, Basant Singh boarded the bus in Khanna. He told Pritam his failing eyesight left him unable to drive his car. He had diabetes and was slowly going blind.

The two old men got down at Bija Bridge and set out on a small road across the fields toward Ghungrali. The freshly watered wheat fields exhaled a damp, earthy smell, and while the sun still glowed on the tall tops of the eucalyptus trees, shadows had fallen on the road's surface. Basant Singh was as self-righteous and opinionated as ever, raging against the Delhi government all the while. "Fertilizer's gone up again. Do you know what I think? This government wants to kill the Jats. You know it as well as I do, Pritamji. From Nehru to Indira Gandhi to this government, they've been crushing the Jats. We Punjabis want state autonomy. So the government won't interfere with Sikhism and will give our farmers cost-price parity. Sikhs ought to get more than this new allotment of two percent of the ranks in the Indian Army too. And Punjab needs all the water it can get. Give up two Punjabi districts just to get Chandigarh? *Bilkool nahi*, absolutely not!" Even with his failing eyesight, Basant Singh kept up on current affairs, with the help of a magnifying glass. As always, aside from newspapers, he read nothing but agricultural or edifying books.

He had strong opinions on everything and went on and on until Pritam interrupted him, saying, "That Bhindranwale spoiled everything."

To Pritam's surprise, Basant Singh vehemently disagreed. "Bhindranwale never spoke one objectionable word! Why, that man always spoke to the point. It is the police who create these *khadkus*. They arrest a young man in a village and take him away and mistreat him. He'll come back a militant. Or they pick up somebody just to ask for money."

"The soldiers don't do that."

"No, they're more disciplined. But mark my words, if the central government doesn't give Sikhs their rights, this trouble won't stop."

"How could a separate state of Khalistan survive?" Pritam asked. "Where would we sell our wheat?"

Basant Singh waved this away impatiently. "There are many countries smaller than Punjab. If we can survive now, we can survive then. Delhi favors Hindus. But if you press a person too hard, he bursts." As they walked, the two old friends kept arguing heatedly until Basant Singh, at last, agreed that Pritam was probably right. "Most Punjabis would settle for autonomy, it's true," he agreed. "With defense and currency for India. India can't live without our wheat and they have forty or fifty times more people." It made sense that India would never let Punjab get away completely.

The talk shifted to farming. As all the village knew, Basant Singh had amassed, with God knows what conniving, fifty-six acres, by far the biggest farm in Ghungrali. But what was to happen to it? Neither of his two sons had chosen to stay in Ghungrali; one was in Canada and the other was a coach at the university in Ludhiana. A grandson looked after things now, but most likely it would be broken up and sold after the old man was gone. Not that Basant Singh was anywhere near giving up the ghost. He still kept up his records of who owned what in Ghungrali. He told Pritam that the village in 1992 had seventy-two tractors, three cars, four jeeps, sixty threshing machines, three combines and over a hundred electrically powered tube wells. He guessed there were about twenty telephones, sixty television sets, forty stereos and a dozen video players. About twenty-five of Ghungrali's young people were abroad, more and more of them Harijans.

As the copse of eucalyptus trees around Ghungrali came into sight, Basant Singh went back to talking about the *khadkus*. "The worst of this terrorism is being done by the government's own agents." Pritam did not believe this but said nothing to challenge him. He wanted to ask Basant Singh's advice about Charan, and told him about his visit to Bhadson and Charan's refusal to give Kuldeep's grandchildren title to his last two acres in Ghungrali. "I'm afraid he will sell those too," Pritam said, "and use the money for opium. If he were going to give to the children he would have done so by now."

"We have the richest land in Punjab in Ghungrali, Pritamji. She should get the two acres in her name and Charan can build her a proper house there."

"It was foolish of him to go to Uttar Pradesh in the first place." Pritam gave a heavy sigh. "My sons would not go, even if they were given a hundred acres each." Pritam sighed.

"Did Charan tell anybody he was going to this village in Uttar Pradesh?"

"Yes. We all advised against it. If he'd stayed here, he'd live comfortably—compared to that jungle in UP, like a king. When he sold the land he should have transferred title at once to Beant's children. He told me six months ago he would do it. The last time he was here he said he would do it. You know he came and took money for the other three acres from Ajit Singh."

Basant Singh listened, smoothing his white whiskers thoughtfully. "You know, Sadhu Singh sat around a good deal. But he also worked hard to bring things from the university and government offices, like threshing machines and the reaper that time." He frowned. "Why does Charan not look after his grandchildren? No, he has taken up religion and enjoys wandering about and takes opium. Did Kuldeep's death affect him so? You know, also, he was an asthma patient for so long and took medicine. I think that led him to opium. But it completely destroys a man's moral fiber."

Pritam shook his head. "I don't know what has happened to Charan. He is like stone. You put stone in the heaviest rain and it is untouched. Opium has made Charan like that. It has hardened his heart." Pritam's voice became despairing. "I fear he will sell these last two acres too. I feel it. I no longer believe him."

"God knows what will happen," sighed Basant Singh. "What he has done is a disgrace."

Pritam nodded. "Charan has lost his honor in Ghungrali." Ahead was the ruined banyan tree and Pritam saw Mukhtar coming from that direction. Basant Singh, who had little time for Harijans, said he would be on his way. As he turned to go, he leaned forward and confided to Pritam in an undertone, "At last the Harijans appreciate me. They know if anyone molests one of their women, we will come and kill them. Someday, Pritamji, you'll see. Ghungrali's Harijans will pay great respect to me." Then he departed.

Pritam greeted Mukhtar. *"Sat Sri Akal."*

"Sat Sri Akal, Sardarji sahib." Mukhtar said he was coming to tell

Pritam that old Chanan, the Mazhbi, was dead; the cremation had been that afternoon. "They found him this morning when his children went to wake him. Just died in his sleep. He worked the whole day yesterday in the fields, came home, said he wasn't hungry, lay down to sleep and in the night he died. Just like that. People are saying that it was a good death. He didn't suffer at all." Pritam said it was a big loss to Ghungrali. He would go to pay his respects to the family. Chanan was a saintly man. The sun was falling lower in the sky. Mukhtar looked at Basant Singh's retreating figure in the dimming light. "Poor Basant Singh," he told Pritam. "Nobody talks to him. He is just an old man going blind."

Across the stagnant pond, not far from the walled courtyard of Pritam's house, a man caught Mukhtar's attention. He was whitewashing an old Muslim grave and had hung blue banners over it. Pritam said it was one of his Jat neighbors who had started to tend the grave and pray there after his baby daughter recovered from a bad fever. He credited Muslim spirits who haunted the grave. After all this time, Ghungrali's Muslims were not forgotten. "An old man came the other day," Mukhtar said. "He came from Pakistan and found an old sealed well near the stadium. 'This well was mine,' he told us. His house was gone but he knew right where it had stood. How he wept."

Mukhtar was worried about terrorism. Bhindranwale had kept to the letter of Sikh scripture when it came to making no distinction between Jats and Harijans, true to Guru Nanak's condemnation of caste: "There are ignoble among the noblest and pure among the despised." He welcomed Harijan followers. Mrs. Gandhi's killer, the subinspector who fired the first shots, was a Mazhbi. Yet, as every Harijan in Ghungrali knew, Mukhtar told Pritam, practically all the *khadkus* were Jats. Sikh militancy was really Jat militancy. A few days earlier, the *khadkus* had sent five men armed with AK-47s and revolvers into Jaspal Banger village, not more than twenty miles from Ghungrali. They shot dead four Harijans, just for favoring one of their own in a village election. *"Dar lugta,"* Mukhtar confided. "There is fear in the village." It was the old caste strife that so clouded the whole of India's future.

Overhead vultures stirred, rustling the banyan tree's last branches. Pritam and Mukhtar gazed up at them. What ugly, rapacious birds they were, Pritam thought with loathing, with their dark plumage and naked purple and orange heads, feeding upon dead putrefying flesh. "Nobody is taking care of the banyan tree," Mukhtar said, interrupting Pritam's dark thoughts. "Look how the roots are exposed. It's dying of old age. These vultures come because it's dying. We should plant a new banyan tree." Something youthful in Mukhtar's tone caused Pritam to look at him. In the fading light, his face looked dark and dusty, and on one cheek there was a smudge of clay from the kiln. Even so, he had hardly aged in twenty years; his hair was still brown and thick and he had an appearance of robust youth. As he often did, Pritam thought how work can keep your health. Mukhtar asked how Pritam's family was.

"Thanks to God, they are united and living a peaceful life." Which reminded him of Charan. He asked Mukhtar if he had heard any news of him.

"He's doing too much wandering, they say. Charan has knowledge of farming. He should stay home and supervise his sons." Mukhtar's handsome features clouded. "Whatever Charan has done that is wrong, if he had remained in Ghungrali I'd go back to work for him. Yes, I swear I would, even after all that has happened. Yes, even now, if Charan came back I would work for him." Like Pritam, surrounded as they were by change and decay, he longed for the certitude and peace of the old days.

Pritam sighed heavily. It had been a tiring journey to Bhadson and back. He could see some of his great-grandchildren outside his gate, waving and jumping about, waiting to welcome him. He knew he was as warmly loved as he loved them. He turned back to Mukhtar. "Charan had a good life in our village. Why did he leave it for that jungle? Why did he abandon these children he left behind?" There were no answers, just the memory of Charan's sad flight. He and Mukhtar parted.

Pritam turned to go home. He felt overcome with extreme weariness, all his earthly years upon him. Across the dusty, flaming Punjabi sky cawing flocks of crows were leaving Ghungrali's rooftops for their nighttime roosts in the fields. He saw a man cutting clover, a bullock cart coming from a well, a huddle of Harijan women carrying bundles of grass on their heads, so alive, so soon subject to decrepitude and decay. And he asked himself, "Was it a glory of a few years only for these people?"

Something stirred overhead and just then still another rotten branch of the banyan tree fell with a great crash and the cracking sounds of splintering wood and ripping rot and the hissing and flapping wings of all the vultures as they rose into the air. Pritam, shaken, stepped backward and stared up to see, not hideous scavengers who feed upon carrion, but beautiful black birds, bright and glittering in the light of the setting sun against the pale blue sky as they wheeled and soared in flight. Dipping their wings, rising higher and higher into the air, they skimmed away, and Pritam, awed by the unexpected splendor of the vultures and stunned by it, was only vaguely aware of Mukhtar turning back to him and the children across the pond crying out and pointing, but more conscious of the man in the field, the cart, the huddle of women, all unchanged, as if the fate of the banyan tree did not matter to them, for a new one would grow in its place. It was like seeing beyond the grave and knowing what would happen to Ghungrali. It would go on, as would its people.

In the short distance home, the beauty and warm comfort of his impression stayed in Pritam's mind. "Let thine own house be the forest, thy heart the anchor . . ." The familiar words of Guru Nanak came to him. "Learn to love, be merciful and forbear." God is truth, Pritam told himself, all He asks is that we till our fields with a plain and simple faith in Him and each other. "As a team of oxen are we driven, by the plowman, our teacher . . ." The Guru's comforting words: live plainly, work hard, speak honestly, oppose wrong, share with the poor, provide for your children, help one another, heal the sick, break bread together. What more could anyone do? ". . . We reap according to our measure, some for ourselves to keep, some to others give. O Nanak, this is the way to truly live."

VIII

Ourselves

THERE WERE giants in the earth in those days," Genesis tells us in the story of Noah, whose times were described as "corrupt" and "filled with violence." Noah himself is seen as "a righteous man, blameless in his generation." That is how I see Pritam, already old when I met him twenty-four years ago, tall, powerfully built, white-bearded, the very picture of an Old Testament prophet. To me, over the years, he came to personify the peasant view of the good life.

Robert Redfield defined this as "an intense attachment to native soil; a reverent disposition toward habitat and ancestral ways; a restraint on individual self-seeking in favor of family and community; a certain suspicion, mixed with appreciation, of town life; a sober and earthy ethic." Redfield:

> Peasants find in life purpose and zest because accumulated experience has read into nature and suffering and joy and death significance that the peasant finds restated for him in his everyday work and play. There is a teaching, as much implicit as explicit, as to why it is that children come into the world and grow up to marry, labor, suffer and die. There is an assurance that labor is not futile; that nature, or God, has some part of it. There is a story or a proverb to assure one that some human frailty is just what one ought to expect; there are in many cases more serious myths to explain the suffering of the innocent or prepare the mind for death. So that although peasants . . . will quarrel and fear, gossip and hate, as do the rest of us, their very way of life, the persisting order and depth of their simple experiences, continue to make something humanly and intellectually acceptable of the world around them.

Among peasants of nineteenth-century England, present-day Maya Indians of Yucatán and ancient Boeotian Greeks, Redfield found the same values given land, work and industry, a common "attitude toward the universe" shared by many traditional villagers like Pritam, old Chanan and Jurek. Others, like Sadhu Singh, saw hard work as something to be avoided at all cost. They were going against an agricultural community's accepted view of "the good life," in the case of the Sikhs, as set down by Guru Nanak, himself a villager, in the early sixteenth century.

Will and Ariel Durant, at the completion of their monumental ten-volume *The Study of History*, published from 1935 to 1967, when they summed up their findings in 1968 in *The Lessons of History*, gave surprising emphasis to agriculture, reminding us that all the elements of civilization can be found in a village: the making of fire and light; the wheel and other basic tools; language, art; the family and parental nurture; social organization, morality and charity.

This agriculture can be of three kinds: *slash and burn*, as in much of Africa and northeastern Brazil, where virgin land is cleared of trees, grass and bush, a hoe or digging stick is used and fields are planted in the ash-enriched soil until yields fall. Or *dryland*, *rain-fed* farming based on the plow, as in Popowlany, Huecorio's upland fields or, increasingly, the Machakos Hills. Or it can be *irrigated*, whether in arid zones like Nageh Kom Lohlah, Sirs el Layyan or Ghungrali or in tropical alluvial fans where water-seeking crops like rice are grown, as in Pilangsari, Nae-Chon or China's Guangdong province.

Whichever he practices, the villager tries as best he can to use his limited resources of land, labor, water, sun, animal power and his own muscles. His land is shrinking: worldwide, the average farm fell from 6½ acres in 1960 to less than 5 acres in 1990. Jurek in Popowlany had 8 hectares, or 20 acres, but half of it was in woods and pasture. Shahhat's mother, Ommohamed, still owned 2 acres of sugarcane, but she improvidently sold off all of the family's inherited land except a date palm garden to marry off her two youngest sons and to enable herself to go to Mecca, just as Shahhat sold his last little patch of pasture to take a second, seventeen-year-old wife. Helmi and Husen had farmed 2-acre holdings with their father but were left virtually landless when the fathers died. Jade's father in Nae-Chon farmed 2.2 acres. Farms in Guangdong province were tiny plots, averaging just half an acre. Huecorio's *ejido* farms were 3 acres. In Africa land was abundant but a family without a draft animal could till only about 2½ acres; 84 percent of African cultivators used hoes because of livestock devastation from the tsetse fly and, rather often, simply because where this plague had been eradicated, there was no inherited custom. In Punjab, Charan sold all but 5 acres of his inherited 15 acres to buy 35 acres of jungle land in an impoverished backwoods. Even Pritam, who was able to add 5 acres to his original 15-acre allotment, divided this between two sons, so each was poorer than he was forty years ago. Respect for property—indeed, as Redfield says, reverence for land—was common among all these villagers. Charan only sold his land in Ghungrali to buy more and cheaper land for his sons. And when Shahhat and his mother sold land for marriages and a religious pilgrimage they were strongly condemned by their neighbors, who predicted, not without cause, the family's ruin.

Village life is based on family and living in groups. Very few villagers live alone, as the 1990 U.S. Census showed 25 percent of Americans do; it was a hardship for Jurek to be without a wife. Mutual help is a necessity; Jurek and Agneshka rushed to help the neighbors get the hay in when it threatened to rain. Everyone in Popowlany pitched in to pick potatoes, just as they did in Helmi's village. Shahhat and Kamil recruited neighbors to cut cane, the women in Machakos said it gave them strength to work together and the elderly Koreans chose to pool their efforts to prepare seedbeds. Nonmechanized farming often needs hands outside the family for planting, weeding and harvesting. In Ghungrali the breakdown of traditional forms of mutual help in favor of expedient monetarized relations between landlord and contractual worker weakened the whole social fabric.

During the 1970 wheat harvest, one of the Mazhbis said, "Where men work, there is God," and I have called religion the core of village culture. To give life and the world meaning, the Polish villagers of Popowlany or the Mexicans of Huecorio have turned to the life and death of Christ, if mixed, respectively, with older Slavic or Amerindian mythology; for the Egyptians and the Javanese the Prophet Muhammad, again subtly leavened for the one by the pharaonic and Christian inheritances and for the other animism and wise and earthy Semar; for the Koreans and Chinese the teachings of Confucius, with shaman, Taoist or Buddhist undertones as the case may be; for the Africans, however nominally Muslim, Christian or pagan, the deeply personal God who lives in the sky and heals and protects them and brings life-giving rain; and for the Sikhs of Ghungrali the rustic rural wisdom of Guru Nanak, however influenced by caste and such Hindu gods as Rama and Sita in perpetual struggle with the evil Ravana. The "unity of mankind" under one God and religion, as preached by Tolstoy and Mahatma Gandhi, also fits in with Redfield's idea of a universal village culture.

George Steiner, one of the best-known Western intellectuals, when he was a visiting professor and I was his student in a course on literature at the University of Innsbruck in 1958 (he was in Austria to finish his *Tolstoy or Dostoevsky*) once told us that the contrast between the rural and urban in the works of Tolstoy "may well be the center of his art." He said, "Tolstoy came to see the distinction between life on the land and life in the city as close to the primordial distinction between good and evil." Dostoevsky, who never came fully to terms with a God who allows the torture of helpless children, does show a great contrast in his "Legend of the Grand Inquisitor," between the urbane old priest, nearly ninety and supremely worldlywise, and the village-like simplicity of Jesus, who returns to earth in Seville during the Inquisition. Arrested, Jesus is accused of having tragically overestimated humanity's ability to bear the agonies of free will. Men are so racked by doubt because Christ has allowed them the freedom to choose between good and evil, to once again eat of the tree of knowledge. Steiner calls this the central theme of the Legend. The Grand Inquisitor makes his ardent prophecy of a total state based on miracles, authority and bread:

> Then we shall give them the quiet humble happiness of weak creatures such as they are by nature . . . They will marvel at us and will be awe-stricken before us . . . Yes, we shall set them to work, but in their leisure hours we shall make their life like a child's game . . . Oh, we shall permit them to sin, too, for they are weak and helpless, and they will love us as children for allowing them to sin . . .

In this famous long passage, the old priest foretells a future when the "weak and unhappy will come crawling to our feet. . . ."

> The most painful secrets of their conscience, all, all they will bring to us, and we shall have an answer for all. And they will be glad to believe our answer for it will save them from the greatest anxiety and terrible agony they endure at present in making a free decision for themselves. And they will be happy . . .

Steiner has written that the Grand Inquisitor's prophecy "lays before us, in precise detail, a summation of the disasters peculiar to our times":

> It does foreshadow, with uncanny prescience, the totalitarian regimes of the 20th century—thought control, the annihilating and redemptive powers of the elite, the delight of the masses in the musical and dance-

like rituals of Nuremburg and the Moscow Sports Palace, the instrument of confession, and the total subordination of private to public life. But like *1984,* which may be understood as an epilogue to it, the vision of the Grand Inquisitor also points to the tawdry cheapness of mass culture, to the preeminence of quackery and slogans over the rigors of genuine thought, to the hunger of men—a hunger no less flagrant in the West than in the East—after leaders and magicians to draw their minds out of the wilderness of freedom.

In a 1993 essay, Steiner grimly asked:

Why the long horror of the twentieth century, with its two world wars (in essential fact, two European civil wars), its totalitarian regimes, its death camps, its return to torture, its burning of books and of human beings? What went wrong, pushing us back toward a bestiality that is now becoming numb habit, be it in Bosnia or in our inner cities?

Steiner went on to speculate:

Homicidal conflict and the unforgiving clash of ideologies—religious, ethnic, social—may simply be the rule in the condition of the human carnivore. It may be that the partial collapse of religious faith in the most developed societies has created a vacuum to be filled not by reason or tolerance, as the Enlightenment had hoped and predicted, but by fanaticism, fake dogmas and psychological instability.

Steiner, who generously provided many insights for my book on Britain ("America is total possibility, Britain is total remembrance"), uses the phrase "most developed societies"—that is, the most urbanized ones. Historians, from Oswald Spengler to Will Durant to Arnold Toynbee to William McNeill, have argued that the city bred irreligion.

I found, somewhat to my surprise, in two conversations I had with him in his final years, that Walter Lippmann shared this view. As he wrote in one of his early works:

The deep and abiding traditions of religion belong to the countryside. For it is there that man earns his daily bread by submitting to superhuman forces whose behavior he can only partially control. There is not much he can do when he has plowed the ground and planted his seed except to wait hopefully for sun and rain from the sky. He is obviously part of a scheme that is greater than himself, subject to elements that transcend his powers and surpass his understanding. The city is an acid that dissolves this piety . . .

As Pritam would say, "God is after our wheat. With these thunder-storms it goes down and becomes shaky at the root." Or Charan's: "These days, if it's rain without wind, it's like God come to earth." Lippmann continues:

> Yet without piety, without a patriotism of family and place, without an almost plant-like implication in unchangeable surroundings, there can be no disposition to believe in an external order of things. The omnipotence of God means something to men who submit daily to the cycles of weather and the mysterious power of nature.

Though the people of Ghungrali, Popowlany, Huecorio and the other villages may differ a lot on the details, they have no doubt that there is an order in the universe that justifies their lives because they are part of it. My grandfather, a New England Quaker who became a doctor and then a Methodist evangelical preacher in the Midwest, had the same faith in divine providence. Modern science shattered that order for my father, a farmer who also became a doctor, as it did for so many of us. Once in Egypt my interpreter grew furious with me after, when he was talking about God, I muttered absently, "If there is a God." Such skepticism that the existence of God can neither be proved nor disproved is rare in villages. And even for agnostics, the needs which religion met still exist.

Either religion itself or a need for religion—what is the meaning of life?—forms the central strand in every culture. Innermost in our own Western Judaic-Christian-Greco-Roman culture is the teaching of a Mediterranean Jewish illiterate peasant villager who lived during the Roman Empire's Augustan age. It was a time, like ours, of a dissolution of popular religion and traditional morality and a vast searching into life's meaning.

In recent years the scholarly quest for the historical Jesus, using modern methods of anthropology, archaeology and textual research, has resulted in a new surge of studies, with Jesus depicted variously as "a magician and healer, as a religious and social revolutionary and as a radical peasant philosopher." What is undeniable to me, rereading the Gospels themselves, is that whatever else he was, Jesus was unquestionably a peasant villager.

Once Pritam says, "What we sow we will someday reap," which sounds Christian. The gentle and humorous founder of Sikhism, Guru Nanak, reveled in agricultural simile and metaphor. One time when he saw Hindus throwing water from the Ganges toward the rising sun as an offering to their dead ancestors, Nanak started splashing it the other way, telling them, "I am watering my fields. If you can send water to the dead in heaven, surely I can send it as far as my village in Punjab." His appeal was to a peasantry, just as was that of the historical Jesus, which tends to be obscured because so soon after his death Christianity became, and stayed, the religion of the urban middle and lower classes. As far as I know, there is no Christian influence on Sikhism. The many similarities come from their shared agricultural roots and common village ways and views.

Biblical textual scholars have come up with a hundred and five aphorisms and parables they feel fairly confident came from the historical Jesus himself. The Gospel of St. Mark, used like the Q Document (for *Quelle*, German for "source") by the authors of the Gospels of St. Matthew and St. Luke, is generally thought to have been composed about seventy years after the death of Jesus, not such a long period of time. I find when interviewing Americans in their eighties or nineties that they often have quite good recall about events in the 1920s. Going over what in Mark is believed to have come from Jesus himself, one is struck by how many metaphors and analogies are drawn from agriculture and village life and by someone familiar with herding and cultivation and the use of plowshares, hoes, sickles, forks and other farming tools. We find allusions to sowers, seeds, birds, vineyards, tenants, laborers, harvests, rain clouds, fishnets, grain, ravens, storehouses, barns, weeds, reapers, foxes, nets, bread baking, sheep, salt, lambs, wolves, sparrows, fields, winnowing, camels, fig trees, fatted calves, jars of meal, wheat, barley, grapes, the list goes on and on.

When Pritam mentioned he was dividing his land equally between his upright son and his ne'er-do-well drunkard son, I thought at once of the parable of the prodigal son. It is easy to picture Jesus and his disciples trudging along a country road in Galilee, Semitic, sun-weathered faces beaded with sweat, touseled black hair and beards, the callused hands, slight stoop and thick wrists and ankles of Mediterranean peasant stock, a ragtag band of the poor, blind, sick and crippled straggling in clouds of dust behind them.

Biblical scholar John Dominic Crossan, who uses cross-cultural anthropology, Greco-Roman-Jewish history and literary research with interesting results, makes much of Jesus's illiterate peasant origins and his emphasis on healing and eating. Not only is there great belief in the supernatural in villages, but I have always found that seemingly

supernatural phenomena do seem to take place remarkably often, especially involving good and evil omens, witchcraft, sorcery, magic,
demons, ghosts, the Evil Eye, faith healing, herbal remedies and pro-
tective amulets and talismans. Villagers tend to prefer traditional
cures and herbs, especially if magic is involved, to modern medicine;
generally—Zofia in Popowlany being an exception to the rule—going
to the doctor is the last resort.

Eating often has spiritual significance in villages. We saw in Ghungrali how breaking bread together is part of Sikhism, as is taking
prasad, the sugary *helwa* Charan ate at the Golden Temple. In Shahhat's village, a small hamlet on the outskirts, Basili, supposedly inhabited by Coptic Christians since their ancestors were converted by the
Apostle Thomas soon after the death of Jesus, the people gather each
Saturday night to sup together at an ancient church out on the desert
and the whole congregation spends the night. A communal feast
called a *slametan* is the core religious ritual in village Java and often
goes with a shadow play.

Crossan in his 1992 *The Historical Jesus* argues that Jesus was essentially a healer and peasant social reformer:

> . . . his work was among the farms and villages of Lower Galilee. His
> strategy, implicitly for himself and explicitly for his followers, was the
> combination of *free healing and common eating,* a religious and economic
> egalitarianism that negated alike and at once the hierarchical and pa-
> tronal normalcies of Jewish religion and Roman power . . . Miracle
> and parable, healing and eating were calculated to force individuals
> into unmediated physical and spiritual contact with God and un-
> mediated physical and spiritual contact with one another. He an-
> nounced, in other words, the brokerless kingdom of God.

The Grand Inquisitor accuses Jesus of having abandoned man not
only to freedom but also to doubt. Unbrokered religion, as among
Muslims like Shahhat and Helmi, African tribals, my Quaker grandfather and Pritam with his rustic Sikh faith, simply says no human agent
can come between an individual and God. Of all Jesus's teachings one
simple commandment mattered—to love God and one's fellow men
—and this was to be judged not in ritual or piety, but solely by its
faithful demonstration in ordinary daily life.

As Dostoevsky saw, the number of human beings capable of autonomous self-responsibility, or of unmediated contact with one another,
much less with God, has always been a minority. For every Pritam

there are many Charans. In Professor McNeill's view, this is the fundamental weakness of the liberal version of human behavior. Christians, certainly Protestants, are supposed to be responsible for saving themselves. But there has always been ambiguity in this tradition. Lippmann told me that in his view the great question ahead was whether "governments can govern" and people "will be willing and able to save themselves." Established moral systems, he said, such as we find in the Mosaic law or the code of Hammurabi, are deposits of custom, rules that lasted from generation to generation because, at least in some rough way, they worked. They worked, said Lippmann, because they were "the broad rules of conduct imposed upon people living close to the soil, upon people, therefore, whose ways of living changed little in the course of generations."

> Whether they thought they could serve God best by burnt offerings or a contrite heart, by slaying the infidel or loving their neighbors, by vows of poverty or the magnificence of their altars, they never doubted that the chief duty of man, and his ultimate chance at happiness, was to discover and then to cultivate a right relationship with a supreme being.

Clinton-era compromise populism, with its visionary, Christian overtones, is testing whether America, having come so far from its rural roots, is governable. What does Jesus, the peasant villager, still have to say to agnostic, postreligious modern man who does not so much deny God as simply the possibility of knowing him?

This radical loss of association with the deepest, village roots of our cultural past is heightened by television, radio, movies, the press and now the whole dizzying multimedia phenomenon, whirling telephone, television and computer into an extraordinary whole. These enormously multiply our awareness of events and people and far-off doings, experiences that are cut off from their causes and consequences, that are only half lived because they are not actually seen or experienced. Our lives are becoming a jarring uproar of ten thousand noises, and amidst these noises, what do we have for the inner ethical guidance religion once supplied?

II

Digitization and fiber optics are creating high-speed networks that will, says Gerald Levin, chairman and CEO of Time Warner, the world's biggest media group, let consumers tune into "anything, any-where, anytime." Television itself will become a powerful supercomputer. This represents a leap of faith that ever-faster, ever-cheaper communication will add to the world's well-being.

Berkeley sociologist Todd Gitlin says television may be "enter-tainer, painkiller, vast wasteland, companion to the lonely, white noise, thief of time," but to "society as a whole, it is the principal circulator of the cultural mainstream." One might add, now that it is so global, the Western cultural mainstream. When Marshall McLuhan in the 1960s put forward the idea that we all now live together in a "global village," television had not yet penetrated, as it did in the 1980s, to most villages. McLuhan:

> Today, after more than a century of electric technology, we have ex-tended our central nervous system itself in a global embrace, abolish-ing both space and time as far as our planet is concerned. The new electric interdependence recreates the world in the image of a global village.

McLuhan saw TV's union of everyone across the world into a "single consciousness" as wholesome and desirable.

When people in a village get together to talk about the weather and the crops, they gossip about each other and have an intense interest in their fellow villagers and a corresponding lack of interest in anything or anyone outside the village. Bill McKibben has sensibly asked, "What aspects of a village can be usefully translated to an almost infinitely larger scale?"

What we are getting is not McLuhan's wholesome global village, but a much more dysfunctional global city. Television's outlook and ethos, produced as it invariably is in cities, are decidedly urban: cos-mopolitan, time-oriented, trendy, subject to shifts in mood and fash-ion, secularized, individualistic, depersonalized, and so on. Professor McNeill says, "The impact of American TV programs on views in foreign countries is one of the great conundrums of our time." We saw how, in the past decade or so, Dhakel and Bawa in Ghungrali, Om-mohamed in Nageh Kom Lohlah and Muhammad Sirhan in Sirs el Layyan, like Jurek in Popowlany, and indeed villagers everywhere, were getting addicted to television. This has happened with stunning speed. Television is only sixty years old, I've just been watching it for forty years, most of the villagers I know less than ten years. *Economist* writer John Heilemann estimates the number of TV sets worldwide has nearly tripled since 1980, 35 percent of them now in Asia, 8 percent in Latin America, 4 percent in the Middle East and 1 percent in Africa. Satellite-TV stations in 1994 numbered nearly three hundred, with seventy more to be launched by 1997. Hong Kong's Star TV now beams BBC, MTV, Prime Sports, English and Mandarin channels to 45 million people from Egypt to Mongolia. In time, we are told, mergers of media, telecoms and computers, based on microprocessors, fiber optics and digitization, will produce 500-channel send-and-receive television, radically altering our lives. "Soon," as Heilemann puts it, "we'll all be cruising down 'information highways.' The multimedia age is at hand." He finds anecdotes supporting McLuhan easy to come by:

> Karen tribesmen huddled around their sets in the Burmese mountains, watching the BBC; a Japanese bond trader at an election-night party, arguing that political reform will not come to his country until it has its own Larry King show; a Zimbabwean guide canoeing on the Zambezi, regaling his charges with vivid descriptions of episodes of "The Simpsons."

Skeptics object, Heilemann admits, to the culturally threadbare quality of these electronic bonds:

> Village life via satellite is reduced to the few things understood by everyone everywhere—war, sports, Big Macs and Levi's. And these are fair points. But even dedicated anti-McLuhanites admit that the spread of television has shrunk the planet, giving farflung people a common base of information that would have been unthinkable at any other time in history.

Even in Africa, I found in 1993 in remote jungle villages that, if no electric power was at hand, villagers used batteries or solar panels; from what I saw, that 1 percent for Africa is way too low. Helmi's hut in the Nile Delta lacked any furniture but a bed and some chests and mats, but there was a TV set recessed into one mud wall. The Gulf War seems to have been the first big news event globally watched by the villagers, though while Americans cheered their high-tech weaponry's performance, the Chinese villagers I happened to be among were appalled by the slaughter of conscripted Iraqi peasants in the retreat—the "turkey shoot"—from Kuwait City. And those films of soldiers in trenches being buried by gigantic earth-moving machinery were viewed with anguish and fury by Muslims.

A great gain from universal television is the way it creates a consciousness of contraceptives and a demand for them among village women. Statistics show this is happening in Thailand (17 persons per set), Morocco (21 persons per set) and Bangladesh (320 persons per set). Bangladesh is the mystery. Fully 86 percent of its 117 million people in 1994 still lived in villages and per capita GNP was just $220 a year, making it among the least likely countries to show a spontaneous drop in human fertility. Yet in 1970–91 the birthrate fell by 21 percent, just as in India's Tamil Nadu state it dropped by more than 25 percent in 1985–91. In both, family planners say TV played a role but so did virtually door-to-door contraceptive marketing.

Professor McNeill cites Greece (4.5 persons per set) as an example of the sharp discontinuity created when American television suddenly erodes generational ties. Greek villagers are now part of an Athens-centered citified universe. Greece's population growth rate is down to 0.1 percent, the rate of a rich urban society, though per capita GNP was just $7,180 in mid-1994. The Greeks had some predisposing characteristics for psychological urbanization besides television. The olives, grapes and wine of its villages, sold for other food, have given Greece a historic market orientation quite unlike, for example, that of Poland, where subsistence villages like Popowlany can pretty much survive on their own pork, potatoes, milk, eggs and cabbages.

"Urbanized" may be too strong a word for what has happened. Young Greek peasants, like the Punjabi Sikhs in Ghungrali, with no land to inherit and no niche in life, tend in hard times to fall back on a tradition of violence. McNeill, who lived for a time in a Greek village, as did Toynbee before him, told me, "I've convinced myself that their guerrilla movement in the Second World War, and the guerrilla war after it ended, down to 1949, came from having villages in which the young had no role."

> There wasn't that much land. There wasn't enough food within the confines of the village to feed the population all year round. They developed various modes of supplementing this. In traditional life, this meant going down to the plains and finding hired work and bringing back food at the end of your time there. Now when opportunities on the plains broke down, what did these young men, partly affected by American television, do?
>
> They put a gun on their shoulder. They came down to the plains and they offered a choice to the villagers there: either share their wealth, i.e., give them food, or be shot. It was very effective.

Greek shepherds, going back to antiquity, fought each other with sticks and stones for pasture grounds, just as seventeenth-century Muslim persecution turned the Sikhs from a pacifist into a martial people, earlier armed with spears and swords, now with AK-47s, whose youths easily turn to violence.

My guess is that in most villages, at least so far, American TV shows are so removed from actual daily life that nobody dares or cares to act on such a model. Television can generate emphatic rejection, as from Pritam, who said he never watched it, to save his eyesight. But the Greek experience is likely to be repeated. McKibben has voiced this fear:

> The global village relentlessly roots out the real villages that still remain, and drains away their content, their information. Even in the poorest countries advertising is inescapable.

In Ghungrali we saw how Nestle's Maggi 2-Minute Noodles were catching on, thanks in part to the enormous popularity of the Hindi soap opera, *Hum Log*, which it sponsored. Arvind Singhal and Everett M. Rogers in a 1989 study, *India's Information Revolution*, warned that television seemed to be encouraging consumerism and widening gaps between urban elites and the poor.

Technology changes our lives in such unpredictable ways, large and small. In my book *Those Days*, an emcee dressed as Uncle Sam at a county fair in 1929 declares to the grandstand crowd through a megaphone:

> Modern times are here to stay, folks. Yes sir-ree. How many of you ever heard of a radio five years ago? Or saw an aeroplane ten years ago? Or owned an automobile 15 years ago?

The first television program I and about 20 million other people saw was Queen Elizabeth II's coronation in Westminster Abbey in 1952. I traveled by sea instead of jets until 1962. I still don't have a computer; the last time I carried my Olivetti portable through airport security the guard asked, "How do you turn it on?"

What sort of message does American television send out to the villages? Very mixed. News shows like CNN are determinedly populist and likely to spread the democratic idea. Asked once what had caused the fall of Communism, Lech Wałęsa pointed to a TV set and said, "It all came from there." Daniel Hallin of the University of California at San Diego observes:

Populism is of course a central part of American political culture; at least since the age of Jackson, politicians, the press and popular culture have paid obeisance to the wisdom of the People, often contrasting it with the corruption and selfishness of those who hold power . . . Television loves nothing more than a story about a "little guy" who stands up to the "powers that be."

Heady stuff in countries like India and China, where, until satellites started beaming down CNN, BBC and NHL, most news was government-produced and focused almost exclusively on the affairs of officials. In China, for example, until Prime Minister Li Peng banned satellite dishes in October 1993, some 15 million households with cable hookups were getting BBC, CNN and MTV from Hong Kong's Star TV. Madonna, Michael Jackson and other pop stars were arriving via the "heavenly thread," the literal translation of "satellite antenna" in Mandarin Chinese. American news sees politics, even war, as a contest; it asks, like King Lear, "who loses and who wins, who's in, who's out . . ." The news has been left even more adversarial by Vietnam, Watergate, Iran-Contra and the Whitewater investigation.

But TV has much more than news. When I was a boy we used to hear on the radio about:

. . . the real life drama of Helen Trent, who . . . fights back bravely, successfully to prove what so many women long to prove in their lives —that because a woman is over thirty—or more—romance in life need not be over.

Soap operas, as *The Romance of Helen Trent* did in the 1940s, still give their viewers what Berkeley's Ruth Rosen calls "emotional release, vicarious wish fulfillment, and advice about how to conduct their lives." Shahhat's mother, Ommohamed, spent hours in her mud-walled entry room watching American soaps. Was she vicariously living the American fantasy with its forbidden love affairs and material richness? Rosen, who is on the University of California faculty, feels soaps can "create an illusion of male-female intimacy that many women seek from baffled and reluctant husbands." Even more so in a Muslim village where women are so sequestered and marriage is so often arranged and such a dogged partnership.

Rosen is writing about the impact of TV soap operas on Americans and suggests that the more they "were forced to confront the anonymity of urban life, the more they mythologized the stability, face-to-face recognition, shared values, and moral accountability of the village."

As the stable small town fades, the soap opera keeps alive its idealized replica, the image of a community in which everyone knows or is related to everyone else, where continuity counts more than transience, where right and wrong are unambiguous, where good triumphs over evil. It is a world dominated by the domestic values of the family.

Prime-time soaps like *Dynasty* and *Dallas*, whose reruns reach global audiences, rely more on sex, money, glamour and fast-paced action than on what Rosen calls "the endless analysis of personal conflict" that characterizes the daytime soaps. For all of them there can be a blurring of the world of the soap and real life, as for Dhakel and the characters of *Hum Log*. This happened in Brazil in 1992 when an actress on one of its enormously popular *telenovelas* was stabbed to death by an actor who played her rejected boyfriend on the day they filmed the breakup of their heated on-screen love affair. After the slaying, Global television, Brazil's largest network, decided to keep running the series. The victim's mother, who wrote the script, decided to keep at it, and viewership rose 30 percent.

In villages, American action cartoons are popular because they are easy to understand, even when violent and antisocial. Author Tom Engelhardt has described such cartoons:

In this struggle between Good and Evil, light and darkness, blondness versus purpleness (or sickly yellowness), blue-eyedness versus glowing red-, purple- or yellow-eyedness, what is at stake is nothing less than "the secrets of the universe" (*He-Man*), "the universe" (*Voltron*), "the destruction of the universe" (*Jayce*), "the ultimate battle of survival" (*Sectaurs*), "the fate of the entire world" (*Robotech*), "the ultimate doom" (*Transformers*) . . .

The actual episodes revolve around a series of evil plans to loose havoc on innocent planets . . . or to trap the hero and deny him his transforming powers, or to stop the mighty robots from being assembled, or to kidnap a friend of the superheroes, or to steal something so powerful, dangerous, radioactive, death-dealing, that it will destroy the earth/planet/galaxy/universe or alternately turn it into a world of slaves/zombies at the service of the Evil Force . . .

All of which results in a series of chases and battles with techno-wonder weapons—space stations, laser beams, harnessed black holes, assorted yet-to-be-invented and never-to-be-invented megaweapons, and a final withdrawal by the forces of evil, uttering curses and threatening to return . . .

Sounds a little like Bill Watterson's Calvin ("We join the fearless Spaceman Spiff, interplanetary explorer extraordinaire, out at the furthest reaches of the galaxy . . . He fires his hyper-jets and blasts into the fifth dimension, into a world beyond human comprehension, INTO A WORLD WHERE TIME HAS NO MEANING!"). Iona Opie, the English authority on children's rhymes and stories, told me she was a great admirer of Walt Disney because he understood children needed something frightening so as to have a happy ending, true for cartoons in peasant villages as well.

More questionable in their impact are TV music videos, whose words, images and music often convey an anticultural rebellion against the older generation. I first saw MTV and one of its first offerings, "Video Killed the Radio Star," in 1983. The rapid and often unrelated images, the same lyrics repeated over and over again—Cyndi Lauper's "Girls Just Want to Have Fun" comes all too readily to mind—the weirdness of Boy George or Michael Jackson, the sheer sexual energy of Tina Turner, mesmerized you. I soon saw that older people were the adversaries—parents, teachers, policemen, judges, any authority figure, any grayhead. There was no cultural continuity across generations; instead full freedom was given to an almost uninhibited expression of adolescent sexuality and selfishness. MTV's disjunctive images and dreamlike feelings—which reached a global viewing audience of 260 million in 1994—while fun, could be explicitly against established, inherited culture, as for example in one Naziesque sadomasochistic video where Billy Idol in his storm trooper's outfit breaks through the stained-glass window of a church by crashing through it on a motorcycle or, more recently, in rap music or any "Beavis and Butt-head" show. Apocalypse is a recurrent theme, just as "Red Rain" invokes nuclear fallout.

Al Gore, with his concern that the sheer numbers of people on earth have begun to disturb global atmospheric and oceanic balances, has some interesting ideas on this. Gore, who has teenage children of the MTV generation, says that we have become "increasingly isolated from one another and disconnected from our roots." And that "we begin to value powerful images instead of tested truths." He talks about finding a way to resist the accumulated momentum of all the habits, patterns, and distractions that divert us from what is true and honest, spinning us first this way, then that, twirling us like a carnival ride until our very souls are dizzy and confused.

In the late 1970s I was in Brazil when a top pop song was "Turn into a Wolfman." Brazil's famous annual pre-Lenten carnival was like a metaphor for total, if temporary, cultural breakdown in the MTV style. In *Villages* I described how anticultural the whole thrust of the carnival celebration could be:

> So, it's *Carnaval* again and let it all explode. Leave St. George; he's nothing but a piece of clay. Leave that phony promise of salvation. Leave those bogus myths of forgiveness, charity and love. This is the here and now, the music is all we've got. So listen to the *trio*'s drumbeats, hear those screaming guitars, see those flashing lights and shadows, c'mon . . . you and me and everybody, take it all in, the whole ear-splitting, all-obliterating din. Let it all combine to break into your mind from without, trampling down all resistance with its force—and when it passes through you the codes and cultures of a lifetime will be annihilated. C'mon, join the mob. *Turn, turn, turn, turn into a wolfman.*

Sex and violence are of course the worrisome exports. The average American child, watching TV about three hours a day, has by the seventh grade seen at least 8,000 murders and more than 100,000 other acts of violence, according to the American Psychological Association. In 1991 the Motion Picture Association of America rated only 16 percent of American movies fit for children under thirteen. Violence and shock-editing have accelerated the past two decades, as has a popular conception that violence in America has become epidemic. Robert Shaye, chairman of New Line Cinema, which produced the *Nightmare on Elm Street* horror films, says, "*Nightmare* is a series of horror films, fantasy, comic-book violence, like *Batman* and *Superman*. Audiences love it." This kind of violent anticulture is such a huge money maker for Hollywood because it needs no translation. Nearly half of all American film revenue in 1994 was earned abroad, much of it from videos. Arnold Schwarzenegger and Sylvester Stallone, worldwide, are the two top American stars. Muhammad Sirhan in Helmi's village said he liked American movies because there was "fighting with police, fighting with planes, fighting with cars." Will villagers commit more violent acts by watching so much of it on TV and in films? The only supportable answer is yes.

Every fourteen minutes someone in America dies from a bullet wound. In 1990 handguns were used to murder 22 people in a country like Britain, but 10,567 people in America; total murders by firearms in 1992 totaled a record 15,377; in 1993 there were nearly 24,000 murders in all. Only Mexico, Brazil, Russia and the Bahamas have higher murder rates. Estimates of guns in America go as high as 200 million and nearly one million handgun crimes take place each year.

A porn explosion has come with videos, AIDS (voyeurism/masturbation is safer sex) and politically correct insistence on fealty to free expression. Pornography that degrades victims and encourages violent conduct has led to an epidemic of sexual violence in America. Milwaukee's killer-cannibal Jeffrey Dahmer's video collection ran to horror movies like *Exodus;* Lionel Dahmer, his father, in his 1994 book trying to make the case that Jeffrey was not an utter monster, asks if exposure to so much media violence, or drugs, alcohol, dysfunctional family life or even faulty genetics might be to blame. The same FBI unit portrayed in both book and film of *The Silence of the Lambs,* a composite of serial killers and kidnappers, took part in the discovery of an actual underground cell where a ten-year-old girl was held captive for sixteen days, some of the time chained by the neck. Both little Katie and her abductor got offers of book and film contracts.

Murder is as old as Cain and Abel and we all meet up with violence in Mother Goose ("When the bough breaks the cradle will fall" or "Along came a blackbird and snipped off her nose"). But the rash of sex crimes, spectacles like the Bobbitt and Menendez trials, and their export worldwide through TV, movies and especially videos is new. American serial killings seem to feed on each other; first the Manson murders, then the Corll slayings of over two dozen youths in Texas, the "Freeway Killings" in Los Angeles or the slaying of nearly forty young women on the Seattle–Tacoma highway. Many are turned into true-crime movies, including the Dahmer and Bundy stories, the Gacey murders in Chicago and the "Hillside Strangler" in Los Angeles. Though none equals the fifty-odd murders of the Russian psychopath Andrei Chickatilo or the over three hundred killings of Pedro Alonso López in Colombia, rage, sadism and a psychopathic need to control or debase others were acted out in all these crimes. Joel Rifkin, who confessed to killing seventeen women—he picked up prostitutes whom he afterward dismembered—said he acted out strangulations inspired by a graphic scene in Alfred Hitchcock's film, *Frenzy.* In his 1994 State of the Union speech, President Clinton said:

Every day the national peace is shattered by crime. In Petaluma, California, an innocent slumber party gives way to agonizing tragedy for the family of Polly Klaas. An ordinary train ride on Long Island ends in a hail of 9-millimeter rounds. A tourist in Florida is nearly burned alive by bigots simply because he is black . . .

Many Americans, fearful about the explosion of violence, were bitterly disappointed by the diversion of Clinton's youth, energy and ideas in the Whitewater affair. Maybe Lippmann was right and America really is getting ungovernable.

Nature or nurture: do you blame criminality on childhood experience, psychic debility or even derangement, or on something culturally going wrong in a society? Nazism showed that ordinary Germans learned not only to kill but ultimately to kill in a routine, and in some cases sadistic, way. Psychiatrist Walter Reich, in a review of Professor Browning's study of the German policemen involved, observes:

> And for a few, the initial horror was replaced by a gory sadism, in which Jews, totally naked, preferably old and with beards, were forced to crawl in front of their intended graves and to sustain beatings with clubs before being shot.

Dr. Reich says he was most disturbed by the capacity of these policemen—"as the ordinary men they were, as men not much different from those we know or even from ourselves—to kill as they did."

> What stands between civilization and genocide is the respect for the rights and lives of all human beings that societies must struggle to protect. Nazi Germany provided the context, ideological as well as psychological, that allowed the policemen's actions to happen.

Though terrorism has eased up in the Punjab now, we saw how the context of a secessionist, quasi-religious cause left young Sikhs able to commit the most atrocious acts without feeling they were violating, or violating only because it was necessary, their personal moral codes. One time in Vietnam I was out on an all-night Marine ambush and at daybreak we discovered the Vietcong had dragged away all their dead but one. One of the Marines asked the platoon commander, who had been reading Thomas Aquinas back at camp, if he could cut off an ear for a souvenir. I remember the anguished lieutenant telling me, "This is a hell of a way to spend a Sunday."

The ethical problem of commercial exploitation of sex and violence was posed by Ruth Slawson, NBC's senior vice president for movies, in discussing why NBC, ABC, and CBS all made films about the Amy Fisher shooting.

> It's crazy. It's self-perpetuating. We all say we don't want to keep on doing these true-crime movies but then the numbers come in and what choice do we have? Obviously the audience wanted to watch it, for whatever reason. I'm happy with the success of our movie. But overall I'm not happy about the state of movies on television.

Compare that to this comment by the mother of a three-year-old who was raped by a twelve-year-old boy after he had seen pornography at summer camp:

> What he saw on those pages not only gave him the ideas of what to do and how to do it, but it gave him the permission to treat females in a degrading and debasing manner.

American images beamed all over the world today, whether big-screen, video or TV, and however glitzy, casually cruel, hip, grim, funny or nasty, tend to exploit sex and violence with insidious effect. It is too early to say what the full impact will be out in the villages, especially once we all get wired up with fiber-optic cable. We do know from our own experience that it can create a psychological context in which aberrant actions, straying from inherited moral standards, lose some of their aberrancy and the unthinkable becomes thinkable, the unacceptable, acceptable.

III

At the end of April 1992, I was about to fly home from Manila. The Philippines were in turmoil; the Americans were pulling out of Clark and Subic. When I entered on the wrong side of his limousine, Ambassador Frank Wisner only half joked, "That's the ambassador's side. Now you'll get shot first." My last night in Manila, the flames of Los Angeles lit up the TV screens. The fires were still burning on CNN in the transit lounge in Seoul. As we landed in San Francisco, our pilot said passengers proceeding to Los Angeles would have to wait; its airport was closed. The taxi drove through an empty city, the driver explaining that Market Street had been looted the night before. I went home across the Bay to Berkeley, under a dawn-to-dusk curfew, just in time to switch on TV and hear Rodney King:

Please, we can all get along here. We can all get along. I mean, we're all stuck here for a while. Let's try to work it out. Let's try to beat it.

The tape was shown over and over: King being dragged from his car, Powell beating him with a baton, Briseno stomping on him, rookie Wind getting in his own baton blows and kicks. On April 30 they had been acquitted.

We heard a lot the next few days about investing in jobs and skills. What to do about the black ghetto culture of defiance, the soaring death tolls of young men who deal in drugs and guns, rising violent crime? Call in, as Washington's mayor appealed, the National Guard?

Blacks are on the frontier of the more general American failure of cultural reproduction. Why? We go back to the truth that no substitute for the rural base of urban culture has been invented. The racial ancestry of most African-Americans is mixed, but with respect to just the African side, as a people they've been twice uprooted: first from a hunting, herding, farming society and then, after being brought to America and used as plantation slave labor until emancipation, being uprooted once again, by the invention of the mechanical cotton picker. Some African cultural traits survive this double uprooting—for example, the mother-centered family and the brokerless religion of a deeply personal God.

Even so, without a rural base, any culture moves gradually toward extinction. Economic and demographic shifts of the past seventy years or so mean that African-Americans are being affected earlier than the rest of us, and, unless the current exodus from rural America is reversed, what is happening to them will eventually embrace our whole society. In the early 1940s, more than 75 percent of African-Americans lived in the South, the vast majority of them rural. As cotton production became mechanized, 95 percent of all black-operated tenant farms—over 350,000 of them—went under in the twenty years from 1950 to 1970. White tenant farms, about a million of them, dropped too, by 70 percent.

This already small number of black farms was halved again in the 1980s, from 243,000 to 123,000, as older farmers went broke, retired or died. In 1988 the Congressional Office of Technology Assessment warned that of 33,250 black-owned farms left, almost all would be lost by the mid-1990s. Where did these dispossessed rural people go? In 1940–80, Chicago went from 8 percent to 40 percent black, Detroit from 9 percent to 63 percent, the District of Columbia from 28 percent to 70 percent. Maybe 60 percent, according to Senator Daniel P. Moynihan, made it into the lower middle or middle class. The rest were isolated in the ugliest, loneliest, most crime-ridden and poorly educated slums in America. For instance, Dan Rather reported on CBS News February 8, 1994, "Nearly all the public housing occupants in Chicago are young unmarried women with children."

This happened just as technology was eliminating the old operator, fabricator, metalworking jobs dependent on strong backs and muscles. The past half-century has seen great scientific breakthroughs, especially in radio astronomy, molecular and solid-state physics, and such technological advances from applying them as space satellites, transistors, computers and rockets. Every advanced society, led by America, is polarizing, with the future bright in electronics, information services and biotech; rewards go to those skilled in high-tech engineering, finance, science and multimedia information. They do not go to those who grow things on farms, or extract, lift or make things in mines, ports or factories. Computer-integrated manufacturing with its microelectronic products and processes is transforming industry with automation, robots, microchips, computers, sensors, software and telecoms. The tools that now matter are these and cameras, scanners, keyboards, telephones, fax machines, computers, switches, compact discs, video- and audiotapes, cables, wires, satellites, optical-fiber transmission lines, microwave nets, switches, televisions, monitors, printers and much more. Global trade and instantaneous data flows matched by almost instantaneous capital flows and the accelerated export of technology are the only ways to stay competitive, even at the cost of mass layoffs. Millions accustomed to earning a good industrial wage have suddenly found themselves jobless or working in a service job at $4, $5, $6 an hour. Hardest hit, partly from racism, more from lack of the newly marketable skills, are African-Americans, particularly men.

When I was helping to cover the Nixon White House in 1968–69, I frequently interviewed Senator Moynihan, then an ex-Harvard professor who was Nixon's urban affairs adviser. America's greatest domestic problem, Moynihan believed, was what he called "the social isolation of the Negro." He said it was caused by postwar economic changes: the mechanization of cotton production, postwar veterans' housing loans and cheap new methods of home construction and the Interstate Highway System. Together they produced a white exodus of homes and jobs to the suburbs. Aid to Dependent Children provi-

sions in the welfare laws unintentionally made things worse by re-
warding fatherless families. The cumulative effect was urban decay,
crime and family breakdown.

Moynihan's proposed solution was a guaranteed minimum income,
or a negative income tax, to enable black families to disperse into the
general population. (When I reported this in the *Star*, Moynihan
phoned and said, "My God, don't use that word 'disperse.' It sounds
like concentration camps.") That was in 1969 and the situation has
grown a lot worse. The 31 million African-Americans, 12 percent of all
Americans, today learn less, earn less, live worse and die sooner than
everybody else. Consider these U.S. Census Bureau figures for 1992:
A black man was six times as likely to be murdered. Homicide was
the leading cause of death for young black men and women alike.
One young black man in four was either in prison, on parole or on
probation, more than there were in college. Blacks were twice as
likely as whites to be jobless. Their median family income was 56
percent of a white family's. Nearly a third of blacks, compared with 10
percent of whites, lived below the poverty line, among them 45 percent of all black children.

In 1972, after my first two years of experimenting with village reporting, including the 1970 Ghungrali harvest, the *Star* asked me to
try the same thing with Americans, moving in with them for a week or
so, following them around and writing down much of what they said
and did. There were about twenty different individuals and families
and it occupied me for much of a year, but the one I remember best,
and used to see now and then, was Clive Gilmore, chosen because at
age twenty-nine he had spent eleven years, or over a third of his life,
in Lorton prison in Virginia. Clive had ties to a rural Virginia community, Dunnsville, which he liked to describe:

> People who have homes there, they've been there for years. There is
> the Chippewa Reservation, coon, deer and rabbit hunting, swimming
> in the Rappahannock River and in Piscataway Creek, oyster hunting
> with tongs and nets. In White Oaks Swamp the fog rolls through the
> hollows like it does in the movies and people still walk for miles and
> miles. There are cookouts and bake sales and a big club where every-
> body goes Friday and Saturday nights.

The key figure in Dunnsville was Clive's grandmother, then in her
seventies, forever cooking and sewing and going to church. Clive said
she was prescient; if she dreamed she saw a hooded figure on a horse

moving toward a neighbor's house, almost certainly a death was at hand.

> She only put in electricity last year. When I go I chop wood for her old iron stove and draw water at the hand pump and chase spiders and crickets from the outhouse. There's an old buggy and flatbed wagon in the yard, you know, and hand-hewn furniture, hooked rugs and tick mattresses in the house. Three bedrooms. Some days I'll drive over to the Shenandoah Valley, maybe to the Luray Caves or the mountains toward West Virginia. It's just about the prettiest part of the country. When you go down to Dunnsville, you don't never want to come back.

A broken marriage took him away from Dunnsville when he was eight, and he lived with his mother in a Harlem tenement and later in a Washington inner-city slum. He studied to be a draftsman, but after a series of menial jobs, or no job at all, he discovered that as a car thief he could earn $600 a night, two or three nights a week. He told me, "I got in with this gang of guys stealing automobiles and stealing parts, and that's been the pattern ever since." The time I spent going around with Clive was to discover a new side of Washington, a rather small underworld where, as in a village, everybody knew everybody else. In 1970 I'd done studies of the Arab underworlds of Casablanca and Paris and it was the same there too. It was a Washington I've hardly set foot in since: Good Hope and Wheeler roads, Martin Luther King Jr. Avenue, Pennsylvania and Alabama near the District Line, East Capitol Street to Eastern Avenue heading into Seat Pleasant, 14th between U and T, 8th and H, 7th and Park, Dupont Circle and the P Street beach.

We did a lot of walking, but kept away from white-dominated areas. Clive said, "If I'm out on the street after dark and see a white woman waiting for a bus, I'll cross to the other side so she won't think some black dude is coming to rob or rape her." Clive was quiet and unassuming, with good manners, an Afro, a muscular physique. He said he'd never been involved in violence; still, if you didn't know him, he was someone you might fear. One time near the Lincoln Memorial, he said, three young men tried to jump him. "Hey, man," he told them. "I'm as poor as you are. I just got out of Lorton." Or he would tell about some dealer he knew: "Six diamonds on his fingers, white and pea-green suit, Electra 225 with TV and telephone, next thing you know, he's busted." What concerned me most was that it seemed like half of Clive's acquaintances we met were ex-cons from Lorton and that at least half could not find a job—in Clive's words, "any lousy job."

In the evening Clive liked to stand on the Potomac's banks across from National Airport with his FM transistor, listening in to the pilots and ground controllers, betting on who would take off or land next, observing the switch from north to south, tallying the arrivals and departures. He'd never flown himself. Once I told Clive it was as if he was looking for something he'd lost. It was true, he said. Clive:

> I had a wagon and I had an airplane. I lost the airplane when we moved away from Dunnsville and never knew what happened to it. Oh, sometimes I'll rummage around the attic down there, you know, through all the old broken stuff, lamps and chairs. That plane. I'm still looking for it. A great metal thing. Painted red. I think it was made in Japan. Tin. Maybe old reworked beer cans.

A younger generation of inner-city blacks no longer even have a Dunnsville in their lives. Two older African-American women I met at the Martin Luther King Jr. Center in Waterloo, Iowa, said commercial television was taking over from inherited culture. Ada Tredwell, whose father had been a sharecropper in the South before coming North to work in a meat-packing plant, said, "The way values keep changing, young people don't know what the rules are."

> There was a time when, if a boy got a girl pregnant, he had to marry her. That was the way we were brought up. Now you look at television and say, "Hey, that's okay. This is okay." And you find yourself changing your life, your standards, your values. It keeps getting foisted on you. You see it enough times, you keep seeing it over and over. And you think: what's wrong with that? So we accept it. There was a time you protested, "Oh, I think it's terrible these kids are getting pregnant or these babies are having babies." Now people criticize you for even objecting. And naturally, the more you accept it, the more acceptable it becomes. And you lose your values. That's what happens.

Martha Nash, the center's director, flatly blamed television for teenage violence:

> You keep drumming it into people in their homes. You keep telling these kids, "This is the way to solve your problems. You don't talk it over. You don't reason. You just blow 'em away . . ." America is in for a lot of social upheaval, social disintegration.

At the heart of this failure of nurture, which can be acute for inner-city black teenagers, is something that affects the whole of American society, the breakdown of the family.

IV

If religion is the heart of a culture and the agricultural community its original basis, the family does most to transmit that culture from one generation to the next. Family breakdown means cultural discontinuity. The arrival of the pill in 1956, a contraceptive that was reliable, easy to use and under female control, gave women the ability to defer childbirth, removing a main barrier to female professional equality. From 1960 to 1980, there was a huge rise of post-pill premarital sex in America, the birth rate halved, the divorce rate doubled and full-time homemakers dropped from three-fourths to one-fourth of all married women. The old image of Dad at the office, Mom in the kitchen and the kids outside playing fits less than one American family in ten. Marriage is coming back, but more couples still choose to live together and even start a family than was the case a generation ago. More of those who do marry later divorce. America has the world's highest divorce rate, 48 percent, followed by Sweden, 44 percent; Catholic Italy and Spain have the lowest, 8 percent. In 1993 *The Economist* reported that in 1973 half of all young American women were married by twenty-one, men by twenty-three; twenty years later the age of marriage had gone up by two and a half years. With more working women, more births out of wedlock and more divorces, a fourth of all American families are now headed by a single parent.

Why do so many families break up? More liberal divorce laws make it easier. There is a huge rise in women with jobs; they formed 32 percent of the workforce in 1956 and earned around a fifth of its total income; now it's 46 percent and well over a third. Two incomes are often needed to keep up a couple's middle-class standards and educate the children. Once wives work, husbands say they do more household chores; in fact, while many men may help shop, do dishes and look after the kids, women still do practically all the cleaning, cooking and washing. This inequity in household chores is the kind of added strain on marriage that along with relaxed laws can sometimes make divorce seem a more attractive alternative than staying together.

Yet divorce hurts everybody. U.S. Census Bureau statistics show that single, divorced or widowed men and women die younger than if they were married, men more than women. *The Economist's* 1993 survey reported that the divorced drink more and spend more time in mental hospitals. Divorce also makes women and children poorer. In 1989, 41 percent of all divorced or separated American women living with children under twenty-one got nothing from their husbands; the rest averaged just $3,000 a year. Separated or divorced women lost about a third of their incomes when their marriages broke up.

If divorce makes men less healthy and women poorer, it is hardest on children. Studies show that children who grow up in a single-parent family are more likely to drop out of school, marry during their teens, have a child out of wedlock or get divorced themselves. With the family in so much trouble in cities—monogamous, divorceless and multichild marriages do better in rural America—there has been a big rise in destructive behavior by young people: school dropouts, drug abuse, vandalism, violence. Estimates of American homelessness now run somewhere about 600,000 on any given night, with 7 million since 1985. These are the mentally ill, alcoholics, drug addicts, drifters, runaways, old people or just helpless people who fall through the supposed safety net. Fifty years ago, parents, grandparents, aunts, uncles, brothers and sisters might have rescued them. When households were larger and cheaper to maintain, it was easier to absorb the drunkard uncle, batty aunt or jobless nephew who couldn't feed his wife and baby. Federal studies confirm that family dysfunction, including physical or sexual abuse, is the prime cause of homelessness among the 500,000 to a million runaway or "throwaway" teenagers.

Yuppie ethics are also to blame for family breakdown. In Professor McNeill's view:

> Instant gratification and a refusal to subordinate one's personal impulse to any larger social solidarity is the way much yuppie behavior strikes me. I do not think a society can thrive or long endure on such a basis.

Pressures on the American family have grown intense. Nurturing is easiest when parents are physically on the scene with their children, as in a village like Ghungrali or Popowlany, or on a farm, or even in a city if parents happen to pursue occupations that keep them at home and can pass skills along to their children. Cultural reproduction breaks down when both husband and wife need to go off to jobs outside the home, often not returning until evening, tired from working, commuting and shopping, and reaching home, likely as not, well

after the children return from school. Cultural influences then become schoolteachers, peer groups and the media. Cecilia Mishoe, a
black first-grade teacher in Washington, D.C., told me, "Parents are
just plain not talking to their children enough." She gave an example:

> They go to the store with their mothers and ask, "What's that? Why
> are they doing that?" Too often the parents ignore the children's ques-
> tions or abbreviate the answers. "Oh, I don't know, honey. Wait a
> minute. Mama's busy." Or they tell them to go watch TV. But a TV
> set cannot answer a question or establish rules or provide the reassur-
> ance of love. An average child should be able to cope, but not all of
> them can.

I spent several days with Mrs. Mishoe's class, a real haven—we took
walks in a park to see the leaves fall. She had a problem child, Billy,
the towheaded son of a Marine sergeant. One day a little girl came
running to Mrs. Mishoe with a bleeding lip after Billy hit her. Sobbing, Billy told Mrs. Mishoe, "She pushed me! My daddy told me if
any kid pushed me I was to hit 'em in the face with my fist." One day
Billy's mother phoned Mrs. Mishoe to say she was taking him out of
school and leaving for California. When Mrs. Mishoe asked Billy
about it, he said, "Oh, yeah, I forgot. We're going to my grandma's
house. My daddy doesn't like us anymore."

Americans who grew up on farms see the failure of nurturing
clearly. Historian Gilbert Fite says, "This is the last generation of
Americans, we older people, who will have any significant hands-on
experience with farming, or a real agricultural life. Those left are so
few they will no longer be numerous enough to provide any rural
leaven in our society." Ada Rasmussen, eighty, a farmer's widow who
ended up living alone in low-income public housing, told me, "Nothing can take the country out of a person." She described growing up
on her father's farm in Pennsylvania; you got a sense of the sun behind the schoolhouse, men moving down the fields of rye and oats
with scythes, a stream that flowed into a little green pool half hidden
in reed grass. "In those days you lived in places you could see, feel,
pin down on a map. I can still remember the road on which I drove
the wagon to town, the church, the fields, the river. It seems more real
than anywhere else I ever lived."

Mrs. Rasmussen said that early on she learned that hard physical
labor was the center of life and that without it "poverty was a dog
whose teeth sank deep." At seventeen, she worked as a hired girl for

neighbors, rising at four o'clock to milk seven cows before making breakfast and starting the chores. For this she was paid three dollars a week. At eighteen she married a farmer with a hundred and four acres. While milking cows, harvesting wheat and corn and mowing hay, she raised four sons and a daughter.

> You know, those years, with my children gathered around me, were the happiest of my life. Nowadays . . . well, I watch the quiz shows and the soap operas and the news. This morning it was all about another rape slaying. I just don't know what's got into people.

Bill McKibben, writing about TV, says that while "people will flee from backbreaking labor at first chance," getting too engaged in "the world of consumption and growth and comfort offered by television" can be just as alienating. Television gives us a semblance of control—we can switch it on and off—but this is false since programming is determined by distant professionals with their own artistic or commercial imperatives.

Only a few Americans today do the kind of hard physical work we saw the Polish, Egyptian, Punjabi and other villagers do. Without it, without father and son, or an older and younger generation, working side by side in the fields, the age-old way by which tradition and skills get handed down is interrupted. In his poem "The Death of the Hired Man," Robert Frost portrays this kind of cultural transmission as the dying hired man remembers working one summer with a college boy:

> He said he couldn't make the boy believe
> He could find water with a hazel prong—
> Which showed how much good school had ever done him.
> He wanted to go over that. But most of all
> He thinks if he could have another chance
> To teach him how to build a load of hay—

In Popowlany, when Jurek recalls he made his first haystack at the age of eight and he is asked who taught him, he says, "Nobody. I just watched the others." Along with skill, discipline and self-reliance were being handed down. Professor McNeill worries that this is being lost in today's city:

> In urban contexts, where the family is not the unit of work or of production, the nurture of the young and the transmission of our cul-

ture has in practice been shifted from the bosom of the family to a far looser and less efficient network of human relationships.

When young people educate each other, all too often what is taught, even if it is not outright antisocial, does not instill values that hard work, practical skills and mutual help are the way to long-term economic prosperity. McNeill:

> In town the youth gangs of our streets provide all the support anyone needs for rebellious behavior; and in some contexts it becomes so entrenched as to defeat formal education and produces young men who are unfit for anything other than criminal activity.

What to do? We might set up some kind of system like the Depression's CCC camps to get these young men off the streets, teach them employable skills and the sort of discipline youthful work brings. A start has been made with more than fifty such "boot camps" across the country, in 1994 housing about 8,000 inmates. But results have been mixed and this is a drop in the bucket when the total male population in prisons, jails and reform schools is 1.3 million, and the biggest inmate complaint is idleness and lack of job training inside prison, or, as among Clive's fellow ex-cons, lack of jobs when they do get out. Also, conceivably, we could monetarize child care—that is, pay mothers so they could earn but stay at home. Or go back to Moynihan's idea of a guaranteed minimum income, to enable people to escape decaying inner cities.

The questions really facing us, in America and all over the world, are: Can we invent a substitute for the shrinking rural base of our increasingly urban sprawl? Can urban living on a long-term basis stabilize for human beings? Can villagelike groups be found within city living that can give our lives the meaning and cultural guidance that rural life provides? Can cities be made humanly and intellectually acceptable to all their inhabitants?

V

Barbara Ward once predicted that the cities were where "all the contradictions will meet, clash and finally explode." She was thinking of the poor nations, but New York and Los Angeles, our greatest marketplaces of ideas and the heart of our media, business, finance and the arts, also have the most violent crime, racial tension, gun battles, drive-by shootings and homelessness.

When I started out to report villages twenty-five years ago, I stopped in Rome to visit the United Nations Food and Agriculture Organization, which was then drawing up a master design to avert world famine. The FAO happens to occupy Mussolini's old colonial ministry in the heart of the ruins of ancient Rome. It faces the Colosseum, with the Circus Maximus on one side and the Baths of Caracalla on the other. The sense of great men, noble speeches, the cries of martyrs and gladiators and the final onrush of barbarians was palpable.

Republican Rome in the third century B.C., Britain in the nineteenth century and America in the twentieth, all peaked at a time when the leaven of rural culture was strong in their cities: a majority of their populations had been nurtured in villages. Without a rural base, a society experiences family breakdown and the beggary and homelessness that go with it, the crime and outcry for more prisons that breed crime, the widening divide between rich and poor and the seeping away of what you might call a culture's emotional authenticity—its kindness, civility and good nature. When two small boys kidnapped and murdered a two-year-old in Liverpool in 1993, forcibly dragging the frightened toddler bruised and crying through crowded city streets without anybody coming to his rescue, the Most Rev. George Carey, Archbishop of Canterbury, demanded in anguish, "We must change this culture of violence and anger." But how? Britain, 90 percent urban, lives in its cities and exemplifies, more than anyplace else, the cultural decline of the West. From T. S. Eliot's *The Waste Land* in 1922, with its ghost city haunted by shadows, to Mike Leigh's 1994 film, *Naked*, with its high-spirited, low-living Johnny from Manchester ("Whatever else you can say about me, I'm not fucking bored"), London has symbolized twentieth-century apocalyptic despair, with its cry for faith and a doomed search, like Johnny's, for a lost wholeness of being. Stand in the chapel at Eton, as in the Roman Colosseum, and listen to the silences.

The past twenty years have seen the computer, telecommunications, automation and biotechnological revolutions come of productive age. They make it overwhelmingly likely that prosperity will grow, if unevenly, as the East Asia of Nae-Chon and China's Guangdong province expand to draw wealth and power into the Pacific, and that the world, if the farming problems of African villages like Fufuo can be solved, will have no trouble feeding itself. The dangerous threshold ahead is less likely to be the exhaustion of resources, pollution or population pressure, but more the rising anarchy and civil disorder in cities caused by a breakdown in an urban culture cut off from its rural base. Such social upheaval can conceivably occur in rich and poor countries alike, and so poison tribal instincts that, as we saw in Popowlany and Ghungrali, civilized people can sing hymns to mass murderers like Hitler or Bhindranwale who are self-evidently criminal psychopaths.

This is why I argue so single-mindedly that we have got to keep enough people on farms and in villages, in America and the world over. All our culture—our institutions of family and property, religion, the work ethic, the agricultural moral code and mutual help—originated in villages. Farming is hard—who would not prefer to sit in Alicja Matusiewicz's drawing room discussing music and art rather than go with Jurek on a cold, rainy morning to milk the cows—I have not, I hope, romanticized it—but agriculture creates societies that work. We miss our rural past as well. Just look how we flee the city for a quiet weekend in the country. How pleasant to set out in a horsecart to spend a sunny summer's day picking hazelnuts among the birches on the Narew River's banks. But saving the countryside is a matter of government. We need in the United States to enact economic policies to save as many farms and small country towns as we can, because the culture of American cities is at stake. I repeat: no substitute for the rural basis of our urban culture has yet been invented.

Professor McNeill cautions that this doesn't mean we cannot find a substitute, just that we haven't.

> A substitute is not clearly visible yet. That's what I would say. Human ingenuity is not that limited. It may take a very long time to emerge. This is a very deep transformation of human life if we're right in saying that we're moving away from the old village—autonomous, local, almost self-contained. As we are. Once farming didn't exist either. I would rank what is happening now with man's transition from a hunter and gatherer into a farmer. This, it seems to me, is the most critical axis of world affairs in our time. Since civilization began, the gap between town and country has been fundamental.

If what we face compares to that earlier transition, we must use our minds to solve problems of the magnitude of learning to place a seed in earth to grow, or finding that an animal can be fed and tamed and not just hunted, or scratching marks on trees and rocks so that those who come behind won't get lost. It means, like the invention of agriculture, husbandry and language, taking purposeful control of our own destiny. Matthew Arnold called culture "the acquainting ourselves with the best that has been said and known in the world, and thus with the history of the human spirit." If we renew our acquaintanceship at its origin, we must look back, past the decaying cities, despite what urbanists like Jane Jacobs may say, past the probably failed experiment of suburbia, past the vanished pioneer settlements, to the rural basis of all our behavior, arts, institutions and beliefs—the village.

The transition from hunting-gathering to agricultural life must have involved very great strains. Getting adjusted to new customs, tools, daily life routines. Suddenly you couldn't eat all the grain you'd collected, but had to save seed for next year, even if it meant sometimes going hungry. Professor McNeill:

> What works tends to propagate itself. If the cities collapse in a kind of civil war, which might happen, or if there are health disasters that bring down human life, there will still be other human beings around and other ways of behaving and other institutional forms that *do* work. In this kind of postindustrial information society—if it sustains itself— these will be found. It may take a hundred years. It may take a thousand years. In human life, just because a problem is there, it doesn't mean there's a solution in the short run. It doesn't mean there's a stone wall either. And I tend to think of it as much more a process of random experiment than selective survival. Those things that work tend to be spread by imitation. And just what will work in our urban jungle isn't very clear yet.

With so much extreme poverty, hunger, shantytown dwelling and joblessness, health disasters would seem to loom larger than pollutional doom or resource exhaustion for so many cities. Until now AIDS has had little demographic impact; worldwide we're still gaining 90 million people a year. But according to Jonathan Mann, the director of the International AIDS Center at Harvard, between 40 million and 110 million are predicted to be infected by the HIV virus by 2000, 42 percent of them in Asia, 31 percent in Africa, 8 percent in Latin America and 6 percent in the Caribbean. In 1992 at least 13 million people worldwide were HIV-positive, 7 million men, 5 million women and the rest children. A rapid spread of AIDS to villages reflects hidden relations with prostitutes or bisexual behavior by men in Asian, African and Latin American cities. Amid fewer claims that AIDS was an imported disease from the decadent West, Egypt in 1992 began a TV campaign with Koranic verses such as "You shall not commit foul sins openly or in secret."

Professor McNeill says a much greater danger to cities than AIDS is posed by upper respiratory diseases spread by droplet transmission or diseases of the alimentary tract spread by feces. McNeill:

> Droplet transmission means an organism that's spread by someone just being in the same room. Little droplets emerge from my nose and mouth and you inhale them. This is the way measles, smallpox, mumps and things are spread. Now a really lethal disease that moves in that fashion would have a catastrophic effect. The notion that medical people could stop it is, I think, naive.

Mutations in a virus can happen quickly and be carried by animals, birds or jet travelers; one theory is that AIDS was first spread by the African green monkey. McNeill finds that cities could act as sinks or sumps for epidemics, and that we may see a return to high death rates.

> I'm surprised it hasn't happened already. In ecological principles, whenever you've got a swarming of one species, it is a rich food source for other organisms. It's an enormous reward for them if they can make the transition into this dense field of food. The concentration of food in our physical bodies for suitable organisms is unparalleled.
>
> There's so many of us. It isn't all consumed directly by human beings and includes the animals we raise as cattle, but 40 percent of the total free energy that comes to the surface of the earth is now diverted, controlled and managed by human beings. Now if that's true, it's an enormous percentage for one species.

I was struck by Professor McNeill's phrase "random experiment." Americans have been pushing on to new frontiers, trying new ways of living, ever since our ancestors landed at Plymouth Rock. Richard Lingeman, in his definitive 1980 history, *Small Town America*, says the idea of "home" for Americans has always stood for both "permanence and transience; civilization, order, and comfort for those on the frontier; a place to be from, that provided identity."

Yet Americans were constantly exchanging realized settled communities back east or in the old world, for the assertion of their individual interests—to better themselves. Most of them, as soon as they arrived in the new place, formed new communities—settlements, rural neighborhoods, villages, towns . . .

The 1960s back-to-the-land movement, with its hippie communes, consciously tried to re-create villages. At one, in Virginia's Blue Ridge Mountains, I found that its forty or so college-educated members, who called each other names like Yellow Sky and Deep Water and lived in tepees, spent their days growing corn, beans and vegetables with hoes. They looked tanned and healthy, but a pretty young woman who had been working on her Ph.D. at the University of Chicago said she suffered culture shock.

> I tried an urban commune but its politics were too radical so one day I put my clothes in a laundry bag and split. I drove a Chevrolet Impala an uncle left me and came here. I got very sick my first two weeks. It can be very damp after a few days without the sun. Just getting back to a city I was all right. It was knowing there was a grocery store on the corner.

What struck me most about the commune, after living in villages, was the lack of family, parents who provided food, shelter and clothing in return for work. A village father's authority has an economic basis. The commune had no substitute, and when one young man, John, said he was going to visit his parents in a Maryland suburb, I asked to go along. They lived in a ranch-style bungalow in a suburb of endless homes exactly the same. His parents were watching a sitcom on TV and John's room was hung with Rolling Stones and Beatles posters. Before we left John's father drew me aside and said, "He's only twenty-one. In a year or two he'll go back to college and marry and settle down." Once, when I used the word "hippie," John admonished me:

> Words like "hippie," "dropout" and "street freak" are a mass-media rip-off and middle-class-value-laden terms. Don't try to put us away in a little box.

The consumer society, I thought, had already done that. No wonder such youths were trying to assert their individuality. A psychologist who worked with them told me many acted as if their often blameless parents were "completely evil."

> It's the only way they know how to assert their own freedom and authority. In most cases they really love and respect their parents. If

the parents remain sympathetic and avoid a direct confrontation, a reconciliation usually follows in time. But if the parents present a flat choice between their values and peer values, the peer values will win every time.

The hippie commune has faded away, but the impulses behind it— a simpler life, back to nature, a need for community, a younger generation's perennial rebellion—are as strong as ever. As a temporary reversal in the 1970s in the steady rural exodus showed, many Americans would live in the countryside if they could. Small towns and farms remain models of a simpler, more congenial society than that of the violent, polluted, traffic-ridden, impersonal cities. On what farms that are left the father-son tie is remarkably strong, 81 percent of American farmers being sons of farmers. But as long as farm productivity goes up through machinery, chemistry, genetic advances and biotechnology, American farms will get bigger and fewer and more small towns will become extinct. As I found in my own rural studies in the Midwest, urban commuters who settled in a former farming village simply brought city ways and views into a bedroom community set in the rural countryside. True rural culture does not emerge if not based on agriculture.

Margaret Mead, toward the end of her life, proposed what she called "an elective village," to which "people move because they want to live there, not because their ancestors have always lived there." In a sense, this has been going on ever since the Puritans sailed to America to escape religious persecution; as John Winthrop famously paraphrased St. Matthew: "We must consider that we shall be a city upon a hill, the eyes of all people upon us." In her 1987 *Cities on a Hill*, Frances FitzGerald gave us four fairly recent examples of McNeill's "random experiments" or Mead's "elective villages": Sun City, a Florida retirement community; the Castro, San Francisco's gay neighborhood; Rancho Rajneesh, the now-defunct New Age commune in Oregon; and Jerry Falwell's Liberty Baptist Church congregation in Lynchburg, Virginia. FitzGerald subtitled her book *A Journey Through Contemporary American Cultures*, but, in my view, none of the four are "cultures"—that is, inherited designs for living—but are instead newly invented conceptions of society that reflect rich, urban, high-technology Western man's new freedom of individual choice about how he will live. Implicit is that such ways of living, like fashions, can come and go, be easily changed, tried, kept or discarded.

(When it comes to being rich, it should be mentioned, Americans, with average incomes of just $23,000, are slipping behind those like the Swiss with $36,000; we now rank eighth in the world in terms of wealth.) While freely chosen patterns of living can have continuity, they do not necessarily provide the same handed-down, ready-made set of solutions to problems that parents teach their children, starting from infancy.

Retirement communities like Sun City, where old people who can afford it pass their fading days playing bridge, shuffleboard and golf, seemingly content in their yellow, pink and white pants suits and Bermuda shorts, were probably inevitable once life expectancies in America rose this century from forty-seven to seventy-two for men and from forty-five to seventy-nine for women. This is mainly due to falls in infant, childhood and maternal mortality. The average woman in 1900 spent much of her adult life childbearing and child rearing. Her life has changed phenomenally. But the average man of sixty today can expect to live just three years longer than he could at sixty in 1900. So he is retiring as soon as he can. Only three-fourths of American men aged fifty-five to fifty-nine and just half of those sixty to sixty-four are still working. FitzGerald predicts that such early retirement may be a temporary phenomenon; as America ages, so will its workforce. Most older people choose to use their relative prosperity to live apart from their children, if nearby. In 1900 only 40 percent did; 80 percent do now. A big drawback to retirement communities is so much infirmity and death. As one Sun City resident told FitzGerald, she was worried about being alone when ill or dying, once "this nice interlude is over."

I live in Berkeley because I happened to inherit a town house there, brown-shingled with garden, picket fence and view of the Bay, in a row of them mostly occupied by older, retired people who bought them twenty years ago when the condominium was built. But it is just north of the University of California campus in a town where the average age seems to be about nineteen. If you can brave all the cyclists, joggers, skateboarders, Nobel laureates, students, and assorted crazies and street people in what sometimes seems like a gourmet lunatic asylum, with outdoor cafés, flower stalls, great bookstores and hiking trails in the hills, all in perpetual fog-cooled sunshine, it is much more life-affirming to be among people of all kinds and ages. I keep close ties with two farm communities in the Midwest—I'll probably end up in one someday—and an uncle, ninety-nine, still runs a tree farm near St. Helena in the Napa Valley, an hour's drive away.

The Castro in San Francisco, like a monastery, the celibate Shaker sect or Egypt's Mamelukes, is fated to biological extinction unless it keeps replenishing its ranks from outside. Since the 1970s tens of thousands of young men settled this neighborhood to create this country's first all-gay settlement with its own commerce, churches, police, politics, choirs, sports teams and sexual mores. There are few women or children about but a preponderance of men in their twenties, thirties and forties with short hair, clipped mustaches, tight blue jeans and bomber jackets. In the Castro's heyday twenty years ago, tourists poured in and gays flocked to its bars and bathhouses in a sexual free-for-all. In 1978 an elected gay city official, Harvey Milk, and San Francisco's mayor, George Moscone, were gunned down in their City Hall offices by Dan White, a former member of the Board of Supervisors, who later killed himself. When a jury returned a verdict against White of "voluntary manslaughter," there were bloody riots. Then came AIDS. In 1994 city officials estimated that 4 percent of San Francisco's people were HIV infected. In 1992, there were 8,263 gay and bisexual men with AIDS, plus just 571 drug users. This is 280 AIDS victims per 100,000 people, compared to only 155 per 100,000 in New York, where the proportion of drug users among patients is much larger, or just 5 per 100,000 in a mid-American city like Youngstown, Ohio. In FitzGerald's words, the Castro's carnival became "the Masque of the Red Death." In a subdued version, the Castro survives as America's first community built by gay liberation, though perhaps less sexual and more mature for having suffered such losses. Even so, Armistead Maupin, the gay author of *Tales of the City*, told FitzGerald as he took her on a tour of the Castro, "I'd never live here. Far too intense."

The first of Maupin's six *Tales of the City* novels, which grew out of a humorous serial on San Francisco life he did for the San Francisco *Chronicle* in the late 1970s and was adapted as a miniseries which ran on PBS in 1994, tells about a group of mainly young people who stay at Anna Madrigal's small apartment house at 28 Barbary Lane on Russian Hill, across the city from the Castro. There is great charm to the story, set in 1976. Frank Rich in the New York *Times* quoted the miniseries scriptwriter, Richard Kramer, as saying Maupin's San Francisco is "a tiny little postage stamp of earth that maybe never existed." Rich's comment:

But it isn't nostalgic sentimentality to believe in Mr. Maupin's ideas. His American city is an extended, improvised and sometimes contentious American family—an attainable community, not a utopia—far more loving than most conventional families . . .

Many of Maupin's characters have such a cheerful innocence and good-natured tolerance that life at 28 Barbary Lane really does suggest that people can find a way to live happily in small, villagelike groups within a city without cramping individual freedom. They are a mixed bag—gay and straight, feminist and male chauvinist, eccentric and conventional, seedy and elegant. While among the young people there is plenty of nude tumbling around in bed, the story's main romance is between a couple that is sixtyish, Mrs. Madrigal and a patrician Republican advertising executive.

Interestingly, as the author takes pains to show us, even as he does so humorously, his two most winning young people—pretty, blond Mary Ann Singleton from Cleveland and gay, free-spirited Michael Tolliver, an ex-Future Farmer of America from Orlando—have been nurtured, as was Armistead Maupin himself in North Carolina, by old-fashioned, highly conventional parents. ("Watch out for fruits," Michael's unknowing father tells him.) When they come to San Francisco to change their lives, they start out with personalities pretty much formed by inherited culture, however much they rebel against it. They are open to a much more various world than the narrower, exclusionary all-gay or all-old societies of the Castro and Sun City. Mary Ann even tells the man who lives upstairs, "You're gentle and considerate and you believe in traditional values," though she soon discovers he makes child pornography. Anguished but still compassionate, she confronts him on the cliffs by the Golden Gate Bridge, and as he backs away and falls into the sea, it is as if we witness Mary Ann's discovery and confident defeat of evil. You get a rush of good feeling from *Tales of the City*, I think, because it is both human comedy and morality play. Its protagonists, simply by being so decent, kindly, humorous and loving, fend off the cruel and corrupt and create order out of disorder.

Bhagwan Shree Rajneesh's Oregon commune, quite another story, no longer exists. In time, the fat, bearded guru, notorious for his fleets of Rolls-Royces and red-clad disciples, was unmasked as a foxy charlatan. Deported, he went back to India, where he died in 1991, and the commune went down in a hail of lawsuits and criminal charges, such as trying to poison the water of an entire town, the Dalles. What made Rancho Rajneesh more than just *National Enquirer* copy was the puzzle why so many doctors, lawyers, accountants, social workers and otherwise seemingly respectable professional people became Rajneeshees. One can also wonder why so many Americans are into the Human Potential Movement or Scientology, or even Zen, TM or est, or encounter groups, tarot card and aura readings, ashrams, Tantric sex, past-life revelations, primal screaming and all the rest of it. Richard Lingeman warns that the search for community can sometimes lead to twisted outcomes:

> "Community" indeed means small town to many Americans—a link to place, a sense of belonging, a network of personal, primary ties to others, homogeneity, shared values, a collective belief in each individual's worth. Such an ideal could be perverted into totalistic community, which could snuff out individuality by probing into the private recesses of the human heart. The models of total community were chilling, mass political movements which subsumed the individual or tight, small religious cults rallied around a charismatic, authoritarian leader.

Cults thrive among the lonely and spiritually rootless; look at Jonestown or the Waco, Texas, cult of David Koresh. The poor in spirit are not always blessed.

Al Gore lists as symptoms of what he feels is a spiritual crisis:

> the resurgence of fundamentalism in every world religion, from Islam to Judaism to Hinduism to Christianity; the proliferation of new spiritual movements, ideologies and cultures of all shapes and descriptions; the popularity of New Age doctrines; and the current fascination with explanatory myths and stories from cultures all over.

The elderly Sun Citians and Castro gays tried to substitute friends for parents and children, especially in cases where children ignored or abandoned elderly mothers and fathers, or families rejected offspring for being gay. Bhagwan Shree Rajneesh went so far as to declare that humanity had "outgrown" the family. In reaction, Jerry Falwell's congregation made a rigid and narrowly defined version of "family values" the banner its Christian soldiers marched behind, something conservative Republicans were quick to pick up from the religious right. Why are fundamentalists who preach the literal truth of the Bible and who prophesy a coming Armageddon making so many converts? Even when they are engaged in such manifestly un-Christian acts as blowing up abortion clinics and shooting doctors?

It is the same Zealotism against change, I think, that we saw in Sant Bhindranwale and his Sikh gunmen. This instinctual reversion to old ways in the face of a superior opponent or idea was described by Toynbee as

> that instinct which prompts a herd of buffalo, grazing scattered over the plain, to form a phalanx, heads down and horns outward, as soon as an enemy appears within range.

Toynbee said that Zealots, acting by instinct, not reason, as they sought refuge in the familiar, could, like Bhindranwale's Sikhs or extreme and unyielding American fundamentalists, drift into violence.

> No doubt if he ever thinks about it—and that is perhaps seldom, for the Zealot's behavior is essentially irrational and instinctive—he says in his heart he will go this far and no farther, he will keep to the law in every other respect and win God's blessing for himself and his children.

Violent and revolutionary as they may be, in all but a few places like Iran, fundamentalists remain, as they do in Punjab, marginal, angry sects opposed to what they see as the wickedness of the larger society about them.

Fundamentalists profit by the sense of older values being lost in the stampede toward feminism, divorce, pornography, drugs, abortion, gay rights and such passing trends as political correctness ("a leftist danger to the very fabric of American life," the Rush Limbaughs chorus to eager audiences). FitzGerald tells about going around New York with Liberty Baptist preachers as they hand out leaflets: "Let's Get the Worm Out of the Big Apple," a battle cry to return to orthodoxy.

Professor McNeill sees much the same thing happening globally. In the University of Chicago's massive four-volume study of fundamentalism, he wrote in 1993:

> The radical instability that prevails worldwide as the human majority emerges painfully from rural isolation and struggles to accommodate itself to the dictates of an exchange economy, gives religious fundamentalists an extraordinary opportunity to channel mass responses either into an angry assault on aliens and infidels or toward peaceful symbiosis with strangers. Both paths are sure to be tried.

It is not easy to be what we might call a true Christian these days. A century ago, one might breeze through life as a smug Victorian, trusting in God and confident of humanity's infinite goodness. Humanism and a liberal "faith of our fathers" went forward hand in hand. In a modern city, "goodness" and "badness" can be hard to define. Do you turn the other cheek to the street mugger or love your neighbor if he pushes drugs at the junior high? Each evening on TV news, we are faced with stomach-wrenching images of burning villages and mutilated bodies in places like Bosnia, or reminders that enough hydrogen bombs are still stockpiled to blow us all sky-high and end life on earth. We do what we can to shape our lives, but some problems are beyond the reach of our mastery or clear responsibility. In the old, isolated village, the choice between good and evil was clear. In a contemporary city, the choice has become as fuzzy as if we were participants at a meeting of stockholders where a single vote counts for little and the moral issues are diffused.

Yet a new situation, such as being stricken by disease or the sudden revelation of horror, can shock our minds to new dimensions and create a compelling need to come to grips with the problem of evil. As I went through the Nazi death camp of Matthausen in 1958, in one whitewashed, odorless, antiseptic hall after another, I heard the guide's voice reciting, "This was the crematorium . . . this the *Vergasungskeller*, the gas chamber . . . this the workroom to extract gold fillings . . . this the experimental laboratory . . . ," until the atrocities surpassed comprehension, and one kept thinking, "Why, why?" When I asked my professor at the University of Vienna, he said that when truckloads of Jews came by on the Ringstrasse bound for Matthausen, *"wir konnten nur hoffen dass sie früh sterben würden;* we could only hope they would die quickly." One felt the same coming upon Vietcong atrocities in Vietnam, such as impaled or decapitated villagers. Liberal Christians might once have affirmed with Goethe's Mephistopheles that "darkness must exist before man has a conception of the light." But the horrors of the twentieth century bring us much closer to Ivan Karamazov, who says just before "The Legend of the Grand Inquisitor": "If the sufferings of children go to swell the sum of sufferings which is necessary to pay for the truth, then I protest the truth is not worth such a price." All too often modern life is like the final image in Ingmar Bergman's classic film *The Seventh Seal*, where the Knight and his court, silhouetted against the sky, are led hand in hand by a black-robed figure, in a writhing Dance of Death toward the Land of Darkness.

"Leave every other kind of knowledge," said Socrates, "and seek and follow one thing only . . . to learn and discern between good and evil." So often, when we explore human behavior, this is where we end up, though in the Polish and Punjabi stories both good and evil emerged more emphatically than I would have expected.

Perhaps a truly lasting "random experiment" or "elective village" continues to elude us because true culture is decided less by moral or personal choice than by its economic basis and that in turn is shaped by technology. Americans, from Puritanism to PC, are forever trying to impose cultural behavior on themselves and others, whereas our true design for living is formed very gradually by such things as stone tools, potters' wheels, reaping machines and water mills, or nowadays the microprocessor, transistor and integrated circuit, jets and space-craft, the pill and the IUD, telephone and television networks, high-yield grain and chemical fertilizer. These are the tools that change the way we live and, consequently, our ideas. As President Clinton has reminded us, "Our problems go way beyond the reach of government. They're rooted in the loss of values, in the disappearance of work and the breakdown of our families and communities."

Agriculture imposes its own rules of conduct upon people who live close to the soil and whose way of life, until very recent years, had hardly changed at all, one generation to the next, for thousands of years. The spread of scientific farming and contraception in the 1960s and 1970s, and television and modern communications in the 1980s, very suddenly altered their economy and culture. Going to the Punjab the first time in 1959, I was lucky enough to observe much of this transformation. Even at that late date, in Punjab and, I think, much of the village world, life's problems were so similar and so often re-peated, the age-old inherited solutions fit. True religious belief, I feel, the heart of human culture with its sense of goodness and morality based upon divine authority, grows best when it is passed from par-ents to children among a village's familiar houses, fields and woods. The annual rebirth of life and the mystery of growth bear witness to a deep permanence in the natural order of things. For most of us—not just Americans but everybody on the planet, and mostly in these past three decades—this continuity of life has been broken in the uncer-tainty of the city or the city's ways of seeing and doing things spread-ing to the villages through television. This could mean a spontaneous drop in fertility rates, as villagers come to know that smaller families mean better futures. But a great majority of the human race, while free of the old rural restraints and conventions we once chafed at, is losing association with its old cultural landmarks.

Our predicament is not unlike that of Jurek or Dhakel, Helmi, Jade or Husen. They have to find ways to keep their values; we have to find ways to restore ours. The deeply religious Muslim like Shahhat, afraid as he is of the twentieth century, or the African woman like Monica Mutuli, compelled to work out a new role for herself, or the agnostic, group-directed Confucians of Nae-Chon, or even the villagers of Huecorio with their dreams of *el norte*, do not, I believe, aspire to be like us. True, if we think of villagers as poorer and more miserable than most of them actually are, since we rarely see them on our TV sets unless they revolt, riot or starve, they tend to see us, not as we see ourselves, in a crisis of spirituality, but, thanks to the fantasy and universal spread of American Coke-jeans-and-Madonna pop culture, as richer and happier than we are.

To a typical villager, America is still a star-spangled wonderland of untold wealth and opportunity, as I've written, "a symbol, an idea, of the good life, of oomph and vitality, freedom and fun." This fantasy, tempered by reality, among immigrants from places like Huecorio, Popowlany and Ghungrali, if they learn English and assimilate, gives America its best chance to stay young and alive and dynamic, for they all bring this vision and their village culture with them. The French actress Jeanne Moreau caught this very well in a 1994 interview:

> This is an incredible country. Maybe because of the way it started
> . . . I walk the streets in Boston and Baltimore and Washington and
> New York, and it's thrilling to me. Everyone is so . . . different. It's
> so mixed.

We need these uprooted villagers. As William McNeill says, "Human beings are not yet adjusted to urban living and may never make the transition. Attracted to it, yes and for sure; but the moth is attracted to the flame." The villagers are not moving from their ways to ours. Rather we are all moving toward a brave new world based upon electronics, new energy sources and scientific wonders yet unknown. Perhaps something close to village life will emerge.

Since life goes on, so do the stories. In 1993 Charan gave title to Kuldeep's children of only one of his two acres left in Ghungrali, wickedly and inexcusably keeping the other himself. Beant and her children live on at his old well in utter destitution. Morality is a matter of individual choice, but it is groups, in the form of villages, that set the moral rules which Charan has broken with tragic finality. Charan now never joins his wife and sons at Chawar Khas but spends all his time at one Himalayan Sikh retreat or another, praying for his salvation. Pritam, a robust ninety-six at this writing, still walks to his fields once a day, his interest in the life around him undiminished. Agneshka writes she and the children—tall and good-looking in a photograph—went back to Popowlany the summer of 1993. Henryk Sadowski who survived Siberia is dead, as is Jurek's father, who came home to spend his dying days. Agneshka writes, "I feel very sorry for Jurek because now he is really alone."

The way and view of life in villages like Ghungrali and Popowlany, so little changed from the day agriculture was invented ten, twelve thousand years ago until just the last twenty-five or thirty years, gave our unstable human society much of what stability it had. Now the people of Ghungrali, Popowlany, Nageh Kom Lohlah, Sirs el Layyan and Pilangsari, Nae-Chon, Huecorio and Kaani, and all the villages like them, quite suddenly find themselves in a new global environment with its fitful televised experiences, many without beginning or end, shocking the senses, stirring the imagination, crowding the consciousness.

Toynbee's sleeper wakes. Drastic cultural disruption awaits us all. We are going to have to take this psychologically unstable, tradition-weakened world as it comes, keep our heads and our nerve and, like Pritam, staying within ourselves unperturbed, pursue a humane and decent life as best we can. "Was it a glory of a few years only for these people?" Will Pritam's question about Ghungrali's future be someday asked of us? We must find a substitute for the old rural basis of our soon-to-be global urban culture. Can we? For the answer, we have this whole good earth, not just our own small hopes and fears, to explore, and knowledge of it, and of its people in their cities and their villages, beckons.

Notes

Acknowledgments

ix *The Rise of the West:* "This is not only the most learned and most intelligent, but is also the most stimulating and fascinating book that has ever set out to recount and explain the whole history of mankind." H. R. Trevor-Roper, *The New York Times Book Review*, 1963, p. 1.

Norman Borlaug: "By showing Asians how to grow more food, Mr. Borlaug has probably done more good for more people than anyone else alive," Richard Critchfield, *International Herald Tribune*, September 8, 1992, Op-Ed.

McNeill, letter to author, February 26, 1983.

McNeill, *Mythistory and Other Essays* (Chicago: The University of Chicago Press, 1986), p. ix.

I The Sleeper Wakes: An Introduction

3 Barbara Ward, quoted by Critchfield, *A New Country: Conclusion of a Two-Year Study*, *The Alicia Patterson Fund*, August 1, 1971, p. 5.

4 E. M. Forster, *A Passage to India* (Orlando: Harcourt, Brace & World, 1924), p. 27.

5 2 million: *1994 World Population Data Sheet*, Population Reference Bureau, Washington, D.C., which shows the global urban population at 43 percent.

6 Robert Redfield, *Peasant Society and Culture* (Chicago: The University of Chicago Press, 1956), pp. 18–19.

W. B. Yeats, *Under Ben Bulben*, IV.

Oliver Goldsmith, *The Deserted Village* (1770).

7 Richard Leakey, quoted by Critchfield, "Science and the Villager: The Last Sleeper Wakes," *Foreign Affairs*, 60th Anniversary issue, Fall 1982, p. 20. Commenting on the theme "what drives individuals and nations," editor William P. Bundy said in an introductory note: "Our two lead articles come at this subject from what could hardly be, on their face, more divergent backgrounds of study and experience. Yet their thoughts come together on significant points, and both Professor McNeill and Mr. Critchfield seem to us to be saying things that are fundamental and perhaps seminal."

Martin Daley and Margo Wilson, "Nature or Nurture? Old Chestnut, New Thoughts," *The Economist*, December 26, 1992, p. 34.

Al Gore, *Earth in the Balance: Ecology and the Human Spirit* (New York: Plume/Penguin, 1992), p. 367.

8 Max Weber, "Religionssoziologie," *Wirtschaft und Gesellschaft* (*The Sociology of Religion*, Germany, 1922).

8   Henry Habib Ayrout, *The Fellaheen* (Paris: Payot, 1938; Cairo: R. Schindler, 1945, translation by Hilary Wayment).

Clifford Geertz, *The Religion of Java* (New York: Free Press of Glencoe/Macmillan, 1960).

McNeill, taped conversation with author, Hartford, Conn., July 25, 1991.

9   Critchfield, *Trees, Why Do You Wait? America's Changing Rural Culture* (Washington, D.C.: Island Press, 1991), p. 203.

McNeill, July 25, 1991, conversation.

Robert Redfield, *Peasant Society and Culture*, p. 77.

10   McNeill, taped conversation with author, Colebrook, Conn., August 1, 1990.

Ibid.

12   V. S. Naipaul, interview, Washington *Post*, Style section, November 19, 1981.

13   Norman Macrae, "America's Third Century," *The Economist*, October 25, 1975, survey p. 19.

TV set data, *1993 Britannica Book of the Year*.

14   Critchfield, "A Great Change Has Started," *The Economist*, March 3, 1979, p. 56.

15   Egyptian data from Critchfield, *Shahhat, an Egyptian* (Syracuse: Syracuse University Press, 1978), xvi.

16   Black death data from McNeill, *Population and Politics Since 1750* (Charlottesville: University Press of Virginia, 1990), p. 2.

Population growth data from Population Reference Bureau, Washington, D.C. *Yearly World Population Data Sheet*, 1975 to 1994, used throughout.

McNeill, "Reconsiderations: Winds of Change," *Sea Changes: American Foreign Policy in a World Transformed* (New York: Council of Foreign Relations Press, 1990), p. 188.

McNeill, *Mythistory and Other Essays* (Chicago: The University of Chicago Press, 1986), p. 62.

17   Ibid., p. 65.

18   George M. Foster: In a famous 1965 article, Foster wrote that "the model of cognitive orientation that seems to me best to account for peasant behavior is the 'Image of Limited Good.' By 'Image of Limited Good' I mean that broad areas of peasant behavior are patterned in such a fashion as to suggest that peasants view their social, economic and natural universes—their total environment—as one in which all of the desired things in life, such as land, wealth, health, friendship and love, manliness and honor, respect and status, power and influence, security and safety, *exist in finite quantity and are always in short supply*, as far as the peasant is concerned. Not only do these and all other 'good things' exist in finite and limited quantities, but in addition *there is no way directly within peasant power to increase the available quantities*." In his preface to the author's *Shahhat*, Foster notes: "We have found that traditional world views, and particularly a zero-sum game outlook—the belief that all good things in life are limited, so that one person's success is at the expense of others—often make it difficult for peasants to take advantage of the new opportunities increasingly available to them." *Shahhat*, p. xi.

Redfield, p. 15.

McNeill, *Mythistory and Other Essays*, p. 67.

19   Redfield, pp. 60–79.

Oscar Handlin, *The Uprooted* (Boston: Little, Brown, 1951), p. 7.

E. K. L. Francis, "The Personality Type of the Peasant According to Hesiod's *Works and Days:* A Culture Case Study," *Rural Sociology*, Vol. X, No. 3 (September 1945), p. 278.

Handlin and Francis quoted by Redfield, pp. 60–61.

Redfield, p. 62.

Ibid., p. 62.

22   Ibid., p. 42.
      Roderick MacFarquhar, "The Post-Confucian Challenge," *The Economist*, February 1, 1980, pp. 67–72.
      "Filial piety": see *The Hsiao King* or *Classic of Filial Piety, The Sacred Books of China.*
24   *The Economist*, quoted by the author in "Of Maharanis and Bartered Brides," Washington *Post, Book World*, May 27, 1990, p. 1.
      Arnold Toynbee, *A Study of History* (Oxford: Oxford University Press, Vols. I–III, 1934; Vols IV–VI, 1954; Vol. XII, *Reconsiderations*, 1961). See also McNeill, *Arnold Joseph Toynbee, 1889–1975*, from *Proceedings of the British Academy*, London, Vol. LXIII (1977), Oxford University Press. In 1989 the author asked McNeill, who worked with Toynbee in London and Oxford in the 1950s, how he summed up Toynbee's achievement. McNeill: "What Toynbee did, in my view, was to enlarge the field of history to make it embrace the whole of humanity. In a way that has not been done before. And this was one of those seismic changes . . . It made *my* mind over." His own work, McNeill said, had focused on technology and ecology, not, like Toynbee's, on religion, and he had failed to interest Toynbee in the cultural findings of American anthropologists like Redfield, whom McNeill had taken a course from at Chicago. McNeill continued, "It isn't true that the history profession has followed in his path. But no one now can think there was no independent history of Asia or any other part of the world before the Europeans discovered it. That's the way it was treated. The timeless East. And he broke that down."
25   Prime Minister Jawaharlal Nehru, from interview by the author for the Washington *Star*, November 19, 1963.
26   Naipaul, *India: A Million Mutinies Now* (New York: Viking, 1991), p. 58.
28   Per capita GNPs taken from 1994 *World Population Data Sheet*.
      Toynbee, *Civilization on Trial* (Oxford: Oxford University Press, 1948).
29   Rice production data from U.S. Embassy, Jakarta.
31   Samuel P. Huntington, "The Clash of Civilizations?" *Foreign Affairs*, Summer 1993, pp. 22–49.
32   Oswald Spengler, *The Decline of the West* (*Der Untergang des Abendlandes*, 1918–22).
      Toynbee, *Civilization on Trial*, p. 39.
33   Ibid., p. 214
      Ibid., quoted by author in *Villages* (New York: Anchor Press/Doubleday, 1981), p. 65.
      Plato, *Critique of Reason*, quoted in *Villages*, p. 70.
34   Aristotle, *Politics*, ii 3, ii 5.

II Winter Nights, Summer Days: After Communism

43   The spelling and pronunciation of Polish proper names defy comprehension by non-Poles. *Puszcza* is pronounced poos'-tah, and Jurek Yoo'-rek. Polish spelling has been used except in the case of Agnieszka, who uses Agnes in New York and is called Agneshka here, the way it sounds and Andre Borowski, who changed his spelling from the Polish Andrzej in America.
57   Historical data on Tykocin and Popowlany from Ewa Wroczyńska, Curator, Tykocin Museum.
62   Adolf Hitler, *Mein Kampf* (Germany: 1924; published in English as *My Struggle*, 1940); written in nine months in jail after the abortive Beer Hall Putsch against the Weimar Republic in 1923. "Ethnic cleansing," like the slaughter in Bosnia, especially among peasants struggling over land, goes way back in history, but Hitler's systematic program of extermination is perhaps the worst example. Since there is a great danger of such ethnic mass murders in the post-cold war world, involving Muslims, Hindus, Jews, Christians or other religious or racial groups, how the Holocaust came to one

small rural community was included in this book. Hitler, quoted by Christopher R. Browning, *Ordinary Men: Reserve Police Battalion 101 and the Final Solution in Poland* (New York: HarperCollins, 1992), p. 10.

63   Browning, pp. 11–12.
       Ibid., p. 13.

64   Heinrich Heine (1797–1856). The opening verse of his famous ballad on the Lorelei theme (1827) can also be translated: "I do not know why I am so sad / I cannot get out of my head a fairy tale of olden times." In his prescient poem "Almansor" (1801), Heine wrote: "Whenever books are burned, men also, in the end, are burned." *"Dort, wo man Bücher / Verbrennt, verbrennt man auch am Ende Menschen." "Halte Ordnung!"*: Such commands, in Gothic script, can still be seen on the walls of the remaining wooden barracks at Auschwitz II, or Birkenau, the Germans' biggest *Konzentrationslager*.

65   "Barbarossa decree": Browning, p. 11.
       The names of Busch, Volkschwein and Schaeffer taken from "Extermination of Jews in Białystok Region in 1939 and 1941–44," a document provided the author by Waldemar Monkiewicz, Curator, Archives on Hitler's Occupation, Białystok, Poland, and confirmed from memory by Alicja Matusiewicz. Since they would only be in their seventies all three are conceivably alive.

69   Browning, p. 85. Professor Browning ends his book: "Within virtually every social collective, the peer group exercises tremendous pressures on behavior and sets moral norms. If the men of Reserve Police Battalion 101 could become killers under such circumstances, what group of men cannot?" McNeill, an army veteran, as is the author, observes, "The army is dedicated to organized murder. You're given weapons and told, 'This is your duty.' Once you're doing it at short range, execution-style, the emotional toll must be considerable. But there is also the emotional argument: 'We're all doing this together. This is our role. This is our duty. We're serving the cause of Serbia or Punjab or Germany or whatever it is." March 26, 1993, conversation.
       Szmul Ismach, *Deposition Number 2735, Katowice Docket, 1945;* copy given the author by the Jewish Institute in Warsaw—Instytut Zydowski, ul Swieverewskiego 65. Szmul—Samuel in English—was born on June 21, 1930, in Tykocin, making him only sixty-four in 1994. He made his deposition just before leaving for London as a war refugee.

77   The Italian film *La Notte di San Lorenzo* (shown in the United States as *The Night of the Shooting Stars*), by Vittorio and Paolo Taviana, depicts the German pullout in the final hours of the war, with the same kind of cruelty and chaos Mrs. Grabowska experienced in Czechoslovakia. Art Spiegelman's *Maus I* and *Maus II* (New York: Pantheon Books and Random House, 1986 and 1991), like Steven Spielberg's 1993 film, *Schindler's List*, as well as a Russian Army documentary made at the time of the liberation of Auschwitz and shown to visitors there, provide a graphic sense of the place and time.

81   The terse four-sentence statement on Chernobyl from the Soviet Council of Ministers, read on the Moscow TV news program *Uremya (Time)* at 9:02 P.M., Monday, April 28, 1986, after the nuclear reactor exploded at 1:23 A.M. on Saturday, sending a fireball into the Ukrainian sky and radioactive clouds over most of Northern Europe, taken from Nigel Hawkes, Geoffrey Lean, David Leigh, Robin McKie, Peter Pringle and Andrew Wilson, *The Worst Accident in the World; Chernobyl: The End of the Nuclear Dream* (London: William Heinemann/Pan Books/The Observer Ltd., 1986), p. 118.

88   *Echo Tykocinskie*, No. 30 (August 1991).

90   Włodzimierz Puchalski, *A Year in the Primeval Forest*, translated by the author's interpreter, Pawel Kraïicz, from a copy in Puchalski's cabin on the Narew River, kept just as he left it by Alicja Matusiewicz.

91   "Stately old poplar trees": Many blew down during a severe windstorm in 1992, ending further debate on their fate.

93   Data on peasantry from Foundation for the Development of Polish Agriculture, Warsaw.

112   *"Żydzi do gazu"*: Reported by the author in "Anti-Semitism in Poland: Never Forgetting," *The Economist*, November 9, 1991, p. 32.

114   Monkiewicz, "Extermination of Jews."

116   "Fear of Germany": Professor McNeill notes that the Germans no longer reproduce themselves. "There are fewer Germans every day. It's a very different situation than existed in the 1930s and the early twentieth century when Hitler made *Lebensraum* an issue."

III   Allahu Akbar: *Two Faces of Islam*

126   Ayrout, *The Fellaheen*, p. 136.

128   The Nile Valley's future: In a June 10, 1976 interview Anwar el-Sadat told the author he favored taking the Nile Valley out of fodder and grain production and into high-value cash crops for export.

135   Leakey, *Origins Reconsidered: In Search of What Makes Us Human*, co-authored by Roger Lewin (New York: Doubleday, 1992), p. 356.

137   Clifford Geertz, *Islam Observed* (Chicago: The University of Chicago Press), p. 18.
Ibid., pp. 16–17.
Naipaul, *Among the Believers* (New York: Alfred A. Knopf, 1981), p. 355.

138   Ibid., p. 168
Ibid., p. 429
Brian Beedham, "Star of Islam," *The Economist*, December 14, 1991, survey p. 3.
Ibid., p. 4.
Hassan al-Turabi, quoted from interview by Jane Perlez, New York Times News Service, from *International Herald Tribune*, January 30, 1992, p. 2.

139   Flora Lewis, "Talking to Islam: We Need to Meet the New Thinkers," *International Herald Tribune*, February 21, 1991, Op-Ed.
Wilfred Thesiger, *The Last Nomad: One Man's Forty Year Adventure in the World's Most Remote Deserts, Mountains and Marshes* (New York: E. P. Dutton, 1980), p. 14.
Peter Theroux, *Sandstorms* (New York: W. W. Norton, 1990), as quoted by Sandra Mackey, "Suburbia Comes to Islam," *The New York Times Book Review*, June 24, 1990.
James Wilde, "Egypt's Writing Colossus," *Time*, December 17, 1990, p. 36.
Naguib Mahfouz, ibid.

140   70 million: Projection by Ahmed Lutvy, economic spokesman, U.S. Embassy, Cairo.
Agricultural data: Clifford Nygaard, Ford Foundation, Cairo; Ahmed Lutvy, U.S. Embassy; and Alan Richards and John Waterbury, *A Political Economy of the Middle East* (Boulder: Westview Press, 1990).
Roy Prosterman, Rural Development Institute, Seattle, in letter to *The Economist* protesting a report on Egyptian land reform, "Killing the Dinosaur," July 25, 1992, pp. 42–43.

143   Upper and Lower Egyptians first contrasted by author in "Egypt's Fellahin, Part I: Beyond the Mountains of Kaf" and "Part II: The Ant and the Grasshopper," *Fieldstaff Reports*, American Universities Field Staff, 1976. The author's most recent treatment of the theme was "Ant and Grasshopper: Tales from Egyptian Villages," *International Herald Tribune*, December 21–22, 1991, p. 4.

150   Robert Stone, "New Barbarians," New York *Times*, March 4, 1993, Op-Ed.

152   Husen: The author's first profile of Husen appeared in the Washington *Star* December 10, 1967. A 252-page illustrated report on Husen's life in both city and village,

"Hello, Mister, Where Are You Going?," was published by the Alicia Patterson Fund, December 1970, and excerpted in *The Golden Bowl Be Broken; Peasant Life in Four Cultures* (Bloomington: Indiana University Press, 1974).

160   Clifford Geertz, *The Religion of Java* (New York: Free Press of Glencoe, a Division of Macmillan, 1960), p. 23.

Ibid., p. 264.

Ibid., p. 23.

Ibid., p. 276.

IV   The Heirs of Confucius: East Asia's Challenge

171   "Strong hand of Japan": For a contemporary view, see F. A. McKenzie, *The Tragedy of Korea* (New York: E. P. Dutton, 1908). McKenzie was London *Daily Mail* correspondent in Seoul. The Korean War from a villager's viewpoint is Ahn Junghyo's novel *Silver Stallion* (New York: SoHo Press, 1990; originally published in Korea, 1976). The author himself served in Korea in 1954–55 as a sergeant in the U.S. Army Corps of Engineers, in Pusan, Taegu and Kunsan, and later spent three years, seven months, 1964–67, as the Washington *Star*'s correspondent in Vietnam, a very different Asian war.

Korea's village peasantry: Genre paintings of peasant life by Korean artists like Shin Yun-bok (1758–?) and Kim Hong-do (1524–57) depict the rural past just as Pieter Brueghel (c. 1525–69) and his family did for Flemish peasants.

174   Confucius: The canonical literature of Confucianism was mostly written during the Chou dynasty (c. 1027–256 B.C.) and gathered into the *Wu Ching* (five classics) during the Han dynasty (202 B.C.–A.D. 220). The *Wu Ching*, traditionally attributed to Confucius either as author or as compiler, include the *Ch'un Ch'iu*, a chronology of Confucius' home state of Lu; the *I Ching*, a system of divination; the *Li Chi*, describing rites and the ideal Confucian state; the *Shu Ching*, historical records, many of them forgeries, and the *Shih Ching*, on peasant life and feudal wars. During the Sung dynasty (960–1279) the quintessence of Confucian teachings was formed into the *Shih Shu* (four books) with the *Ta Hsueh* (great learning), *Chung Yung* (doctrine of the mean), the *Lun Yu* or *Analects* of Confucius as we know them, and the *Book of Mencius*, named for Meng-tse (371?–288?), after K'ung Fu-tzu (551?–479 B.C.), the most noted Chinese Confucian philosopher.

179   Buddha: Indian prince Siddhartha Gautama (563–483 B.C.), called the Buddha, founded Buddhism as a religion and philosophy. Buddhism entered Korea in the fourth century and became the state religion under the Silla dynasty until it was replaced by Confucianism in 1392, enjoying a comeback only in recent years.

189   Park Chung Hee, quoted by Roderick MacFarquhar, "The Post-Confucian Challenge," *The Economist*, February 9, 1980, p. 70.

190   MacFarquhar, p. 67.

Jim Rohwer, "When China Wakes," *The Economist*, November 28, 1992, survey p. 3.

Napoleon, quoted by Rohwer, p. 18.

191   McNeill, taped conversation with author, August 1, 1991.

MacFarquhar, p. 68.

McNeill, August 1, 1991.

MacFarquhar, p. 71.

192   Andrew Cowley, "Where Tigers Breed," *The Economist*, November 16, 1991, survey p. 6.

Lee Kuan Yew, quoted by Cowley, p. 6.

Lee Kuan Yew, quoted by Rohwer, "When China Wakes," pp. 17–18.

193   Toynbee, Jane Caplan condensation of *A Study of History*, 1972, p. 415.

194 Yuan Long Ping, conversation with author at second symposium on hybrid rice, International Rice Research Institute, Los Banos, Philippines, April 24, 1992. The author nominated Dr. Yuan for an Alan Shawn Feinstein World Hunger Award, which was presented to him at a ceremony at Brown University April 14, 1993.
China's economic data from International Rice Research Institute, 1993.

195 Rohwer, p. 4.

196 Brian Beedham, "Three People's China," *The Economist*, December 31, 1977, p. 39. Sulamith Heins Potter and Jack M. Potter, *China's Peasants: The Anthropology of a Revolution* (Cambridge: Cambridge University Press, 1990), pp. 21–22.

197 Potter and Potter, pp. 327–28. See also "The South China Miracle," *The Economist*, October 5, 1991, pp. 21–24, and "The Overseas Chinese: A Driving Force," *The Economist*, July 18, 1992, pp. 21–24.

199 Beedham, "Three People's China," p. 35
Ibid., p. 39.

200 McNeill, taped conversation with author, Hartford, Conn., March 26, 1993.
"One-Child Family System": The author reported it was failing in many villages in "China's Miracle Rice: A New Rivalry with West," *International Herald Tribune*, June 17, 1992, Op-Ed.

201 Population Crisis Committee: See Barbara Crossette, "Population Policy in Asia Is Faulted," New York *Times*, September 15, 1992.
Deng Xiaoping, quoted by Roderick MacFarquhar, "Deng's Last Fling," *The New York Review of Books*, December 17, 1992, p. 22.
Ibid.

202 Rohwer, "A Billion Consumers," *The Economist*, October 30, 1993, p. 21.
Lee Kuan Yew, quoted by Rohwer, pp. 21–24.

203 Brian Beedham, "The West's Mistake Was to Relax After the Cold War," *International Herald Tribune*, May 9, 1994, Op-Ed.
Joseph Levenson, "Marxism and the Middle Kingdom," *Diplomat*, September 1966, p. 48.

V You Can Go Home Again: Migration

207 Population data: "Census Reveals Changes As It Paints a Picture of Metropolitan America," New York *Times*, August 1, 1992, p. 7. See also Michael Elliott, "The Shadow of the Past," *The Economist*, September 5, 1987, survey pp. 1–22, and Christopher Wood, "Into the Spotlight," *The Economist*, February 13, 1993, both on Mexico.

208 Per capita GNP: *1994 World Population Data Sheet.*
Alan Riding, *Distant Neighbors: A Portrait of the Mexicans* (New York: Vintage Books, 1986; originally published by Alfred A. Knopf, 1984), p. 538. See also "Mexico's Second-Class Citizens Say Enough Is Enough," *The Economist*, January 8, 1994, and "The Revolution Continues; the Clash in Mexico," *The Economist*, January 22–28, 1994.

209 The off-the-cuff estimate of 850,000 Mexicans legally and illegally entering the United States the past year comes from Dr. Jorge A. Bustamante, president, Colegio de la Frontera Norte in Tijuana. Bustamante cautions this is just an informed guess as nobody really knows.

210 Redfield, *Tepoztlán—a Mexican Village* (Chicago: University of Chicago Press, 1930).
Oscar Lewis, *Life in a Mexican Village: Tepoztlán Restudied* (Champagne: University of Illinois Press, 1951).
Redfield, lecture, Cornell University, 1952.
Lewis, *Five Families: Mexican Case Studies in the Culture of Poverty* (New York: Basic Books, 1959), *The Children of Sanchez: Autobiography of a Mexican Family* (New York:

Random House, 1961) and *La Vida: A Puerto Rican Family in the Culture of Poverty—San Juan and New York* (New York: Random House, 1966).

211　D. H. Lawrence, quoted by Gene Lyons, "Inside the Volcano," *Harper's*, June 1977, p. 42.

212　Bernal Díaz del Castillo, *True History of the Conquest of New Spain* (1632), quoted in ibid., p. 41.

　　　Hugh Thomas, *Conquest: Montezuma, Cortés and the Fall of Old Mexico* (New York: Simon & Schuster, 1994), quoted by Christopher Lehmann-Haupt, "A Portrait of Cortes as Bold, Even Funny," New York *Times*, March 3, 1994, B2.

214　For the story of Tzintzuntzan, George M. Foster, *Empire's Children: The People of Tzintzuntzan* (Mexico City: Imprenta Nuevo Mundo, 1948), also published by the Smithsonian Institution.

227　"The Real Case for NAFTA": See "Eat Your NAFTA," lead editorial, *The Economist*, November 13, 1993, p. 16.

　　　Eric R. Wolf, *Peasant Wars of the Twentieth Century* (New York: Harper & Row, 1969), p. 3.

　　　Emiliano Zapata, quoted in "Reversing the Revolution," *Time*, December 23, 1991, p. 40.

229　Norman E. Borlaug, interview by the author, El Batán, Mexico, February 21, 1987.

　　　Toribio Medina Salazar, quoted in "Reversing the Revolution."

230　McNeill, *Population and Politics Since 1750*, p. 1.

　　　Ibid., pp. 25–26.

231　McNeill, March 26, 1993, conversation with author.

　　　George Foster, quoted by Redfield, *Peasant Society and Culture*, p. 41. In a Berkeley conversation April 7, 1993, Foster told the author in reference to Mexican villages, "What's happened to peasants? What do we call them now? Tzintzuntzan has more than twenty satellite dishes. They're no more peasants than I am."

　　　Redfield, p. 42.

232　Octavio Paz, quoted by Lyons, "Inside the Volcano," p. 44.

234　David Hays-Bautista, quoted by Elliott, "The Shadow of the Past," p. 20.

　　　Hispanic population data from "Census Reveals Changes As It Paints a Picture of Metropolitan America," p. 20. See also Latino National Political Survey, quoted in the New York *Times*, December 15, 1992, p. 1, and David Gonzalez, "Mexican Migrants Crowd New York," New York *Times*, May 19, 1991.

235　"Visiting Englishman": quoted from "Columbus's Children," *The Economist*, December 26, 1992–January 8, 1993.

VI　*Have You Seen the Edge of the Sky? Africa's Special Farming Problems*

239　Karen Blixen (pseudonym: Isak Dinesen), *Out of Africa* (New York: Random House, 1984, originally published 1937), quoted by the author in "What Is Going Wrong in Africa?" Washington *Post*, August 6, 1982, Outlook section, p. C1.

　　　Truman Capote, *Music for Chameleons* (New York: Random House, 1981), pp. 252–53. That Kamande was alive and in bad condition came to the author's attention during a 1981 visit to Kenya through a story by Wariara Gachie, "The (Real) Kamande Story," *Weekend Standard*, Nairobi, September 4, 1981. Gachie reported that Blixen erroneously called Kamande "Kamante" in *Out of Africa*, though he was a central figure. In a 1937 review Britain's *Guardian* called the book "a brilliant study of Negro life and thought."

240　Income data from *1994 World Population Data Sheet*.

　　　See the author's *Villages* for a description of Nuba tribal life in the Nuba Mountains of southwestern Sudan, pp. 29–41, and Dinka life in the Sudd swamp, pp. 221–24, both presently threatened by a genocidal "holy war" waged against them by Khartoum's fanatic Muslim fundamentalist rulers.

241 Monica Mutuli, profiled by the author in "Kenya: You Have the Soil and Your Own Energy," cover story, *UNICEF News*, issue 101, 1981.
Ernest Hemingway, "The Snows of Kilimanjaro," from *The Snows of Kilimanjaro and Other Stories* (New York: Charles Scribner's Sons, 1986, a Scribner Classic/Collier edition, originally published, 1927), p. 27.
Ibid., p. 28.

246 McNeill, *The Rise of the West: A History of the Human Community* (Chicago: The University of Chicago Press, 1963), p. 12.

251 See the author's report on the 1984 United Nations Sahel trip, "Even the Vultures Have Fled," *The Economist*, April 14, 1984, p. 51.

253 C. P. Snow, lecture, Westminster College, Fulton, Mo., November 12, 1968.

254 Norman Borlaug, taped conversation with the author, El Batán, Mexico, February 11, 1987.

255 Richard Leakey, *Origins Reconsidered: In Search of What Makes Us Human* (New York: Doubleday, 1992), coauthored with Roger Lewin.

256 C. Peter Timmer, "Food Price Stabilization: The Relevance of the Asian Experience to Africa," June 1992. Professor Timmer of Harvard gave this paper at the International Conference on Agricultural Development Policy Options for Sub-Saharan Africa, sponsored by the Sasakawa Africa Association, Airlie House, Warrenton, Va., August 23–25, 1992.
McNeill, *Sea Changes*, p. 172.

257 Ryoichi Sasakawa: This 1985 telephone conversation was quoted by Borlaug at the August 1992 Airlie House workshop on feeding Africa. The author's first article on Borlaug's initiative was "To Improve African Crops," New York *Times*, April 4, 1985, Op-Ed. The author's "The Greening of the Dark Continent," *The Economist*, March 14, 1987, p. 42, reports Borlaug's early problems with Global 2000, former President Jimmy Carter's foundation in Atlanta, which also received Sasakawa support.

260 Crop production figures for Sudan and Ghana provided by Borlaug at the Airlie House workshop.

261 Fertilizer data from Borlaug.
"Resistance from the World Bank": Early in the Reagan-Bush years pressure was brought on the World Bank to adopt free-market "structural adjustment" policies, a shift from the bank's old "welfare" role under Robert McNamara's leadership. See "World Bank Under Fire: The Reagan Team Mounts a Full-Scale Attack on the Bank's 'Uneconomic' Loans to the Third World," *Newsweek*, September 14, 1981, or Hobart Rowen, "Clausen, Resisting U.S. Pressure, Backs More Third World Loan Aid," Washington *Post*, October 3, 1981.

262 Kevin Cleaver: See "Making Agricultural Extension Work in Africa," paper given at the Airlie House workshop, when he was Chief of Agriculture, Africa Region, World Bank.
Jimmy Carter, closing remarks, Airlie House workshop.
The author's account of the Airlie House workshop: "Time for a Green Revolution to Save Africa," *International Herald Tribune*, September 8, 1992, Op-Ed; and the same article, expanded and given almost the entire Monday Op-Ed page, "Bring the Green Revolution to Africa," New York *Times*, September 14, 1992. Both reported the confrontation between Borlaug and Carter on the one hand and the World Bank on the other over whether to subsidize fertilizer in Africa. On October 3, the *Times* published four letters critically responding: Cleaver ("grossly distorts the nature of World Bank assistance to African agriculture"); G. Edward Schuh, Dean, Humphrey Institute of Public Affairs, University of Minnesota and a former head of agricultural programs at

the World Bank, who co-chaired the Airlie House workshop with Borlaug ("a mislead-
ing and ultimately mischievous characterization of a very difficult situation"); Walter
Coward and Robert W. Herdt, directors, respectively, of Rural Poverty and Resources,
Ford Foundation, and Agricultural Sciences, Rockefeller Foundation ("He is incorrect
to state that the Ford and Rockefeller Foundations have 'phased out their agricultural
programs' "), the two foundation staffers responsible for administering the research
grants for this book; and Ruth Katz, a former Peace Corps volunteer in Africa ("Has
he forgotten the devastation caused by these technologies?"). The *Times* received
more letters, including one from Michigan State University professor Carl Eicher,
than they ran. Masataka Minagawa, General Manager of the Sasakawa Africa Association, at once faxed the author from Tokyo: "We support you and Dr. Borlaug."
Borlaug himself phoned Herdt at the Rockefeller Foundation to object to his letter to
the *Times* and was drawn into a heated argument with him. In a letter on November
11, 1992, Borlaug reassured the author, as quoted in section VI, that he was right. See
also, "In Africa, Avoidable Disaster," *International Herald Tribune*, August 19, 1993, on
the author's report on another workshop on feeding Africa, this one in Cotonou,
Benin, and subsequent talks with Cleaver and McNamara in Washington. For
Borlaug's role in launching the green revolution, see *Villages*, pp. 307–17.

265 World Bank study: "Africa: A Flicker of Light," *The Economist*, March 5, 1994, p. 22.
Edward Jaycox, ibid., p. 23.
Anonymous bank official, ibid., p. 23.
Oxfam, ibid., p. 21.
The Economist, ibid., p. 21.
Ishrat Husain, ibid., p. 21.

266 Borlaug, conversation with author, August 26, 1992.
Borlaug, letter to author, November 11, 1992.

VII The Banyan Tree: The Last of the Peasants

270 Guru Nanak, *Guru Granth Sahib*, sacred scripture of the Sikh religion, translation of
verses by Khushwant Singh.

271 *Chowkidar:* Watchman.

273 *"Sat Sri Akal!"*: "God is truth!"—the common Sikh greeting.

278 *"Allah-o-Akbar!"* "God is most great!"—the common South Asian rendering of the
Islamic *tekbeer*, usually written in English among Arabs as *"Allahu Akbar!"* See Edward
Lane, *Manners and Customs of the Modern Egyptians* (Cairo: Livres de France, 1836),
p. 80.

286 "Skeletons": Still there in 1994.

290 Wolf Ladejinsky: See his pioneer studies, "The Green Revolution in Punjab: A Field
Trip" and "The Green Revolution in Bihar—the Kosi Area: A Field Trip," published,
respectively, in Vol. IV, No. 26 (June 28, 1969), and Vol. IV, No. 39 (September 27,
1969), *Economic and Political Weekly;* also his "How Green Is the Green Revolution?"
Vol. VIII, No. 52, Review of Agriculture (December 29, 1973), *Economic and Political
Weekly;* also *Agrarian Reform As Unfinished Business: The Selected Papers of Wolf Ladejinsky*
(Oxford: Oxford University Press, 1977, published by the World Bank). Ladejinsky,
the architect of postwar land reform in Japan and Taiwan, wrote of Basant Singh,
without naming him ("The Green Revolution in Punjab," p. 14): "He is one of the
big farmers who with the help of a farm management specialist from the university
keeps detailed accounts of all his operations and has no reluctance to exhibit them."
Still true, despite Basant Singh's failing eyesight, in 1994. Like the author, Ladejinsky was an ardent fan of McNeill's *The Rise of the West*.

294 "Mazhbis": Since they came to Sikhism earlier, they have a higher standing with the

Jats than the fairer-skinned Chamars. Khushwant Singh, in his otherwise definitive two-volume *A History of the Sikhs* (Princeton: Princeton University Press, 1966), has very little on the role of caste in Sikh villages and "Mazhbi" and "Chamar" do not appear in his indexes. In several conversations with the author, Khushwant Singh, India's foremost Sikh novelist and commentator, who is from a distinguished and rich urban family, treated caste as a socioreligious curiosity, even though caste broods over Sikh village life.

295   "Scythians": Just the author's theory.

298   *Gurdwara:* Sikh temple, from the word *guru.*
      Sarpanch: Village chief who heads the *panchayat,* a five-member elected village council, *panch* meaning "five" in Hindi.

299   *Charpoy:* String cot.

300   *Raja:* Prince.

308   *Chapatti:* Unleavened bread, usually served hot right from the griddle; northwestern India's staff of life.

309   *Wallah:* "One," as in "Ghungrali *wallah,*" one from Ghungrali, or "black-turbaned *wallah,*" somebody in a black turban.

317   *Lavi:* Age-old tradition whereby harvesters were paid each night with all the grain they could carry home on their heads.

322   *Dhoti:* White cloth, tied diaperlike, a common form of Hindu male clothing; not worn by Sikhs or Muslims or Westernized Hindus.
      Bilkool nahi: An emphatic no, commonly used.

324   *Salwar kameez:* Long shirt and loose pants worn by women in northwestern India, Pakistan and Afghanistan, sometimes with a veil, usually brightly colored.

327   "Anna": Old coin, a penny; today the word "paisa" is used; when the author was first in India thirty-five years ago it was called *naya paisa,* "new money." *Kooch paisa nahee* is a much-heard phrase meaning "I have no money."

337   *Pandit:* Brahman priest or teacher, whence Pandit Nehru.

346   "Crows": In Punjab all crows migrate diurnally, staying in villages by day and fields by night, a phenomenon the author has seen nowhere else.

349   "Bapuji": Literally "Father," but often used also for "Grandfather," which properly is "Dadaji." Mahatma Gandhi was called Bapu by his followers.

354   Gurcharan Singh Tohra: Mark Tully, chief of the New Delhi bureau of the BBC, describes Tohra as "a cunning but unsophisticated politician with Communist connections," *Amritsar: Mrs. Gandhi's Last Battle* (London: Pan Books, 1985), co-authored by Satish Jacob, p. 72. See also Tully, *No Full Stops in India* (London: Penguin Books, 1991), especially Chapter 5, "Operation Black Thunder," pp. 153–80; and *From Raj to Rajiv: Forty Years of Indian Independence* (London: BBC Books, 1988), co-authored by Zareer Masani, based on a BBC documentary series. In a conversation in New Delhi on January 7, 1992, Tully told the author, "The Sikh tradition of farming has in some way broken down and that means there are lots of footloose and idle young men. An educated farmer's son won't go back and farm. He thinks it's below his dignity. But where does he get a job? I mean, there aren't enough jobs going, you know. So many become terrorists." Tully, born in Calcutta and educated in England, is probably the most knowledgeable source on the Punjabi struggle.
      Sant Bhindranwale: See Tully and Jacob, Chapter 4, "The Rise of Sant Jarnail Singh Bhindranwale, *Amritsar,* pp. 52–64; Khushwant Singh, Chapter 19, "Prosperity and Religious Fundamentalism," *A History of the Sikhs,* Vol. II, pp. 319–41; and Naipaul, Chapter 8, "The Shadow of the Guru," *India: A Million Mutinies Now,* pp. 420–89. For an excellent concise history of Sikhism, see Khushwant Singh, *The Sikhs* (Delhi: Lustre Press, 1984), photographs by Raghu Rai, pp. 11–45.

372   Bhindranwale's speech: The author used both a tape-recorded sermon translated by

Tully and Jacob, *Amristsar,* pp. 112–13, and what Charan, who was in the audience at Dheru, could remember.

373 *"Choli chuk":* Obscene epithet, quoted by Charan from memory.

376 Bhindranwale quoted from Tully and Jacob, *Amritsar,* p. 72.
Indira Gandhi, quoted from display, Indira Gandhi Museum, 1 Saftarjang Road, New Delhi.

380 Mogul emperor Jehangir, quoted from Tully and Jacob, ibid., p. 19.

381 Baljit Kaur: Details on slaying, *Time,* June 18, 1984, p. 18.

382 Subhash Kirpekar: In 1961–62 the author's student at the graduate school of journalism, Hislop College, Nagpur University. A photograph of Kirpekar interviewing a Nagpur rickshaw *wallah* is on the cover of the author's textbook, *The Indian Reporter's Guide* (Bombay: Allied Pacific, 1962), and an investigative report by Kirpekar is reprinted in full in a chapter on crime reporting, "Prohibition Offences on Increase; Sale of Tonic Widespread." In 1994, thirty-two years later, Kirpekar was parliamentary correspondent, *The Times of India,* New Delhi, and one of India's best-known journalists. His interview with Bhindranwale, the last the Sant would ever give, was reconstructed after two taped conversations between Kirpekar and the author on March 18 and 22, 1992. This interview, Bhindranwale's last contact with anyone outside the Golden Temple, is also described in Kirpekar, "Punjab Riddle," *Indira Era: A Symposium,* D. R. Mankekar, editor (New Delhi: Navrang, 1986), pp. 131–56. See also Kirpekar, *The Punjab Story* (New Delhi: Roli Books International, 1984). Kirpekar did not disclose he had seen Bhindranwale's dead body on his return to the Golden Temple until the 1992 conversation with the author.

385 "At least sixteen hundred people . . . never accounted for": Tully and Jacob, p. 191.
"Bhindranwale was alive": Both Charan and the author's interpreter in Punjab, Yadvender Singh, still had doubts in 1994 that Bhindranwale was really dead. Photographs of his body have been published, as in Tully and Jacob, p. 130.

387 *The Economist,* "Death of an Empress," November 3, 1984, p. 9.
"A little island": From display, Indira Gandhi Museum; Mrs. Gandhi's residence has been left just as it was on the day she died, except for exhibits of photographs and framed excerpts of speeches and letters. The author first met Indira Gandhi in 1962 when A. M. Rosenthal, then covering the India-China war for the New York *Times,* asked him to do a short profile of Nehru's daughter as requested by New York. Rosenthal did not think much of the first draft and sent the author back to rewrite it, with the advice: "Be subjective, not objective." The author continued to meet Mrs. Gandhi occasionally until mid-1970 when, after a falling-out over Kashmir, whenever she was in power, except for two weeks in 1974, she banned him from India for the rest of her life.

388 H. Y. Sharada Prasad, known by the author when he was Prime Minister Morarji Desai's press secretary when he interviewed Desai in 1978, provided this eyewitness account of what happened in the garden the morning Mrs. Gandhi was killed by her Sikh bodyguards. Sharada Prasad, a soft-spoken, kindly person, was originally Mrs. Gandhi's press secretary, then Desai's, then Mrs. Gandhi's again, and finally Rajiv Gandhi's before he retired after holding the job more than a quarter-century. When the author asked him if he liked Indira Gandhi, Sharada Prasad replied, "I wouldn't have stayed with her all those years if I hadn't. She was a remarkably well-read, cultured woman who could talk on anything." Sharada Prasad headed the committee that created Mrs. Gandhi's remarkably well-done museum.
Peter Ustinov, quoted by William K. Stevens, "Gandhi, Slain, Is Succeeded by Son; Killing Laid to 2 Sikh Bodyguards; Army Alerted to Bar Sect Violence," New York *Times,* November 1, 1984, p. 1.

390   "Death toll": Both Tully and Khushwant Singh, in separate conversations with the author, March 1992, put the total death toll close to ten thousand.

393   *"Hum Log"*: See Arvind Singhal and Everett M. Rogers, Chapter 4, "The *Hum Log* Story," *India's Information Revolution* (Newbury Park, Calif.: Sage Publications, 1989), pp. 88–125.
       "Maggi 2-Minute Noodles": ibid., pp. 76–78.

397   "So when sin soils": Khushwant Singh translation, *The Sikhs*, p. 23.

398   Death toll: Official government of India figures.

399   K. P. S. Gill, quoted in "Punjab: Rule of the Gun," cover story, *India Today*, January 15, 1991, p. 26.

401   "Ignoble among the noblest": Khushwant Singh translation, *The Sikhs*, p. 22.

411   *Patwari:* Rural official who keeps land records.

414   "Too much water": Expert opinion in India is divided on the water issue. B. G. Verghese, *Waters of Hope: Himalaya-Ganga Development and Cooperation for a Billion People* (New Delhi: Oxford & IBH Publishing Co., 1990), argues that the melting snows of the Himalayas could provide irrigation and power to the densely populated, still-parched Gangetic Plain. "It is a very, very old challenge, but not impossible," Verghese, a highly respected veteran Indian journalist, told the author in a March 1992 interview. "For much of India, the green revolution is still to come." Indira Gandhi, in letters shown to the author by Dr. Borlaug, blamed entrenched caste and landlord interests for agricultural failures in eastern Uttar Pradesh, Bihar and Orissa, India's poorest region. In Punjab, where the water table has dropped, some professors at Punjab Agricultural University warn that excessive irrigation might lead to some areas of Punjab reverting to the near-desert of the 1940s.

418   Opium: The story of Saroop's nephew, Buldev, who helped Surjit save her farm in 1970 when her husband was addicted to opium and her sons were small boys, is told in *Villages*, pp. 110–19.
       Chandigarh: The disputed capital of Punjab and Haryana states, a curiously graceless town designed by Le Corbusier.

421   *"Dar lugta"*: "There is fear." Once out in the fields, where no one could hear, Bawa also told the author this, using the same phrase, *"Dar lugta*, Dick sahib."

VIII   Ourselves

427   Genesis 6:4.
       Ibid., 6:11.
       Redfield, *Peasant Society and Culture*, p. 78.
       Ibid., p. 74.

428   Will and Ariel Durant, *The Lessons of History* (New York: Simon & Schuster, 1978).

430   George Steiner, lecture, Leopold Fraenzens University, Innsbruck, Austria, 1958, from the author's handwritten notes as a student.
       "The Legend of the Grand Inquisitor," In Fyodor Dostoevsky, *The Brothers Karamazov* (London: Penguin Books, 1958), p. 296. Originally published in Moscow in 1879–80.
       Ibid.
       Steiner, *Tolstoy or Dostoevsky* (London: Penguin Books, 1967, revised edition; originally published in the United States in 1959), p. 307. See the author's interview with Steiner, *An American Looks at Britain* (New York: Doubleday, 1990), pp. 10–11, 38–39, 55, 76–77, 116, 231–34, 239, 242, 246, 251–53, 259–61, 263–64, 317, 334–35, 340, 405, 448.

431   Steiner, review of *The Cultivation of Hatred* by Peter Gay, *The New Yorker*, October 25, 1993, pp. 127–30.

Walter Lippmann, *A Preface to Morals* (New York: Macmillan, 1929), pp. 62–63.

432 Ibid., p. 63

433 John Dominic Crossan, *The Historical Jesus: The Life of a Mediterranean Jewish Peasant* (San Francisco: HarperCollins, 1992), pp. xiii–xxvi.

434 Ibid., p. 422.

435 Lippmann, from one of two conversations with the author, in Washington in 1967 and in New York in 1968.
Lippmann, *A Preface to Morals*, p. 134.

436 Todd Gitlin, "Introduction: Looking Through the Screen," *Watching Television* (New York: Pantheon Books/Random House, 1987), p. 3
Marshall McLuhan, quoted by Bill McKibben, "What's On?" *The New Yorker*, March 9, 1992, p. 66.
McNeill, *Sea Changes*, p. 178.

437 John Heilemann, "Feeling for the Future," a survey of television, *The Economist*, February 12, 1994, p. 3.
Ibid., p. 4.

438 Data on contraception: Quoted in "A Smaller, Better World," New York *Times*, editorial, January 11, 1994.
McNeill, March 26, 1993, conversation with the author.
Ibid.

439 McKibben, p. 68.
Singhal and Rogers, *India's Information Revolution*, p. 85.
"Modern times": Quoted from Critchfield, *Those Days: An American Album* (New York: Doubleday, 1986), p. 267.
Lech Wałęsa, quoted by Heilemann, ibid., p. 4.
Daniel Hallin, "Network News: We Keep America on the Top of the World," *Watching Television*, pp. 14–15.

440 "Helen Trent": Quoted from *Those Days*, p. 374.
Ruth Rosen, quoting Herta Herzog, "Soap Operas: Search for Yesterday," *Watching Television*, pp. 14–15.
Ibid., pp. 45–46.
Ibid., pp. 47–48.

441 Ibid., p. 49.
Ibid., p. 51.
"Stabbed to death": "Brasília Journal: A Slaying That's Right Out of Soaps," New York *Times*, January 1, 1993, p. 4.
Tom Engelhardt, "Children's Television: The Shortcake Strategy," *Watching Television*, pp. 88–89.

442 Bill Watterson, *The Essential Calvin and Hobbes* (Kansas City: Andrews and McMeel, 1988), p. 105.
Al Gore, *Earth in the Balance*, p. 367.

443 Ibid.
"It's *Carnaval* again": *Villages*, p. 15.
American Psychological Association data quoted by Ken Auletta, "What Won't They Do," *The New Yorker*, May 17, 1993, p. 45. Also rating of Motion Picture Association of America, ibid.
Robert Shaye, quoted by Bernard Weinraub, "Despite Clinton, Hollywood Is Still Trading in Violence," New York *Times*, December 26, 1993, p. 1.

444 Joel Rifkin, murder method described by Joyce Johnson, "Annals of Crime: Witness for the Prosecution," *The New Yorker*, May 16, 1994, p. 42.
Bill Clinton, State of the Union Speech, January 25, 1994.

445   Walter Reich, "The Men Who Pulled the Triggers," *The New York Times Book Review*, April 12, 1992, p. 26.

"Hell of a way": From Critchfield, "The Battle for Five Mountains: Under a Searing Sun, GIs Stalk an Unseen Enemy," Washington *Star*, November 23, 1965. The story was in series cited by the Overseas Press Club of America when it presented the author with its award for "best daily newspaper or wire service reporting from abroad during 1965" for his coverage of the Vietnam War.

446   Ruth Slawson, quoted in "TV Movies of Amy Fisher Are Hits on 3 Networks," New York *Times*, January 5, 1993. Harry Stein, a *TV Guide* columnist, responded to Slawson's comment, "What choice do we have?": "Actually, the choice is simple. If it's really that painful, quit. Otherwise, have the grace to shut up."

"Mother of a three-year-old": Quoted by Associated Press report, "Anti-Pornography Fight Seeks to Mobilize Women," San Francisco *Chronicle*, January 18, 1993.

447   Rodney King, quoted from the Oakland *Tribune*, May 2, 1992, p. 1. King, speaking to radio and television reporters in Los Angeles the day before, also said, "People, I just want to say, can we all get along? Can we stop making it horrible for the older people and the kids?" King left an indelible image on the American psyche.

Black farm data: Congressional Office of Technology Assessment, 1988.

448   Senator Daniel P. Moynihan, interviewed by the author in 1969 when Moynihan was President Nixon's urban affairs adviser.

449   "Sounds like concentration camps": quoted in *Villages*, p. 360n.

Clive Gilmore, "How We Live—7: Clive Is Still Looking," Washington *Star*, February 12, 1972, p. A-1.

450   Ibid.

451   Ibid.

Ada Tredwell, quoted by the author in *Trees, Why Do You Wait?*, p. 233.

Ibid., p. 234.

452   Family data from "Family Values: The Bargain Breaks," *The Economist*, December 26, 1992.

453   McNeill, letter to author, November 24, 1990, quoted in *Trees, Why Do You Wait?*, p. 245.

454   Ada Rasmussen, "How We Live—6: Old Woman Alone," Washington *Star*, February 11, 1972.

455   McKibben, "What's On?," p. 79. This *New Yorker* article later adapted in *The Age of Missing Information* (New York: Random House, 1992).

Robert Frost, lines from "The Death of the Hired Man" quoted from *Collected Poems of Robert Frost* (Garden City, N.Y.: Halcyon House, 1942), p. 52.

McNeill, *Trees, Why Do You Wait?*, p. 245.

456   Barbara Ward, "The End of an Epoch?" *The Economist*, May 27, 1972, pp. 66–76. See also Ward, "The Fat Years and the Lean," *The Economist*, November 2, 1974, p. 19. In the only interview the author had with Ward, in August 1969, she argued that the West suffered from a failure of the imagination when it came to helping poor nations: "Foreign aid has simply got to go up if we want to do it in time." She repeated the theme of her 1972 *Economist* essay, which ended with an appeal to recognize the unity of our planetary existence: "As E. M. Forster once put it, with his customary modesty, 'Only connect.' It is not a bad motto for a humanity that must hope it can learn to survive."

458   McNeill, taped conversation with the author, Colebrook, Conn., August 1, 1990.

459   Matthew Arnold, *Literature and Dogma*, preface to the 1873 edition.

Dr. Jonathan Mann, quoted in "Researchers Report Much Grimmer AIDS Outlook," New York *Times*, June 4, 1992, p. A8.

460   Egypt's television campaign: Reported by Reuters, March 24, 1993.

McNeill, taped conversation with the author, Hartford, Conn., July 25, 1991.

Richard Lingeman, *Small Town America* (New York: G. P. Putnam's Sons, 1980), p. 479.

461 "Culture shock": Commune member quoted by the author in "Dropping Out," Washington *Star*, May 14, 1972, p. D1.

Ibid., p. D4.

Ibid.

462 Margaret Mead, *Village Viability in Contemporary Society*, edited by Priscilla Copeland Reining and Barbara Lenkerd (Boulder: Westview Press, 1980), pp. 29–31.

Frances FitzGerald, *Cities on a Hill: A Journey Through Contemporary American Cultures* (New York: Simon & Schuster, 1986), partly from articles in *The New Yorker*, 1981, 1983.

463 Ibid., p. 243.

464 AIDS data from San Francisco Department of Public Health, quoted in "AIDS in San Francisco Hit Peak in '92, Officials Say," New York *Times*, February 16, 1994, p. A8.

Ibid., p. 87.

Armistead Maupin, *Tales of the City*, series of six novels on life in San Francisco based on a serial published in the San Francisco *Chronicle* in the 1970s. The first novel adapted as a television miniseries for Britain's Channel Four and broadcast by PBS's *American Playhouse* on January 10–12, 1994.

465 Frank Rich, "San Francisco Paradise Lost," New York *Times*, January 12, 1994, Op-Ed.

466 Lingeman, p. 475.

Gore, p. 367.

467 Toynbee, *Civilization on Trial*, p. 203.

Ibid.

FitzGerald, p. 191.

McNeill, "Epilogue," *Fundamentalism and Society: Reclaiming the Sciences, the Family, and Education*, Vol. II of the Fundamentalism Project, edited by Martin E. Marty and R. Scott Appleby (Chicago: University of Chicago Press, 1993), p. 573. In a letter of January 25, 1993, McNeill wrote the author he was discussing "the role of change in peasant communities and the religious implications thereof" with "an angle of vision on contemporary affairs close to yours—indeed dependent on your writings in some considerable measure." It was heartening and a relief to know that the extended dialogue on the ideas in this book with the great University of Chicago historian was not entirely one-sided, though I suspect he is being more generous than reality warrants.

468 *The Brothers Karamazov.*

469 Socrates, as quoted by Plato, *The Last Days of Socrates* (*The Apology, Crito* and *Phaedo*) (London: Penguin Books, 1954).

470 "A symbol": quoted from *Villages*, p. 334.

Jeanne Moreau, quoted by Bernard Weinraub, "For Jeanne Moreau, Life Is the Perfect Role," New York *Times*, January 3, 1994, p. B2.

McNeill, letter to the author, May 2, 1993.

Index

RICHARD CRITCHFIELD is the author of nine previous books, including three on villages, *The Golden Bowl Be Broken*, *Shahhat* and *Villages;* two social histories of rural America, *Those Days* and *Trees, Why Do You Wait?;* a political study of Vietnam, *The Long Charade;* and *An American Looks at Britain.* Former Asian correspondent of *The Washington Star* and a longstanding contributor to *The Economist* and *International Herald Tribune,* he has reported on villages for over thirty years. In 1981–86 he was one of the first MacArthur Fellows. He received an Overseas Press Club award for his reporting on Vietnam, and awards from the Ford, Rockefeller and Alicia Patterson foundations. He lives in Berkeley, California.